A History of the Restoration and Conservation of Works of Art

To the memory of Caroline Villers and Gerry Hedley,
with love and gratitude.

Alessandro Conti

A History of the Restoration and Conservation of Works of Art

Translated by
Helen Glanville

ELSEVIER

AMSTERDAM · BOSTON · HEIDELBERG · LONDON · NEW YORK · OXFORD ·
PARIS · SAN DIEGO · SAN FRANCISCO · SINGAPORE · SYDNEY · TOKYO
Butterworth-Heinemann is an imprint of Elsevier

Butterworth-Heinemann is an imprint of Elsevier
Linacre House, Jordan Hill, Oxford OX2 8DP
30 Corporate Drive, Suite 400, Burlington, MA 01803, USA

First edition of this work published by Electa 1988
This edition of *Storia del restauro e della conservazione delle opere d'arte* by Alessandro Conti is
published by arrangement with Elsevier Ltd, The Boulevard, Langford Lane,
Kidlington OX5 1GB, UK, 2007.

British Library Cataloguing in Publication Data
A catalogue record for this book is available from the British Library

Library of Congress Cataloguing in Publication Data
A catalog record for this book is available from the Library of Congress

ISBN: 978-0-7506-6953-5

For information on all Butterworth-Heinemann publications
visit our web site at http://books.elsevier.com

Typeset by Charon Tec Ltd (A Macmillan Company), Chennai, India
www.charontec.com
Printed and bound in Italy

07 08 09 10   10 9 8 7 6 5 4 3 2 1

Table of contents

Preface

It is now accepted that there are many ways of relating the history of art. Traditionally, following the model established by Vasari in the sixteenth century, scholars have been concerned with origins, with artists and their lives, and with the development of style: then in the twentieth century art historians have investigated the role of patrons, market forces and the reception of works of art, but in spite of this wider remit the emphasis still falls upon the period when a work was first created and its initial reception by the audience for whom it was made. Alessandro Conti's *A History of the Restoration and Conservation of Works of Art* traces another history, which is the story of what has happened to works of art over the centuries. Hermeneutics has shown that interpretation is historically contingent, always evolving and conditioned by previous interpretation: what this groundbreaking book lays out is nothing less than a hermeneutics of conservation. In attending to the neglected history of the alteration and survival of works of art over time it achieves two key goals. The first is to make us critically aware of how knowledge and response to the art of the past are framed by the interventions, physical and intellectual, of previous generations. The second is to demonstrate that the survival or afterlife of paintings and sculpture – and sometimes their destruction – is a vital constituent of a wider cultural history.

Meticulously based upon a close knowledge of primary sources from Italy, France and England, both documentary and visual, this book traces the history of the preservation, alteration and adaptation of art from the Middle Ages to the end of the nineteenth century. The long time-frame gives the narrative its special value. Allowing his sources to speak for themselves, Conti elucidates the motives – religious, political, aesthetic and commercial – for conserving, repainting, emending, reframing, adapting or repositioning a work of art, and he explores how these motives shifted from period to period. His accounts of the "modernizing" of earlier altarpieces at the end of the fifteenth century, or the reframing of miraculous paintings in the early seventeenth century, illuminate the history of taste and of sacred images. The many instances detailed here of famous artists, such as Guercino in the seventeenth century or Canova at the turn of the nineteenth, emending earlier paintings and sculpture, remind us of what some period-based surveys neglect, namely that the history of art is shaped by a pattern of interleaving, of revisiting, of obstinate survivals, unexpected marriages and metamorphoses. Conti's achievement is to have recovered so many forgotten voices and to have orchestrated them in a narrative at once nuanced in detail and broad in scope.

Almost every one of today's debates about the cleaning, the reintegration and the presentation of pictures or sculptural monuments has been rehearsed in the past by artists and curators with a precise understanding of the historical vicissitudes the paintings in their charge had undergone, and the difficult choices that had to be made to preserve them for the future. Of course, the decisions that they made were coloured by the values of their time, but to read the reports of one of the heroes of this book, Pietro Edwards, who oversaw the conservation and cleaning of paintings in Venice around 1800, is to realize how much there is to learn from earlier witnesses. Indeed, Conti's discerning account of shifts in emphasis between the eighteenth century and the nineteenth century is particularly compelling. Shrewdly he observes that the most discerning curators and artist–conservators of the eighteenth century conceived of material and image as an essential unity, whereas in the nineteenth century, as the Romantic idea of individual expression gained the upper hand, so the apprehension of technique as integral to the nature of the work of art was eroded. Today, many contemporary artists, using an unprecedented assortment of materials, found or fashioned, alert us once again to the unity of substance and image. To ponder the story that Conti presents is to realize that matter and feeling – the material of art and what has been done to it over the centuries – are inextricably entwined. This book is much more than a history of conservation: it is a history of art that crucially complements the history of origins and makers.

Paul Hills

Introductory essay: "Relativity and restoration"

Helen Glanville

> *"Let us just speak of what would be seen by*
> *observers in different frames of reference. No*
> *one 'observer' is more 'right' than another …*
> *no one human view is truer than any other. All are relative …"*
> Albert Einstein

There never seems to have been a time when restoration has not been the stuff of controversy. Differences which seem at times unbridgeable separate the vocabularies and opinions of artists and non-artists, art-historians and schools of restoration entrenched in their opposing positions. Anglo-Saxon and Italian approaches have, since the cleaning controversies of the 1960s, been especially at odds, to the extent that Conti and Brandi – both authors of seminal works if the practising restorer is to have what Leonardo termed "rudder and compass"[i] – have only just been translated into English.[ii] The fact that they have, is, I hope, an indication of a change of climate within the field of restoration as well.

The seemingly irreconcilable differences which separate the different approaches to cleaning and restoration[iii] are as profound as those which separated the Newtonian, atomist supporters of light as particles, and the convinced defenders of the wave theory of light. The comparison is not a spurious one, as I hope to show.

Perception and the duality of light

Newton established that light was made up of a stream of discrete particles, and his authority was such that although Thomas Young had proposed an "undulatory theory" of light as early as the end of the eighteenth century, "when he discovered facts in optics which Newton's theory was incompetent to explain",[iv] it was not until the mid-nineteenth century that this wave theory of light was accepted and indeed completely supplanted Newton's.

---

[i] "Those who are in love with practice without knowledge are like the sailor without rudder or compass and who can never be certain whither he is going", *The Notebooks of Leonardo da Vinci*, ed. Jean Richter, 2 vols (New York, Dover Publications, 1970), p. 18. The original text is printed by the side of the translation.

[ii] Alessandro Conti's revised, enlarged edition of *Storia del restauro* which is here translated appeared in 1988; the first edition in 1973. Cesare Brandi's *Teoria del restauro* first appeared in 1963.

[iii] See the Glossary for the definition of these terms within my frames of reference.

[iv] That is the phenomenon of diffraction, when light bends round corners if the obstacle is small enough. John Tyndall, *Six Lectures on Light*, London, 1895 (lectures delivered in the USA 1872–1878).

It is well over half a century, in the wake of Einstein's discovery of relativity and special relativity,[v] since quantum physics has proven experimentally that the physical world is one of ambiguity in which light is made up potentially of both particles and waves *at the same time*, and its behaviour as one or the other (its actuality) is dependent on the observer and the context in which it is observed. Classical Newtonian science is founded on the distinction between the observer and the observed, a divide which is crucial to its "objectivity"; an understanding of the material world in terms of quantum physics differs fundamentally from this, in that the observer is part of the very reality observed or measured, and dictates the observation in a way which is not as yet completely understood.

This is borne out by the most famous and difficult to comprehend (in the deepest sense of the word) experiment in quantum physics: the double-slit experiment (see Fig. A). In this experiment, a stream of photons (units of light) is emitted from a light source. Just in front of the light source the experimenter erects a barrier with two open slits which allow the photons to pass through. On the other side of the barrier he or she places either two particle detectors or a wave detector (a screen), with which to observe the photons after they have passed through the slits. If the experimenter has placed particle detectors on the other side of the screen, the photon behaves like a particle: it follows a definite path through one of the slits and strikes one particle detector. If, however, the physicist replaces the particle detector with the screen, the photon behaves like a wave: it travels through both slits and contributes to an interference pattern on the detector screen.

That is, if the physicist looks for a particle, a particle is found. If he or she looks for a wave, that is what is found. This means in effect that all observation, every intervention, and even the results of a "scientific" experiment, are subjective.

The kind of measurement in an experiment, the conditions in which light (or the work of art) is observed, the approach chosen by the scientist in his or her experiment or the restorer in the restoration, will dictate which kind of actuality will be plucked out of the sea of possibilities, and be observed.[vi] Nothing can be perceived or measured outside some context, and the nature of what is perceived will be determined by this context: this is the essence of the change brought about in our understanding and perception of the material world by Einstein's theories of relativity and special relativity. In this quantum world antithetical positions are equally valid in that they are both potentially held within observed reality: both aspects are necessary for any full description of the nature of light, of matter, or of any phenomenon including the work of art, all of which are organized wholes which are greater than the sum of their parts.

---

[v] For all aspects which relate directly to the theories of relativity and quantum physics, I have relied heavily on the following volumes, which are directed by the physicist to the layman: *Who's Afraid of Schrödinger's Cat?* (Ian Marshall and Danah Zohar, 1997), *The Evolution of Physics* (A. Einstein and L. Infeld, Cambridge University Press, 1938), *The Meaning of it All* (R. Feynman, Penguin, 1998).

[vi] A quantifiable, particulate reality made up of photons, for instance, in which 1 particle + 1 particle = 2 particles, or an indeterminate reality, made up of the wave-like aspects which, as Einstein says, traverse time and space, in which 1 wave + 1 wave = another wave.

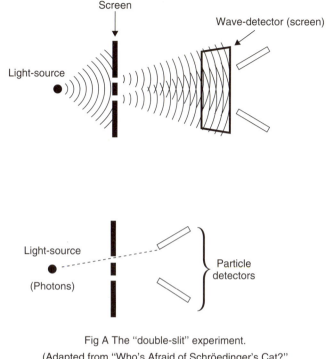

Fig A The "double-slit" experiment.
(Adapted from "Who's Afraid of Schröedinger's Cat?"
– I. Marshall and D. Zohar, 1997)

A.

Bearing this in mind, the importance of going back to the sources, of knowing the context within which the works we are restoring were created, becomes paramount. How did the artist himself perceive his work? What was the context not only for his choice of materials, but also of the meaning of the work? By what means was "inert matter directed to a spiritual end?",[vii] and what were the frames of reference at that moment in time? These are dynamic questions which cannot be measured or reduced: the indeterminate "wave" aspect of reality, without which our understanding and perception is not complete.

The materials of painting and their perception

From its early beginnings in the first laboratories attached to museums and academic institutions in the 1930s, the discipline of what is now often termed "technical art history", the investigation and analysis of the materials and techniques of artists, has been gathering momentum. It looks to analyse scientifically and define the measurable "particulate" elements of which works of art, and in particular paintings, are made. For paintings, until fairly recently, there

---

[vii] W. Holman Hunt, *The present system of obtaining materials in use by artist painters, as compared with that of the Old Masters*, Journal of the Society of Arts, 23 April 1880, p. 499.

was a broad division between the investigation of inorganic materials (the majority of pigments) and that of the organic materials in which these were bound and applied.[viii] There is now a decided move towards an understanding of their interaction, rather than just their individual natures. Documentary research in this field has been limited by comparison, and on the whole has concentrated on the analysis of technical treatises and related texts: what I would also term research of the "particulate" aspects of the reality of paintings, of the materials used originally, but from written texts rather than the paintings.

Textual evidence from earliest times[ix] indicates the awareness that colour was not solely dependent on the physical and chemical nature of the pigment, but also on the nature of the light in which it was seen, and its context: an awareness that colour was as much a question of perception as an intrinsic quality of the material. Philippe de la Hire, for instance, makes this very clear in the following passage:

> "Painters are well aware of pigments which appear much brighter in candlelight than in daylight, and several others which on the contrary although very bright in daylight, completely lose their beauty by the light of a candle. For example, vert-de-gris has a very beautiful colour by candlelight, and when its colour is not very strong, that is when it is mixed with a great quantity of white, it appears of a reasonably fine blue colour. Reds which contain some lake pigment also appear very bright by candlelight, whilst others, such as minium and vermilion, appear dull."[x]

A passage from Malvasia's "*Lives of Bolognese Artists*", in which he describes the practice of Guido Reni, shows this same awareness of the interrelationships of pigments and light:

> "certain purplish and bluish tints mixed into the half-tones and in the flesh ... such as one sees in delicate skins, which appear diaphanous almost, and even more so and more clearly, when light falls on them, especially when it comes through a window, especially a glass one, as everyone can very well observe, as his observations are not fanciful inventions ... but new observations neglected by the older masters".[xi]

Some idea of the alteration in one's perception of a work according to the light in which it is seen, can be gauged from Leonardo's *Virgin of the Rocks* in the National Gallery in London;

[viii] I. Rawlins, *Natural Philosophy and the Fine Arts* in *Aesthetics and the Gestalt* (Nelson, 1953), p. 55: "The characteristics of the scientific method is to isolate a particular band of truth ... namely a strip containing that which can be measured ... but there are other truths, incapable as yet of metrical conquest, perhaps for ever so ...".

[ix] For instance, *The Optics of Ibn Al-Haytham* (Al Hazan) Books I–III (translated and with a commentary by A. I. Sabra, Warburg Institute, London, 1989). In particular, Chapter 4 of Book I, dealing with colour perception, saturation, illumination, etc. Written in the eleventh century, translated into Latin (with important omissions in the late twelfth/early thirteenth century); translated into Italian in 1341 by Guerruccio di Cione Federighi and by Risner, a Swiss, in 1572. Poussin, amongst others, knew the treatise (Félibien, *Entretien V*, p. 320).

[x] Philippe de la Hire, *Mémoires de, mathématique et physique* (Paris, 1694), pp. 235–236. Quoted in the original in Glanville, *Veracity, verisimilitude and optics in painting in Italy at the turn of the seventeenth century*, Italian Studies Vol. LVI, 2001. Michael Baxandall's use of this source in *Patterns of Intention* (YUP, 1985) first drew my attention to it. See also Félibien, *Entretien V*, p. 623.

[xi] Carlo Cesare Malvasia, *Vite de' pittori bolognesi* (Bologna, 1678), II, p. 80: "*certi lividetti, e azzurrini mescolati fra le mezze-tinte, e fra le carnagioni ... quali si osservano nelle carni delicate, che rendono un certo diafano, ma più poi, e evidentemente, qualora il lume cade sopra di esse, passando in particolare per finestre chiuse, massime di vetro, come ciascuno può molto bene osservare; non essendo le sue invenzioni chimeriche ... ma nuove osservazioni da gli antichi trasandate*" (quoted in Glanville, 2001). Deriving from Aristotle's observations of nature originally, through Leonardo's observations and deductions, used by Rubens and Velasquez amongst others, re-emerging with Goethe's *Theory of Colour*, and then into nineteenth-century practice.

seen in reproduction, we can appreciate the volume of the figures set within the craggy cove melting into the deep translucent shadows, and the landscape airily disappearing into the distance. When we see it in the flesh, say in the morning light, when the light levels in the gallery are not low enough for the artificial lighting to switch itself on, there is a feeling of disappointment almost. The light scattering off the picture surface makes the painting look greyish, the colours unsaturated[xii] and flat: there is no depth, the illusion of space is want-ing and the painting does not sing out to you. If you are lucky enough to be there when the London sky clouds over and the artificial lighting comes on, this is less diffuse and warmer, and therefore nearer in its effects to the strong, directional, tungsten lighting which is used when photographing paintings. Because this light penetrates the broken-up surface of the varnishes and the dark coruscated pigments, it restores to them some of the transparency required in order to give the illusion of volume on a flat surface. This depends, amongst other things, on the use – and the perception – of warm transparent shadows. From the time of Leonardo onwards, for all artists whose aim was to not to copy things as they were or were known to be in the mind's eye, but as they were perceived in nature, in order to give an illusion of reality,[xiii] pigments and paint were handled to this end.

Gainsborough's portraits as well as his landscapes "were often wrought by Candle-Light, and generally with great force and likeness. But his painting room, even by Day (a kind of darkened Twilight) had scarcely any Light, and your young friend has seen him, whilst his subjects have been sitting to him, when neither they nor the pictures were scarcely dis-cernible".[xiv] What comparable effect of the paintings can we expect when such paintings are then hung either in the diffuse light of day, or in the evenly distributed artificial light, as is cus-tomary in many museums and collections today? Such lighting is only suitable for some works (in the sense that these were the conditions envisaged by the artist in order for his work to have the intended effect); it is not suitable for those painted in low, directional warm lighting, such as candle light or gas light, nor for those which aimed at the dissolution of the flat pic-ture surface, to engulf the observer in their deception of real space, negating the observer/observed distinction.

Gainsborough's letters also show how particular he was about where and how his paintings were hung in order that they should be seen as he wanted them to be seen. Writing in 1757 to a client, for instance: "I should be glad [if] you'd place your picture as far from the light as possible; observing to let the light fall from the left".[xv] When I had the opportunity of having Gainsborough's *The Linley Sisters* in the photographic studio whilst carrying out a "technical examination", because the light fell from the left in this painting

---

[xii] See Glossary and diagrams.

[xiii] A paraphrase of Galileo in a letter to the painter Cigoli, 26 June 1612, where he speaks of sculptors copying things as they are, and painters as they appear to be: *"quelli imitano le cose com'elle sono, e questi com'elle appariscono"* (quoted in E. Panofsky, *Galileo as a Critic of the Arts*, The Hague, 1954).

[xiv] Ozias Humphry papers, Royal Academy of Arts Library, London. HU/1/20-40, p. 37. Quoted in Glanville, *Gainsborough – Artist or Artisan?* In "A Nest of Nightingales – Gainsborough's *Linley Sisters*", catalogue of the exhibition, Dulwich Picture Gallery, 1988.

[xv] *The Letters of Thomas Gainsborough* (Ed. Woodall, 1963), letter no. 24, 24 February 1757, to a client in Colchester, possibly Mr Robert Edgar. It is worth noting that in John Senex's translation of Leonardo's *Treatise on Painting*, which appeared in 1721, is included Leonardo's dictum, "Painting should only be view'd from one single place" (p. 25).

also, I tried lighting it with only one source of light, from the left, and with the shutters of the photographic light half-closed to moderate its intensity. The result was astonishing: the flat picture surface disappeared, and the sisters sat and stood within their leafy bower, the shadowy air surrounding them. Not sitters against background, but figures within and of the landscape.[xvi] Gainsborough's use of an artifice such as candlelight, which is not after all "natural" for a landscape setting, "far from weaking the truth of imitation, [it] gives more truth to what the artist imitates after nature".[xvii]

Disegno and *colore* and the cleaning of paintings

Newtonian science is atomistic, quantum physics is essentially holistic. That is, where the atomist believes that any whole can be broken down and analysed into its constituent parts, the holist maintains that the whole is greater than the sum of its parts.

Translated into the field of painting, we find this duality formally formulated by Vasari, in his opposition between *disegno* and *colore*. It has often been reduced to an opposition between Raphael/Michelangelo and Titian, between the painting of Florence and that of Venice, the depiction of the "Ideal" and that of "brute" nature.

Leonardo can be found at the roots of this bifurcation. In his writings, he provided so many of the precepts which would form the basis of the theoretical knowledge, the *scientia* required of the artist. Alongside the Classical heritage brought to light in the form of statues providing models of the "Ideal", and the Classical texts in which painting stood alongside poetry and music as a liberal art, these would form the basis of Vasari's concept of *disegno*. In his practice, guided by his detailed observations of natural phenomena and perception, Leonardo laid the ground for *colore*. His unfinished paintings show monochrome blocking in of the tonal relationships between light and shade as found in nature, which would then be translated into colour in the subsequent paint layers. As confirmed by his observations, no outlines in nature and therefore none in his paintings, and every part related to the whole and to each other through the unifying action of light. The artist, through his skill, and by the same means as in nature, becomes the artificer of the illusion of nature on a flat surface.

Disegno would form the foundation of the Academies:[xviii] precepts and rules, copies from line engravings of the "Old Masters" and then from the Antique; piecemeal at first (ears, noses and other appendages), working up to a whole made up of these parts, and only then would students be let loose on nature; by this time they could only see its manifestations through the eyes of others.

"He who can go to the fount does not go to the vessel" would exclaim Leonardo.[xix] Direct experience and observation of nature, not as relayed through accepted authorities, whether authors or artists: this would form the basis of the new "science" and, in the arts,

---

[xvi] Even the pigments used by Gainsborough work to this end, analysis showing the same pigments used by him in flesh, drapery and landscape, a physical link between the figures and their setting.

[xvii] The power of such illusions is difficult for us to understand from the perspective of our own visual culture in which we are constantly being asked to enter fictional worlds in photographs and films. The frame of reference of Gainsborough's time is quite different.

[xviii] With the exception of that early and great Academy, *L'Accademia degli Incamminati* (of those finding their path), founded by the Carracci in Bologna in 1581.

[xix] Leonardo, *On Painting* (Ed. M. Kemp, Yale University Press, 1989).

of the Venetian school of painting, which for Vasari was the epitome of *colore*. Whereas the part played by paint was minimized in the Florentine schools, because of its material qualities which linked it to the mechanical arts to the extent that the mark of the brush was actively avoided,[xx] the Venetian school and its later "followers" (if one can apply such a term to Rubens, Van Dyck, Velasquez or Gainsborough!) made paint their means of expression. Reynolds, describing Gainsborough's practice, spoke of his way "of forming all the parts of the picture together: the whole going on at the same time, in the same manner as nature creates her works".[xxi]

The extent to which this opposition between the piecemeal and the indivisible whole was alive for whole generations subsequent to Vasari can be found not only in seventeenth- and eighteenth-century texts relating to painting (Félibien and De Piles, for instance), but also in other fields, for instance in this literary critique by Galileo opposing what was, for him, the unsatisfactory piecemeal construction of Tasso's epic poem *Gerusalemme Liberata* (which he likened to a painting made out of marquetry, in contrast to the oil used by Ariosto to "paint" his *Orlando Furioso*:[xxii] Tasso "patch[es] together disjointed concepts which have no connection or relation to one another, so that his narrative is closer to a picture made out of inlaid marquetry (*pittura intarsiata*) than one painted in oil; because the marquetry is made up of a medley of small pieces of differently coloured wood, which can never sweetly merge into one another and harmonize (*accoppiarsi*) as they have hard edges and because of the diversity of colours, the figures can only appear crude, dry and without relief and volume. Whereas in the work painted in oil, the outlines softly merging, one passes from one tint to the next, so that the painting appears softly rounded (*morbida*), in relief, with both force and volume. Ariosto (*sfuma e tondeggia*) … whilst Tasso handles his work in a fragmentary, dry and crude manner …".[xxiii]

The cleaning of paintings of the "Venetian" school, in the broadest sense of term, that is those works which are painted as a whole and are more than a sum of their parts,[xxiv] accentuates the problems which face the restorer when cleaning. The materials of which the painting is made will have inevitably, as Hogarth pointed out, aged differentially, and in different ways, altering the original relationships. Seventeenth- and eighteenth-century sources suggest that this element – the effect of age on pigments – was taken into consideration by artists, in much the same way as viewing distance and the application of varnish.[xxv] The Venetian restorer Pietro Edwards, to whose admirable work Conti deservedly devotes a whole chapter of this volume, speaks thus of the problem:

[xx] See directives in Armenini, for instance (Giovan Battista Armenini, *De' veri precetti della pittura*, 1586, Einaudi, 1988).

[xxi] Sir Joshua Reynolds, *Discourses on Art* (Ed. Robert R. Wark), Yale University Press, 1975, *Discourse* XIV, l. 147

[xxii] The parallels between poetry and painting; Horace's *ut pictura poesis* (as in painting so in poetry) was a cultural commonplace from the Renaissance onwards.

[xxiii] Galileo Galilei, *Opere Complete*, Vol. IX, p. 63.

[xxiv] Conti 2007, Chapter VI, p. 214 Lanzi, in a manuscript note in the library of the Uffizi, remarked that "the Venetians, even the modern ones, have an advantage over the other schools [of painting] in that they give unity to a work, imagining it as a whole with all its passages of light, so that the eye easily follows its lines and runs over the picture from top to bottom. Mister Pietro Edwards asserts that when having on occasion to cut down paintings because of the owners' will, it was as difficult to do on a work belonging to the Venetian school as it was easy to do it on works from other schools, where the composition is often piecemeal and not thought out in its integrity (*insieme*). Here, Edwards is obviously making a distinction between private and public practice.

[xxv] For instance, Roger de Piles *Cours de Peinture par Principes* (Gallimard, 1989; first published 1707), p. 129.

"the masses of some of the strongest shadows as well as those of certain draperies which hardly contain any lead white in the paint mixture, in these old paintings will darken because of their nature, nor is there any hope of reviving them through cleaning …

The liquids and the varnishes used in the restoration of these kinds of paintings, rather than reducing the darkness of those shadows, in fact increase their force. Therefore, if the practitioner begins and continues the operation, cleaning the highlights and then the half tints, cleaning them as one might say until they look freshly painted, the final result will be a severe loss of balance between the highlights, which will appear exceedingly shrill, and the deep shadows, without any intermediate gradation in tone".[xxvi]

Every cleaning operation, now as then, begins with what are known as "cleaning tests": these are carried out to establish the relative solubilities of the varnish layers and the underlying paint, and the optical effects on the materials being tested. These tests are first carried out either on areas rich in lead-white (lead-white forms a much tougher paint film with oil than the pigments used in the shadows) or on the more vulnerable areas of shadow.[xxvii]

We have seen how in the double-slit experiment, the initial choice made by the physicist in experimental procedure will determine the behaviour of light in the experiment. The approach which leads the restorer to one or other of the above options in cleaning will, in the same way, fundamentally influence what will be the final appearance of the painting. Gauging first the condition and strength of the shadows leads on to a level of cleaning in the lights relative to the harmony between the various elements. Speaking of canvases by Francesco Bassano and Tintoretto, Edwards notes that "we had to leave several areas undercleaned, so as not to lose the most prized excellence (*pregio*) relating to the union of colours, that is their harmony". Warnings of the dangers of imbalance to the final harmony of work from an overindulgent use of white pigment by the artist are found consistently in the art literature from Alberti through to Eastlake.[xxviii] When the decision is made to begin cleaning areas rich in lead-white first, because the strength of the lights, and hence the modelling, is treated by the artist in relation to the strength or colour of the shadows, it will prove difficult for the restorer to preserve a balance, and this will be reflected in the final effect.

This is not to say that works which have been conceived in a more piecemeal fashion, such as works of the Florentine school or, leaping into the nineteenth century, Pre-Raphaelite paintings as opposed to the works of the Impressionists, are not concerned with harmony; but the meaning of "harmony" in the context of these paintings is different, because the context has changed. As Reynolds so perceptively remarked, bracketing together those two seventeenth-century inheritors of the dispute between *colore* and *disegno*, Rubens and Poussin: "Yet however opposite their characters, in one thing they agreed; both of them always preserving a perfect correspondence between all the parts of their respective manners; in so much that it may be doubted whether any alteration of what is considered as defective in either, would not destroy the effect of the whole".[xxix]

[xxvi] Conti 2007, Chapter VI, p. 206.
[xxvii] I am grossly simplifying what is an exceedingly complex and lengthy procedure, but this is the essential difference between two approaches.
[xxviii] For instance, see Félibien, *Entretien V*, p. 687.
[xxix] Reynolds, 1975, *Discourse V*, Dec. 1772, l. 312.

Harmony

"Harmony" is a homonym: that is, a word (and concept) which although preserving the same outward appearance, will alter in meaning according to the context in which it is found or used. It is relative to its own frame of reference. As de Piles wrote in 1707, "… all the objects which enter into a painting, every line and every colour, all the lights and all the shadows are only large or small, strong or weak by comparison".[xxx] This is true of all works, whatever antithetical category one may wish to place them in. Conti quotes a fascinating extract from the restoration report written by Molteni, the great nineteenth-century Milanese restorer, on the cleaning of Raphael's *Marriage of the Virgin* (Fig. 149) in the Brera in Milan. Painted on a white ground, which in itself emphasizes flatness, this painting in Vasarian terms epitomizes the concerns of *disegno*. Molteni, like Edwards in the previous century working on Venetian paintings, began the cleaning of the painting with the areas which had darkened most over time, in order to bring back the relationship between the figures and their background, a relationship which the uneven accretions of "patina" had inverted,[xxxi] making a nonsense of the artifices used by Raphael for the spatial construction of the painting. On completion of the cleaning, some areas had been left untouched (the flesh, for example) and other areas had been cleaned to different degrees.[xxxii]

All effects of light, and therefore colour, are relative; in painting as in music, what we are sensitive to is the interval which separates them,[xxxiii] the relationship between them rather than the note or colour itself. You can transpose a melody into another key, but if you change the intervals between the notes you will lose the melody or, should you still recognize it, you will wince, as it is out of key and dissonant. To change the relationship between colours in a painting will have the same effect. Artists themselves would use musical terminology when trying to express in words the way they handled colours and the effects they were trying to achieve (or avoid). Poussin spoke of "modes" for his paintings, different "keys" of colour being suitable for different subjects;[xxxiv] Barocci of "tuning" and "harmonizing" his work;[xxxv] Gainsborough of the jarring of bright colours placed out of harmony, like wrong notes, making "noise" rather than music in a painting.[xxxvi]

> "A music master who is tuning a lute or a harp … he cannot teach you to tune them by telling you to turn the pegs a certain number of times. It is the ear that must judge their harmony when they are plucked. Similarly for colours, it is eye that must be the judge …".[xxxvii]

[xxx] Roger de Piles, *Cours de Peinture par principes* (1707), ed. Thuillier, Gallimard, 1989, p. 65. My translation.

[xxxi] Conti, 2007, Chapter VIII, pp. 296, 300 (Fig. 149). For Molteni, this "patina" of time was a concrete addition, an "accretion" rather than an alteration of the original materials, as Conti points out.

[xxxii] What Gerry Hedley would later term "selective cleaning" (see Glossary).

[xxxiii] E. Gombrich, *Art & Illusion: The Psychology of Pictorial Representation* (Phaidon, 1960), p. 46. My debt to this book is immense.

[xxxiv] *Nicolas Poussin: Lettres et propos sur l'art* (Ed. Anthony Blunt, Paris, 1964), pp. 124–125, Letter to Chantelou, 24/XI/1647.

[xxxv] Asked by Guidobaldo Duke of Urbino what he was doing, pointing to the painting on which he was working, he replied: "Sto accordando … questa musica". G. B. Bellori, *Le vite de' pittori, scultori e architetti moderni* (1672) Ed. Evelina Borea (Turin, Einaudi, 1976).

[xxxvi] *The Letters of Thomas Gainsborough* (Ed. Woodall, 1963), Letter No. 34 to David Garrick, 1772.

[xxxvii] André Félibien, *Entretiens sur les vies et les ouvrages des plus excellents peintres anciens et modernes* (Vols I and II, Paris, 1685, 2nd edn), p. 676. My translation.

Where Félibien refers to the artist, Edwards makes the eye of the observer the ultimate judge of a cleaning: "if the paintings of Francesco Bassano and those by Tintoretto could be seen in the disharmonious state in which they would find themselves if not cleaned in the fashion indicated above, they would excite the contempt (*dispetto*) of even the most mediocre connoisseur, even if during the cleaning, the original paint of the artist had rigorously been preserved with the greatest scruple".[xxxviii]

A very interesting report which Cavenaghi wrote when asked to sit on a committee judging the controversies surrounding the cleaning of paintings in the Florence Galleries in 1910, shows that for him as for Edwards, for a cleaning to be considered successful, it was not sufficient not to have removed any original material. This is in marked contrast to later criticisms, which lean heavily on the premises that original material has been removed from the painting during cleaning: "It was not the glazes which were removed in this painting, nor any other original physical material, so it is not really correct to say that the painting has been ruined. Rather, one should lament … that the restorer – either through an excess of scruple or because deficient in sensitivity for art – but in any case failing in his duty, was not able to restore to the painting, after cleaning, the balance of its overall harmony".[xxxix]

Edwards goes a step further, recognizing the relative quality of the term and its use within specific frames of reference, and is at ease with the ambiguity which we, despite Einstein, still find hard to cope with in what is still, essentially, a Newtonian vision of reality and of the work of art. "Only remain a few words to say relating to the harmony of the aforementioned works after their restoration. This element cannot be as easily defined in words, as it can be felt in the flesh. Harmony in painting has not, as yet, been reduced to mathematical laws as has that of sounds; for almost all of men it is still a matter of feeling. Furthermore, as we are dealing with an old painting, we must not think to give back to the work a harmony of colour as this should be, *intrinsically*, but rather as it was practised by the author of the work, *as it would have appeared according to his own judgement*. Otherwise, we would be removing a characteristic difference between the various styles of past masters".[xl]

Restoration and authenticity

Restoration as a practice involves the intervention of the restorer on the surface, the image of the painting. Both Brandi and Conti have attempted to rationalize the various approaches open to a restorer when confronted with an incomplete and/or damaged image which has suffered through the passage of time and/or the effects of man.[xli] These approaches differ not only in the degree of intervention, but more fundamentally in their perception of the nature and meaning of the work of art, and therefore in the ultimate "end" of restoration.

[xxxviii] Conti, Chapter VI, p. 206.
[xxxix] Conti, Chapter IX, p. 374.
[xl] Conti, Chapter VI, p. 212. The emphases are mine.
[xli] Cesare Brandi's distinction is between the "positive" and "negative" actions of time.

Conti distinguishes among three basic approaches: restoration as conservation (that is, abstention or an archaeological approach), aesthetic restoration (invisible retouching and reconstruction through analogy) and visible restoration (for want of a better term in English, which is in harmony with the original, yet clearly distinguishable).[xlii]

As has been the case intermittently through time,[xliii] restoration today involves in-painting (the brush of the restorer confining its actions to the losses in the original paint layers) rather than repainting or over-painting, indicating a concern to preserve the authenticity and integrity of the artist's hand; reversibility[xliv] of the materials used for retouching is another criterion, so that in the future the solutions and interpretations proposed by the present restorer on the painting can be removed easily[xlv] and different solutions replace them. There will be as many different solutions and interpretations as there are restorers, and therefore the original work will look different in each case.

In a manuscript or an incomplete text, these interpretations of the contents of *lacunae* are clearly marked, with brackets for example, as being the work of another; there is no confusion in the mind and eye of the reader as to authorship, no ambiguity, and the insertion of another person's critical interpretation of the missing portions of the text will not affect the original. The completed text will not be a translation of the original.

Not so with paintings: whatever the solution applied by the restorer, the perception of the original will be affected by the treatment of the *lacunae*, whether these be individually tiny, constituting the wear of the picture surface with time, or large areas of damage and loss.[xlvi] Nothing can be either lost or added without altering the effect, and hence perception of the whole.

The work of art is more than a sum of its parts, whether speaking in terms of a quantum entity or a *Gestalt*,[xlvii] in Hegelian terms of a "higher reality born of mind",[xlviii] or intuitively as an artist. Conti quotes from a letter by Goya[xlix] in which the artist speaks of the historical unrepeatability of the artist's touch, which means that even the original artist could not replace a touch on his own painting, because that instant in time has passed and material and the mind that moved it are one and cannot be separated: "the spiritual and the

---

[xlii] See the Glossary for definitions of these approaches. I am using Conti's broad distinctions, but without certain of his undertones; for instance that linking aesthetic restoration to nineteenth-century Lombard practice. The English equivalents, because not homegrown, are clumsy and inadequate in their descriptive qualities compared with the Italian: *restauro di tutela, restauro amatoriale* and *restauro di accompagnamento.*

[xliii] See Conti, for instance Chapters V and VI.

[xliv] See Glossary for definitions of these terms.

[xlv] Using solvents which are limited in their action and effects on the paint layer.

[xlvi] See note 42.

[xlvii] I. Rawlins, *Aesthetics and the Gestalt* (Nelson, 1953) p. 62: "… a picture is a Gestalt; modification, subtraction, addition implies a disturbance of balance and new relations between the parts are called for if equilibrium is to be restored".

[xlviii] Hegel, *Introduction to the Philosophy of Fine Art* (trans. Bernard Bosanquet, London, 1886), p. 13: "Art liberates the real import of appearances from the semblance and deception of this bad and fleeting world, and imparts to phenomenal semblances a higher reality, born of mind. The appearances of art, therefore, far from being mere semblances, have the higher reality and the more genuine existence in comparison with the realities of common life".

[xlix] Conti, 2007, Chapter VII, Note 3, p. 263.

sensuous side must in artistic production be as one"[1] or the paint, the pictorial element, is nothing more than adornment, a decoration.

Restoration as conservation (*restauro di conservazione o di tutela*)

The idea that replacing a part that has been lost or damaged compromises historical authenticity and makes of the work of art or monument an object belonging to everyday reality, a sum of its parts any of which can be replaced if missing, underlies the approach to restoration which has at times been called archaeological, or restoration as conservation.

Only conservation of the material structure is to be carried out, with no attempt being made to integrate or complete the image (restoration). Within these parameters, this approach can also include the introduction within the image, in portions lost or badly damaged, of an intervention which is in itself blank and of indeterminate colour, what is termed a "neutral" restoration (see, for instance, Fig. 172).

This approach makes of the work of art an instrument of instruction and learning, an historical document which can be studied and analysed, and the material authenticity of which can be confirmed. Championed by Cavalcaselle in the nineteenth century, this abstention from reintegration of the losses also came to the fore in the twentieth century, perhaps as a reaction to the excesses of reconstruction and restoration of the intervening years.

Cesare Brandi saw this approach as giving pre-eminence to the historical, material authenticity of the work, at the expense of the aesthetic aspects of the work. In his analysis of the role of the restorer and of restoration in general, Brandi used the principles of *Gestalt* psychology to inform and define the principles of intervention. A work of art (like a *gestalt*) is more than a sum of its individual components, just as music is a more than a sum of its constituent notes. It is an organized whole whose parts have an intrinsic relationship, and it is these relationships to which we are sensitive: the intervals separating the notes which give them relative values and the organization which makes of notes music rather than a cacophony.

Our perception will also accord such relative values as "foreground" and "background"[li] to elements within the work so that a damaged area, or one which has been left blank or been given a neutral tonality, can leap to the foreground in our mind's eye, relegating the original picture to the status of background. Brandi sees the restorer's task as inverting this order of things – bringing the original back into the foreground, restoring to the work its expressive potential as a work of art, so that it is more than just an historical document to be analysed in its component parts, for that is not the end of an work of art. In Hegel's words:

> "For the work of art ought to bring a content before the mind's eye, not in its generality as such, but with this generality made absolutely individual, and sensuously particularized. If the work of art does not proceed from this principle, but sets in relief the generalized aspect with the purpose of abstract instruction,

---

[1] Hegel, *Introduction to the Philosophy of Fine Art* (trans. Bernard Bosanquet, London, 1886), p. 74: "the spiritual and the sensuous side must in artistic production be as one. For instance, it would be possible in poetical creation to try and proceed by first apprehending the theme to be treated as a prosaic thought, and by then putting it into pictorial ideas, and into rhyme and so forth; so that the pictorial element would simply be hung upon abstract reflections as an ornament or decoration".

[li] I. Rawlins, *Aesthetics and Gestalt* (Nelson, 1953), and E. Gombrich, *Art and Illusion* (Phaidon, 1960), p. 46.

then the imaginative and sensuous aspect is only an external and superfluous adornment, and the work of art is a thing divided against itself, in which form and content no longer appear as grown in one".[lii]

Aesthetic restoration (*restauro amatoriale*)

If conservation–restoration only recognizes the value of a work of art in its historical and documentary authenticity, aesthetic restoration looks to present the image in its entirety (rather than wholeness), and to reintegrate and reconstruct losses so that these are not discernible to the naked eye. The restorer has interpreted what is missing; but that this is an interpretation and not the work of the original artist is not clear; the observer may not perceive that the work is damaged.[liii] The damage incurred may be severe, of considerable size or importance, and involve reconstruction of missing areas "by analogy", or be widespread small losses and wear of the paint surface, the result of the passage of time on the fabric of the paint, which are in-painted and give the paint an un-aged appearance.

Consciously or unconsciously, this is an attempt to turn back the clock, to go back to an "original" untainted state: the Garden of Eden evoked and invoked by Origen in the opening page of Conti's book. It is an imagined authentic past re-created by the restorer in the present. The damages and ageing inflicted by time on the work are erased, or rather masked, by the restorer's brush. This desire to re-create a lost age in its concrete manifestations, an age which is past and therefore not susceptible to the fluxes and chaos of contemporary events, seems to come to the fore (as both Ruskin and Conti point out) in times of particular unrest, almost as a form of escapism.

Because the restorer, like the artist, must "stand[s] within this reflective world and its conditions, and it is impossible for him to abstract from it by will and reserve",[liv] restoration cannot but modernize, interpreting according to its own frames of reference, so that these re-creations tell us more about the time in which they were carried out than the times and concerns of the original artist.[lv] As Conti says (and Edwards before him), if the frame of reference for the restorer in his approach to the restoration of the work of art is the cultural context and taste of his own time rather than that of the artist himself, then the restoration will be a reflection of this "simply updating to new visual demands",[lvi] and because the frames of reference change with passing taste and generations, the restoration – like a translation – will date and not last. The original meaning, its power to move us through its material expression across the centuries as a living work, will have been lost.

[lii] Hegel, *Introduction to the Philosophy of Fine Art* (trans. Bernard Bosanquet, London, 1886), p. 97.

[liii] This is true in a great number of cases, even when there is extensive documentation accompanying the restoration, of which the general public can be largely unaware when looking at a restored work.

[liv] Hegel, *Introduction to the Philosophy of Fine Art* (trans. Bernard Bosanquet, London, 1886), p. 19.

[lv] Umberto Eco, *Mouse or Rat? Translation as Negotiation*, Orion Books, 2004, p. 82. As with paintings, "translation is always a shift, not between two languages but between two cultures …. A translator must take into account rules that are not strictly linguistic but, broadly speaking, cultural. Translators, even when trying to give us the flavour of a language and of a historical period, are in fact *modernizing* their source".

[lvi] Conti, 2007, Chapter IX, p. 375.

By its very nature, retouching is a meticulous task, and cannot be carried out other than in a piecemeal fashion: detail by detail, whether reconstructing large areas of loss, or areas of wear and abrasion where the losses are minuscule. The restorer has no choice but to focus on the detail.[lvii] Heisenberg's "uncertainty principle" has shown that if we focus on the particle-like properties of a quantum entity (in this instance the painting), we gain a good sense of the isolated part at the expense of the whole; if we focus on the wave-like qualities, we have a sense of the whole but lose our ability to focus on the part or the particular.[lviii] As has so often been the case, the antithesis between these two aspects was understood long before it received scientific confirmation. Félibien, looking at Dürer's work, commented that the latter had not taken into consideration, when making such detailed studies for each element, that when put together these would have a quite different effect.[lix] When confronted with the Pre-Raphaelite truth to detail of Holman Hunt's *The English Coast* (1852), Théophile Gautier remarked how "the painting which seems [appears] the most false is precisely the most true".[lx]

Truth in detail, and truth of the whole: one is description, the other evocation. One is the approach of the Pre-Raphaelites and the other of the Impressionists. These are fundamentally different world views, one particulate and the other indeterminate, and both necessary for a full description of matter.[lxi]

Visible restoration (*di accompagnamento*)

"The art of imitation is two-fold. One aspect of it in the use of hands and mind in producing imitations, another aspect the producing of likenesses in the mind alone" (Apuleius).[lxii]

The practical side of aesthetic/invisible restoration involves the careful imitation of original paint in colour and texture[lxiii] (by the use of hands and mind, as Apuleius says). Imitation is a meticulous task, and even if carried out with knowledge of the original technique, will suffer from the heaviness inherent to the process, "for he who imitates the work with much attention will produce a laboured thing".[lxiv] This is as true in restoration as it is in painting: and the

---

[lvii] One does, however, have a choice as a restorer in how one works: in-painting over the entire painting at the same time, or completing one area before moving on to the next.

[lviii] See *Who's Afraid of Schrödinger's Cat?* (Ian Marshall and Danah Zohar, 1997), p. 182, and I. Rawlins, *Aesthetics and the Gestalt* (1953), pp. 218–221. See also the double-slit experiment on Fig. A, p. xi.

[lix] André Félibien, *Entretiens sur les vies et les ouvrages des plus excellents peintres anciens et modernes* (Vols I and II, Paris, 1685, 2nd edn,) *Entretien IV*, p. 534, "*Il n'a pas pensé en étudiant chaque chose en particulier, qu'elles font un autre effet toutes ensemble …*".

[lx] Quoted in Casteras and Craig Paxon, *Pre-Raphaelite Art in its European Context* (AUP, 1995), p. 43.

[lxi] Albert Einstein, *The Evolution of Physics* (Cambridge University Press, 1938): "… in the case of light waves and photons, it was shown that every statement formulated in the wave language can be translated into the language of photons or light corpuscles. The same is true for electronic waves".

[lxii] Philostratus' *Life of Apollonius of Tyana* (quoted by Gombrich, *The Image in the Clouds*, in *Art & Illusion* (Phaidon Press, 1960), p. 155.

[lxiii] The texture matching that of the surrounding paint is provided by the fill. See Glossary.

[lxiv] Marco Boschini in the posthumous preface to "*Descrizione de tutte le pubbliche pitture de la Città di Venezia*", Venice, 1733, p. 11 (quoted in Gombrich, *The Image in the Clouds*, in *Art & Illusion*), p. 167. See also Goya's letter, note 3, Chapter VII, in Conti, 2007.

dangers of diligence (or over-diligence) so often referred to in texts on art, of not knowing where to stop, are as present for the restorer as for the artist.

On a small scale, invisibly in-painting a loss in a paint film is, from an optical point of view, a tautological exercise which does not take into account the mechanism of perception. The mind's eye will automatically compensate for losses, bridge the gap and read the image as whole, just as the ear will do in music, because both painting and music are organized wholes. That this is so was recognized long before the time of *gestalt:* Gainsborough, writing to a friend, described how in painting just as in music, your eye should be able to predict the next note of the melody[lxv] .... And if note or paint is not there, what is missing will be provided by the mind's eye or the inner ear. Gombrich quotes a wonderful example of a tenor, knowing he could not reach the top note of an aria during a performance, simply leaving it out, and the audience not noticing as they had provided the missing note themselves;[lxvi] had he sung the note, and it had been slightly off or in any way inadequate, the audience would have immediately picked it up (and their perception of the whole aria would in fact have been altered). As in music, so in painting ...

With large areas of loss, we have seen how "neutral" solutions will float in front of the original (Fig. 172), and invisible reconstructions will relegate the work of art to the status of an object belonging to everyday life, by materially replacing what has been lost. For Apuleius' "imitative faculty" of the mind to come into action, it is the areas of damage that must first be relegated to the background, so that the expressive potential of the original image is brought to the foreground once more. Neither of the antithetical approaches discussed above do this, in that both are "stronger" than the original and interfere with or impede this expressive potential.[lxvii] Brandi, in his development of the technique of *tratteggio*,[lxviii] wanted to provide a rationalized approach which would at the same time respect the historical authenticity of the work and its expressive potential as a work of art to provide a solution which would be neutral in the true sense of the word – that is, relative in colour and tonality to the paint in its immediate vicinity, as well as being in the "background" of the original. As mediation between two antitheses, it could not be and cannot be other than a compromise. As with other more individual truly neutral solutions adopted by different restorers over time, which are on analysis immediately distinguishable from the brush of the artist, these solutions, at the normal viewing distance for the work in question, allow the work to be observed as a whole, and "to make an impression on the imagination and feeling"[lxix] of the observer that the original artist intended. As with all restoration work, the success of this endeavour cannot be separated from either the manual skill or the sensibility of the restorer.

Conti gives a very good example of a restoration of a badly damaged Fra Bartolomeo, restored in 1872 (see Figs 163, 164). The losses are pushed back, visually speaking, so as not

---

[lxv] *The Letters of Thomas Gainsborough* (Ed. Woodall, 1963), N. 53 to William Jackson: "One part of a Picture ought to be like the first part of a Tune; that you can guess what follows, and that makes the second part of the Tune and so I've done ...".

[lxvi] Gombrich, *Image and Eye*, p. ??.

[lxvii] To use an analogy from the world of structural conservation, they are like the cradles applied to the reverse of panels which should allow the panel to move, but in fact in many instances distort the original support and can cause it to split and fail, because the intervention of the restorer is stronger than the original.

[lxviii] *Tratteggio* is a technique of hatching, carried out in either watercolour or pigments bound with varnish, which is used to integrate losses in a visible but not disturbing way.

[lxix] Hegel, *Introduction to the Philosophy of Fine Art* (trans. Bernard Bosanquet, London, 1886), p. 103.

to be prominent, and the restorer has provided a reconstruction by the side of the original, stimulating the onlooker's eye as to what is missing in the original work. At no point is the authenticity of the material structure in question, or the expressiveness of the original tampered with. Each observer provides his or her own solution. Reynolds' insights into how Gainsborough's captured "likeness" and "truth" in his portraits eloquently express this interaction between observer and observed which is so fundamental to the visual arts and a quantum vision of reality:

> "Though this opinion may be considered fanciful ... it is presupposed that in this undetermined manner there is the general effect; enough to remind the spectator of the original; the imagination supplies the rest, and perhaps more satisfactorily to himself if not more exactly, than the artist, with all his care, could possibly have done. At the same time it must be acknowledged there is one evil attending this mode; that if the portrait were seen, previous to any knowledge of the original, different persons would form different ideas".[lxx]

Such solutions imply an acceptance of the relationship which binds the observed (the work of art) and the individual observer, and of the "imitative faculty" aspect of human perception. Imitative, invisible retouching, on the other hand, imposes on the work of art the viewpoint of one observer only (the restorer/director of restoration) in a material fashion on the fabric of the work, thus precluding the observer from being able to superimpose or replace this with his or her own interpretation.[lxxi] To put this into a wider contemporary context, it could be seen as another symptom of the politics of a "nanny-state society", where choices are made on behalf of the individual, and ready-made solutions are provided for ease of consumption, rather than trusting or encouraging each to provide his or her own interpretation. A decision is made on behalf of the observer.

Ian Rawlins, who was appointed the first Scientific Adviser to the National Gallery in London in 1934, in an article first published in 1950,[lxxii] spoke of the "unity in essentials between the arts and the sciences", adding that such a condition implied "a precondition, and that is the existence of a common language". Over half a century has passed since that time, and this unity in essentials is still separated by the lack of a common language between the arts and sciences, so that they do indeed have the appearance of being antitheses. Antitheses that Hegel saw as having "in all time and in manifold forms preoccupied and disquieted the human consciousness, although it was modern culture [in our times as well as his] that elaborated them most distinctly, and forced them to the point of unbending contradiction";[lxxiii] this is true within the field of restoration as it is in so many others.

Einstein's theories allow for the equal validity and coexistence of contradictory views. The fundamental importance of the frame of reference within this new non-mechanical view of the world, when transferred into the field of restoration, brings to the fore the importance

---

[lxx] Sir Joshua Reynolds, *Discourses on Art* (1975), Disc. XIV, 10 December 1788, l. 412–421 (also quoted by Gombrich in *The Image in the Clouds*, in *The Image and the Eye*, p. 168. Gombrich also quotes a wonderful phrase from a Chinese treatise on painting: "Idea present, brush may be spared performance"!

[lxxi] Heisenberg's "uncertainty principle": one cannot measure both the position of a photon or an electron (the particle-like aspect) and its momentum or movement (the wave-like aspect) at the same time, only one or the other. In fixing one, the other is lost.

[lxxii] I. Rawlins, *Aesthetics and Gestalt* (Nelson, 1953), p. 66.

[lxxiii] Hegel, *Introduction to the Philosophy of Fine Art* (trans. Bernard Bosanquet, London, 1886), p. 103.

for the restorer of having access to the sources: not only material, but also documentary. In eliminating the distinction between the supposed objectivity of science as compared to the subjectivity of art, and shifting the emphasis in the understanding of the behaviour of particles and charges in physics away from their intrinsic nature[lxxiv] to that of their nature in relation to each other and to particular conditions, Einstein rejoins artists in their understanding of the nature and handling of materials they used to create works "to make an impression on the imagination and the feeling …".[lxxv]

Having begun this essay with words by Einstein, I should like to end in the same fashion. Speaking of the new vision of reality which his theories had brought about, he says:

"A new reality was created, a new concept for which there was no place in the mechanical description …. But it would be unjust to consider that the new theory destroys the achievements of the old. The new theory shows the merits as well as the limitations of the old theory, and allow us to regain our old concepts from a higher level …. To use a comparison, we could say that creating a new theory is not like destroying an old barn and erecting a skyscraper in its place. It is rather like climbing a mountain, gaining new and wider views, discovering unexpected connections between our starting-point and its rich environment. But the point from which we started out still exists and can be seen, although it appears smaller and forms a tiny part of our broad view gained by the mastery of the obstacles on our adventurous way up".[lxxvi]

[lxxiv] A. Einstein and L. Infeld, *The Evolution of Physics* (Cambridge University Press, 1938), pp. 157–158.
[lxxv] Hegel, *Introduction to the Philosophy of Fine Art* (trans. Bernard Bosanquet, London, 1886), p. 103.
[lxxvi] A. Einstein and L. Infeld, *The Evolution of Physics* (Cambridge University Press, 1938), p. 159.

Notes from the translator

As a translator, my challenge has not been dissimilar to the one I have faced as a restorer for the past twenty-five years: to be true to the spirit as much as to the letter of a work, and transmit as truthfully and coherently as possible its meaning, to a generation which belongs to a different culture or time to that of its original author. It also implies that the personality of the translator/restorer remains invisible or at least unobtrusive, to the degree that the work does not appear to be either a translation or a restoration. You, the public and reader, are in both instances the best judges of the degree to which this is successful.

In the jargon of translators, a translation can be either text or reader orientated, which immediately tells you that translations, like restorations, are a personal interpretation and rendition, however well informed. They can aim to be true to the spirit and letter of the original, or attempt to convert this original into a language that is accessible to the widest possible contemporary audience.

With Hegelian support, I can state that – like the artist – the translator and the restorer cannot but reflect the times they live in, willingly or unwillingly. If reader/observer orientated (that is, reflecting the present times), all translation, whether of a text or on a painting, will to some degree be a modernization, and as such is liable to become out of date. Both the translator and the restorer aim to be as true as is humanly possible to the original, with an understanding of the context within which the work was created, so that in the translation/restoration the materials (whether words or paint) have similar meaning and effects.

The scope and erudition of Alessandro Conti's book are such that my task as a translator has been two-fold: to translate Alessandro Conti's own text and commentary in a manner which would be accessible to readers, whilst retaining the characteristics of his style, and to translate the wealth of documentary material with which the majority of English readers will be completely unfamiliar in such a way that the texts nevertheless retain the flavour of the times in which they were written. I did not want a fourteenth-century text to sound, or read, like an eighteenth-century one, nor that either text be reduced to twenty-first century easy-speak.

Like Conti, I strongly feel that for restoration to move forward in its practices, it is absolutely essential to return to the sources: the documentary sources in their language of origin. Because of this, wherever possible, I have included the original text, or else the particular term by the side of my interpretation, in order to allow readers who possess Italian, French or Spanish to make their own judgement, and for those who do not, to provide some guiding lights in the vocabulary that they may encounter when reading contemporary texts.

The original impetus for this translation was my increasing despondency at the fact that over the past twenty years, I have had fewer and fewer students with anything other than their maternal tongue; because of this, students have been unable to consult first hand documentation relating to works of art, and argumentation and practice have relied heavily on received and perceived material, with no consequent advances in learning and knowledge in this field.

The chilling thought was that there would be no new generation of scholars who would be able to balance the knowledge acquired from first-hand material sources (from the progress in the technical analysis of the materials of works of art themselves) with progress in the uncovering and deciphering of contemporary documentary sources from the times, both technical and cultural. Language is a tool of scholarship within the field of restoration.

Restoration vocabulary and terminology in Italian are much richer, and have more shades of meaning than in English, reflecting the long tradition which, like its art, lies at the foundations of restoration practice and theory in the West. Single words, like pigments, change hue depending on their context and the light in which they are seen, and such words I have also given in their original as well as in English.

I hope it is indicative of the present climate that the present volume by Alessandro Conti, which is the only comprehensive attempt to chart the history of restoration in any language, should see the light of day in English, within two years of Cesare Brandi's equally comprehensive *Theory of Restoration* (Nardini, 2005), which deals with the philosophical and theoretical bases of the same: more than a quarter of a century since they were written.

Navigational notes

The notes at the end of each chapter are Alessandro Conti's, and therefore the "I", both in the notes and in the chapters (except, of course, within a direct quotation), refers to Conti's own thoughts and opinions. The footnotes at the bottom of each page are mine, and therefore the "I" in these reflects my thoughts and feelings, either as a translator or as a restorer.

At the end of the book you will find a glossary, which has been drawn up to clarify some of the terminology associated not only with the material and optical properties of paintings, but also with conservation and restoration treatments. It is not exhaustive by any means, and concerns only paintings, and mainly easel paintings at that, which are my particular field of expertise. For a glossary of relevant terms to sculpture, I refer you to Nicholas Penny's excellent *The Materials of Sculpture* (Wiley, 1993). To all those interested in translations of the human spirit, I recommend Umberto Eco's *Mouse or Rat? Translation as Negotiation* (Orion, 2004).

Helen Glanville

Acknowledgements

I should like to thank all friends and colleagues who have supported me in their various and multiple ways over the past two years, and without whose help I could not have brought the project to completion, as well as the enthusiasm and receptiveness of my students – past and present.

In particular, I thank Claudio Seccaroni and Isabel Horovitz for their linguistic, critical and moral support over the years as well as during this project; John Wilkinson, Fiona and Tim Clarke, Angela Hall, Amanda Paulley and Mick Doran, Babeth and François Calmettes, Yannick Lintz and Georges Lampel, Marie-Thérèse François-Poncet and Muriel Boulmier for enabling me to keep body and soul as one over the protracted period of the project; Helen Weston, Isabel Horovitz, Alice Tate-Harte, Tanya Glanville-Wallis, Mary Bustin, Michael Komanecki, Rhona Macbeth, Nicholas Penny and Victoria Leanse for their critical readings; also Nana Kuprashvili, Jacqueline and Thurloe Conolly, Jean-Pierre Haldi, Jean Woodward, Spike Bucklow, Libby Sheldon, Alison Wright, Ashok Roy, David Bomford, Helena Attlee and Alex Ramsay, Candida and Giles MacDonogh, Justin and Fiona Mundy, Karen and Merlin Unwin, Matthew and Elvira Wauchope, Susie and Bill Crawley, Barbara Canepa. Finally, my infinitely patient offspring, who sincerely hope not to hear the words "translation" and "relativity" again, for a very long time.

My thanks also go to the Churchill Memorial Trust Fellowship, which in 1981 funded me to study the theories and practice of restoration in Italy, to the London Library, without whose existence and understanding I could not have survived as an independent researcher, and to my editor Stephani Allison for being so supportive, and such a good midwife.

Responsibility for any errors or misunderstandings is, of course, mine alone.

Helen Glanville

1

Towards restoration

1. Some notes on its ancient origins

The great architect–restorer, Eugène Viollet-le-Duc, referring to the Latin terms *"reficere"*, *"instaurare"*, *"renovare"*, immediately specifies that these terms do not mean to restore, but to recover or make afresh. He observes, with a conscious self-satisfaction in his own set of values so characteristic of the nineteenth century, that both the concept and the practice [of restoration] are modern. The conclusions of the great architect–restorer are not belied by Pliny's accounts of the various events and misadventures surrounding the conservation of famous works of art: when we examine the sources, they would seem to indicate that works of art were considered more as trifles (*"ludicrae"*) to delight the ear and the eye (*"ad voluptatem aurum atque oculorum"*), as Seneca observed, rather than being instances of a figurative discourse, bearing a cultural message.[1]

The problems associated with images pertaining to Christian worship are of a different nature: and this is without taking into account problems more purely anthropological, such as considerations on the nature of objects of worship and their transmission. When Origen in his *Thirteenth Homily on Genesis* compares man to an image painted by God, on which man himself has then painted the earthly image with its vices, like colours hiding the original paint, it becomes clear that images were preserved with appropriate repainting from the very earliest times. The practice of maintaining icons through repainting, respectful of the iconography of the image, shows us the most usual method of conserving an image; the importance of the example expounded by Origen, is that it shows that in the first half of the third century, this practice was sufficiently widespread for him to be able to extract from it an easily accessible moral fable.[2]

Of even greater significance is what is implicit in Origen's comparison between the original image and the one repainted by man with all his sins. With reference to the transmission of images, it allows one to clarify a concept which is even now central to the vision of restoration and its aims, and which is as deeply rooted in the Biblical tradition of the garden of Eden as it is in the myth of the Golden Age: the return to a primitive state which is better than the present one. The deep roots of this vision in both mythology and Western religious tradition allow us to understand (and this we can observe on a daily basis) how dangerous this vision can become when restoration is approached without an adequately critical spirit: indeed, it induces one to pass over the concept of the ageing of materials, and often will impose the model of a return to the original (*ripristino*), whatever the cost.

1. Head of Livia, reused in the
Herimankreuz; Cologne, middle
of the eleventh century. Cologne,
Diocesan Archiepiscopal
Museum.

2. Antonio da Faenza, remount-
ing of a head of Tiberius; 1581.
Florence, Museo degli Argenti.

3. Coppo di Marcovaldo,
Madonna; with repainted heads
dating from the end of the
thirteenth century. Orvieto,
Museo del Duomo.

Moreover, transferral, survival and new context for a work of art are not all one and the same thing: we need only look at the long history of the reuse of antique fragments in the Middle Ages. Without again running through a subject that has already been adequately covered, I should only like to mention the head of Livia, which was used in the ninth century for the *Herimankreuz* in Cologne, because it lends itself easily to comparisons with similar salvage operations that occurred within the compass of sixteenth-century collecting, such as the head of Tiberius in the Museo degli Argenti in Florence. In its new context, the head of the *Herimankreuz* takes on the meaning of the head of the Redeemer: its use as such may have been suggested by the recognition of its formal perfection, or else by its suggestive qualities of the past glories of Rome, and the collapse of paganism and its replacement by the new Christian faith. It exemplifies how a different context can give new iconographic meaning to the recovered fragment, and imbue it with new ideological values. Tiberius' head, adapted in 1581 to fit a new rich and ornate gold mounting by Antonio da Faenza, may have been interpreted and treated more or less respectfully, but has nevertheless been presented according to the subject attributed to it; it testifies to the existence of an ancient world that can serve as an example, but is no longer retrievable. Restoration can only repropose iconographic or formal values, to a fragment which is in itself an artistic or a historical rarity.[3]

1, 2

The reworking (*rifacimenti*) of altarpieces from the end of the Middle Ages presents us with a wide spectrum of adaptations, renewals and repaintings; an artist charged with the maintenance of a painted panel would find it difficult to refrain from some little touch of repaint, perhaps to brighten the colours that the cleaning had not sufficiently revived, or else to bring the painting up to date iconographically or in line with the prevailing taste of the day. With the onset of the use of X-radiography as an analytical tool, more and more images have been discovered beneath the ones we see; a number of scholars now fear to manoeuvre their way round this minefield, after so many thirteenth-century panels have been found to have been repainted at a date insidiously close to that of their creation, leading to many errors in chronology.

For example, Coppo di Marcovaldo's *Enthroned Madonna* in Orvieto serves as a lynchpin in the reconstruction of the Master's œuvre, and it is on this work that the appraisal of the artist as a precursor to Cimabue now rests. During the recent restoration of the work at the Istituto Centrale del Restauro, it was discovered that the principal heads had been completely repainted, probably as the result of damage caused by fire. It seems to me that no other conclusion can be put forward (and in this I differ from those directing the restoration) but that the repainting was carried out in the last years of the thirteenth century by a painter who had seen the work of Cimabue. His presence can be detected especially in the neck of the Madonna, with its closed, harmonious outline resembling that of a Greek vase, and in the Romanesque, almost succulent, foliage of the crown.[4]

3

The most venerated panels might be subjected to multiple repaintings, as can be seen in the half-length figure of Saint Dominic in the Fogg Art Museum (Cambridge, Massachusetts), a fragment from a Sienese work painted not long after the canonization of the saint in 1233. The earliest repainting of the head dates from the decade after 1260, whilst the third (which constitutes the present image) was painted about twenty years after that, and can be attributed to the workshop of Guido da Siena. The hands have also been painted over at least once, and even the tunic has at some point been brought up to date; finally, the gilded halo seems to be a punched decoration dating from the fourteenth century.[5]

4

*4. Circle of Guido da Siena,
Saint Dominic; palimpsest
panel, Cambridge (Mass.), Fogg
Art Museum.*

In recent times, this type of intervention has led to various misunderstandings and difficulties in dating, as happened, for instance, after a series of errors surrounding the figure of Agostino Veracini, whose work it is impossible to recognize with any certainty in a series of reconstructions in the Greek manner. As to what the philosophy should be regarding any possible intervention on these repaintings (which should at all events be one that avoids their destruction), has been expounded on with great clarity by Giovanni Romano. It should be borne in mind that copies and falsifications of thirteenth-century paintings of a satisfactory standard are a very recent twentieth-century phenomenon (for instance, the Volpi *Madonna*, exhibited in 1937 in the Giotto Exhibition). The *Madonna dell'Impruneta* (painted in 1758 by Ignazio Hugford in imitation of the no longer visible image) is a good example of the limitations of eighteenth-century artists struggling with the style of the Early Masters, despite having a passionate devotion to their art.[6]   5, 6

With the onset of the fourteenth century, it became possible to link works of art on which can be seen ancient restorations with documentary accounts that give a relatively detailed picture of the work undertaken, especially in the instance of the Tuscan cities that have been more intensively studied by art historians and archivists. In Pisa, for example, we see this in the frequent references to the repairs carried out on the frescos in the Camposanto; from the earliest references in 1371 to the point when, in 1523, il Solazzino works on the *Inferno*, a restoration to which Vasari also refers.[7] Restorations can be seen in Siena on works that still exist and are often of great renown, such as those carried out by artists of the stature of Duccio or Simone Martini. The latter, in 1321, repainted eight of the most important heads in the *Maestà* of 1315 in the Sala del Mappamondo: a complex case, not least in the chronology of its execution, on which the recent restoration under the direction of Alessandro Bagnoli should shed some light. Whether or not the repainting is linked to conservation problems, it is nevertheless an intervention that brings the work into line with more modern taste.[8]

The most considerable reconstructions that can be considered satisfactory from the point of view of uniting the old *intonaco*[i] with the new can be seen in such famous works as   7
Ambrogio Lorenzetti's *Buongoverno* and the *Guidoriccio da Fogliano* by Simone Martini. It is somewhat surprising that between the time of Cavalcaselle and 1955, the reconstruction in Lorenzetti's fresco was never taken into account, and that it is only during the most recent restoration that the extensive earlier intervention on Simone Martini's masterpiece was noted. The reconstructed part of the *Buongoverno* lies in the section where the wall representing the well-governed city meets the wall decorated with the allegorical figures: whether it was as the result of the violence of one of the turmoils of 1356 or 1368, or the obliteration of figures linked to the old regime once the new government was in place, a significantly large area was reconstructed by Andrea Vanni, with technically excellent results.

The other fresco is, instead, an example of a complete reconstruction, including the application of a new *intonaco*, of the whole area representing the castle of Montemassi. It was executed in a manner so faithful to the original that no scholar, viewing it from below, had ever noticed either the difference, or the hesitations in the handling, which are now evident even in reproduction. It is likely that the offending *intonaco* was knocked down, once the castle painted on it had either been traced or copied in some other manner. It also

---

[i] *Intonaco* is the final layer of very fine plaster, into which the artist would paint with pigments (powdered colours) in water. This is what is commonly known as *fresco* technique; that is, the colour is applied onto "fresh" plaster.

5. Early twentieth century fake; Madonna and Child. Formerly Florence, Volpi Collection.

6. Ignatius Hugford, Madonna and Child; imitation of a thirteenth century panel, 1758. Impruneta, Pieve di Santa Maria.

7. *Simone Martini, Guidoriccio da Fogliano
at the siege of Montemassi, detail; integrated
at the end of the fourteenth century. Siena,
Palazzo Pubblico.*

seems clear that whoever executed the reconstruction still shared the Trecento vision of space: there was no correction of the characteristic perspective construction of that time, nor any overturning of the planar construction, resulting in a representation of Montemassi that is entirely in keeping with the architecture of the stories of Beato Agostino Novello. Thus, this is not an iconographic reworking, as is the case in Lorenzetti's work, but a true integration, once the damaged *intonaco* had been replaced, and which everything suggests is faithful to the original.[9]

The documents in the Opera del Duomo in Siena bear witness to the continuing upkeep of the polychrome sculptures and painted panels in the cathedral. The note of a payment made to one Martino di Bartolomeo on 3 November 1404, for the panel of the altar of the wood-carvers and stone-masons: "to which I put back some colours and saints" ("*a la quale rimessi cierti colori e santi*"), gives us a good idea of the spirit in which this work was undertaken. Martino's intervention was seen as bringing the altarpiece in line with the new demands of worship, changing or adding figures of saints and recovering the colours that no longer carried out their optical function, to use the terminology of modern restoration. This intervention occurred only, and because of, the function of the panel as an object of worship, and as part of the furniture that brought prestige to the cathedral.[10]

In Florence, the Strozzi papers ("*spogli strozziani*") record the ongoing restoration of the mosaics in the Baptistry, common maintenance practice for such decoration, whilst in 1392, Benedetto degli Albizi asked Niccolò di Pietro Gerini to "complete and repair" ("*compiere e racconciare*") a *Deposition* in San Pier Maggiore, of which he left us an interesting record when adding "and it was painted by Maso the painter, a great master".[11]

2. Gothic polyptychs, and frames "in the Antique style"

The attendant parts complementing the works of the Early Masters, in addition to alterations dictated by changes in usage,[12] resulted in a kind of intervention which, by the middle of the fifteenth century in Florence, was not unusual; that is the squaring up of cusped polyptychs within rectangular frames. The spandrels between sections were filled, and pilasters in Renaissance style were added, as well as friezes inspired by the new architectural style. Contemporary documents term these new frames adornments "*all'antica*" (in the Antique style), and it was Offner who had already drawn attention to them as examples of "early modernizations".[13]

Giotto's *Baroncelli Coronation* was modernized in Ghirlandaio's workshop with the specific intent of preserving the figurative elements of a master who enjoyed great prestige among the humanists, and who was still the object of study by artists, as we can see from Michelangelo's youthful drawings which can be dated from these very same years. What was no longer of any great interest was the Gothic frame, which we can imagine being similar to that of Giotto's polyptych in the Pinacoteca in Bologna. The *predella* was preserved in its original length, the main sections brought closer together, eliminating the pinnacles that divided them, and the cusped arches cut down. Only in the central section was an original part of the painting cut: the upper portion of the throne and the coronation with *L'eterno fra angeli*, and this is the fragment that is now in the museum in San Diego, California. The sections were brought together in a beautifully carved and gilded frame, with two pilasters and a frieze decorated with heads of cherubs. More heads of cherubs were painted in the spaces

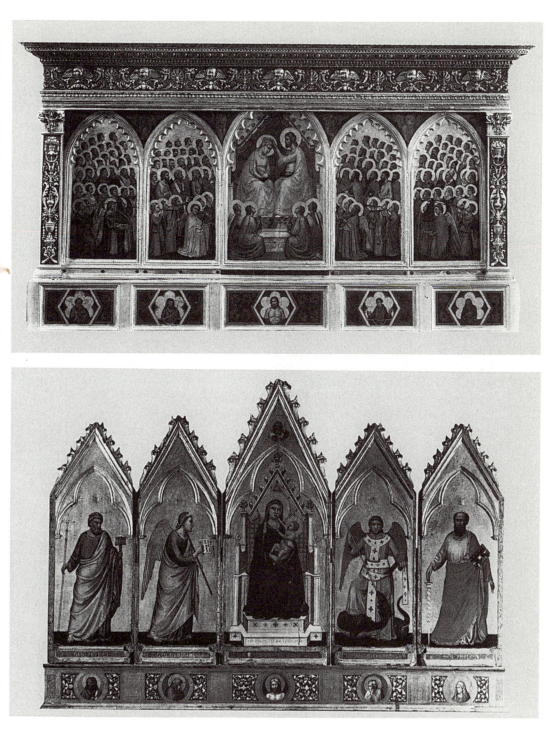

8. Giotto, *Baroncelli Coronation; polyptych reframed by Domenico Ghirlandaio, Florence, Santa Croce.*

9. Giotto, *polyptych. Bologna, Pinacoteca Nazionale.*

10. *Beato Angelico, Saint
Dominic Altarpiece; reframed
by Lorenzo di Credi in 1501.
Fiesole, San Domenico.*

11. *Beato Angelico, Saint Mark; after the removal of Lorenzo di Credi's repainting. Chantilly, Musée Condé.*

12. *Beato Angelico, Saint Matthew, with Lorenzo di Credi's repainting, 1501. Chantilly, Musée Condé.*

created between the cusped arches and the new frame, without any loss in the quality (which one might have expected in such small-scale intervention), which is worthy of Ghirlandaio himself. The actual painting did not undergo any modernization, and the recent restoration did not find any repainting that might be ascribed to Ghirlandaio's intervention.[14]

The care and intelligence with which this painting by Giotto was conserved and (in its own way) enhanced, by eliminating the Gothic woodwork, demonstrates an approach in which there is a distinction between the painting and the object as a whole; a distinction that we still have difficulty in resisting when making the decisions that are often inevitable in the field of restoration. However, it also demonstrates the high quality of these "early modernizations", which are usually presented with a more craft-like concreteness, and preserve the devotional or heraldic–devotional character [of the work]. This is what we find in Neri di Bicci's *Ricordi* which, in 1472, for instance, referring to a panel by Tommaso Soderini in San Frediano, tell us: "altered (*fe' racconciare*) the cusps of the arches, repainted (*rifece di nuovo*) four new cherubs, retouched and repainted almost all of the old figures, and turned San Frediano into Saint Margaret".[15]

The last great example of a polyptych adapted to fit a new frame in the style of the Antique, and by an artist highly acclaimed in his profession, is the reframing in 1501 by
10–12
Lorenzo di Credi of the panel by Beato Angelico in San Domenico in Fiesole. The sections of the old polyptych were regrouped to make a single panel, with an architectural background opening out onto a landscape which replaced the original gold, and the whole then reframed in a large frame in the Antique style. The only areas to be repainted were the throne of the Virgin, the new background and some minor adjustments in terms of perspective. The small figures of the saints, originally painted inside the old Gothic columns, were inserted within the pilasters of the new frame, adapting them to small niches in perspective. I suspect that it is only at this point in time that the *Gloria Celeste* (now in the National Gallery in London) became the *predella* of the work.[16]

In Bologna, Francesco del Cossa repainted (*rifa*) the fourteenth-century fresco of the *Madonna del Baraccano*; he preserved the central section, and then developed an intermediary style between his own and that of the original work, which can be seen in the handling of the folds of the drapery of the central figure. However, the architecture and the landscape background are in complete accord with his painting style in that period (the fresco dates from 1472), for instance in the Griffoni Altarpiece. A similar approach can be seen in Graffione's only documented work, the Madonna, which he adds to the Saints by Baldovinetti in Sant'Ambrogio, in Florence in 1485. This is not much help from the point of view of a stylistic identification of the artist, because of the way in which he tries to integrate his own style with that of Baldovinetti; the iconography and the compositional traits are no longer those of the earlier master, but the chiaroscuro is completely coherent with that of the original figures.[17]

Giannicola di Paolo, in Perugia in 1519, found that he had partly to repaint the *Pala*
13
dei Disciplinati by Giovanni Boccati which he proceeded to do, constructing figures in a style not his own, making concessions to the more archaic style of the fifteenth-century master. However, in his desire to appear archaic, his handling became so awkward that it is easy to discern the vast areas of repainting.[18]

Not so many years later, artists of different stature would soon be demonstrating quite different levels of attention [to the detail], and interpretation of styles not their own, although outside the compass of attempts at conservation or renovation of the paintings of the Early Masters. Moretto gave a perfect imitation of the Gothic style in the embroidered

13. *Giovanni Boccati, Pala dei Disciplinati; detail with the repainting by Giannicola di Paolo, 1519. Perugia, Pinacoteca Vannucci.*

figures on the copes of the Doctors of the Church in the Frankfurt Altarpiece, whilst in the *Saint Luke* in the Church of San Giovanni Evangelista in Brescia, he inserted an icon which reproduced with complete accuracy the stylistic elements of the Greek manner. Rosso Fiorentino represented a small Madonna, in the old style, in the background of his *Portrait of a Young Man* in Naples, with an overall effect which is characteristic, although the poor state of conservation of the painting means that it is not possible to verify the extent to which the new consciousness of "manner", of style, had led him to analyse and then construct the image in a stylistically different manner.

There is no doubt, however, that what we now have before us is a consciousness of *"maniera"* as a system to be used in the construction of an image. It would, before long, be present in Vasari, with all its implications of organic unity and homogeneity as prerequisites for any intervention that alters or makes good (*risarcisca*) a painting. This unity and homogeneity must be present in order for restoration to take on a different physiognomy to that of the painter's normal activity.

3. Adaptations and renovations at the turn of the sixteenth century

Palatine Manuscript 1001 is one of the finest collections of recipes in the Biblioteca Nazionale in Florence; it is written both in Latin and in a Venetian dialect that gives us an indication of its origin, and contains various recipes directed towards the cleaning of paintings. The date of 1561 scribbled on the flyleaf allows us to turn to this text to verify which were the materials and the procedures used in the sixteenth century, and probably also in the preceding century, when a panel appeared excessively dark and one wished to "lighten" it. For example: *To brighten up old gold and pictures:*[ii]

> "Take the finest lime and cover it with three fingers of water in a glazed container, and let it dissolve thoroughly with the aid of a stick, and then let the mixture clear. When it is clear, distil it twice with a retort and keep it to one side. Then take ashes from soft wood and mix them together, and if the mixture is strong, so much the better. Take two *inghistere* [measures] of this mixture and five pounds of white soap, finely grated, and with a sponge you will make it dissolve thoroughly in this lye, and then distil it all two or three times, the more the better. Having done this, you mix together three pounds of water made up with the ashes and soap, and one of lime water; when you want to use it, first of all

[ii] *Al dar el lustro all'oro vecchio e alle pitture.*

"*Abbiate calcina viva perfettissima, sopra la quale vi metterete tanta acqua che avanzi tre ditta di sopra, e di queste metterete in un vaso vedriato et faretela disfar molto bene con una bachetta, poi lassate schiarire, quando sarà chiara fattela distilar per lambico doi volte e serbatela, poi pigliate cenere di legna dolce et farette una lissia comuna, et se la sarà forte la sarà meglio assai; di questa ne piglierete due inghistere et sabon bianco libre cinque rassato sottilmente et con una sponga lo farette disolver in detta lissia bene, poi distilate detta mattera doi o tre volte, et quanto più tanto sarà megliore; fatto questo mescolerete insieme libre tre di acqua fatta di cenere et sapone et libra una di acqua di calcina; et quando vorrete adoprarla, prima netterete bene la tavola dalla polvere, poi con una sponga bagnerete nel sievo predetto e preparato. Bagna la tua opera fin a che la vederai bella, da poi con acqua chiara et netta lava la tua opera dalla maistra, da poi lassate secare et con la bocha al fondo sopra calcate con il bambaso gli darete il lustro. Ma nottate che bisognandovi lavare le figure tanto che venghino nette, di fare con tanto destrezza et modo che non li levicate il colore, et quando saranno seche datali sopra della chiara d'ovo che non sia sbattuta, item se l'ovo sarà sottile basterà solamente la maistra*".

clean all the dust from the panel, then you will wet a sponge with the aforementioned and previously prepared tallow. Keep washing your work until it is beautiful, then with clear and pure water wash away the mixture; allow it to dry and, using cotton wool, with the remnants in the recipient, shine it up. Note, however, that having to wash the figures so that they appear clean, you must do this with such skill and in such a manner as not to remove the colour; when the painting is dry, pass over it a hand of egg-white which has not been beaten; similarly, if the egg is very thin, the mixture will be sufficient [in itself]."

It is a question of being able to emulsify sufficiently well the alkaline substance with the fatty or proteinaceous components, which allow the process to be slowed down or regulated: the care and skill of the painter were of course the determining factors for keeping the operation within the desired limits. Other recipes also indicate the use of honey, presumably as a substance that would keep what would later be termed the "corrosive substances" in suspension, and limit the depth of their action. Present-day restorers use similar methods when they wish to control reagents, in order to obtain the level of cleaning that seems to them to be the most appropriate for the painting entrusted to their care:

Method of renovating paintings on panel or on walls or on gold, which are old and they will appear new:[iii] "Take a new, glazed cooking pot and put into it a pound of black soap and an *inghistera* [measure] of a mixture made of strong ash and quick lime as you know how, then boil it until the soap has dissolved, and then remove it from the fire. Have to hand a glass of strong white vinegar, three whole eggs and an ounce of common salt, and having put everything into a bowl mix it just as though you were making a broth. Take a lira's worth of white honey, and mix it well with the other ingredients; when you are ready, you will be able, either with the finger or the brush, to quickly spread the mixture on the figures and the gold. Have the sponge to hand and wash it away, but see that the sponge is imbibed with weak lye, which is better than water. When you are wetting [the surface], make sure the mixture or the water is clean and pure, and work quickly with the sponge and lightly, and you will make the paintings appear as newly painted; if you wish to clean them, take white of egg and fig's milk, mix well as you know how, and then proceed."

To do the same:[iv] "Take one pound of the finest white soap, two ounces of ammonium salts, three ounces of white cherry gum, as much well water as is required, let everything dissolve thoroughly and then use as above."

[iii] *Modo di rinovar piture sopra tavola o vero in muro et sopra oro che siano vechie pareranno nove: "pigliate una pignata invedriata nova et mettetevi dentro una libra di sapon negro et una inghistera di maestro fatta di cenere forte e di calcina viva come sapete, dipoi farete bollire fino ch'el sapon sarà disfatto, poi levatelo dal foco, poi abbiate un gotto d'aceto forte bianco, tre ovi con la chiara et rosso et una oncia di sal comune, et ogni cosa posta in un cadino, messeda come proprio voleste farti brodetto, poi torete lira una di miel bianco et con le predette cose mescolatelo ben insieme, et quando vorete operare sarete presto con il dito o con il pennello in onger le figure e l'oro, et subito abiate la sponga et lavarate, ma fatte che la sia bagnata in lissia dolce ch'è meglio che in acqua, et quando bagnerrete, fatte che la lissia o l'acqua sia netta et chiara et siate presto in adoprar la sponga et operar però leggermente, et farete le vostre opere come se fusse fatta da novo; se le vorete mondificar, pigliarete chiara d'ovo et late di fico, et messedate bene come sapete et operate".*

[iv] *Al medesimo: "Recipe fior di sapon bianco libre una, sal d'armoniaco oncie doi, gomma di cerese bianche oncie tre, acqua di pozzo netta quanto basti, et farete risolver ogni cosa bene et operate come è ditto sopra".*

14. *Piero della Francesca, Saint Jerome; with the repainting dating from the early years of the sixteenth century. Berlin Dahlem, Staatliche Museen.*

15. *Piero della Francesca, Saint Jerome; after the removal of the repainting dating from the early years of the sixteenth century. Berlin Dahlem, Staatliche Museen.*

Or else: *To clean figures painted on a wall or on a panel so that they appear new*:^v
"Take oak ash and the same quantity of quick lime and mix everything together, making a warm lye. Then take some honey, black soap, yolk of egg (equal quantities of each), and make sure that everything is well bound together, then rub with this tempered mixture which is proven [to work]; if the figures are painted on wood, only the mixture is necessary, and then to wash them with a sponge".[19]

Naturally, one or other of the recipes would have been chosen according to what was compatible with the technique of the figures requiring cleaning (painted or sculpted), and also according to the speed required for the results. A slower and less hazardous method might be chosen not only to avoid the risk of damaging an important painting but also, from a more craftsman-like point of view, in order to save on the time which the repainting of an abraded area would have taken, with all the added problems of making new parts fit in with the old.

It is from precepts such as these that we can better understand what happened at the beginning of the sixteenth century to Piero della Francesca's *San Jerome*, now in Berlin. Up to the restoration carried out between 1968 and 1972, the presence of sixteenth-century paint covering much of the little panel which was dated 1450, had been noted, but it was thought that the work that had been left unfinished had then been completed at the turn of the sixteenth century. The highly abraded paint surface that emerged on removing the overpaint made it clear that the repainting had been a means of correcting the excesses of the cleaning; repainting showing great respect towards the figure, as well as the niche carved out of the rock containing books and the cartouche with the signature, but more freedom in the landscape, and with the trees "restored" exclusively to fulfil their iconographic function. The most evident stylistic updating (which led to misunderstandings by Bode, and a doubt on the authenticity of the work on the part of Longhi) can be seen in the sky, in which the clouds that articulated the depth of the painting (as they do in the *Baptism* in the National Gallery, London, and in *The Battle of Constantine*, Arezzo) were painted over. The author of the repainting replaced the highly developed spatial definition of the sky painted by Piero della Francesca, which was typical of fifteenth-century taste, with a *sfumato* which, following the norms of early classical taste, from the intensity of the far sky becomes paler by degrees towards the horizon.[20]

More often, it is only a question of a change in taste that leads to modifications in a painting and to the elimination of some detail that is disturbing because of its antiquated appearance: Michiel, for instance, when describing a Giovanni Bellini in the house of Antonio Pasqualino on 15 January 1532 (it is difficult not to think that he is referring to the *Madonna Frizzoni* in the Museo Correr in Venice). He notes the repainting by Catena, observing the pictorial merits of the work, but without passing comment on the problem of different hands:

"The half-length figure of Our Lady, much smaller than life, painted in glue-size (*a guazzo*), was by the hand of Giovanni Bellini, reworked (*riconciata*) by Vincenzo Catena, who replaced the textile in the background with a blue sky. It is many years since he did this and it is clearly outlined, with the strong highlights

---

^v*A far nette le figure dipinte in muro et in tavola che pareranno nuove:* "*Recipe cenere di rovere et tanta calcina viva et messedate ogni cosa insieme, poi fattene lissia caldata, poi pigliate del mile, sapon negro, et rosso di ovo, tanto di uno come dell'altro et fatte che ogni cosa sia insieme incorporate, poi con questa lissia distemperata et con questa frigate ch'è cosa provata: se le figure fussero di legno, basta solamente la lissia et con una sponga lavarle*".

poorly blended with the half-tints; nevertheless it is a work worthy of praise for
the grace of the heavens, for the drapery as well as the other parts".[21]

Repainting could aim to give a more traditional air to a painting, as well as updating it; this
can be seen very well in the *Orazione nell'Orto* in the predella of Raphael's *Colonna Altarpiece*,
which was entirely in keeping with the reputation of the "simple and venerable" women, as
Vasari described the nuns of Sant'Antonio in Perugia, for whom it was painted. A comparison with the small cartoon of the Pierpoint Morgan Gallery and with the X-radiograph
shows that the *Orazione dell'Orto* is rendered easier to read with the flying cherub replacing
the original chalice, and that greater impact is given to Christ's profile, which originally was
too foreshortened for the image to be read easily by an uneducated eye.[22] The small adjustments are the work of an Umbrian painter, contemporary of Raphael, rather than by the
master himself. However, it is not always easy to distinguish between autograph alterations and
those carried out by an assistant, a follower or a trusted collaborator of the artist. I am thinking
of works that remain in the artist's studio for a long time and are picked up again at a later date,
as was the case with Correggio's unfortunate *Madonna del Coniglio*: all the final adjustments,
made by the artist himself, were removed during the wretched restoration of 1935.[23]

    There are times when the alterations or reworkings revealed by the X-radiographs, ultra-
violet or infrared examinations, cannot be interpreted except as being by the hand of the artist,
the author of the original version. In order not to destroy these autograph re-elaborations, it
would suffice, as a philosophy of conservation, to remember the principle that does not allow
for restoration (overpaint) to be removed unless it can be proven to be such through dating.
I am thinking, again, of a particular example: Paolo Uccello's *Madonna and Child* in the National
Gallery of Ireland, Dublin, in which the removal of the blue veil covering the Virgin's head
attenuated the look of a "Peasant Virgin", to use Alessandro Parronchi's vivid expression. This,
on its own, can explain why either the commissioner, or Paolo Uccello himself, had opted for
a solution in which the Virgin's head played a less active role within the character of the image,
which otherwise has more in common with a perspectival theorem than an object of devotion.

    Although the repainting covered some areas of damage, a later date is not possible
because no-one would have taken the trouble to imitate the style of Paolo Uccello (even allowing for recognition of the authorship of the panel, as well as the ability and the understanding
to do so), at a time when repainting alterations were still largely a matter of bringing works up
to date. The veil that was removed shared precisely those stylistic characteristics that many prefer to attribute to the "Maestro di Prato", as distinct from Paolo Uccello. At the end of the
nineteenth century, when the little panel first entered the art market, we find it in the Bardini
Collection with an attribution to Lorentino di Arezzo; such a solution, already confirmed by
the earliest photographic images, would never have been considered at a time pre-dating the
insertion of the panel within the works of either Paolo Uccello or the "Prato Master".[24]

    At times it can be a much more straightforward case of taste dictating an autograph
repainting, as in the case of the portrait by Antonello da Messina in Berlin, once upon a time
dated 1478. We are indebted to Longhi for identifying the sky and the landscape as old
repainting: to the stylistic elements ("the projected shadows in the head are too strong to
have been conceived in 'plein air'") are added the optical behaviour and physical characteristics of the paint with which the sky and landscape are rendered, typical of overpaint. They
lack luminosity, because of the original black paint that continues to show through, whilst
"to make a bit more room for the landscape (nevertheless somewhat curtailed) the right
shoulder has been dismantled so that it no longer has the perspectival weight found in the

16. *Paolo Uccello, Madonna and Child; after the removal of the autograph repainting. Dublin, National Gallery of Ireland.*

17. *Paolo Uccello, Madonna and Child;*
with the autograph repainting. Dublin,
National Gallery of Ireland.

18. Giovanni Bellini, Madonna Frizzoni; with the sky repainted in the sixteenth century. Venice, Museo Correr.

19. Correggio, Madonna del Coniglio; with autograph repainting. Naples, Museo Nazionale di Capodimonte.

20. Correggio, Madonna del Coniglio; after the removal of the autograph repainting. Naples, Museo Nazionale di Capodimonte.

master's other portraits." However, on close examination of the painting, one can detect that the lead-white or lead-tin yellow highlights on the hair are in fact painted over the sky; despite its incongruities, the repainting is clearly autograph. Should we want to express our dissatisfaction, we will have to limit ourselves to suggesting Jacobello da Messina as the author of the landscape, or else find other solutions within Antonello's workshop.[25]

In the light of what in the idealist theory of restoration is called the "aesthetic case"[vi] (*"istanza estetica"*), the conservation of a reworking executed by the artist himself (or within his workshop) is not a foregone conclusion, as the original painting often has an effect of

---

[vi] I am using here the translation of *"istanza estetica"* as it appears in the recent (and long overdue) English translation of Cesare Brandi's *Teoria del restauro*. (*Theory of restoration*, ed. Giuseppe Basile, trans. Cynthia Rockwell, Nardini Editore/Istituto Centrale per il Restauro, 2005.)

greater freshness, whilst the reworking will have the material dullness, the opacity, characteristic of overpaint. It is, I believe, giving way to temptations of this kind, that in 1967 the lunette forming the pinnacle of the Pala Felicini by Francia (*Dead Christ with Angels*) was returned to its initial state, which is dated 1494. This involved the removal of the complete repainting of the work that was executed in the later style of the painter, probably towards 1515, when other adjustments were also made to the central section of the altarpiece as can be seen in the cleaning test on the right shoulder of Saint John the Baptist. If the quality of Francia's earlier painting aesthetically justifies such a debatable course of action, one must nevertheless note that the solvents and reagents used to remove the second painting did cause an impoverishment of the 1494 paint layer, with some areas of damage that are now particularly noticeable in the most visible wing, belonging to the angel on the right.[26]

4. The restoration of frescos

The problem of the conservation (*manutenzione*) and the substitution of cycles of frescos when these have reached an extreme degree of disrepair can be followed clearly in the Venetian documents of the Palazzo Ducale from as early as 1409, when it was noted that in the Sala del Maggior Consiglio "much has been lost in the paintings"; however, the Ufficiali al Sal "have [had] these paintings restored with the money of the community, which could be done for an expense of less than two hundred ducats".[vii] A deliberation of the Senate of 9 July 1422 reiterated the necessity of entrusting a painter with the upkeep of the paintings which "fall apart as we speak", "for the everlasting glory and praiseworthiness of such solemn, ceremonial works and for the honour and glory of our lord and city".[viii] On 1 September 1474, Gentile Bellini's offer was accepted, to maintain the paintings of the Sala del Maggior Consiglio "in good condition" ("*ben in conzo*") without other remuneration than the concession of the first available brokerage of a warehouse ("*sanseria de fondego*"). And, in 1479, when Gentile was in Constantinople, the task was entrusted to Giovanni Bellini.

When, in 1515, Luca Luchini (assistant to the deceased Gentile and to Giovanni Bellini) offered his services for the maintenance of the paintings in the Sala del Maggior Consiglio, he was no longer referring to the late Gothic frescos, but to canvases painted by the Bellinis, by their assistants, and to the canvases by Alvise Vivarini and Carpaccio: there came a moment in time when, to preserve the order in the hall, it became necessary to replace the paintings which were too damaged. In this instance, the move was also made from fresco to canvas. In Lorenzo Malipiero's *Annali Veneti*, Gentile and Giovanni Bellini were not referred to as having painted anew, but as having restored the *Battaglia dei Veneziani con Barbarossa*; this concept of restoration would mean that still today, in the canvases by Tintoretto, Bassano, Veronese and his heirs, we would be seeing the same hall as originally decorated with the frescos of Gentile da Fabriano and Pisanello, at least inasmuch as they celebrated the same episodes of Venetian history. Or again, in the Sala dei Giganti di Liviano in Padua, we would have before our eyes the cycle of *Illustrious Men*

[vii] "*multum destruitur in picturis*"; "*dictas pictures faciant reaptari dedenariis nostril communis cum quam minori sumptu fieri poterit nontraseunda summum ducatorum ducentorum*".

[viii] "*cadunt in dies*", "*prolaudabili et perpetua fama tanti solemnissimi operis, et pro honore nostril dominii et civitatis nostrae*".

21. Antonello da Messina,
Portrait of a Young Man. Berlin
Dahlem, Staatliche Museen.

22. Ambrogio Lorenzetti, Il Buongoverno; detail with the integration by Pietro di Giovanni Orioli, 1492. Siena, Palazzo Pubblico.

(*Uomini Illustri*) which the Carrarese commissioned in the fourteenth century, in the frescos renovated by Domenico Campagnola and his assistants in 1540.[27]

The making good of lost parts, or the renewing of areas of perilously attached *intonaco*, necessarily involved interventions that one could class as restorations because of the need to harmonize the new areas with the original, using techniques adapted to match the original paint application, and imitating some of the stylistic features, even if not showing a real understanding of the style. In 1467, when Benozzo Gozzoli worked on the *Maestà* by Lippo Memmi in San Gemignano (and this is after Bartolo di Fredi's additions in the second half of the fourteenth century), he imitated the pointed feet of Trecento painting in the figure of Saint Louis, and reproduced the friezes and the uncial script (already obsolete) of the original inscriptions with great care.[28]

Analogous, but also more complex in his capacity to achieve a balance between his own style and that of the original, is the manner in which Pietro di Giovanni Orioli carried out the vast integration on the extreme right of Ambrogio Lorenzetti's *Buongoverno*. Until the recent clarifications on the identity of Orioli by Alessandro Angelini, the portion repainted in 1492 had been confused with the later restorations by Girolamo di Benvenuto: the earlier restoration follows the stylistic characteristics of the fourteenth-century master in the depiction of the mountains, especially in the way that they are profiled along the horizon against the ultramarine of the sky. More than one detail bears comparison with the landscapes by Orioli, for instance the *Sulpicia* in the Walters Art Gallery, Baltimore, which, despite some hesitation in the handling, eliminate any possible doubt on the authorship of the integration in the *Buongoverno*.[29]

During the Renaissance, accounts have also reached us of the transfer of frescos: Michiel in the house of Alessandro Cappella in Padua recalled seeing "the head of Saint John in fresco on wall, by the hand of the Florentine Master Cimabue, now placed in a wooden frame, which was removed from the church of the Carmelites when it was burnt down". This is one of many examples of the removal from a fresco of small sections of the *intonaco*, such as we encounter in all periods, and which were carried out when demolition or whitewashing was impending. Often, the loss of a head in a fresco revealed when the whitewash was removed indicated that an attempt had been made to remove such painted "crusts". There are countless examples, right up to Stendhal writing in 1837 about the Papal Palace at Avignon, where the occupying soldiers had been busy cutting out "heads by Giotto" from the fourteenth-century frescos, in order to sell them to passing tourists.[30]

Quite other is the aim of the *trasporti a massello*[ix] of wall paintings. The earliest such transfer for which we have documentation is that of Piero della Francesca's *Resurrection* in Sansepolcro, transferred from one wall to the other of the Palazzo Comunale, presumably around 1474, when building work was being carried out. The surface is well preserved, the only verifiable damage being in the loss of part of the columns which framed it in perspective.[31]

That both Vitruvius and Pliny the Elder should refer to painted walls being moved from Sparta to Rome in 59 BC probably made of the operation yet another example of a *paragone* in which the architects of the Renaissance pitted themselves against the Ancients. In a manuscript that can be attributed to Baldassare Peruzzi, in which he deals with the merits of brick walls (which is exactly the same context in which Vitruvius speaks of the transfer of mural paintings),

---

[ix] *Trasporto* or *stacco a massello* is a different method of detaching frescos from their original walls, as the painted plaster is removed along with part of the wall. With the technique of *strappo*, only the painted "crust" is removed.

he noted: "In my city Siena, a work worthy of great admiration, eighteen foot across and twelve foot high, of wonderful and ancient paintings, cut out and transferred to a new location in the residence of the Merchantia."[32] From the fifteenth century onwards, the transfer of frescos *a massello* was practised, and destined to have a long life right up to the attentions devoted to it by Forni in 1866, even if the practice did not always have the felicitous results we can see in Piero della Francesca's *Resurrection*; it was Mengs who made the point that: "in similar cases, it always happens that with the fresh damp, and with the salts in the plaster, that a kind of encrustation forms, covering the frescos and making them apparently disappear".[33]

Notes

1. E. Viollet-le-Duc, 1854–1868, p. 14. The most systematic collection of information on restorations carried out on works of art in Greek and Roman times is that put together by Michelangelo Cagiano de Azavedo, 1952 and 1965. I do not share the views of Giuseppe La Monica, who sees in the interventions dating from Antiquity of which we know, veritable prototypes of every type of subsequent intervention in the field of restoration; see *Ideologie e prassi del restauro*, Palermo, 1974. The problem of whether or not the figurative arts are simply hedonistic in their content is closely linked with whether the artist is considered to be a cultural agent or not. Limiting myself to a few quotations from a restricted spectrum of easily consulted sources, see the anthology edited by F. Coarelli, *Artisti e Artigiani in Grecia*, Bari, 1980. The reference to Seneca comes from *Ad Lucilium epistulae morales*, letter 88, paras 21–23. See the discussion of further examples in Conti, 1973, pp. 31–32 and 208.

2. Origen, *In Genesim homil. XIII*. Among the medieval icons on which repaintings have been found see P. Cellini, *Madonna di San Luca in Santa Maria Maggiore*, Rome, 1943; A. Morassi, *Capolavori della pittura a Genova*, Milan–Florence, 1951, pp. 27–28; C. Bertelli, *La Madonna del Pantheon*, in "Bollettino d'Arte", 1961, pp. 24–32; I. Toesca, *L'Antica Madonna di Sant'Angelo in Pescheria a Roma*, in "Paragone", n. 227, 1969, pp. 13–18.

3. On the reuse of marbles and other ancient materials see Greehalg, 1984; Settis, 1986, pp. 383–410. On the head of the *Herimankreuz* see R. Wesenberg, *Das Herimankreuz*, in *Rhein und Maas. Kunst und Kultur 800–1400*, catalogue of the exhibition, Cologne 1972–1973, II, pp. 167–176. For an important example of votive layering in goldsmithery, on the reliquary of Saint Faith of Conques, see Gauthier, 1977.

4. The most recent repainting is strong and of good quality, so much so that it has been attributed to the "Maestro della Madonna di San Brizio" by Miklos Boskovits (*Intorno a Coppo di Marcovaldo*, in *Scritti Procacci*, 1977, pp. 94–105). However, I am not sure that I am in agreement in attributing to this master a painting which I consider influenced by models deriving from Cimabue in around 1280. The Istituto Centrale del Restauro proposed an absurdly late date for the reworking of the work based on its being executed in an oil medium, see Cordaro, *Il problema dei rifacimenti e delle aggiunte nei restauri ...*, in "Arte Medievale", 1983, pp. 263–276; *Dalla raccolta alla musealizzazione*, edited by G. Testa and R. Davanzo, Todi, 1984, p. 14; J. Polzer, *The Virgin and Child enthroned from the Church of Servites in Orvieto*, in "Antichità viva", 1984, n. 3, pp. 5–7. I shall not go into the arguments raised by Annarosa Ciofi Luzzato and Laura Conti, for whom the presence of oil is linked to its use as a medium in the repainting, excluding its ancient use in the upkeep of works of art. The deduction of a date beyond the fifteenth century which is echoed by Polzer, and that of Cordaro who sees the oil repainting as "much later", both forget the discussion of oil as a medium in Cennini and even in Theophilus, demonstrating a rather surprising lack of information on ancient techniques.

5. G. Stout, *A Puzzling Piece of Gold-leaf Tooling*, in "Notes" in the Fogg Art Museum, 1929, pp. 141–152; C. Gomez Moreno–A. K. Wheelock–E. H. Jones–M. Meiss, *A Sienese St Dominic Modernized in the Thirteenth Century*, in "The Art Bulletin", 1969, pp. 363–366. The punches used for the fourteenth-century repainting also occur in the works of Ugolino di Nerio, see M. S. Frinta, *Note on the Pounced Decoration of two early Painted Panels in the Fogg Art Museum*, in "The Art Bulletin", 1971, pp. 306–307. The *Saint Francis* signed by Margarito in the Pinacoteca in Arezzo suffered a similar fate, the original image, which is visible in the X-radiograph, painted over after an interval of maybe twenty years. See A. M. Maetzke, *Nuove ricerche su Margarito d'Arezzo*, in "Bollettino d'Arte", 1973, p. 108.

6. Romano, 1984, p. 30, with references to the most notable mistakes. An instance of two superimposed paintings which was resolved through the separation and recovery of both paintings, thanks to the presence of an intermediate layer of varnish separating the two, is that of a small cross in the Museo Bandini in Fiesole, described in Procacci, 1953.

7. Vasari, 1568, I, p. 184; F. Bonaini, *Memorie inedite intorno alla vita e ai dipinti di Francesco Traini*, Pisa, 1846, p. 103; L. Tanfani Centofanti, *Notizie di artisti tratte da documenti pisani*, Pisa, 1898, pp. 193, 279, 448; Lupi, 1909, p. 54; Papini, 1909, pp. 441–457; M. Meiss, *The Problem of Francesco Traini*, in "The Art Bulletin", 1933, pp. 159–160.

8. I. Hueck, *Fruhe Arbeiten des Simone Martini*, in "Munchener Jahrbuch", 1968, pp. 29–60. For some of the most important examples see: P. Bacci, *Fonti e commenti per la storia dell'arte senese*, Siena, 1944, pp. 136–137; C. Brandi, *Il restauro della Madonna di Coppo di Marcovaldo nella chiesa dei Servi di Siena*, in "Bollettino d'Arte", 1950, pp. 160–170; E. Carli and C. Brandi, *Relazioni sul restauro della Madonna di Guido da Siena del 1221*, in "Bollettino d'Arte", 1951, pp. 248–260; L. Tintori–E. Borsook, *Gli affreschi di Montesiepi*, Florence, 1969; L. Bellosi, *Jacopo di Mino del Pelliciaio*, in "Bollettino d'arte", 1972, p. 75.

9. On the *Buongoverno* see: Cavalcaselle–Crowe, 1864–1866, III, note 1 p. 224; Brandi, 1955. The repainting of the *Guidoriccio* was discovered as a result of the recent restoration campaign, in the wake of the interest prompted by the grotesque hypothesis that it is not by the hand of Simone Martini. See M. Seidel, "*Castrum pingiatur in Palatio*", in "Prospettiva", n. 28, 1982, p. 24.

10. G. Milanesi, *Documenti per la storia dell'arte senese*, I, Siena, 1854, pp. 285, 651; V. Lusini, *Il Duomo di Siena*, I, Siena 1911, notes 9, 36, 59, 60 pp. 238 and following, notes 37, 63, 77, 140, 143 pp. 317 and following; P. Bacci, *Fonti e commenti per la storia dell'arte senese*, Siena, 1944, p. 164.

11. Milanesi, in Vasari, I, 1878, note 2 p. 628; G. Milanesi, "Nuova Antologia", 1870, pp. 13 and following, reprinted in *Sulla storia dell'Arte Toscana. Scritti vari*, Florence 1873, p. 339. For the restoration of mosaics carried out in Florence see: Milanesi, in Vasari, *Vite …*, I, Munich, 1911, p. 323. Interventions for the maintenance and the adaptation of mosaic works in the Middle Ages have received fairly extensive coverage in the literature. To cite only a few of the most important: Riolo, 1870, pp. 7–9 and 40; Gerola, 1917; J. Wilpert, *Die Romischen Mosaiken und Malereien der Kirchlichen Bauten vom IV bis XIII Jahrhundert*, Freiburg, 1917; Ricci, 1930–1937; G. Bovini, *L'aspetto primitivo del mosaico teodoriciano raffigurante la "Civitas Classis"*, in "Felix Ravenna", 1951, April, pp. 57–62; C. Bertelli, *Un antico restauro nei mosaici di Santa Maria Maggiore*, in "Paragaone", n. 63, 1955, pp. 40–42; Matthiae, 1967. On the restoration of mosaics in the fifteenth century see: Vasari, 1568, I, p. 381; Milanesi, in Vasari, III, 1878, note 1 p. 274; L. Fumi, *Il Duomo di Orvieto e i suoi restauri*, Rome, 1891, pp. 18–114, 140–164; A. Bellini Pietri, *Guida di Pisa*, 1913, p. 142; Kennedy, 1939, pp. 237–238, 249–251; Ponticelli, 1950–1951, pp. 123–126; H. W. Kruft, *Domenico Gagini*, Munich, 1972, p. 248.

12. It is worth recalling the custom, common at the time of Lorenzo Monaco, of outlining the most ancient crucifixes (see Conti, 1973, p. 210).

13. R. Offner, *A Corpus of Florentine Painting*, III, V, New York, 1947, note 10 pp. 88–89; B. Berenson, *Homeless Paintings*, ed. London, 1969, pp. 44–45; G. Sinbaldi–G. Brunetti, *Pittura italiana del Duecento e del trecento*, Florence, 1943, n. 145; B. Klesse, *Der Meister der Hochaltars von San Martino a Mensola*, in "Mitteilungen des Kunsthistorischen Institutes in Florenz", 1959, pp. 245–252; U. Procacci, *La tavola di Giotto sull'altar maggiore della chiesa della Badia fiorentina*, in *Scritti di storia dell'arte in onore di Mario Salmi*, II, Rome, 1962, pp. 17–20, 38–43; Marcucci, 1965, pp. 48, 50, 111; F. Guidi, *Per una nuova cronologia di Giovanni di Marco*, in "Paragone", n. 223, 1968, p. 36; M. Boskovits, *Appunti su un libro recente*, in "Antichità viva", 1971, n. 5, p. 9; Conti, 1981, pp. 40–41; G. Ragionieri, *Fra adattamento e "restauro": polittici e cornici all' "antica"*, in *Domenico Ghirlandaio. Restauro e storia di un dipinto*, catalogo della mostra, Figline Valdarno, 1983, pp. 24–26.

14. F. Zeri, *Due appunti su Giotto*, in "Paragone", n. 85, 1957, pp. 75–87; Ragionieri, op. cit. On Ghirlandaio's willingness to undertake minor commissions and for interventions on older paintings in his workshop (such as the Galli Dunn polyptych by Taddeo Gaddi in the Metropolitan Museum, New York) see: Vasari, 1568, I, p. 462; G. Carocci, *Il museo di Firenze antica*, Florence, 1906, p. 16; Conti, 1979, p. 153; A. Conti, in *Domenico Ghirlandaio. Restauro e storia*, op. cit., p. 7; C. Caneva, in *Capolavori a Figline*, catalogue of the exhibition, Figline Valdarno, 1985, p. 46. The lack of success which could result, technically, from inexperience in this type of work can be seen in the reworking of the faces of the Virgin and the Child in the altarpiece painted by Botticelli for Sant'Ambrogio, for which Berenson proposed Perugino as the author, see *Un Botticelli dimenticato*, in "Dedalo", 1924–1925, pp. 17–41.

15. On Neri di Bicci's various interventions on the panels of Early Masters, see: Milanesi, in Vasari, III, 1878, notes pp. 85–86; E. Borsook, *Documenti relative alle cappelle di Lecceto e delle Selve di Filippo Strozzi*, in "Antichità viva", 1970, n. 3, pp. 3–20; B. Santi, *Dalle Ricordanze di Neri di Bicci*, in "Annali della Scuola Nazionale Superiore di Pisa", classe di lettere, 1973, pp. 175–177; Neri di Bicci, 1976, pp. 19, 35, 66, 222, 353, 357, 382–383.

16. Vasari, 1568, I, p. 360; J. Pope-Hennessy, *Fra Angelico*, London, 1974, pp. 189–190; U. Baldini, *Contributi all'Angelico: il trittico di San Domenico a Fiesole e qualche altra aggiunta*, in *Scritti Procacci*, 1977, pp. 236–246.

Lorenzo di Credi is also responsible for the addition of the griffins in the frame of the monument to Sir John Hawkwood by Paolo Uccello, see: Milanesi, in Vasari IV, 1879, note 5 p. 568; Reymond, *L'architecture des peintres aux premières années de la Renaissance*, in "Revue de l'Art", 1905, p. 48 and note 1.

17. Baraccano's fresco was detached in 1969 by Ottorino Nonfarmale. On this subject, see the entry in *Arte e pietà*, catalogue of the exhibition, Bologna, 1980, n. 1, pp. 145–147. The fourteenth-century image is not, however, by the hand of Lippo di Dalmasio, but is the work of an earlier master, relating to some of the works by "Pseudo Jacopino". On Graffione see: Kennedy, 1938, pp. 248–249; Conti, in "Paragone", n. 223, 1968, pp. 18–19.

18. U. Gnoli, *Giannicola di Paolo*, in "Bollettino d'Arte", 1918, pp. 41–42; M. Bacci, *Il punto su Giovanni Boccati*, in "Paragone", n. 231, 1969, note 13 p. 33.

    In Umbria, at the turn of the century, many panels were modernized: for instance, the repainting (close to Caporali in style) of the *Madonna* by Duccio in the Pinacoteca in Perugia, the face of the Madonna in the altarpiece by Boccati now in Budapest, the repainting of the fourteenth-century *Madonna* stolen in August 1970 from Santa Maria Maggiore in Spello; see: F. Santi, *Galleria Nazionale dell'Umbria*, Rome, 1969, p. 43; M. Bacci, *Il punto su Giovanni Boccati*, in "Paragone", n. 233, 1969, note 31 p. 19; E. Lunghi, in *Pittura in Umbria tra il 1480 ed il 1540*, Milan, 1983, p. 142.

    In Naples, the *Saint Anthony of Padua* in San Lorenzo Maggiore is an interesting example of the persistence of the old practices of bringing paintings up to date: the figure of the saint, close in style to the work of the "Maestro di San Giovanni da Capestrano", is accompanied by putti by the hand of Leonardo da Besozzo. Both can be ascribed to the date (repainted) of 1438, and can probably be dated to about twenty years later, see: Celano, I, pp. 120–121; F. Bologna, *Il Maestro di San Giovanni da Capestrano*, in "Proporzioni", 1950, p. 93 and note 39 p. 98; F. Bologna, *Napoli e le rotte mediterranee della pittura*, Naples, 1977, p. 109. Often, the repainting carried out by artists in the early part of the sixteenth century will be read in a devotional key, as was the case in Bolognese restorations attributed to Francia by Malvasia (1686, pp. 239, 287) and by Oretti (ms B 30 in the library of the Archiginnasio in Bologna, c.385 v.); or, in Naples, for Andrea Sabatini (see De Dominici, 1742–1743, I, pp. 192, 195; II, pp. 43, 57; *IV Mostra di Restauri*, Naples, 1960, p. 151; P. Giusti–P. Leone de Castris, "*Forastieri e regnicoli*". *La pittura moderna e Napoli nel Primo Cinquecento*, Naples, 1985, pp. 131–132).

19. The manuscript Pal.1001 is described in *I codici palatini della R.Biblioteca Centrale di Firenze*, Rome, 1890–1940, II, pp. 476–477; a selection of recipes found in the Palatine manuscripts should be published in an edition edited by Gabriella Pomaro, to whom we owe many of the transcriptions. The precepts quoted in the text are from c.41, where we also find: "Take as much refined linseed oil as you require and as you will need, and you will always keep some [ready] refined. This is the manner in which you refine it: first you will take some bread, some ground glass and the oil and you will mix them well together and you will boil them up mixing them as much as is necessary, and then you will put it out at night into the cool air, where you will leave it for nine nights, then drain it and it will be cleaned/refined. *Il modo di lavar [Manner in which to clean]*. Take sand and grind it fine, then take clean water and mix well together and wash using sponges."

    Modo di nettar figure e tavole dipinte dorate o non di marmoro, di legno, di rilievo: "*Recipe oglio di seme di lino purgato quanto volete et quanto vi farà bisogno et ne torrete sempre del purgato. Il modo di purgarlo è questo: prima torete una molessa di pane, vetro pesto e l'oglio et messolate insieme e fatte bollir messedando tanto quanto bisognerà, poi la metterete la notte al sereno et lassatelo per nove notte, poi colatelo et sarà purgato. Il modo di lavar. Pigliate rena et pestatela sottilmente, poi pigliate acqua pura et chiara e messedate insieme et con sponga lavate*".

20. W. von Bode, *Der heilige Hieronimus ... von Piero della Francesca*, in "Jahrbuch der Preussinschen, Kunstammlungen", 1924, pp. 201–205; Longhi, 1963, pp. 219–220; R. Oertel, "*Petri de Burgo opus*", in *Studies in late Medieval and Renaissance Painting in honor of Millard Meiss*, New York, 1977, pp. 342–351; various opinions and facts relating to the events surrounding the *Saint Jerome* are to be found, albeit with rather confused conclusions, in E. Battisti, *Piero della Francesca*, Milan, 1971, note 72, pp. 467–468, II, pp. 5–6.

21. Michiel, pp. 149–150. We also have photographs taken before and after restoration of Giovanni Bellini's *Madonna Fodor*; a restoration which was careful to remove the embellishments introduced by a sixteenth-century painter close in style to Domenico Campagnola, thus revealing the young Giovanni Bellini's landscape, in all its original sparseness.

22. D. A. Brown, *Raphael and America*, Washington, 1983, pp. 120–121. The main sections of the *Colonna Altarpiece* had also been reworked in such a way as to facilitate their reading (in a traditional sense). But these reworkings were much later in date, as I was able to establish in the documentation, kindly made available to me by Keith Christiansen, see also J. M. Brealey in an appendix to K. Oberhuber, *The Colonna Altarpiece*, in "Metropolitan Museum Journal", 1977, p. 91; F. Zeri–E. E. Gardner, *Italian Paintings, Sienese and other Central Italian Schools*, New York, 1980, p. 76.

23. R. Causa, *Deux inedits du Corrège*, in "L'Œil", January 1968, pp. 13–17, C. Gould, *The Paintings of Correggio*, London, 1976, p. 229 (with the absurd claim of affinities between the portions removed and the hand of Alessandro Mazzola).

24. E. Sindona, *Una conferma uccellesca*, in "L'Arte", n. 9, 1970, pp. 67–107, note 1 p. 103; A. Parronchi, *Paolo Uccello*, Bologna, 1974, pp. 21–22. When considering the repainting which was carried out very soon after the original painting, in addition to stylistic considerations one must take into account the information on the painting technique, which Giovanni Urbani communicated to me on 16 September 1970, see Conti, 1973, pp. 211–212.

    The new elements which bring one back once more to an early dating of the *Battles of San Romano* (L. G. Boccia, *Le armature di Paolo Uccello*, in "L'arte", n. 11–12, 1970, pp. 55–91; C. Volpe, *Paolo Uccello a Bologna*, in "Paragone", n. 365, 1980, pp. 3–28) suggest that one should examine with renewed care the adaptations undergone in the distant past by the three panels, as they may well have been executed by Paolo Uccello himself at the time of the their removal from the old Medici houses to be installed in the new palace built by Michelozzo. For their identification see: U. Baldini, *Restauri a dipinti fiorentini*, in "Bollettino d'arte", 1954, pp. 227–235; A. Parronchi, *Paolo Uccello*, Bologna, 1974, pp. 33–34; Conti, 1988, pp. 74–78.

25. See Roberto Longhi's introduction to the first edition of this volume (pp. 16–17); the hypothesis of the execution of the "pentiment" by Jacobello is due to Fiorella Sricchia Santoro (*Antonello e l'Europa*, Milan, 1986, pp. 139, 170).

26. The main section of the *Pala Felicini* may have already undergone some "modernization" towards 1500, probably after damage incurred during the unfortunate events in which the church of the Misericordia was involved, at the beginning of the sixteenth century, see: R. Rossi-Manaresi–J. Bentini, *The Felicini Altarpiece …* in *La Pittura nel XIV e XV secolo*, 1983, pp. 395–422.

27. L. Malipiero, *Annali veneti dall'anno 1457 al 1500*, in "Archivio storico italiano", serie I, VII, 1844, p. 663; Cavalcaselle–Crowe, 1864–1866, IX, note 1 p. 70; G. Lorenzi, *Monumenti per servire alla storia del palazzo ducale di Venezia. Parte I, dal 1253 al 1600*, Venice, 1868, pp. 52, 53, 57, 85–86, 88–89, 91, 92, 162–163, 182, 309; Olivato, 1974, pp. 13–16. On the iconographic programmes of the canvases in the Ducal Palace, see W. Wolters, *Der Bilderschmuck des Dogenpalasts*, Wiesbaden, 1983. On the *Sala dei Giganti* in Padua, see M. M. Donato, *Gli eroi romani tra storia ed "exemplum"*, in *Memoria dell'antico nell'arte italiana*, II, Turin, 1985, pp. 103–106.

28. L. Bellosi, in *Mostra di opere d'arte restaurate nelle provincie di Siena e Grosseto*, catalogue, Genoa, 1981, n. 4, pp. 24–31.

29. For the identification of Orioli, see A. Angelini, *Da Giacomo Pacchiarotti a Pietro Orioli*, in "Prospettiva", n. 29, 1982, pp. 72–78; on his restorations and those of Girolamo da Benvenuto in the Sala della Pace, see: G. Milanesi, *Documenti per la storia dell'arte senese*, Siena, 1854–1856, II, p. 392; Milanesi, in Vasari, I, 1878, note 1 p. 528; Cavalcaselle–Crowe, 1864–1866, III, note 1, p. 224; A. Angelini, *Pietro Orioli e il momento "urbinate" della pittura senese del Quattrocento*, in "Prospettiva", n. 30, 1982, p. 43 and note 26 p. 39; Angelini, 1982.

    The unity of style, even in the iconographic adjustments, can also be found in the restoration carried out by Fogolino on the frescos of the *Mesi* in the Torre dell'Aquila in Trento. Bernardo Clesio wrote to his overseers from Prague on 25 May 1534 recommending that the paintings "should not differ in any detail, and in all the areas in which, because of humidity or for some other reason, the figures are coming away, see that some composition is put in their place, so that one does not have to repeat the operation several times. If the need arises, give Master Marcello more workers, as we have written", see A. Morassi, *Come il Fogolino restaurò gli affreschi di torre Aquila a Trento*, in "Bollettino d'Arte", 1928–1929, pp. 337–367. For other reworkings (*rifacimenti*) either by or attributed to Fagolino, see L. Puppi, *M. Fagolino*, Trento, 1966, pp. 18, 30, 44, 46.

30. Michiel, p. 40; E. Castelnuovo, *Un pittore italiano alla corte di Avignone*, Turin, 1962, p. 159 (extract from the *Mémoires d'un touriste*, 1839): "the soldiers detach from the wall and sell to the *bourgeois*, the heads painted in fresco by Giotto … the red outlines of the original drawing are still visible on the walls"; "*les soldats détachent du mur et vendent aux bourgeois les têtes peintes à fresque par Giotto … les contours rouges du dessin primitif sont encore visibles sur les murs.*"

31. C. Tolnay, *La Résurrection du Christ par Piero della Francesca*, in "Gazette dea Beaux-Arts", 1954, note 1 pp. 35–36; E. Battisti, *Piero della Francesca*, Milan, 1971, II, pp. 33–35, which is a rich mine of information, indicating, against his own conclusions, that the *Resurrection* was at one time transferred "*a massello*".

32. Vitruvius, II, 8–9; Pliny, XXXV, 173; A. Parronchi, *Un manoscritto attribuito a Francesco di Giorgio Martini*, in "Atti e memorie dell'Accademia toscana di Scienze e Lettere La Colombaria". XXXI, 1966, pp. 165–213.

33. Mengs, 1783, pp. 155–156; cited in Merrifield, 1846, p. 115.

2

Conservation of works of art in the sixteenth century

1. The restoration of ancient statues

The practice of reusing [ancient sculpture] as filling material was for a long time destined to coexist with the earliest interventions that might be described as "restorations"; that is, with interventions that sought to give back to ancient fragments the completeness that would enable an improved aesthetic appreciation and, more often than not, a subject matter without which the figure would remain illegible, in terms of a representation linked to the fundamental requirements of "history". Fifteenth-century Venice was the city that presented the richest array of examples of the traditional reuse of materials, this reuse gradually turning into solutions that could be classed as restoration, at least in the sense of the word during the Renaissance.

What to make of the fine statue representing *Saint Paul* in an eighteenth-century niche in Campo San Polo? The ancient statue has in fact a head in the style of the Bon workshop, not seemingly overconcerned with problems of imitating the style of the original: completed in this manner, the whole was inserted into the lunette of the Gothic portal of the church of San Polo. And can the insertion of a Roman bust in a niche decorated in the style of Bartolomeo Bon in Calle Bon or dell'Arco, be simply considered the reuse of material?

Restoration of a kind can be detected in the head, thought to be of Plato, "with the tip of the nose made of wax", which Niccolò and Giovanni Bellini sold to Isabella d'Este in 1512, and which originally formed part of the inheritance of Gentile Bellini. As often the case in Venice, in the context of its relationship with the Antique, there was no end of stories, veiled with a particular mystery, such as that of the *Berlin Ephebus* discovered on Rhodes, which was apparently completed with a bronze foot that Bembo had found in Padua, which fitted it to perfection (at least, that is the tale passed on to us by Enea Vico).[1]

It is difficult to find such a wealth of examples elsewhere; there is little that can be reconstructed of Vasari's "endless antique heads placed above doors", which we are told were restored by Donatello (we know that these were, at least in part, put in order by Verrocchio) for Palazzo Medici. In the marble sculptures that are still in existence, or which passed into the Grand Duke's collections, we can no longer identify these first adaptations, which were substituted as the taste in collecting changed. We know only that the "the white antique marble depicting Marsyas, placed at the entrance to the garden" (restored by Donatello, according to Vasari), corresponds to the sculpture which is now in the Uffizi, but the attribution of the restoration still requires verification. The other *Marsyas*, given to be restored to Andrea Verrocchio and now lost, was praised by the great sixteenth-century historian for the way in which "it had been worked with so much judgement and skill, that certain fine white veins which were in the red stone, were engraved by the artist so as to look like nerves, such as are seen in flayed flesh. These must have made this work, when first finished, very life-like".[2]

The completion of an antique fragment required first of all a correct or plausible interpretation of the missing parts, and then their execution in a "manner"[i] that was in keeping with the antique original. Problems would arise when the interpretation of the fragmentary parts seemed to challenge any possibility of comprehension, as is shown by this passage by Ludovico Castelvetro, which has only recently come to the attention of art historians:

"Not many years ago, during excavations in Rome, a large and beautiful marble sculpture of a River [God] was brought to light, its beard broken, and partly missing. Judging by the portion which remained around the chin it seemed that the beard, had it remained intact and taking account of the proportions, should have reached down to the navel. However, the point of the beard could be seen at the top of the figure's chest, not descending any further; all were perplexed, and no-one seemed able to imagine what the beard must have looked like originally. Only Michelangelo Buonarroti, that sculptor of rare and wonderful brilliance, who was present, quietly engaged in his own thoughts, understood how it must have been, and said: "Bring me some clay". With the clay that was brought, he fashioned that part of the beard which was missing, in proportion with the fragment remaining; when added, it reached down to the navel. Then, tying it in a knot, he clearly showed how the point of the beard would then only reach the top of the chest, in the identical place where the point of the broken beard remained. Thus, to the great admiration of all who were present, he demonstrated what the missing beard had looked like, and how it had been knotted".[3]

23, 24   The description of the sculpture allows one to identify it as *Tigris* (*Arno* at the time of Clement VII), which is now in the Vatican Museums, restored with its lordly knotted beard. In this instance, as in the case of the *Laocoon*, which is much better known and documented through copies, drawings and sketches, as well as real attempts at integration, the restoration consists primarily in the interpretation of the original appearance of the now mutilated figure. But once this interpretation had been resolved (which was only possible in the above example, for an artist of the intelligence of Buonarroti), there still remained the problem of which of the options, some more and some less faithful to the original, should be used in the completion of the work.

25   The original position of the arm of the *Laocoon* was understood right from the beginning, when it was discovered in 1506; Amico Aspertini's drawing in the sketchbook in the British Museum was faithful to it, as was the copy executed by Baccio Bandinelli between 1520 and 1525. However, the problem did not present itself in terms of simple reconstruction or faithful renovation (*ripristino*). If one really wanted to show the original to its best advantage, emphasizing its merits (its quality, we might say), rather than simply carrying out

---

[i]Vasari's term "*maniera*" is usually translated by the terms "manner" or "style", and incorporates both the aspects of physical handling of the material and the stylistic elements represented.

a faithful integration, a case could be made for enhancing its "grace" (*grazia*); that is, its sense of movement and rhythm, beyond a slavish imitation of nature. That is what Montorsoli would do, with the outstretched arm in clay with which he replaced the wax arm of Baccio Bandinelli's first restoration. The intrinsic value of this choice is amply testified by its confirmation with each successive restoration, when Agostino Cornacchini refashioned Montarsoli's clay arm in marble between 1725 and 1727, as well as those carried out after the Napoleonic requisitions. Winckelmann, who was well aware of the different position [of the arm] envisaged by the original authors, observed that "the arm bent back over the head would in some way have detracted from the work, dividing the spectator's attention".[4]

Vasari refers to the principle of "grace", when recalling the arrangement given by Lorenzetto to the antiquities restored for the courtyard of Cardinal Andrea della Valle: "within the courtyard he arranged columns, antique bases and capitols, and distributed around the basement, piles of ancient fragments [carved with] stories. On an upper storey, beneath some of the larger niches, another frieze made up of antique fragments; above these, he placed statues – also antique and of marble – which, although they were not intact, some headless or missing an arm and some with no legs at all, that is all missing some portion, he nevertheless managed the whole thing very well, having had excellent sculptors replace all the missing parts. And this is why other gentlemen, following this example, had many antiquities restored; for instance the Cardinals Cesis, Ferrara, Farnese – in short – all of Rome. And it is true, these antiquities have much more grace when restored in this manner, than have those imperfect trunks, or those limbs – headless or in some other respect defective or incomplete".[5]

It is not by chance then, that from the sixteenth century, a sculpture such as the *Torso Belvedere* was left incomplete without reintegrations. Even in its extreme incompleteness, the sense of movement, indeed the "grace", which permeates the work, allowed the figurative message to appear clearly, despite the work's fragmentary state. The restoration of the *Laocoon* with the outstretched arm intervened within the original composition of its ancient authors, thus giving it better "*disegno*".[ii] And this is the attitude that we find behind another famous episode, involving the lower portion of the legs of the *Farnese Hercules* which were completed by Guglielmo della Porta, a restoration that was not removed when the originals were discovered, on the advice of Michelangelo (according to Baglione).[6]

It is also in this vein that we should understand Benvenuto Cellini's intention, his desire to "serve" the master of antiquity who had executed the youthful torso that is shown him by Cosimo I and which formed the basis of the *Ganymede* which is today in the Bargello: "… I do not recall ever having seen amongst the fragments of antiquity, a work of such beauty representing a young boy, nor so finely fashioned. For this reason, I am offering to restore it for Your Renowned Excellency: the head, the arms and the feet. And I shall make him an eagle so that he shall be known as a Ganymede. Although it really does not suit me to cobble together sculptures, because that is the work of cobblers who do it rather badly, the excellence of this master requires that I should serve him".[7]

[ii] "*Disegno*" is like "*grazia*", a concept intrinsic to sixteenth-century art theory, and connected in particular with Vasari. "Grace" as a translation of *grazia* is not too problematic. "*Disegno*" refers specifically to the theoretical aspects of art (in all its concrete manifestations; that is, drawing, painting, sculpture, architecture, etc.), absent from any "craft", which is considered to be purely manual.

23. The Tigris or the Arno; with the integration based on Michelangelo's model. Rome, Musei Vaticani.

24. Marteen van Heemskerk, the niche with the statue of the Tigris. Berlin Dahlem, Staatliche Museen, Kupferstichkabinett.

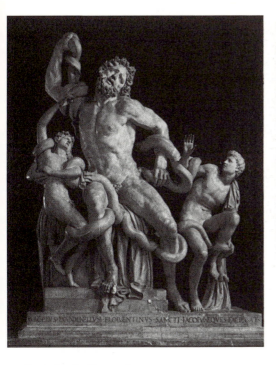

25. Baccio Bandinelli, copy of the Laocoon. Florence, Galleria degli Uffizi.

26. Laocoon; restored with the arm outstretched. Rome, Musei Vaticani.

Underlying all the older restorations, there was also the problem of how to harmonize these with the [original] marble, and the treatment of their finish. Often the surface would be polished, abraded, sometimes even chiselled to blend together the old parts with the new, but also in order to remove the more degraded part of the surface, making it more solid with a view to its future conservation. The use of marbles of a different nature to that of the original was the norm rather than the exception for integrations, to the extent that Raffaello Borghini in his *Riposo*, after having spoken of the putty to be used to "stick the parts together", then went on to describe the method of giving "antique colour to marble":[iii]

> "Some take soot, and put it onto the fire in vinegar, or else in urine, until it reaches boiling point; then they strain it, and use the liquid with a brush to tint the marble. Others take cinnamon, and some cloves and boil them in urine, and the more they boil [it], the darker the colour, and with this warm mixture they give one or two coats to the marble. Others (because there are many

iii "... *alcuni pigliano della filligine, e la pongono al fuoco in aceto, overo in orina, tanto che abbia levato bollore; poscia la colano, e di detta colatura con un pennello tingono il marmo. Altri pigliano della canella, e de' garofani, e gli fanno bollire in orina, e quanto più bollano, tanto si fa più oscura la tinta, e di questa così calda danno una, o due volte sopra il marmo. Altri (perchè si trovano marmi antichi di diversi colori) per poter meglio contraffargli, prendono più colori da dipintori, e gli vanno mesticando insieme con oglio di noce, fin che trovino il colore che desiderano, facendone prova sopra il marmo, e di questo danno, dove fa luogo, per far unire il marmo nuovo coll'antico".*

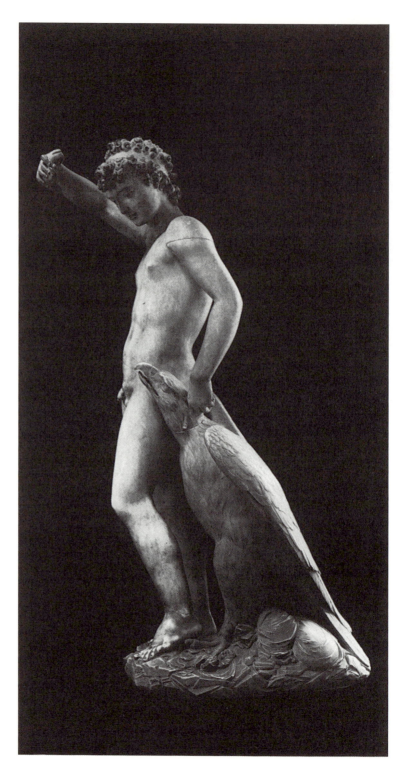

27. *Benvenuto Cellini,*
Ganymede; integration of an
antique marble sculpture,
1548–1549. Florence, Museo
Nazionale del Bargello.

differently coloured marbles), to better counterfeit them, take many painters' pigments, and mix them with walnut oil, until they have the colour they are looking for, trying it out on the marble. And this they use, where necessary, to harmonize the new marble with the old".[8]

Small bronzes and small sculptures fashioned out of precious materials also underwent restoration: Duke Cosimo, when excavations brought to light the *Chimera* of Arezzo (1554), used to amuse himself by cleaning the small bronzes which had been found alongside it, and Cellini would help him by completing the missing parts of the figurines. But Cellini had already restored antique bronzes: in 1546 "the bronze man of fear" (in reality pseudo-antique), and in 1548 a figure for which he had created a horse. In the Museo Archeologico in Florence, there are numerous small bronzes from the Medici collection which were reintegrated in the sixteenth century, especially heads completed with busts of gilded metal and precious stones. Amongst them should be noted an antique torso, Herculean in type, which has new legs, right arm and left forearm, as well as an adolescent head.[9]

2. Giorgio Vasari: works of art and the passage of time

In the sixteenth century, we begin to find observations relating to the conservation of works of art, in writers on art. Michiel, for instance, would observe how in the house of Leonico Tolomeo in Padua, the "portrait of Leonico himself as a young man" by Giovanni Bellini was now all "flaked away (*"tutto cascato"*), yellowed and obscured", and would refer frequently to antique fragments in Venetian palaces, but shown as they were, and not as part of a decorative scheme; rather in the way they can be seen in Lorenzo Lotto's *Portrait of Andrea Odoni* in Hampton Court. In addition, in a work as elaborately drawn up and rich as Vasari's *Lives*,[10] we find a vast field of discussion related to the problems and expectations connected with conservation, and the possibility of survival of works of art.

Despite the Neo-platonic myth of even the waves and the wind respecting Raphael's *Spasimo di Sicilia*, Vasari was well aware of the dangers to which works of *"disegno"* were exposed, "as even marbles and the most eminent works of men are at the mercy of fortune".[11] To remain within the scope of works in the "modern manner", the loss of the preparatory model for a *Venus* by Sansovino, destroyed during the Florence flood of 1557, was to be lamented, as was the extreme damage suffered by Perino del Vaga's *Deposition* which, we are told, would have been "one of the most priceless works in Rome", had it not been submerged during the flood which followed the Sack of Rome: "the water softened the gesso and swelled the wood so that, whatever the water had reached, had peeled right away, so that little of it could now be enjoyed. Rather, one was filled with pity and regret, to see it [in such condition]". Raphael's *Madonna del Cardellino* found itself engulfed when Lorenzo Nasi's house collapsed in 1548: "none the less, having found the pieces amongst the rubble of the ruin, Batista (son of Lorenzo, and a great lover of art) had them put back together as best one could". In 1527, when the Medici were hunted out of Florence, "during the fighting for the Palazzo della Signoria, a bench was thrown from the building onto those who were attacking the door; as luck would have it, the bench hit one of the arms of Michelangelo's *David*, and broke it into three pieces." These pieces were gathered up by Giorgio Vasari and Cecchino Salvati, who were boys at the time, and preserved in their homes, so that in 1543 Duke Cosimo was able to have the three pieces reattached with copper pins.[12]

To ill-fortune then, one must add neglect, as well as the ignorance of those who were unable to understand the importance of a work, especially if in the "old style",[13] or out-and-out vandalism as in the case of the soldiers during the siege of Florence in 1530, who destroyed the marble sculptures prepared by Benedetto da Rovezzano in San Salvi, for the chapel of San Giovanni Gualberto in Santa Trinita.

Often, prized works, such as frescos or buildings, were destroyed out of the necessity to make way for new constructions or decorations; a habitual occurrence, not to be deplored when a work of greater "*disegno*" replaced a lesser one, that is one in the old style or simply one inferior in quality. If such occurrences were to be accepted as inevitable, in as much as bound to the wheel of fortune, as with all human endeavour, Vasari, in a rather more sinister light, also presents us with such works that have been wilfully damaged or destroyed through the envy of artists. Amico Aspertini was reputed to have damaged the antiquities which came within his reach or which he drew; Baccio Bandinelli was thought to have used for his own work certain marbles from San Lorenzo on which Michelangelo had already begun to rough out some figures, had broken into pieces the *Hercules and Anteus*, which Montorsoli had been working on for the Villa Medici in Castello and, worst of all, he had torn into pieces the cartoon for the *Battle of Cascina*.[14]

Confronted with so many incidents that could endanger a work of "*disegno*", it was well to have in mind the advantages that a good technique could bring in terms of the conservation of a painting, the drawbacks resulting from poor choices. Some of the most significant works in the modern manner had [already] darkened excessively through the use of lamp black ("*nero di stampatori*") in the darks: the *Marriage of Saint Catherine*, for instance, by Fra Bartolomeo, Raphael's *Transfiguration* in which the artist had used the pigment almost "through caprice", the panel in Santa Maria dell'Anima by Giulio Romano "because the black, although varnished, dies as it is by nature thirsty, whether it is carbon black, or burnt ivory, or lamp black, or burnt paper".[iv] The poor outcome of the use of lamp black is – of course – for readers of Vasari, almost proverbial, although it seems to me legitimate to ask to what degree should one indeed regret the alteration of this colour, and whether Vasari's annoyance does not principally reflect his opposition to the cold tonality of the shadows in which it was used: less soft, seeming not to share to any degree that brown and enveloping character obtained through painting in the oil medium, that he himself so clearly appreciates in the introduction to the *Vite*. That is, the position he took was an indication of taste, which made him attribute defects in the behaviour of a colour, when in reality, the chromatic choices made [by the artist] were, above all, different from his own.[15]

Good technique would, on the other hand, sometimes favour the preservation of a work; for instance, Rafaellino del Garbo's *Resurrection*, painted in oil, escaped damage from the lightning which struck its frame, so that it can still be seen today in the Galleria dell'Accademia in Florence, in good condition, but in a fine mid-sixteenth-century frame, which obviously post-dates the lightning damage. But if the panel by Rafaellino was simply another example of the excellence of the oil medium, some of the new expedients used by artists to improve the longevity of their works, or preserve their original appearance, did not always meet with Vasari's approval; for instance, Beccafumi's choice of tempera as a medium

---

iv " *conciosia che il nero, ancora che sia verniciato, fa perdere il buono, avendo in sè sempre dell'alido, o sia carbone, o avorio abruciato, o nero di fumo, o carta arsa*".

for the execution of the altarpiece in the Oratory of San Bernardino in Siena, or Sebastiano del Piombo's paintings on stone, of which he denounced the excessive weight.[16]

Copies were made, in order to preserve the memory of works of art, which in themselves were, sooner or later, destined to disappear (as had happened with the works of Antiquity); Vasari recounts how he had Aristotele di Sangallo reproduce in oil a drawing from the cartoon of the *Battle of Cascina* by Michelangelo, "as paper is so easily damaged"; whilst the copy of Leonardo's *Last Supper* was useful to him in order to understand the original, of which, he says in 1566, he could only make out "confused blots".[17] Another way of transmitting the memory of such works of "*disegno*" was to write about them. Vasari lingers with pleasure on the churches in Arezzo, and their works of art, destroyed during the construction of the Medici fortress, and on the buildings knocked down for the defence of Florence during the siege, such as the monastery of San Giusto alle Mura, described at length in the *Life of Pietro Perugino*.

The restorations that occupied his attention most, were the completion of ancient statues, the renovation of mosaic cycles, and the repainting of frescos and panel paintings, about which he was always vexed. Referring to the cherub which had suffered from the damp, and which Sodoma had repainted in Signorelli's *Circumcision* in Volterra, he observed: "it was repainted much less finely than the original"; and that "it would be better at times to preserve the work of excellent masters half ruined, than have them retouched by those who are less able". Of the panel by Fra Angelico in Fiesole, which was enlarged by Lorenzo di Credi, he noted that "perhaps, because it appeared to be deteriorating, it was retouched by other masters, and looks worse", not revealing, out of respect perhaps, the name of the artist who carried out the intervention. On the other hand, he seemed happy enough to name a minor artist such as Solazzino as the author of the repaintings on the *Inferno* in the Camposanto at Pisa. Elsewhere, the author of the repainting remained anonymous, perhaps because he was too second-rate, such as the one responsible for repainting Giotto's *Annunciation* in Santa Croce ("with little judgement on the part of he who commissioned the work to be done"), or else the artist who had in "in a poor manner transformed" ("*in mala maniera condotto*"), a fourteenth-century fresco in the Chiostro Verde in Santa Maria Novella, by repainting a city and a landscape as background to a Crucifixion between two Dominican friars: a repainting which can still be seen in old photographs, and was removed – a questionable choice – when the fresco was transferred from the wall. Confronted with the interventions of such painters, who obviously were excluded from the circle of the most excellent artists dealt with in the *Lives*, rather than it being a question of old or modern manner, it was rather that of "bad style" ("*mala maniera*"), as is suggested by the fate of two tabernacles by Jacopo del Casentino which were remade by "a worse master than Jacopo had been": objectively, falling short of the "greater art" one would rightly expect of a work in the modern manner.[18]

Considering the poor light in which Vasari presents the restoration of paintings, it does not seem like chance that he should put forward as authors of restorations (*rifacimenti*) artists such as Sodoma (a master very far removed from the model of the artist put up for imitation), or Giuliano Bugiardini, who had harmed rather than helped the *Battle Scenes* painted by Paolo Uccello in Casa Bartolini in Valfonda: the latter, a painter in whose *Life* is highlighted the foolishness of an artist whose lines of reasoning continued to reflect the stylistic preoccupations of the beginning of the century, without ever coming near to the greatness and the "grace" of the modern manner.

Moreover, as overpaint and the original paint must always appear different both in handling and for reasons of technique, it is impossible even for the author to obtain satisfactory results when taking up one of his works again after a period of time. When Giovanni da Udine, commissioned by Pius V, retouched what he had painted in the first Loggia at the time of Raphael, "it was an ill-judged mistake, because retouching it *a secco* made it lose all those masterly touches, which had been drawn from Giovanni's brush when he was in his prime; and he lost that freshness, that boldness, which originally had made it such a rare and precious thing".

It was unseemly that a painting, even if painted in the old manner, should be besmirched by an artist of lesser worth than its author, as had happened in the case of the tabernacles by Jacopo del Casentino. On the other hand, there was also the case of works considered so clumsy that an artist who replaced them with works in the "*buona maniera*" became praiseworthy; as was the case with the group of figures by Rustici over the north door of the Baptistry, which took the place of "certain awful marble figures … which had been made … in 1240".[19] In the same way, we find Vasari presenting himself as deserving of praise, for his restorations (*rifacimenti*) to the parish church of Arezzo:

"Moved by Christian devotion, and by the affection in which I hold this venerable collegiate and ancient church, and because it was in this church that, when decked in my first youth, I took my first instruction, and that it contains the relics of my ancestors, I was moved – as I have said – by these reasons, and by seeing it in so derelict a condition, to restore it in such a manner that one could say that from being dead, it returned to life. In addition to having brought light to it (it had been very dark) by enlarging the existing windows as well as making new ones, I also moved the choir, from the front where it occupied a large portion of the church, to behind the altar, to the great satisfaction of the canons".

The altar was also completely refurbished (*rinnovato*) by Vasari: from the altar table, to the baldachin and the altarpiece, all executed at his own expense, so that one cannot even use economic factors to explain the contradiction between his behaviour as an historian and as a restorer. In addition, his opinion on the architecture of the Aretine parish church (referring to the façade and attempting to insert it within a historical perspective) was that "not only is it outside the good old order ("*buon ordine antico*"), but outside almost all canons of true and rational proportions".[20]

Vasari considered that at times it was necessary to destroy works that were too damaged, a practice also recommended by authors of the Counter-Reformation when sacred images were beyond repair, or no longer fulfilled their function as objects of devotion. The principle of decorum remained the same, but in Vasari this concerned not only the devotional aspects, but also the lost figurative dignity of the object. These were the "good reasons" for which the heads painted by Sodoma beneath the frescos of Monteoliveto were removed, as "from some of these heads the eyes had been removed, whilst others had been defaced".

His engagement in promoting the good style ("*buona maniera*") in the "arts"[v] inevitably led to the replacement of works that may have been of historical importance and good in parts (in particular, displaying certain ingenuities of "invention"[21]) with sculptures or paintings

---

[v] Literally, the arts of design, the arts which have an intellectual foundation. See footnote i.

in the modern manner, which could be appreciated in their entirety, thus benefiting the creators [of such works] and contributing to the diffusion of the taste for works in the *buona maniera*. A panel in the old manner could simply give up its pre-eminent position to a work in the new and "better" style, such as that of Pietro Lorenzetti, in the Aretine parish church, with figures judged to be "really beautiful and executed in an excellent manner". This was moved after Vasari's renovations, to "the altar of Saint Christopher at the entrance of the church".

When it came to frescos, the problem became serious, as it was seldom worthwhile, or indeed possible, to undertake the complex task of transferring them *a massello*.[vi] In the Stanze, Raphael had destroyed the existing mural paintings; Michelangelo's *Last Judgement* took the place of three frescos by Perugino as well as two lunettes from the series of *The Ancestors of Christ* painted at the time of the vault. Vasari records as a perfectly normal occurrence the fact that he knocked down some grotesques by Morto da Feltre (the importance of which can be deduced by the fact that he found them worth mentioning at all in the *Lives*) in the Palazzo della Signoria in Florence. Of Raphael, who had not destroyed the ceiling painted by Perugino in the Stanza dell'Incendio, or the cornices by Sodoma in the ceiling of the Stanza della Segnatura, Vasari observed that he showed himself to be "goodness itself and modesty". It is in such a manner that in the Vatican of Pius III, a chapel with frescos by Fra Angelico was demolished, whilst under Pius IV, Taddeo Zuccari's *Labours of Hercules* were lost in the renovation of the Belvedere, and the *Apostles* in the Sala dei Palafrenieri, painted in monochrome earth colours by Raffaello and Giovanni da Udine, were actually destroyed (except for a few strips of flesh).[22]

Of the great Florentine churches in which Vasari was responsible for the arrangement of the new altars once the rood-screens had been demolished, as well as the restructuring of the decoration of the lateral naves, Santa Maria Novella was badly impaired by the restorations carried out in the nineteenth century, which destroyed all of the sixteenth-century ones. Today, we can judge Vasari's attitude towards the works he ran into during his renovation, by his adaptation of the wooden panelling by Baccio d'Agnolo in the main chapel, with back rests for the new choir, for instance; or the way in which he protected the main figures of Masaccio's fresco of the *Trinity* against which he placed an altar in 1570, taking care that the transverse bars of his altarpiece of *The Madonna of the Rosary* did not lead to the chiselling away of the painted wall.[23]

The altars of Santa Croce, from which the altarpieces were removed after the flood of 1966, have shown the differing behaviour of Vasari and other younger painters when confronted with the fourteenth-century works which they were covering with their new works; the remains of frescos, although mutilated in order for the transverse bars to be embedded in the wall, are only found behind the works of Vasari, Alessandro del Barbiere and Andrea del Minga. Behind the other altarpieces, the frescos have been chiselled away completely, including the remains of Ghirlandaio's fresco of the *Storia di San Paolino* which would have been behind Santi di Tito's *Crucifixion*. In the case of Vasari's *Pentecost*, the first of the panels to be installed (in 1568), there is evidence to suggest that an attempt was made to detach parts of Giotto's fresco of the *Crucifixion*, more damaged now (with losses in the most important areas) than any of the other frescos found behind the altars in Santa Croce.[24]

[vi]With part of the wall attached. (See Glossary.)

3. Events involving works of art in the sixteenth century

With the exception of provisions taken for the simple conservation of works of art, or the references to Andrea del Sarto's frescos (the Tabernacle of Porta Pinti, as well as the *Last Supper* of San Salvi) which the vandals of the siege of 1530 did not have the heart to destroy, Vasari refers several times to "*trasporti a massello*", which give us a good indication of what, especially during the demolition of the rood-screen, was considered to be worth saving.[25]

The most obvious instances were those dictated by devotional interests, even if linked to figurative aspects rather than those of worship: for instance, in Arezzo in 1561, Spinello Aretino's painting of *Our Lady who Offers the Christ Child a Rose* [is saved]: a work in which, according to Vasari, "simple grace which holds of modesty and sanctity . . . draws men to hold it in utmost reverence". Otherwise, we see that the works which were saved were almost exclusively fifteenth-century ones; neither the *Martyrdom of Saint Mark* by Stefano in the Cappella degli Asini from the rood-screen of Santa Croce, nor Taddeo Gaddi's *San Jerome*, Giotto's *Saint Ludovico* nor a youthful fresco by Fra Angelico in Santa Maria Novella survived Vasari's readaptations of these churches, although in the *Lives* they are remembered with a certain amount of interest. In Ognissanti, on the other hand, Ghirlandaio's *Saint Jerome* and Botticelli's *Saint Augustin*, which were by "the door leading into the choir", were transferred, fastening them "with irons". Similarly, around 1568, in Santa Croce, the fresco by Domenico Veneziano depicting *Saint Francis and Saint John the Baptist* was also transferred using a metal armature, a band ten or so centimetres wide.[26]

In Parma in the sixteenth century, Correggio's *Annunciation* was transferred (with mediocre results as Mengs recorded), as was his *Coronation of the Virgin*. The first transfer of the *Annunciation* took place when the church in which it had been painted was demolished in 1546 in order to build the fortress, and subsequently it was again transferred, this time to the church of the Annunciata, which Giambattista Fornovo began building in 1566. The shallow dome with the *Vergine ed il Redentore che la incorona*, first brought to the Ducal oratory in La Rocchetta, and then moved in the eighteenth century to the Palatine Library, was originally transferred in 1587, when the apse of the church of San Giovanni Evangelista was built further back to allow for the new placement of the choir.[27] In the new apse, the fresco was copied by Cesare Aretusi and, as well as the principal figures which were transferred *a massello*, some sections of the surface *intonaco* painted with the heads of angels were also detached in the age-old custom of preserving some memory of frescos that were to be hidden or demolished. Similar circumstances, I believe, surround the rescue of the "putto" painted by Raphael, now in the Accademia di San Luca in Rome. It is to this, or to a similar fragment, that Cavazzoni was probably referring when he spoke of "a small putto, painted in fresco, brought from Rome by the hand of Raphael of Urbino" in the house of Count Battista Bentivoglio in Bologna.[28]

In the earlier generations of Mannerists, there was still a live attachment to the paintings of the fourteenth and fifteenth centuries. A generation later it would become unthinkable to hear a painter confess to have "learnt much" as a boy when copying two figures, wasted away through humidity, by Giovanni Toscani in the Duomo of Arezzo, "studying the manner of painting of Giovanni, and the shadows and colours of that work". Of even greater interest, in that sense, is Vasari's tale of Perino del Vaga's visit to Florence in 1523, and his attempt to pit himself against Masaccio. He executed a *Saint Andrew* to accompany Masaccio's *Saint Paul*, right up to the cartoon stage, to demonstrate that in Rome one knew how to

28. *Correggio, Annunciation, detail; transferred with part of the original wall in about 1546. Parma, Museo Nazionale.*

29. *Correggio, Coronation of the Virgin; fragment transferred with part of the original wall in about 1587. Parma, Pinacoteca Nazionale.*

30. *Cesare Aretusi, copy of the Coronation by Correggio. Parma, San Giovanni Evangelista.*

*31. Raphael, Putto;
transferred in the six-
teenth century. Rome,
Accademia di San Luca.*

match the style ("*paragonare*") which the Florentines believed no-one had surpassed "[neither] in the relief, nor the resolution, nor the practice". Massaccio, therefore, still represented a valid paragon and important point of comparison.[29]

It is therefore significant that we find Perino as a protagonist in the rescue of a *Madonna* by Giotto, which would otherwise have been lost in the demolition of the old basilica of Saint Peter's. In his *Life of Giotto*, Vasari limits himself to referring to the "beauty" of the work (a relative "beauty" of course, only such as one might expect to find in a fourteenth-century painting), which had led to its being transferred. In the *Life* of Perino, on the other hand, Vasari focused on two elements that were to become topical from the sixteenth century onwards, when rescuing the work of an Early Master: historical interest and a certain civic "*pietas*" [in this case] for his compatriot Giotto:

> "The old walls of that church were falling into ruin, and as the masons were con-
> structing new ones for the building, they came to a wall on which were painted
> *Our Lady* and other works by Giotto: Perino and his great friend the Florentine
> doctor Niccolò Acciaiuoli, in whose company he was, having seen it, were both
> moved with pity for this painting. They prevented it from being destroyed and,
> moreover, having had the wall cut all around it, they had it secured with metal
> [bands] and beams, and then had it placed beneath the organ of San Piero,
> where no altar or other work had been ordered. And, before the wall which sur-
> rounded the Madonna was demolished, Perino copied the Roman senator Orso
> dell'Anguillara, who had crowned Messer Francesco Petrarca [Petrarch] on the
> Campidoglio, who had been painted at the feet of this Madonna. Also the stuc-
> chi, and decorations around the Madonna, and a memorial to another Niccolò
> Acciaiuoli who had also been a Roman senator. Perino immediately put his
> hand to making drawings and, helped by his young assistants, and by Marcello
> Mantovano who was a relation, the work was carried out with great care".[30]

Historical interest, if not linked to the history of the figurative arts, was not in itself suffi-cient to preserve works of art; ancient customs, effigies of famous characters and other docu-ments could also, and more simply, be transmitted as copies. Of a fresco by Bruno and Buffalmacco in Santa Maria Novella, which would be destroyed not long after the *Lives* had been written, in works which Vasari himself directed, he observed:

> "This painting, although not very beautiful is nevertheless worthy of some praise,
> taking into account the drawing by Buonamico and the invention, and particu-
> larly because of the variety in dress, the visored helmets and the armours of the
> time. I made use of them in some of the histories I painted for Duke Cosimo,
> in which I needed to represent men armoured as of old, and other details per-
> taining to that time, which greatly pleased His Illustrious Excellency and others
> who saw it. And from this, you can judge how much capital can be made from
> the inventions and the works of these Early Masters … ".

Artefacts that were less bulky than frescos, such as the *cassoni* attributed to Dello Delli, were more likely to be preserved as historical documents: many citizens preserved these in their homes, preferring them to modern furniture, as did Vasari himself "because it is good to keep some memory of these ancient things". In the new apartments that he had built for Duke Cosimo in the Palazzo della Signoria, examples were kept "which are by the hand of Dello himself, and which are and always will be worthy of admiration, for the men and women in all the varied costumes of the times which one sees in them".[31]

The favourite kind of historical documentation, following Paolo Giovio's example, was portraits of famous men. Vasari recalls effigies copied from frescos that were due for demolition, and copies executed for Giovio's museum such as certain heads painted by Fra Angelico in the chapel destroyed under Paul III, or others which Raphael instructed to have copied from the frescos of Piero della Francesca and Bramantino, before pulling them down to make way for his own frescos in the Stanze. Of the earliest examples of interpretations taken from "portraits" copied from frescos of the thirteenth and fourteenth centuries, we have no record, as the pieces that have survived from Giovo's collection are of more recent date; while the copies of the copies executed by Cristoforo dell'Altissimo for Cosimo I are too far removed from the original to give us an idea of how a good sixteenth-century artist might have interpreted a passage derived from the work of an Early Master.[32]

But the most pressing problems, and those closest to the preoccupations for the conservation and for the enhancement of works of art, which, in time, would develop into restoration, can be found in the attention that is already required by the great examples of the modern manner. In the Sistine Chapel, the first of the cleaners ("*mundatores*") officially charged with the regular dusting of the frescos was L'Urbino – Francesco Amadori – a servant of Michelangelo. A "*motu propriu*" of Paul III of the 26 October 1543 entrusted him with the lifelong task of maintaining the beautiful paintings ("*pulcherrimae picturas*") (those completed in the Sistine Chapel, and those in progress in the Pauline Chapel) "free of dust and other dirt such as from the smoke of candles which are used during the holy services".[vii] A seventeenth-century cleaning of the frescos, known through a passage found in certain copies of the Mancini manuscript, gives us an idea of the cleaning techniques used: "Under Pope Urban VIII, the paintings in the palace known as Sisto's [that is, the Sistine Chapel], were cleaned, and this is the order of procedure: having removed the loose dust from each figure with a linen cloth, the dust and other worse filth was carefully removed with slices of bread worth a *baiocco* or less, rubbing with care and in some places, where the dirt was more tenacious, then lightly wetting the bread, thus returning the paintings to their pristine beauty without in any way damaging them. This handiwork was carried out by Master Simon Laghi, gilder of the palace, and was begun in January 1625 …".[viii]

Gaspare Celio was probably referring to this cleaning when lamenting that the fifteenth-century paintings in the Sistine Chapel "with wanting them to look fresher, are no longer what they were". As a result of the subsidence of 1565, an actual reintegration of the *intonaco* [and hence paint layer] had been necessary in the vault painted by Michelangelo. Between 1566 and 1572, the vast loss in the *intonaco* in *Noah's Sacrifice* was made good by a little known painter: Domenico Carnevale da Modena. If one examines the restoration without insisting on a comparison with Michelangelo's original, it is difficult not to be impressed by the qualities of this sixteenth-century master. For the reconstruction of the figures, it is possible that he was able to make use of drawings or other graphic documentation, whilst in the handling of the paint he showed the ability – particular to restorers – not to imitate the

34

---

vii "*a polveribus et aliis immunditiis etiam ex fumo luminarium quae in celebratione divinorum in utraque capella fient*".
viii "*Sotto Papa Urbano VIII furono rinettate le pitture della cappella di palazzo detta di Sisto, e l'ordine che si tenne fu questo, che spolverata figura per figura con un panno di lino se gli levava la polvere con fette di pane a baiocco o altro piu vile stropicciandolo diligentemente, e tal volta, dove la polvere era più tenace, bagnavano un poco detto pane e così ritornarono alla loro pristina bellezza senza ricever danno alcuno. Questa manifattura fece mastro Simon Laghi, indora-tore di palazzo, e fu cominciata di gennaro 1625 …*".

original technique, but to make allowances in his integration for his work to be seen from below. To do this, Carnevale used large strokes, as featureless as possible, with which he reconstructed an image which is somewhat anonymous in as much as it did not have any distinctive handling characteristics of its own, but which succeeded admirably in fitting in with the original paint.[33]

The episode recalled by [Ludovico] Dolce of a restoration by Sebastiano del Piombo in Raphael's Stanze (no longer identifiable) is well known. The Venetian writer wished to underline the particular difficulties of harmonizing the differing styles of the two artists. During the Sack of Rome, soldiers had "with little respect lit a fire for their own use in the rooms painted by Raphael, and either the smoke, or they themselves, had damaged some of the heads. Once the soldiers had left, and Pope Clement returned, he was so troubled that such beautiful heads should remain damaged, that he had Sebastiano repaint them."

When Titian visited these rooms in the company of Sebastiano del Piombo "with both his mind and his eyes fixed on Raphael's paintings which he had not seen before, having reached the part in which Sebastiano had repainted the heads, he asked him who had been so ignorant and presumptuous as to besmirch those faces [with paint], not realizing that it was Sebastiano himself who had reshaped them, but only seeing the unseemly difference between the other heads and these".[34]

If the reconstruction appeared as a smear, it would seem permissible to deduce that was because of the alteration that it had already undergone with the passage of time, so that it no longer harmonized with the original. The alteration therefore emphasized the difference in handling, in brushwork, in style, all of which could not originally have been so evident; it also underlined a fundamental disagreement, in which a more highly cultured tradition, more closely linked to artists, will always prefer visible damage, which only interferes to a limited extent with the painting, and does not disturb the "the inner eye" (*l'intelligente*) [to restoration].

At what level, and to what degree did the problem of respect of authorship present itself, is suggested by the differing fates of two unfinished panels depicting *The Adoration of the Magi* in the second half of the sixteenth century in Florence; that is, in a city in which there was an abiding tradition of care and respect for those works of art which were recognized as being of importance. One of these was Leonardo's famous painting which passed from the house of Amerigo Benci to the collection of Francis I in the Casino of San Marco: its unfinished status as a work of art precluded its use as an altarpiece, but made of it a precociously collectable object. It was therefore left in its unfinished state, which sixteenth-century taste was already prepared to accept as an example of Leonardo's style, on whose *chiaroscuro* (which was moreover of exceptional figurative concreteness) no intervention was possible.

The other *Adoration of the Magi* was the one that Giovanni Antonio Sogliani had kept in his studio for many years without ever completing it; when sold at his death as "old stuff" to Sinibaldo Gaddi, it was completed by the very young Santi di Tito and placed in the Gaddi Chapel in San Domenico, such an intervention being necessary in order for the painting to reach its destination. Neither is any attempt made to intervene in the unfinished sections of Raphael's *Madonna del Baldacchino*, and these are still easily distinguishable (and constitute an invaluable guide to an understanding of his technique). These would also be left untouched when Cassana enlarged the panel at the end of the seventeenth century. Therefore, when the works [concerned] were by Leonardo or Raphael, there was no intervention: but

32

33

32. Leonardo da Vinci,
Adoration of the Magi.
Florence, Galleria degli Uffizi.

33. Giovanni Antonio Sogliani,
Adoration of the Magi; com-
pleted by Santi di Tito. Fiesole,
San Domenico.

when a painting was by Sogliani or, in the case of Bronzino's great altarpiece for the nuns of the Conception, when there were circumstances in which the wishes of the commissioners were more strongly heard, the painting would be completed.[35]

From what Dolce recalled of Titian's reaction to Sebastiano del Piombo's retouchings on the frescos of the Stanze, and from what we learn from Leonardo's *Adoration of the Magi* about the respect that was obligatory when confronted with even the unfinished state of a work of art that was universally accepted as such, we can better understand the unease felt when confronted with the problem of intervening on the most important painting in the modern manner: Michelangelo's *Last Judgement* with Daniele da Volterra's famous retouchings. After *The Last Judgement* was unveiled at the end of 1541, the criticisms that would be directed towards it found an authoritative voice in the renowned letter by Pietro Aretino of 1545. But it was not until the pontificate of Paul IV (1555–1559) that the possibility of direct intervention on the painting in order to modify it was considered. Such a possibility was discussed at the actual sittings of the Council of Trent, and at the beginning of 1564 a commission was put into place, specifically to amend the paintings of the Apostolic Chapel. The retouching work did not then begin until after the death of Michelangelo, which occurred on 17 February of that year.[36]

The choice of Daniele da Volterra was made with great tact; he was the artist closest to Michelangelo, and his intervention would have been seen to be the least injurious to the memory of Michelangelo.[37] It would be difficult to imagine how such a task could have been carried out with more discretion, especially in view of the fact that at first a demolition of the fresco had been proposed. The figures of San Biagio and the ample draperies of Saint Catherine's dress were completely repainted in fresco technique, given the ambiguity

34. Michelangelo, *The Sacrifice; detail with the figures integrated by*
Domenico Carnevale, 1566–1572. Rome, Palazzi Vaticani, Sistine Chapel.

to which their position lent itself in the eyes of the worldly. No more than thirty draperies were added, and they were not all by the hand of Daniele da Volterra, as the names of others who intervened on the fresco are known: Girolamo da Fano and Cesare Nebbia in the sixteenth century, in a tradition that was to be renewed right up to the eighteenth century.[38]

Vasari, in the first edition of the *Lives*, made no mention of the problem regarding the alterations that might have to be made on the fresco; it is only in 1568 that he referred to it in the *Life of Daniele da Volterra*: "as Pope Paul IV wished to demolish the *Last Judgement* by Michelangelo because of the nude figures which, he felt, showed the shameful parts in too immoral a fashion, cardinals and men of judgement were of the opinion that it would be a great shame ('*gran peccato*') to destroy them, and they found a solution, that Daniele should fashion some thin draperies to cover them, which task he then finished under Pius IV with the repainting of Saint Catherine and San Biagio, as it seemed that they were not represented with honesty".

According to Vasari, Michelangelo himself was open to suggestions that might resolve the displeasure created by the "shameful parts" which were depicted "too immorally". The master, who was occupied in the building of Saint Peter's, had word passed to Pius IV that "it was a small thing, quickly sorted: he should [concentrate] on sorting out the world, as with paintings this was quickly done". That Michelangelo was amenable to have small changes made in order to make the *Last Judgement* more acceptable, was already known when Gaspare Celio first mentioned the name of Braghettone[ix] for Daniele da Volterra, referring to the work he carried out on Raphael's *Isaiah* in Sant'Agostino, after it had been damaged by a sacristan at the time of Paul IV: it was "retouched by N. called Braghettone because he covered up the obscene parts of the figures in Michelangelo's Judgement by order of the aforementioned Pope, and with Michelangelo's consent"; retouching carried out on the figures "so that the owner would not have them destroyed".[39]

Although Celio represents a rather late source in relation to the events to which he is referring, he nevertheless nicely reflects the ambiguous nature that such a problem presented in the years preceding the corrections: a bad reputation and discredit for the person who intervened on the work of art of another (hence the nickname *Braghettone*), and on the other hand the consent of Michelangelo for what appeared to be the lesser evil, when confronted with the intentions of the "master", Paul IV. It is this double position that is characteristic of the Counter-Reformation: on the one hand, a desire to strengthen the importance of the position of the artist and his autonomy within a strictly professional compass, while at the same time avoiding the creation of unseemly images or ones containing "errors"; that is, images which through their visual message allude to positions condemned by the Church.

Resolving the problem with the application of "thin draperies", in itself a simple solution and respectful of Michelangelo's composition, nevertheless took twenty-three years, taking place at a moment when the figure of Michelangelo was being rehabilitated in Counter-Reformation circles, which leaves more than one question unanswered surrounding these events. But with this, we find ourselves already at the centre of the problems that would be characteristic of the post-tridentine period, when new attention directed towards the image as an object of worship and as a means of doctrinal divulgation led to a series of

---

[ix] *Braghette* are breeches; punning on Daniele da Volterra's activity, clothing nude people.

positions destined to coexist and interweave with that which, in a different field of action, was the conservation and restoration of works of art.[40]

4. Catholic reform and the Counter-Reformation

For the person approaching the events surrounding the conservation, adaptation and restoration of our artistic heritage from the point of view of its present position, the Counter-Reformation (with its prescriptions for the cleanliness of the place of worship and of its furniture, the devotional correctness and efficacy of its images, and the requirement for their correction should they be "badly made", even in a figurative sense), must appear responsible for many of the present ills, in the form of repaintings, arbitrary reductions and changes in context. Exhibitions of restored works are never without some example of a fourteenth-century panel, or fifteenth-century fresco, sometimes even a more recent canvas, which has been freed from devotionally inspired overpainting. It is only recently that an attitude has developed towards these repaintings (*rifacimenti*), which recognizes that they have, nevertheless, some historical significance. Before removing them, questions are beginning to be asked, as to whether their removal is really compensated for by the improved legibility of what is presumed to be the original work.

There are few works that have suffered a devotional restoration without their strictly figurative elements being in any way interfered with, and it is these elements that specifically concern the art historian. It is also true, however, that it is thanks to their life as devotional objects that some of the works of the Early Masters have survived, although cut down, repainted, inserted within Baroque stucco work, and for a period of about 300 years having at most a purely documentary interest.[41]

Devotional adaptations and modernizations often proceeded along the same lines as those carried out in the fourteenth and fifteenth centuries, but with a different purpose, in that now one was acting with the respect owed to paintings which were fully recognized as works of art; it goes without saying that these works would belong to the modern manner, or to the period immediately preceding it. There coexisted, therefore, up to the rediscovery of the Early Masters, two differing spheres of interest towards what we consider now, without distinction, works of art.

The devotional interest is primarily directed to the iconography, which is what characterizes the worship of images. These were to be considered not as objects, but as "symbols of objects"; as cardinal Paleotti tells us, "so that they take on the condition of that which they represent":[42] it is neither the painting nor the sculpture which is conserved, but the image, which could, at a pinch, survive in the form of a copy, bound to its original only by the iconographic elements related to its worship. The antiquity of the work, as demonstrated by the old panel, the signs of age or the style of the painting, were of marginal interest; documentation perhaps, secondary to the iconographic legibility which remained the main focus, although it might well contribute to what we would call, in our language, the aura of the image.

In the other sphere, we find such works as Raphael's frescos, Leonardo's *Adoration of the Magi* or Michelangelo's *Last Judgement*, around which an area of respect was taking shape, encompassing non-intervention or interventions justified by serious reasons of suitability or conservation; an area, in other words, which would slowly develop into that of

35, 36. Twelfth-century
Romanesque Master, fragments
of a Madonna and Child; devo-
tional mounting dated 1851.
Farfa, Abbey.

restoration. Obviously, the two areas were not mutually exclusive: even in an intervention on a devotional image, workmanship required that the painter's alterations should not be a blot on the original, and that his work be in keeping with the style of the older work. On a work of recognized figurative worth, it could happen that an intervention became necessary in order to correct an "error", as was the case with Tintoretto's *Annunciation* in San Mattia in Bologna, in which the Christ child was painted out; he had been represented on his way towards his mother as though already made incarnate, an error formally condemned by Pope Benedict XIV.[43]

The tradition discrediting restorations on paintings, already in evidence in Vasari, was well to the fore in Gaspare Celio's notes on the paintings of Rome published in 1638, where we can detect the continuation of this tradition which, at least in the written word, insisted on the negative aspects of restoration. In a few instances, his observations were due to the coarseness and incompetence of the interventions, but the controversy easily extended to restoration in general: the paintings by Pellegrino da Modena in San Giacomo degli Spagnoli were ruined under the pretext of renovating them, "which is the gravest mistake"; the *chiaroscuri*[x] at the base of the Stanze della Segnatura "were" by Perino del Vaga, "as one

---

[x] Literally, works painted in *light and shade*; monochromatic works, usually painted with one earth colour (*terretta*), such as green earth or yellow ochre.

37. *Giulio Romano, Madonna and Child with Saints; restored for the first time by Carlo Saraceni after 1598. Rome, Santa Maria dell'Anima.*

can still see in a few small areas, although they have been restored"; and it is "injurious in the extreme" to refresh frescos as was done in the apse of Sant'Onofrio. A small chamber painted in fresco by Raphael and Giulio Romano in the Villa Lante on the Janiculum "was retouched, that is – ruined"; Cesura's *Deposition* in Trinità dei Monti "was badly ruined, nothing remains but the composition". He alluded also to the restoration carried out by Carlo Saraceni on the altarpiece by Giulio Romano in Santa Maria dell'Anima, specifying that "it was ruined by the river when it flooded, under Clement VIII [1598], and afterwards they did not make good the damage, but ruined that which the river had not touched". As a borderline case of tampering, the mutilation of the pudenda of Michelangelo's *Christ* at the Minerva by a religious maniac ("despite the fact that it was covered by a cloth") was cited. Celio's distrust of restorations reached the point where, when talking about paintings which have been cleaned, he would refer to them in the past tense, as though irretrievably lost. But none of these works, with the exception of the apse of San Onofrio and a tempera panel of *Saint Francis Receiving the Stigmata* in San Pietro in Montorio (present whereabouts are unknown) pre-dated the modern manner. As it seems highly unlikely that hurried jobs were not also carried out on older paintings, Celio serves as witness (also because of his links as an artist with Padre Valeriano, and the Counter-Reformation problems surrounding the image) to the fact that two distinct areas had come into being: that of works of art (which did not preclude them also fulfilling the function of devotional images), and that of old images, which were of no figurative interest, and were subjected to the practices associated with the transmission of devotional images.[44]

It was Baglione, an artists' biographer (a category which is now indissolubly linked to the philosophy of the respect owed to the work of art) who would recount with complete equanimity the activities of Father Biagio Bietti, illuminator, preparer of blue pigments, painter: "If by chance a badly painted sacred image fell into his hands ... he would repaint it with the utmost zeal; and for greater reverence, he would endow it with the better grace of art and devotion (*buona grazia d'arte e devozione*)". Although of a later date, the restoration of Beato Angelico's canvas painting of the *Virgin and Child* in Santa Maria sopra Minerva, helps us greatly to understand with what iconographic adjustments and embellishments father Bietti might have sought the "greater artistic grace and devotion" mentioned by Baglione.[45]

In the light of the problem of correcting images which were "badly done", it is noticeable that of the Early Masters which have reached to us, those which are stylistically the most expressive, and have the strongest tendencies to a profane gothicism, those furthest removed from Giotto's regularity, are also those that have had the lowest survival rate. To what extent did the unseemliness of the best of the Bolognese fourteenth-century school, for instance, or the overtly wordly fantasies of the Lombard Gothic, contribute in putting them outside the laws of propriety and decorum required of images during the Counter-Reformation? And did their evident "deformities", in the context of seemliness ("*convenientia*"), lead to their destruction at every possible opportunity: every time the renovation of a building was allowed, or a modernization to prevailing taste, or the visit of a particularly zealous bishop? In Italy, there had not been one particular moment of general or immediate purging; rather, the selection had occurred over a period of time, mingled with all the changes in taste of the seventeenth and eighteenth centuries. If you were now to travel across the Marche or Emilia Romagna, you would quickly come to realize how many of the medieval churches – in the name of cleanliness, seemliness, newness of décor – had already been renovated with the complete destruction of their wall paintings, by the first half of the nineteenth century.

Where the contrasting positions of the Catholics and Protestants had more direct religious and political implications, in the Netherlands for instance, you see a more system-atic campaign of correction of images.[46] The problems of the conservation of these images and their use by the Catholics are dealt with very lucidly in the treatise *De Historia Sanctarum Imaginum et Picturarum pro vero eorum usu contra abusus* by Giovanni Molano, published in Louvain in 1594, a veritable "*summa*" which places itself against the arguments of the Protestants, who were against images or even iconoclasts.[47] In the context of the conserva-tion of images (seen as "books for the simple-minded"[xi]), any suggestion of lack of clarity had to be avoided, for instance if through neglect there were losses, or accrued dirt. On this problem, Molano shows his knowledge of religious culture by quoting Athanasius and Saint Jerome, and even the pagans who set the example for the care with which paintings should be conserved.

As far as reckless or unskilled cleanings undertaken in the name of the cleanliness of the place of worship (remember the monks and the sacristans mentioned by Celio), Molano used as a deterrent the incident of Marcus Junius who had ruined a panel by Aristides through poor cleaning, and with this anecdote from Pliny, endowed the discussion with nobility, at the same time removing it from the realms of possible contemporary contro-versy. As a positive example, he cited the restoration that he saw as a child of a Crucifixion in the beguinage of Diest ("full of art and pity"[xii]), carried out in such a way that "it was in no way different after the restoration than before", except for the fact of having regained its original appearance.[xiii] With this, he once more picked up the old theme that we find in the fathers of the Church, which refers to the return to a primitive state which is better than the present. The painting is returned to a condition which is nearer to that in which it was left by its artist–creator, no different to man himself, who will "better" in direct proportion to how near he is brought to the state of Grace he was in, before Original Sin.

From an Italian perspective, Molano represents a text of religious culture which was surely read and assimilated, as it was written in Latin; but it was only from a distance that the great upheaval of Protestant iconoclasm, with all its repercussions not only for conservation but also in the approach to images as works of art, was followed. During the wars of religion in the sixteenth century, many paintings which were recognized as having the status of works of art were removed from churches and installed in public palaces (as symbols of local pres-tige), or acquired by the middle classes for their homes: for the first time an altarpiece (or a portion of it) was transformed into an object forming part of the decoration, or part of an art collection (*quadro da collezione*). The rescue operations occurring in these circumstances allow us to find the names of all the greatest artists of northern Europe of the fifteenth and sixteenth centuries: Dürer's *Deposition* in the church of the preachers in Nürnberg was bought by Hans Ebner for his private house; in Antwerp, the Tryptych of Saint John by Quentyn Metsys was bought by Martin de Vos and then by the municipality; in 1566 Van Eyck's Ghent Altarpiece was brought to the Town Hall in order to protect it from the Calvinists. In some of Europe's most cultured towns, such as Basle, not only Holbein's

40, 41

---

xi "*idiotarum libri*".

xii "*plena pietatis et artificii*".

xiii "*non videretur aliter differre ab antique, quam sicut ipsa antique imago differebat a se ipsa, cum primum depicta fuerat*".

38. Beato Angelico, Madonna
and Child; after the removal of
the devotional repainting.
Rome, Santa Maria sopra
Minerva.

39. Beato Angelico, Madonna
and Child; with the devotional
repainting dating from the early
seventeenth century. Rome,
Santa Maria sopra Minerva.

40. *Jean Prevost, detail from*
The Last Judgement. Bruges,
Municipal Museum.

41. *Jean Prevost, detail from*
The Last Judgement; with the
repainting by Pieter Pourbus,
carried out in 1550. Bruges,
Municipal Museum.

paintings of religious subjects, but also older works the quality of which was evidently recognized, such as Konrad Witz's *Saint Leonard Altarpiece*, survived the Reformation.[48]

The "idols" were mostly represented by statues, and these survived only rarely. Notwithstanding the rescue operations, the losses must have been immense for paintings too, especially amongst the older works: one need only consider the rarity of Dutch paintings pre-dating the sixteenth century. The memory of this was still fresh when Van Mander was compiling the list of all the works that were either destroyed by the iconoclasts or removed from churches during the wars of religion. Bewailing the ignorance of the destroyers, but nevertheless with an outlook of religious tolerance, he abstained from a discussion of the prime motives that led to the violence against these works of art.

Baldinucci, who used Van Mander for his entries on Flemish and Dutch painters in the *Notizie*, provides an amusing contrast, written as it is by a personage tied to the court of the extremely devout Cosimo III, proposing a veritable catalogue of the misfortunes of the arts (*arti del disegno*) amongst the heretics. Divine intervention, the miracle, becomes *de rigueur*: when Anne Boleyn throws a portrait of Thomas More by Holbein out of the window, Divine providence intervenes to save it. Or else, during the fire in the Pardo in 1608, a canvas by Titian, filled with satyrs and shepherds, has the obvious fate (had it been an object of devotion), but that it should escape destruction by the flames was completely abnormal, as it was described as "very profane".[49]

Although perhaps marginal to the Counter-Reformation, it would be difficult to exclude the problem of lascivious figures, which is certainly not new, and is linked primarily to the kind of enjoyment derived from these images. As Baldinucci himself reminds us, the nudity in Artemisia Gentileschi's *Inclination* on the ceiling of the gallery in Casa Buonarroti was painted over (and with great skill) by Volterrano, because of the "chaste eyes" of Leonardo Buonarroti's numerous children. Had the children not had ease of access to the room dedicated to the *fasti michelangioleschi*, the nudes could have been left uncovered without incurring any problems.

Although Ottonelli and Berrettini in their treatise fulminate against the paintings which make of the galleries and the studies of many gentlemen "rooms belonging to the Emperor Heliogabus ... rather than to a modest and Christian knight or Prince", in general their presence could be justified within certain limits. Mancini, who was a doctor, mentioned that the sight of such images was beneficial to married couples when engaged in procreation: it sufficed that such images should not be exhibited to the sight of "children, unmarried girls, nor to outsiders or the scrupulous".[50]

The cause of the many repaintings on particularly profane nudes was to be found in events in the owners' lives or in individual circumstances, rather than in the history of ideas. The most ancient repainting on Bronzino's famous *Allegory*, now in the National Gallery in London (which was removed [during cleaning] in 1958), probably dated from when the painting was given to François I of France, a clear distinction being made between the contemplation of a nude figure and that of details which were too overtly descriptive. At other times, it was a figure which in itself did not appear to be unseemly in any way that found itself altered, such as the portrait of Florence's Barbera (a famous courtesan) included by Borghini in the works of Puligo, which was transformed by Giovambatista Deti from being a singer into a Saint Lucy, repainting the attributes "to the satisfaction of his lady". Or else it was simply a portrait to which one wished to give a different subject matter, that of a saint or an allegorical figure, as happened in the case of the famous Raphael in the Galleria

42. *Artemisia Gentileschi,*
L'Inclinazione; with the
draperies added by Il
Volterrano. Florence, Casa
Buonarroti.

Borghese, in which a young girl (to whose chastity the unicorn clearly alluded) was transformed into a Saint Catherine, with a plausible attribution to Sogliani.[51]

Notes

1. See: G. Lorenzetti, *Venezia e il suo estuario ...*, Rome, 1956, pp. 294, 363, 400–401; C. M. Brown, "*Una testa di Platone antica con la punta del naso in cera*", in "The Art Bulletin", 1969, pp. 204–211; M. Perry, *A Greek Bronze in Renaissance Venice*, in "The Burlington Magazine", 1975, p. 209; W. Wolters, *La scultura veneziana gotica*, Milan, 1976, cat. N. 203; D. Pincus, *Tullio Lombardo as a Restorer of Antiquities*, in "Arte Veneta", 1979, pp. 29–42 (he attributes to the Renaissance master the making good of the Grimani *Muse of Philiskos* which, however, seems to date from too late in the sixteenth century, and recalls different Antique models to those habitually used by him).

2. Vasari, 1568, I, pp. 331, 483–484; L. Beschi, *Le antichità di Lorenzo il Magnifico: caratteri e vicende*, in "Gli Uffizi, Quattro secoli di una galleria", Atti del Convegno (Florence, 1982), Florence, 1983, pp. 161–176 (in particular, see pp. 166 and 169). See "Palazzo Vecchio", 1980, n. 642, p. 314, for a bust which accompanies a head of *Alessandro Severo* exhibited in the Palazzo Vecchio, which demonstrates a solution analogous to that of the "modern" heads, and which could have been used in the fifteenth century to mount antique heads also.

3. L. Castelvetro, *Poetica d'Aristotele vulgarizzata ...*, ed. Bari, 1978, I, pp. 287–288; Collareta, 1985; *Michelangelo. Studi di antichità*, edited by G. Agosti and V. Farinella, Turin, 1987, pp. 41–43.

4. As well as the works dealing with the restoration of antiquities in Rome, see: Vasari, 1568, pp. 429, 611, 623–624, Winkelmann, 1783, II, p. 242; A. von Salis, *Antike und Renaissance*, Ehlenbach-zurich, 1947, pp. 136–153; A. Prandi, *La fortuna del Laocoonte dalla sua scoperta nelle terme di Tito*, in "Rivista dell'Instituto di Archeologia e di Storia dell'Arte", 1954, pp. 78–107; E. Vergara Caffarelli, *Studio per la restituzione del Laocoonte*, ibid., pp. 29–69; F. Magi–C. Bertelli, ad vocem *Laocoonte*, in "Enciclopedia dell'arte antica", IV, Rome, 1961; M. and R. Hertl, "*Laokoon*", Munich, 1962; M. Bieber, "*Laokoon*", *The Influence of the Group since its Discovery*, Detroit, 1967; H. H. Brummer, *The Statue Court in the Vatican Belvedere*, Stockholm, 1970; J. Paul, *Antikenerganzung unt Ent-Restaurierung*, in "Kunstchronik", 1972, n. 4, pp. 86–90; Oechslin, 1974, pp. 3–29; M. Winner, *Zum Nachleben des Laokoon in der Renaissance*, in "Jahrbuch der Berliner Museen", 1974, pp. 83–121; Haskell–Penny, 1981, n. 50, pp. 337–343; H. W. Kruft, *Metamorphosen des Laokoon*, in "Pantheon", 1984, pp. 3–11; Pray Bober-Rubinstein, *Renaissance Artists and Antique Sculpture*, Oxford, 1986, n. 122; Rossi Pinelli, 1986, pp. 183–190 (and also, note 3 p. 184, a further bibliography).

5. Vasari, 1568, II, p. 134; Rossi Pinelli, 1986, pp. 197–198.

6. On restorations in Rome, see: Vasari, 1568, II, pp. 365, 680–681, 753, 843; Baglione, 1642, p. 151; Richardson, 1728, III, pp. 213–215; De Rossi, 1826, p. 26; R. Lanciani, *Storia degli scavi di Roma*, II, Rome, 1903, pp. 161, 180–182; Enciclopedia dell'arte antica, VII, Rome, 1966, pp. 951–954; Boselli, 1967, pp. 86–87; Howard, 1968, pp. 402–403; C. Schwinn, *Die Bedeutung des Torso von Belvedere ...*, Frankfurt, 1973; Haskell–Penny, 1981, p. 123; G. Martines, *Silla Longhi e il restauro della Colonna Antonina*, in "Roma e l'arte e la cultura del Cinquecento", atti del corso (1982), Rome, 1985, pp. 174–209; Rossi Pinelli, 1986, pp. 194–201, 209–214, 218–220. Destruction of buildings in order to recuperate materials and maintenance of antique buildings in sixteenth-century Rome, are discussed in P. Fancelli, *Demolizioni e "restauri" di antichità nel '500 romano* in *Roma e l'antico nell'arte e la cultura del Cinquecento*, op. cit., pp. 357–403.

7. B. Cellini, *Vita*, II, 69, 72, 73. On the restorations in Florence in the second half of the sixteenth century, see: M. Neusser, *Die antikenerganzungen der Florentiner Manieristen*, in "Wiener Jahrbuch fur Kunstgeschichte", VI, 1929, pp. 27–42; G. Mansuelli, *Restauri di sculture antiche nelle collezioni medicee*, in "Il mondo antico nel Rinascimento", proceedings of the symposium, Florence, 1956, pp. 179–186; Rossi Pinelli, 1986, pp. 214–216.

8. R. Borghini, *Il Riposo*, Florence, 1584, pp. 157–158. On the subject of the washing or treating of the surface of antique statues, see the examples cited from the Uffizi by Luciano Berti (*Il restauro delle sculture*, in "Il restauro delle opera d'arte", proceedings of the symposium, 1968, Pistoia, 1977, pp. 177–178).

9. B. Cellini, *Vita*, II, 87; Vasari, 1568, p. 70; R. Bianchi Bandinelli, in *Enciclopedia dell'arte antica*, III, Rome, 1960, p. 498; E. Plon, *Benvenuto Cellini*, Paris, 1883, p. 385. Neusser, op. cit., n. 12, p. 31; C. Albizzati, in *Enciclopedia Italiana*, XXIX, 1936, p. 134. The small bronze in the Museo Archeologico to which I am referring is n. 2284.

10. Michiel, pp. 38, 189, 238–239. There is a vast literature devoted to the subject of Vasari as a restorer and destroyer of works of art; see: A. del Vita, *Opere distrutte e salvate da Giorgio Vasari*, in "Il Vasari", II,

1928–1929, pp. 155–156; C. A. Isermeier, *Il Vasari e il restauro delle chiese medievali*, in "Studi vasariani", proceedings of the symposium, Florence, 1950, pp. 229–236 (he makes clear that in the Duomo of Arezzo, it was the opposition of the workmen and the canons that prevented Vasari from substituting the Gothic altar with a canopy of his own; it also highlights the political motives underlying the destruction of the rood-screens and the new layout of Florentine churches); Procacci, 1956 (in particular, attention is drawn to the importance of the renown given to the Brancacci Chapel by Vasari's text, resulting in its survival, especially during the eighteenth century); Previtali, 1964, pp. 3–21 (specifically emphasizes historical relativism, and the connection, through Michelangelo, with fifteenth-century tradition; this connection will no longer be felt by the following generation). Because of the ease with which one can find the examples I refer to in the indexes of the main editions of Vasari, I will only give references for the least obvious.

11. On the *Spasimo di Sicili*a, see 1568, II, p. 79. Van Mander (1604, 1884 translation, pp. 100–101) refers to a similar episode occurring with Rogier Van der Weyden's *Deposition* which is today in the Prado. The platonic theme of the strength of art even when confronted with the ignorant ("a multitude made up partly of peasants and partly of soldiers") is clearly evident in Benedetto Varchi's tale of the unsuccessful attempt to destroy Andrea del Sarto's *Last Supper* at San Salvi; see *Storia Fiorentina*, X, ed. Cologne, 1721, p. 292: "when their destruction reached the place where stood the refectory in which Andrea del Sarto had painted a Last Supper, they all, suddenly – as if they had lost the use of their arms and tongues – stopped, and became silent, and full of an unaccustomed amazement, were not willing to continue their work of destruction. And it is for this reason, that we can still see today in that place, and for those who have some understanding, with even greater amazement, one of the most beautiful paintings in the world". A similar way of presenting the episode is to be found in the 1550 edition [of Vasari's *Lives*] (p. 765): "Truly a great honour to this art which, completely mute, without a word, has the strength to temper the fury of arms, and suspicion, inducing reverence and respect even in those who are not of our profession, who know its worth". However, when Vasari refers to the same incident in the 1568 edition (II, pp. 165–166), the work is only saved because of "the presence of the leader guiding them, and who perhaps had heard speak of it".

12. For further information and documentation on the conservation of these works, see: J. Shearman, *An Episode in the History of Conservation*, in "*Scritti Procacci*", 1977, pp. 356–364; L. Vertova, in "The Burlington Magazine", 1972, p. 496; A. Lensi, *Palazzo Vecchio*, Rome, 1929, p. 109.

13. I, pp. 96, 122–123, 168, 213.

14. II, pp. 215, 425, 439, 618, 725.

15. The panel by Caroto depicting the *Presepio* in San Giorgio in Verona was flaking away because of a poorly bound ground layer; the *Saint Vincent Ferrer* by Baccio della Porta had cracked all over because it had been painted "onto fresh glue with fresh colours". For the drawbacks of lamp black see Eastlake, 1847–1869, I, pp. 462, 466; II, p. 174. Gettens and Stout (*Painting Materials*, New York, 1942) do not mention any particular alterations associated with lamp black.

16. II, pp. 378, 345; see also p. 255 on the use of varnish by Torbido, who was of the opinion that varnish made panels age more quickly, "and therefore when painting used varnish in the darks, and certain refined oils".

17. II, pp. 537, 559–560; the copy by Fra Girolamo Buonsignori, after its adventurous past during the suppressions and nineteenth-century collectionism, now finds itself in the abbazia di Vangadizza near Badia Polesine, and contrary to the opinion held by Vasari, has been attributed, not very convincingly, to Giovan Francesco Caroto (F. Trevisani, *Restauri in Polesine*, catalogue of the exhibition, Milan, 1984, pp. 92–132).

18. II, p. 599, I, pp. 91 and 146; II, p. 529; II, p. 984. However, while still a boy, Vasari had been guilty of just such an intervention, when working with Angelo di Lorentino, retouching a chapel by Giovanni Toscani in the Duomo of Arezzo (I, p. 192).

19. II, p. 599. The information is, at least in part, the result of a misunderstanding, as on the north gate, before the sculptures by Rustici, there had been a group (of which a fragment still exists) by Andrea Pisano.

20. I, pp. 91, 146; C. A. Isermeyer, *Die Cappella Vasari und der Hochaltar in der Pieve von Arezzo*, in "Festschrift fur C. G. Heise", Berlin, 1950, pp. 137–153.

21. S. Alpers, *Ekphrasis and Aesthetic Attitudes in Vasari's Lives*, in "Journal of the Courtauld and Warburg Institutes", 1960, pp. 190–215.

22. On works destroyed or lost during the renovation of buildings, see also I, p. 396; II, pp. 251, 391.

23. M. B. Hall, *Renovation and Counter Reformation: Vasari and Duke Cosimo in Santa Maria Novella and Santa Croce*, Oxford, 1979.

24. A. Conti, *Frammenti pittorici in Santa Croce*, in "Paragone", n. 225, 1968, pp. 18–20. Vasari's reputation for destroying works of art was already flourishing in the seventeenth century, when a manuscript in the

Biblioteca Nazionale in Florence records the information, which Giuseppe Piacenza would use in 1817, that it had been Vasari's intention to knock down Francesco Salviati's frescos in the Sala di Camillo in the Palazzo Vecchio, to substitute them with a cycle of his own: see Ms Magl. XVIII, 11 (c. 31r) in the Biblioteca Nazionale di Firenze, and G. Piacenza, in Baldinucci, V, 1817, note 1 p. 223.

25. On the tabernacle of Porta Pinti, see II, pp. 159–160.

26. 1568 I, pp. 215–216; the fresco is still in existence in the little church of Santa Maria Maddalena in Arezzo, see P. P. Donati, *Spinello: note e inediti*, in "Antichità viva", 1967, n. 2, pp. 13–14. See Vasari, I, pp. 127, 141, 180, 359, where he cites the works that were not saved during the demolition of the rood-screens. On the works which on this occasion were transferred *a massello* (with part of the wall, or else as simple "crusts" of paint layer), see also Vasari (I, pp. 388, 458, 471), Bocchi–Cinelli, *Le bellezze della città di Firenze*, Florence 1677, p. 318; M. B. Hall, *The "Tramezzo" in S. Croce, Florence and Domenico Veneziano's Fresco*, in "The Burlington Magazine", 1970, pp. 797–799.

27. Vasari, 1568, II, p. 17; Mengs, 1783, pp. 155–156; C. Ricci, *Correggio*, Rome, 1930, p. 147; A. O. Quintavalle, *La R. Galleria di Parma*, Rome, 1939, p. 113; A. O. Quintavalle, *Un disegno del Correggio scoperto nello stacco dell'affresco dell'Incoronata*, in "Bollettino d'Arte", 1937–1938, pp. 80–88; C. Gould, *The Paintings of Correggio*, London, 1976, pp. 246, 268. The remarkable technical abilities in the linking of walls, demonstrated in the segments of the spherical vault painted by Correggio, are also attested by Vasari when referring to the king of France's (Louis XII) project, to remove to his own country, Leonardo's *Last Supper* (II, pp. 6–7).

28. F. Cavazzoni, in *Una guida inedita del Seicento Bolognese*, ed. R. Varese, in "Critica d'arte", n. 108, 1969, p. 25. The putto in the Accademia di San Luca has all the prerequisites for having been transferred a very long time ago; see Pico Cellini, *Il profeta Isaia di Raffaello e il putto dell'Accademia di San Luca*, in "Bollettino d'Arte", 1960, pp. 93–95, which brings to mind Vasari's allusion (1568, II, p. 73) to a first painting of the fresco begun in a different location to the pilaster in a chapel.

29. I, p. 192, II, pp. 356–357.

30. I, p. 124; II, pp. 366–367. For the drawing by Perino del Vaga which shows the decoration destined for this Madonna (Berlin, Staatliche Mussen, K. d. Z. 5166), see E. Parma Armani, *Perino del Vaga*, Genoa, 1986, p. 332.

31. For works cited for the historical interest of portraiture etc, see Vasari, 1568, I, pp. 161–162, 257, 258, 354–355, 361.

32. E. Muntz, *Le Musée de portraits de Paul Jove*, in "Mémoires de l'Académie des inscriptions et belles lettres", XXXVI, part II, 1900, pp. 294–343; A. Santangelo, *Museo di Palazzo Venezia-Catalogo-I dipinti*, Rome, 1948, pp. 3–4. P. O. Rave, *Das Museo Giovio zu Como*, in "Miscellanea Bibliothecae Haertzianae", 1961, pp. 275–284; M. Giaconcelli, *L'antico museo di Paolo Giovio in Borgovico*, Como, 1976; P. L. De Vecchi, *Il museo giovano e le verae imagines*, in "Omaggio a Tiziano", catalogue of the exhibition, Milan, 1977, pp. 87–93. In this sense, a portrait of *Michele di Lando* is interesting; a high-quality panel to be attributed to Perino del Vaga, between the fourth and fifth decades of the sixteenth century, one of the oldest examples of the Giovioesque fashion for portraits copied from Early Masters, published in Conti, 1973, p. 62. The series of portraits belonging to Giovio pre-dating those by Cristofaro dell'Altissimo for Cosimo I (Vasari, 1568, II, pp. 868–869) was copied by Bernardino Campi for Giulia Gonzaga; see A. Lamo, *Discorso intorno alla Scoltura ed alla Pittura*, Cremona, 1584, p. 53.

33. The first damage to the Sistine Chapel ceiling may date back to the fire which destroyed part of the roof in 1544; see A. M. Corbo, *Documenti romani su Michelangelo*, in "Commentari", 1965, pp. 115–116. On the various interventions that are known so far, see Celio, 1638, p. 33; Steinmann, 1901–1905, II, pp. 757–763 (one should note, however, that the "mundator" referred to on 18 August 1557 is simply a cleaning contractor) and p. 783; E. Steinmann, *Zur Restauration der Fresken Michelangelos in der Sixtinischen Kapelle*, in "Museumkunde", 1905, pp. 226–229; G. Mancini, *Modo tenuto per rinettare le pitture della Cappella di Sisto nel Palazzo del Vaticano*, in "Bollettino dell'Istituto Centrale di Restauro", n. 7–8, 1951, p. 99; E. Camesasca, in R. Salvini, *La Cappella Sistina in Vaticano*, Milan, 1965, pp. 152, 187; G. Colalucci, in *The Sistine Chapel. Michelangelo Rediscovered*, London, 1986, pp. 262–263 (deductions on the interventions carried out by the first restorers of the Sistine ceiling, interpreting the information according to the criteria guiding him in the controversial intervention led by him on Michelangelo's frescos).

On Domenico Carnevale da Modena (1524–1579; in Rome between 1566 and 1572), see A. Lugli, *Carnevale, Domenico*, in Dizionario Biografico degli Italiani, XX, 1977; Conti, 1986, pp. 77–81, 169, and, for further attributions, C. Strinati, *Marcantonio dal Forno nell'Oratorio del Gonfalone a Roma*, in "Antichità viva", 1976, n. 3, p. 19; the information on his integrations within the vault of the Sistine Chapel go back to Giovanni Bottari, in Vasari, *Vita di Michelangelo Bonarroti*, Rome 1760, pp. 176–177, and Bottari, 1759–1760, II, pp. 360–361. Tolnay (*Michelangelo, II, The Sistine Ceiling*, Princeton, 1945, ed. 1949, p. 30 and note 11 p. 133) identifies as the work of Domenico Carnevale, God's left hand in *The separation of the earth from the waters*; the reasons for which this hypothesis does not seem tenable, are to be found in Conti, 1986, p. 78.

An instance of equal importance would have been the renovation (*rifacimento*) by Lorenzo Sabatini which Gaspare Celio refers to for the *Coronation of Charlemagne the Great* in the Stanza dell'Incendio (1638, p. 37); instead, it should be considered an error of misinformation, or an attribution made by Celio to whom the figure probably appeared so close in style to that of Sabatini as to be considered by his hand. Cavalcaselle did not note any restoration (Cavalcaselle–Crowe, 1882–1885, II, pp. 58–59); see now F. Mancinelli, *Raphael's "Coronation of Charlemagne" and its cleaning*, in "The Burlington Magazine", 1984, p. 404.

34. L. Dolce, 1557, in Barocchi, 1960–1962, I, p. 151; Cavalcaselle–Crowe, 1882–1885, II, p. 312; L. Dussler, *Sebastiano del Piombo*, Basle, 1942, pp. 112, 213; R. Palucchini, *Sebastiano Viniziano*, Milan, 1944, note 45 p. 123; M. Hirst, *Sebastiano del Piombo*, Oxford, 1981, note 104 p. 147. The various hypothetical identifications, somewhat uncertain after so many successive restorations on the frescos of the *Stanze*, have on the whole been suggested by the vicinity of a chimney to one or other of the frescos.

35. On the provenance of Leonardo's *Adoration of the Magi*, see the observations in the catalogue *Palazzo Vecchio*, 1980, pp. 248, 301. On Sogliani see Vasari, 1568, II, p. 190; on the Bronzino destined for the nuns of the Concezione, L. Berti, *Un ritrovamento: la "Concezione" del Bronzino*, in "Rivista d'Arte", 1951–1952, pp. 191–193. Vasari also refers to some blue drapery which Ridolfo del Ghirlandaio had completed on a *Madonna* by Raphael destined for Siena, and which has often been identified with *La Belle Jardinière*, an identification which is to be discounted; see *Raphael dans les Collections Françaises*, 1983, p. 83.

36. On this problem and the relative testimonies, see Barocchi, 1962, III, note 563, pp. 1254–1297, note 585, pp. 1377–1390, IV, note 659, pp. 1614–1617; for more detailed information on the retouching, see Biagetti–De Campos, 1944, pp. 144–145; C. de Tolnay, *Michelangelo, V, The Final Period*, Princeton, 1960, pp. 98–99; Camesasca, op. cit., p. 239; R. De Maio, *Michelangelo e la Controriforma*, Bari, 1978, pp. 17–45.

37. M. Calì, *Da Michelangelo all'Escorial*, Turin, 1980, p. 169.

38. Biagetti–De Campos, 1944, pp. 141–142, 146; Camesasca, op. cit., pp. 239–240. One should also bear in mind that the pavement of the presbytery was raised between 1578 and 1585, destroying the lower part of the fresco which did not contain any figures; for the band that was lost from the *Last Judgement*, compare the engraving by L. Vaccari (ibid., p. 133) and Venusti's copy of 1549, which is today in the Museo Capodimonte in Naples.

39. Vasari, 1568, II, pp. 683, 760–761; Celio, 1638, pp. 16, 101.

40. See Calì, op. cit., pp. 138–141 in particular. See Romeo Di Maio's important observations in *Michelangelo e San Carlo*, in "Prospettiva", n. 43, 1985, pp. 57–58.

41. On the problems surrounding the fortunes of the Early Masters from the sixteenth to the nineteenth centuries, see Previtali, 1964.

42. G. Paleotti, *Discorso sopra le immagini sacre e profane*, Bologna, 1582, in Barocchi, 1960–1962, II, pp. 199–200; the passage is cited by Francesco Abbate in the introduction of the fine 1965 anthology.

43. See Anna Maria Maetzke's discussion on the subject of a similar repainting (although concerning an Early Master) of Andrea di Nerio's *Annunciation*, in *Arte nell'Aretino*, catalogue of the exhibition (Arezzo, 1974–1975), Florence, 1974, p. 56.

44. Celio, 1638 (facsimile edition, edited by E. Zocca, Milan, 1967), pp. 16, 27, 37, 39, 43, 65–66, 85–87, 92, 101, 117 (see Abbate, 1965, pp. 46–47). See F. Zeri, *Pittura e Controriforma*, Turin, 1957, pp. 67–71; Abbate, 1965, pp. 38–44. On the altarpiece by Giulio Romano (which was the object of many successive restorations), see A. Ottani Cavina, *Carlo Saraceni*, Milan, 1968, pp. 81, 117.

45. Baglione, 1642, p. 318; Abbate, 1965, p. 39. Su Biagio Betti; see the entry by M. Chiarini, in the *Dizionario Biografico degli Italiani*, IX, 1967, pp. 712–713. The canvas by Beato Angelico in the Minerva is published in *Per la salvezza dei beni culturali in Italia* (acts of the so-called "Commissione Franceschini"), Rome, 1967, III, plate CCVIII. For other restorations to works by Beato Angelico which also show devotional aspects, see: A. Conti, in "Paragone", n. 223, 1968, pp. 5–7; J. Pope-Hennessy, *Fra Angelico*, London, 1974, pp. 193, 197.

46. In Bruges, for example, in a *Last Judgement* by Jan Prevost, such a fine painter as Pieter Pourbus, between 1549 and 1550, paints out certain religious figures, who are being tormented with the grotesque punishments of Flemish hells typical of the early years of the century. In the edicts of 1540 and 1550, Charles V in fact denounced disrespectful images not only of saints, but also of the clergy. See Marijnissen, 1967, II, note 30 p. 339; for other episodes relative to Flemish painting, see Conti, 1973, p. 216.

47. Del Molano; see *De Historia Ss. Imaginum et Picturarum pro vero earum usu contra abusus*, Lovanii 1594, II, XLIII (Of the history of the holiest images and paintings in order to [make] a true use of them and against their abuse] (see Abbate, 1965). See the quotation from Athanasius, which is extremely significant in showing

the Counter-Reformation's position with respect to paintings: "When what is painted onto a panel, must be newly painted or made [afresh] because the image has been erased due to dirt or carelessness, it must be carried out in such way, in order that it could again be renewed with the same materials and panels: in fact [if] it is painted in the same form and materials, it is not destroyed, but this better allows [to restore] the same state it had before".

48. Coulton, *Art and Reformation*, Cambridge, 1953; R. H. Bainton, *The Reformation of the Sixteenth Century* (1952) translation Turin, 1965, p. 85; for examples of works rescued from iconoclastic destruction, see, in brief: N. Von Holst. *Creators, Collectors and Connoisseurs*, London, 1967, p. 78.

49. Van Mander, 1604, trans. 1884, I, p. 53, 62, 90, 109, 160, 355, 356, 403; Baldinucci, 1681–1728, ed. 1845–1847, II, p. 238, 271, IV, p. 11.

50. F. Borromeo, *De Pictura Sacra*, Mediolani, 1625, Book I, Chapters V, VI, XIII; O. Lelenotti da Fanano–B. Prenetteri [G. D. Ottonelli–P. Berrettini], *Trattato della Pittura e scultura, uso et abuso loro*, Florence, 1652, p. 295; Borghini, 1584, p. 116; Mancini, 1956, p. 143.

51. Borghini, 1584, p. 396. Examples of this type of portrait by Poligo can also be found in Berenson's indexes (*Italian Pictures of Renaissance–Florentine School*, London, 1963, plates 1413, 1414); Baldinucci, 1681–1728, ed. 1845–1847, III, pp. 713–714. Lately, on the portrait by Raphael, see C. Bon Valsassina, in *Raffaello nelle raccolte Borghese*, catalogue of the exhibition, Rome, 1984, p. 25.

BOOK ORDER

THE BRITISH MUSEUM 12020.001

Supplier   Dawson Books (UK)   Order
Order Date   08/05/2007   Item
Quantity   1   ISBN
Unit Price   34.99   Curre
Instructions

Author   CONTI, ALESSANDRO
Title   HISTORY OF THE RESTORATION AND CONSE

Volume   NEW TITLE   Edit
Format   Publ
Shelf Mark

Site
Fund
Loan Type
Quantity   1

3

___

Some local traditions in Italy

1. Bologna and Carlo Cesare Malvasia, Naples and Bernardo De Dominici

The devotional tradition which favoured interventions and even modernizations on paintings, and more specifically on early works, and the tradition in which respect was shown when treating the works of the great masters, would intertwine and influence one another in various ways throughout the seventeenth century. It is not possible really to trace a line of demarcation between these two traditions, as it would vary according to circumstance: whether the painting was seen as an object of worship and part of the church furnishings, or whether it was characterized as a work of art. Moreover, at what point in that nebulous time which is the Classicism of the end of the fifteenth century can one say that the "good style" ("*buono stile*"), in all its fullness, began to be recognized?

In Malvasia's *Pitture di Bologna*, he shows us clearly the strength of the Bolognese tradition of miraculous images, which was revived with the Counter-Reformation; he refers to more than seventy Madonnas transferred from one wall to another, attributing this custom to much earlier times, as though the Bolognese bishops of ages past had been ecclesiastics of the Counter-Reformation, wishing to revive the worship of images.[1] One of the guidelines offered by Malvasia with regard to ancient paintings was that of "poor taste" ("*basso gusto*"): with such an identification, it is not difficult to imagine the destruction that was meted out to such works, or how they were adapted to a better style. But the other criterion is that of their "curious genius", which renders some of his pages so vivid, such as the one in which he describes a now lost *Nativity* by Vitale da Bologna.[2]

Alongside this situation, which reflects the general attitude towards the Early Masters, one can discern a tradition of confidence towards modern painting, linked to the custom of the best qualified artists retouching the works of beginners, or of other painters who, turning to these masters, would have their paintings enlivened with some masterly touch. No need to recall how the idea of these final touches by the hand of either Guido Reni or Annibale Carracci was often, within the tradition of collecting, an expedient to lend prestige to workshop productions; but what is interesting within our discussion is the vitality of this tradition in the pages of Malvasia. Referring to Guido Reni: "There would be an infinite number, if one were to draw up a complete account of all the final touches [carried out by Reni]; because it seemed that this great soul found no greater pleasure than to undertake such work, for simple thanks and not gain, and this made of him a teacher to all. Many [paintings he retouched] for Brunetti, his pupil; these, after his death, went to the

Marquis Bernardino Paleotti. Many for Gallinari, and for Sirani; for instance those of the old man, and the woman school teacher. For Ercolino, and Saulo Guidotti, who also had many originals. For Procurator Lemmi, the Silenus which had been an Arianna, sold to Mastri who then sent it to France where he was given two hundred scudi for it. The four seasons for the embroiderer, another version of it going to the Signori Conti Castelli, in whose room the original had been painted. The two philosophers sold to His Highness of Modana, for the sum of two hundred scudi. For Marchese Cospi the Cleopatra copied from the original, painted for His Serene Highness, now the Cardinal of Tuscany. Another, in the house of the deceased Marchese Angelelli. The Annunciation in the church of Santa Maria della Vita, and many, many retouched for Alessandro Barbieri, for the lame barber whose name was also Alessandro, for Domenico Cappellaro, for his little Marco, and so on".

It becomes obvious then, that it was not considered unseemly for the prestige of a master such as Reni to manifest itself in such a way. Outside of Bologna, such a practice would not have been described in such detail: one need only think of Bottari who, arguing on the subject of the restoration of frescos, had to resort to the authority of Saint Cyprian in order to demonstrate how offensive it was for a painter to lay his brush on the work of a colleague.[3]

Guercino was particularly prone to intervening on the works of others, in both the ancient and the modern manner, as well as on his own paintings when they required some repair or modernization. His account book confirms what Scannelli tells us: that when his early paintings were criticized for their "excessive darkness", he himself "in order to do his utmost and satisfy the majority, especially those who demanded the work with money, had made the paintings more legible using a lighter manner". The theme of respect between artists would return in Scannelli, when he recorded Guercino's refusal to complete the Certosa di Sant'Anna in Bologna, an altarpiece left unfinished by Reni, having "at all times held its author in due reverence". On the other hand, the account book does show Guercino, in early 1643, working on a *Saint Jerome* by Reni in the possession of the merchant Ludovico Mastri, and then on a *Saint Matthew* which Reni had begun. Referring to the *Saint Jerome* by Reni, Malvasia specified that "it was given to Giovan Francesco Barbieri to complete, but he [Mastri] never considered it to be by his [Guercino's] hand, but by [Reni], and he paid for it with this in mind".[i]

Staying as his guest, Guercino had retouched many paintings for Filippo Aldovrandi; and in 1652, the account book registered the intervention on a *Madonna with Saint Joseph* by Titian for Cardinal Cibo, legate to Ferrara. In any case, his activities in the field of restoration and adaptation were well attested by his repainting of an altarpiece by Dosso Dossi, executed for the Duke of Modena towards 1650. Notwithstanding the very precise indications given by the annotators of the nineteenth-century edition of the *Felsina Pittrice*, which allow one to identify this painting with the great *Immaculate Conception* of Dresden, scholars of Dosso Dossi, embarrassed by the apparent anomaly of the classicism of this work, have always attributed this to the collaboration of his brother Battista. In this case, however, the distinction between the hands of the two brothers becomes marginal in comparison to the massive intervention of the painter from Cento, which is evident although not verifiable, since the altarpiece was destroyed in the bombing of Dresden at the end of the Second World War. From the photographs, one can safely identify the hand of Guercino in areas in which he was not faithful to the original

43

---

[i] *"fatto poi finire al Signor Giovan Francesco Barbieri, mai si trovò che per mano di esso lo volesse, ma si bene del suddetto, e con tale rispetto solo pagarlo".*

43. Dosso Dossi, The Immaculate
Conception; restored by Guercino
towards 1650. Dresden.
Gemäldegalerie. (destroyed)

composition: for instance, in the figures of the Father of the Church in the centre, who is pointing to the sky, and the two figures of the Virgin and God the Father.[4]

To what extent the admission that a master was prepared to retouch a painting (whether
with the aim of restoring it or modernizing it) was linked to a question of principle can easily
be established if we compare the tone of the information given us about one and the same
artist by different biographers, representing the purist tradition to different degrees. Baldinucci
makes no mention of the information given by Malvasia about the poor results of the varnish
applied by Reni to his own oil painting in the cloister in San Michele al Bosco, nor on the circumstances in which he had applied the finishing touches to a *Madonna and Saints* in Palazzo
Sacchetti in Rome, which had been "blocked in" (*sbozzata*) by Titian. He summarizes and
interprets the Bolognese writer, affirming that Guido Reni "would fall into a rage when he
heard that a painter had dared touch the paintings of Old Masters, even if torn and damaged,
something that he would never agree to do". The passage Baldinucci is referring to is the one
in which Malvasia records the respect in which Reni held ancient paintings "because of their
age and devotion" (*per certa venustà e devozione*), as well as recounting the episode [which
occurred] in Ravenna in which he had been enraged by the retouching carried out on some
figures by Livio Agresti in the church of San Spirito Santo, to the extent that "he had added
blows to the rebuke" meted out to the unfortunate charged with the task, but there is no principle suggesting that this was a generally held attitude.[5]

Amongst other masters responsible for repaintings or restorations were Lionello
Spada, the Cavalier Franceschini who is thought to have repaired the image of the Christ
child in the *Madonna di Galliera*, and Felice Cignani in the fifteenth-century frescos of the
Cappella Bentivoglio in San Giacomo Maggiore. Much of the information cannot be verified on the paintings themselves, as these have been either recently restored or else dispersed; but the tradition carried on, and was well documented throughout the eighteenth
century, as can be seen from the protests against the worst of the botchers working on
paintings exhibited in public spaces, protests recorded in the various editions of *Pitture di
Bologna* as well as in the manuscripts of Marcello Oretti.[6]

Bernardo De Dominici was, according to Giannone, a repairer of old paintings, so it is
not surprising that he gives us an extremely well-articulated account of the renovations ("*rifacimenti*") undergone by the paintings in Naples, a city with a maritime climate ill-suited to the
conservation of paintings.[7] One of the principal factors leading to interventions on paintings
which had deteriorated (or which required devotional adjustment) was the Neapolitans' lively
cult of images, which easily led to cleanings, periodic oilings and repaintings. Of a panel by
Silvestro Buono in San Gregorio Armeno, De Dominici affirms that he was unable to see it,
notwithstanding considerable efforts to find it, "so that I surmised that it had been removed or
been retouched by Giovanni Bernardo Lama, as was the case with those which were in San
Pietro ad Ara and in the [church of] the Santissima Nunziata, as well as the one in San Niccolò
alla Dogana which, because they were in such poor condition, had to be largely repainted, so
that they no longer appeared to be by him to the eye of the onlooker. A misfortune which
occurs frequently, at times even to the works of the most renowned masters, so that the paintings lose the reputation of being by the hand of the master, although the greatest honour must
always go to him who is responsible for the composition".[8]

Overpaintings and restorations could also be carried out only a few years after the
completion of a painting. Battistello's two canvases of the *Torture* and *The Decapitation of
San Gennaro* in the Certosa of San Martino were found in appalling condition once the

wretched seventeenth-century repainting (which had even altered the composition) had been removed; entrusted in the 1970s to the attentions of Antonio De Mata, many other paintings from the Certosa revealed repaintings which could be dated to only twenty or thirty years after the original execution of the works. In Ribera's *Deposition*, a much travailed composition, a seventeenth-century restoration had already moved the nail in the background to a parallel position in the foreground; of *The Nativity* by Battistello, companion piece to *The Adoration of the Magi*, only the composition of the original was preserved.

A few of these canvases serve as evidence that the repainting was not always carried out by those who De Domenici terms "botchers" ("*guastamestieri*"): the two lateral paintings by Caracciolo depicting *Saint John the Baptist* and *San Gennaro* had been repaired, strengthening the dark backgrounds (in the *Saint John* the suggestion of a landscape can now be made out), the damaged parts repainted, for instance the upper portion of the Precursor's cane. A restoration of this kind had also been carried out on the lunettes depicting the founders of the religious orders by Finoglia, the repaint only having a tendency to darken the general tonality of the painting. Sometimes the authorship of the restorations or adaptations can be traced to some of the best artists active in Naples: Battistello, when painting the frescos in the chapel in Santa Maria la Nova in which hangs the *Saint Michael* by Paolo Pino, painted in some   44, 45

44. *Marco Pino, Saint Michael;*
with the addition and the patination
by Battistello Caracciolo. Naples,
Santa Maria la Nova.

45. *Marco Pino, Saint Michael;*
during restoration. Naples,
Santa Maria la Nova.

additional figures of devils in the lower section of the painting, and harmonized the original section with the new with a dark glaze, which nevertheless did not cover the halo surrounding the Archangel's head, as can be seen in old photographs.[9]

Lanfranco, using tempera, repainted the corbels of his cupola in the church of the Gesù Nuovo, which had been blackened during a fire, and it is not surprising to find the name of Luca Giordano (an artist renowned for painting in the manner of other artists) amongst those entrusted with restorations: he was responsible for repainting the head of a Madonna in a *Holy Family* by Andrea Vaccaro, which had suffered "because the ground of the painting had cracked", and in the altarpiece by Lanfranco in Sant'Anna dei Lombardi (which is now in the church of the Rosary at Afragola) he modified two saints, adapting himself to the style of that master, and "he imitated Lanfranco's manner so well – Celano tells us – that it is impossible to distinguish if one is not in the know".[10]

This tradition of restoration often executed with great bravura, but always balanced between renovation and repainting (*ripristino e ridipintura*), carried on into the eighteenth century: amongst examples that were carried out in his own time, De Dominici referred to the repainting of the sky and clouds in the ceiling by Corenzio in Santa Maria di Costantinopoli, after which it was found to have "much more beauty". Gennaro Greco, a landscape painter in fresco, successfully transferred to the use of the oil medium when restoring a perspective. Paolo de Matteis, when painting the side panels which were to accompany a work by Sabatini in Sant'Anna di Palazzo, also laid his brush on the sixteenth-century central panel; and his pupil Domenico Guarino, as well as restoring landscapes by Domenico Gargiulo and paintings by Corenzio in the Certosa di San Martino, [in the church of] the Incoronata, also restored the frescos by Roberto di Oderisio, which at the time were believed to be by Giotto.[11]

If one bears in mind how, as recently as in the previous century, in some cases (take the additions to the *Negation* and the *Liberation of Saint Peter*, two small paintings by Cavallino in the church of the Gerolimini), the canvas used had just been a strip from some old painting, then it is easier to understand the admiration felt by De Domenici when he referred to how Francesco Solimena, in order not to touch the original sketches, had "transferred onto another canvas" the unfinished compositions on biblical subjects which Luca Giordano had begun for the Duke of Ascalona; or how he had chosen to paint on canvas certain figures of apostles, in order not to destroy the frescos of Giacomo del Po in Santi Apostoli. The respect of the works by other artists had become, by this time, a trait of professional ethics, which an esteemed master could no longer ignore.[12]

When confronted with the conservation of ancient paintings, De Domenici's position was still linked to a consideration of their relative value: substitution was legitimate, when the new painting would be a better one, although this might lead to the loss of mural paintings. The passage that best illustrates this point refers to the frescos of Agostino Tesauro in the Chapel of Sant'Aspreno in the Duomo in Naples, which have recently been recovered from under the very repaintings which De Domenici lamented:

"One can see the stories and the ornaments which have been painted anew by an able but not skilled pupil of Solimena, by order of the present prince of Monte Miletto Don Leonardo Tocco, who wished them to be modernized and enriched; he has added gold highlights to the decoration, and completely repainted them. And you can see … how much excellence they have lost through having new colours laid over them; if one really wished to bring them up to date in order to improve them, then there was our renowned Francesco Solimena who would have consoled us for the loss of these esteemed paintings, by the acquisition of some of

46. *Giovanni Lanfranco, Madonna
and Child and Saints; with the
repainting by Luca Giordano.
Afragola, Chiesa di Rosario.*

his priceless works, which are as truly worthy of immortality as he is. But it is the misfortune of Naples, to seem to be congenitally disposed towards having the many paintings by the aforementioned great artists (which are to be venerated because of their antiquity), modernized by the hand of idiot painters (we call them botchers) rather than restored by worthy and skilful men".[ii,13]

Already in the seventeenth century, we find the profession of restorer becoming distinct from that of painter; De Dominici records as a painter specializing in restorations, a certain Giacomo di Castro (a pupil of Battistello who had become a follower of Domenichino):

"As Naples was at that time full of lovers of our arts, and with this delighting in paintings, they had him repair many of these works; some – which were almost dead and considered as lost – he brought back to life with his secrets; and Giacomo took up this work as he saw that some [practitioners] ruined rather than repaired paintings; and, more importantly, rather than retouching them, they had plastered them over, so that they lost the beauty which had been painted there. And this is what had happened to a head painted by Titian, which was in a sorry state, belonging to a Lord of the House of Capua, a certain Giacomo. Having seen the damage he tried to remedy it. And it is thus that he took up this work, and becoming excellently skilled in the knowledge of the different styles of the artists, because he had their brushwork before his eyes, with his hands he would treat these works so that he became very knowledgeable, as was also the case with Nicola di Liguoro who from childhood was his apprentice, and Antonio di Simone who was a disciple to Luca Giordano ...".[iii]

We know that Giacomo di Castro cleaned the paintings of the Monte di Misericordia in about 1670; as yet, no restoration has been found by the hand of the other two restorers mentioned by De Dominici–Nicola di Liguor o and Antonio di Simone. A very attractive portrait of Di Simone as a painter/philosopher was painted by De Dominici in his *Life of Luca Giordano*, printed in Rome in 1728; "drawn by his genius, he also applied himself to the repair of pictures, especially by Old Masters", becoming a connoisseur and collector [as a result].

"In fact, transforming himself into a figure of antiquity, he himself became an object of curiosity to the curious who would visit him, as he would appear to be

---

[ii] "*Si veggiono da capo le storie e gli ornamenti rinovati da uno scolaro, pratico ma non perito del Solimena; il quale per ordine dell'odierno principe di Monte Miletto Don Leonardo Tocco, che ha voluto modernarle ed arricchirle, lumeggiando con oro i suoi ornati, le ha tutte da capo ridipinte. Ma vedesi però ... quanto pregio abbian perduto per i nuovi colori soprappostovi; se si modernar si volevano, per migliorarle, vi era il nostro celebre Francesco Solimena che con le acquisto delle sue preziosissime, e degne dell'immortalità, come egli è veramente. Ma la disgrazia di Napoli par che abbia per connatural costellazione che molte pitture dei mentovati artefici, venerande per loro antichità, sian modernate da' più sciocchi pittori (che guastamestieri da noi vengono nominati) più tosto che da' valenti uomini rifatti*".

[iii] "*Essendo allora Napoli piena di amatori delle nostri arti e con ciò dilettantissimi di pittura, gli fecero moltissimi quadri accomodare, ed altri che erano come opere morte tenuti perduti, li ravvivò con suoi segreti; essendosi Giacomo messo a fare tale mestiere, per aver veduto che alcuni guastavano più tosto, che accomodavano le pitture: e, massimamente, impiastrandole in vece di ritoccarle, facevano perdere quel bello che vi era dipinto; come accadde alla testa di un ritratto di Tiziano, assai malconcio, che un Signore della Casa di Capua possedeva, il quale, chiamato Giacomo, e veduto quel danno, cercò al possibile di rimediarlo. Ed allora fu ch'egli a tal mestiere si diede; laonde acquistò una pratica eccellentissima nel conoscere le maniere de' pittori perchè sotto l'occhio aveva il pennelleggiare di quell'autore, e con le mani trattava quella pittura onde ne divenne intelligentissimo, come lo furono Nicola di Liguoro suo discepolo sin da fanciullo ed Antonio di Simone, che fu discepolo di Luca Giordano ...*".

more worthy of curiosity than the copious antique objects that he would show as copies to his visitors. He himself appeared as one of those philosophers of Antiquity, surrounded by books and antique objects, wearing about the house a medieval-looking wide-sleeved coat with four or more caps on his head, or else – at times – a curiously shaped paper hat, according to his need or if his head felt too hot. In other words, leading a philosopher's life, full of knowledge and information, especially relating to painters (much of which he shared with me), loved by his friends, valued by the nobility and esteemed by all. His lungs having become asthmatic, and only eating food if he happened to see it or if he suddenly remembered, notwithstanding that this did him no good, and not wishing to see in this any warning to his health, he was struck down with a high fever, and not many months ago he passed on to a better life at the age of seventy-two".[iv,14]

2. Florence and Rome

The repainting of pictures was not favoured by Tuscan authors writing on art, and, remaining faithful to Vasari's concept of "*disegno*", they are also careful to recommend conservation for earlier works pre-dating the modern manner in painting. Within the literary tradition, Masaccio was very much present (although often confused with Filippino Lippi in the cycle of frescos in the Carmine), as well as the artists active at the turn of the sixteenth century to whom Vasari had guaranteed renown, and Andrea del Sarto.

In his *Ragionamenti delle regole del disegno*, which was published around the same date as Vasari's work, Alessandro Allori mentioned in passing the cleaning in 1565 of the frescos in the Brancacci Chapel in the Carmine, as well as Agnolo Gaddi's cycle in the main chapel of the church. And in 1627, a certain Giuliano Fratellini, having discovered a secret method of cleaning paintings, noted that this method had then been used with good results on the frescos by Ghirlandaio and Filippino Lippi in Santa Maria Novella. Baldinucci referred to the cleaning in 1688 of the two equestrian portraits by Paolo Uccello and Andrea del Castagno in the Duomo in Florence: "not having removed any brightness of colour" their paintings remained as we "had seen and enjoyed them for so long beforehand".[15]

Apart from these restorations which show the continued interest in fifteenth-century works, in March 1590 a sum was paid to Alessandro Allori for having directed the "cleaning" ("*rifioritura*") and restoration of Ridolfo del Ghirlandaio's frescos in the chapel of Palazzo Vecchio, as well as the frieze by Cecchino Salviati in the Sala di Camillo, the whole

---

[iv] "*Anzi, transformandosi egli in una figura antica, era curioso oggetto a' curiosi che lo visitavano dappoichè appariva egli più curioso che non apparivano degne di curiosità le cose antiche che in copia a molti dimostrava. Così sembrava uno di que' filosofi dell'antichità, circondato da' libri e cose antiche, usando per casa una veste a foggia di schiavina e portando in testa quattro o più berette, e talvolta una sola di carta di figura curiosa ne costumava, secondo ne sentiva il bisogno o che la testa se riscaldava. Insomma, menando vita filosofica, pieno di cognizioni e di notizie, particolarmente de' pittori (delle quali molte da lui avute abbiamo), amato dagli amici, prezzato da' nobili e stimato da tutti, fatto asmatico di pulmoni, appetendo il cibo checchè vedeva o che li veniva in mente, tuttochè male notabile li recasse, non volendo sentire in ciò ammonizione alcuna, fu assalito da febbre acuta, e, non ha molti mesi, ch'è passato da questa a miglior vita in età d'anni settantadue*".

operation taking thirty-nine and a half days. For other paintings which have very old retouchings (such as the *Deposition* from the Compagnia del Tempio dell'Angelico), we can date the restoration from the fact that the works were submerged in the flood of 1557: extensive restorations of the paint layer can be seen in Fra Bartolomeo's and Giuliano Bugiardini's *Deposition* which is now in the Palazzo Pitti, and in Andrea del Sarto's *Madonna of the Harpies*, in which the whole of the lower section which was present until the recent restoration, was the work of an artist who had replicated with a good deal of understanding the style of the original.[16]

Baldinucci, when not deploring the quality of interventions on paintings by past masters, only mentioned the activity of restoration if this element was useful in the understanding of the character of a particular artist. This is the case, for instance, with Carlo Dolci, a pious and modest man, who during his sojourn in Innsbruck had retouched for the Archduchess of Austria "several devotional paintings, created by worthy men, which time had spoiled".[17] At times, the restorations seem to indicate a certain *pietas* for the Old Masters (of the kind shown by Vasari towards Perino del Vaga): when Pope Urban VIII granted the Church of the Santissima Annunziata in Florence the privilege of four penitentiaries, a commemorative stone was erected:

> "When the builders and labourers made the holes in the wall beneath the loggia so as to be able to erect scaffolding and comfortably place the inscription, one of the them was so thoughtless as not to realize that on the other side of the wall, in the small cloister, were the wonderful stories from the life of San Filippo Benizzi, painted by Andrea del Sarto. He dug through the entire thickness of the wall, emerging on the other side with the result that two of the most beautiful heads along with part of the chest, painted by that great master in the story of the resurrection of the child, fell to the ground ... Having heard this, Passignano rushed to the scene and having searched for the fallen pieces with great care amidst the rubble, retrieved them and with the greatest diligence, put them back where they had come from, so that the heads were once again almost as beautiful as they had been originally, with only the finest hair cracks visible at the joins. And thus, that which was seen then with great anguish by lovers of art, because of Passignano's skill, is today looked at with wonder."

Giovanni Bottari recounted a similar incident concerning Cecchino Salviati's fresco in the Palazzo Vecchio representing *Camillo attacking Brenno*, in which – in one the fallen participants – one can still detect the joins in the *intonaco* where Baldassare Franceschini (il Volterrano) picked up and replaced the fallen pieces.[18]

In Baldinucci's *Vocabolario toscano dell'arte del disegno*, the term *"rifiorire"* clearly makes the distinction between these integrating interventions, whether conservation or restoration, and the retouching, reworking or reconstruction which were always condemned whether or not they were arbitrary:

> "Almost to flower as new: extremely colloquial term which is used by the common people to describe their unbearable foolishness in having old paintings covered with a new layer of paint if they have been somewhat darkened with the passage of time, and usually by the hand of some unskilled practitioner, which not only removes the beauty of the painting, but also any appreciation of its antiquity. One could term to restore, or to repair or to bring back to a state of well-being, the remedies applied to small sections of a painting even by one of

47. *Andrea del Sarto, Madonna of the Harpies; showing the sixteenth- and seventeenth-century integrations. Florence, Galleria degli Uffizi.*

48. *Andrea del Sarto, detail from A Miracle of San Filippo Benizzi; showing the heads restored by Passignano. Florence, Chiesa della Santissima Annunziata, chiostro dei Voti.*

the greatest masters, where paint has been lost or otherwise damaged, which it is easy for a skilled hand to carry out; and as far as the painting is concerned, it only seems that one is removing that defect – however small – which disfigures and ruins the work. However, there are many, and not entirely lacking in expertise in the field of art, who have been of the opinion that great paintings must never be retouched even a little or at all, not even by those skilled in the practice because, whether immediately or with time, and to whatever extent or degree, the restoration will always become visible; it is also true that a painting which is not pure, untouched, will always be accompanied by a poor reputation".[v]

---

[v] *"Quasi di nuovo fiorire; termine volgarissimo che usa la minuta gente esprimere quella sua insopportabile sciocchezza di far talvolta ricoprir di nuovo colore, anche per mano di maestro imperito, qualche antica pittura che in processo di tempo sia alquanto annerita, con che toglie non solo il bello della pittura, ma eziandio l'apprezzabile dell'antichità. Direbbesi restaurare o resarcire o ridurre a bene essere, il raccomodare che si fa qualche volta alcuna piccola parte di pittura anche d'eccellente maestro, che in alcun luogo fosse scrostata o altrimenti guasta, perchè riesce facile a maestra mano; e alla pittura, non pare che altro si tolga che quel difetto che, quantunque piccolo, par che le dia molta disgrazia e discredito. Molti però, non del tutto imperiti dell'arte, sono stati di parere, che l'ottime pitture nè punto nè poco si ritocchino, anche da chi si sia, perchè, essendo assai difficile che, o poco o molto, o subito o in tempo, non si riconosca la restaurazione, per piccola che sia; è anche vero che la pittura che non è schietta va sempre accompagnata con gran discredito".*

In addition, the manner in which Baldinucci referred to the cleaning of paintings (another way of making them "reflower") was quite rightly brought up at the time of the "cleaning controversy":

> "This term *rifiorire* has also been understood by ignorant people as the practice of cleaning old paintings; which at times is carried out with the same lack of restraint as might be employed in rough-hewing a piece of marble. They do not take into account that it is often the case that the nature of the priming or ground layer is unknown, as is that of the pigments employed by the artist (and earth colours are much less susceptible to the action of lye or even milder cleaning agents than pigments artificially made). Not only do they endanger these paintings by losing with the cleaning the glazes, the half-tones and also the finishing touches, which constitutes their perfection; but they could flake off all in one go. I recall this happening to a fine self-portrait by Giovanni di San Giovanni, in oil on canvas. Maybe because the ornamentation required attention, it first went to a skilled gilder who, wanting to clean it, used the same method he had previously used on many paintings. Cleaning accomplished, almost immediately the priming and the paint began to flake off and fall to the ground in tiny pieces, and soon nothing of the original beautiful picture remained but the canvas and the stretcher".[19]

In his search for authoritative figures that he could use to back his position against restorations, the description Baldinucci gave of Passignano is significant. He described him as an artist who "held the art he practised in the highest esteem, and the works of skilled artists in high regard; because of this he would refuse to lay a finger on their creations, nor would he tolerate anyone else doing so"; to the extent that he refused do allow the traces of the casting to be removed from a bronze Crucifix by Prospero di Brescia, as well as not allowing it to be cleaned "as it seemed to him that no one but the artist could carry this out satisfactorily".

The concern that he showed in the search for the fragments of Andrea del Sarto's fresco and their reinstalment demonstrated the esteem in which he held Old Masters. However, the image we have of an artist respectful of the works of others is refuted by a documentary source which revealed that in 1618 he "paints" (*colorisce*) the panels of Sant'Agnese by Andrea del Sarto in the Duomo in Pisa, whilst Gaspare Celio related that the altarpiece in the Cappella degli Angeli in the Gesù, which was "by" Federico Zuccaro, "had been ruined by the Cavaliere Passignani". Baldinucci himself, having described this attitude a few pages earlier, then goes on to mention in passing a panel in the old manner, with much gold ornamentation, which Passignano was repairing during his stay in Venice. This brings one back once again to the almost universally accepted demarcation between respectful interventions on paintings in the *buona maniera*, and the freedom of intervention in the renovation of paintings in the old manner.[20]

The position characteristic of Baldinucci, with all the exceptions one might expect to find in practice, is in some way reflected in the respect shown in the enlargements carried out to Florentine altarpieces between the sixteenth and eighteenth centuries. In the church of Ognissanti, the *Assumption* by Francesco Traballesi was enlarged with an arched top by the addition of two angels, one of the Santi di Tito's most pleasing creations; in San Giorgio alla Costa, the *Conversion of San Giovanni Gualberto* by Passignano was adapted to Foggini's renovated altar, by the addition of a shaded coulisse, which created the illusion that the scene was taking place through an arch; whilst at the Carmine, Gregorio Pagani's

Adoration of the Magi was given an addition that perfectly matched the perfection of the surface of the original, which makes it one of the best preserved paintings in Florence.

In Rome also, renovations and restorations are often considered activities unsuited to a great master. Baglione joins Celio in deploring the restoration of the panel by Giulio Romano in Santa Maria dell'Anima, which was carried out by an artist for whom he had little regard (in terms of both his art and his behaviour), Carlo Saraceni: "wherever he had intervened, Giulio's hand was no longer apparent, and all the masters were very unhappy that he [Saraceni] should have dared to lay a hand with so little restraint, on so precious a work".[21]

For artists living at this time, even the partial reworking of one of their paintings by a colleague could become a question of honour. Pietro da Cortona, compelled by Pope Innocent X to cover the nudity of the Christ child in a painting by Guercino which had been presented to the Pope by Prince Ludovisi, "wrote a letter of apology to Giovanni Francesco [Guercino], protesting that he had been compelled to ruin his painting". Guido Reni, according to Bellori, "rightly complained" of the "excessive impudence" of Lanfranco who had replaced Reni's angel in the *Vision of Saint Ildefonso* with the figure of a Virgin by his own hand, in the Cappella Paolina in Santa Maria Maggiore; a reworking (*rifacimento*) executed at the request of the same Pope, once Reni had returned to Bologna.

Artists who, like Federico Zuccaro, insisted on both the antiquity and the nobility of the art of painting (it was Zuccaro who first cleaned the *Nozze Aldobrandine* when this renowned Roman wall painting was first unearthed) extended this point of honour to encompass the defence of past masters. According to Baglione, "it happened that the painting of Saint Luke by the hand of Raphael, which the artist had donated to this place [the Accademia di San Luca], having incurred some damage was given to Scipione da Gaeta, a worthy member of the Academy, be put into order; he carried out the repairs and then, as he was accustomed to do in his own works, he painted in a card beneath the figure, with his name. Federico, seeing this, and taking note of Scipione di Gaeta's presumption, destroyed the card and his signature, and covered him with insults, so that they came to blows, and it took much effort to calm them down. This is how zealously he guarded the honour of the great masters and of the excellent works of art".[22]

Giambattista Marino, writing to Bernardo Castello in 1604, felt obliged to apologize for having had Il Cavaliere d'Arpino retouch a *Venus* which had arrived in Rome in poor condition. A number of observations by Giulio Mancini show us a world more closely linked to collecting than to the conservation of paintings in churches. Mancini belongs wholly to the tradition that is critical of reworkings (*rifacimenti*), and we find him lamenting the retouching of more ancient works as well, such as those in the apse of San Lorenzo in Lucina (possibly), and on the *Paradiso* by Antonio Pastura in the Infirmary of Santo Spirito in Sassia. However, in his discussion on the conservation (*manutenzione*) and presentation of paintings, he shows himself not to be averse to the application of varnish, nor indeed to the cleaning of paintings. Speaking of varnish, he cites the precedent of Apelles' use of *atramentum* as described by Pliny the Elder, and asks himself how it could be suitable for paintings with tempera as the medium, such as those painted by the ancients, when modern usage of varnish was exclusively on paintings with oil as their medium. However, in San Giacomo degli Spagnoli, he had seen a painting which could no longer be enjoyed, restored with: "I know not what material, perhaps based on a varnish or maybe something else". He felt that the cleaning of paintings should be entrusted to "intelligent men with a knowledge of what constitutes dirt on paintings, of the variation in pigments in different areas of the painting, for instance in the flesh, or in the draperies containing black pigment, and in other parts, as different pigments will suffer to different degrees from the cleaning process. Should there be such a master with knowledge of these distinctions, then I would recommend cleaning, as one can see in the altarpiece of the Birth of Marcello Santa Maria della Pace, which was cleaned recently and has come back to life. If no such master is available with this discernment, I would recommend leaving them as they are".[vi,23]

From all over Italy and Europe, artists and their clients came together in Rome, each bringing their own customs and practices. As perhaps can be seen more clearly in Venice, alongside the various practices concerned with the conservation (*manutenzione*) of paintings, there is the tendency, associated with collecting, to improve and embellish works of art. Paul Brill repainted the landscape in a *Story of Saint Benedict* by Baldassare Peruzzi in the garden of San Silvestro in the Quirinale; Francesco Cozza restored paintings in private collections, as did Angelo Caroselli, who "held many secrets for the cleaning, and imitation of past styles (*maniere*)". This activity was one which often resulted in minor reworkings or additions, such as the small Christ figure painted in by Cigoli in a *Saint John in the Desert* by Annibale Carracci in Casa Chigi, a collection which also records in its inventory a *Nativity* by Sodoma and a *Venus Cutting her Nails with a Cherub*, both retouched by Ventura Salimbeni. Of Borgognone, Baldinucci goes as far as to say that "for a certain sculptor", he worked on some portraits by Velasquez which had been left – apparently – unfinished, and that he completed them.[24]

In the case of frescos, an example might be the repainting of Sebastiano del Piombo's *Polyphemus* in the Sala dei Pineti in the Farnesina, carried out in the middle of the seventeenth century, as well as the cleaning of the Sistine Chapel and the restoration of Raphael's *Sybils* in Santa Maria della Pace, of which we have the details in a letter written by Fabio Chigi in 1627. The intervention became necessary due to the staining caused by the oiled paper used by copyists in tracing:

> "Because this is a jealously guarded activity, I shared [the information] with monsignor Mancini, as well as with Giovanni Lanfranco and Cavalier Giuseppe D'Arpino, both excellent painters. I followed the procedure adopted in the Vatican, where the Sala Regia, which had become unrecognizable with the accumulated dust of years, was cleaned in the following manner, and now can be enjoyed to the full in all its painted details. We began with the Prophets above, continuing beneath the cornice with Raphael's *Sybils*, and then proceeding in the following manner: with the bread from a country loaf, suitably moist inside and at times warmed, if necessary, the painting is rubbed, removing all the dust and the counter-effects of smoke, the air and time. Finally, a thin layer of glair is applied which revives the colours wonderfully".[vii,25]

---

vi "*uomini intelligenti che conoschino la sordidezza della pittura, la varietà del colore a parte a parte, come per esempio nel color delle carni, in quello dei panni con il nero, et altrove, che per distinzione di colore pate più o meno dell'esser lavata. Pertanto quando vi fosse artefice che sapesse questa distinzione, io loderei lavarle, com'è visto nella Pace quell'altare della Natività di Marcello lavato a quest'anni che s'è ravvivato. Ma quando non vi fosse maestro con quell'Avvedutezza, io le lascerei.*"

vii "*Questo, perchè era negotio geloso, l'ho comunicato con monsignor Mancini, con Giovanni Lanfranchi e col Cavalier Giuseppe d'Arpino, pittori eccellenti, et ho seguito l'esempio del Vaticano ove la Sala Regia, che per la polvere di tanti anni non si riconosceva, è stata rinettata in questa maniera et ora si gode ottimamente in tutte le sue parti dipinte. Si è cominciato a' Profeti di sopra e si seguirà di sotto il cornicione alle Sibille di Raffaello; e si fa in questa maniera: con pagnotte da contadini alquanto umidi dentro, ovvero, ove occorre, calde, si frega la pittura e si leva tutta la polvere e contrattione del fumo, dell'aria e del tempo; di poi se li dà una mano sottilissima di chiara d'ovo la quale ravviva i colori mirabilmente.*"

In his *Lives*, and in the manuscript annotations in the margins of a copy of Baglione, Bellori also referred to several examples of paintings which had suffered through poor cleaning or repainting: for instance, Domenichino's frescos in San Luigi de'Francesi, his panel in San Lorenzo degli Speziali, the *Tabitha* by Baglione in Saint Peter's which was retouched – and ruined – by the artist himself.[26] However, in such a melting pot of diverse traditions as was Rome, it was Bellori who would become the author who, leaving behind the tradition which unconditionally condemned all restorations, and through his keen appraisal of the restoration work carried out under the direction of Maratta on Raphael's frescos in the Stanze and the Loggia di Psiche, opened up the debate on the restoration of the painted image (*restauro pittorico*), which was to involve some of Europe's most artistically cultivated authors of the eighteenth century.

In Florence, the attitude of respect towards tradition and towards the masters of old which we found in Baldinucci, in the eighteenth century led to some notable interventions on the older paintings of the Tuscan school. In 1730, Giovanni Bottari, in his preface to Raffaele Borghini's *Riposo*, paused to comment on the conservation of good and ancient paintings, specifically using as examples paintings from the sixteenth-century school which corresponded to his taste, in contrast with the modern styles: "every one affected and mannered". The Old Masters, when they lacked art, compensated for their lack with a close attention to nature, and left behind them works which were worthy of study for these qualities and for the "great treasure chest of old costumes and manners of the time". Nevertheless, the earliest of these works referred to by Bottari were still the frescos of the Brancacci Chapel, for which he wished more respectful behaviour from the faithful who would light candles and hang *ex voto* to the miraculous Madonna on the altar.[27]

The interest in the beginnings of painting remained alive in certain local traditions, for instance in the restorations which continued on the frescos of the Camposanto in Pisa (between 1665 and 1670, it was Zaccaria Rondinosi who worked on them, and in 1728 the Melani brothers, who were painters of perspectives and printmakers). This would eventually lead to an important intervention, such as the revision of the frescos in the Capellone degli Spagnoli in Santa Maria Novella by Agostino Veracini between 1731 and 1733, and of the Rinuccini Chapel in Santa Croce in 1736.

A pupil of Sebastiano Galeotti and of Sebastiano Ricci, Veracini produced paintings in an eclectic style, sometimes of note because of their high degree of culture, if not for any great pictorial beauty. In the Cappellone of the Spagnoli, it was his restorations on which Ruskin paused to remark, in his *Mornings in Florence*. For a long time, they led to perplexity and confusion, as, for instance, the addition of Giotto's Campanile in the *Via Veritatis*, or the edifice in the *Pentecost* painted in the vault. Almost all these additions were removed in the restoration which took place around 1965; during the restoration of the Rinuccini Chapel which took place during this same period, accurate photographic documentation was carried out which allows one to follow in detail the work of the eighteenth-century restorer.

It is worth noting that Veracini would repaint the damaged parts of frescos, but would   49, 50
confine himself to the architecture and the backgrounds, whilst abstaining from "improvements" to the figures: he added mullioned windows to the end of the nave in the Temple of Jerusalem in the *Cacciata di Giovacchino*, simplified the coffered ceiling in the House of the Pharisee, painted over the now tarnished metal leaf of the cutlery in the *Conversion of the Magdalen* and *Christ in the House of Martha and Mary*; but in the case of the figures, with the exception of repainting some of the drapery, he only touched the hand of the youngest apostle participating in the feast of the Pharisee. Finally, as was also the case in the Capellone

49. *Giovanni da Milano, detail of the Meeting at the Golden Gate; with the repainting by Agostino Veracini, 1736. Florence, Santa Croce, Rinuccini Chapel.*

50. *Giovanni da Milano, detail of the Meeting at the Golden Gate; after the removal of the repainting by Agostino Veracini. Florence, Santa Croce, Rinuccini Chapel.*

*51. Matteo di Pacino, Noli me
tangere; with the repainting by
Agostino Veracini, 1736.
Florence, Santa Croce,
Rinuccini Chapel.*

*52. Matteo di Pacino, Noli me
tangere; after the removal of the
repainting by Agostino Veracini.
Florence, Santa Croce,
Rinuccini Chapel.*

degli Spagnoli, he repainted in light blue the ultramarine of the backgrounds, interpreting
them naturalistically, as skies. The proximity of Giovanni da Milano shows up the wretched-
ness of the eighteenth-century restoration, whilst on the works of Matteo di Picino (that is,
"the Master of the Rinuccini Chapel"), the outcome of Agostino Veracini's restoration is not
displeasing: for instance, the leafy fronds with which he transformed the garden in the *Noli
me tangere*, the abolition of a spatially ineffective wall replaced with a blue sky, and various
divagations of a vegetable order.[28]

    Some of his restorations have received critical approbation, for instance the additions
to Botticelli's *San Barnaba* altarpiece, which are thought to be compensating for an earlier
mutilation. It should not be necessary to point out the eighteenth-century character of his
paint handling, which can clearly be seen, for instance, in the shepherd's dog in the *Incontro
alla Porta Aurea* by Giovanni da Milano, were it not for the fact that until Erling Skaug's verification of the punchmarks it had been generally assumed that the tondo representing *Christ*
painted in the centre of the vault of the Rinuccini Chapel was the product of the eighteenth-
century restoration. Such a conclusion can easily be disproved if one looks at Veracini's awk-
wardness in the restoration of a supposed Cimabue, a *Madonna* by Bernardo Daddi now in
the Accademia, restored in 1750.[29]

    An even greater ability than Veracini's in adapting to the style of painters pre-dating
the modern manner can be seen in the restorations of Ippolito Maria Cigna di Volterra, who
was responsible for the 1732 repainting which, until 1966, covered part of Signorelli's
Circumcision in the National Gallery in London. Still in existence is his restoration of Luca

51, 52

53

54

55

*53. Sandro Botticelli,
San Barnaba Altarpiece; with
the enlargement by Agostino
Veracini. Florence, Galleria
degli Uffizi.*

54. *Giovanni da Milano, the
Redeemer. Florence, Santa
Croce, Rinuccini Chapel.*

55. *Bernardo Daddi, Madonna and Child, detail; restored by Agostino Veracini in 1750. Florence, Galleria dell'Accademia.*

56. Luca Signorelli, Annunciation;
restored by Ippolito Cagna, 1731.
Volterra, Pinacoteca Civica.

56   Signorelli's *Annunciation* in the Pinacoteca in Volterra, which was struck by lightning in 1731; a work which, as we now see it, is glazed with brown tones quite foreign to the taste of the painter from Cremona, and which was described by Cavalcaselle as one of the artist's "most graceful and pleasing" works.[30]

3. Venice

In Venice, during the sixteenth century, we encounter the usual adaptations and repaintings, such as that on the panel by Antonio di Negroponte in San Francesco della Vigna, with its addition of an Eternal Father in the style of Diana; whilst in the *Sacra Conversazione* by Lotto in the Museo Capodimonte in Naples, a child Saint John the Baptist in the style of Bassano has replaced the donor who was being presented by Saint Peter the Martyr. Other

57, 58   alterations were dictated by changes in taste: in the *Crucifixion* by Giovanni Bellini now in the Museo Correr, the kind of aviary filled with cherubim above the arms of the Cross must have appeared too medieval even for a devotional picture, and it was concealed beneath a cloudy sky. But not always does one find such an understanding of the painting to be altered; the *Pietà* in the Ducal Palace (also by Giovanni Bellini) was squared up in 1571 by a painter traditionally identified with Farinati. A landscape was added to it without any attempt being made to harmonize it with the fifteenth-century style of the painting, in addition to which, it was set out with an extremely high vanishing point, which is completely out of keeping with the original figures which are seen from below.[31]

     A more advanced taste was shown in the 1611 repainting (although it was also

59, 60   reworked in the nineteenth century) carried out on the *Saint John the Baptist* and the *Saint Matthew* by Alvise Vivarini in the Accademia in Venice; removed by Pellicioli in 1949, it was characterized by the presence of a lamb in the style of Veronese at the feet of the Baptist. Sixteenth-century examples of restorations such as these which finished by distorting the original were also mentioned by Zanetti: in the Library in San Marco the figures of Mars and a cherub which were repainted by L'Aliense in a "Giorgione", a fragment of the school of Bonifacio which is today in the Accademia, representing a *Madonna and Child with Saint Rosanna and Saint Catherine*. In San Martino in Murano, "the panel on the High Altar was by Tintoretto, but it was restored by Palma; a Bishop Saint is by Tintoretto, and also the figure of a poor man, but the rest is almost all by Palma"; in the Scuola Grande della Misericordia, Il Padovanino had restored the *Madonna della Misericordia* by Veronese, adding a cherub which does not appear in the engraving of the painting by Agostino Carracci.[32]

     These interventions were often the result of the necessity of repairing damage, as was the case, one imagines, with the reworking by Paris Bordone of the *Tempest* by Palma Vecchio in the Scuola Grande di San Marco. In the Scuole, moreover, the adaptation of series of canvases to new decorations or new surroundings was a fairly frequent occurrence. In 1551, those by Carpaccio in the Scuola di San Giorgio degli Schiavoni were moved from the upper room to the ground floor, and it must have been at this point in time that in

61   *The Story of Saint George Baptising the Pagans* the opening for the door in the bottom left section of the painting, beneath the famous group of musicians, was painted in with a summary but nevertheless intelligent intervention. In 1544, in the Scuola di San Giovanni Evangelista, some of the canvases had to be adapted to their new positions, and Titian's advice was sought: "a man whose experience is known to all", and he suggested that "the canvases

57. *Giovanni Bellini,*
Crucifixion; with the sixteenth-
century repainting. Venice,
Museo Correr.

58. *Giovanni Bellini,*
Crucifixion; after the 1947
restoration. Venice, Museo
Correr.

*59. Alvise Vivarini, Saint John the
Baptist; with the seventeenth- and
eighteenth-century repainting. Venice,
Gallerie dell'Accademia.*

*60. Alvise Vivarini, Saint John the Baptist;
after the 1949 restoration. Venice, Galleria
dell'Accademia.*

61. *Vittore Carpaccio, Saint*
George baptizes the pagans; with
the reframing of the the opening
for the doorway, c. 1511.
Venice, Scuola di San Giorgio
degli Schiavoni.

should be cut from the bottom, which would reduce them from four to one and a half, and this cut would not damage the aforementioned canvases in any way". Carpaccio's painting, with the famous view of Rialto, with the cut in the lower left-hand section which was badly reintegrated in the seventeenth century, gives us an idea of the effects of the reduction in size which occurred in the sixteenth century.[33]

The recipes in the Venetian manuscript in the Biblioteca Nazionale in Florence have reminded us of the materials in use in the sixteenth century, whilst two seventeenth-century manuscripts published in 1849 by Mary Merrifield direct us rather towards the methods used in Venice, and elsewhere, in the cleaning of paintings: these were the Codex 992 of the University Library in Padua, and Giambattista Volpato's *Modo da tener nel dipinger*. Volpato clearly defined the attitude which even such a minor painter as he would have had when confronted with requests to intervene on old paintings. In fact, the younger of the two apprentices, between whom the imagined dialogue takes place, asks how to clean certain smoky paintings which he had seen in the master's studio:[viii] "It must be some trick to play a friend or patron, because good pictures either never are washed or the owners perform the operation themselves; and it is not merely a mechanical operation, because the pictures are easily spoiled, for if washed too much, those last retouchings which are the perfection of the work are effaced, and I have seen many paintings spoiled in this manner, by ignorant persons who know not what mischief they do. And I have even seen them wash paintings on panel and canvas in such a way that after being washed, they have scaled off, because the gesso underneath was affected by the moisture, and swelled; therefore it is great folly to wash good paintings."

If cleaning is inevitable, then "Take some ashes, which have been sifted very fine that there may not be any pieces of charcoal or any large substances which may scratch the picture; put them into a small pipkin with pure water, and with a sponge spread them all over the painting, and clean it by moving about the sponge gently, then wash it off quickly with pure water, because the ashes corrode the colour. Afterwards wash it well with clear water, dry it with a linen cloth, and then varnish it with white of egg."

Oilings are to be avoided "for the oil is not good for pictures, except on their backs when they are scaling off, as I have told you; and in proof of this, see the *Saint Peter the Martyr*, at Venice, who having been oiled so many times by sacrilegious blockheads who have copied him, is so spoiled and blackened, that there is no telling what sort of face he has, and yet I recollect when he was beautiful, and you may observe the children, which being above reach of similar influences, are in excellent preservation".[34]

"Commercial restoration" enjoys a reputation which is sufficiently bad for me not to have to dwell on its inadequacies. In the eighteenth century, with the diffusion amongst collectors of the "grand taste" for Italian painting and, in particular, for sixteenth-century Venetian painting, Venice had become a great centre for the commerce of art, where all the practices associated with the art market such as cleaning, adaptation, repainting and falsification were carried out. And it is in the seventeenth century that altarpieces began to be acquired by the great collections, especially the princely ones; for instance, those by Andrea del Sarto in Florence, or the Correggios in Modena, and these have been kept in their

---

[viii] These passages are Mary Merrifield's original translations of the Volpato text, not my own, and can be found alongside the original text in the recently republished Dover Edition of the original 1849 edition.

original monumental dimensions, without having been painfully cut down because of their excessive size, unlike Antonello da Messina's *Pala di San Cassiano* for instance, or even a *Marriage of the Virgin* by Palma Vecchio which Ridolfi refers to, in the home of Luigi Quirini.[35]

Thefts were also potentially linked to an art market that had to be kept stocked; Boschini referred to Moretto's *Nozze di Cana* which had been stolen from the convent of Santi Fermo e Rustico near Vicenza: "… as the painting was vast, the thieves in their haste, were not able to keep it intact, so that rolling it up as best they could, they damaged it disfiguring the human figures. After some time, the painting was found, like a bloodless corpse, as though lacerated by cruel knife wounds, so that it looks worse from its scars than a body afflicted with leprosy …".

A better fate was suffered by Paolo Veronese's *Ascension* in San Francesco in Padua; only the figure of Christ now remains in the original church, integrated within a work by Pietro Damini. The *Apostles*, stolen in 1625, quickly found their way into the collection of   62, 63 Lord Arundel and then, after passing through various other collections, now find themselves in the National Gallery in Prague.

Volpato, notwithstanding the declarations in his manuscript, must have had good first-hand experience of the restoration and preservation of old paintings, in view of the event which is referred to by Verci in precisely this context of thefts and the improper appropriation of paintings. In Feltre, not long after 1674, he appropriated two altarpieces by Jacopo Bassano in the churches of Tomo and Rasai; under the pretext of restoring them, he made copies of them which he then substituted for the originals "having had the especially clever idea of oiling the reverse of the originals, asserting that thus they would be protected from the injuries of time, the object in truth being to confound the smell of fresh paint emanating from the copies". The matter would only be cleared up in 1682 and, although Volpato was convicted, the pictures were not recovered, and eventually found their way to the Alte Pinakothek in Munich.[36]

Amongst all the Venetian painters of the Seicento, the best known for his restorations (as well as for his copies of the Old Masters) was Pietro Vecchia. The contest between him and Father Time, which we encounter in the *Carta del Navegar Pitoresco*, also clearly shows the taste for patina which was widespread amongst seventeenth-century lovers of art:

"Il Vecchia halted Time and said: hey,
What do you think you're up to with your glazing?
Are you trying to make painting immortal?
Stop, I want you to stay and be astonished.
And he shows Time a really dark canvas
And says to him: for how long, have you been working away
To make a patina over these colours,
So that this painting becomes old?
And Time replies: for more than a hundred years
I have been studying, and trying to paint on
That which the brush was unable to supply,
And there I think I know more than you do.
Ah no, there you are wrong, Vecchia replies:
I want to rub out what you have done;
And here is the proof. And lo and behold, in one fell swoop

62. *Paolo Veronese, Apostles; stolen from the church of San Francesco in Padua in 1625. Prague, National Gallery.*

63. *Paolo Veronese and Pietro Damini, Ascension; integrated in 1625. Padua, San Francesco.*

The painting is cleaned, making it new and shiny
And then Time said: I know
That what I have done can quickly be undone.
If you were as quick in the making [it old],
I would bow down to you and wish you good-day.
And indeed Vecchia, in his old way,
Careful, diligent and industrious,
Gloriously shames Time,
And returns the picture to its pristine state in no time at all".[ix]

ix "*El Vechia ferma el tempo e dise: olà/Cosa pensistu a far col tuo velar? Vustu forsi Pitura inmortalar?/Ferma, che voi che ti resti incantà./E mostra al tempo una tela scura,/Col dirghe: quando xe, che ti laori/a far patina sora sti colori,/Perchè vechia deventa sta pitura?/Responde el tempo: l'è cent'ani, e pi,/Che studio e che me sforzo a colorir/Quel che'l penelo no*

The *Madonna and Saints* by Battista Franco in San Giobbe, which Zanetti recorded as having been restored by Vecchia, cannot be traced in order to verify his methods; but Giorgione's *Pala di Castelfranco* is recorded by Nadal Melchiori as having been restored by Vecchia in 1674, aided by Melchioro Mechiori who, without "touching it with a brush, but solely cleaning it and fixing certain portions which had lifted, wonderfully returned it to its original state".[x] These "lifting portions" corresponded, it would seem, to the inserts of the paint layer which were transported onto canvas and then reattached to the panel; most of the left-hand side of the face of San Liberale was treated in this way, a restoration which is one of the most important testimonies of the origins of the process of transfer.[37]

Vecchia was also active as a painter; in the *Carta del Navegar Pitoresco*, after the contest with Time over cleaning and artificial ageing, he demonstrated his ability in the execution of original works. Michele Piera, however, is recorded by Boschini solely as a restorer:

"That repairing paintings damaged
in accidents, or some mishap,
with such skill and grace
you cannot tell where they are repaired.
Because in a city like this one,
In which there are millions of paintings,
If there was no one to care for them worthily
It would be a real shame".[xi,38]

The letters from Grand Prince Ferdinand of Tuscany to Niccolò Cassana, a painter who bought paintings for him in Venice and was his habitual restorer, demonstrated clearly the nature of the adaptations that restorers of picture collections often found themselves having to perform:

"Signor Niccola – he writes in September 1698 – a painting has fallen into my hands which appears in good taste as far as the animals and the rest are concerned; it only seems lacking [in taste] in the figure, which I would like covered with a tasteful tint, but keeping the same attitude. The drapery, shirt and head-dress you may repaint to your taste; I should also like that the two heads of the cadavers to be covered, both the woman's and the man's, but I should like you to paint everything from nature, because it is this that I ask you, that will make a fine picture".[xii,39]

---

ha possù suplir./Dove pretendo saver più de ti./Misier no, misier no, replica el Vechia:/Te vogio depenar quel che ti ha fato; vegno ala prova. E là presto, int'uno trato,/El neta el quadro, che ognun se ghe ispechia./Alora dise el tempo: so anche mi,/Che a desfar quel che ho fato se fa presto./Se in l'operar ti fussi così lesto,/M'inchinerave e te daria 'l bondì./El Vechia, con la strada vechia aponto,/Propria, particular, industriosa,/Fa una vergogna al tempo gloriosa,/E torna el quadro in pristino int'un ponto."

[x] *"senza ponervi pennello, ma solamente col nettarla et attacarvi certi fogli sollevati la resero mirabilmente nel primiero stato".*

[xi] *"Che xe conzar I quadri danizai/Da l'acidente, o da qualche desgrazia,/Con tanta bela industria e tanta grazia,/Che nons'acorze dove i sia conzai./Perchè int'una Città come xe questa,/Dove gh'è milioni de piture,/Si non ghe fusse de ste degne cure,/La sarave una pena manifesta".*

[xii] *"Signor Niccola ... mi è capitato un quadro che mi è parso per gli animali, et il restante, di buon gusto; solo manca nella figura, quale vorrei mi ricoprisse di una tinta dig ran gusto, però nella stessa medesima attitudine. Et il panno, e camicia, e acconciatura di testa rifatela a vostro gusto; come anche vorrei che le due teste di morto, sì di femmina che di uomo le ricoprisse ma tutto vorrei, che vedesse dal vero, perchè con questo che vi avviso facciate che si riduce un buon quadro."*

The adaptations of paintings to "good taste", or to the requirements of the galleries of the great, take us quite naturally and easily from Venice to the world of European collectors in the Age of Absolutism.

Notes

1. For a more detailed discussion of the examples of restoration and repainting cited in Malvasia, and more generally, in the Bolognese tradition, I refer you to the first edition of this volume. For the transfer of images, see Malvasia, 1686, pp. 67, 253, 299. A not inconsiderable nucleus of transferred images was brought together in the Chiostro delle Madonne of the cemetery of the Certosa, from the churches which were suppressed in the last years of the Kingdom of Italy. On these, see I. Massa, *Le Madonne della Certosa di Bologna*, in "Strenna storica Bolognese", XX, 1970, pp. 129–157; G. Guidicini, Ms Gozzadini 269 in the Biblioteca dell'Archigennasio di Bologna (additional issue, up to 1814, c. 31).

2. On the taste for the Early Masters in Malvasia, see: 1678, I, p. 26; R. Longhi in "Paragone", n. 5, 1950, pp. 23–24; Previtali, 1964, pp. 53–59; F. Arcangeli, *Natura ed espressione nell'arte bolognese-emiliana*, catalogue of the exhibition, Bologna, 1970, p. 29; in 1678 (I, p. 27) he lamented the "fearless clumsiness" (*baldanzosa goffaggine*) of the workmen, who, with a certain malignant glee, took pleasure in whitewashing over the works of the great and worthy artists of the past, and in 1686 (p. 93) the fact that "with such great loss to art", the frescoed arches beneath the colonnade of San Giacomo Maggiore had been walled in.

3. 1678, II, p. 51; see also pp. 24, 28–29, 33, 43, 50; Malvasia, 1686, pp. 40, 204, 247, 291, 312; C. Celano, 1692, II, p. 92. For examples of retouching by other Bolognese artists, see: Malvasia, 1678, I, pp. 196, 355, 357, II, p. 8; F. Baldinucci, *Lettera di F. B. fiorentino ... nella quale si risponde as alcuni quesiti in material di pittura ...*, in *Opere*, III, Milan, 1809, p. 333; *Le pitture di Bologna*, Bologna 1706, p. 71. For the reference to San Cipriano in Bottari, see 1754, p. 244.

4. For the many passages in Guercino's book of accounts (published on pp. 307–343 of the 1841 edition of *Felsina* Pittrice) in which restorations or retouchings are referred to, see Conti, 1973, pp. 218–219. Of particular importance are the comments on 30 April 1643, 14 July 1652 (retouching of the Titian for Cardinal Cibo with *"The Virgin with Saint Joseph"*), of 2 September 1662, on the addition of the figure of the Virgin in the painting with Saint Philip Neri in the *Madonna di Galliera*. See also: F. Scannelli, *Microcosmo della Pittura*, Cesena, 1657, pp. 74, 115; Malvasia, 1678, II, pp. 42, 263, 265, 267, 271; Malvasia, 1686, pp. 48–49; notes in Malvasia, 1678, ed. 1841, II, note 2, p. 310; *Omaggio al Guercino*, catalogue of the exhibition, Cento, 1967, n. 9 (radiographs confirming the presence of a first laying in of the head of Christ in the *Cattedra di San Pietro*), n. 16 (retouchings removed from *Cristo risorto che appare alla Madre*, probably those noted on the 5 September 1653 in Guercino's account book); J. Plesters, in *Rapporto della Soprintendenza alle Gallerie di Bologna*, Bologna, 1968, pp. 59–62; D. Mahon, in *Il Guercino*, catalogue of the exhibition, Bologna, 1968, nn. 28 and 63.

   On the *Immaculate Conception*, which had been in Dresden, see Malvasia, 1678, II, p. 267; J. C. Calvi, in *Malvasia*, 1678, ed. 1841, II, p. 294; notes in *Malvasia*, 1841, II, note 51 p. 294; A. Mezzetti, *Dosso e Battista ferraresi*, Milan, 1965, pp. 79–80; F. Gibbons, *Dosso and Battista Dossi*, Princeton, 1968, pp. 238–239.

5. Bellori, 1672–1696, p. 10; Malvasia, 1678, II, pp. 12, 55–56, 64; Baldinucci, 1681–1728, ed. 1845–47, IV, p. 28.

6. Malvasia, 1678, II, p. 182 (letter from Francesco Albani of 1653 on the restoration of one of his own paintings damaged in an attempt to steal the painting); Malvasia, 1686, p. 86 (Felice Cegnini, see A. Ottani Cavina, in *Il tempio di San Giacomo*, Bologna, 1967, note 30 p. 131); *Le pitture di Bologna*, Bologna 1706, p. 323 (Antonio Burrini); *Le pitture di Bologna*, Bologna 1776, p. 111 (Leonello Spada); *Le pitture di Bologna*, Bologna 1792, p. 12 [Madonna di Galliera restored (*risarcita*) by Cavalier Franceschini].

7. O. Giannone, *Giunte sulle vite de'pittori napoletani*, Naples, 1941, p. 95. For the bad effects of Naples' climate, see C. Celano, 1692, I, pp. 267, 277; III, pp. 20–30, 123; De Dominici, 1742–1743, I, pp. 85, 126–127; II, pp. 276, 304.

8. De Domenici, 1742–1743, I, p. 192. Similar characteristics can be seen in other examples of interventions recorded by De Domenici, see: I, pp. 172–173, 190–191, 194; II, p. 157. For adaptations of paintings and restorations (including transfers *a massello*), of a devotional character, see: Celano, 1692, I, p. 272; II, pp. 43, 207; III, pp. 78–79, 82; De Dominici, 1742–1743, I, pp. 84–85, 191, 195; II, pp. 60, 61, 161, 196, 324; III,

pp. 107, 442, 458. For works which underwent restorations to bring them up to date devotionally, see: *III mostra di restauri*, Naples, 1960, pp. 51–53. However, a verifiable example makes us aware that De Dominici might be explaining away certain stylistic conventions with which he was not familiar, through the hypotheses of retouching or repainting, as he does for the *Crucifixion* by Domenico Fiasella in San Giorgio dei Genovesi (II, pp. 300–301; see R. Longhi, *Gentileschi padre e figlia*, in *Scritti giovanili*, Florence, 1961, p. 282; F. Bologna, *Caravaggio 1610*, in "Prospettiva", n. 23, 1980, pp. 38–39).

9. With the exception of the *Torture* and *Decapitation of San Gennaro* (IV *Mostra di restauri*, op. cit., pp. 71–72) by Caracciolo, I owe the identification of ancient restorations on the paintings of the Certosa di San Martino to Antonio de Mata, who was restoring them when I was preparing the 1973 edition of this volume; a friend the memory of whom is as bright now as then when I followed him in his work. Some examples received commentaries from R. Causa, *Musei Napoletani: restauri a San Martino*, in "Arte illustrata", n. 39–40, 1971, pp. 17–27; a request made to Lanfranco in 1638 to retouch his own works, at the wish of the prior, helps us to understand the spirit in which these repaintings were carried out in the Certosa (see N. F. Faraglia, *Notizie di alcuni artisti che lavorarono nella chiesa di S. Martino e nel tesoro di S. Gennaro*, in "Archivio storico per le provincie napoletane", 1885, pp. 441–442 and 457–458). On the *Saint Michael* by Marco Pino, see *III Mostra di restauri*, op. cit., n. 9.

10. On Lanfranco, see: Bellori, 1672, p. 388–390; De Dominici, 1742–1743, III, p. 50.
     For Luca Giordano, see: Bellori, 1672, p. 379; Passeri, 1673, pp. 161–162; Celano, 1692, III, pp. 8–9; De Dominici, 1742–1743, III, p. 142 (note in the margin), 345, 430; Cochin, 1758, I, pp. 170–171; A. Griseri, *Luca Giordano "alla maniera di ..."*, in "Arte Antica e Moderna", 1961, pp. 417–438; O. Ferrari–G. Scavizzi, *Luca Giordano*, Naples, 1966, I, p. 125 and note 22 p. 132; II, pp. 182, 217; Ferretti, 1981, pp. 137–138, 142; E. Schleier, in *Civiltà del Seicento a Napoli*, catalogue of the exhibition, Naples, 1985, n. 2137, pp. 333–336.

11. De Dominici, 1742–1743, II, p. 296; III, pp. 536, 546–547, 553–554.

12. *III Mostra dei restauri*, op. cit., nn. 18–19; another instance of an enlargement being made using fragments from another painting is mentioned in G. Previtali, *Frammenti di Tanzio a Napoli*, in "Paragone" n. 229, 1969, pp. 42–45; an important example of excessive confidence in the treatment of paintings of excellence, is that of the *San Vito* in the church of Santi Marcellino e Festo, obtained from a *Venus and Mars* by Battistello, hiding (with the appropriate repainting, which probably dates from the beginning of the nineteenth century) the figure of the goddess (see *Civiltà del Seicento*, op. cit., n. 2. 24, pp. 210–211). On the respect which Solimena showed towards the work of other artists, see: De Dominici, 1742–1743, III, pp. 431, 589, 595; F. Bologna, *Francesco Solimena*, Naples, 1958, pp. 260–261; Ferrari–Scavizzi, op. cit., I, pp. 187–188. De Dominici, 1742–1743, I, p. 199 (the author of the repaintings was Filippo Andreoli; see P. Giusti–P. Leone de Castris, *Forastieri e regnicoli*, Naples, 1985, p. 228). For the attitudes taken towards the loss or the dispersal of Old Masters, see Celano, 1692, I, pp. 163–164; De Dominici, 1742–1743, I, pp. 33–34; II, pp. 40, 55.

13. De Dominici, 1742–1743, I, p. 199 (the author of the repainting was Filippo Andreoli; see P. Giusti–P. Leone de Castris, *Forastieri e regnicoli*, Naples, 1985, p. 228. For positions held with respect to the loss or dispersal of ancient works of art, see Celano, 1692, I, pp. 163–164; De Dominici, 1742–1743, I, pp. 33–34; II, pp. 40, 55.

14. B. De Dominici, *Vita di Luca Giordano*, in G. P. Bellori, *Le vite de'pittori, scultori ed architetti moderni*, Rome, 1728, pp. 391–392; De Dominici, 1742–1743, I, p. 126; II, pp. 289–291; III, pp. 448–449; Ghelli, 1788, pp. 276–277 (Giacomo di Castro remembered as Giacomo Costa); S. Ortolani, *La mostra della pittura napoletana dei secoli XVII–XVIII–XIX*, Naples, 1938, p. 74; M. Cagiano di Azavedo, *Una scuola napoletana di restauro nel XVII e XVIII secolo*, in "Bollettino dell'Istituto Centrale di Restauro", n. 1, 1950, pp. 44–45; R. Causa, *Opere d'arte del Pio Monte di Misericordia*, Cava dei Tirreni–Naples, 1970, pp. 35–37.

15. A. Allori *Ragionamenti delle regole del disegno*, Florence, Biblioteca Nazionale, Ms Palatino E. B. 16.4 cc. 33v–34r (this passage was kindly brought to my notice by Detlef Heikamp); Baldinucci, 1681–1728, ed. 1845–47, I, pp. 441–442, 496; Forni, 1866, pp. 435–439. Another cleaning of the Ghirlandaio frescos is noted by Bottari, 1730, note 2 p. 281. Alessandro Allori, in 1582, draws up a balance of the work undertaken at Poggio a Caiano and annotates his interventions on the frescos of Andrea del Sarto, Franciabigio and Pontormo: on the latter he repaints "the sky" (*l'aria*) and it is interesting to note that he terms a *rifacimento* the enlargement that he carries out on the two former frescos, with the attitude – almost that of a sculpture restorer – who does not differentiate between the remaking of a lost part, and the amplification with something

which nevertheless did not exist beforehand, but which obliges him to emulate the style and the "grace" of the work (*I ricordi di Alessandro Allori*, ed. I. B. Supino, Florence, 1908, pp. 28–29).

For other significant episodes and comments, see Baldinucci, 1681–1728, ed. cit., III, p. 86; Cavalcaselle–Crowe, 1864–1866, II, notes pp. 82 and 86; G. Milanesi, I, 1878, notes pp. 381, 514; II, 1878, note p. 8; Lupi, 1909, pp. 55–59; Papini, 1909, p. 451; Luca Signorelli Exhibition, Cortona–Florence, 1953, p. 109; W. Mostyn-Owen, review of the Luca Signorelli exhibition, Burlington Magazine, XCV, 1953, p. 274.

16. A. Lensi *Palazzo Vecchio*, Milan–Rome, 1929, pp. 136, 255; Conti, in "Paragone", N. 223, 1968, pp. 11–13. The inpainting of the losses of *The Virgin of the Harpies* must have been corrected when the panel entered the collection of the Grand Prince Ferdinand of Tuscany in 1704.

17. Abbate, 1965, pp. 42–43. Baldinucci, 1681–1728, ed. cit., III, pp. 436–437; V, p. 353.

18. Baldinucci, 1681–1728, ed. cit., III, pp. 441–442; Bottari, 1730, p. XII.

19. Vocabolario toscano dell'arte del disegno, Florence, 1681, *ad vocem*; quoted by Gombrich, 1962, p. 52.

20. Celio, 1638, p. 40; Baldinucci, 1681–1728, ed. cit., III, pp. 447–448, 449; L. Tanfani Centofanti, *Notizie di artisti tratte da documenti pisani*, Pisa, 1898, p. 155; J. Shearman, *Andrea del Sarto*, Oxford, 1965, p. 272.

21. Baglione, 1642, p. 146 (on the vicissitudes undergone by this panel, see as well as the Celio cited on p. 54, J. Lohninger, *S. Maria dell'Anima*, *die Deutsche Nationalkirche in Roma*, Rome, 1909, note 1 p. 101; Corbo, 1969, p. 242).

22. Malvasia, 1678, II, pp. 269–270; Bellori, 1672 and 1672–1696, ed. 1976, pp. 382, 512–513; Baglione, 1642, p. 124. The information regarding Federico Zuccaro's cleaning the *Nozze Aldobrandini* is found in his *Idea de' pittori, scultori et architetti*, Turin, 1607, book I, p. 37.

23. G. Marino, in Abbate, 1965, pp. 45–46; Mancini, 1956, pp. 145, 185, 285.

24. Bellori, 1672, ed. 1976, p. 96 (on this painting, which is now lost, see D. Posner, *Annibale Carracci*, London, 1971, II, p. 59; M. Chappell, *Missing Pictures by Ludovico Cigoli*, in "Paragone", n. 373, 1981, p. 85; M. Chappell, *Ludovico Cigoli and Annibale Carracci*, in *Per A. E. Popham*, Parma, 1981, p. 140); Passeri, 1673, p. 193 (on the activity of Caroselli in the style of other painters, see Ferretti, 1981, p. 139); Baldinucci, 1681–1728, ed. 1845–1847, III, p. 27, V, p. 206; Pascoli, 1730–1736, II, p. 67; V. Golzio, *Documenti artistici sul Seicento nell'archivio Chigi*, Rome, 1939, p. 282. For information regarding other restorations carried out in Rome, see: De Dominici, 1742–1743, III, pp. 533–534 (Paolo de Matteis who repainted one of Filippino Lippi's *Sybils* on the vault of the Carafa Chapel in Santo Maria sopra Minerva, see C. Bertelli, *Il restauro della Cappella Carafa in S. Maria sopra Minerva a Roma*, in "Bollettino dell'Istituto Centrale di Restauro", 1965, pp. 145–195); Titi, 1763, I, pp. 131, 191; Piacenza, VI, 1820, p. 439, note 1; J. Hess, in Passeri, 1673, ed. 1934, note 2 p. 51, 1 p. 294, 10 p. 298, 6 p. 309 (Raffaello Vanni, in 1662, restored various altarpieces from the altar in Saint Peter's).

25. Bottari (1759–1760, II, note 1 p. 470) observed that the *Polyphemus* by Sebastiano del Piombo had been repainted by a second rate artist, whilst Cavalcaselle (1882–1885, II, note 2, p. 242) referred to Giampaolo Marescotti (responsible for the decorations on the pilasters of the Sala dei Pianeti) for some retouchings on the neighbouring *Galatea* by Raphael. On the recent restoration, see A. Mignosi Tantillo, *Restauri alla Farnesina*, in "Bollettino d'Arte", 1972, pp. 33–43; A. Angelini, *La Loggia della Galatea alla Villa Farnesina a Roma*, in "Tecnica e stile, esempi di pittura murale del Rinascimento italiano", Cinisello Balsamo, 1986, pp. 95–101. For the letter by Fabio Chigi on the restoration of Raphael's *Sybils*, see Cavalcaselle, 1882–1885, II, note p. 252; the damage caused by a cleaning, which resulted in Giacomo Frey desisting from engraving the fresco, are recorded in Bottari, 1754, note p. 245. The damage caused by copyists is also recorded with reference to a small copper painting by Annibale Carraci; see Bellori, 1672, ed. 1976, p. 95.

26. Bellori's annotations are reproduced in the facsimile edition of Baglione, edited by Valerio Mariani (Rome, 1935, pp. 383, 402).

27. G. Bottari in Borghini, 1584, ed. Florence, 1730, pp. VII–XVI; U. Procacci, *Di uno scritto di Giovanni Bottari sulla conservazione e il restauro delle opere d'arte*, in "Rivista d'Arte", 1955, pp. 229–249; in "Bollettino dell'Istituto Centrale di Restauro", n. 23–24, pp. 131–145.

28. See above, note 15, for the interventions on the frescos of the Camposanto in Pisa. On Veracini, see: F. M. N. Gabburri, ms Palatino E. B. 9. 5 of the Biblioteca Nazionale di Firenze, vol. 1, p. 270; G. M. Mecatti, *Notizie istoriche riguardanti il Capitolo … di Santa Maria Novella*, Florence 1737, pp. 29–36; G. Richa, *Notizie istoriche delle chiese fiorentine*, Florence, 1754–1762, I, pp. 63, 322; III, pp. 88, 92; IV, pp. 138, 200; VII, p. 65; VIII, p. 313; X, p. 340; I. M. Cigna, ms B 5 of the Biblioteca dell'Archiginnasio di Bologna, cc. 54r., 54v.,

70v. (restoration of the frescos by Giovanni Balducci, 1747, and the *Fall of Saint Paul* by Domenichino in the Duomo di Volterra); Lanzi, 1809, I, p. 281. G. Aiazzi, *Ricordi di storici di Filippo di Cino Rinuccini*, Florence 1840, p. 311; [F. de Boni], *Biografia degli artisti*, Venice, 1840, p. 1069; M. Marangoni, *La pittura fiorentina del Settecento*, in "Rivista dell'Arte", 1912, pp. 61–102, R. Offner, *Corpus of Florentine Painting*, sect. III, vol. IV, New York, 1934, pl. LIII; Thieme–Becker, 1940; M. Ciatti, *Una sconosciuta tavola antica ed un restauro del 1753*, in "Rivista d'arte", 1984, pp. 373–376. For a more detailed discussion of this bibliography, consult pp. 222–223 of the first edition of this volume.

29. R. Salvini *Tutta la pittura del Botticelli*, Milan, 1958, II, pp. 45–46; M. Gregori, *Giovanni da Milano nella Cappella Rinuccini*, Milan, 1965, p. 5; M. Boskovits, *Giovanni da Milano*, Florence, 1966, p. 38; L. Vertova, *Restored Works of Art in Florence*, in "The Burlington Magazine", 1972, p. 499. The punching, typical of the works of Giovanni da Milano, on the Redentore of the Cappella Rinuccini, has been examined by Erling Skaug, who also comments, rightly, on the unfinished state of the tondo; see *The Rinuccini Tondo*, in "Atti del convegno sul restauro delle opera d'arte" (1976), Florence, 1981, pp. 333–339.

30. Information on Cigna can be found in: F. M. N. Gabburri, ms cit. Bibl. Naz. Firenze, vol. III, p. 1725; Cavalcaselle–Crowe, 1864–1866, VIII, p. 457 and note 2 pp. 457–458. Milanesi, III, 1878, note 2 p. 273; K. Busse, in Thieme–Becker, 1912; M. Davies *National Gallery Catalogues. The Earlier Italian Schools*, London, 1961, pp. 479–480; *The National Gallery January 1965–December 1966*, London, 1967, pp. 55 and 117 in *Mostra del Restauro, catalogue of the exhibition*, Pisa, 1971, n. 10 p. 47. Another possible intervention by Cigna on a work by Signorelli is described in the catalogue *Momenti d'arte a Volterra*, Volterra, 1981, p. 26.

At a later date, towards 1788, one could mention the enlargement in the style of the original, of the *Assumption* by Bartolomeo della Gatta in San Domenico in Cortona. However, he never comes anywhere near in his ability to imitate the Early Masters to the painter from Volterra; see A. M. Maetzke, in *Arte nell'Aretino*, catalogue of the exhibition, Arezzo, 1979, pp. 51, 54.

31. R. Palucchini, *Mostra di Giovanni Bellini*, Venice, 1949, nn. 40 and 50; G. Marachier, *Il Museo Correr di Venezia. Dipinti dal XIV al XVI secolo*, Venice, 1957, p. 45; E. Merkel, *Una ricerca per Frate Antonio Falier da Negroponte*, in "Quaderni della Soprintendenza ai beni artistici e storici di Venezia", n. 8, 1979, pp. 45–47; the traditional attribution to Farinati of the reworking on the Pietà in the Doge's Palace is now rightly questioned by Loredano Olivato (1974, note 8 p. 15).

32. V. Moschini, *Nuovi aspetti di opera famose*, in "Bollettino d'Arte", 1949, pp. 165–166; R. Longhi, *Ritorni e progressi su Alvise*, in "Paragone", n. 229, 1969, p. 39, in *Opere Complete*, X, Florence, 1978, pp. 149–150. For the reworkings cited by Zanetti, see 1733, pp. 153 (see also Marconi Moschini, 1962, pp. 34–35), 394, 455.

33. In 1560 four canvases of the Scuola di San Giovanni Evangelista also underwent a cleaning. See N. di Carpegna, *Il restauro dei Carpaccio di S. Giorgio degli Schiavoni*, in "Arte Veneta", 1947, pp. 67–68; Marconi Moschini, 1955, pp. 57, 96; Marconi Moschini, 1962, pp. 165–168.

34. Merrifield, 1849, pp. 750–752 (Dover Edition, 1999); the Volpato manuscript in the Biblioteca Remondiniana di Bassano is dated by Merrifield not long after 1670, see pp. 721–725 and p. 751–753; in addition to the passages cited in the text, see also the observations on grounds and their conservation on pp. 731 and 733.

35. As a guidance to the dates of entry of altarpieces into the Princely collections, one should bear in mind that Andrea del Sarto's panels in Florence coincided with the arrival of Mary Magdalen of Austria (that is, before 1631); the works by Correggio in the Gallery in Modena between 1638 and 1649 (Venturi, 1882, pp. 225–230). On the events leading up to the dismemberment of the San Cassiano Altarpiece, see *Kunsthistorisches MuseumGemaldegalerie*, I, Vienna, 1965, pp. 2–3; C. Ridolfi, 1648, I, p. 120, on the fragment by Palma Vecchio.

36. On the thefts see: C. Ridolfi, 1648, I, p. 128 (the landscape from Lotto's *Marriage of Saint Catherine* in Bergamo was cut out and stolen by a French soldier); Brandolese, 1795, pp. 249–250 (see E. A. Safarik, *Torzo Veronesova vrocholnéhodila v Narodni galerii v Praze*, in "Umeni", 1964, pp. 387–413, on the restoration of the Prague fragment); M. Boschini, *Breve instruzione*, in Boschini, 1660, ed. Venice–Rome, 1966, pp. 716–717; G. B. Verci, *Notizie intorno alla vita e le opera de'pittori, scultori e intagliatori della città di Bassano*, Venice, 1775, pp. 251–253; Ferretti, 1981, pp. 148–149 (see here, pp. 149–150, as well as the problems of simulated thefts, and the copies which were substituted in place of the originals).

37. Boschini, 1660, pp. 501–502; Zanetti, 1733, p. 416; Ferretti, 1981, pp. 142–145. On Vecchia's restoration, and others on the Pala di Castelfranco, see: A. Morassi, *Giorgione*, Milan, 1942, pp. 76, 165 (canvas inserts

considered by Pellicioli to date from the sixteenth century, during his restoration of 1934); N. Melchiori, *Notizie di pittori ed altri scritti*, Rome, 1964, p. 135 (restoration by Antonio Medi in 1731); G. Bordignon Favero, *Le opera d'arte e il tesoro del Duomo ... di Castelfranco*, Castelfranco, 1965, pp. 26–29; *La pala di Castelfranco Veneto*, catalogue of the exhibition, Milan, 1978 (see in particular, L. Lazzarini on p. 48 for the dating of the paint transferred onto the canvas inserts); Merkel, 1981.

38. Boschini, 1660, pp. 584–586.
39. G. Fogolari, 1937, p. 166 (the painting is identifiable with a *Circe* mentioned in a letter of 11 April 1699).

4

Gallery pictures

1. Reductions in size and enlargements

Reconstructing the events which had led to the mutilation of Mantegna's *Dormitio Virginis*, Roberto Longhi was to observe that "in the sixteenth and seventeenth centuries, predominant taste, which was decorative and courtly *par excellence*, adjusted itself to the mutilation of paintings with the same spirit as it hurried to enlarge them with additions (please note the many clumsy enlargements of Venetian pictures in the Louvre or the Prado, etc.): that is, on every occasion, for the most banal requirements of the distribution or architecture of a gallery, whether to make related paintings of different formats 'go' together, or to fit in with the scheme and the dimensions of the plasterwork, or the mouldings, or even to make the painting fit as a decorative panel over a door, and so forth."

Such operations had already been carried out for the Duchess of Ferrara by Bastianino between 1586 and 1588 (added and filled, and other adjustments with oil paint)[i] on twenty-three paintings attributed to sixteenth-century painters from Ferrara (amongst these Dosso Dossi's *Magi*), as well as works by Raphael, Mantegna and Correggio. In 1540 at the court of François I, Primaticcio received payment for having cleaned the panel by Raphael depicting the *Holy Family*, also *Saint Michael, Saint Margaret* and the *Portrait of the Vice-reine of Naples*. In England, between 1588 and 1589, George Gower was to be found repairing some of the paintings belonging to Elizabeth I in Whitehall.[1]

In the seventeenth century, there are references to painters restoring or adapting pictures in all Princely collections: Hans Van Achen worked on the paintings belonging to Rudolph II, Johann Georg Fischer transformed the wings of Dürer's *Paumgartner Altarpiece* for Maximilian of Bavaria, into that observatory almost of landscape and botanical detail, which could be seen in the photographs pre-dating the cleaning of the painting by Hauser. As soon as the Gonzaga paintings acquired by Charles I arrived from Venice, they were entrusted to Hieronimus Laniere, a painter who was also known for his fakes. It is from Théodore de Mayerne that we know that they had been blackened by the vapours of sublimated mercury to which they had been exposed during the voyage and, when taking notes on the methods used in their cleaning, he observed that it had only been possible to recover the paintings in oil.

---

[i] *"zunta e istucati et altri accomodamenti di colorj a olio"*.

In Spain, in 1625, Vincente Carducho enlarged three paintings by Titian; and Velasquez himself, as well as having reworked, sometimes after an interval of many years, some of his old Court portraits, enlarged and repainted the equestrian portraits of Philip III and Margaret of Austria by Bartolomé Gonzales. In his turn, he had his own works adapted to new formats, for instance the *Mercury and Argus* in the Prado.[2]

In France, no documentation relating details of the conservation of the Royal collections seems to have been preserved before the time of Louis XIV, at which point we do find reports relating to the restoration, enlargement and reduction of paintings. In 1665, Baudin Yvart restored the *Conversion of the Magdalen* by Veronese, which had been given as a gift by the Venetian Republic; in 1665 Jean Baptiste Cany cleaned a painting depicting *God the Father* by Albani which he was copying, Gabriel Blanchard worked on a work by Guido Reni in 1686, and Titian's much distressed *Sacra Conversazione* (which had arrived from Rome in 1665) was repaired by Pierre Mignard in 1691. The activity of one Gueselin is recorded solely as a restorer, working on paintings by Raphael, by Poussin and by Albani in 1685 and in 1688, on Titian's *Venere del Pardo*, one can assume with poor results as the painting was then handed over to Antoine Coypel, for it to be put it back in order.

In 1681, Charles Lebrun became "*garde des tableaux*", a position in which he was followed by René Antoine Houasse and then Antoine Paillet, who from 1699 was entrusted with the cleaning of the paintings and the ceilings of Versailles. Nicolas Bailly succeeded him in the position of "*garde*", and in 1722 his duties were set out by the Duke d'Antin: to check the paintings, not allow them to be either moved or copied without permission, and to indicate to the [picture] cleaner Stiémart the works on which he was required to intervene. In order to fit in better with the architecture and the furnishings of Versailles, many paintings were to undergo additions which, for the most part, were removed between 1784 and 1789; others have remained in place to this day, or until recent restorations. The orders of the Sun King did not even give way before the models of Antiquity: not even the *Venus* donated by the city of Arles to the King could escape adjustments by Girardon.

Some paintings were given a round or oval format which, at the time, was found more tasteful; for instance, Guido Reni's panel depicting *Il Disegno e la Pittura*, which was made into a perfect tondo, amplifying the background against which the figures were set, so as to allow the eye to rest, before taking aboard all the details of the idea that the painting was expressing. Other compositions felt to be too crowded or cramped, such as Lotto's *Christ and the Adulteress*, or Parmigianino's probable *Self-portrait*, were made larger. It was in this search for balance between figure, background and frame, conforming to the dicta of classicism, that portions of the original were at times also removed, as in the case of the *Mona Lisa* at an unspecified moment in time, when it was relieved of the two columns which stood against the light, framing the portrait and giving depth to the landscape in the background.

Even in 1756, Francesco Algarotti was lamenting the fact of having witnessed in Vienna the mutilation of paintings by the hand of Titian himself. And when one thinks of paintings that have been mistreated in the past, does one not immediately think of certain Venetian paintings in Imperial Collections such as Giorgione's *Laura*, or Bellini's *Circumcision* which was turned into an oval, or Parmigianino's *Girl in a Turban* which was reduced to a square containing only the head, as though in Imperial Collections there existed a more insistent and deliberate cruelty in this type of operation?[3]

In Florence, Grand Prince Ferdinand entrusted his paintings to the Venetian Niccolò Cassana, to whose advice we owe such enlargements as that on Rubens' huge canvas *Satyrs and*

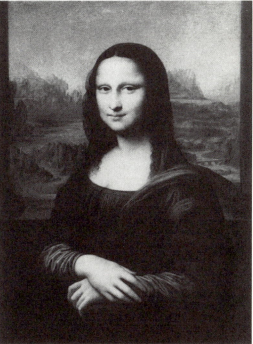

*64. Diego Velasquez, Mercury
and Argus; with gallery enlargement. Madrid, Museo del
Prado.*

*65. Guido Reni, Il Disegno e la
Pittura; with an enlargement
dating from the second half of
the seventeenth century. Paris,
Museé du Louvre.*

*66. Copy of the Mona Lisa,
Leonardo da Vinci; with the
columns in the background which
have been mutilated in the original. Paris, Museé du Louvre.*

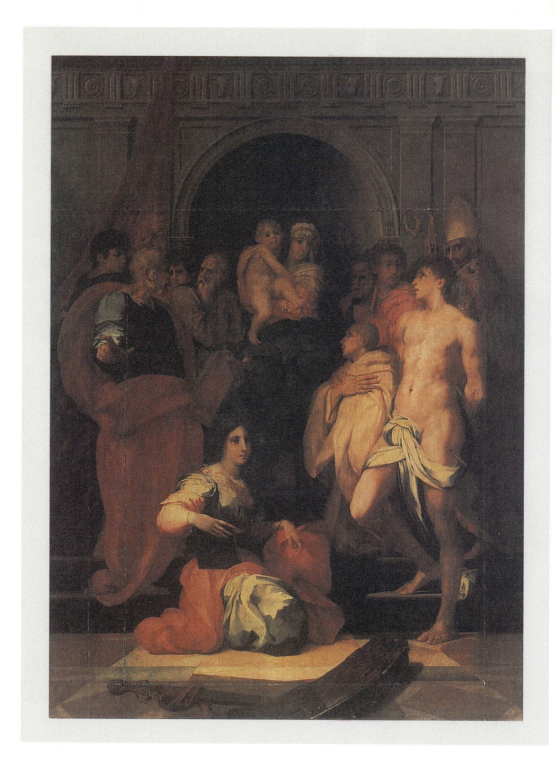

67. *Rosso Fiorentino, Pala Dei;*
with the enlargement by Niccolò
Cassana. Florence, Galleria
Palatina, Palazzo Pitti.

Nymphs, Raphael's *Madonna del Baldacchino* or Rosso Fiorentino's *Pala Dei*. Cassana's letters serve as a good introduction to the spirit in which a glittering Prince such as Ferdinand   67, 70
saw these "gallery" adaptations: a kind of framing device almost, which allowed paintings
to cohabit, adapting themselves to the requisites of the "grand taste". In 1699 he wrote to him
thus: "I would be grateful if you could pay a quick visit here, in order to restore the painting
by Parmigianino (the *Madonna dal Collo Lungo*), which has already been all filled, and the
Baptism of Paul, which was glued to the stretcher, so that much of it has been painted onto
the stretcher itself, and as it will now have to be removed [from it], it will be necessary to
make canvas inserts, and then repaint these portions which cover the stretcher, which are
of considerable size …".

A certain respect for the original seems, however, to have prevented mutilations, and
sometimes suggested rather timid solutions such as that to the *Pala Dei*, which was enlarged
on all sides but without additions which would give the composition, which is very tight,
that added breath which Louis XIV's *gardes des tableaux* were able to obtain [with their
additions]; the *Madonna del Baldacchino* by Raphael and the *Christ amongst the Evangelists*
by Fra Bartolomeo were adapted so as to be of the same format, with the Raphael being given   70, 71
an additional strip along the top and [strips] reframing the central portion of the painting
by the friar. The operation received the approval of Richardson who, in 1722, observed that
the two panels seemed made to hang together; they seemed to suit each other in every possible way, even in their tonalities.[4]

The problems associated with the general effect of the whole and the adaptation of
works of art to contemporary taste were obviously not confined to the sphere of galleries.
With the same spirit they also encompassed church furnishings, altarpieces and funerary
monuments. It was not infrequent to find that when a frame was renewed, the renewal was
accompanied by enlargements or reductions, especially to give the canvases or the panels
the rounded profile of Baroque frames; this is what happened to Lorenzo Lotto's *Madonna
del Rosario* in San Domenico in Cingoli, or Palma Vecchio's *Saint Peter the Martyr* in Alzano
Maggiore; referring to the latter painting, already in 1793, Giacomo Tassi observed that "it
had been square in shape with a magnificent old gilded frame. Those monks have altered it
into an arched, smaller and badly conceived [shape], so that this work of art, so precious,
finds itself in some way maimed." It was not by chance that, as early as 1775 and in Bergamo,
Andrea Pasta should have been wishing that "rectangular panels should not be rounded off,
nor should semicircular works be broken up with angles or other bizarre inventions which
destroy the formal majesty of a work and diminish the background …". However, at times,
the results could be surprisingly original: for instance, the *Risen Christ* by Palma Vecchio
(part of the polyptych of Serinalta), which was enlarged around 1760 with the most extra-   68
ordinary decoration, almost *chinoiserie* in its taste, which was removed a few years ago,
the result of a decision which I find difficult to understand, as well as not being in agreement with it.[5]

Palma's creation was eminently suited for insertion within a completely different context, and we need only remember the most famous of these precedents: Borromini's forced
insertions of the funerary monuments in the Lateran. The great architect's wish would have
been to rebuild the basilica completely. The fact that the new building included the old
transept and englobed the old walls within the new building was not of his volition, but a
mark of respect for the tradition of conservation of funerary monuments encouraged by the
Counter-Reformation, which had found renewed vigour with the cardinals of the Barberini

68. Jacopo Palma il Vecchio,
*The Risen Christ; with the
enlargement, dating from
around 1760. Serinalta,
Santissima Annunziata.*

69. Francesco Borromini,
*Memorial to Sergius IV. Rome,
San Giovanni in Laterano.*

family; to the extent that, once the Basilica had been restructured, it was only under Alexander VII that the fragments containing the old memorials were remounted.

Borromini plays on the evocative power of the fragments, but tries to camouflage, as far as he is able, their figurative peculiarities which were not modern: for instance, the exquisite funerary memorial to Sergius IV, in which he makes the sculpture with the portrait of the pontiff disappear within a wonderful cornice of stars, placing it as an oval between two cherub-herms. In instances where the whole structure was unable to absorb these antique figures because their stylistic peculiarities are just too far removed from the Grand Style or from the taste capable of producing grandiose effects, then the fragments were inserted within smaller complexes adapted to provoke surprise in the onlooker, such as the statue in the funerary monument to Annibaldi di Arnolfo, surmounted with a moulding of death represented by a winged skull, sporting a beard and wearing a crown. Or the fragments of the tomb of Cardinal Giussano, put back together alternating cosmatesque elements and heads in relief, or else the great *custodia* in which is mounted the fragment of the fresco depicting Boniface VIII attributed to Giotto.[6]

But how can one repair, bring up to date and adapt paintings to a more modern taste without these integrations, retouchings and enlargements becoming so many blotches disfiguring the original, rather than breathing into it a fresh and modern air? This was to become the dominant theme in the world of restoration in the seventeenth and eighteenth centuries: the desire to adapt paintings to the dictates of a more reliable taste, without disfiguring them with patches and incoherent additions. Against the backdrop of the tradition of respect for paintings characteristic of Roman writers on art, it is worth considering the letters written in 1604 by Giambattista Marino to Bernardo Castello, and the unfortunate events surrounding the *Venus* which arrived in Rome damaged, and which was given to the Cavalier d'Arpino to repair. Out of what appears at times to be the rather suspicious professional dignity characteristic of painters of the time in Rome, which led to them to specify that the work had been retouched by the Cavalier d'Arpino "in his own hand" and "in some not really noteworthy places", there emerges the crux problem which he encountered in his intervention: that is, that it "would prove extremely difficult to imitate the style, and to make fresh and new colours appear indistinguishable from those tempered by another hand".[7] The difficulty arose (and arises) from the impossibility of imitating the manner of another master; but also, independently, from the problem of freshly applied colours drying with different effects than those achieved by Castello with his oils and his mixtures, which would inevitably have been different from those used by the Cavalier d'Arpino.

With this we already find a clear formulation of the central problem which would characterize the restoration "*di accompagnamento*"[ii] right up to our own day, when, with a unilaterality worthy of other causes, the absolute necessity of the visibility of these integrations will often be theorized upon. Mimetic restoration, on the other hand, demands invisibility: the problem arises because, on acquiring its own patina with age (which will inevitably differ from that of the original), the restoration will become materially distinguishable and intrusive [with time].

69

[ii] Literally, "which accompanies", that is, a restoration which is in harmony with the original, but is making no attempt to be mistaken with it. It is not invisible.

The maintenance of gallery paintings would also lead to the diffusion of restoration practices. During the first half of the seventeenth century, Theodor Turquet de Mayerne, in his great collection of recipes and secrets gathered from the painters at the Court of Charles I in England, reported on some of the methods advised for the cleaning of paintings, some of which were reminiscent of the methods found in the Venetian collection of recipes from the sixteenth and seventeenth centuries, but also containing interesting and different approaches, such as the cleaning of a painting by pouring warm glue onto the surface and then peeling it off when cold ("see if this can be removed without damaging the work", adds de Mayerne).[iii] Or again:

> "A painting dirty with dust can simply be washed with a sponge and fresh water
> (squeezed out), and then put in the sun for an hour or two. The sky and the far-
> off landscapes painted with smalt, [ultramarine] ashes, massicot and lead white,
> become lighter with this method. But where there are organic greens (*scudegrün*)
> and lake colours, both water and sun will harm them; so these parts of the paint-
> ing must be covered with paper glued on top of them. Trees and other greenery
> painted using an organic yellow (*schitgeel*) and massicot are also of this number".[iv]

Whilst in an earlier recipe de Mayerne noted that cleaned paintings should be varnished using egg-white, which could simply be removed with fresh water every time it was necessary to clean the painting from newly accrued filth, on the advice of Soreau (probably the painter Jean Sorge), he then goes on to warn that this could be harmful as: "it is an enemy of some colours, and will kill them". Also reported are methods to be used in the unrolling of paintings which have been long rolled up without damaging them, and various remedies for flaking and cracking paint. In 1632 Van Dyck advised him:

> "In order to repair an oil painting which is flaking and to preserve it from the
> damp of the walls, you must brush the reverse with umber lightly ground with
> oil, which will dry quickly. This is necessary for paintings which have a glue
> ground and water bound paint."[v]

De Mayerne also reported on other methods of application of oil and glue-based substances to the reverse of paintings which would become the notorious *"beverone"*[vi] of the eighteenth century.[8]

It was not a big step to go from these applications of glue and oil to the reverse of canvases, to lining. In the second half of the seventeenth century, one comes across various definite references [to the practice]: in 1688 the *Venere del Pardo*, as well as being restored, was lined with the old system using sand, which would only be abandoned by French restorers

---

iii "*Voyes si cela se peult reiterer sans endommager la piece*".

iv "*Un tableau saly de poussière soit simplement lave avec une esponge pleine d'eau estrainte, puis soit mis au soleil pour une heure ou deux. Le ciel et les païsages esloignés faicts avec esmail, cendre, masticot, et blanc de plomb, par ce moyen s'esclaircissent. Mais la ou il ya du scudegrün, et de la lacque, le soleil et l'eau y nuisent equalement; par tant ces parties du tableau doibuent estre couvertes de papier collé dessus. Les arbres et les aultres verdures qui se font avec le schitgeel et le masticot sont de ce nombre.*"

v "*Pour raccomoder un tableau à l'huile qui s'escaille, et pour le contregarder de la moiteur de la paroy, il fault passer par derrière de la terre d'ombre broyée fort clairement à huile qui sèchera bien tost. Ceste invention est necessaire aux tableaux dont l'imprimeure est faitte avec colle et avec couleurs à eau.*"

vi Beverone was a mixture of organic substances, which could also include eggs and vinegar as well as the glue and oil mentioned by De Mayerne, made up to the personal recipe of the restorer, which seems to have been used both as a brightening agent on frescos.

in the second half of the eighteenth century. In 1698 one finds a fairly exhaustive list of paintings in the Royal Collections which were destined to receive this treatment: some Titians, a Veronese, Quimper's *Saint Sebastian* and the Charleville *Assumption* by Annibale Carracci, Reni's *Flight into Egypt*, which is now in Brussels, two [works by] Domenichino, one by Guercino, Pietro da Cortona, a few Valentin [de Boulogne] and a Van Dyck. In Italy there are even earlier references [to the practice]: in 1683 the Chigi family pay their colourman ("*coloraro*"), Nicola Cariol, for the lining onto a fine canvas of Lanfranco's *David*. In 1684, a lining is envisaged for the restorations carried out by Giambattista Rossi on a number of the canvases in the Sala del Maggior Consiglio in the Ducal Palace, and as early as 1672 Bellori recorded a lining entrusted to Maratta of Annibale Carracci's *Nativity of the Virgin*, which now hangs in the Louvre.[9]

2. "Time the Painter"

Admiring the perfect harmony ("*accompagnamento*") obtained by hanging together Raphael's *Madonna del Baldacchino* and the panel by Fra Bartolomeo, the aspect that Jonathan Richardson found particularly felicitous, was the homogeneity of their relative tonalities. This is a quality that we can no longer appreciate today, since the *Risen Christ* by Fra Bartolomeo was transferred onto canvas in Napoleonic times, and is no longer in the good condition of the Raphael.[10] However, we should not imagine that the two panels would have had the same tonalities originally; it is very likely that this concurrence had been obtained through various varnishings and opportune tonings. The colour of gallery paintings also presented problems when it came to their insertion within the schemes of the rooms they would decorate: works by different artists could lead to discordant, or at least displeasing, effects. It was felt that a predominant hue was preferable, especially as the public had become accustomed to the unifying tonality of seventeenth-century painting. This often resulted from the use of coloured grounds which, with time, became predominant absorbing the paint layer, and first encountered, with all the well-known attendant conservation problems, in the works of painters active in the beginning of the century, such as Ludovico Carracci or Passignano.

The simplest way in which works differing too radically in hue could find a unity (whether internal or overall) was through the darkening which time conferred through the yellowing of the oil medium and, if present, the varnish. A yellowish or brown, warm tonality developed, which lowered the highlights and lightened the dark backgrounds, which was found so pleasing that artists would seek to imitate it, and became used to considering the effect of their paintings in the light of these [future developments], when time, through the settling of the materials, had rendered them sweeter.

In 1657, Prince Leopold de'Medici sent back to Paolo del Sera, a Florentine art dealer in Venice, an *Adoration of the Shepherds* by Veronese which del Sera had proposed as an acquisition: "Your Serene Highness and my Lord and Master – del Sera replied – I have received the kind letter that Your Serene Highness addressed me, together with the painting by Paolo Veronese which I see was not to your liking …, I would imagine in any case, that the excessive freshness of the painting troubled you, because it is a fact that the patina which time gives [a painting] is very enticing, and gives a certain union which is pleasing. Speaking of which, Signor Niccolò Ranieri has *Four Seasons* by the hand of Bassano the

70.Raphael, Madonna del bal-dacchino; with the enlargement by Niccolò Cassana. Florence, Galleria Palatina, Palazzo Pitti.

71. Fra Bartolomeo, The Risen Christ among the Evangelists; reframed by Niccolò Cassana, trans-ferred by Foucque in 1806. Florence, Galleria Palatina, Palazzo Pitti.

Elder, extremely naturalistic, but because they come from a villa and are so well preserved that they seem to have been completed yesterday, he has never managed to sell them for their true value. These are matters of taste, and each desires to satisfy his own ....”[vii]

Still in Venice, in 1660 Boschini showed his appreciation of the effects of time on paintings:

"All things Time uncovers
that is clear, and we know it:
but Painting against Him
with a transparent veil will cover itself, […]
and indeed this is what happens to Painting:

[vii] *"Serenissimo mio signore et padrone … ricevo la benignissima lettera di Vostra Altezza Serenissima … et insieme il quadro di Paulo Veronese, che vedo non essere stato di suo gusto …, as ogni modo, mi immagino che la troppa freschezza del quadro abbia dato fastidio, perchè in effetto quella pattina che dà il tempo è una cosa che alletta assai, e dà una certa unione che piace, et a questo proposito il signor Niccolò Renieri ha quattro Stagioni, di mano del Bassan Vecchio, realis-sime, ma perchè sono uscite di una villa e sono conservate così bene come fatte adesso, non ha mai trovato da farne esito al prezzo che veramente vagliano. Sono cose che consistono nel gusto, et ognuno vuol sodisfare al suo proprio …".*

The Patina of Time has two effects,
Colours become always more perfect,
And the handling more worthy of esteem".[viii]

Félibien is the author who best allows us to understand the effects on paintings of the alteration which occurs in the oil medium with the passage of time: "I will again say that it is for this very reason, this great harmony amongst the colours, that excellent works painted in oil, and executed a long time ago, present themselves with greater strength and beauty; this is because all the colours with which they have been painted have had the time to blend together, to merge and to mix, as the more liquid and moist portions of the oil medium dry out".

The concept of "Time the Painter", who intervenes to add harmony to paintings, became commonplace among connoisseurs at the end of the seventeenth century. In 1694, John Dryden concludes a long poem addressed to Sir Godfrey Kneller on this very theme:
"For time shall with his ready pencil stand,
Retouch your figures with his ripening hand;
Mellow your colours, and imbrown the tint;
Add every grace which time alone can grant;
To future ages shall your fame convey,
And give more beauties than he takes away."

In 1711 Joseph Addison dedicated a page of the "Spectator" to this subject (*A Dream of Painters*), which Algarotti referred to in his letter of 1744, in which he complained of those who removed from the paintings of Titian and Tintoretto "the blending, the glazing, and that precious patina that imperceptibly unifies the tints, making them sweeter and softer, and which alone can give paintings that venerable [appearance] of age that time alone brings, working with the finest brushes, with incredible slowness, as he appears to the Spectator in his picturesque vision".[11]

We have already met Boschini describing the contest between Pietro Vecchia and Time, with the painter being able (once the paintings had been cleaned) to return to them the look of age which so pleased the collectors. It is likely that, to this end, he would have made use of some sort of artificial patina, or pigmented varnish, of the type well known to seventeenth-century painters who, like Vecchia, were imitating Old Masters. Referring to Terenzio of Urbino, Baglione specified that he was one of those painters who liked to pass off his own work as old, "by way of some good drawing, he so ground away with his pigments, that out of somewhere his works appeared; and. having painted them, he then would then expose them to smoke, and by covering them with varnishes in which some pigments were mixed, he made them appear as though they were hundreds of years old".[ix]

[viii] "*Tute le cose el Tempo descoverze;*
questa xè cosa chiara, e la savemo:
ma la Pitura contra lu medemo
d'un velo trasparente el la coverze, [...]
Così intravien aponto a la Pitura:
La Patina del Tempofa do efeti,
i colori vien sempre più perfeti,
e in mazor stima l'istessa fatura".

[ix] "*per via di qualche buon disegno, tanto pestava co' colori, che da qualche cosa le faceva apparire, e, dopo esser dipinte, le appiccava al fumo, e con certe vernici miste con colori che sopra loro dava, faceale parere immagini per tratto di centinaia d'anni al tempo avanzate.*"

Bartolomeo Manfredi also imitated "the styles of others", especially that of Caravaggio, using "certain secrets of varnishes and pigments mixed with oil".[x] To this world (from the techniques of which would develop what would become the principle practices of restoration) also belonged the Ferrarese painter Giuseppe Caletti, imitator of Titian and the Dossi: "not only did he imitate the composition when he so wished – specified Lanzi – but also the colour and brushwork which is so difficult. He also succeeded in counterfeiting that patina of antiquity that time adds to paintings, increasing their harmony."[xi,12]

These painters working on the very edges of falsification testify clearly to the use of pigmented varnishes, "mixed with pigments" (*miste a colori*). Nor was there a clearly defined boundary between varnishes and oils to be used as binding media or as a finish for the colours. During the "cleaning controversy" at the National Gallery, it was Otto Kurz who directed the discussion towards the intention of painters with regard to the effects of their paintings with time, and onto whether or not total cleanings[xii] should be carried out. The problem is important, but not so much because of the use of pigmented varnishes to simulate the passage of time on new paintings, but rather because of the testimonies reminding us that artists could execute works, bearing in mind the settling (*assestamento*) with time of the pigments, media and varnishes used.

It is this aspect of "Time the Painter" that those involved with restoration today should not forget, and on which attention was focused during the eighteenth century, well beyond the admiration for the darkened varnishes of the "black masters" referred to by Hogarth.

Already Malvasia, referring to Guido Reni, was commenting that: "And in the end he wished [to paint] thus, and in contrast to past good masters he ventured to use lead white immoderately, unlike his master, Ludovico Carracci, who used to say that one ought to reflect for a whole year before even laying down one stroke of white. And there is no doubt that with every day that passes we see his feelings confirmed: where the paintings of the others lose so much with the passage of time, his improve with the yellowing of his lead white, acquiring a certain patina which reduces the colours to a true and good natural appearance; where the others darken to excess, and in that smoky darkness become uniform, no longer allowing one to see or distinguish the volumes, the half-tints, and the principal highlights".[xiii]

Scannelli confirmed this information relating to Reni's attitude, but unlike Malvasia, was not capable of comprehending his stance. In any case, Bolognese painters were well aware of the problem; Zanotti referred to a similar attitude on the part of Donato Creti, who in his use of colour was "much more daring" (*ardito*) than his masters Cantarini and

---

[x] *"certi suoi segreti di vernice e colori ad olio impastati"*.

[xi] *"non solo imitò il disegno, quando volle ..., ma il colorire, ch`è si difficile. Vi seppe contraffare ancora quella patina di antichità che il tempo aggiunge alle pitture e le fa crescere in armonia"*.

[xii] "Total" cleaning implies the removal of all layers which are not considered to be original. (See Glossary.)

[xiii] *"Egli alla per fine ha voluto far così, ed al contrario de' buoni maestri passati s'è arrischiato a oprar smoderamente la biacca, a porre giù una sola pennellata della quale, soleva avvisar Ludovico suo maestro, bisogna pensarvi un anno intero; e certo che si osserva ogni dì più avverarsi il suo presagio, che dove le pitture de gli altri perdono tanto col tempo, le sue acquisteriano ingiallendosi quella biacca, e pigliando una certa patina, che riduce il colore ad un vero e buon naturale; ove l'altre annerendosi troppo, ed in quella affumicata oscurità uguagliandosi, non lasciano conoscere e distinguere il più e il meno, le mezze tinte, e i lumi prinicipali"*.

Pasinelli, believing that "where possible, colours must show themselves as they are by their nature, and as far as art will allow, leaving to time the patina that it will in any case give, and which when added to that counterfeited by the painter, instead of increasing the beauty of the work, plunges them into darkness and blackens them".[xiv,13]

If we find Reni or Creti confident in the settling and ageing of materials with time, rather than conscious of their deterioration, this aspect is instead emphasized and its potential irreversibility noted, by William Hogarth in 1753, in his polemical advocacy for modern painting as opposed to the myth of the "black masters":

> "When colours change at all it must be somewhat in the manner following, for as they are made some of metal, some of earth, some of stone, and others of more perishable materials, time cannot operate on them otherwise than as by daily experience we find it doth, which is, that one changes darker, another lighter, one quite to a different colour, whilst another, as ultramarine, will keep its natural brightness even in the fire. Therefore, how is it possible that such different materials, ever variously changing (visibly after a certain time) should accidentally coincide with the artist's intention, and bring about the greater harmony of the piece, when it is manifestly contrary to their nature, for do we not see in most collections that much time disunites, untunes, blackens, and by degrees destroys even the best preserved pictures".[14]

Luigi Crespi, on the other hand, in two letters written in 1756 and addressed to Francesco Algarotti, developed an argument dealing explicitly with the problems of restoration. Referring to the darkening of paintings, and having specifically dealt with the drawbacks caused by the absorption [of colours] by the ground, he goes on to protest that one should not entrust paintings to "those who pretend that with such cleaning they can restore them to how they were originally painted", and then moves on to a veritable dissection of the risks of cleaning:

> "It should be known that all great men of this profession [painting] have always (some more, others less, but all without exception), and I repeat – always – worked on the foreground and the background of their paintings, this being one of the most important elements for the relief of the figures to be effective. Now, although it is perfectly possible to achieve this foreground and background during the actual painting by altering the vivacity of the tints, brighter and paler according to requirement, nevertheless it is not always possible to achieve it at one go, without having to come back to it when finishing. And then, by means of glazes, half-tints, shading, to make recede, gradually, what needs to be [behind]. Moreover, such skilful professionals have always achieved the concord, harmony and union of the whole; and this concord, harmony and union can only be achieved in the finishing of the painting.

> "This means that the foreground and background, the concord, harmony and union of a work does not consist in the body of the colour, nor in particular pigments or solid applications of colour, but in the thinnest of glazes, simplest

---

xiv "*ove si può I colori abbiano da mostrarsi quail son di lor natura, e quanto l'arte può consentire, dovendo lascia, dic'egli, al tempo la cura di dar loro quella patena, che loro in ogni modo vuol dare, la quale aggiungendosi a quella che da principio finge il pittore, invece che di accrescere bellezza all'opere le adombra troppo, e annerisce*".

shadings, and an almost misting over [of the paint surface]; sometimes it consists in the mere dirtying of the paint surface with an uncleaned brush, as can
be distinguished by any careful and diligent observation of the paint surface.
Who is it who cannot see that by cleaning a dark painting, one which is filthy
and yellowed and other such things, who is it who cannot understand that all
this concord and all the art used [to achieve it] will go to the devil during the
cleaning? And, having lost this harmony, and such recession, of what worth is
the painting now to an intelligent eye? It is worth nothing at all, lacking two of
its principal and necessary qualities.

"But, would it not be possible to remove the filth, the rankness, the surface dirt
on an old painting, to clean it and restore it to how it was, without removing any
of the above, and therefore without detriment to the painting? It is possible,
but do not expect it with the materials used by picture-cleaners, nor hope for it
considering the quality of the people who become picture-cleaners".[xv,15]

As an artist Crespi still showed himself attached to the dark tonalities of his father Giuseppe
Maria, the kind of painting which predominant taste would move away from as the century
progressed. The effects of "Time the Painter" would be increasingly appreciated within the
limits of a settling of the original materials used, rather than anything that those imitating
Old Masters in the seventeenth century could produce with their coloured varnishes. In
1762 in his *Saggio sopra la Pittura*, Algarotti limited himself to noting the greater union that
was brought to paintings by the passage of time, and then confronted the problem from the
viewpoint of a youth approaching the work of art by comparing the artifice of painting with
the reality of nature:

"A painting which one sees many, many years after its completion, appears as it
would when freshly painted but as though through a veil, or rather as though in
a mirror in which the light had misted over. It is reliably thought that Paolo
Veronese, whose care was above all for the beauty and what one might call the
clamour of his colours, left to time the task of bringing harmony to his paintings and, to a certain degree, seasoning them. But the majority of past masters
did not allow their paintings into the public eye, unless they were duly finished

---

[xv] "E dunque da sapersi che gli uomini grandi d ital professione hanno sempre (chi più, chi meno, ma però tutti), hanno
sempre procurato l'innanzi e l'indietro de' loro quadri, come una dele cose più necessarie per il rilievo delle figure. Ora
un tale avanti e un tale indietro, benché ottenere si possa, e si possa fare nel tempo istesso che si dipigne, col tenere, dove
più vive le tinte, e dove meno, secondo il bisogno, contuttociò, non sempre in tutto e per tutto si può ottenere, onde non
sia poi necessario nel finirsi il quadro, a forza di velature, di mezzetinte, di ombreggiature, l'andar mandando degrada-
mente indietro ciò che bisogna. Hanno inoltre sempre tali valenti professori procurato l'accordo, l'armonia e l'unione del
tutto insieme, il quale accordo, armonia ed unione non si può fare che sul finirsi del quadro". "Perchè dunque e l'avanti
e l'indietro, l'accordo, l'armonia e l'unione, non consiste in corpo di colore, o sia in colori, e tinte di corpo, ma in sottilis-
sime velature, ombreggiature semplicissime, ed appannamenti superficialissimi, e talvolta in semplici sporcature fatte col
solo pennello sporchetto, come dall'ispezione oculare diligentissima si riconosce; chi non vede che ripulendo un
quadroscuro, insudiciato, ingiallito e cose simili, chi non vede che tutto questo accordo e tutta questa arte usata, se ne va
con la ripulitura alla malora? E, perduta una tale unione, ed una simile degradazione, cosa vale più il quadro all'occhio
intelligente? Nulla affatto, mancandogli due cose delle principali e necessarie". "Ma e non si potrebbe levar il sudiciume,
il rancico, lo sporchetto a un quadro antico, ripulirlo, e renderlo tale quale egli era, senza punto levare alcune delle suddette cose, e però senza pregiudizio del quadro? Si può, ma non si speri con ciò che adoperano i ripulitori de' quadri, nè
si speri dalla qualità delle persone medesime che fanno i ripulitori".

and seasoned with their own brush. And I do not know if the *Cristo della Moneta* or the *Nativity* by Bassano have profited or lost, by the continued retouching of Time over the past two hundred years or more. Impossible to determine. But the young student will be able to amply compensate for the damage suffered over the years by the examples [he wishes to study], by going back to nature and the original, which never loses its flower of youth and does not grow old, and which itself served as model to his examples".[xvi]

With even more directness, Liotard, in 1781, examined paintings from the point of view of naturalness, and observed that the "ignorant" (that is, he who is not an expert on the matter of paintings) would always find himself ill at ease in front of paintings which had grown with time, whilst the artist would take pleasure in finding the beautiful colour of the original through all the alterations. If this man ignorant of art should see side by side a painting by Albani and its copy, "if he should he dare to express his opinion, he will prefer the copy and will take it to be the original and, in relation to the original, he is right. The copyist has avoided copying the colours which have darkened, and moreover has steered clear of the brown tonality which time has laid over the original. The copy is nearer in its tonality to the light colours found in nature, and it is with this that the ignorant man is struck, because he is unable to recognize the true [painting] when disguised. A painter will distinguish the original from the copy, art guides him and his expert eye distinguishes truth beneath the mask which covers it and destroys everything".[xvii,16]

To bring this digression to a close, and to make it clear that this is no enslavement to a taste for yellowed varnishes, Lanzi can remind us how the vision of colour ("*il colorito*") was articulated as a result of these experiences: "The amateur will never become skilled unless he has seen many works by the same [master] and taken note of the kinds of colours that he loves most, how he distributes them, brings them together and deadens them. Which are his local colours, and what the overall tonality used by him to harmonize the colours. In Guido[Reni] this is light and as though of silver, in Titian and his followers golden, and so on …".[xviii,17]

[xvi] "*Un quadro che veggasi dopo molti e molti anni che è fatto, apparisce quale vedrebbesi fatto di fresco a traverso di un velo, ovveramente dentro a uno specchio di cui fosse appannata così un poco la luce. É assai fondata opinione che Paolo Veronese, badando sopra ogni altra cosa alla vaghezza dei colori e a ciò che si chiama strepito, lasciasse al tempo avvenire la cura di mettere ne' suoi quadri un perfetto accordo e, in certa maniera, di stagionarli. Ma la maggior parte de' passati maestri non lasciarono uscire al pubblico i loro dipinti, se non dal loro proprio pennello istagionati e compìti. E non so se il Cristo della Moneta o la Natività del Bassano, ricevuto abbiano più di pregiudizio o di utile dal continuo ritoccargli il ha fatto, per così dire, il tempo da due e più secoli in qua. La cosa è a determinarsi impossibile. Ma ben potrà il giovane studioso compensar largamente il danno che per lunghezza d'anni abbiano patito i suoi esemplari, col ricorrere al naturale ed al vero, che ha sempre il medesimo fior di giovanezza e non invecchia mai, il quale agli stessi suoi esemplari fu di esempio.*"

[xvii] "*Se osa esprimere la sua opinione, troverà migliore la copia e la prenderà per l'originale e, in rapporto al vero, ha ragione. Il copista ha evitato di copiare i colori che si sono anneriti ed in più ha evitato di imitare il tono bruno che il tempo ha steso sull'originale. La copia si avvicina più ai toni chiari della natura, ed è questo che colpisce il profano, che non riconosce più il vero quando è mascherato. Un pittore distinguerà l'originale dalla copia, lo guida l'arte ed i suoi occhi esperti scorgono il vero sotto la maschera che lo copre e che distrugge tutto.*"

[xviii] "*Il dilettante non giunge mai a farne pratica che non abbia vedute molte opera di uno stesso e notato seco qual genere di colori ami egli fra tutti, come gli comparta, come gli avvicini, come gli ammorzi; quali siano le sue tinte locali; quale il tono generale con che armonizza i colori. Questo, quantunque sia chiaro e come d'argento in Guido e ne' suoi, dorato in Tiziano e ne' tizianeschi e così degli altri ….*"

3. The restoration of Antique sculpture

In the sphere of collecting, we see a continuation of the tradition which had established itself in the sixteenth century, of restoring and completing Antique sculpture. Indeed, their restoration and their intended destination followed precepts which immediately allow us to grasp the level of importance accorded to them. First, when the sculptures were exhibited in special loggias or galleries alongside paintings, they were accorded the status of true works of art. Their restoration, which could be largely interpretative, and their choice as a collector's item, could also depend on a taste for combining different materials, rather like in a *Wunderkammer*; for instance, at the beginning of the seventeenth century in the Borghese *Zingara* (which is now in the Louvre) a marble torso integrated with bronze in a restoration probably carried out by Nicolas Cordier, although in the past this was attributed to Bernini.[18]

Then there was the band of sculptures destined to complement the architecture of villas and palaces, the restoration of which became almost a matter of routine. In Rome especially, where it was easy to come across fragments of Antiquity, façades, courtyards and perspectives were decorated with statues often put together from pieces of differing origin. It is within this area of sculpture used as decoration, or else as insertions within garden schemes, that "pastiches" were created, using fragments which everybody recognized as being extraneous to one another.

A practice that grew in strength during the sixteenth century, which would now define restoration (although to our eyes still rather free), and was quite distinct from the simple reuse of materials as in the past, was that of always claiming for the statues of antiquity a subject drawn either from mythology, or from Greek or Roman history, or else to reinstate them as allegorical figures. A few interesting Roman examples such as Nicolas Cordier's *Saint Agnes*, which used an antique alabaster torso, or the antique bust that Bernini and Algardi completed in order to make the statue of Carlo Barberini in the Palazzo dei Conservatori, are to be considered as isolated examples.[19] The interpretation and the realization of a subject with a precise name and significance was indeed one of the aspects which linked restoration to antiquarianism, and which endowed it with particular dignity.

An esteemed restorer such as Orfeo Boselli in the *Osservazioni della Scultura Antica* observed that restoration, and the ability to do it well, "is not something for an indifferent intellect as others believe, but rather for an enquiring mind, so varied and sublime that it entices the greatest in the art. One must attempt to recognize the Antique statue, which Virtue or God or character it represents, to be able to follow its bearing, and give it the required attributes to hold; then to give it its due proportions, and most importantly to follow the antique style, if any one can attempt so much".[xix,20]

As was the case in the sixteenth century, at times restoration became an opportunity to present and comment rather than reconstruct the Antique sculpture and, alongside examples in which the aim was to be in harmony with the original (for example, the right arm

---

[xix] *"Non è cosa da mediocre ingegno, come altri si crede, anzi di speculatione, tanto varia e sublime che aguaglia, le magiori del arte. Poichè si ricerca il conoscere la statua antica, qual virtù, deità o personaggio rapresenti, per secondare il portamento, et darli in mano segni convenienti; darle la debita proportione; et quello che più importa accompagnar la maniera antica, se alsuno si può promettere tanto".*

72. The "Zingara" Borghese;
restored by Nicolas Cordier.
Paris, Musée du Louvre.

73. Ippolito Buzzi, head of an
Aphrodite. Rome, Museo
Nazionale Romano, Ludovisi
Collection.

74. Alessandro Algardi, head of
the Athena Ludovisi (Minerva)
1626–1627. Rome, Museo
Nazionale Romano.

75. *Ares Ludovisi; restored by
Gianlorenzo Bernini, 1633.
Rome, Museo Nazionale
Romano.*

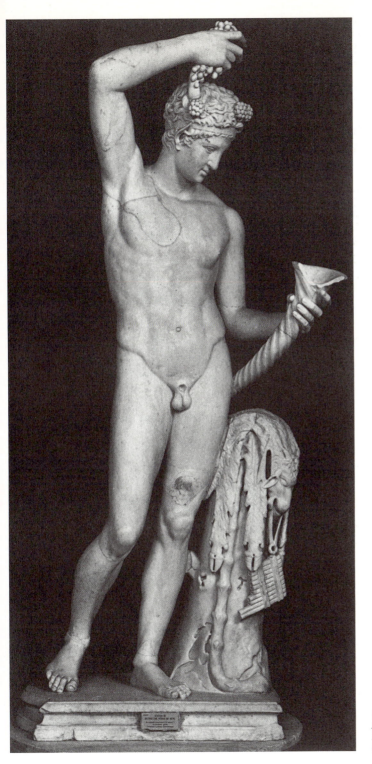

76. *Satyr; restored by Alessandro
Algardi, 1626–1627. Rome, Museo
Nazionale Romano, Ludovisi
Collection.*

73   of the *Dying Galata* executed by Ippolito Buzzi, who was the Ludovisi's restorer until 1623),
one also encounters sculptors who preferred to remain distinct from the antique; for instance,
Bernini in the mattress for the Borghese *Hermaphrodite*, which is now in the Louvre, or
75   the putto he added in 1623 to the *Ares Ludovisi*. Two restorations executed by Algardi for the
Ludovisi between 1626 and 1627, the *Lampadoforo* and the *Minerva*, clearly demonstrate
the difference between a completion which presented and reconstructed the antique fragments [in a manner] far removed from any possible original and, in the *Minerva* (although
74   only the torso was original), a completion which aimed to remain faithful to it.[21]

Decorative pastiches were put together without any attempt at reconstruction nor
indeed of seeking inspiration from an original, and pieces of different provenance were joined
together; Boselli, who himself had undertaken this kind of work, noted that poorly qualified
sculptors recomposed statues which "look like the monsters in Horace's *Ars Poetica*". Often
the result of these, the most current restorations, leave us with a sense of unease, because of
the assembly of antique fragments within a space which is, consciously or unconsciously, tied
to the new malleability of Baroque sculpture: an unease which one never feels even in the
freest integrations of the sixteenth century. This can be verified in a great many of the palaces
in Rome, and to cite but one example which is easily accessible, in the statues disposed along
the grand staircase of Palazzo Barberini. Miraculous results can also be seen, for instance
79   Ercole Ferrata's transformation of the *Faun with Kid* which is today in the Prado, into a modern work; also in one of Algardi's best known interventions, such as the completion of
77   *Hercules and the Hydra* in the Capitoline Museums, which demonstrates the difficulty of
attempting to integrate the severity (both expressive and spatial) of Antique sculpture with
the impetus imposed upon it by seventeenth-century restoration, when this has taken the
road of reconstruction.[22]

However, the fact is that all the principal sculptors were involved in the restoration or
in the reconstruction of important statues; again it was Boselli who noted: "Of our contemporaries, Cavalier Bernino must be praised for having made a foot, the fingers of a hand,
75   and a putto for the Gladiator [that is the *Ares*] which already resides, well loved by the
Empress Faustina, in the palace of the Villa Pinciana of the Ludovisi. Cavalier Algardi
should also be praised for the restoration of a statue of Mercury, for which he made feet
and an arm, which can be seen in the same villa. Nor will I be silent about the figure of a leaping Faun belonging to the Signori Rondanini, which François du Quesnoy from Flanders
made good with thighs, legs, arms and a head, harmonizing with the original in the most
marvellous way."[xx]

Algardi had a long apprenticeship as a restorer in the country residence of the
Ludovisi, and he directed the work on the antique statues in the Villa Doria Pamphili; but
it was Duquesnoy who, out of all the contemporaries, was most renowned for his excellence
as a restorer, for the *Rondanini Faun* and for a *Minerva* in oriental alabaster which
he restored for Ippolito Vitelleschi, completing it with "a head armed with a helmet, the

---

[xx] "*De i nostril coetanei, va laudato il Cavalier Bernino per aver fatto un piede, dita di mano, et un Amorino al Gladiatore
[cioè Ares] che siede già amato dalla imperatrice Faustina nel palazzo della villa Pinciana de Ludovisi. Così il Cavalier
Algardi per la ristauratione di una statua di Mercurio, al quale rifece piedi e braccio, nella istessa villa esistente. Non tac-
erò la figura di Fauno saltante de' Signori Rondinin, risarcito dal nominato Francesco Quesnoi Fiamengo, al quale sono
rifatte coscie, gambe, braccia e testa, a meraviglia accompagnata la maniera antica.*"

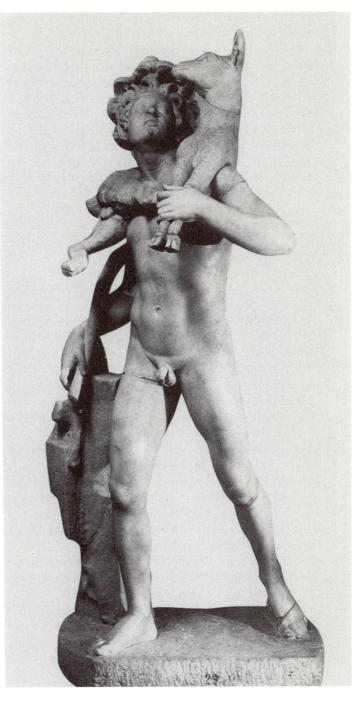

77. *Hercules and the Hydra; restored by Alessandro Algardi. Rome, Capitoline Museum.*

78. *Ercole Ferrata, Head for a Venus. Florence, Galleria degli Uffizi.*

79. *Faun with a kid; restored by Ercole Ferrata, c. 1676. Madrid, Prado Museum.*

hands and feet in Corinthian metal extracted from melted down medals", as detailed by Bellori.[23]

The identification of restorations on sculptures is not always an easy task, as the earliest integrations have been replaced by others which were thought to be more faithful to the original, or better suited for insertion of the work within a desired scheme: the legs of the *Barberini Faun* – attributed to Bernini and executed in plaster by Giuseppe Giorgetti and Lorenzo Ottoni in 1679 – were replaced by Vincenzo Pacetti in the Neo-classical era, with new legs in Greek marble. Similarly, Baldinucci referred to various details of the substitution of the Mannerist restoration of a Venus in the Uffizi (a head "not nobly held, and with a long neck"), with an integration carried out by Ercole Ferrata, which was then itself substituted during the restorations carried out from the eighteenth century onwards.[24]

4. Pictorial restorations: Carlo Maratta

At the end of the seventeenth century, in the same way that Antique statues were at times restored by the greatest sculptors, a prestigious painter such as Carlo Maratta would take upon himself the restoration of some of the most important paintings in Rome. This was no longer purely an occasional occupation but, as Bellori would show, a constant concern for the models of the Neo-classical tradition for which the Papal city was, in artistic terms also, the capital of the Catholic world, a tradition within which Maratta himself had a well-earned place.[25]

It is in this juncture in which we find both Classicism and Rationalism, rather than in themes typifying the Counter-Reformation, that we can distinguish the weighty Catholic contribution to the formation of an awareness of the conservation and restoration of works of art. Unlike Cavalier Franceschini, who himself restored the Christ child in the *Madonna di Galliera* in Bologna, Maratta did not turn to making devotional interventions of a personal nature, but acted within the compass of a conservation programme which (beyond the principles of non-intervention which now distinguished the fine artist when confronted with restoration problems) looked to return to their pristine integrity the masterpieces of the tradition to which he himself belonged. Alongside the operations that could be classed as simple conservation, there was also a tendency towards renovation (*ripristino*), towards the recuperation of an original state that was better than the deteriorated state in which these works had come down to us, a tendency guided by a certain academic spirit which allowed that once the good principles on which these images had been founded were mastered, it became possible to integrate and reconstruct them coherently, even if this reconstruction were not identical to the original.

Maratta's first restorations dated back to 1672; still episodic in character, nevertheless they already revealed his concern with the conservation of fine old paintings. Bellori recounted how on a devotional visit to Loreto, "he found that the best altar paintings in the church were in very poor state and in danger of being lost if not attended to immediately; particularly Annibale Carracci's *Nativity of the Virgin*. This damage, precautions not having been taken, was caused by the great number of bats nesting behind the wall and covering the reverse of the canvas with their filth. So that he (out of the veneration he felt towards this great master), accelerated the remedy, and not considering that simply lining the canvas and backing it with a panel was sufficient, also moved [the painting] to a safer place …".[xxi]

The paintings which Maratta had moved to the sacristy for their better conservation were the aforementioned altarpiece, Barocci's *Annunciation*, and a painting by Lorenzo Lotto (*Saint Christopher, Saint Roch and Saint Sebastian*), which he had "cleaned and brought back to a good state".[xxii] The spirit of *"pietas"* which characterized such interventions is made very clear when Bellori observed (referring to the Gallery in the Palazzo Farnese and the Loggia di Psiche) that: "The benefit accorded to posterity through the excellence of the works that eminent men of the past leave behind for our education is so great, that one cannot help but feel pain at the ingratitude towards their benefactors, in leaving their works to perish miserably".[xxiii,26]

This activity of Maratta's should in fact be inserted within the biographical model of an exemplary professor, who does not despise the works of the ancients, but rather ensures their survival, "venerating" great masters such as Annibale Carracci and bearing a memory full of gratitude towards his own master, Andrea Sacchi, whose fresco in San Giuseppe a Capo le Case he restored. It is a form of respect which led to embarrassment when Innocent XI required him to cover up the neckline of Guido Reni's *Madonna che cuce* in the Quirinale; he found himself "embarrassed, having on one hand to obey the Pope, and on the other not having the courage to lay a hand to cover even one stroke made by such a great man. Being in all his actions careful and prudent, he thought of a subtle way out of his predicament, obeying the pontiff whilst leaving the work intact. Having therefore taken pastels of earth colours, ground with gum, with them he painted the veil over the breast of the Virgin as the Pope wished, so that it would last; but whenever one should wish to remove it, with a sponge the original paint would reappear".[xxiv]

Bellori also recounted how in the work carried out in the Farnesina, in the Loggia di Psiche, Maratta restored "the outlines and the paint" with "a little lapis and pastel", to the extent that the *Encyclopédie*, in a brief report on the masters of the Roman school, would already see the problem in an eighteenth-century perspective, in terms of the reversibility of the restoration: Carlo Maratta had not wished to carry out the restoration in anything else but pastel, so that it could be removed at any time and replaced by a master who was more worthy of placing his brush by that of Raphael, than he was.[27]

These restorations responded to a vision of Rome as the capital of Neo-classicism which could not fail to render them acceptable, even from an official viewpoint: under Innocent XI,

---

[xxi] *"trovò in chiesa I migliori quadri degli altari mal ridotti ed in pericolo di perdersi se non vi si fosse rimediato; particolarmente la Natività della Vergine di mano di Annibale Carracci. Questo male, causato per negligenza in non provedere, derivava dalla gran quantità delle nottole ch'annidavano dietro il muro, in modo che infracidavano la tela, ond'egli per la venerazione che professa a questo gran maestro, accellerò il rimedio, e non giudicando sufficiente il foderar la tela e munirla con tavole, pensò di collocarla in più sicuro luogo …".*

[xxii] *"ripuli e ridusse in buono stato".*

[xxiii] *"E cosi grande il benefizio che gli uomini insigni recano a' posteri con l'eccellenze dell'opere che lasciano per loro ammaestramento, che non si può sentire senza dolore l'ingratitudine che usano a' li benefattori con lasciarle miseramente perire".*

[xxiv] *"confuso, dovendo da un canto ubbidire il papa, dall'altro non avendo ardire di por mano e cancellare ne' meno un tratto di sì grand'uomo, essendo egli in tutte le sue azioni ben prudente ed accorto, pensò ad una finezza d'ubbidire al pontefice e lasciar l'opera intatta. Pigliati dunque colori di pastelli di terra macinate a gomma, con essi dipinse il velo sopra il petto della Vergine come voleva il papa, in modo che rimane durabile; e, quando si voglia torre con la sponga, ritorna il colore di prima".*

Maratta was named "custodian" of Raphael's frescos in the Vatican Stanze and Loggie, and in 1693 he also became "custodian" of the Sistine Chapel. The Duke of Parma's agent could not but entrust to him the direction of the restoration of the Carracci Gallery in Palazzo Farnese, and Raphael's Loggia in the Farnesina. Of all this activity, the best known (apart from the restoration of pictures such as the panel by Giulio Romano in Santa Maria dell'Anima, in 1682) were the operations carried out on the frescos in Palazzo Farnese and in Raphael's *Stanze*.[28]

The restoration of the frescos consisted primarily in consolidation, as the principal cause of the damage was a "crack reaching from top to toe of the vault, which divided the width into two, extended down the walls to the floor, and had produced many more hair-line cracks, so that all the intonaco had detached from the vault, and even more from the south-facing wall on which Andromeda was painted, where it was already beginning to fall in pieces. Smaller pieces were also falling away from the vault itself. The second type of damage was an efflorescence of saltpetre over the part where Aurora and Cephalus were painted, which extended also to the medallions and the adjacent nudes".[xxv]

For the structural consolidation of the building, the consultant was Carlo Fontana: four chains were placed beneath the floor and four over the top of the vault. The efflorescence of saltpetre had as its origin "the coming away of the travertine cornice above the four exterior columns, and as the wind swept rain would bring the water onto this cornice, this penetrating through the gaps where the cornice had come away, would wet the wall. The humidity would then communicate itself to the interior, and saturate the medium and the pigments of the paintings. Future damage was taken into consideration when laying slabs of marble over the travertine stone of the cornice, extending half a palm inside the wall, making sure that they sloped away from the wall and overlapped one another at the joins".[xxvi]

For the *intonaco* (what Bellori calls "*colla*"), which was coming away, Gianfrancesco Rossi (who Maratta had chosen to carry out the work) used a "new and wondrous invention", which secured it to the wall in the manner of a silk or woollen cloth, with T- or L-shaped nails. For each of the nails he would follow this procedure:

> "Before inserting it [the nail] he would find the area which was most needy, rapping it with his hand to hear the sound and reverberations of the void, and where the colours were darkest, he would drill a hole with the utmost care, to the required depth for the strongest bond, he would fill it with a gesso paste. Then, choosing a nail of the length required by the hole, he would thrust in the nail up to the surface of the *intonaco*, in which he would embed it in order to hide the head or the sides of the nail. Having completed this operation, he would wait for the *intonaco* to dry, which the use of the gesso had wet around the nail, and then he would go over it with washes of watercolour in complete

---

[xxv] "*una crepatura da capo a piede della volta, che segando per mezzo la larghezza si stendeva giù per i muri sin al pavimento, ed aveva prodotto molti peli più piccoli, di modo che s'era staccata quasi tutta la colla della volta, e molto più quella del muro verso mezzo giorno ove è dipinta l'Andromeda, e già cominciava a cadere a pezzi, sì come n'andavano cadendo alcuni pezzetti della volta stessa. Il secondo mancamento era una fioritura di salnitro in quella parte ove è dipinta l'Aurora, e Cefalo, che si stendeva anco a' medaglioni e a' nudi contigui*".

[xxvi] "*dalla staccatura del travertino, che forma la cornice sopra le quattro colonne esteriori, perchè le piogge a vento portavano l'acqua sopra detta cornice, e quella insinuandosi nelli spazi di detta stuccatura, veniva ad aspergere il muro e a communicare l'umidità alla parte interiore ed a inzuppare la colla et i colori delle pitture; che però fu previsto al male futuro con mettere sopra il travertino della cornice tavole di marmo, e stenderle mezzo palmo dentro il muro, con avvertenza che stassero in pendenza verso il fuori, e si sopraponessero nel congiungersi l'una con l'altra*".

accord with the missing colour and matching the remaining paint, which – once dry – was barely distinguishable".[xxvii]

According to Bellori, there were one thousand and three hundred nails inserted in the gallery in the manner described above, and a further three hundred in the vault of the *gabinetti* painted by Annibale Carracci. In good reproductions, it is possible to make many of them out, most of them inserted in shaded parts or flat tints.[29]

Pictorially speaking, the restoration of the Loggia di Psiche was much more demanding in that it was a question of restoring the paint itself in the areas that had deteriorated most:

> "Raphael's loggia, although older, has been treated by the passage of time with more respect than by the inclemency of the air. Although the vault has cracked, and also has hair-like cracks, and the intonaco has come away in several places, nevertheless as these cracks are now stable, there has been no need to draw the walls together, nor to restore the walls, but simply to reattach and nail the detached intonaco in the same manner as was done in the Carracci gallery, using 850 nails in the process.

80

> "The damage caused by the air to this loggia is much more extensive as, having been exposed to the open air for about one hundred and forty years without the protection of the wooden panelling and glass which now fill the spaces between the pilasters, it was at the mercy of the night air, and of turbid and foggy days, and especially the north winds which would bring the rain right inside [the loggia]. From this, it is easy to comprehend the damage done to the colours, which have lost all their vivacity, and especially to the half-tints which have largely disappeared, and all the backgrounds which have blackened to such an extent that one cannot tell that they had been painted with that fine blue which one could just perceive in less exposed or better applied areas. But because this is a damage too difficult to put right without offending the beliefs of those who would rather consent to the complete loss of a prized painting than allow the slightest touch from a different hand – even if skilled and excellent – it is certainly a common misconception to believe that one can do nothing but conserve as best one can what time has left behind, and the revered relics of such wondrous works".[xxviii]

---

xxvii *"Prima di conficcarlo andava scoprendo il luogo più bisognevole, percotendolo con la mano per udirne il suono e'l rimbombo del vano. E dove erano le tinte più scure, faceva con somma diligenza un buco col trapano, penetrando sin dove conveniva per rendere più forte l'attaccatura, e poi l'empiva di pasta di gesso. Indi, scelto un chiodo della lunghezza, che richiedeva la profondità del buco, ve lo conficcava dentro sino alla superficie della colla, ove faceva il suo incastro per nascondere il capo del medesimo chiodo, o siano le coste laterali di esso. Fatta quest'operazione, lasciava che s'asciugasse la colla, che l'uso del gesso aveva bagnata intorno al chiodo, e poi v'andava sopra con certe acquerelle di tinta tutta somigliante a quella di prima e corrispondente alle parti rimaste della pittura, quasi rese asciutte, s'univano così bene che non era possibile ritrovarvi un divario imaginabile".*

xxviii *"La loggia di Raffaello, benchè più antica, è stata rispettata dal tempo più di quello, che abbia fatta l'inclemenza dell'aria, perchè se bene la volta aveva ancor essa le sue crepature, e i suoi peli, e la colla fatti i suoi staccamenti in più luoghi, contuttociò, essendo già pervenute le sudette crepature alla loro consistenza, non vi è stato bisogno di restringere, o di ristorare muri, ma solamente di riattaccare, et inchiodare la colla nell'istessa maniera, che si è fatto della galleria d'Annibale, con mettere in opera 850 chiodi. Il danno fatto dall'aria a detta loggia è stato molto più considerabile, perchè, essendo stato per centoquaranta anni in circa aperta senza il riparo, che oggi si vede di tavole, e vetri ne' vani degli archi tra pilastr, o e l'altro, n'è accaduto che sia stata sempre in potere dell'aria così notturna, come de' giorni torbidi, e nebbiosi,*

80. *Annibale Carracci, The
Triumph of Bacchus and
Ariadne; detail with the metal
staples inserted during the
restoration directed by Carlo
Maratta. Rome, Palazzo
Farnese, Gallery.*

To the description of the methods used in the restoration, Bellori felt it his duty to add various observations on the necessity and the need for the restoration of the image:

"It is however true that future generations will not be of the same mind as our scrupulous contemporaries, if only the vestiges of those parts will come down to them, which they will know had been perfect in our own or recent times; they will think us uncharitable or maybe even unjust that we denied painting that courtesy which is customary towards sculpture, which often sees its statues restored with fresh legs or arms or even heads to hold together the mass, and the rest of the figure. With this in mind, Signor Carlo Maratti, with the approval of the aforementioned Signor Felini and other knowledgeable men, renovated all the backgrounds using as guidance those fragments which remained intact, as we have mentioned above; and then, seeing many figures perish abandoned by their strength and moving spirit or the loss of the midtones, or the greater crudeness of the shadows, or else the complete fading away of the light in their eyes, we are pleased to register here each of the reparations undertaken by the same Signor Maratti, so that our contemporaries as well as future generations will know the obligation that is due to the conserving genius of this great man. The figures which he repaired are the ones mentioned below, that is: Bacchus and Hercules in the Feast of the Gods; in the Council of the Gods, Mercury who is holding a cup out to Psyche and Cupid, who is embracing the self-same Psyche whose head he also repaired; almost the whole of the north wall with the corbels and paintings above the arches, and in particular the portion in which Psyche is borne up to the heavens by cupids, and the putti bearing the Gods' *imprese* in the same way as in the corbels opposite he brought back from the state of mere vestiges the figures of Jove and the suppliant Venus. All of which has been carried out with such judgement and such skill that it would be difficult for any of the professors to discover the whereabouts of the modern handiwork if he did not already know it ..., such is the concordance of the modern with the ancient, and such was the effort this great man into finding the precise sites where the original tints still existed. And I know that when he could not be absolutely certain of his knowledge because of the complete absence of vestiges, he would then draw from the statues of Antiquity, as he did for instance in the case of the Antinous and the torso of the Hercules Belvedere, from which Raphael had drawn the above figures.

"In truth, who examines the events of this great restoration will have to confess the aforementioned signor Felini was right to say: that a century will not always have the good fortune of having a Carlo Maratta, and will wish then for what we have now".[xxix]

81

---

e de' venti specialmente aquilonari, che portavano le piogge anco colà dentro. Da questa notizia è facile a comprendere il danno fatto a i colori, che hanno perduta la loro vivacità, e soprattutto alle mezze tinte, in gran parte sparite, et universalmente a tutti i campi, che erano diventati così neri, che appena si conosceva esser stati formati con quel buono azzurro, che in qualche parte o meno sposta, o meglio tinta, pure si vedeva. Ma perchè questo è un male troppo difficile a repararsi senza offendere la superstizione di alcuni, che consentono più tosto alla caduta totale di una pittura egregia, che a mettervi un puntino di mano altrui, benchè perito, et eccellente, è certo un inganno comune a credere che non si possa far altro che attendere a conservare al meglio, che si può gli avanzi del tempo, e le venerate reliquie di così mirabili lavori".

xxix "è però vero che i posteri non saranno del sentimento de' scrupolosi moderni, perchè se giungeranno a' tempi loro appena gli embrioni di quei parti, che sapranno esser stati a' nostri dì, o poco avanti così perfetti, ci riprenderanno di poca carità,

To the reconstruction aspect of the restoration was added the problem of inserting these paintings into an appropriate whole, in that the white or single-tint walls which characterized the Renaissance loggia did not seem to provide an appropriate setting for the painted vault; in addition to which the work could be considered unfinished, as the festoons remained interrupted before the cornice against the "intention of the work". In order to support the vault and give a completed appearance to the loggia, Maratta would instruct Domenico Paradisi and Giuseppe Belletti to execute a monochrome decoration: "the festoons were finished, and painted down to the cornice, and then the lunettes were also painted, imitating the under-arch paintings on the opposite side, so excellently painted by Giovanni da Udine, and the windows and cornices, which complete the aforementioned arches. Moreover, all that can be seen today from the cornice to the floor, was painted in monochrome abstaining from painting figures but only architectural effects, out of respect for the vault. And so that the loggia could appear as a fully formed gallery, two more doors were opened of the four, which can be seen from the head and the foot [of the gallery] with their blocks of African marble. The shafts of these doors made anew with veined walnut, so that everything is in wondrous harmony, and pleases the eye right up to the uppermost stroke". [xxx,30]

One of Maratta's assistants, Bartolomeo Urbani, documented the restoration to Raphael's *Stanze* carried out between 1702 and 1703.

In every room the lower portions of the frescos had been badly damaged, worn away and disfigured with gashes and inscriptions, to the extent that in the stanza of Heliodorus it had been necessary for Maratta to give drawings in order to completely repaint the *trompe l'œil* yellow monochrome reliefs; in the *Stanza dell' Incendio*, all the lower portions of the figures of the kings who had been of good service to the Church had been lost, and in the

82

---

*e forse d'ingiustizia che si sia negato di fare alla pittura quella cortesia che s'usa verso la scoltura, la quale vede frequente-
mente ristorate le sue statue col rifacimento della gambe, o delle braccia, e talvolta della testa per sostenere il massiccio, ed
il resto della figura. Su questa considerazione, il signor Carlo Maratti con l'approvazione di detto signor Felini, e d'huomini
savi ha rinovati tutti i campi, accordandoli a quel segno, che mostravano quei pochi antichi rimasti intatti, come s'è detto
di sopra, e poi vedendo perire molte figure abbandonate dalla forza, e spirito primiero o con l'ammissione delle mezze tinte,
o con la crudità divenuta maggiore nelli scuri, o nel totale svanimento della luce degli occhi, ci piace registrare quivi tutte
l'individue riparazioni fatte dal medemo signor Maratti, acciò tanto i moderni quanto i posteri sappiano l'obligazione, che
devono al genio conservatore di questo grand'uomo. Le figure adunque da lui aggiustate sono l'infrascritte, cioè; il Bacco e
l'Ercole nella Cena de' Dei; nel Concilio de' Dei il Mercurio, che stende la tazza a Psiche, et Amore, che abbraccia la
medesima Psiche, e la testa di essa; quasi tutta la parte settentrionale ove sono li peducci e soprarchi, e particolarmente la
Psiche portata dagli Amorini in Cielo, et i putti che tengono l'imprese de' Dei, sì come ne' peducci opposti ridusse da uno
stato deplorato al segno, che si vede, il Giove, e la Venere supplicante. Il che è statoeseguito con tanto giudizio, e con tanta
perizia, che non darebbe l'animo certamente ad alcuno de' professori ritrovare quali siano gli aiuti dell'opera moderna, se
non l'avesse inteso …, tale è l'accompagnamento del moderno con l'antico, e tale è la fatica che ha fatta questo grand'uomo
per andare a ritrovare i siti precisi, ove stavano le tinte primiere, sapendo io che dove egli non poteva assicurarsi bastante-
mente dell'eccellenza della sua cognizione per la mancanza totale de' vestigi si poneva a disegnare statue antiche, come fece
in particolare dell'Antino e del torso dell'Ercole Belvedere, d'onde Raffaello prese le suddette figure. Veramente chi essam-
ina l'evento di questa bella riparazione confesserà che detto Signor Felini diceva con molta grande ragione che il secolo non
avrà sempre la ventura d'avere un Carlo Maratti, onde abbia a volere allora, ciò che si può adesso".*
*xxx "si sono compiti i festoni, e tirati giù sino alla cornice e dopo si sono dipinte anche le suddette lunette, imitando i sotto-archi
della parte opposta, fatti così eccellentemente da Giovanni da Udine, e il naturale delle invetriate, e delle cornice, che chiudono
gli archi suddetti. Di più si è dipinto a chiaroscuro tutto quello, che oggi si vede dalla cornice sino a terra, contendentosi in semplici mostre d'architettura senza figure per il rispetto dovuto a quella volta. Et acciò la suddetta loggia diventi una galleria for-
mata, si sono aperte altre due porte delle quattro, che vi si vedono da capo, e da piede con i loro conci d'africano, e i fusti delle
suddette porte fatti di nuovo con noce venata, onde il tutto fa un accordo mirabile, et appaga l'occhio al più alto segno".*

case of two of them, it was even impossible to work out their posture. In addition, their out-lines in white had been badly repainted, as had been the entire lower section of the *Stanza della Segnatura*, probably in the restoration criticized by Gaspare Celio. All the disfigurements in the lower portions were blocked out and repainted by Maratta's young assistants, taking care "in no way to detract from that which is preserved, but only colouring those portions which required it, and that the old be well matched in the appearance of the colour, so that nothing should appear renovated".[xxxi]

In the *Stanza della Segnatura*, all the repainting on the base of the frescos was removed and the reconstruction of the architectural ornaments and the grotesques was entrusted to Domenico Belletti, whose works are "so fine, and accompany without being in any way inferior to the works preserved and dating from the times of Raphael". Taja, referring in par-ticular to the *Sala di Costantino*, makes clear that the monochromes painted in earth pigments were repainted using as a guide ancient engravings, and specifically notes that the women clad in the "heroic" fashion in the *Stanza dell'Incendio di Borgo* were "reawakened and exe-cuted by the brush of Signor Carlo [Maratta] himself".

83

After the completion of this work, there were still the large stories to clean, which Maratta put in the hands of Pietro Tosini "renowned for his skill in this work". It is of this cleaning that Bartolomeo Urbani wrote:

"Work began in the room in which Giulio Romano had painted the story of the apparition of the Holy Cross to Constantine; it was wonderful to see the cleaning of that painting. It seemed, as one removed the dirt, that jewels were being brought to the light, and one saw again the beauty of those colours and how the figures seemed to regain their liveliness. Seeing one part cleaned and not the other, it appeared all the more manifest because of the contrast, and the Pope took much pleasure in the work, and as it progressed would continually send people to look. The paintings were being brought back to the light from having been buried not only under dust but also in some instances injured by the smoke as could be judged when, where there was dust, the white cloths which were used to wipe dry the paint-ings after these had been moistened or wetted with wine, would appear as though they had been placed in mud; and when soot was encountered, then they became dark, almost black, and this was the case in the *Stanza dell'Incendio* in the case of the story painted above the fireplace and which was therefore in very poor condition. The same was the case in the *Stanza dell'Attila* in the story of Heliodorus, which was similarly placed above the fireplace, so that it was believed that as soldiers had been in these rooms in the time of the Sacking by the Bourbons, they must have uncon-cernedly lit great fires, which had reduced the paintings to such a poor state. In the *Stanza dell'Incendio*, the wooden door had also suffered and had to be made anew, similar to the old one which had been put into place at the time of Leo X. To the left of this door were a number of monochrome grotesques of great beauty, but in very bad condition, having even had torches extinguished on them as everybody could tell from the soot left behind, and the wax which was still attached to the wall. A similar state of affairs was found in the neighbouring room, near the door, where

---

[xxxi] *"non punto pregiudicare a quello che si ritrovava conservato, ma che solo colorissero I luoghi dove erano bisogno, e che si accompagnasse bene l'antico nella forma del colore, in guisa che non apparisse rinnovata cosa alcuna ..."*.

81. Raphael and assistants, detail of the Loggia di
Psiche; restored under the direction of Carlo Maratta.
Rome, Farnesina.

82. *View of the Loggia di Psiche, with the decoration of the walls, carried out under the direction of Carlo Maratta. Rome, Farnesina.*

FAVETE·LINGVIS·ADVENAE
IN·ARCIS·QVAE·STABAT·OPPVGNATIONE
TORMENTA·EXPLOSA
ISTVD·ET·QVAE·PROXIMA·SVNT
HAVD·TEMERE·RESARCIENDA
DETRIMENTA·INTVLERVNT
ANN·MDCCIV

83. *Gaudenzio Ferrari, detail
of the Assumption of the
Magdalen; with the loss left
visible, 1704. Vercelli, San
Cristoforo.*

the wooden partition (*bussola*) at the entrance stood. His Holiness had this one and the other one in this room, as well as the one in the *Stanza dell'Incendio*, removed because they obscured the light [falling] on the paintings."[xxxii]

Bartolomeo Urbani's report also referred to the criticisms of certain "malicious people", which resulted in Maratta documenting the condition of the paintings prior to his intervention: he had the lower section of the *Stanza della Segnatura* copied in its original state with the repaintings, and in many areas would have liked to leave "a small portion of each condition [encountered] in its uncleaned state, so as to confound with hard evidence those opposed to his cleaning", but at the request of the Pontiff himself, Clement XI, he confined himself to leaving only "a small section of those ornaments with the old rusty colour", near the entrance to the *Stanza della Segnatura*.[31]

I remember my perplexity, at the time I was working on the first edition of this book, when Longhi observed that Maratta must surely have restored the *Loggia di Psiche* better than the restorer who was at work on it at the time of writing. How could one possibly think that a painter who (notwithstanding all his declarations on retouchings carried out in pastel) would nevertheless carry out his spottings over the original fresco paint layer, and whose integrations spilled over to cover original paint without a second thought, could possibly be found preferable to a restorer who, suitably equipped and controlled scientifically, was at that moment in time proceeding with careful consolidation and accurate in-painting; that an intervention which at times was close to a repainting, should be considered preferable to a "modern" restoration?

I do not know whether Longhi's objections were valid for the *Loggia di Psiche*, but that his apparently paradoxical position might not have been without foundation is the conclusion I have now reached, taking into consideration the interventions on the vault of the Sistine Chapel executed during Maratta's "custody" between 1705 and 1710, and then the material and chromatic robe with which it has been invested in the present restoration. Maratta delegated to assistants and to minor figures the execution of restorations which he saw in a perspective very different to one of our conservation interventions; his aim was to find a way of returning the image first and foremost to its "idea", but also with the material and optical characteristics that were most appropriate to this "idea".

[xxxii] "*Fu incominciata l'opera nella salad a quella storia dipinta da Giulio Romano che rappresenta l'apparizione della Croce a Costantino; fu cosa mirabile il veder ripulire quella pittura, parea, mentre si levava quel fango, si scoprissero tante gioie, e ravvisarsi la bellezza di quei colori, ed accrescersi lo spirito a quelle figure, e vedendosi ripulita una parte, e non l'altra, appariva più manifesta per l'opposizione, ed il papa ne ebbe grandissimo piacere e, proseguendosi il lavoro mandava continuamente persone a vederlo, tornando alla luce quelle mirabili dipinture sepolte, non solo nella polvere, ma anche in parte offese dal fumo, come si vide, imperocchè dove era la sola polvere venivano i panni bianchi, che si adoperavano per asciugare dopo che si era bagnato, o inumidito col vino, come se fossero stati posti nel fango, e quando incontravasi il fumo divenivano oscuri, e quasi neri, e ciò avvenne nella Stanza dell'Incendio in quella storia, che è sopra il camino, che si ritrovava perciò in pessimo stato, siccome ancora nella stanza dell'Attila nella storia d'Eliodoro, che similmente è sopra il camino, onde si stimò che, essendo ivi stati i soldati nel tempo del Sacco di Borbone, questi senza alcun riguardo vi facessero gran fuoco, che avea quelle pitture sì mal condotte; si ritrovò ancora nella Stanza dell'Incendio la porta di legno, che avea molto patito, e bisognò farla di nuovo, come la antica, che vi era stata posta in tempo di Leone X, ai lati di questa porta vi erano alcuni grotteschi di chiaro oscuro di meravigliosa bellezza, ma così mal conci, che sopra di essi v'erano fin state ammorzate le torcie, e si conoscea da tutti per la negrezza lasciatevi, e per la cera, che ancor era attaccata, simile inconveniente era anche nella sala appresso la porta, dove era la bussola; che fu tolta per ordine di Sua Beatitudine insieme con altra qual v'era, e quella della Stanza dell'Incendio perchè toglievano il lume alle pitture*".

Never would a restoration carried out by Maratta have accepted effects such as the ones visible on the figure of Joel where the purple gown and the red cloak are no longer balanced. Either the cleaning or the saturation caused by the materials ill-advisedly used to protect has disturbed the material relation between the two colours, and the indigo comes out dazzled, giving it the [tonal] value of a light which no longer allows it to work alongside the deep modelling of the mantle. A Maratta would, obviously, have lowered the tone or else had that zone which resulted unbalanced at the end of the cleaning, repainted. But he, with his experience as a painter, would also have immediately been able to choose a finishing material that would not have altered the balance, in terms of materials and luminosity, between the various media used in the wall painting: *fresco*, lime and *secco*.[32]

5. Controversies over Carlo Maratta

Whilst the restoration of the *Stanze* did not particularly become the object of controversy, the restoration of the *Loggia di Psiche* became the focus of a debate which lasted through the greater part of the eighteenth century, so that it became *de rigueur* even for travellers to express an opinion on Maratta the restorer. He had felt himself authorized to complete the images basing himself on a Classical and prescriptive analysis of the work of art which, as such, must follow norms that can be acquired through proper method. The figures of Bacchus and Hercules redrawn from the Antique on the vault recovered the essential elements of the images, and the underlying "idea" found full expression despite the rather clumsy handling and a few unavoidable variations.

The negative judgements were mostly linked to probable changes and to the difficult legibility of the frescos which, until the restoration directed by Giulio Aristide Sartorio in about 1920, had backgrounds of deep ultramarine, as can also be seen in the false tapestries in the vault of the *Stanza di Eliodoro*, and in early echoes of the *Loggia* such as the frescos in the Eroli Chapel in the Duomo of Spoleto. This archaic trait, characteristic of artists of the early part of the sixteenth century, was therefore misunderstood by visitors such as president de Brosses, who had no hesitation in ascribing it to Maratta's retouching, But the relative success of the criticisms, as a question of principle, was also closely linked to a less academic vision of painting, more appreciative of its material qualities and its creative aspects, and the unforeseen and therefore unrepeatable elements of the painterly process, which therefore could be neither imitated nor "accompanied" [by the restoration].

Jonathan Richardson found it impossible to make any judgement on the *Loggia di Psiche*: "as this work had deteriorated, it was retouched; and there are some places which have been completely repainted by Carlo Maratta who, although an excellent Master, far from putting back in order Raphael's work which had been ruined over the long passage of time, has ruined it even more than Time has or could have done. It may be that Maratta's work now does not appear as it did then, that the colours have darkened or changed over time. But whatever the case may be, whether the project was poorly planned or insufficiently well executed, the fact of the matter is that the work as a whole, as we see it today, does not correspond in the slightest degree to our conception of the work of Raphael".

Even the brick-like colouring of the flesh contrasts too vividly with the ultramarine which is believed to have been applied by Maratta: an effect which "shocks the eye". President de Brosses reiterated that "the colouring is execrable, reddish and completely lost", and that the ultramarine used by Maratta in the backgrounds makes them come forward and increases the natural hardness of Giulio Romano's colour.[33]

The official positions, on which Bellori focused, could not but be favourable towards an artist who had taken such care to preserve the tradition of the great masters who had been his artistic models. Bearing this position in mind helps one to understand the different stance taken by Giovanni Bottari; in 1730 he referred to the *Loggia di Psiche* as "having been retouched, has lost much". On moving to the capital of the Papacy, in his *Dialogo sopra le tre arti del Disegno* of 1754, he brings forward Maratta himself as a character, dealing with the subject of restoration, and makes him the advocate of a "middle way". Paintings must be neither washed using "a thousand secret potions" nor retouched and repainted (as poor restorations are worse than naturally caused damage), nor should they be left to perish. And if their lordly owners are often responsible for having poor restorations carried out, and even being pleased with the results, this is because "where before the works were dull, after [the restoration] they appear with brighter colours which, being striking to the sight, easily leads them astray":[xxxiii] to take pleasure in a painting is not the same as being knowledgeable about it. Various examples of poor restorations are given, but the *Loggia* is not included among them. The author of a letter on varnishes published in Rome in 1788 finds it "very odd that one should have introduced Maratta in these *Dialoghi* to speak on the subject of restoration".[34]

Luigi Crespi, in 1756,[35] confronted the problem of the retouching of frescos in a more general context; Maratta's interventions are used by him solely as a point of departure in an exposition of all the reasons why an "intelligent" man could only be opposed to such restorations. First of all, it was impossible to restore a fresco because "… either the missing parts are reconstructed using *buon fresco* (if it is indeed possible to do so), or in a *secco* technique, or finally with pigments bound in lime, but [the restorations] will always be distinguishable from the original, and it will never be possible to perfectly match the hues, the *patina* or the freshness …".[xxxiv]

Other observations concern the comparison (*paragone*) with those objects of antiquity which were revered for their archaeological or historical importance, and a discussion of the different approaches to the restoration of paintings and sculpture. On the subject of medals, he made the following observations: "If a person when confronted with an antique medal, the rareness and antiquity of which is signalled by the patina or the loss of some portion of the medal, should want either to have it cleaned or to have the missing portion replaced, would he not be condemned by all antiquaries and experts? Would not a person who went to the trouble of having antique lettering 'adjusted' on a memorial stone be ridiculed?"[xxxv]

[xxxiii] *"dove prima le pitture erano smorte, dopo le veggiono d'un colorito più vivo, il quale dando loro negli occhi, facilmente gl'inganna".*

[xxxiv] *"… o si rifacciono de' pezzi mancanti a buon fresco (dato che si possano rifarre), o si rifacciano a secco, finalmente si rifacciano co' colori mescolati con calce, sempre si deve riconoscere il rifatto dall'antico dipinto, e però giammai si otterrà l'intento di perfettamente uguagliare le tinte, la patina e la freschezza …".*

[xxxv] *"Chi volesse ad una medaglia antica, la cui rarità e segno di antichità fosse o la mancanza di qualche parte di essa, o la patina, chi volesse, dico, o ripulirla, o farle aggiungere quel pezzo che vi mancasse, non sarebbe egli da tutti gli antiquari ed intendenti condannato? Chi si prendesse la briga di far accomodare un antico carattere in una memoria o lapide, non si renderebbe egli ridicolo?"*

Bellori's invitation to show to paintings the same "courtesy" that was habitually extended towards sculptures led Crespi to distinguish between the appropriateness of the integration of missing parts in statues, and the inappropriateness of such interventions on paintings: "as it is a question of adding legs, arms, heads, hands and the like, etc., which might be missing on a statue, these are additions which in no manner interfere with the original to which they are added, in no way deforming it, and can be at any point in time removed at pleasure without the original incurring any damage".[xxxvi] Moreover, the "outline" of a sculpture could be imitated more easily than that of a painting (in which are found both outline and colouring), and the new parts in a statue could be well matched by patinating them, which is something that could not be done in paintings. In paintings one ended up, in order to match the restoration to the original, by laying hands on the "original paint". As a writer and painter linked to the tradition of dark paintings characteristic of the beginnings of the century, Crespi also pointed out the impossibility for his contemporaries of adapting their style to that of the Old Masters to be restored:

> "If there existed in our day and age someone who by studying with this purpose in mind the masterly techniques of our great men of the past, endeavouring to imitate them, would then hazard to retouch the works to which he related most closely, then maybe one might just be able to tolerate this intervention, although it would still be worthy of censure. But completely different styles are being studied, not the strong chiaroscuro but the tender style of the sweet and delicate; not the grandeur of the outline but the delicacy and detail of the background; not the boldness of the brush but diligence and high finish. And even worse, one hears with horror, all day long, these same professors with the greatest and unbelievable audacity criticizing as extravagant the boldness of the outlines of Michelangelo and of Tebaldi, the painterly touch of Guercino in his early works and of Caravaggio, the brightness of the colours of Carracci, and advising their young disciples to be careful and distance themselves [from these], as though vices within the profession …".[xxxvii]

And Crespi too, having categorically denied the possibility of a technically satisfactory restoration, then focused on the distinction between the painter and the restorer: an artist could be "skilled and excellent in his own style", but completely incapable of retouching a work executed in a different style to his own. In 1756, this professional distinction was one of the principal clarifications in the field of restoration, which was arrived at from a variety of different directions.

[xxxvi] *"trattandosi d'aggiungere gambe, braccia, teste, mani e simili, ec., le quali manchino ad una statua, trattasi d'un'aggiunta che per niente tocca l'antico cui s'aggiunge, per niente il difforma, e può ad ogni ora levarsi a piacimento senza lesione del vecchio".*

[xxxvii] *"Se vi fosse a' nostri dì chi, studiando di proposito le magistrali maniere de' nostri valorosi uomini, e procurando d'imitarle, si azzardasse, a seconda delle maniere cui più si approssimasse, di ritoccarle, pur pure si potrebbe soffrirlo, benchè in questo caso ancora sarebbe cosa degna di biasimo, ma nel vedersi che tutt'altre maniere si studiano, non la forte del chiaroscuro, ma la debole del delicato e tenero; non la grandiosità del contorno, ma la delicatezza ed il minuto de' contorni, non la prontezza del pennello, ma lo stento ed il finimento; anzi nell'udirsi con raccapriccio tutto dì criticare da' medesimi professori con somma e inaudita baldanza, per stravagante l'arditezza del contorno dei Buonarroti e de' Tebaldi, la macchia della prima maniera de' Barbieri e Caravaggi; il forte del colorito del Carracci, e da tali esempi guardarsi, non solo come da tanti vizi nella professione, ma insinuarne l'allontanamento ne' giovani discepoli …".*

Notes

1. L. de Laborde, *La Renaissance des arts à la cour de France*, Paris, 1858, pp. 403–404; A. Venturi, *Quadri in una cappella estense nel 1586*, in "Archivio storico dell'Arte", 1888, p. 426; R. Longhi, *Risarcimento di un Mantegna* (1934), in *Me Pinxit e questi caravaggeschi*, Florence, 1968, p. 72; J. W. Goodison, *George Gower, Serjeant Painter to Queen Elizabeth*, in "The Burlington Magazine", 1948, note 15 p. 264; Kurz, 1962, pp. 56–57.

2. Turquet de Mayerne, in Berger, 1901, p. 124; R. and S. Redgrave, *A Century of British Painters*, London, 1866, ed. 1947, p. 4 (see also p. 5 for the pleasing recollection of the "domestic picture cleaning" carried out by itinerant craftsmen who went from one country house to the other); C. Justi, *Velasquez e il suo tempo* (1888), trans. Florence, 1958, pp. 462–463, note 2 p. 710; Stübel, 1926, note 4, p. 125; H. Tietze–E. Tietze Conrat, *Der junge Dürer*, Augsburg, 1927, p. 47 (see H. Tietze, *Genuine and False*, New York, 1948, pp. 26–27 for the figure of Saint Eustace in the *Paumgartner Altarpiece* with the repainting by Fischer); J. Moreno Villa, *Como son y como eran unos Tizianos del Prado*, in "Archivio Español de arte y arqueologia", IX, 1933, pp. 113–116.

3. Apart from particular references, for all the paintings in the French Royal Collections, and for their restoration, see Engerand (1899), whose analytical indexes allow easy access to the various works concerned. See also: B. Lepicié, *Catalogue Raisonné des tableaux du Roy*, II, Paris, 1754, p. 221; Engerand, 1900; Cagiano de Azavedo, 1948, pp. 36–37; K. Clark, *The Nude*, Harmondsworth, 1956, ed. 1964, pp. 80–83; G. Briganti, *Pietro da Cortona*, Florence, 1962, p. 224; for Algarotti, see the letter of 10 August 1756, in Algarotti, 1781, VII, p. 51.

4. Vite, V, Siena, 1792, note pp. 326–334; Fogolari, 1937 (p. 175 for the letter quoted in the text); M. Chiarini, in Richardson, 1728 (I ed. 1722), I, pp. 125–126; G. Richa, *Notizie istoriche delle chiese fiorentine*, IX, Florence, 1761, p. 28; G. della Valle, in Vasari, *Artisti alla corte granducale*, catalogue of the exhibition, Florence, 1969, pp. 63–65; *La Galleria Palatina*, catalogue of the exhibition, Florence, 1982, pp. 42–49. Il Cavalcaselle (1882–1885, I, note 1 p. 403) notes retouchings and glazings on the *Madonna del Baldacchino*, but these cannot be seen now; the panel, which is unfinished, is in exceptionally good condition.

5. G. Tassi, note to F. M. Tassi, *Vite de'pittori, scultori e architetti bergamaschi*, Bergamo, 1793, note 1 p. 101 and note 2 p. 102; Pasta, 1775, pp. 9–10; ed. Longhi, 1964, p. 50.

6. M. Dvořák, *Francesco Borromini als Restaurator*, in "Kunstgeschichtliches Jahrbuch der K. K. Zentralkommission", I, 1907; A. Blunt, *Borromini*, London, 1979, pp, 141–154; P. Portoghesi, *I monumenti borrominiani della Basilica Lateranense*, in *Borromini nella cultura europea*, Bari, 1982, pp. 325–383.

7. In Abbate, 1965, pp. 45–46, see p. 72.

8. In Berger, 1901, pp. 124–128, 322, 324–326, 338.

9. Bellori, 1672–1696, ed. 1976, p. 603; Cavalcaselle–Crowe, 1877, II, note p. 319; Engerand, 1899, p. 71 in particular the materials paid to widow Lange for the lining of the *Venere del Pardo*, "glues, sand and marouf": V. Golzio, *Documenti ... nell'archivio Chigi*, Rome, 1939, p. 290; Olivato, 1974, pp. 21–23, 105 (here, p. 98, a possible reference to the use of canvas in restoration in a request from Pietro Vecellio in 1608, which one should bear in mind when considering the origins of lining, but the interpretation of which still remains problematic).

10. Richardson, 1728 (I ed. 1722), I, pp. 125–126. Fra Bartolomeo's panel was transferred onto canvas by Fouqué in 1806 (Emile Mâle, 1979, pp. 241–242).

11. Boschini, 1660, p. 8, as well as the passage cited about Pietro Vecchia; A. Félibien des Avaux, *Entretiens* (1666–1668), ed. 1688, II, p. 240; J. Dryden, *To Sir Godfrey Kneller*, vv. 174 and following, ed. J. Kingsley, London, 1961; J. Addison, *A Dream of Painters*, in "The Spectator", 5 June 1711; Algarotti, 1781, VII, p. 5; Kurz, 1962, pp. 58–59; Muraro, 1962, pp. 475–477. See Conti, 1973, p. 226, for further indications on the letters in which Veronese's painting mentioned by De Sera is discussed.

12. On Terenzio da Urbino, see: Mancini, 1956, pp. 257–258; Baglione, 1642, pp. 156–157; J. S. Gaynor–I. Toesca, *S. Silvestro in Capite*, Rome, 1963, p. 106; Ferretti, 1981, pp. 138–139. On Manfredi: Baglione, 1642, pp. 158–159. On Caletti: Lanzi, 1809, V, p. 266; E. Riccomini, *Il Seicento ferrarese*, Ferrara, 1969, pp. 41–47; Ferretti, 1981, pp. 145–146; Conti, in *Sul restauro*, 1988, pp. 58–60.

13. F. Scannelli, *Il microcosmo della pittura*, Cesena, 1657, p. 114; Mavasia, 1678, II, p. 59; G. P. Zanotti, *Storia dell'Accademia clementina*, II, Bologna, 1739, p. 120; Kurz, 1962, p. 58; Mahon, 1962, p. 466.

14. W. Hogarth, *The Analysis of Beauty* (1753), New Haven–London, 1997, note pp. 91–92. The acquisition of the *Sigismonda* by Francesco Furini as a presumed Correggio (now in the collection of the Duke of Newcastle) gave rise to one of Hogarth's particularly ironic comments on the "*black masters*", see C. McCorquodale, in *Painting in Florence 1600–1700*, catalogue of the exhibition, London, 1979, p. 76. Hogarth's position can be

understood more clearly, if one also bears in mind his observation on how colours "will appear to be more united and mellowed by the oils they are ground in" (idem., p. 91).

15. Crespi, 1756, in Bottari, ed. Ticozzi, II, pp. 429–432. For a critical position taken with regard to the cleanings in Bologna during the eighteenth century, also see Ms B30 by Marcello Oretti in the Biblioteca dell'Archigennasio, which is referred to in: G. Zucchini, *Abusi a Bologna nel secolo XVIII in material di quadri*, in "L'Archigennasio", 1949–1950, pp. 45–82.

16. *Saggio sopra la pittura* (1762), see Saggi, edited by G. Da Pozzo, Bari, 1963, p. 8384; Liotard, *Traité des principes et des règles de peinture* (1781), ed. Geneva, 1945, pp. 144–153.

17. Lanzi, 1809, ed. 1968, p. 26.

18. Haskell–Penny, 1981, pp. 505–508; on the restorations of Nicolas Cordier, see: S. Pressouyre, *Les trois Graces Borghèse du Musée du Louvre*, in "Gazette des Beaux-Arts", LXXI, 1968, pp. 148–160; Haskell–Penny, 1981, pp. 33–34; S. Pressouyre, *Cordier Nicolas*, under the heading, in *Dizionario Biografico degli Italiani*, XXIX, 1983.

    On the restoration of Antique sculpture in general, see Boselli, 1978 (Book V, Ch. XIII), ed. 1967, pp. 86–96; De Rossi, 1826, pp. 27–30; A. Muñoz, *La scultura barocca e l'antico*, in "L'Arte", 1916, pp. 129–160; Cagiano de Azavedo, 1948, Ch. II; Howard, 1968; I. Faldi, *Il mito della classicità e il restauro delle sculture antiche nel XVII secolo*, in *Barocco fra Italia e Polonia*, Acts of the symposium, Warsaw, 1977, pp. 57–69; Ferretti, 1981, pp. 160–161; L. Dolcini, *Per una storia del restauro delle sculture*, in "OPD Restauro", 1986, pp. 16–18; Rossi Pinelli, 1986, pp. 221–229.

19. Muñoz, op. cit., p. 143; R. Wittkower, *Gian Lorenzo Bernini*, London, 1966, p. 196; J. Montagu, *Alessandro Algardi*, New Haven–London, 1985, pp. 398 (the restoration of a now lost fragment, as Saint Cecilia), 402 (on the statue of Carlo Barberini; one should bear in mind that, for the same destination on the Campidoglio, in 1593 Ippolito Buzzi had completed in a similar manner an antique figure with the head of Alessandro Farnese).

20. 1978, ed. 1967, p. 86.

21. On the Ludovisi sculptures (the polishing with pumice and nitric acid used by Algardi in the restoration of the marble statues which can be seen, particularly heavy-handed on the *Galata morente*) and, in general, on the artists who intervene [on them], see: De Rossi, 1826, pp. 26–29; R. Wittkower, op. cit., pp. 178–179, 191–192; Bruand, 1956; G. A. Mansuelli, *Galleria degli Uffizi – Le sculture*, I, Rome, 1958, pp. 65–66; A. Nava Cellini, *L'Algardi restauratore a villa Pamphili*, in "Paragone" n. 161, 1963, pp. 25–37; M. Heinbürger Ravalli, *Alessandro Algardi scultore*, Rome, 1973, pp. 53–57 (the Ludovisi Collection); Haskell–Penny, 1981; B. Palma, *I marmi Ludovisi: storia della collezione* (*Museo Nazionale Romano. La scultura*, edited by A. Giuliano, I, 4), Rome, 1983, pp. 19–38; B. Palma–L. de Lachenal, *I marmi Ludovisi* (*Museo Naz.*, op. cit., I, 5), Rome, 1983; J. Montagu, *Alessandro Algardi*, New Haven–London, 1985, pp. 11–15, 22, 398–402; *Il Galata capitolino*, edited by M. Mattei, Rome, 1987.

22. Cagiano de Azavedo, 1948, p. 30; Hovard, 1968, pp. 403–405; Heinbürger–Ravalli, op. cit., pp. 58–59; Haskell–Penny, 1981, p. 123 and n. 37; J. Montagu, op. cit., p. 400. Some of the restorations for Palazzo Barberini have been identified by Jennifer Montagu (*Antonio and Gioseppo Giorgetti Sculptors to Cardinal Francesco Barberini*, in "The Art Bulletin", 1970, pp. 278–298) but, executed towards 1670 with a strongly classicistic bent, they differ from those to which I allude in the text.

23. Bellori, 1672, ed. 1976, p. 300; Passeri, 1673, pp. 112–113; J. Hess, *Notes sur le sculpteur François Duquesnoy*, in "La Revue de l'Art", LXIX, 1936, pp. 26–27; A. Nava Cellini, op. cit., p. 27.

24. Baldinucci 1681–1728, XIII, pp. 441–445; Montesquieu, *Voyage d'Italie*, Bordeaux, 1894, II, p. 330; in Œuvres Complètes, Paris, 1964, p. 355; Muñoz op. cit., p. 158–159; Mansuelli, op. cit., n. 317; H. Keutner, *Die Bronzevenus des Bartolommeo Ammanati*, in "Münchener Jahrbuch der Bildenden Kunst", 1963, pp. 79–92 (and for various restorations carried out in the Galleria di Firenze by Foggini, see R. Herbig, *Barocke Restaurierung antiker Marmorstatuen in Florenz*, in "Mitteilungen des Deutschen Archeologischen Instituts, Römisches Abteilung", 1961, pp. 187–197); Rossi Pinelli, 1981, note 13 p. 54.

25. Rome's identity as the artistic centre for the Catholic world is well demonstrated in the footsteps taken by Paolo Alessandro Maffei (*Raccolta di statue antiche e moderne*, Rome, 1704, p. VIII), quoted by Orietta Rossi Pinelli (1981, p. 221). See my comments in 1979 (pp. 245–251) and in 1981 (pp. 45–48). On the relationship between classicism, rationalism and Catholic thought, it would be useful to reread the stimulating study by Paola Santucci, *Poussin. Tradizione ermetica e classicismo gesuita*, Naples, 1985.

    Maratta showed a technical training well adapted for restoration, which can also be seen in his remarkable ability in retouching some of his own works, for instance *The Adoration of the Shepherds* in the Quirinale, and *The Death of Saint Francis Saverio* in the Church of the Gesù, see Bellori, 1672–1696, ed. 1976, pp. 609, 618; A. Mezzetti, *Contributi a Carlo Maratti*, in "Bollettino dell'Istituto di Archeologia e Storia dell'Arte", 1955,

p. 343; see also the references to his repainting in the early eighteenth-century inventory published in *Il Cardinal Alessandro Albani*, 1980, pp. 27–28.

26. Bellori, 1672–1696, ed. 1976, pp. 602–603; Bellori, 1695, p. 81.

27. Bellori, 1672–1696, ed. 1976, pp. 553, 603, 616, 639, 649; *Encyclopédie*, entry for *Ecole Romane*, ed. Livourne, V, 1772, pp. 303–304; A. Sutherland Harris, *Andrea Sacchi*, Oxford, 1977, n. 80, p. 100 (on the *Dream of Saint Joseph* which still exists, but repainted, in San Giuseppe a Capo le Case).

28. On the "custody" of Maratta, see Bellori, 1672–1696, ed. 1976, pp. 647–649. For various restorations attributed to Maratta, see: F. W. von Ramdohr, *über Malerei und Bildhauerbeit in Rom*, II, Leipzig, 1782, pp. 72–73 (background of the *Ganymede* by Damiano Mazza, which is now in the National Gallery, London); J. Lohninger, *S. Maria dell'Anima …*, Rome, 1909, p. 101 and note 1. The attribution to Maratta of the restoration of the *Dea Barberini* which is referred to by Winckelmann is a traditional one, see Cagiano di Azavedo, *La Dea Barberini*, in "Bollettino dell'Istituto di Archeologia e Storia dell'Arte", 1954, pp. 108–111, in *Cultura e tecniche artistiche*, Milan, 1986, pp. 57–60.

29. *Della riparazione della Galleria del Carracci nel Palazzo Farnese e della loggia di Raffaello alla Lungara*, in Bellori, 1695, pp. 81–83; M. Cagiano di Azavedo, *Il primo uso delle grappe metalliche per fermare gli affreschi*, in "Bollettino dell'Istituto Centrale di Restauro", n. 7–8, 1951, pp. 99–100.

30. Bellori, 1695, pp. 83–86; Bellori, 1672–1696, ed. 1976, p. 649. On other interventions, especially those concerning the securing of the intonaco with nails, on Raphael's *Galatea* and on Peruzzi's frescos in the Farnesina, see: Bellori, 1695, pp. 83 and 86; Titi, 1763, I, p. 35; A. Mignosi Tantillo, *Restauri alla Farnesina*, in "Bollettino d'Arte", 1972, p. 35.

31. The report by Bartolomeo Urbani (the other assistants under the direction of Maratta were Pietro de' Pietri, Andrea Procaccini and Gian Paolo Melchiorri) is published in Bellori, in the edition edited by M. Piacentini in *Le vite inedite* (Rome, 1942, pp. 143–148); in *Ritratti di alcuni celebri pittori del secolo XVII …*, Rome, 1731, pp. 237–246. On this restoration, see also: A. Taja, *Descrizione del Palazzo Vaticano* (ante 1750), cod. Vat. 9927, c. 193; Bottari, 1754, p. 229; Cavalcaselle, 1882–1885, II, note 1 pp. 175–176, III, note 2 p. 63; R. Redig de Campos, *Relazione dei laboratori di restauro*, in "Rendiconti della Pontificia Accademia Romana di archeologia", 1957–1959, pp. 273–306.

32. See G. Colalucci, in *The Sistine Chapel, Michelangelo Rediscovered*, London, 1986, pp. 263–264; Conti, 1986, pp. 73–74.

33. Richardson, 1728, III, pp. 189–190; De Brosses, 1739–1740, II, pp. 178–179.

34. Bottari, 1730, note p. 317; Bottari, 1754, pp. 232–245; G. G. D. R., 1788, p. 245. For other opinions on Maratta's restorations, see: Titi, 1763, I, p. 35; Piacenza, 1768–1820, II, 1770, note 96 p. 348; Orsini, 1876, pp. 302–303.

35. Crespi, 1756, pp. 387–417.

5

Eighteenth-century restorations in Italy and France

1. The origins of the transfer of frescos

The tradition of transferring frescos *a massello*[i] was very much alive in the eighteenth century, and was carried out in all cities in Italy. Luigi Crespi referred to them as operations which guaranteed the survival of paintings without disfiguring them. As an example, he referred to Ludovico Carracci's *Ecce Homo* in the Oratorio dei Filippini, not without lamenting the addition of two soldiers in the background painted in by Donato Creti, as well as the reframing, both of which he felt lessened the success of the operation. This type of transfer was usually put in the hands of sculptors, as it required the ability to avoid damage during the process, through the splintering or breaking up of the piece of wall or of the thin skin of *intonaco*, rather than knowledge of the behaviour of this paint layer when put into contact with either adhesives or solvents. At Herculaneum, the transfer of the mural paintings of antiquity found during the excavations was entrusted to the sculptor Canart. For painted surfaces of considerable size, the *trasporto a massello* became the responsibility of architects or engineers, and those carried out in Florence under the direction of Peter Leopold by Niccolò Gasparo Paoletti achieved considerable renown: the "*Volticina*" attributed to Matteo Rosselli in the villa of Poggio Imperiale in 1773, and the tabernacle depicting the *Flight into Egypt* by Giovanni da San Giovanni, which was transferred from the Palace of the Crocetta to the Accademia delle Belle Arti in 1783.[1]

Truly noteworthy examples of the transfer of paintings attached to the section of wall they were painted on (and without the removal of the entire wall) were those undertaken in Rome by Niccolò Zabaglia, which caused stupefaction by their sheer size: these were altarpieces from Saint Peter's, which were transferred to the Certosa di Santa Maria degli Angeli in order to be replaced with mosaic copies. In 1727, Romanelli's *Presentation of the Virgin* and the altarpiece painted on slate by Pomarancio of the *Punishment of Ananias and Saphyra*, in 1736 the *Martyrdom of Saint Sebastian* by Domenichino. In 1743 *I Castelli e ponti di Maestro Zabaglia* was illustrated with a series of engravings reminiscent of those in the *Encyclopédie*,

---

[i] Frescos transferred *a massello* were detached along with the plaster and part of the wall on which they were painted. When transferred with the *stacco* technique, only part of the plaster was detached along with the image, whereas when strappo was the method used, only the pigmented layer making up the image was detached, leaving the plastered wall behind. (See Glossary.)

84. *Ludovico Carracci, Ecce Homo; transfer "a massello" from the beginning of the eighteenth century. Bologna, Santa Maria di Galliera.*

85. *Method used for the transfer of Dominichino's Martyrdom of Saint Sebastian, from "Castelli e ponti di maestro Niccolò Zabaglia". Rome, 1743.*

whilst Saverio Bertinelli referred to him to give an idea of those early architects, illiterate but expert in construction, who brought about the renaissance of the arts after the millennium, in their capacity to emulate: "with the aid of machines and wonderful inventions the most enlightened mathematicians, without ever having studied, and without being able to read".[2]

A completely different method to the *strappo* of the fresco by means of cloth or paper glued to the surface was given in the slim volume by Carlo Ruspi, a minor practitioner of the art of detaching frescos (*estrattista*) and copyist of Old Masters, active in Rome during the nineteenth century. Having described one of the usual methods of detaching a fresco, he went on to describe a "method adopted in Naples":

"They first chase a square around the painting, whatever the size required, and then embed a solid stretcher built in the manner of a case which is made to penetrate into the wall, to whatever thickness of wall one wishes to remove. They then cover the entire painting with a wetted sheet so that it remains stuck to the surface, and covering it with a plank the same size as the painting, as though it were a cover, they attach it to the stretcher with metal screws but allowing an inch or so between it and the painting. They then fill the gap with liquid gesso and

once it has hardened, with suitable metal files they detach the *intonaco* containing the painting, or else saw through the wall to the appropriate depth".[ii]
The abbot of Saint-Non also referred to Naples in his description of the method employed in the second half of the eighteenth century to remove the paintings at Herculaneum: "Having made incisions with a small hammer around the painting which is to be transferred, one ensures as far as is possible that the four sides are at right angles; after which one lays onto it four lengths of wood which are held in place and held together, by long metal screws. Having completed this operation, the wall is sawn from behind, and the painting removed taking the precaution of doubling it up with a panel made out of slate or some such material ... All middle-sized paintings have been detached without suffering any damage. They only require to be supported with an edging band of wrought iron, and to double the support with this slate".[iii]

De Dominici referred to the *estrattisti* Nicolò di Simone and Alessandro Maiello, who specialized in the transfer of flaking paintings on panel onto canvas; only one mural painting is mentioned by him, a lunette painted in tempera by Battistello in the Church of San Giuseppe in Chiaia, which was transferred onto a "large panel" in 1720. Their method, however, was not applicable to works executed in true fresco technique: with their "wonderful secret mixture" they were only able to "remove the painted skin" (*scrostare*) of wall paintings, "as long as these were painted in oil".[3]

At the beginnings of the eighteenth century, a proper method of peeling a fresco off the wall (*strappo*) was discovered by Antonio Contri of Ferrara. Lanzi himself recorded his activities:

"After experimenting for a whole year, he developed a glue or pitch (whichever term you prefer), which he applied onto a canvas the size of the painting he wished to transfer. Having applied it to the painting, and pressing on it with a wooden mallet, he would then cut the plaster around the painting, and apply a well-supported panel onto the canvas, so that the glue would set, and evenly. After a few days he would skilfully detach the canvas from the wall, which would take the painting with it. Having laid it flat onto a table, he would apply to its reverse another canvas onto which he had applied a stronger mixture than to the front. He would then cover the whole work with a pile of sand, which would apply pressure equally over the whole surface; after a couple of weeks he would

---

[ii] "*Praticano dapprima una traccia quadrata attorno alla pittura, sia di qualunque grandezza, e v'incastrano un solido telajo di legno costrutto a mo' di cassa il quale penetri nell'interno del muro tanto quanta è la grossezza del masso che tagliare si voglia. Coprono appresso l'intiera pittura con un foglio di carta inumidita, affinchè vi resti attaccata; e collocandovi sopra una tavola grande quanto è il dipinto fatta a forma di coperchio, la fermano attorno al detto telajo con viti di ferro, in guisa però che rimanga scostata dal dipinto un'oncia o più. Ermeticamente compaginato tal coperchio, gettano nel vano tra questo e la carta del gesso liquido e, poi quasi indurito, con lamine di ferro acconcie traggono fuori l'incollatura che contiene la pittura oppure segano in quella grossezza che vogliono*".
[iii] "*Dopo aver inciso a piccolo colpi di Martello il muro attorno al dipinto che si vuole trasportare, si fa in modo, per quanto è possibile, che i quattro lati stiano ad angolo retto; dopo di che vi si appoggiano sopra quattro liste di legno contenute e fermate da lunghe viti di ferro. Compiuta questa operazione, si sega il muro da dietro e si toglie quindi il dipinto prendendo la precauzione di controfondarlo con una tavola di una specie di ardesia o di lavagna ... Tutti i dipinti di mediocre grandezza sono stati staccati senza soffrire alcuna alterazione. Non si deve che sorregerli con un bordo di ferro battuto e controfondarli con questa lavagna.*"

return to the two canvases, would remove the first with warm water, and on the other canvas remained the painting which he had detached from the wall".[iv] Cavazzoni had seen one of his interventions in 1729, and had been very much surprised to find that it was not the case of "the crust of painted plaster" being detached, but rather the detachment of the pigment itself "of which no trace remains in the plaster except for a few signs where the colour had been densest and darkest"; he was also astonished that the first mixture (*segreto*), which resulted in the removal of the pigment from the *intonaco*, should then be "overcome" by the other mixture, with which it had been attached to the new canvas.

It was Barrufaldi who gave the most detailed information on Contri. His first entirely successful experiment with the technique had been carried out on part of a frieze depicting buildings and battle scenes in Palazzo Schinchinelli Manfredi in Cremona: three battle scenes and a few monochrome figures. In the same city, Contri had also transferred "a life-size standing figure of a very beautiful woman, placing a burning firebrand in her mouth, probably representing Portia, the famous Roman matron", which Bernardino Campi had painted above a fireplace; this was the most extensive of his transfers.

In 1728, he was given the opportunity to carry out other *strappi* in Ferrara: the abbot of San Giorgio offered him the transfer of the *Feast of Balthazar*, a mural painted in oil by Tommaso Laureti, which because of its size could not be detached "all in one go, as indicated and required by the nature of the secret mixture employed". And finally, it was Baruffaldi himself who offered him the opportunity of transferring onto canvas two of the fourteen heads painted by Domenico Panetti which were detached with a skin of *intonaco* from a *Story of Saint Maurelio* destroyed during the reconstruction of a new chapel in San Giorgio. Contri chose two heads of "equal size looking at one another", asking only to be given a wooden stretcher and two pieces of stiff cloth. After two weeks or so, Baruffaldi was presented with a basket containing the stretcher with "the cloth nailed to it, with the two heads which seemed to fit so well that they seemed to have been painted there in the first place: in addition (and this is the most awe inspiring), the two pieces of wall which had been given to him were included separately, without their skin and deprived of every vestige of colour except that of the plaster, the remains of the tracing, and some shadows of the initial colour."

The Ferrarese writer was particularly astonished because, "as the above paintings were executed either in glue-size or fresco technique, and not in oil, hardly anything remains on the surface of the wall, as the plaster absorbs all the moisture and the pigment; and yet the entire painting appears here, just as it was originally, but fresher and without the dust which with time had accumulated on it".[4] We do not know of any treatise on the technique by Contri, but in the eighteenth century transfers were not a rarity. In Cremona too, there are two putti and a portrait of *Curzio Rufo* in the picture gallery, which were transferred in 1776, too tardy a date to be able to relate them to Contri's technique.[5]

---

iv "*Varie esperienze tentate per un intero anno gl'insegnarono a formare una colla o bitume che si voglia dirsi, che disten-deva sopra una tela pari alla pittura che volea trasferirivi. Applicata alla pittura, e calcatela ivi con mazzuola di legno, tagliava la calce all'intorno, e applicava alla tela una tavola ben appuntellata, perchè il lavoro facesse presa e venisse uguale. Dopo alcuni dì staccava destramente dal muro la tela, che traeva seco la pittura; e, distesala in piana tavola, le applicava posteriomente un'altra tela inverniciava di una composizione più tenace della prima. Indi ponea sopra il lavoro un cumulo di arena, che ugualmente in ogni punto lo comprimesse; e dopo una settimana rivedeva le due tele, distaccava la prima con acqua calda, e allora rimaneva nella seconda tutto il dipinto tolto dal muro*".

2. The earliest transfers from panel

In one of his family letters from Italy (dated 1740, but written several years later), De Brosses referred to an artisan in Rome who transferred oil paintings from either panel or canvas onto new supports: a modest operator, who would return the old canvas or the worm-eaten panel alongside the transferred painting, and who had no knowledge of pictorial restoration (*restauro pittorico*). His method was not suitable for frescos, and for the transfer of panel paintings he would charge three times the amount that he charged for canvas paintings. In the Palazzo Pamphilii, De Brosses had seen examples of transferred paintings which as a result were in excellent condition. However, the president observed, such a discovery would have been particularly useful for frescos, which were more at risk from the environment in which they found themselves, than other kinds of painting. It was possible, for paintings in oil, that this artisan might also have undertaken transfers from copper and glass: "He glues his painting, from the paint side, onto something which is both flexible and rigid, with a preparation of which he holds the secret; then he completely imbibes the painting with a liquid which detaches the paint layer from its old panel or canvas. Then he patiently rolls both painting and the old canvas until they are completely detached from one another …. Having done this, he once more lays out the painting and attaches it to a new canvas (it was not made clear to me whether with or without the priming layer). Then, with a similar artifice, he detaches the painting from the layer to which he had attached it to make it stronger".[v]

In 1769 Joseph-Jérôme de la Lande would refer to a certain Domenico Michelini as the author of the transfer (executed in 1729) of a canvas depicting a *Child* by Titian, in Palazzo Altieri in Rome. A Michelini in Rome was also mentioned by Luigi Crespi as a good restorer and, in 1721, Charles-François Poerson told of having packed some paintings into cases in Rome, to be sent to France, with the assistance of Cavalier Luti and Signor Domenico "who is excellent in the reparation of paintings: it is he who has the skill and the secret of removing the paint layer from a painting, and attaching it to a new canvas in the most incredible manner; but as I have seen this with my own eyes, I cannot doubt it." Michelini's signature and the date 1714 were found on the reverse of the *Road to Calvary* by Paolo di Giovanni Fei, now in Memphis (published by Adolfo Venturi in 1906).[6]

In Italy, in the early eighteenth century, there were thus several operators who carried out transfers: the Maiellos in Naples, Signor Domenico, the artisan visited by President De Brosses, as well as Contri who discovered a secret [process] different to theirs, which enabled him to detach frescos from plaster. Francesco Maria Riario was different from these artisans, but a very imprecisely defined character: a dilettante of noble stock, who dedicated himself to the study of optics, to physics and to the restoration of old paintings. In 1751, the "Mémoires de Trévoux" referred to a Riario who could not, chronologically, be the same man who was a pupil of Tiarini, and who Gaetano Giordani recorded as having died in 1676,

---

[v] "*Incolla il suo quadro, dalla parte della pittura, su di un corpo che sia flessibile e rigido con un preparato di cui ha il segreto; poi imbibe a fondo il quadro con un liquido che distacca la pittura dalla sua vecchia tavola o dalla sua vecchia tela. Dopo di che egli arrotola con cura e con pazienza sia la pittura che la vecchia tela finchè non siano interamente distaccate l'una dall'altra … Fatto questo, distende di nuovo la sua pittura applicandola su di una tela nuova (se con l'imprimatura o no questo non mi è stato detto), poi con un arteficio, probabilmente, più o meno analogo, distacca, la pittura dal corpo al quale l'aveva incollata per darle maggior consistenza.*"

having executed a few transfers. The Riario of which we hear talk in France was supposed to have transferred various views by Le Sueur painted on plaster in the Hôtel Bouillon; the "Mercure de France" in 1756 referred to a Riario as "an Italian gentleman, a proficient painter and very expert in physics, medicine, chemistry, optics etc. …", who in 1741 had given a seminar on [the process] of transfer in Brussels.[7]

It is not coincidental that so much of the information on transfers carried out in Italy should come from French sources, as it was in France that this interest in the mechanical arts manifested itself always more clearly, and was one of the inspirations behind the *Encyclopédie*. In the preliminary discussion to that great work, d'Alembert makes the distinction between the mechanical and the liberal arts:

"As the mechanical arts depend on manual operation and are, if I might be allowed to use the term, subject to a kind of blind practice, they have been left to those men whom prejudice has placed in the lowliest positions. Indigence, which has forced these men to apply themselves to such [mechanical] tasks, more often than their desires or inclinations might have directed, has subsequently become a reason for despising them, so much does it harm that which it accompanies. As far as those operations of the free spirit are concerned, they have become the prerogative of those who have felt themselves privileged by nature. However, the superiority of the liberal arts over the mechanical ones, because of the travail they demand of the spirit and because of the difficulty of excelling in them, is sufficiently compensated by the much greater usefulness which, by and large, the latter procure us. It is this very utility which has pushed us to reduce them to purely mechanical operations, in order to facilitate their access to a greater number of men. But society, although it must duly respect the great geniuses which illuminate it, must not revile the hands which serve it … and what difference is there really between a head filled with unconnected facts lacking any order or usefulness, and the instinct of a craftsman reduced to mechanical execution?"[vi]

Diderot analysed the distinction between the liberal and the mechanical arts even more radically under the heading "Art": "although there is some foundation [for this distinction], it has had a bad effect, debasing highly respectable and highly skilled people and reinforcing in us a tendency towards laziness, which has already led us to believe too easily, that to apply oneself with constancy and continuity to particular material tasks was in some way to detract from the dignity of the human spirit; and that to practise or even just to study the mechanical arts entailed lowering oneself to study things which were laborious, the meditation

---

[vi] *"Les Arts Méchaniques dépendans d'une operation manuelle, & asservis, qu'on me permette ce terme, à une espèce de routine, ont été abandonnés à ceux d'entre les hommes que les préjugés ont placés dans la classe la plus inférieure. L'indigence qui a forcé ces hommes à s'appliquer à un pareil travail, plus souvent que le goût & le génie ne les a entraînés, est devenue ensuite une raison pour les mépriser, tant elle nuit à tout ce qui l'accompagne. A l'égard des opérations libres de l'esprit, elles ont été le partage de ceux qui se sont crus sur ce point les plus favorisés de la Nature. Cependant, l'avantage que les arts libéraux ont sur les arts mécaniques, par le travail que les premiers exigent de l'esprit, & par la difficulté d'y exceller, est suffisamment compensé par l'utilité bien supérieure que les derniers nous procurent pour la plûpart. C'est cette utilité même qui a forcé de les réduire à des opérations purement machinales, pour en faciliter la pratique à un plus grand nombre d'hommes. Mais la société, en respectant avec justice les grands génies qui l'éclairent, ne doit point avilir les mains qui la servent …. quelle différence réelle y-a-t-il entre une tête remplie de faits sans ordre, sans usage, sans liaison, & l'instinct d'un artisan réduit à l'exécution machinale?"*

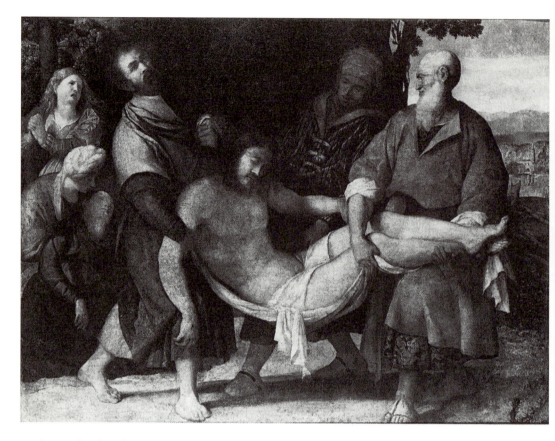

86. Jacopo Palma il Vecchio,
Deposition; transferred onto
canvas by Robert Picault in
1748. Brussels, Musées Royaux.

of which was ignoble, the exposition difficult, the commerce dishonourable, the number without end, and the value minimal. On one side of the scales lay the true advantages of the most sublime sciences and the most honoured arts, and on the other the mechanical arts, and you will note that the esteem in which one and the other are held is not distributed proportionately to the advantages, and that the men who have done their best to make us believe that we are happy have been much more highly praised than those who have done their best to truly make us so".[vii,8]

[vii] *"cette distinction, quoique bien fondée, a produit un mauvais effet, en avilissant des gens trés estimables & trés utiles, & en fortifiant en nous je ne sais quelle pareses naturelle, qui ne nous portrait déjà que trop à croire que donner une application constante & suivie à des expériences & à des objets particuliers, sensibles & matériels, c'était déroger à la dignité de l'esprit humain; & que de pratiquer ou mêmed'étudier les arts mécaniques, c'étqit de s'abaisser à des choses dont la recherche est laborieuse, la méditation ignoble, l'exposition difficile, le commerce deshonorant, le nombre inépuisable, & la valeur minutielle … Mettez dans une balance les avantages réels des sciences les plus sublimes & des arts les plus honorés, & dans l'autre côté ceux des arts mécaniques, & vous trouverez que l'estime qu'on a faite des uns & des autres, n'ont pas été distribuées dans le juste rapport de ces avantages, & qu'on a bien plus loué les hommes occupés à faire croire que nous étions heureux, que les hommes occupés à faire que nous le fussions en effet."*

87. *Paolo di Giovanni Fei,*
The Road to Calvary; transferred
onto canvas by Domenico
Michelini in 1711. Memphis,
Brooks Memorial Art Center.

Not even the Jesuits distanced themselves from this climate of interest in the mechanical arts; in fact, their *"Mémoires de Trevoux"* were one of the sources which followed the first interventions of the restorer Robert Picault with the greatest attention and detail. It was he who, with the transfer onto canvas of a few great pictures, adequately answered the expectations of the contributions to progress of the mechanical arts.

Already "cleaner of the Royal bronzes and gilding", according to an article in the Mercure de France of 1746, his first experiments in the field went back about six years. Between 1744 and 1745, he had transferred murals by Antoine Coypel in the Château de Choisy; in 1747, when the Ambassadors' staircase was demolished in the Château de Versailles, he transferred the *Taking of Cambrai* by Van der Meulen, which had been painted on plaster. In 1748 it was the *Deposition* by Palma Vecchio, which today hangs in Brussels, and a painting attributed to Parmigianino. It was with reference to this particular painting that Picault noted how, with the possibility of renewing the transfer of the support whenever it became necessary, a painting underwent an operation which "perpetuates painting, and renders artists immortal with the very aspect of their works" through repetition of the process, he hoped in the future to be able to execute them more rapidly, and hoped that the King would come to his aid so as to permit him to buy tools such as roller-presses which for the moment he could not afford.[9]

Between 1749 and 1750, Picault transferred Andrea del Sarto's *Charity*, describing the operation in a memorandum presented alongside the invoice: "A painting by Andrea del Sarto of 1518, representing Charity … painted on an oak panel made up of four boards secured and glued together, measuring 5 feet 10 inches in height, and 4 feet 2 inches in width. Which painting was removed and transferred from its panel onto canvas, having first removed and repaired thousands of retouchings which had been used to secure the areas of lifting paint, which were countless, and which masked the pure brush of Andrea del Sarto, all of which was extremely difficult, and had to be done with incredible care. After all these interventions, the painting was solidly glued to a well stretched piece of raw canvas onto an extensible stretcher. The work took about nine months, both day and night".[viii]

The restoration of the paint layer of del Sarto's *Charity* was carried out by another restorer, the renowned Collins. A letter from the Academy of Painting to Charles Coypel dated 7 June 1756 spoke of the general admiration induced by the exhibition of the transferred painting side by the side with its old panel support: "The call was unanimous to use the same means to prevent the ruin of Raphael's *Saint Michael*, which is deteriorating with every day which passes".[10]

[viii] *"Un tableau pein par André del Sarte en 1518 représentant la charitez … pein de sure un panneaut de bois de chainne de quatre planches assemblés et collez portant 5 pieds 10 pouces de aux sur 4 pié 2 pou de large; la quel peinture a été enlevé été passée de sure bois sur toile après avoir oté et réparez des milliés de repeins qui servais à retenir tous les endroits tréfilez qui aitoye sans nombre é qui empaichais de voir le pur pinceaut d'André d'Elsarte, se qui ma coutez des peines et des soins incroyables. Après toutes ces opérations a étez maroufleé sur une toile, écru, bien tendue sur un chassis clef. Ouvrage de près de 9 mois ten de jour que de nhuis."* The spelling is that of Picault.

The *Saint Michael* and the *Holy Family of François I* were the most famous paintings in the Royal Collections; despite this, they were continually subjected to the normal comings and goings of the paintings in the royal *guarderobe*, and in 1749 a report addressed to the director of the *Bâtiments* spoke of their state of conservation in the following terms:

"The *Holy Family* and the *Saint Michael* by Raphael, the two paintings which require the greatest care amongst all of those in the King's possession, are painted on panel. This means that, together with the weight of their frames, they are exceptionally heavy and as a result, difficult to handle; when the furnishings of the great apartment at Versailles are changed, they are moved to the picture store, and suffer all the more during these moves as the paint is lifting in many areas and flaking off, which is inevitable in paintings on panel. The *Saint Michael* has been so ill-treated in the past that it has had to be retouched repeatedly in several places. The *Holy Family* is still pristine and untouched, but it is unlikely to remain in this condition for long, and it is to be feared that one day one may be forced to transfer it to canvas by means of the new secret method practised by Picault. However, as this is an extreme remedy to which one resorts as late as possible, it would be to its advantage to preserve it to ensure, or to give the order that, whatever the change in the décor and furnishings, the paintings remain where they are, or else that a place to store them is found on the same floor in the château as close as possible to the apartment, without removing them to the store in the Hôtel de la Surintendance".

On 28 November 1750, the Academy of Painting examined the *Saint Michael* in order to decide what measures should be taken for its conservation, and whether Picault, after his treatment of the Andrea del Sarto and the mural painting by Van der Meulen, should also be entrusted with the Raphael, for the painting to undergo the same treatment. The examination showed that considerable paint loss was imminent, and that, if one were to repair the painting leaving it on its present support, "one would not only have to retain the old repaints, but also add new ones", renewing these in the future, so that in the course of a few years nothing would remain visible of the original work. By entrusting it to Picault to be transferred, "one would preserve all that remains untouched of Raphael, but also ... as the aforementioned Monsieur Picault also has the secret for removing overpaint, one could bring back to the light indications of the outlines and the colours." In order to be convinced of this advantage, one need only think how "when there was flaking in one part of the painting, he who was entrusted with the restoration, in order to harmonize the painting, would repaint the entire area, which is what happened in particular to the figure of the crushed demon in this painting by Raphael. Whilst now, one recalls the missing areas with dots of paint."

On 10 January 1751, an exhaustive report was drawn up of the state of conservation of the painting before the transfer: this was signed by Coypel, Portail, Charles Vanloo, Lépicié, members of the Royal Commission on Painting. D'Alembert, in the introduction to the *Encyclopédie*, in the discussion on the progress of the arts, had declared that Raphael and Michelangelo had brought the fine arts "to such a pinnacle of perfection that it remained unsurpassed to this day"; it would have been inconceivable to find a more exacting and important restoration than that of the *Grand Saint Michel* – one of the great creations of the human spirit – in France during that period. The very detail of the report drawn up prior to the transfer is an indication of the seriousness with which its restoration was considered.

88, 89

88. Raphael, Grand Saint Michel; transferred onto canvas by Robert Picault in 1751, *and transferred again onto another canvas in 1777. Paris, Musée du Louvre.*

89. *Raphael, Grand Saint
Michel, detail. Paris, Musée du
Louvre.*

Covered with countless repaints, especially in the darks, the *Grand Saint Michel* continued flaking, and in many places the white ground on which it had been painted was left showing: "it is not difficult to see that this painting is in a most deplorable state, especially in the lower section, that is from the knee of Saint Michael and below. From above the knee, including the whole of the sky, the drapery and the landscape, although very damaged, these [areas] have been preserved more purely, but you could not find two square inches of paint which are not either flaking, or have been already clumsily restored".

In the midst of all this enthusiasm, the first objections made no impact. In a letter dealing with the Royal paintings exhibited in the Palais du Luxembourg dated 10 December 1750 and published in the "*Mémoires de Trévoux*" of the following January, the originality of Picault's process was put into question. The author of the letter referred to both the ceiling painting by Le Sueur transferred from the Hôtel de Bouillon by Riario and the interventions seen by De Brosses in the home of Prince Pamphili in Rome. And yet the following month, in the same publication, appeared the *Observations sur l'art de conserver les ouvrages de peinture qui menacent ruine* by Father Berthier, which referred to Picault and his work in the most glowing terms. Paintings, in general, were lost as a result not of the deterioration of the paint layer, but of the support; there could be no doubt that Picault, having successfully treated Andrea del Sarto's *Charity*, would have the same success with Raphael's painting, the panel of which – as Pliny recounted of the *Venus* by Apelles – was "consumed by dry rot" ("*consenuit carie*"). Masterpieces must be safeguarded from the injuries of time, and whenever it should become necessary, the *Saint Michael* could be transferred again.

The actual method used in the transfer was also related: "A considerable length of time is spent by Monsieur Picault preparing to remove a painting from its support. This precious skin, if we can use such a word, belongs so inherently to the material which supports it, that only a fire, a very great fire together with the solutions which make up the secret, can successfully bring about – and only just – this operation …. The new support which receives what has been separated from the old support, is imbibed with a strong composition termed '*maroufle*', and the painted figures, set onto this adhesive, acquire an extraordinarily strong attachment to the new support. They become identified with it, so to speak, they form an almost indissoluble whole; and it is this which makes one say that paintings, thus transferred, acquire a second life, longer than their first. When only part of the support has perished, Picault is able to carry out a partial transfer, which allows for the repair of the panel or the wall, and then for the reattachment of the temporarily transferred painting, back into its original position".[11]

In the course of 1751, the Royal Collections also entrusted him with the transfer of a tondo attributed to Leonardo and, both the Academy of Painting and the "*Mémoires de Trévoux*" were full of admiration for the work carried out on a Madonna by Raphael in the collection of the Duke of Orleans.[12] At the end of the year, having completed the work on the *Saint Michael*, the restorer addressed a memorandum to the *Direction des Bâtiments* in which he detailed the difficulties of the task, in answer to those who reproached him his extortionate prices and had wondered, ironically, whether perhaps he used gold in the process. He pointed out that he had had to work uninterruptedly both night and day, having to renounce sleep; in fact, during the eight months taken to transfer the *Saint Michael*, for three of them he had not lain down to sleep. The Van der Meulen, the Andrea del Sarto and the tondo thought to be by Leonardo for which he was asking payment had taken twenty months of work, during which he had risked his health because of the nitrous and sulphurous substances which he had been obliged to inhale during the process.

The sums requested by Picault were substantially reduced, and as the reduction was to be expected, one cannot not use this fact to demonstrate Picault's greed: of the seven-thousand lire asked for the Van der Meulen, he received three-thousand, the Andrea del Sarto was paid two-thousand five-hundred rather than six-thousand, and the Leonardesque tondo one-thousand two-hundred rather than the original two-thousand five-hundred. Even the *Saint Michael* was paid seven-thousand rather than the eleven-thousand lire requested. Although the payments were reduced as well as being late, in May 1752 Picault was granted an annual pension of one-thousand four-hundred lire, and then on 7 October, the Academy of Painting expressed its satisfaction with the successful transfer of the Raphael: "the works of the Old Masters will be safeguarded from the injuries of time and will take on a new life thanks to a secret [process] which we cannot ever praise highly enough."

On 18 October 1752, the *Saint Michael* was exhibited to the public in the Palais du Luxembourg. As 1752 progressed (this was the year that the *Encyclopédie* was sequestered), Picault's star rapidly declined, and his substitution in the contracts for the restoration of the Royal pictures was accompanied by a literature increasingly hostile towards the restorer. On 10 December, his requests for payment were rejected by Marigny in the following terms: "The more I have examined your four bills, and had them examined by others, the more I find your prices disproportionate in relation to the finest works commissioned by the King from our best artists. It is both astonishing and indecent that you should ask as much – if not more – to remove a painting from its panel and put it onto a canvas, as the artist originally received to execute it. Once you had discovered your secret [method], for which you have been amply recompensed, what possible intellectual effort was required [from you] to carry out your operation?"[ix,13]

3. Polemics surrounding Robert Picault

The objections regarding the limited "intellectual effort" required for Picault to actually carry out his transfers are to be found again in Jacques Gautier d'Agoty's responses to the articles in the "*Mémoires de Trévoux*". His observations on *L'art de conserver les belles peintures* are an answer to the article of February 1751, and describe in minute detail the method of an Italian "virtuoso", operating in Marseilles, who had transferred a *Judith* thought to be by Domenichino, on which Gautier had then restored the painted image (*restauro pittorico*). Differing in this from Picault, the aforementioned virtuoso had transferred the painting by destroying the [original] support, without therefore acting directly on the paint layer:

"This Italian had skilfully laid his painting (despite its great size) face down onto a large and smooth panel, and having cleaned it [the reverse] well, softened the canvas with boiling water; when this canvas was sufficiently softened, he turned the painting over onto the same large panel so that he was now able

---

ix *"Plus j'ai examiné ou fait examiner vos quatre mémoires moins j'y trouve de proportions entre vos prix et ceux des plus beaux ouvrages que le roy a fait faire aux meilleurs artistes. Il est aussy étonnant qu'indécent que vous demandiez autant et peut-être plus pour lever un tableau sur bois et le mettre sur toile que l'auteur n'a eu pour l'execution. Votre secret trouvé et dont vous avez été amplement recompensé, quelle dépense de génie faites-vous pour votre opération, de la patience des soins et un peu de charlatanisme en font les plus grands frais."*

to stretch it with his arms and nail it all the way round. The painting being thus well stretched and secured, he applied a hand of hot glue onto it, covering it with a piece of worn canvas the same size as the painting. Having stuck this canvas to the painting, he then proceeded to nail it down all the way round, then exposing the painting to the sun to make it dry as quickly as possible.

"The Italian then removed the painting held between the two canvases, and nailed it face down with its original canvas on top. Having made a border out of wax all the way round, and having placed the panel on a perfectly level surface, he covered the original canvas with a 'second' water, that is, etching acid mixed with pure water, the dosage adapted so as not to consume the painting (this is easy to check, as when you place a finger into this 'second' water, it should not yellow). He allowed the 'second' water to work until the canvas had been consumed, which could be seen when it detached easily. At this point he poured off the 'second' water into earthenware bowls, and with a spatula removed the threads out of which the canvas had been made, thus freeing the layer of paint which remained attached, face down, onto the worn canvas I spoke about earlier.

It is not difficult to guess what the 'virtuoso' did next: he cleaned off the paint layer with fresh water and a dried it with a soft sponge, allowing it to become perfectly dry. The following day he passed a hand of glue on the painting into which he had added a little distilled alcohol or spirits of wine ('*acqua-vite*') to make it stronger, and in this manner, with the greatest of ease attached the painting onto its new canvas, being careful to press it all over with his hands to ensure that the canvas was perfectly adhered to the painting in all places.

He then took the precaution of applying pressure to the whole, with slabs of lead or marble, or some such material, whilst every so often wiping the reverse of the canvas with a cloth to prevent it from sticking to these slabs. Having dried the whole, he removed the nails to detach the first canvas from the panel; having done this he then turned it over once again and with the 'second' water moistened the worn canvas which covered [the painting], which was very easy to do at this point. Finally, he removed any remaining glue from the surface of the painting with some warm water and when it was dry, I painted in the heads and the draperies which were missing. The Italian told me that when the paintings are on panel, the process is much the same, and that with the painting face down, it is easy to remove the deteriorated wood. When the wood has not deteriorated, then it is thinned with a plane to a thickness which can be corroded away by the 'second water' with ease ...".

Already in these observations Gautier brings up the problem of whether Picault's operation was to be considered an art as suggested by the Jesuit Berthier, or simply a secret, and goes on to discuss this problem at length in his observations in *L'art de conserver les belles peintures*, in which he examines the responses to the "*Mémoires de Trévoux*" of February and April 1752.

Between that which cannot be considered anything else but a *secret*, and which Picault used to transfer paintings, and an *art*, there is the same difference as between the discovery of a remedy and surgery. In February 1752 the Jesuit publication responded with a review of the first edition of Gautier d'Agoty; a work which, predictably, would give rise to one of those literary debates which would be fruitful to both the arts and the sciences. Father Berthier made the point that Picault's invention shared elements of the *secret*, in its recipe for the mixture or potion used to detach paintings from their support, but also of an *art* in all the judgement and discernment required to bring about the successful outcome of the operation. Speaking of the *Saint Michael*, which had been exhibited to the public in Versailles in April 1752, Berthier observed that "all the Court, and all of Paris bear witness to the success of this artist [Picault]".

The subsequent edition of Gautier's book included an eighth observation which was articulated around two questions: whether Picault's method was to be considered an art, and whether it was to be preferred to the method practised in Marseilles. The first response, rather than being addressed to the Jesuit, seems to have been directed to d'Alembert's (and especially Diderot's) observations on the distinction between the liberal and mechanical arts as it appeared in the first volume of the *Encyclopédie*: "If the qualities which Father Berthier attributes to Monsieur Picault really were as he describes them, then the arts would become confused with secrets, secrets with trades, and trades with the lowliest occupations. Artists are not workmen, they are learned men (*savants*) who manipulate the chisel and the graver, the brush and the burin, the set-square and the compass, and who construct a pleasing pattern with sounds and rhymes".

True artists were to be considered "*savants*"; just as a surgeon was required to have knowledge of anatomy and medicine, the painter must have knowledge of the laws of nature and anatomy, the sculptor or engraver cannot be ignorant of the animal form, nor the architect of mechanics, and so forth. If they did not have this fundamental knowledge, they were artists in name only. Picault, in order to carry out his transfers, did not require any knowledge of philosophy, nor did he have to be either a doctor or an astronomer or a mathematician. It did not seem [likely] that the secret of transferring paint layers would one day lead him to the practice of a science, as he was neither a painter nor a draughtsman, and his knowledge consisted solely in the practice of his secret [method].

The care and attention which he was obliged to take in the execution of his transfer process were comparable to the caution taken by the stone-cutter in the fear that a rock of exceptional size might squash him; and just as the stone-cutter did not move outside his condition as a non-artist despite the preciosity of the materials he worked with, so, when evaluating Picault's activity, it was of no consequence whether he was transferring works by Raphael and Michelangelo, or the signs on the bridge of Nôtre-Dame: his place was alongside that of the picture cleaners and framers.

Moving on then to discuss whether Picault's method was to be preferred to that of the Italian "virtuoso", Gautier then pointed out that the latter removed the old support without acting on the paint layer, that is, without the softening of the paint film which was unavoidable with Picault's method, and which then ran the risk of either expanding it or contracting it to excess, and had as its only advantage the preservation of the worm-eaten and splintered panel. The only inconvenience of the method practised in Marseilles was that it could not be used on wall paintings for which (specifying that they must be painted in oil), Gautier put forward the following method of transfer, which he said was used by Picault:

"Paintings executed in oil on plaster must be washed thoroughly with spirits of wine, and the dust and smoke which may have altered them over time, removed with care. Then, over the next few days, depending on the requirements and the aridity of the paintings, one must moisten them with spirits of turpentine so as to give them a certain plasticity and unctuousness which is absolutely necessary to the crusty layers of old paint. Having completed this operation, and when you feel that the painting has regained some of its youth, you apply a warm and evenly bound layer of strong Flanders glue to the paint, and then do the same to a fine canvas (linen canvas from Flanders if you can), and attach this canvas onto the painting you wish to detach from the wall.

If the painting is thin and very much on the surface, you can simply use paper in the place of canvas, adhering this to the painting in its stead; but if the painting is large and the paint impasted and thick, then it is absolutely essential that you use canvas, and well stretched canvas at that. It must be secured all the way round with nails to prevent it shrinking, and you must allow it to dry for twenty-four hours. You will notice that the edges of the painting, as soon as the canvas is dry, will detach from the wall, especially if you put a stove in its vicinity or if the sun falls upon it.

In order to complete the operation (an operation which according to Father Berthier is admired by the whole of Paris), you carefully detach the canvas from the wall which brings away the oil paint with it; in the areas where the paint is too well attached – which happens not infrequently – you wet the wall with the "second" water, and with the aid of a spatula knife, you skilfully with one hand detach the piece of plaster, whilst pulling on the canvas with the other. With a little patience, you will be able to remove a painting twenty toise[x] in length, should the case arises; and if it is necessary to remove it section by section in pieces, you will then take the appropriate measurements. The detached paint layer glued to the canvas from the front can be softened as one wishes, and can be attached easily to the backing for which it is destined. When one is quite sure that the painting is well secured to this backing, one proceeds with the operation with the spirits of wine as I have described with reference to the method of the Italian."

The recent examination of Andrea del Sarto's *Charity* has shown that this method, necessary for mural paintings, was not the only one used by Picault, and that both his and Father Berthier's declarations on the use of heat and nitrous and sulphurous substances [for this transfer] had some factual basis. It would seem that he had in fact used fumes of nitric acid to act on the materials of the priming, which required great care in preventing them also acting on the paint layer. The grey discolorations, and the greenish haloes in the sky of the painting, would seem to suggest that perfect control had not always been possible. As for the "*maroufle*", the conclusion was that it had contained colophony and calcium-based resins, and that its composition was not a guarantee of durability; indeed, the absence of any proper priming layer helps us to understand why these paintings had to be retransferred after only a few decades.[14]

The attacks on Picault were not limited to these discussions; for other restorers the priority was to take his place in the transfer of paintings in the Royal Collection. In the Salon of 1752, widow Godefroid – their customary restorer – exhibited some examples of her transfers onto canvas, of paintings in the collections of Crozat and the Comte de Caylus; in the following year, when Picault was asked to undertake the transfer of a portrait of a man by

---

[x] An old French lineal measure, a little under two metres in length.

Joos van Cleve (at that time attributed to Holbein), she offered to do it for five-hundred rather than eight-hundred lire. The painting was handed over to her in March 1753, and in June of the following year she received the authorization to exhibit the restoration in the Salon.

The result of this situation was that a few years later Monsieur de Vahiny, referring to Picault's requests for payment, would observe that the restorer had received a substantial pension, and that it was five years since he had worked for the Bâtiments, having requested seven-thousand lire in payment for the *Saint Michael*, and as much again for two other old pictures in the Royal Collection which had been entrusted to him. Of these "old pictures", de Vahiny observed that "art lovers were all in agreement that it would be much better to use twenty-thousand lire to acquire two fine new pictures from one of the great masters, which would remain fresh, whole and in good condition, than to spend twenty-one-thousand lire to have two old pictures transferred onto canvas, which having undergone this process, would then not be worth a hundred scudi apiece."

Such were the impressions of Portail and the lamented Lepicié; the latter, surprised by the excessively high price which Monsieur Picault expected to receive for his work, and convinced that the "remedies" which Monsieur Picault allegedly employed in his operations were nothing but a swindle, in 1752 expressed the opinion that Monsieur Picault's bill was not [to be considered] as that of a pharmacist, but of a charlatan. To demonstrate that he was right, he turned to Madame Godefroid, asking her whether or not she could carry out the transfer of old frescos and panel paintings. She replied to Monsieur Lepicié that she indeed she could carry out this operation at his convenience, telling him in all good faith that whole secret lay in warm water and patience.[15]

To criticize Picault became commonplace: everybody, now, recalled others who had experimented in the transfer of panel and canvas paintings onto new canvas [supports]. It was during this period that President de Brosses' letters were gathered together and published, and it must surely be the case that the information on the poor craftsman in Rome who could transfer paintings onto canvas, but was unable to reintegrate the losses, was suggested by the success of those who, like Picault, would leave the restoration of the painted image (*restauro pittorico*) to others (Collins for the Andrea del Sarto, for instance). In 1755, in the *Mémoires de la Société Royale des Sciences et Belles Lettres* of Nancy, a letter was published from the Chevalier de Solignac on the transfers carried out in that city as early as 1736 by Léopold Roxin, a painter at the court of the Duke of Lorraine: with the exception of frescos, this painter was confident in his ability to transfer any painting. In an appendix to the letter, the *Mémoires de la Société Royale des Sciences et Belles Lettres* also published a description of the transfer which Gautier d'Agoty had watched, and related the experiments which a certain Credo, member of the Société Royale, had carried out in its wake. Using a much diluted acid (*acqua seconda*) he had succeeded in entirely removing an old canvas, without decomposing it as had the craftsman in Gautier's description, hence reducing the risk to the paint layer from the its effects. With the identification of the correct solvents, it would become possible to carry out the transfer of paintings from whatever support: "it is to be supposed, that with experience one will succeed in multiplying and simplifying the methods used to conserve, transfer, renew and perpetuate the precious works of the great masters".[16]

In January 1756, the "*Mercure de France*" published an anonymous letter from Brussels, on the transfers carried out by Riario in 1741, accompanying the report with the most malicious inferences that changing times could suggest. The reports of restorers and amateurs who had transferred paintings, and the description of the methods most suited to the operation would become increasingly frequent: the "*Mémoires de Trévoux*" of 1755 and 1756 refer to a certain Sauvages, canon of Verdun; Antoine-Joseph Pernetty in the *Dictionnaire portatif de la peinture* published in 1757, confesses himself unfamiliar with the method employed by Picault, although knowing how to transfer a painting from one panel to another. The following year, Dossie's *The Handmaid to the Arts*, also described a method used in England to detach oil paintings from the canvas or the panel on which they were painted, and of transferring them in their entirety, without damage, onto new supports. In 1756 both the entry for "*Tableau*" in the *Encyclopédie*, and the treatise on the pigments for use in enamel and porcelain by Didier-François d'Arclais de Montamy (published posthumously by Diderot), described the same method of transferring paintings onto a new canvas.[17]

But Gautier also recognized the fact that Picault's method was the only one suited to the transfer of mural paintings. He denied that it was a method that could be used for frescos, even though, for anyone with even the most summary knowledge of the transfer of frescos, the analogy between the Picault's method as described by Gautier and the technique of *strappo* is evident. In both 1745 and 1747, Picault had gone to Fontainebleau in order to look at some of the paintings which would require transfer in view of the King's projected renovations in his apartments; despite all the controversy, in October 1756 he received the order to return and once more examine these paintings, and between February and September of the following year he transferred the frescos by Primaticcio in the Chambre de Saint-Louis, and some of the monochrome paintings from the ceiling of the Galerie de Diane. All these frescos are now lost, but in 1793 Picault's son Jean-Michel reported some of these fragments to be in his possession. The many experiments in the transfer of paintings that took place in the second half of the eighteenth century prevent us now from extracting indications from his text as to the details of the practice of transfer in the middle of the century. It would not seem, however, that the transfer of mural paintings during this period underwent huge developments, and the balance of the pros and cons of the process that one finds in Jean-Michel Picault's text gives an adequate idea of the quality of those first transfers undertaken by Picault (the father). The principal drawbacks seem to have been that: "all ceiling paintings or other compositions painted on plaster which have been transferred onto canvas, are no more than a thick crust of paint glued onto a new support, which, if examined closely, makes one think that this painted surface attached onto canvas cannot last. On the other hand, if you go and look closely at the ceiling painted by Vouet in the home of Monsieur Donjeux (it was thought to be by Le Sueur), judge for yourself the effects that one can expect from this operation, from what I have achieved in this field."

In order to achieve a good result, it should be borne in mind that: "Paintings on plaster (of a quality justifying the transfer) are the only paintings which, when transferred onto canvas, should take on its weave-pattern, because the effect of the toothed trowel used by the mason results in formless deformations on the picture surface. This means that there is a hundred per cent improvement when the painting has been properly separated from its support and transferred onto canvas, in that it becomes smooth and malleable and takes on the weave pattern of the new support. Of this, I can give you proof."

Of the technique used to detach true frescos, and on the drawbacks of the process, Jean-Michel Picault observed: "The paintings carried out in fresco technique and transferred onto canvas, can also take on the canvas weave without any loss in their effect nor in their beauty. This is because the surface of this kind of painting has the least finish (*smalto*) and subtlety (*finezza*) of any, as the lime and sand plaster surface on which the painting is executed is only applied to the area that the painter can cover in a single day. This means that as soon as the wall is partially plastered, the painter only has time to try and incise the outlines of his cartoons onto it, etc. The result is that the extremely liquid colours which he uses, impregnating the sand of this plaster, leave no glaze (*smalto*) on the surface of this type of painting. The very few worthwhile frescos executed in France have certainly not put our restorers in a position to be able to transfer them. In 1757, my late lamented father received the request from Monsieur de Marigny to go to Fontainebleau in order to transfer seven frescos which were the decoration of the Salle Saint-Louis, which he proceeded to do. These paintings were by the hand of Primaticcio, Niccolò dell'Abate etc. They represented the history of Troy. Three of these frescos were twelve feet long and six feet high, and I now have a few fragments of these paintings in my possession".[18]

4. The "tableaux du roy"

The frequent restorations (cleaning, lining, removal of retouchings) left their mark on many of the paintings in the old Royal collection, both before and after their acquisition. One need only think of the *Antiope* by Correggio, weakened in the shadows, flayed in the sky, worn away the length of the seam which crosses the whole length of the canvas, and reduced to a mere vestige of what the original painting must have been in the area of lion's skin on which the putto lies, and in the feet of the sleeping woman. L'Engerand reports a restoration on this painting around 1780, carried out by Hoogstoel (who cleaned it in only six days), and a removal of repaints by François-Ferdinand Godefroid in 1786; and it is by no means certain that these were the first interventions. On the other hand, it would seem that none of the better preserved paintings entering the Louvre from the Royal Collections, such as Correggio's *Marriage of Saint Catherine* (of which Lepicié in 1754 had remarked that it would have been difficult to find a better conserved painting) or the *Belle Jardinière*, the *Petit Saint Michel*, or the *Saint George* by Raphael had undergone restoration in the eighteenth century.

    We do not have documents dating from the first half of the eighteenth century which allow us to follow the activity of restorers in any structured way; there is no doubt, however, that paintings were lined (as is implied by the report by the Academy of Painting of 1750 on the measures to be taken for the conservation of the *Saint Michael* by Raphael), and retouched to stop the flaking of the paint. The possibility of not having recourse to these measures was one of the reasons why Picault's transfers were so popular; as he also possessed the secret for the removal of the overpaints, these operation revealed once more "*le pur pinceau*" of the artist, limiting the retouching to the areas of loss.[19]

    In 1748, at the time when the documents from the Bâtiments du Roi first allow us to follow the activities of the restorers, we find that Marie Jacob Van Merle (*la veuve Godefroid*) and François-Louis Collins, one of the most renowned restorers of the time, were being employed. The promptitude of Godefroid's reaction to the novelty of the transfer process gives us an idea of how jealous she was of her position, to the extent that at her death in 1775, d'Angiviller does not nominate a successor, in order to prevent the restoration of the King's pictures becoming a monopoly, and to allow him the freedom of choosing the most appropriate restorer in each case. It was the restorers working at the end of the reign of Louis XVI – the various members of the Grandpré family, Martin, Hoogstoel, Godefroid

90. *Raphael, Holy Family of*
François I; transferred by Jean-Louis
Hacquin in 1777. Paris, Musée du
Louvre.

91. *Raphael, Holy Family of François I, detail. Paris, Musée du Louvre.*

(the son) – whose methods came under attack from Jean-Michel Picault and Jean-Baptiste Lebrun in 1793. There was, no doubt, some polemical exaggeration in their statements ("they have ruined everything they have touched"), but it is nevertheless significant that an official document such as the Rameau inventory of 1784 should lament the damage suffered by some of the paintings at the hands of Grandpré.[20]

Many of the paintings restored by Godefroid and Collins are not, on the other hand, in particularly poor condition. Around 1750, the year part of the Royal Collection was opened to the public and exhibited in the Palais du Luxembourg, they undertook a great number of restorations: these included Titian's *Madonna of the Rabbit* and the *Venus del Pardo*, Veronese's great *Conversion of the Magdalen*, and some works by Poussin (all of which had been restored in 1749); Rubens' *Village Fair* and *Madonna in Glory* were both cradled[xi] in 1750. In 1751, many of the most important works in the collection were lined and restored: Titian's *Lady with a Mirror*, Veronese's *Crucifixion*, Guido Reni's four *Stories of Hercules*, *David playing the harp* by Domenichino, Lanfranco's *Coronation*, the *Portrait of Alof de Vignancourt* attributed to Caravaggio, Valentin de Boulogne's *The Fortune Teller*. In 1750, Collins restored Holbein's *Portrait of Anne of Cleves* and *The Burning Bush* by Francisco Collantes, on his own. In 1753 a commission was set up which included Silvestre, Vanloo, Boucher and Lepicié, in order to oversee the cleaning of Rubens' Marie de' Medici cycle, an operation which Godefroid repeated in 1768, on occasion of the visit of the King of Denmark.

By collaborating with Collins, and after 1760 with Guillemard, widow Godefroid also ensured the successful outcome of the restoration of the image. She did not make herself particularly available for the transfer of paintings (especially when these were of a certain size), despite her alacrity in 1753 to take on the transfer of the *Portrait* by Joos van Cleve. In 1766, the decision was taken to detach a ceiling painting by Vouet in the Château de Vincennes; Picault was consulted, and then Godefroid, in the hope of being quoted a more modest price. She pointed out that the operation was in fact more complicated than she had at first anticipated, and success was not guaranteed, as the work had been painted directly onto the plaster, without a priming layer. The work would eventually be entrusted to Jean-Louis Hacquin for the sum of six-hundred lire.

90, 91   In 1774, Raphael's *Holy family of François I* began to flake; Picault was being considered for the transfer from the panel when Godefroid intervened, suggesting that one should be wary of those who used mysteries and quackery in order to persuade: she herself had always opposed the transfer because the work was painted on cedar which was not liable to attack by woodworm (in fact the transfer was being considered not because of the poor condition of the support, but because of the flaking of the paint layer), and she felt that the damage was simply the result of the painting having been hung above a fireplace. Why not entrust her with the work, and she would only charge a thousand lire rather than ten-thousand? This panel, also, would be transferred three years later by Hacquin.[21]

The recommendation which Louis-Joseph de Bourbon, the Prince de Condé, gave the Bâtiments in 1741 made clear what were the interventions for which Jean-Louis Collins was held in high esteem, "His particular talents lie in the repainting and spotting in (*punteggiare*) of old paintings in the areas in which they have been damaged, the cleaning, the

---

[xi] Cradling: when a wooden grid (the cradle) was secured to the reverse of the panel, which often had been thinned in preparation, with the purpose of keeping the panel flat. (See Glossary.)

92. Correggio, Leda; recomposed from a number of fragments by François-Louis Collins and Marie-Jacob Godefroid, 1753–1755. Berlin Dahlem, Staatliche Museen.

painting of additions in the style of the appropriate master, as well as the removal of old restorations where these have been poorly executed, or where they now form blotches which no longer match the original colours".

Other contrasting aspects are emphasized by Mariette: "In essence his talent consisted in making copies of Flemish paintings; but he was even more skilful in their cleaning, and for this he had been chosen for the care of those belonging to the King, together with widow Godefroid. Whatever his skill, there was always a risk involved with the paintings that passed through his hands, because each cleaned painting is effectively a ruined painting; this is something that art dealers do not wish to admit, but is nevertheless true. He also vaunted himself as a great connoisseur, which he was, but only of Flemish paintings."

93. *Raphael, Holy Family of Canigiani; with the repainting by François-Louis Collins, about 1755. Munich, Alte Pinakothek.*

94. *Raphael, Holy Family of Canigiani; after removal of the repainting by François-Louis Collins. Munich, Alte Pinakothek.*

The catalogue of the Fonspertius sale of 1747, referring to one of two paintings by Nicholas Berchem, specifically mentioned that it had been "artistically enlarged to make it the same size as its companion" by Collins. In other words, a restoration which fitted with traditional gallery practice, far removed from such consideration as the nature of works of art as expressions of genius, or the means of their transmittal in all its modulations, which characterized Picault's transfers. We are in that area which the *Encyclopédie Méthodique* of 1788 stigmatized, observing that "the dealer, expert in all the expedients of his profession, has his paintings retouched, repainted, and opportunistically gives them either the respectable character of antiquity, or the dazzling freshness of a less imposing epoch".

Highly illuminating are Collins' remarks in 1749 when offering the Royal administration a *Crucifixion* by Rubens, which today hangs in the Louvre: "A further circumstance which should sway in favour of the acquisition, is that the subject corresponds to the one which was to be commissioned for the church of Saint Louis at Versailles, with Saint Louis at the foot of the cross. By good fortune, Saint John is in this case draped in red, and has much of the character which it is customary to give to Saint Louis, with this difference – if one dares to say such a thing – that this figure is much nobler. One need only add a crown at the feet of the cross, and dash off a few fleur-de-lys on the drapery".

From the inheritance of Charles Coypel, Collins had persuaded them to buy the fragments of Correggio's *Leda*, which Louis d'Orleans had cut into pieces as well as having the two principal heads removed; under his direction, widow Godefroid then reunited them, and Jacques François Lyen (a painter specializing in copies from the Old Masters) integrated the missing part, painting it in anew (*rifacimento*). However, it is Collins' intervention on Raphael's *Holy Family of Canigiani* (executed around 1755, for the Elector of Palatine for whose gallery in Düsseldorf he was the Inspector) that is a particularly significant episode for an understanding of his success. Collins covered two unfinished groups of putti in the clouds with an unbroken sky. His intervention was so successful that Wölfflin (in *Classical Art*), discussed the composition of the *Holy Family* without taking into account the eighteenth-century restoration, which is in itself significant, whether he neglected to check the easily verifiable history of the painting, or simply forgot the episode at the moment of writing. Until 1983, no gallery director had had the courage to prefer Raphael's composition (which had always been known from copies, as well as identifiable in the X-radiograph) to the eighteenth-century adaptation which, as Wölfflin unintentionally confirms, so perfectly interpreted the spirit of classicism which was expected in a work by Raphael. Unfortunately, Collins, far removed from the questions of reversibility which would soon feature in any discussion on restoration, in order to make the repainting adhere better, had abraded much of the figures of the putti beneath his sky.[22]

Although widow Godefroid would not take on the transfer of very large paintings, it was not often that Picault was turned to: in 1757, for the frescos at Fontainebleau, in 1774 he was consulted for the transfer of the *Holy Family of François I*, a project which was finally carried out by Hacquin three years later. In 1767, the *Saint John the Evangelist* by Innocenzo da Imola (which was thought to be by Raphael) was entrusted to him, and he signed and dated the transfer on the reverse of the canvas: "Painted in 1510 by Raphael of Urbino; in 1773, the painting was separated from its priming which remained adhered to the panel, and fitted to this canvas by the artists Picault, father and son".[xii]

In 1766, new paint losses were noted on the *Saint Michael*, a painting which even after its transfer continued to be moved, every year, from the stores at Versailles to the Salle de Mercure (where it hung between Easter and All Saints), so that a new transfer had to be undertaken. Picault offered his services free of charge, making it clear that these losses might correspond to the areas of repaint, or else to those in which he had been unable to completely remove the original priming and that surely this was to be expected in one of his earliest attempts.

Between 1775 and 1777, there was an exchange of letters and meetings to discuss the yielding up of Picault's secret to the direction of the Bâtiments; Picault's last letter, dated 22 March 1777, bore a note from the Royal administration to the effect that, as he had refused to part with his secret even for very advantageous terms, and taking into account his high prices, the Comte d'Angiviller had decided to use Hacquin in his stead, whose working methods were known. In a letter dated 30 October 1776, d'Angiviller had rejected Picault's offer to go back and work again on the *Saint Michael*: "I hold no prejudice against your method, as I have no knowledge of it, but at present I am extremely satisfied with that practised by Monsieur Hacquin, which is fast, safe and very cheap when compared to yours; so that, from every aspect, it is his method I would prefer …".[23]

[xii] "*En 1510 peint par Raphael d'Urbin; en 1773, la peinture a été séparé de l'impression restant sur bois et adaptée sur cette toile par Picault artistes; père et fils*".

95. Eustache Le Sueur, Phaeton
obtains the Chariot of the Sun;
transferred by Jean-Louis Hacquin,
1777. Paris, Musée du Louvre.

The widow Godefroid exited from the scene in 1775; at this time Hacquin received a huge commission of Royal paintings that were to be either transferred or lined.[xiii] He had already in the past received intermittent employment from the Royal administration: he was asked to transfer the ceiling painting by Vouet (probably the very same one that Jean-Michel Picault referred to as being in the possession of Monsieur Donjeux in 1793); in 1766, to transfer onto a new canvas Laurent de la Hire's *Crucifixion*, and in 1768 Domenichino's oval, *Timocles and Alexander*. Other jobs show closer links with his old profession of cabinet-maker,

---

[xiii]In the process of transfer, the painting will lose its original support (panel or canvas), sometimes also its ground layer, before being attached to a new support. In lining, the original canvas support is preserved and attached onto a new canvas support. (See Glossary.)

96. Eustache Le Sueur, *Phaeton*
obtains the Chariot of the Sun,
etail. Paris, Musée du Louvre.

*97. Eustache Le Sueur, The
Death of Raimond Diocrès,
detail; transferred by Jean-Louis
and François-Toussaints Hacquin.
Paris, Musée du Louvre.*

such as the cradling of panel paintings: in 1770 Pierre, first painter to the King, wrote to
Marigny to inform him that Rubens' panel *The Village Fête* had split, almost certainly
because of the poor cradling that it had undergone over thirty years before (in fact, it was
Godefroid who had cradled it in 1750); for two-hundred lire Hacquin proposed to attach
one of his "new cradles, which are mobile and prevent accidents occurring to the wood when
the seasons change."

In 1771, Hacquin had transferred *The resurrection of Lazarus* by Sebastiano del Piombo
from the Orléans Collection (which now hangs in the National Gallery), with results which
must be considered good, in view of the size of the panel and the impossibility of getting
back to those responsible for the serious imbalance due to poor cleaning. In 1777, paintings
were entrusted to him which required either consolidation of the paint layer or restoration,
including some paintings on copper; also a work by Feti on a piece of slate which had split,
and for which he made a cradle; paintings to transfer onto canvas such as *Louis XIII* by

Philippe de Champaigne and Raphael's *Saint John the Baptist;* the *Saint Michael* to be transferred for the second time, and various panels (a Guercino, a Luini, a *Flight into Egypt* attributed to Rubens of which Hoogstoel had restored the image) and most importantly, the *Saint
Margaret* and the *Holy Family* by Raphael. In the same year he also undertook the transfer
of Eustache Le Sueur's ceiling painting *Phaeton obtaining the chariot of the Sun,* which had   95
been acquired by the Bâtiments with his other paintings in the Hôtel Lambert; he also
transferred various paintings by Jouvenet in the Hôtel Saint-Pouange.

It is just as difficult to get a clear idea of the restorations undertaken by Jean-Louis
Hacquin as it was with those of Robert Picault, as almost never he the first or the only
restorer to have worked on the paintings. The recent restoration of the *Holy Family of
François I* found it in a reasonable state of preservation for a painting which had undergone
the transfer process, although the dissonances revealed [during the cleaning] make one
understand why Jean-Michel Picault had included it amongst the paintings used as examples to demonstrate the damage inflicted by cleaning on the harmony which both the artists
and time had given to paintings. The report on the conservation of the *Saint Michael* and
the *Saint Margaret,* drawn up by Jean-Baptiste Lebrun in 1797, in which he proposed to
entrust the works to Jean-Michel Picault, noted that their deterioration was due not to the
paint layer, but to the glue-based priming which was applied during the transfer and which
was reacting to changes in humidity; the report also lamented the fact that in the operation
the paintings had lost the smoothness characteristic of paintings on panel, the paint layer
becoming imprinted with the weave of the canvas.

The *Observations* which Jean-Michel Picault circulated in 1793, describing the drawbacks of the restoration of paintings, often served to highlight the negative aspects of the
techniques used by the Hacquin. For instance, referring to the transfer of mural paintings,
he lamented the fact that when detaching the entire paint layer, traces of the trowel remained
imprinted as well as the weave of the new canvas support, an effect which can be seen in   96
the ceiling painting by Le Sueur transferred from the Hôtel Lambert.

Of the majority of paintings transferred onto canvas without the required skill, he
remarked that: "all the paintings which have been transferred from panel onto canvas have
lost the clarity (*correttezza*) and purity of their colours, their smoothness (*smalto*), their
freshness of touch, their transparency, etc., in that the paint has taken on the weave of the
canvas for which it was not made. This canvas weave produces a quantity of deformations
on the surface of the paint which tones down the handling and the touch of the master,
destroying their true impact. Look at all the paintings transferred from panel onto canvas.
Look at the paintings from the Charterhouse and weep; and now examine Raphael's *Holy
Family* and judge it with honesty."

These paintings from the Charterhouse were the *Stories of Saint Bruno* by Le Sueur   97
which, when acquired by the Royal Collections in 1776, were transferred by Hacquin for six-
hundred lire each. They were already in rather poor condition, and when they were moved
in 1802 from the Musée d'Art Français to the Galerie du Luxembourg, they were entrusted
to new restorers. Moreover, it would not seem that the transfers were carried out with the
greatest of care: in 1784, François-Toussaints Hacquin showed Pierre that mice, attracted by
the glue in the new supports, had damaged some of the paintings in his laboratory in the
Louvre: a *Saint Sebastian* by Guido Reni, a *Galatea* by François Van Loo, an *Aeneas and Anchises*
by Charles Van Loo, and three of the *Saint Bruno* stories by Le Sueur.[24]

5. Experiments in the physics and chemistry of painting

In 1787 François-Toussaints Hacquin proposed the use of "oil and resin-based materials" for the restoration of paintings "which would not be susceptible to being affected by humidity, and which would be more viscous". Lebrun, on the other hand, in 1797 would criticize the transfers by Hacquin (the father) of the *Saint Margaret* and the *Saint Michael*, for their use of improper materials, such as the glue-based primings (*fondi di colla*) which reacted to variations in humidity.[25] As the techniques were new, and one could not rely with confidence on a long tradition of professional use, attempts were made to justify the use of the new techniques through a study of the materials employed in the light of the new sciences of physics and chemistry. A study which, before being directed towards restoration, had turned its attention to the whole subject of painting technique, with experiments being made to try and find new pigments and new binding media[xiv] which would guarantee the durability of the works of genius, and would prevent their alteration [with time].

As Hogarth would remind us, these experiments would highlight an important concept for the understanding of the problems related to the conservation of works of art: that is, that time can bring irreversible changes to colours, excessive absorption of colours by the priming layers, and changes in the chemical structure of the pigment. A codified and rational knowledge of the materials used would thus allow one to control and limit these possible alterations, beyond the literary concepts of Time the Consumer and, more positively perhaps, of Time the Painter.

In 1749, for instance, Jean-Baptiste Oudry had advised against the use of ochre-coloured grounds (as these hardened the shadows) as well as that of white grounds (which weakened the shadows and the half-tones by absorbing them); in 1751, the Petit de Bachaumont would refer to the alterations occurring with time, in particular those seen in the skies of Veronese's paintings which had darkened because they had been painted using azurite ashes [as the pigment] rather than ultramarine. In 1782, Jean-Baptiste Pierre (not without a certain spirit of contentiousness) remarked that a Greuze proposed for acquisition by the Royal Collection had lost its glazes (*velature*), and now had a hardness of appearance which it would not have had originally: "Paintings which are impasted improve with time, whilst those which only have an apparent harmony are ruined".[26]

The approach to techniques through the physical and chemical definition of the materials employed resulted in an extraordinary cycle of publications which, over the span of the eighteenth century, saw many craft techniques translated into the new, exact terminology. These publications were for the most part in French, the language which allowed adequate diffusion throughout the cultured milieux of Europe, a diffusion which perhaps through its publicity, in some measure compensated the authors for the loss of some of their secrets. With his observations on materials that were also relevant to paintings, it was in the context of these issues that Watin (or rather the "*savant*" whom he as an artist–varnisher had approached for the drafting of the text) took up his position in his manual on varnishes.

[xiv] All paint (when dry) is made up of two distinct elements: the pigments (coloured powder) and the binding medium which, as the word implies, binds together the particles to make a film. Glue-size, egg-yolk and oil are all traditional binding media. (See Glossary.)

The inspiration animating the author of the text can be perceived clearly from both the language and the observations used in the criticism of the poorly produced compilation known as the *Manuel du Vernisseur*, which had appeared only a few years earlier: "I am astonished that in such an enlightened century, in which the light of reason is beginning to penetrate into the recesses of even the darkest workshop, in this century in which the artist abandons routine, and is programming and perfecting his art, that one should dare to present as elements of the art of varnishing the greatest absurdities, to put forward as excellent procedures the most pitiful results; and that one should dare to state to posterity with this ridiculous document, that this – in 1722 – was the sum total of our knowledge on varnishes".[27]

The problem of a binder that would alter less with time than oil was linked to the research on the encaustic technique[xv] used for painting by the ancients, and the verification of its qualities. In France, one of the earliest enthusiasts of the research into this particular technique was the Conte de Caylus, according to whose instructions a head of Minerva was painted in 1745. His experiments were not linked solely to his antiquarian interests, but also to the concern that oil altered and yellowed with the passage of time. The rediscovery of encaustic painting also led to a dispute as to who, in the wake of Pliny, had been responsible for this rediscovery: Caylus or Bachelier, who had used it to paint a *Zephyrus and Flora*. The *Encyclopédie* had an entry for the technique, and an illustration which showed the instruments required for its practice. A wax medium was also suggested as a retouching medium[xvi] in Pernety's *Dictionnaire portatif.*[28]

In the second half of the century, such was the popularity of the encaustic medium (kept alive by the recent discoveries at Herculaneum) that Mengs would note that the paint in the *Madonna of Saint Jerome* ("*Il Giorno*") by Correggio in the Galleria Nazionale in Parma "has an impasto and a fatness in the paint, which one finds in no other, and at the same time is executed with a limpidity which is very difficult to preserve when using so much paint; but what is most difficult in this type of impasted painting, is to preserve the truth of the tints, and it seems almost not to have been applied with a brush, but fused together as though molten wax".[xvii] And it is in fact in Correggio's home town of Parma that a whole series of painters such as Gaetano Callani or Giuseppe Baldrighi used wax as a medium for some of their most important works.[29]

There were many publications on the techniques of the ancients, and alongside these were the continuing discussions around the discrepancy between the various different encaustic techniques proposed, and the technique described by Pliny. Goethe, in his *Journey to Italy*, mentioned the experiments with encaustic painting that he had watched in the house of Consigliere Reiffenstein, and Lanzi, after running through all the various

---

[xv] That wax was used by the ancients as a binding medium for pigments was known; what was not clear was the "technique", that is the method of application of the paint, as wax is only liquid enough to apply when hot, or when dissolved, in solution. (See Glossary.)

[xvi] The search was on for a medium that could be used for the retouching of paintings that would not darken with time. This was spurred by the oil retouchings of the past, which were now clearly visible as disfiguring blots on restored paintings, and were also difficult to remove.

[xvii] "*ha un impasto e una grossezza di colore che non si vede in verun'altra, e nello stesso tempo è fatta con una limpidezza che è molto difficile conservare usando tanto colore; ma il più difficile di questo genere di pittura così impastata è la verità delle tinte, e il vedere che i colori non sembrano posti col pennello, ma come se fossero stati fusi insieme a guisa di cera sul fuoco*".

experiments with the technique which took place in the eighteenth century, concluded with the following words:

> "Without speaking of the chemists who have contributed with their luminaries to the advancement of this art, the Roman school began in a certain way to educate it, make it grow, bringing it to maturity. At that time lived Councillor Reiffenstein, friend of Mengs and Winckelmann; a man of the purest taste in the Arts, and always surrounded by a quantity of artists (*artefici*) who received from him either advice on artistic matters, or commissions from foreigners, private individuals or crowned heads. He began to propose now one, now another technique of encaustic painting and soon had his cabinet full of paintings on canvas, on wood and on various stones, which had already undergone every possible trial, being buried or submerged, exposed to all weathers none of which caused any damage whatsoever. After this, the new discovery was disseminated through many publications, and then across the cities of Italy and foreign kingdoms. Whole rooms would be painted in encaustic, for instance the one which Archduke Ferdinand, governor of Milan, had decorated in this manner in his villa in Monza. For the moment, this technique seems more successful when used for ornamentation and in landscapes, rather than in the painting of figures. Everybody agrees that it has not yet reached that degree of refinement and softness which the ancients achieved with their use of wax, and the moderns with their use of the oil and the glazing technique. But where many are working together to refine it, it can be hoped that a Van Eyck may yet rise for this technique, who would find – or rather perfect – that which all the painters in the world have so long desired".[30]

The limitations of a technique based exclusively on the use of wax are clearly shown by Lanzi, and there was no shortage of writers who appeared perplexed by the new technique. As early as 1775 Charles-Nicolas Cochin, ironically and with great wit, mocked the investigations into the techniques of the ancients using what today would be termed destructive methods of analysis. Imagining in the "Mercure, June edition of the year 2355", a "report" on the investigations of a passionate English experimenter, Mr Truthlover, into the darkening of paintings, he observed:

> "Not only does he prove it with some apposite quotations from old sources, but this curious researcher has thought it necessary to make sure of his findings by the use of chemicals to decompose a number of paintings that he found artistically less important. It is difficult to decide what to admire most: his zeal for important discoveries, or his generosity in sacrificing paintings (which are nevertheless important because of their rarity and age) for the public good. He makes the observation that eighteenth-century paintings are much less darkened than those of the seventeenth: a statement which at first sight, does not seem to pose any great problem, as after all there is a century between them. But Mr Truthlover, who is not to be satisfied as common people might be with initial conclusions, has gone further in his quest. He believes that the difference in the darkening of the oil between works of the two centuries is too great …".[31]

Artists like Angelika Kauffmann and, principally, Sir Joshua Reynolds, were passionate experimenters with new techniques; Horace Walpole ironically proposed that Reynolds should only be paid for his paintings by instalments, and only as long as the painting remained in good condition.[32] Walpole's jokes apart, it must be said that the research was not always directed to really useful ends: new suggestions were for *"peinture eludorique"*, and both milk and blood serum had been proposed as alternative paint media, all from the pens of scientific investigators who did not seem able to recognize [the importance] of the material qualities of paint.[33]

In fact, these experiments, in addition to being seen in relation to the search for a longer lasting paint medium which would not alter with the passage of time, should be understood in the context of that extraordinary sensibility to the relationship between the material and the image, which is characteristic of the eighteenth century. I should like to illustrate this point using a marginal piece of evidence, a report which appeared in *Antologia Romana* in 1781, on a fixative for pastels, which was presented by Loriot to the Academy of Painting in Paris:

> "It will not however be necessary to repeat the application more than three times, although further applications cannot in any way cause damage. But why do this? The end of these applications is to simply bind together the pastel particles, which are nothing else but powder, so that they can neither come away nor change, and to achieve this, no more than two or three applications are necessary. It is possible that someone may think that to continue, may result in being able to dispense with covering the pastel with glass, as is the custom; in this they would be quite mistaken, just as they would be mistaken in thinking that further applications might allow them to handle and rub the paint surface as wished. Further applications would only result in the pastel painting losing at least one of its most prized qualities, that is, its velvety surface and softness".[34]

6. A century of varnish

The sensitivity to the materials of painting which transpires so clearly in the article in "Antologia romana" in its remarks on the "velvety surface and softness" of pastels is also apparent in the discussions which ignite at the end of the century on the use of varnishes. That essential varnishes[xviii] would provide a medium particularly well suited to the restoration and conservation of paintings was one of the results of the codification of the materials and the procedures resulting from eighteenth-century experimentation, which would then become characteristic of the practice of the restoration of paintings. This is perhaps a less showy result than the transfer or the *strappo* of frescos, but it is in no way less decisive for the ultimate fate of many works, and not always in a positive way, as we can observe daily.

The effects of a varnish on an oil-based paint were well described by Antonio Franchi in 1739 to demonstrate "The nature of the 'dying' (*prosciugare*)[xix] of colours in painting". His comments immediately transport us into that climate of observation of the physical

---

[xviii] Essential varnishes are varnishes which are made by dissolving a resin in a solvent, and which dry by evaporation of this solvent, turpentine for instance. They remain fairly soluble, and therefore do not cause the same problems in varnish removal as do oil varnishes which, as their name implies, contain oil as well as resin. This means that they become insoluble with time, cannot be dissolved with solvents but have to be broken down using caustic materials, as well as darkening substantially more with time. (See Glossary.)

[xix] *Prosciugare*, literally drying out, occurring, as the text says, when the medium binding the pigment is "sucked out" of the paint. Certain pigments, blacks and organic reds, are particularly prone to this effect, which leaves the surface of the paint matt and unsaturated. (See Glossary.)

phenomena associated with the figurative arts, which is characteristic of the eighteenth century. He observed: "You will always observe it occurring on canvases which have been freshly or recently primed, and on surfaces and materials which have a spongy nature such as wood and the like; and you will never see it on canvases which are fully dry, or when you paint on glass or other dense or compact bodies."

Spongy materials absorb the oil which gave freshness to the colour, and induce a change in the surface: "the surface changing from smooth and transparent which it was when the paint was fresh, to rough and misty; therefore this surface must necessarily change colour, as we will demonstrate. The same occurs when we pour water onto a dry brick pavement;[xx] such a pavement, being light red in colour, soon becomes of a much darker colour. Where does the new colour derive from? Not from the water: being colourless itself it cannot pass colour on, conforming to the axiom *Nemo dat quod non habet* (no-one gives what they do not have). But if the water does not provide the colour, we must affirm (if we do not wish to concede the impossible, that is, that effects exist that have no cause) that this change in colour must be due to a change in surface configuration. This same effect we see when we give a coat of varnish to a painting which has 'died'; itself colourless, the varnish will give back that unctuous quality to the paint surface which it had lost through the penetration of the oil into the spongy, rarified material. By thus altering the configuration of the surface, you bring back its original and true colour".[xxi,35]

By 1788, when varnish was at the centre of the controversies ignited by the publication of Philipp Hackert's famous letter, it becomes clear that it was not used universally, and that many artists painted their works with a view to presenting them with a final protective layer of either egg-white varnish or some other material, which the famous German landscape painter considered damaging. The varnish under discussion was one based on mastic dissolved in spirits of turpentine, which Watin already considered to be the only one suitable for the conservation of paintings; its formulation was the consummation of a century of impassioned experimentation, and indicative of a taste which took pleasure in surface gloss, which was to be read according to a veritable and very specific code. The success of the varnish was confirmed when Watin observed that the word "brings to mind the concepts of *éclat* (brilliance) or *lustre* (sheen) to which we should maybe add that of durability: so, for instance, one speaks metaphorically of giving a coat of varnish to a speech or a thought: that is, to give them a form which is brilliant, solid and durable."

If we look back over the entire episode of varnishes, we can see that this gratification had its origins in the experiments carried out in order to verify and then adapt the composition

---

[xx] Leonardo had used the same example in his description of the optical effects of varnish, in his treatise on painting (See Glossary).

[xxi] "*trasmutandosi con ciò tal superficie di liscia e tersa che era mentre I colori eran freschi in rozza e appannata; dunque detta superficie deve per necessità mutar di colore, siccome di fatto vediamo seguire. E in questo caso accade come vediamo accadere nel versar l'acqua sopra un pavimento asciutto di mattoni. Tal pavimento, essendo di color rosiccio chiaro, diventa tosto di colore molto più scuro. Or che gli dà questo nuovo colore? L'acqua no perchè ella non avendo colore, non glielo può dare, conforme l'assioma 'Nemo dat quod non habet'. Ma se non glielo dà l'acqua, dunque è necessario affermare (se non vogliamo concedere l'impossibile, cioè effetti senza causa) che glielo dia la mutazione di disposozione della superficie. Questo medesimo effetto lo vediam ancora nel dar la vernice a' quadri prosciugati; poichè rendendosi con essa (la quale non ha colore) quell'ontuosità alla superficie de' colori, e in consequenza quella tersezza che ella aveva perduto nella penetrazione dell'olio entro i detticorpi rari e spugnosi, e con ciò diversificando e variando la disposizione della medesima superficie, fa ritornar in essa il vero e proprio suo colore*".

of traditional oil-based [varnishes] in the light of a whole series of related trials undertaken
to find a product with which to imitate chiaràm, the Chinese varnish. This would take us
right back into a world which pre-dates the Enlightenment debate on the mechanical arts,
and the experimentation in physics and chemistry with which, during the eighteenth century, the materials and processes of traditional arts would be verified, and a world to which
the Jesuit Filippo Bonanni can provide a good introduction. When, in 1720, he published
his *Trattato sopra la vernice detta comunemente cinese*, Bonanni had no idea that he was entering the field of ideological values. His was still a world of dilettanti, of seventeenth-century
experimenters and craftsmen who could not hide their secrets from him. The highly transparent varnishes "required to cover or glaze paintings" were made according to recipes based
on sandarac (*sandaracca*), oil of turpentine (*olio di abezzo*), lac resin (*gomma lacca*), copal resin
given to him by "a German knight" or "a Franciscan friar" expert in the manufacture of paper
flowers, or even an artisan of the Via de' Coronari.[36]

Watin's manual, on the other hand, as it appeared in the second edition of 1773, showed
itself to be fully conscious of the debate on the mechanical arts and their usefulness, showing
perhaps an all too great awareness of the merits of arts such as that of the painter–decorator
(the "*peintre d'impression*"), arts devoted if not so much to the necessities, at least to the pleasures of civilized life. *L'Art du peintre, doreur, vernisseur* made pleasurable reading with its brilliant style and clear exposition, both of which were particularly well suited to attract an amateur
public. It is quite evident that the text has been written by a man of letters and not by a craftsman, however cultured or at ease with an elegant clientele he might have been.

Bonanni's world was by now very far removed, also because of the completely different relationship existing between the practice of the "artist" and the scientific verification
of his materials. His knowledge of the materials he used was no longer based on practical
experience, nor did it use casual terminology, but was derived from the laws of physics and
chemistry. The definition of oil, for instance, was not simply that of a liquid obtained by
pressing (whether scorpions or flowers), but a substance which behaved according to a particular set of physical and chemical rules.

Even the description of the varnish suitable for use on paintings is interesting in its
choice of wording: what appears clearly is an awareness of an activity which one might term
restoration and a conscious conservation (*manutenzione*) of the work of art, quite different
from routine maintenance (*manutenzione*) or simple adaptation to a change of usage.
Amongst the criteria which distinguish it, it is not difficult to identify the one which we now
term reversibility:

"Varnish on paintings is used solely to bring back colours and to conserve them,
not to impart colour or to give them a gloss that would prevent one from distinguishing the subject; it must not be opaque, but colourless, light and sweet.
The varnishes containing spirits of wine cause flaking of the paint layer; those
containing oil being too highly coloured and too opaque muddy them (*li impastano*), forming a veil over the bright colours of draperies and preventing them
from being cleaned, as their removal would also remove the original paint.
Because of these drawbacks, both spirit-based and oil-based varnishes have
been rejected for use on paintings. To make a good varnish which would perfectly feed a canvas and preserve the colours in their original state, and which
can be removed without the painting incurring damage, you need to make
it with mastic and turpentine which you will dissolve together in spirits [of

turpentine], filtering it and allowing it to clarify. You will then be able to use it on paintings; you need to make it well; I sell one which is much sought after".[xxii,37] Pietro Edwards, on the other hand, remarked that with such a composition the varnish would lack "the permanent solidity which we seek in true varnishes", and asked himself whether one could really term it such. Its success was neither immediate nor unanimous, through the continued existence of old traditions such as the use of oil in the Gallerie di Firenze, and it would seem that it is to these practices that Lanzi was referring in the following passage: "according to the most recent observations, the paint is not damaged if one uses mastic and spirits of turpentine; oil is damaging to old paintings, the new never blends in with the old, and after a little time, every retouching is transformed into a blot".[38]

Also present were the negative aspects of physicochemical research on the materials of art, of experimentalism at all costs, such as the passion for flower oil of the Director of the Dresden Gallery referred to by Burtin;[39] but, most effective against an indiscriminate and generalized use of varnish, was a sensitivity to the materials of painting, which did not always find the effects of varnish acceptable.

The controversy resulting from Hackert's letter showed an attention to the material qualities of paint (not always suited to the application of a varnish), which had never been so much in evidence as in the eighteenth century. Impastos, glazes, finishing touches all contributed to a veritable code, which was followed even by such unassuming writers as Luigi Crespi. The entire century saw a continual transformation of the mechanics of painting, every artist proposing his own solution for that which we abstract and call the image; the variations in style could not be separated from the specific choices made in the priming, the oil, and whether or not to finish with a varnish (and, then, which varnish?). The dark tonalities of Crespi's paintings could never be imitated with Nattier's materials, nor were the greys, pinks and browns of the latter, compatible with the impastos of the Italian master.

Style could only be changed as a result of deliberate choices made at each of the material stages of the creation of the picture. Recollect Bellotto, who in Dresden and Vienna abandoned the rosy tonalities characteristic of Canaletto, to turn to a colder tonality better adapted to a more rigorous optical vision; and then his return to the darks, as though he were a painter belonging to the earliest part of the century, in the Polish paintings. Or else, in full Neo-classical mode, Gavin Hamilton's paintings in Palazzo Braschi with their yellow varnish: a perfect example of the desire to wipe out the "dominance of matter" ("*jattanza della materia*"), as Brandi put it.[40] And it is yielding to this sensitivity to the material qualities of paint that some of the great masters will turn to the exclusive use of pastel or, even further removed from the great traditions, watercolour.

The solution recommended by Hackert, immediately embraced by many with great enthusiasm, was found to be wanting by one artist, who thought it oversimplified. In the

---

xxii "*La vernice dei quadri non serve che per richiamare i colori e conservarli, non per colorarli o per dare loro una brillantezza che impedirebbe di distinguere il soggetto; si deve poi evitare che sia opaca, ma deve essere bianca, leggera e dolce. Quelle a spirito divino fanno screpolare i colori; quelle ad olio li impastano essendo troppo colorate e troppo opache, formano una velatura sui colori vivi dei panneggi ed impediscono di pulirli, dato che con esse si rimuoverebbe anche il colore: questi inconvenienti hanno fatto rifiutare tutte le vernici a spirito e le vernici grasse per i quadri. Per fare una buona vernice, che nutrisca perfettamente la tela, conservi i colori nel loro stato e che si possa togliere senza danneggiare i dipinti, componetela con del mastice e della terebentina, che farete fondere assieme nell'essenza; filtratela e lasciatela schiarire. Potrete usarla sui quadri: bisogna saperla fare bene; io ne vendo una molto ricercata.*"

"Giornale delle Belle Arti" in Rome, a riposte promptly appeared, thought to have been penned by Raimondo Ghelli. In the article, he emphasized the poor quality of the restorations carried out by Anders, the restorer who Hackert had introduced to the Neapolitan court, especially those on Titian's *Danae*; he defended the use of egg-white and, as examples of good restoration, he put forward the work carried out by signora Margherita Bernini on the paintings in the Galleria Giustiniani in Rome. Thus is born a small-scale debate on the cleaning and varnishing of paintings, with a letter in defence of Hackert (initialled G.G.D.R.) appearing in October 1788 in the "Memorie per le Belle Arti", and a series of polemical articles which remained unpublished until 1876, disseminated by Baldassare Orsini.[41]

The guardian spirit to whom appeal was made by the author of the riposte to Hackert, and by the author of the brief piece favouring varnish which appeared in the "Memorie per le Belle Arti", was Mengs. Had he used varnishes, and if so, which; and, seeing the results, would he have carried on using them? In the panorama of Neo-classical Rome under Pius VI, it was a question of choosing between the "placidity" of non-varnished colour, and the brilliance and different homogeneity which the painting acquired with a varnish.[42]

Previsions and expectations often led the discussion far from the actual paintings restored, for instance when Ghelli described the effects of the bad cleaning which he felt must inevitably precede the varnishing: "by washing the paintings with corrosive liquids, all the parts which contain mineral colours such as lead white, blues (*l'azzurro*)[xxiii] and the like, are brought back to their initial lightness as though they had never been tempered with oil. The parts containing earth colours or [plant] juices are left deadened. Then you apply the varnish: the earthy parts deepen greatly, whilst the mineral parts remain blanched and calcined; and now we have a painting which has left behind the sweet harmonies imagined by its author. In order to harmonize such discords, paintbrushes are brought to hand, and with these the ruination of the painting is complete".[43]

In Perugia, Hackert's letter was published in defence of Francesco Romero's intervention on Perugino's *Resurrection* and Raphael's *Coronation*, and it is this which gave rise to Baldassare Orsini's strong reactions. The two panels were to undergo another restoration only a few years thence, as a result of the French requisition, and with that disappeared any possibility of verifying the results of the eighteenth-century restoration; it is quite likely that Romero did rely on the glazings and retouchings denounced by the writer from Perugia, in order to remedy the disharmonies caused by the saturation of the original colours with the new varnish. Not so long ago, we were also to witness a less than satisfactorily programmed restoration on Perugino's *Deposition* in Palazzo Pitti, and its fifteenth-century oil (the glazes having been removed during a restoration in the Napoleonic era) did indeed exhibit: "the excessive whiteness of the horizon which kills the figures", while "the colour in the most clamorous section strikes the eye with a more vibrant light than it did before".

The good reversibility of mastic meant that it was almost universally adopted as a varnish, and was particularly well suited to routine conservation. In the nineteenth century, the generalized use of mastic as a varnish would more often than not be accompanied by the addition of oil to give it a "golden glow", or else to make it less transparent. The original brilliance which could be out of tune with the age of the painting would be dampened

---

[xxiii] *Azzurro*: the nomenclature of pigments is always a problem, depending on the context, the author's background, etc. In this instance the author is probably referring to either lapis lazuli or azurite.

down, and the differences in saturation muffled, all those bad effects which Baldassare Orsini had lamented in Perugino's restored paintings.

In a more oil-rich painting, the effect of the varnish is that described by Antonio Franchi, such as can be seen, for instance, in Titian. It is true that the Master himself could have prevented differences in saturation by applying an intermediate layer of glue or egg-white between the paint and the varnish layer. But even late works such as the extraordinary *Apollo and Marsyas* of Kromeriz (now in the National Museum in Prague), made up of the blotches, touches and clots of paint which so astonished Vasari, would behave according to the same laws. However, having seen a few unvarnished Titians such as the *Saint Jerome* in the Escurial (Madrid), which I was lucky enough to do in 1977, one can appreciate all the material beauties of paint which are normally drowned in varnish, and understand that this indeed is the happiest state for a canvas by Titian: the dark blue of the background, the pink of the Saint's drapery which is at once transparent and opaque are beauties which can only be appreciated when seeing the painting in the flesh. If such were the examples before them, we cannot but sympathize with the Neo-classical polemicists so opposed to the varnish of Philipp Hackert.

Notes

1. G. Cavazzoni Zanotti, in *Le pitture di Bologna*, Bologna, 1706, p. 4; *Le pitture di Bologna*, Bologna, 1732, p. 55; G. Marangoni, *Istoria dell'antichissimo oratorio ... di San Lorenzo nel Patriarchio Lateranense ...*, Rome, 1747, p. 219; L. Crespi, in Bottari, 1756, pp. 411, 414; Piacenza, II, 1770, p. 232; G. Ratti, *Descrizione delle pitture ... dello Stato Ligure*, Genova, 1780, I, p. 337; F. Milizia, *Memorie degli architetti antichi e moderni*, Bassano, 1785, pp. 292–294; G. del Rosso, *Memorie per servire alla vita di Niccolò Maria Gasparo Paoletti*, Florence, 1813, pp. 25–29, 33–36; Cavalcaselle–Crowe, 1864–1866, VIII, pp. 308–309; Venturi, 1882, p. 327; O. Kurz, *A forgotten masterpiece by Lodovico Carracci*, in "The Burlington Magazine", LXX, 1937, p. 81; Cagiano de Azavedo, 1948, p. 71; *Mostra dei dipinti restaurati della Pinacoteca Ambrosiana*, Milan, 1956, p. 11; for other examples see Conti, 1973, pp. 228–229.

2. de Brosses, 1739–1740, II, p. 261; *Castelli e ponti*, 1743; Bottari, 1759–1760, II, p. 18; Titi, 1763, I, p. 10; G. P. Chattard, *Nuova descrizione del Vaticano*, Rome, 1762, I, pp. 45, 120; de la Lande, 1769, IV, p. 383; S. Bettinelli, *Del risorgimento d'Italia negli studi, nelle arti e ne' costumi dopo il Mille*, II, Bassano, 1775, p. 198; Matthiae, 1967, p. 415. Of Zabaglia, we know of an unfortunate attempt he made to transfer the mosaics of the Lateran Triclinium in 1735; for the tradition from which this experiment could have derived, see Mancini, 1956, p. 47; Taja, ms cit., c. 311 r.; Piacenza, I, 1768, note 1, p. 158; Ricci, 1930–1937, II, p. 12; entry for *Provenzale, Marcello*, in Thieme–Becker, 1933; Cagiano de Azavedo, 1948, p. 26.

3. De Dominici, 1742–1743, II, pp. 195–196, 287–288; R. de Saint-Non, *Voyage pittoresque ou description des royaumes de Naples et de la Sicilie*, 1782, cited in Guillerme, 1964, note 20 p. 147; G. Sigismondo, *Descrizione della città di Napoli e i suoi borghi*, Naples, 1788, II, pp. 244, 332; C. Ruspi, *Metodo per distaccare gli affreschi dai muri e riportarli sulle tele proposto dal cavalier Carlo Ruspi e pubblicato per cura di Ercole Ruspi*, Rome, 1864, pp. 12–13; O. Giannone, *Giunte sulle vite de' pittori napoletani*, Naples, 1941, pp. 49, 51, 85; [Ghelli], 1788, p. 279. For his activity as an *estrattista*, we should mention Nicola Lapiccola, a painter from Crotone and active in Rome, see: Zani, *Enciclopedia metodica ...*, part I, XI, Parma, 1822, p. 250; G. Ceci, in "Thieme–Becker", 1928.

4. C. Cittadella, *Catalogo Storico de' Pittori e Scultori Ferraresi*, Ferrara, 1782, IV, pp. 102–113; G. Baruffaldi, *Vita di Antonio Contri ferrarese pittore e rilevatore di pitture dai muri*, Venice, 1834; G. Barrufaldi, *Vite de' pittori e scultori ferraresi*, Ferrara, 1844, I, pp. 189–192; II, pp. 338–359; G. P. Cavazzoni Zanotti, in Baruffaldi, op. cit. I, 1844, pp. 39–40 (a letter which can be dated to 1737 for the allusion to Niccolò Baruffaldi); Lanzi, 1809, V, pp. 276–277.

5. A. Puerari, *La Pinacoteca di Cremona*, Florence, 1951, p. 88.

6. C. F. Poerson, in *L'Académie de France à Rome d'après la correspondance de ses directeurs*, in "Gazette des Beaux-Arts", 1869, 2°, p. 85; de Brosses, 1749–1750, pp. 262–264; L. Crespi, 1756, pp. 434–435; de La Lande, 1769, IV, p. 156; A. Venturi, *La galleria Sterbini in Roma*, Rome, 1906, p. 26; Thieme–Becker, 1930; F. R. Shapley, *Paintings from the Samuel Kress Collection, Italian Schools XIII–XV Century*, London, 1966, p. 61;

Il Cardinale Alessandro Albani, 1980, pp. 42–43 (Albani inventory dating from the beginning of the eighteenth century, which refers to paintings transferred by a certain Carlo Monti).

7. See: "Mémoires pour l'histoire des sciences et des beaux-arts" (Mémoires de Trevoux), January 1751, pp. 110–111; *Lettre écrite de Bruxelles sur le secret de transporter les tableaux sur de nouveaux fonds et de les réparer*, in "Mercure de France", January 1756, 2°, pp. 174–185; Zani, *Enciclopedia metodica …*, Parma, 1817–1824, XVI, pp. 90, 283; Giordani, 1830, note 6, pp. 36–37.

8. Didérot and D'Alembert, *Encyclopédie ou Dictionnaire raisonné des sciences, des arts et des métiers*. Vol. I, Paris, 1751, pp. xiii, 714.

9. "Mercure de France", July 1746, pp. 112–116; December 1750, 1°, pp. 150–151; Engerand, 1899, pp. 108, 131, note 1, p. 430; Engerand, 1901, p. 626; Fierens–Gevaert, *Correspondance de Bruxelles*, in "Gazette des Beaux-Arts", 1919, pp. 330–331; Marot, 1950, pp. 248–249; Emile-Mâle, 1982, p. 221.

10. *Lettre au P. B. J. sur les tableaux exposés au Luxembourg*, in "Mémoires de Trévoux", 1751, pp. 110–111; Milanesi, V, 1880, note 2 p. 30 (another transfer in 1842); Lépicié, I, 1752, pp. 52–54; *Procès verbaux de l'Académie Royale de Peinture et de Sculpture 1648–1793*, VI, Paris, 1885, pp. 216–217; Engerand, 1899, p. 35 and note 1; Marot, 1950, pp. 249–250; Emile-Mâle, 1982, pp. 223–231. We also have references to another painting by Andrea del Sarto, a Madonna mentioned in the sale of the Principe di Conti in 1779, which Picault is said to have transferred onto glass "to show both sides" (*Hommage à Andrea del Sarto*, catalogue of the exhibition, Paris, 1986, p. 45).

11. "Mémoires de Trévoux", 1751, pp. 456–457; 1752, pp. 762–764; Courajod, 1869, pp. 374–375; Guiffrey, 1879, pp. 407–417; *Procès verbaux de l'Académie*, op. cit., VI, 1885, pp. 216–217, 236–237, 241–243, 284, 335; Engerand, 1899, pp. XIX, 12–17; *Raphael*, 1983, pp. 433–434, 441–443. The report on the state of conservation before the transfer of 10 January 1751 is published by Guiffrey (pp. 408–412), by Engerand, and in the first edition of this volume (1973, pp. 330–331).

12. "Mémoires de Trévoux", 1752, pp. 340–341, 762; *Procès verbaux de l'Académie*, op. cit., VI, 1885, p. 284; Engerand, 1899, pp. 6–7. Two Madonnas by Raphael which were in the Orléans Collection, and were transferred during the eighteenth century: the *Mackintosh Madonna* in the National Gallery in London (which can plausibly be identified with the painting in question, and suffered considerable damage in the process, see Cavalcaselle, 1882–1885, II, p. 146 and note 1, p. 147) and the *Madonna della palma* in the National Gallery, Edinburgh. For the latter, Waagen (*Treasures of Art in Great Britain*, London, 1854, p. 27) specifically states that it was damaged during a transfer carried out by Hacquin.

13. *Lettre au P. B. J.*, op. cit., in "Mémoires de Trévoux", pp. 110–111; *Observations sur l'art de conserver les ouvrages de peinture qui menacent ruine*, ibid., pp. 452–465; "Nouvelles Archives de l'Art Français", s. III, XIX, 1903, pp. 27, 28; Marot, 1950, p. 251 (letter from Marigny to Picault of 10 December 1752).

14. Gautier d'Agoty, 1753, I, pp. 176–184 (in *Observations sur l'histoire naturelle, sur la physique et sur la peinture*, Tome premier, II partie, Paris, 1752, pp. 128–130; Gautier d'Agoty, 1753, I, pp. 184–204; Emile-Mâle, 1982, p. 227 and notes 31–33, p. 230 (with an analysis of the materials by Jean Petit).

15. The painting by Joos van Clève is the one which is now in Nantes (see L. Benoist, *Ville de Nantes-Musée des Beaux-Arts Catalogue et guide*, Nantes, 1953, p. 75), not to be confused with the painting with a similar subject in the Louvre (E. Michel, *Catalogue raisonné des peintures … Peintures flamandes du XVème siècle*, Paris, 1953, p. 75); on its transfer, see Engerand, 1899, p. 226; Marot, 1950, p. 251–252. A method which may resemble that used by Widow Godefroid is described by Paillot de Montabert (1829–1830, IX, p. 703). For Vahiny's report on Picault's "Mémoires", see Engerand, pp. XXIV–XXV.

16. *Lettre de M. le Chevalier de Solignac à M. Freron, sur les tableaux du Sr. Roxin*, in "Mémoires de la Société Royale des Sciences et Belles-Lettres de Nancy", III, 1755, pp. 236–250; Marot, 1950, pp. 241–247.

17. "Mémoires de Trévoux", 1755, pp. 552–553; 1756, pp. 570–572 (on the canon Sauvages de Verdun, see Marot, 1950, p. 267); "Mercure de France", January 1756, 2°, pp. 174–185 (eulogy of the restorer Dumesnil from Brussels, and Collins' reply: 1756, 2°, pp. 170–177); A. J. Pernety, *Dictionnaire portatif de peinture et gravure avec un traité pratique des différentes manières de peindre*, Paris, 1757, p. 498; R. Dossie, *The Handmaid to the Arts*, London, 1758, II, pp. 381–387; D. d'Arclais de Montamy, *Traité des couleurs pour la peinture en émail et sur la porcelaine …*, Paris, 1765, pp. 223–229 (a translation appears in Secco-Suardo, 1866, pp. 339–342, which was not included in subsequent editions).

18. On the transfer of the frescos in the Chambre Saint Louis in Fontainebleau, see Picault's letter as published by Engerand (1899, pp. 624–628); on this transfer, and the method used, see also: "Feuille nécessaire", Paris, 1759, p. 280, in "Revue universelle des arts", XVIII, 1863–1864, pp. 137 and XIX; 1864, p. 140; Picault, 1789, articles XXIV and XXV.

19. Apart from specific indications, in general see: Engerand, 1899 and 1900; Marot, 1950, pp. 255–264.

20. See the criticisms of these restorers by Jean-Michel Picault and David in 1793 (Picault, 1793, ed. 1859, p. 34; Emile-Mâle, 1956, note 3, p. 392). On Grandpré, see Engerand, 1899, pp. XXIV, 154, 157, 197; 1900, p. 606; on Hoogstoel, Engerand, 1899, pp. XXVI, 7, 12, 241; 1900, pp. 580–581, 607. Amongst the initiatives taken in the field of the restoration of paintings in the last years of the reign of Louis XVI, one should remember that between 1784 and 1789, several of the paintings, enlarged at the end of the seventeenth century, were returned to their original size; amongst them, Raphael's *Double Portrait* and Titian's *Man with Glove* and *Woman with a mirror.*

    Obviously, the diffusion in France of restoration was not restricted to the paintings in the Royal Collection; we have references to the restoration of paintings in the churches in Paris, of the cleaning of the paintings in Nôtre-Dame (in 1732, by Achille René Grégoire, and in 1781, by François-Ferdinand Godefroid), of transfers (for instance, a *Nativity of the Virgin* by Valentin de Boulogne belonging to the Dominicans in the rue Saint-Jacques Dubucquoy in 1778), see: "Revue universelle des arts", 1860, pp. 134–135; Marot, 1950, p. 248; "Revue universelle des arts", XVIII, 1863–1864, p. 138.

21. P. J. Mariette, *Abecedario*, V, Paris, 1858–1859, p. 189; L. Arbaud, *Mademoiselle Godefroid*, in "Gazette des Beaux-Arts", 1869, I, p. 39; Courajod, 1869, p. 375; J. Guiffrey, *Joseph Fernand Godefroid, maître peintre*, in "Nouvelles Archives de l'Art Français", 1883, pp. 395–417; Engerand, 1899; Engerand, 1900; *Correspondance de M. de Vandières, Marquis de Marigny*, in "Nouvelles Archives de l'Art Français", série III, XIX, 1903; pp. 11–12, 40, 42, 45, 49, 78, 166, 172, 213, 267, 269–270; XX, 1904, pp. 46, 47–48, 109; entry for *Godefroid, Joseph-Fedinand*, in Thieme–Becker, 1921; Marot, 1950, pp. 251–253 (observations on Raphael's *Holy Family*), 255–262.

22. E. F. Gersaint, *Catalogue raisonné des bijoux, porcelaines, bronzes … tableaux provenans de la succession de M. Angran, Vicomte de Fonspertius*, Paris, 1747, pp. 193–194; "Mercure de France", April 1756, 2°, pp. 170–174; P. J. Mariette, op. cit., I, Paris, 1851–1853, p. 386; Engerand, 1899; Engerand, 1900 (pp. 606–607, on Rubens' *Crucifixion*, n. 2082 in the Louvre); "Nouvelles Archives de l'Art Français", III, XIX, 1903, pp. 43, 78, 170; Stübel, 1926, p. 129; Marot, 1950, pp. 259–260 (presentation of the Prince of Condé). On the *Leda* by Correggio see: E. Dacier, *La vente Charles Coypel d'après les notes manuscrites de P. J. Mariette*, in "La revue de l'art ancien et moderne", LXI, 1932, pp. 61–71; E. Freron, *L'Année Litteraire Année MDCCLIV*, IV, Amsterdam, 1754, pp. 95–96; *Encyclopédie méthodique Beaux-Arts*, I, Paris–Liège 1788, pp. 83, 252; Marot, 1950, pp. 267–268; Guillerme, 1964, pp. 69–70 and note 31; C. Gould, *The Paintings of Correggio*, London, 1976, pp. 194–195. On the *Holy Family of Canigiani*, see: Cavalcaselle, 1882–1885, I, note 2, p. 307; von Sonnenburg, 1983, pp. 13, 39–41.

23. Guiffrey, 1879, pp. 414–417; Engerand, 1899, pp. 14, 15, 18; Marot, 1950, pp. 253–254; *L'école de Fontainebleau*, catalogue of the exhibition, Paris, 1972, p. 176.

24. On Raphael's *San Giovanni Battista*: Lepicié, 1752–1754, I, p. 89 (quality revealed with the cleaning by Stiémart); *Raphael*, 1983, p. 434. On the second transfer of the *Saint Michael* (relined by J. M. Picault in 1800) and on the *Saint Margaret*: Paris, Arch. Musées Nationaux, *Procés-verbaux de l'Administration du Musée central des Arts*, 18 fructidor an V (4 September 1793), and P 16, 15 October 1797 (cited by G. Emile-Mâle, 1956, note 1, p. 406); Cavalcaselle, 1882–1885, note 2, pp. 107–108. On the *Holy Family of François I*ᵉʳ, J. M. Picault, 1793, articles XIV and XX, Engerand, 1899, p. 17. On the ceiling attributed to Vouet in the Château de Vincennes, see: Picault, 1789, article XXIV; Engerand, 1900, note 3, pp. 634–635; "Nouvelles Archives de l'Art Français", s. III, XX, 1904, p. 49. On the ceiling by Le Sueur transferred from the ceiling of the Hôtel Lambert: F. Villot, *Notice des tableaux exposés dans les galleries du Musée National du Louvre. Ecole Française*, Paris, 1978 (9th ed.), p. 359; J. J. Guiffrey, *Lettres et documents sur l'acquisition des tableaux d'Eustache Le Sueur pour la collection du roi (1776–1789)*, in "Nouvelles Archives de l'Art Français", 1877, pp. 318–322; Engerand, 1900, pp. 580–582. On the transfer of the *Saint Brunos* which remained interrupted at the death of Jean-Louis Hacquin in 1783: Picault, 1793, article XX; Millin, 1806, III, p. 435; Guiffrey, op. cit., pp. 295–318; Engerand, 1900, pp. 574–577. On other works: Guiffrey, op. cit., note 1, p. 321; Engerand, 1899, p. 167 (*Alexander and Timocles* by Domenichino, restored by Collins in 1750), 241, 367–368; Engerand, 1900, pp. 606–607, 631; "Nouvelles Archives de l'Art Français", op. cit., 1904, pp. 150, 152, 212, 215; C. Gould, *National Gallery Catalogues, The Sixteenth-Century Venetian School*, London, 1959, note 1, p. 79.

25. Marot, 1950, pp. 263–264; Lebrun, op. cit. in note 42, p. 349.

26. J. B. Oudry, *Discours sur la pratique de la peinture et ses procédés principaux* (1749), in "Cabinet de l'amateur", 1861–1862, p. 182; [Petit de Bachaumont], *Essai sur la peinture, la sculpture et l'architecture*, 1751, pp. 30–31; in "Archives de l'art français", 1873, p. 391.

27. Watin, 1773, pp. 6–7.

28. See Conti, 1973, p. 235 for a review of the opinions on the mosaic in the eighteenth century. For the redis-covery of encaustic, see: Caylus, *Reflexions sur quelques chapitres du XXXème livre de Pline*, II, *du genre et l'espèce des peintures anciennes* (1732), in "Mémoires de l'Académie des inscriptions et belles lettres", XXV, op. cit. in Guillerme, 1964, note 1, p. 26; Monnaye, *Encaustique* entry in *Encyclopédie*, Paris, 1751–1752, ed. Livoune, V, 1772, pp. 558–565; A. J. Pernety, *Dictionnaire portatif*, Paris, 1757, pp. 499–500; Guillerme, 1964, pp. 177–178; M. Simonetti and M. Sarti, in Baroni, Sarti, etc., 1973, pp. 19–20.

29. Mengs, 1783, II, p. 157; Baroni, Sarti, etc., 1973.

30. J. Fratrel *La cire alliée avec l'huile ou la peinture à l'huile-cire, trouvée à Mannheim par M. Charles, baron de Taubenheim*, Mannheim, 1778; V. Requeno, *Saggi del ristabilimento dell'antica arte de' greci e de' romani pittori*, Venice, 1784; "Giornale delle belle arti", Rome, 1786, pp. 65–67, 131–132, 137–140; A. M. Lorgna, *Discorso sopra la cera punica*, in "Opuscoli scelti", XVI, 1793; A. Fabroni, *Antichità, vantaggi e metodo della pittura encausta*, Rome, 1797; Lanzi, 1809, V, pp. 278–283; J. W. Goethe, *Italianische Reise*, 24 November 1786; Merrifield, 1849, pp. C–CII; G. Secco-Suardo, *Della pittura ad encausto, ad olio ed a tempera*, in "L'Arte in Italia", 1871, pp. 69–72, 82–85, 119–123; G. Secco-Suardo, *Alcune idee sulla pittura degli antichi*, ibid., 1872, pp. 65–69, 81–83, 100–103.

31. C. N. Cochin, *Œuvres diverses ... ou Recueil de quelques pièces concernant les arts*, Paris, 1771, I, pp. 121–144; Guillerme (1964) refers to a certain Roquet, as critical of the encaustic method advocated by the Count of Caylus, in *L'art nouveau de la peinture au fromage ou au ramequin inventée pour suivre le louable projet de trouver graduellement des façons de peindre inférieures à celles qui existent*. (The new art of painting with cheese or with the ramekin, invented in order to follow the praiseworthy project of gradually finding techniques of painting which are inferior to those already in existence.)

32. Eastlake, 1847, pp. 444, 538–546; Guillerme, 1964, p. 20 and note 34, pp. 20–21; see the discussion on Reynolds' technique in the exhibition catalogue *Sir Joshua Reynolds 1723–1792*, Paris, 1985; London, 1986.

33. L. B. Guyton de Morveau *Recherches pour perfectionner la préparation des couleurs employées dans la peinture, lues à la séance publique de l'Académie de Dijon du 15 mai 1781*, ms 237 of the Ecole des Beaux-Arts in Paris (op. cit. in Guillerme, 1964, pp. 174–176); J. Senebier, *Mémoires physico-chimiques sur l'influence de la lumière solaire pour modifier les êtres des trois règnes de la nature*, Geneva, 1782; F. Carbonnel, *Su un nuovo genere di pittura col siero del sangue*, in "Opuscoli scelti", XXII, 1803, pp. 297–302; Guillerme, 1964, pp. 173, 176, 184, 194. Dealing more closely with restoration: N. Martelli, *Sulla maniera di restituire il colore perduto alle antiche pit-ture a fresco*, in "Opuscoli scelti sulle scienze e sulle arti", VII, Milan, 1784, pp. 97–99.

34. *Metodo discoperto del Signor Loriot per fissare i colori delle pitture a pastello*, in "Antologia romana", VII, 1780–1781, pp. 251–255; the experiment had been carried out on what was thought to be the self-portrait of Rosalba Carriera in the Louvre (*Venise au dix-huitième siècle*, catalogue of the exhibition, Paris, 1971, n. 37).

35. A. Franchi, *La teorica della pittura*, Lucca, 1739, pp. 169–171.

36. Bonanni, 1720, pp. 74–75; Watin, 1773, p. 187; Hackert, 1788; [Ghelli], 1788; G. G. D. R., 1788. Referring to Chinese varnish, Bonanni (p. 72) writes: "... it is never used on paintings, but rather serves as a base, on which one then works with gold and paint, as it is not transparent but opaque so that, when it has become black, it will cover anything, even darkened silver; and if one is making it of a different colour, mix it with this same varnish, which always has body." Among the numerous references and items of information which make Bonanni's *Trattato* so precious, and insert it within a context which is not yet characteristic of the eighteenth century, I should like to pick out the reference to Fioravanti for the varnish used by the Turks to varnish their bows and quivers, also the reference to copaiba oil, the description of amber varnish "procured from a chemist from Augsburg", the recipe received from the medallist Ferdinand Saint Urban, or Coronelli's varnish, which was suitable for the varnishing of globes.

37. Watin, 1773, p. 240; by now Tingry (1803, pp. 156–158) is already giving his compositions in grams, and for an important picture he advises a varnish composed of 366.86 grams of cleaned and washed mastic, 45.85 grams of pure turpentine; 15.28 grams of camphor; 152.85 grams of ground glass and 1.0057 grams of spirits of turpentine. The composition of Hackert's varnish (mastic dissolved in spirits of turpentine) is recorded in a memorandum published by Incerpi, 1982, pp. 348–349.

38. Edwards, 1786, Gino Lanzi, 1809, 178, note 221 (see Incerpi, 1982, on the use of oil in the Galleria di Firenze).

39. Burtin, 1808, I, pp. 432–437; Stübel, 1926, pp. 131–135. Of the two Riedels who worked in the Gallery in Dresden, Gottfried (the father) impregnated all the pictures with a siccative oil which darkened them, to the extent that in some paintings by Veronese he then had to repaint the skies. With his son Anton, who succeeded him in 1755, the siccative oil becomes a "chymisches oel" with which he impregnated the paintings entrusted

to him with the greatest diligence, until his death in 1816. De Burtin particularly lamented the consequences of this impregnation in the instances of Correggio's *Night*, and *Madonna di San Giorgio.*

40. Brandi, 1963, ed. 1977, p. 102.

41. Hackert, 1788; [Ghelli], 1788; Orsini, 1876. One should remember the poor results, in Naples, of the varnish applied onto the paintings in Herculaneum, by the pioneer Stefano Moriconi; see de la Lande, 1769, VI, p. 113; M. Cagiano de Azavedo, *Vernici settecentesche sulle pitture di Ercolano*, in "Bollettino dell'Istituto Centrale di Restauro", n. 1, 1950, pp. 40–41. On Anders, see: A. Filangieri di Candida, *La Galleria Nazionale di Napoli*, in *Le Gallerie Nazionali italiane*, 1902, pp. 225–226; Thieme–Becker, 1907. The "Giornale delle belle arti" has various references to Margherita Bernini, see: 1784, p. 136 (*San Diego* by Annibale Carracci, in San Giacomo degli Spagnoli in Rome); 1785, p. 219; 1786, pp. 351–352 (*Cleopatra before Octavian* and *Persian Sybil* by Guercino, in the Galleria Capitolina, Rome; 1788, pp. 269, 283, 287 (note 1: thinks highly, in his comparisons, of Batoni, who never used varnish), 288–290 (restorations in the Galleria Giustiniani in Rome).

42. See also the brief response initialled G.G.D.R. (Giovanni Gherardo de Rossi?) which appeared in the "Giornale delle belle arti" (1788, pp. 343, 345), where it was mentioned that Hackert's varnish had damaged a landscape by Claude in the Galleria Colonna, Rome, and that the anecdote relating that Mengs had mistaken a retouching by Anders for an original portion by the hand of Domenichino was proven to be untrue.

43. [R. Ghelli], 1788, p. 269.

6

Venice and Pietro Edwards

1. The "public paintings"

During the course of the seventeenth century, the restoration of the paintings in the public palaces of Rialto consisted still, in the case of paintings which were too far gone, in their replacement: in the Biblioteca Marciana, the tondos by Bernardo Strozzi and Padovanino replaced those by Battista Franco and Zelotti; in the Sala dello Scrutinio, at the end of the century, four canvases by Palma Giovane, Benedetto Caliari, Francesco Bassano and Domenico Tintoretto had been replaced. Edwards himself, in the case of paintings which were too damaged, excluded them from his reports, as their restoration would have involved a complete repainting: in such cases, he suggested replacing the paintings with new ones.[1]

Edwards' preliminary reports made it quite clear that because the Ducal Palace was used as a seat of government, this resulted in a whole range of "disorders" that prevented the good preservation of the canvases; moreover, there was frequent damage caused by the infiltration of various forms of humidity: "rain and ice … wet the walls, the tiles, the canvas, and dampen the glue [size] and the gesso [ground]", bewails Giovambattista Rossi in 1684, referring to Tintoretto's *The Venetian Ambassadors meet Barbarossa at Pavia*. And it is the maintenance of the building, and the prevention of such damage that is discussed in one of Edwards' finest manuscript texts: *Dissertazione preliminare al piano di custodia da istituirsi per la possible preservazione e per il miglior mantenimento delle pubbliche pitture* (Preliminary discussion for the plan to make the conservation possible and improve the maintenance of public paintings).

It is against this background of damage incurred as a result of the life led in the Ducal Palace, and in particular damage resulting from the lack of maintenance of the roofs and floors, that one needs to consider the conservation (*manutenzione*) and restoration activities carried out on the "public pictures"; it is also in the light of these circumstances that one can comprehend why, right until the time of the direction of Pietro Edwards, it was always the same canvases that were put forward for restoration.[2]

Traditionally, the restoration of the canvases had been entrusted to painters, often to minor painters such as Giovambattista Rossi who, in 1677 and then again in 1684, was busy with the restoration of the works in the Sala del Maggior Consiglio and the Sala dello Scrutinio, which were rendered necessary by the infiltrations of the thawing snow, as well as restretching ("*imbrocadura*") of Tintoretto's *Paradiso*. Although contested by "rumours", such repairs were officially approved by Carlo Loth, Antonio Zanchi and Niccolò Cassana, who nevertheless made clear his reservations, which were probably suggested by his experiences as a restorer, of which his letters to the Grand Prince of Tuscany are such eloquent evidence. From 1686 onwards, Rossi was officially charged with the preservation of the public paintings from dust and from other accidental damage, and his reports show him to have been particularly careful of conservation measures (*provvedimenti di manutenzione*).[i] In 1694, when confronted with the need for some retouchings on Tintoretto's ceiling in the Sala del Maggior Consiglio, he requested permission to proceed "with the assistance of accredited painters" to the colouring of a probable addition with "blue water" ("*l'acqua celeste*"), and to intervene on the "poles, flags and carpets which are damaged in the middle of painting" and on some of the heads "which have rotted". At his death in 1704, the care of the public paintings passed into the hands of Vincenzo Cecchi, who is not known to have been active as a painter, and during whose incumbency important restorations were passed on to masters such as Niccolò Bambini, who was responsible for the restoration of Tintoretto's ceiling in the Sala delle Quattro Porte in 1714.[3]

When the time came to choose a successor to Cecchi in 1724, the College of Painters requested the office of the monthly checks on the Public Paintings; the Magistrati al Sal, who were responsible for the cost of the upkeep of public buildings, raised the objection that:

> "At first sight the tasks must appear as prized and lofty inspections, with regard to the inestimable worth of that which is inspected; but when considered more closely, you see that actually that these are fairly primitive operations ... such as shaking off the dust, removing spiders' webs, looking over the frames and reattaching any loose fragments on these, checking from month to month if there is any deterioration or damage visible on the canvases, or if there is damage to the figures, or other such things .... We cannot persuade ourselves that renowned professors should wish to demean themselves by carrying out such mechanical and burdensome work. Either they have been misinformed as to the nature of the ministry that they aspire to, and then, having graciously accepted the position, they will then disdain to carry out the task out of a sense of dignity. Or else they have decided to put lowly craftsmen in their place .... Which means that what has to be decided, is not so much whether this care should be shouldered by the College of Painters, but rather whether the selection of a representative to carry out these duties should be devolved to them, rather than being the onus of public authority ...".

Moreover, the Provveditori al Sal also suspected that from the method chosen by the painters to be remunerated for the job – reduction of their annual taxation – that it was "the undertaking reflecting the interest of those few" who bore the brunt of the charges, the most important painters, "the furthest removed from this lowly practice"; they also feared that the absence of a single responsible person for the operation would lead to great disorder. Nevertheless, the task was entrusted to the college with a decree from the Senate, on 14 September 1724.[4]

After another decree by the Senate on the restoration of public pictures of 19 June 1727, three paintings from the Ducal Palace were entrusted to Sebastiano Ricci. According to Edwards, it was only after his remarks that "you needed no less theoretical knowledge to clean an old painting, than had been necessary to its author [for its creation]", that even more highly qualified painters began to become involved in the restoration of paintings. However, regular restorers would undoubtedly have been minor painters; Edwards' reports

---

[i] What we would term measures of "preventive conservation".

refer to an Agostino Letterini for the work on Veronese's ceiling in the Sala del Consiglio dei Dieci, or else regret the retouchings carried out in oil by Pietro Cardinali, the painter who was trusted most in the restorations of the paintings in the Palazzo Ducale: on a Leandro Bassano and on the *Taking of Zara* by Domenico Tintoretto in the Sala del Maggior Consiglio, and on the paintings of the Sala dello Scrutinio. Expressions of satisfaction were addressed in 1739 to Cardinali as an active restorer, for his restoration work in Santa Maria Maggiore, in the Salute, and in the Sala del Consiglio dei Dieci, to the extent of that he was asked to present estimates for the Sala delle Quattro Porte and for the ceiling of the Sala del Collegio: all works of which Edwards had been critical of the earlier restorations.[5]

The reports from the Collegio dei Pittori to the Provveditori al Sal, from 1748 to 1759, almost always referred to the same paintings: Tintoretto's *Paradiso*, a few works by Bonifacio in Rialto, the Veronese in the ceiling of the Sala della Bussola. The *Paradiso* was restored in 1755 by Francesco Fontebasso, with results that Edwards used as an example of the poor use of public funds. Beginning to emerge is the situation which would lead Edwards to make the distinction between "worthy painter" ("*valente pittore*") and "skilled restorer" ("*perito restauratore*").[6] The Veronese would require a further restoration in 1762, the year in which the report enumerated so many public paintings requiring restoration, that the sheer volume of work led to the attachment of a list of "professors" suitable for the task; the list shows us that many of the principal painters in Venice were active as restorers. We find Gasparo Diziani, Fabio Canal, Giuseppe Angeli, Giacomo Guarana and Giuseppe Nogari. Some of these had carried out noteworthy restorations: Giacomo Marieschi had worked on the paintings of the Sala del Tribunale del Consiglio dei Dieci, and on the majority of the works by Bonifacio in the Stanza dei Provveditori agli Ori e Argenti in Zecca; Giuseppe Bertani, well known as a restorer, had repaired the paintings in the Corpus Domini; Gaetano Zompini all the paintings on the walls of the *albergo* in the Scuola di San Rocco. Domenico Maggiotto had worked on an altarpiece in San Pietro di Castello, and "looked after paintings for His Excellency the Noble Gasparo Bragadin, the Noble Francesco Vendramin at the Maddalena, His Excellency English resident, the English Consul the Count Bonomo Algarotti. In the *cancelleria* of the Scuola della Carità, and many others which he sent to Moscow".[7]

Ten paintings would indeed be entrusted to Domenico Maggiotto (amongst which the ceiling of the Sala della Bussola by Paolo Veronese and *The Fall of the Manna* by Bonifacio in the Magistrato del Pro' fuori di Zecca), with the instructions that he was to line and restore them without the use of the paintbrush. Giuseppe Angeli, who had declined the commission to restore the paintings himself, considering it a task "far removed and quite different from painting", was instead supervising the restoration, verifying that "the paintings were not cleaned imperfectly so that the most delicate outlines, tints and shadows remained hidden and confused within the dark foreign patina; or else that through insisting too much on its separation, those masterful strokes of art be worn down and removed along with it, as can happen all too easily. In this way, pitifully losing either through one method or the other, in the overall and complex appearance of these wondrous canvases, the harmony and accord for which they are most prized".[ii][8]

98

[ii] "*o imperfettamente le pitture non fossero ripulite, sicchè I più delicati lineamenti, tinte, ed ombreggi, non ne rimanessero, anche dopo il fatto, dentro la estrania pattina confusi, e nascosti; o per troppo insistenza all'incontro di separare oltre quanto convien, questa pattina, quei tratti maestri dell'arte non ne fossero insieme logorati e perduti, come pur troppo agevolmente avvenir potrebbe; restando così perdute miseramente e per l'uno e per l'altro modo, nel complesso, ed aspetto universale di queste tele ammirabiliquell'armonia, e concordanza, che ne formano il pregio maggiore.*"

*98. Bonifacio Veronese, The Fall of the Manna;
restored by Domenico Maggiotto, 1762, under the
direction of Pietro Edwards, 1780-1781 (with the
nineteenth century squaring up). Venice, Gallerie
dell'Accademia, on deposit with the Fondazione
Giorgio Cini.*

The restoration of public paintings under the direction of the College of Painters must have been an untidy affair; in 1777, a "private communication" on the subject, requested by the Senate from the Riformatori dello Studio di Padova (and of course drawn up by Edwards), brought to attention the fact that: "the outcome of their requests never fulfilled the true needs of the affair, nor their wishes. And this because, overwhelmingly, their differences of opinion and their prospects of private advantage were in continual conflict with the production of a straightforward plan which could be used to carry out this important work. Therefore, the work which should have been commissioned on almost all the paintings in the aforementioned palaces either to prevent imminent damage, or to repair damage which had already occurred, not only was restricted to very few of the myriad needy canvases, but also (and this is even more painful) the commissions in almost all cases were given to such a pitiful choice of artist, that as much as imminent ruin in the remaining works awakens compassion, so the great majority of restored works rightly moves all true lovers of the fine arts to indignation".[9]

As might be expected, it was not only the paintings in the public domain which underwent restoration; paintings in private collections, churches and schools were also being restored. Gasparo Diziani restored the small altarpiece by Tintoretto in San Gallo and, most probably the Giovanni Bellini in Santi Giovanni e Paolo. In 1733, in the Scuola Grande di San Marco, Giuseppe Zanchi (with the attached condition that he should not use the brush "imaginatively") restored the *Paris Bordone* and the *Tempest* attributed to Giorgione; in 1738, Cardinali worked on the Tintoretto, and on the canvases by Bellini and Mansueti.[10]

As a rule, the large canvases were secured onto a wooden support rather than stretched over a stretcher to keep them taut: the *Storie di Sant'Orsola* by Carpaccio would only be given a stretcher in 1753 and in 1754 the Carpaccios in the Scuola degli Schiavoni were also put onto stretchers. In the Scuola di San Giovanni Evangelista, the canvases were still not on stretchers in 1784, when the inspector, Mengardi, worked on them; this is the same Mengardi who, in 1791, pointed out the difficulty of removing *The Apparition of Saint Mark* by Tintoretto when Vivant Denon was engraving it in the Scuola Grande di San Marco, as it was nailed to its panel support.[11]

The frequent interventions on the paintings that hung in churches, which were not always executed with the accuracy one might wish, and especially the sale of works of art which at times fetched ridiculously low prices,[12] together with the neglect in which were kept so many masterpieces, induced the Consiglio dei Dieci to nominate an inspector of public paintings. Their choice fell on Anton Maria Zanetti the Younger (12 July 1773), who prepared the list of paintings to be bound by the new legislation in Venice and the surrounding islands. These works would no longer to be allowed to be either moved, nor entrusted to restorers without "public permission"; for each church or Scuola, lists were compiled on forms ("*stampiglie*") with the lion of Saint Mark. Every six months the inspector had to notify the State Inquisitors of any future removals or displacements of works of art, notify them of any paintings requiring restoration, then make sure that this was carried out and finally approve the results of the restoration. The works put forward for restoration in Zanetti's reports (1773–1778) were not many: he had, to use our vocabulary, a very keen sense of the choices available in restoration. He thought that paintings were lined more than was necessary, observed that time did not benefit paintings, but that restoration was a perilous remedy "to be resorted to only in the case of imminent ruin, in order to prevent the loss of an illustrious work". Zanetti also put forward as candidates for restoration seventeenth-century works such as *The Nativity* by Carlo Roth in San Silvestro, and two works by Liberi. The most demanding restorations were those on sixteenth-century works: Tintoretto's *Last Supper* in San Simeone Grande (carried out by Bertani), the *Paris Bordone*, the *Tempest* attributed to Giorgione, and the Tintorettos, all of which were in the Scuola di San Marco; the *Saint Barbara* by Palma Vecchio in Santa Maria Formosa (entrusted to Bertani), the *Saint Peter the Martyr* and the *Last Supper* by Veronese in Santi Giovanni e Paolo. Of the fourteenth-century works, he had the polyptych by Giovanni Bellini in this same church restored, and it was during this operation that the gilded inset was inserted into the lunette, which can still be seen today in the place of God the Father which was moved to the *albergo* of the Scuola di Vincenzo Ferrer.[13]

From 1779 to 1795, the inspector was Giovanbattista Mengardi. Giovanni Maria Sasso, engraver and the habitual restorer employed by the British Consul Udney, was one of the practitioners to whom he entrusted the restoration of the church paintings, putting him forward in 1780 for the restoration of the two works by Bellini in San Michele on Murano, the triptych now in Düsseldorf, and the *Resurrection* in Berlin (thought to be by Cima da Conegliano). For the work on the two Girolamo di Santa Croce di Santa Ternita[iii] he put forward Maggiotto (1780), as he also did for the restoration of the Pordenone in San Rocco, which he eventually restored himself in 1783. Quite frequently it would seem, it was the inspector himself who would carry out the restorations: two altarpieces by Carpaccio and by Bonifacio Veronese which were moved from Sant'Antonio di Castello to San Barnaba, a number of large canvases in the Scuola di San Giovanni Evangelista, the Cima da Conegliano now in Berlin, and other paintings in the *scuola* of the silk weavers, *The Marriage at Cana* by Padovanino in the convent of San Giovanni di Verdura in Padua, the works by Tintoretto in Santa Margherita and Santa Maria Materdomini, the *Last Supper* by Veronese in San Sebastiano.[14]

For the restoration of the altarpieces by Carpaccio and Bonifacio which had been moved to San Barnaba, Mengardi used the professional services of Giuseppe Bertani, who on 10 December 1783 would observe that his request for fifty *zecchini* was honest and reasonable, as the Bonifacio Veronese was missing heads and hands, and one whole figure was almost entirely lost; on the other hand, Carpaccio's *Martyrdom of the Eleven Thousand* was still in good condition, although a blue pigment used in the cuirasses had altered in certain areas.

On the subject of the slow progress of the work on five large fifteenth-century canvases in the Scuola di San Giovanni Evangelista, on 1 June 1784, Bertani pointed out that "up to now, the canvases have only been lined: still to be done are the most important and necessary aspects, that is the filling, and then employing the brush only where it is strictly necessary, an operation which is not insignificant due to the quantity of architecture and tiny figures in the painting, which require maximum accuracy, so as to retain their innate character".[15]

In the final years of his incumbency, it would increasingly only be notifications of restorations which Mengardi would approve: Antonio Marinetti would work on the altarpiece by Luca Giordano in Santo Spirito (now in the Brera), Giambattista Canal on the paintings in the Scuola del Sacramento attached to San Giovanni in Bragora, and Antonio Pavona was chosen to clean Tintoretto's *Resurrection* in San Cassiano. In Mengardi's last reports, one continually encounters observations on the poor state of conservation of the Basaiti, the Bellini and the Carpaccio in San Giobbe, panels which he had offered to restore as far back as 1784. Especially in the case of the Basaiti, his notes would become ever more pressing from 1787: the paint layer was flaking and falling onto the altar table, and its removal for restoration

---

[iii] Now S. Trinità.

would be complicated by the necessity of having partly to demolish the altar, an expense in which the Foscarini patrons were unwilling to engage. When the panel was moved at the time of the suppression, in order to avoid this demolition, part of the panel was sawn. A similar situation occurred with the Veronese in Sant'Antonio in Torcello: the nuns did not wish to undergo the expense, until in 1792, Bertani and Baldassini repaired it at their own expense.

In the last years of Mengardi's activity, Edwards also attended to the care of some of the paintings in churches: the two altarpieces by Palma Giovane in Santa Lucia, the Veronese in Torcello, the paintings in San Giobbe, the Giovanni Bellini in the Chiesa degli Angeli in Murano. The last would be between 1796 and 1797, Francesco Maggiotto would be the last to fill the office of Inspector of Public Paintings, and his reports simply picked up on Mengardi's last observations, with only the occasional addition, such as the notification of the poor state of conservation of the *Madonna* thought to be by Giovanni Bellini in Santa Maria Maggiore (that is, the Mantegna now in the Brera, Milan), and the authorization for a few restorations.[16]

On 24 July 1773, the Senate was looking to extend the measures taken for the works of art in public collections to those in churches within the jurisprudence of the state (such as the churches of the Redentore and the Salute) and on the mainland. Mengardi, who was a Paduan by birth, would occasionally mention the state of emergency in which works found themselves in his native city, and would then refer to the principal restorer of frescos working there: Francesco Zannoni da Cittadella. That measures had been in existence for some time on the mainland can be deduced from the fact that in 1755 a nephew[iv] of Gregorio Lazzarini, Santo, from San Vito al Tagliamento, was requesting that the care and restoration of the paintings in the districts of Friuli, Carnia, Cadore and the Bellunese, be entrusted to him on the strength of the excellent results he had achieved in the restoration of the *Deposition* by Basaiti in Sesto al Reghena, carried out in 1745 and now in the Hermitage in St Petersburg.

Other information, for instance that relating to Giambettino Cignaroli, who restored a panel by Francesco Buonsignori in San Bernardino in Verona, or Antonio Medi, who in 1731 worked on Giorgione's altarpiece in Castelfranco Veneto, shows the republic's interest extending to the conservation of works of art on the mainland. In Padua, in 1795, Brandolese would lament the poor quality of the restorations; Moschini's guide of 1817 recorded the "little honour" that Mengardi attracted, when he added an angel to an altarpiece by Domenico Tiepolo, as well as various other mistreatments of paintings such as the poor restoration by Luca Breda of the frescos by Giusto in the Baptistry, and the abysmal one by Domenico Sandri (1786) in the chapel of Giusto al Santo, resulting in the blackening which to this day mars the colours of these marvellous stories.[17]

Historically, the most significant figure amongst the restorers working outside Venice was undoubtedly Francesco Zannoni, especially for his activity on fourteenth- and fifteenth-century frescos. From Brandolese we have the following information: "Diligent, and erudite artist. He should not be judged by the merit of the works of which he is the author, which perhaps because of their excessive diligence and studiousness appear of little merit, but rather by his worth in giving back life to the works of those excellent Old Masters, preserving their original character, at which he was incomparable. Because of this, he was able to glean the praise of even those who were sworn enemies of modern botchers ("*rappezzatori moderni*"). He died in Padua where he had lived for a long time, at the age of seventy-two."

[iv] *Nipote*: can mean either nephew or grandson.

99. *Late Gothic Master, detail
of the frescos of the Salone; with
the repaintings by Francesco
Zannoni, 1762 and following.
Padua, Palazzo della Ragione.*

100. *Late Gothic Master, detail
of the frescos of the Salone; after
the removal of the repaintings by
Francesco Zannoni. Padua,
Palazzo della Ragione.*

Zannoni restored the frescos of the Scuola del Santo (1748), put back into order the
paintings of the Salone in 1762, worked on the chapel of San Felice al Santo in 1772–1773, as
well as on various sixteenth-century cycles of devotional interest. His hand can be recognized
in the vault in San Giovanni Evangelista in Ravenna, on the *Evangelists with the Fathers of
the Church*, which in Vasari's times was thought to be by Giotto. In the Salone, he revised the
frescos using as an iconographic guide the manuscript of Pietro d'Abano's *Astrolabius*. Where   99, 100
the figures had been framed in architraved recessed panels, removing the trefoils he adapted
the panels to fit in with the other paintings, giving a decorative homogeneity to the whole
without, however, departing from the antique style that suited the original architecture.

On the same subject of the relationship between Gothic painting and architecture,
referring to the chapel of San Felice al Santo, decorated with Altichiero's frescos, he observed
in 1772, that "everything is wonderfully coherent, the building erected according to the rules
of Romanesque architecture, the architect being in perfect possession of this art, except for
in the ornamentation the art of which had been lost by the thirteenth century, and the sim-
plicity of the style would not allow modern counterparts".[18]

The figure of Zannoni is also interesting because of the interest he showed in the
paintings of the Early Masters; but it is in 1775, in the introduction to the *Pitture di Bergamo*
by Andrea Pasta, that we are confronted with the most significant testimony to the importance of conservation (*tutela*) in the territories pertaining to Venice. Zannoni's attitude of
well-justified diffidence towards the practice of restoration probably brings him closer to
Anton Maria Zanetti than to Pietro Edwards, whilst his full respect for paintings as devotional objects did not prevent him from making a number of observations that firmly place
this doctor from Bergamo within the Enlightenment. Paintings by illustrious artists (and he is
thinking of Lotto, Cavagna, Talpino), "must be considered as one of the principal ornaments

of the city, and also as a school always open to young students". Pasta accepted additions to altarpieces but not their mutilation, deplored devotional repainting and the application of metal halos, and advised against cleaning which he found unnecessary whilst a painting "could still be seen". For prized paintings he advised careful maintenance (*manutenzione*)ᵛ (dusting, attention to sources of humidity, curtains to protect paintings from direct sunlight, removal of paintings from chimneys), as well as "a good lining applied by a skilled and loving hand". His concepts, as a doctor, demonstrated that the move from the tradition of workshop secrets to the new language of chemistry had already occurred: "analysing" the solvents used in cleaning one would find traces of the paint removed from the painting, whilst "salts", "oil" or "resin" varnishes have become the new terms of reference.

Varnishes were to be avoided because "with the progress of time they turn the whites yellow, the yellows brown, the blues turn greenish, and other colours degenerate into unpleasant and dirty tints", varnishes which, in line with the theme of Time the Painter, must not be confused with patina which he defined as that "which is produced by the action of the environment, which with time deadens (*mortificando*) the boldest colours, making them mutually more harmonious and in tune with one another. Such a patina is also given by time to bronzes and marbles: one would never find an antiquary, however coarse he might be, who would think that he is improving his antique medals or his marble sculptures, by having them cleaned up, so as to acquire that cleanliness that they had when just made coined or sculpted."

2. The direction of Pietro Edwards

In 1770, a further intervention on Veronese's ceiling in the Sala della Bussola was deemed necessary. A decree of the Senate of 6 June 1771 established that the restoration should be entrusted to "the renowned skill" of Giuseppe Bertani, leaving the decision of whether or not the public paintings should always be entrusted to him for restoration, to the Riformatori dello Studio of Padua. Notwithstanding the official form in which the commission was entrusted, personally to Bertani, there was no shortage of intrigue aimed at providing him with insufficiently qualified collaborators: so much so, that in the end he refused the public commission.

Even a connoisseur such as Zanetti, who was cautious in the extreme in advising restoration, remembered with admiration the discreet restoration of the Tintoretto in San Simeone Grande by the most esteemed restorer in Venice, "the master of all restorers", as Edwards called him: Giuseppe Bertani. Around 1750, he was responsible for the restoration of the *Pesaro Altarpiece* by Titian, a painting which would undergo more ample and controversial restoration in 1782. This restoration, and the one of the *Saint Barbara* by Palma Vecchio in Santa Maria Formosa, were so famous that as late as 1812, Edwards would use them as examples of successful restorations to whoever was critical of any repair to old paintings. In 1788 Bertani restored (under the supervision of Edwards) Veronese's *Family of Darius* in Casa Pisani in San Polo (the painting has been in the National Gallery of London since 1857), the restoration of which brought back to light the blue sky from beneath the yellowed varnishes, and for which he was paid 148*zecchini*.[19]

Pietro Edwards was himself a restorer: in 1776 he had worked on Veronese's roundel painted in tempera on *intonaco* on the ceiling of the Sala dell'Anticollegio, a painting which

---

ᵛ What today we consider measures of "preventive conservation".

had been damaged during previous restorations and of which nobody wanted to undertake the restoration, in which he secured the *intonaco* with metal staples; one of Veronese's least fortunate works, still today changed by the presence of darkened retouchings. In about 1777, the head of the eldest of the Magi was cut out and removed from Bonifacio Veronese's *Adoration of the Magi*, in the Ducal Palace (now in the Sala degli Stucchi): Edwards replaced it with another head which can all too clearly be seen now after successive restorations have revealed the whole. His son, Giovanni Edwards, passed on an unfounded story based on tradition only, when he told Mrs Merrifield that at the same time, the principal head in Titian's *Triumph of Faith* had also been replaced.

Pietro Edwards was born in Loreto ("by accident", we are told by Moschini), in 1744, into a Catholic family which had left England after the revolution of 1688. He was a pupil of Gasparo Diziani, and some of his devotional paintings (a *Sacred Heart*, a *San Luigi Gonzaga*) were disseminated through engravings. His son, Giovanni, seems almost to congratulate himself on the fact that all the various governments, before and after the fall of the Republic, had found in his father a consultant of undisputed seriousness and professional competence, useful to their politics of art. Since 1767 he had been a member of the Liberal Collegio di Pittura, and from 1775 of the Veneta Accademia; as well as being Director for the restoration of public paintings, he was also Secretary of the Liberal Collegio between 1778 and 1783, the year in which he resigned because of the "evil practices of those artists". In 1779 he was consulted over the project for a public gallery which would bring together all the best paintings in Venice, and the Inquisitori di Stato entrusted him with the examination of the paintings in various churches, although this was Mengardi's task. His activity within private collections is documented in the various inventories drawn up for the division of property.[20] With his availability as an expert, with the seriousness which is apparent in the reports documenting his work, it was not surprising that in the confusion surrounding the restoration of public paintings, the Riformatori dello Studio of Padua, after Bertani's resignation from work, should look to him for indications and suggestions to put some order in this activity. With the decree of the Senate of 3 September 1778, he was therefore entrusted with the organization of the restoration of all the public paintings, as well as the paintings in the Ducal Palace and the public offices of Rialto.

The financial and organizational aspects, as well as the regulations to be followed during restoration, were fixed in two contracts regulating the duties of the professors who executed the work, and the inspector who controlled them. No other professor could be added to the list, which consisted of Bertani, Giuseppe Diziani and Niccolò Baldassini, who were allowed four assistants, as well as being able to use the services of the inspector in his capacity as a restorer. Every substitution in the body of helpers could only take place with the consent of the authorities, and within the limits proscribed by the regulations. The three professors were under the supervision of the inspector, who had the power to remove any assistant that was not found to be equal to the task in hand. The duties of the professors were as follows:

"I) To repair the paintings put into their care without impairing their virgin state (to use the words of the professors), if they are untouched, that is not degraded either in the body nor the surface of the paint layer. II) To remedy all the damage caused to the painting by the lack of skill of other picture cleaners, but always within the limits of the possible, and refusing all charlatan deceptions. III) To solidly fix all the paint which is detaching, and about to be lost from its priming. IV) To flatten paintings on panel when these are warped, and to mend them when they are in any way split or broken, without that these mends should be then visible. V) To prevent the future infestation of old panels by woodworm, and to make good any such damage caused to the reverse of the panel. VI) To transfer just the painting – undamaged – from the old panel or canvas, onto another new panel or canvas, when it becomes clear that the old support is no longer restorable. VII) To line the paintings which are in need of lining, and to remove old linings from paintings which are prejudiced by the presence of old linings; in general to strengthen the support of each work according to its need. VIII) To remove aged smoke and dirt; crazed, yellowed and cracked (*sobbollite*) varnishes; stains of every sort; the filthiness of blackened oil layers on the surface; the countless and resistant insect droppings which can only be removed with the aid of a needle; and in general, to remove everything which impedes the free perception of the beauty of the paint layer (*colore*). IX) To remove all the non-original retouchings covering untouched paint, and to uncover it without causing damage to the original. X) To find once again the original appearance of all the colours which have altered when these alterations are not of the pigments themselves, as is the case with almost all the darks. XI) To put back all areas of lost paint without covering original paint, so that the repair should not be visible. XII) To repair (*risarcire*) areas which have been torn or lost such as heads, hands, draperies, etc., always imitating the style of the author. XIII) To give back the natural feel (*sapore*) of the painting, by returning to it the freshness lost through excessive aridity, and through all the other ills to which paintings are prone, to all of which – even if they have not all been enumerated in the present text – the professors must minister the possible remedies. XIV) And finally, they agree not to use materials on the paintings which cannot be removed at will by practitioners of the art."

The work was to be estimated dividing the paintings into three classes: at twenty, fourteen and eight lira per square foot. The measurements were to be taken in the middle of the sides, leaving aside any irregularaties of shape which might either augment or reduce the surface area of the painting. The professors had at their charge the expenses of collaboration, transport and materials, with the exception of new stretchers if these were needed, and the cost of eventual repairs to the "niches" of the paintings. If the restorations were not deemed successful, the expenses would be lost as well as payment, and there might be other personal penalties if "malice" were proved. The three restorers also renounced all other work, as they were guaranteed the monopoly of the restoration of public paintings.

First of all, the inspector had to draw up a written report of all the damage noted, and then to evaluate the restorations present on a painting, so as to avoid judgements by the professors, "either in the hiding of damage having completed the commission, or using palliative expedients that only superficially resolved the problem". He then had to allot individual paintings to one of three classes:

"*First class*, or paintings in extreme need [of attention]: major paint loss and in the noble parts of the work. Non-acceptable restorations over most of the painting. Powdery paint, vulnerable, and falling away in most of the painting. Both drying cracks (*sobbolimento*) and darkening in the majority of the painting. *Second class*, or paintings gravely in need of attention: to this class belong works which have the above deterioration but to a lesser degree. *Third class*, or paintings in lesser need of attention: paintings which are simply dirty, with a paint layer which can be fixed simply with pressure from the reverse, and which do not show to any great degree the deterioration and damage noted in paintings in the first and second class."

The transfer of a painting onto a new support implied that the painting belonged to the first class; during the procedure the inspector had to ensure that any damage which was only discovered during the restoration was not overlooked. As far as the restoration itself was concerned he had to guarantee the following:

"I) That in order to speed up the work, corrosive substances were not used which might endanger the untouched quality of the painting and corrode the paint layer. II) That the consolidation of flaking paint is carried out before passing onto other arduous operations, and that this fixing is stable and solid, and should it not be successful in the first instance, that the operation be repeated until [such is the case]. III) That lining is not omitted in order to avoid the expense of a costly new canvas, and that this should always be of a finer weave than the original, otherwise they do not bond well together. IV) That one does not omit to carry out the transfer of the painting onto another support when it already belongs to the first class because of other damage, and if such a procedure is deemed necessary. V) That one does not neglect to remove all the dirt and the varnishes from a painting when this operation is not in any way dangerous, or there is no reason not to do so, as at times does happen. VI) That old retouchings are not left in the places where they have altered in colour, and where there is some hope of uncovering original paint. VII) That in applying the necessary retouchings, one never goes beyond the margins of the damage (*corrosioni*), either from a lack of diligence or through a desire to speed up the lengthy operation. VIII) That no professor, even with the good intention of improving on the original, remove anything of the original, nor add anything of his own; nor should he remove or add inscriptions. IX) That all the mechanical operations be executed with every possible diligence, and therefore that the linings, pressings, stretching, filling, and every other such intervention, as the success and longevity of the restoration, also depend heavily on these material aspects. This also means that the season in which the work is carried out will influence the result, as will the style and practical technique of the artist being restored, as well as the site in which the painting will be hung. X) Finally, he will make observations on all aspects which deserve reflection, and will require the professors to do the same, offering them advice without however falling into odious pedantry."

In addition, there were the policing aspects of the inspector's job: to see to it that the restorers did not take the works home with them, that when it was dark they only worked on "manual things", that nobody made copies of works under restoration or that strangers had the keys to the laboratory. In addition he had to check on the skills of the assistants, and ensure that they were only employed on the most basic tasks. And finally, he had to present the report of the work which had been carried out and evaluate it according to the pre-established method, organizing the division and continuous efficiency of the restoration, so that the Provveditori al Sal were not bothered by "trifling quarrels". The inspector did not share in the benefits of the professors (except for when he actually collaborated in the work), but he was remunerated with a fixed sum for every painting, four lire per square foot.[21]

In 1785, Edwards presented a report of the work carried out up to that date, detailing the price, the works restored, those excluded from restoration and those still awaiting it.

Reports dating from 1778 to 1785, addressed to the Provveditori al Sal, detailing estimates or treatments carried out, are easily accessible. The first report, which is particularly detailed in its description of all the damage observed, refers to Veronese's ceiling in the Sala della Bussola:

> "The large painting in the centre represents Saint Mark in glory with the three theological virtues in the lower section of the painting. Almost half of the surface of this painting has been foully repainted in oil by a reckless, and also unskilled, hand, and the repaints are not confined to areas where the paint was missing, but also cover areas of original paint. So that for a loss which was no bigger in circumference than a bean, one often finds an area spanning a hand's width, smeared in this manner. The greater part of this clumsy repainting is also not at the same depth as the original paint, the whole surface of the painting appearing uneven, rugged and deformed, so that even the most inexperienced eye can judge of the appalling condition of the work. To demonstrate the extreme ignorance of those who laid their hands on this work in the past, and the extreme diligence required to restore it (*ripristinarla*), it suffices to say that having noticed an extreme clumsiness in the design of an angel reclining to the right of the saint, I immediately had the repaint removed to try and establish who was responsible for such an unpardonable error, and to my surprise as well as that of the worthy operators, we discovered that a thigh and leg had been added, pure invention [on the part of the restorer]. The original paint as well as a large part of the repaint are no longer attached to the ground (*fondo*), and are coming away from the support; and a good part of what one terms glazes (*svelature*), the final ephemeral touches of the master, were grazed (*sfiorate*) during the clumsy cleaning with corrosive substances, which scraped away (*raschiarono*) the brightness of the colour and upset the harmony of the work; this can be seen particularly clearly in the little putto holding up the book for the Evangelists, and in the other two angels to the right of the saint. On the reverse of the canvas, there are two patches detached from the canvas, which may have occurred as the result of a defect in the nature of the glues used in the process. The original canvas of the painting was also damaged by rain falling on areas which had not been lined, but the damage is not extensive."

In addition to the central canvas, which was to be requisitioned by the French and can be seen today in the Louvre, there were also the monochromes and the surrounding decorative canvases:

> "The painting described above is surrounded by eighteen other canvases all painted in *chiaroscuro* of various tints. The two largest pieces represent symbolic figures of Victory, and their condition reflects in every aspect that of the aforementioned painting, except that the repainting is even more free, not to say fearless, and the paint has not come away from the support. Then there are two oblong monochromes, painted in a very restrained tonality, representing the triumphal entry of one of the emperors: imaginary scenes painted to appear as Roman bas-reliefs. These two works do not seem to be entirely by the hand of Veronese, although this may be because they have been distorted by the choices taken by the restorer during cleaning, which have altered the appearance to the extent that one can no longer clearly distinguish the hand; but of this we will be able to judge better during progress of the work. As well as the aforementioned

101. Paolo Veronese, Saint Mark
and the Theological Virtues;
restored under the direction of
Pietro Edwards, 1778–1779.
Paris, Musée du Louvre, from
the Sala della Bussola in the
Ducal Palace, Venice.

distortion of the brushwork (*pennello*), it also seems that in these two works three or four small figures have been entirely lost from the canvas.   10

A third, small *chiaroscuro* is in similar condition: in it we see the figure of an emperor seated on a throne, with a group of warriors in conversation with a few old men wearing togas, without being able to recognize any elements referring to a particular story. However, one should note that all *chiaroscuri* described, and the others which accompany them, all allude to the siege and capture of Brescia, and that the artist treated the subject without any observation of dress or customs, as is indeed the case on other occasions. The three small oblong canvases of similar size, and similar subject matter to those described above, are in a better state of preservation, and their principal defect lies in the natural darkening of the tints and also, maybe, in the use of a little artificial patina which we suspect was applied to all, in order to hide the damage done to some through injudicious cleaning.

Four smaller paintings represent resounding fame. They are painted in a *chiaroscuro* with high contrast, as though imitation stucco work, and their most serious injury lies in having been overly cleaned and appearing blanched (*biancastri*). They were also particularly disfigured (*imbrattati*) by flies, more so than any other canvas on the ceiling, which may be due to their having had a varnish applied after cleaning which contained ingredients particularly attractive to flies; and as the paint is very thin in these little works, as indeed it is in the other *chiaroscuri*, so the action of the liquid deposited by the flies – always rather corrosive – has eaten through the very thin layer of paint through to the canvas.

There remain six little pictures wonderfully painted with the heads of six lions in a yellowish hue, and as luck would have it, the person who laid hands on the other paintings which I have been describing, somehow forgot these little works and they escaped the devastation which, to my great chagrin, I will have on many occasions have to report to your Excellencies, unpleasant things which the duties of my office cannot dispense me from relating. In doing so, the shortcomings of past methods will show themselves always more clearly: the ignorance, and the exclusive control of the person who carried out the work and he who approved the operations, as well as the importance and the usefulness of our present caution."

Having described the state of the canvases, Edwards went on to give the estimates for the work which needed to be carried out: "Having described the state of the above paintings, I must also share with your Excellencies the information relating to the restorations which must unfailingly be carried out, so that by using these details to compare with the work of the restorers, one will be able to form a judgement as to the reasonableness or imperfection of the work. *First*: the paint layer in the first three paintings must, on completion of the work, be stable, fixed and solid as though they were new paintings. *Second*: the three aforementioned paintings must be lined in their entirety, and not just with patches as at present. *Third*: all the repaint must be removed whether it covers losses or original paint, because in both cases they have been applied badly, not only in their handling, but also in the medium used to bind it, which has now darkened and turned yellow. *Fourth*: the fourth, fifth and sixth paintings require the aforementioned diligent – and essential – interventions mentioned above. So that these do not become the fruit of individual judgements (*arbitri*), I think it is necessary to detail some of the areas which require intervention most urgently.

102. *a, b. Paolo Veronese,*
monochromes, details;
restored under the direction
of Pietro Edwards, 1779.
Venice, Ducal Palace,
Sala della Bussola.

They are as follows: in the central portion of the ceiling, all of the glory behind the figure of Saint Mark, almost all the clouds in the painting (in which at present all one sees is confusion and clumsiness without distinction in the brushwork nor in the lights, and under which most of the original, untouched paint is still present), the head, left shoulder, both arms and both hands of the figure of the saint, the aforementioned angel reclining to the right of the saint as well as a further angel in that same section, a third unclothed angel seen from behind supporting the saint, the profile and the shoulder of the figure of Charity, an arm of the figure of Hope and the veil of the one symbolizing Faith. In addition to these important sites, there are also a great number of other repaints to be removed, as well as many others to be replaced which I will not go into detail so as not to make this report even longer than it is already. Suffice it to say that in the figures of the two Victories it is no longer possible to say which is the most damaged area; in one of the Triumphs, all the outlines of the small figures have been altered and that in the sixth painting, there is a band the length of the painting, three fingers wide, which goes from one end of the painting to the other, which requires to be completely cleaned of its overpaint. *Fifth*: the four little figures in the paintings representing the Triumph have to be put back in the style of the artist so as not to lose the rest of the work. *Sixth*: it is almost superfluous to have to speak of the soot, the patination, the blotches which will have to be removed from these paintings, as it is clear that the intervention must include these operations. Rather, I will make a point of mentioning that as these paintings were overcleaned in the past, except for the lion-heads, and that the *chiaroscuri* were painted very thinly, and – as one says – *alla prima* (that is, without preliminary blocking in (*abbozzo*), one must not expect that the highlights will become much lighter, not that certain areas of the paintings will alter significantly especially in the case of the *chiaroscuri*. In these paintings, it would not be possible to entirely clean away the smoke and the natural and artificial patinas, which have insinuated themselves within the thin surface of the paint, without disturbing and dissolving the original paint and doing it some injury: and anyone who maintains the contrary is a fraud. Instead, one will have to remove the upper and external part of these accretions, leaving, so to speak, a very thin layer of the oldest, and it is in this which lies the great difficulty, and the skill, of the work. *Seventh*: the irregular and scaly surface of the paintings must be reduced to perfect uniformity, particularly in the case of the first three paintings. *Eighth*: similarly the irregularities of gloss and absorbency which depend on the difference of the underlayer, now a fill, or canvas, original paint or overpaint, must be entirely removed, and must appear with uniformity of liveliness and zest (*sugo e sapore*) in the whole of the work".

Such detailed reports give an idea of the criteria followed by the restoration studio under Edwards' direction, as well as the care taken by him in the examination of the works of which he undertook the restoration.[22]

3. The laboratory at Santi Giovanni e Paolo

The restorations directed by Edwards were rarely the first to be carried out on paintings from the Ducal Palace or those of Rialto, and seldom were they not subjected to further interventions which, at times, make one regret the wisdom of eighteenth-century practitioners. At the end of the Republic, in 1797, work was still being carried out on a few of the paintings from the Ducal Palace; as early as 1793, further work had been deemed necessary

on certain paintings from the Magistrato del Sal which had already been restored in 1779. Some of the work undertaken by Edwards must certainly have been revised in Paris after the requisitions of 1798, and many others during the Kingdom of Italy, in the adaptations which the paintings had to undergo in order to fit the new Royal palace, or the villa di Strà, or when removed to the new picture galleries at the Accademia in Venice, or Brera in Milan. Many of the works by Bonifacio from the Rialto were reframed at that time.[23] Certain of the paintings remained in the state in which they had been left after the eighteenth-century restoration, until the time in which one was able to photograph them.[24] Finally, other interventions date to the last years, and often the cleaning has only revealed the pitiful condition which Pietro Edwards had in part masked through partial cleaning, glazing and retouching. In the case of other paintings, although we are not absolutely sure that they have not been restored   103
at least superficially since, they are still in a condition close to that in which they were left after the eighteenth-century restoration: in particular, amongst the works by Bonifacio, the *Dispute with the Doctors*, which now hangs in Palazzo Pitti in Florence, where it arrived as an exchange after the Restoration. It shows very clearly the results of a varnish treatment, adapted to accompany, and with time to accentuate, the natural yellowing of oil, but with   104
transparent materials which would not render the painting opaque.

Amongst the paintings which best illustrate Edwards' criteria is the canvas by Andrea Busati, which is now in the deposits of the Accademia, which was taken for restoration from the Magistrato delle Ragion Vecchie in 1783. On completion of the restoration, Edwards made the following observations: "The painting by Busati awakens the pride of one of the professors in particular, who worked on it more than the others, and that was Signor Diziani. Over and above the cleaning and the new cohesion introduced into the paint which had been crumbling away in tiny particles, I beg your Excellencies to examine in particular the sky, of which entire areas were missing, the tree behind Saint Francis of which only the tips of some of the branches remained apart from the outline engraved in the gesso ground, and the greater part of the habit of the saint which was also only known from the outline in the ground. I would happily invite the most severe critics to try and find in what way the restored areas differ from the original ones, and how one could have made this picture more beautiful, more delectable (*saporito*) and closer in condition to a new and freshly painted work."

The eighteenth-century restoration is indeed evident not only in the tree behind Saint Francis, but also (alongside areas which are clearly original such as the sphinxes on the back of Saint Mark's throne) in a large proportion of the landscape with the city towers reflect-   105
ing in the water, which allows one to follow Diziani's brush which interprets Renaissance painting with paint made with varnish.

Tintoretto's *Madonna dei Tesorieri* was restored in 1780; of this work, which is one of the most sober of the opus of this sixteenth-century master (and one of the works in which the colours have remained most in harmony), the final report observed:
> "The depth of darkness, the drying out of the paint (*prosciugamento*), and the dust which has almost become one with the painting, do not allow me to judge whether or not this work has been restored in the past. The gravest visible injury is the loss of paint in many areas, and principally in the draperies; nevertheless, I like to think that this work will be astonishing, and all the more so, as in a certain way, it will be rediscovered afresh. There is a black drapery which should go back to being green, and another one – also black – which should become a deep purplish-red (*pavonazzo*). Of the latter, however, I cannot yet give the go-ahead to

103. Bonifacio Veronese,
Dispute with the Doctors;
restored under the direction of
Pietro Edwards. Florence,
Galleria Palatina, from the
Palazzo dei Camerlenghi di
Rialto, Venice.

104. Andrea Busati, Saint
Mark between Saint Andrew
and Saint Francis, detail; with
integrations by Giuseppe
Diziani, 1783. Venice, Gallerie
dell'Accademia, deposits.

105. *Jacopo Tintoretto, La Madonna dei Tesorieri; restored under the direction of Pietro Edwards, 1780. Venice, Gallerie dell'Accademia.*

the practitioners, as we have not yet established whether this colour is painted in body-colour or with glazes."

Few paintings have reached us in better condition than Veronese's large canvas painted to celebrate the battle of Lepanto in the Sala del Collegio, and the two figures – white statues in pink niches – which flank it; it is a painting which, even with the slight yellowing of the varnish, would seem to show us the best possible state in which to present his paintings. In the report accompanying the estimate of the work required on the painting, Edwards observed:

"The hand of unskilled restorers did not play a part in the damage suffered by these paintings, or maybe only with the solution (*lavacro*) that has rubbed some of the tints a little in the background. For the rest of the painting, the damage one encounters is due to the passage of time, and to the incredible thinness of the paint layer (*colorito*) used by the master in these paintings. The thinness of the paint, as well as having given easy access to the activity of the surrounding air, and to the introduction of smoke and the absorption of the minute particles of dust which have become part of the painting, makes the retrieval of such paintings exceptionally difficult. At the end of the restoration, in order to judge the skill (*intelligenza*) of the professors, one will have to study whether or not the glazes, the half-tones, the full-bodied paint (*pasta*) in the flesh-painting, the sweetenings (*sfumature*) with the brush which those in the art world call rubbings (*sfregazzi*), and generally all those final touches of the work, have in any way suffered from the cleaning and the other operations which are directed to recapture the beauty (*vaghezza*) of these three divine paintings. One will have to leave out of this examination the background of the large canvas, as well as the head of the principal page, because it would seem that in these areas some damage has already occurred at the hands of others. If the restoration of these paintings is perfectly successful, which I have every reason to believe, this will serve as one of the best

pieces of evidence to demonstrate the singular skill of the people who are destined to this enterprise, and of the great utility of their art when it is practised with
good judgement. There are other less important points to make with reference to
these works, but I will confine myself to the necessity of lining the large canvas
although it is at present in an excellent state of preservation. This may seem paradoxical, but it is something which I will continue to justify whenever asked."

Of the restoration in 1779 of Tintoretto's great canvas representing *The Presentation of
Doge Mocenigo* in the Redentore, Edwards had the following reflections: "the original work
was repainted at least three times, and three times it was thought that the original paint
layer applied by the artist had been discovered beneath this triple layer of restoration which
covered the entire painting. The superimposition of all these layers of paint had resulted in
such an overall darkening of the whole, that for several days, even after the removal of the
filth from the smoke and other superficial accretions, one still could not fully understand
the distribution of the figures, the colour of the draperies nor the intention of the master.
Over and above the difficulty of always working in this perilous darkness, with the constant
fear of making a mistake, one also had to overcome the problems caused by the extreme
cracking (*sobbollitura*) of the original colour, the surface of which was completely uneven,
rough, bumpy, covered in minute breaks so that the new paint from the restoration had
tenaciously introduced itself and taken hold in these irregular sinuousities, and it seemed
almost impossible to extract it without completely ruining the painting from top to bottom.
Nevertheless, we succeeded in cleaning it from these filthy additions, and the original coun-
tenance of the painting was revealed as was also the reason that had induced restorers in the
past to lay hands on it: and one must confess, that even at that time the painting was in the
most appalling condition .... I will not try to put about that the practitioners have magically
and wholly created even those parts which no longer existed on the canvas, but I will say
that the many substitutions which were required seem to me to be entirely reasonable, and
executed in a manner that would have pleased the artist himself. Similar praise is merited by
the other elements of this laborious task, the progress of which has entailed such detailed
work and so many repeated and burdensome applications, exercising such artful precautions, so much mechanical handiwork and such an exercise of learning, that a full account
would be an abuse of Your Excellencies' tolerance."

Of the works restored in the eighteenth century of which we now have only photographic evidence, Giovanni Bellini's *Deposition* in the Ducal Palace was brought back to its   106
fifteenth-century format by Pellicioli in 1948. Edwards wanted to avoid its restoration, and
in 1783 he observed: "In this restoration, it will be the case of working both on the addition
and the original. The former was executed by a mannered and completely unskilled painter,
whilst the former is in Giovanni Bellini's driest manner. How can one possibly imagine that
one can clean this work, and bring it back to life whilst keeping the immense distance
between the two manners hidden? While the smoke, the stains, the blackness and the pre-
conceptions of the public made one look at this painting with veneration, its deformities
remained hidden, but once the cleaning has removed the confusion, one will notice the vul-
garity of the addition, and one will think it the result of our work. Moreover, it should be
added that the original part is so rubbed and worn that the artist's outlines in the shadows
can barely be seen, and consist only of the darkened ground layer".[25]

The "chapters" relating to the duties of the inspector and of the restorers never give
any details of the actual methods to be used during the restoration, to the extent of not even

106. Giovanni Bellini,
Deposition; with the enlarge-
ment and the repaintings of
1571, restored under the direc-
tion of Pietro Edwards, 1783.
Venice, Doge's Palace.

mentioning that the retouching and integration [of missing parts] were carried out in varnish colours. It is true today also that the majority of restorations take place in more or less accepted secrecy, so it is not surprising that the restorers employed by the Venetian state did not divulge their methods. Without attempting to identify the various mentions of methods of restoration which one finds in Edwards' writings or in texts relating to him with the methods followed in the restoration of public pictures, one can nevertheless draw from these a fairly exhaustive picture, if not of the nature of the materials used, at least of the criteria followed in their use.

Mrs Merrifield would recall how for lining, the paint layer would be protected with a facing of paper and flour paste, and the canvas stretched onto a "terraced" floor; the lining would be applied with a mixture of flour paste, Flanders glue and ox gall, and attached not using hot irons but (using the old method) with hot sand which was poured onto the reverse of the canvas, beginning in the centre to a certain thickness, so that by eliminating air bubbles, the painting would in the end remain under equal heat and pressure. The Busati in the Accademia in Venice enables one to examine a lining carried out in 1783.

As was mentioned in the report relating to the large canvas by Veronese in the Sala del Collegio, these restorers were quite clear that lining served not only to consolidate the old canvas, and to fix the paint to it: referring to the large canvas by Leandro Bassano in the Sala del Consiglio dei Dieci, Edwards remarked that a new lining was necessary "in order to keep in hand the overall cracking which because of the thickness and hardness of the paint, and the deformations from the creases in the canvas, could not be durably and correctly flattened without this aid". In 1787, he hoped by lining to "preserve the vivacity of the faded colours (*smontato colorito*)" of Titian's *Descent of the Holy Spirit* in the Salute.[26]

Restoration work also included the transfer of works from panel and from canvas, an intervention which Edwards always tried to avoid in order to also preserve "the external characteristics of the original". It is because of this that he observed, referring to a little Madonna attributed to Raphael in the Sala dei Capi del Consiglio dei Dieci with a split panel, that it would be an easy solution to transfer it onto a new support, but that he would do what was necessary to find some other method of restoring it. Three tondos by Veronese in the ceiling of the Library had suffered through humidity and, in a report dated 4 June 1784, their transfer onto a new support was envisaged, should the lining not prove sufficient. In the summer of 1971, I was able to confirm that this operation had only been carried out in the case of *Song*, in which one can see signs of the weave of the new canvas, whilst the tondo representing *Honour*, although it had a huge restoration in its centre and a large tear, was indeed left on its original support.[27]

The answer to the question put to him by the architect Giannantonio Selva on the manner of cleaning oil paintings ["which are on the whole in good condition and one simply wished to clean them superficially with some simple and universal solution (*'lavacro'*)"], without giving the details of any secrets or complex procedures, is a good illustration of the conclusions on cleaning methods, which Edwards had reached by 1802:

"If the paintings are essentially in good condition, as is maintained, then one should not try to improve their condition with the use of any universal cleaning solution (*lavacro generale*), neither simple nor mixed, neither weak nor strong. The cleaning of paintings is an absolutely essential part of the highly complex art of their restoration, and indeed can only be really carried out only when the painting is in good condition. But this cleaning has nothing in common with that blessèd idea of a universal cleaning fluid, which is suggested by a lack of knowledge and experience. Applications of even pure cold water, over the whole area of the painting, especially if this is extensive, are seldom without bad consequences, whilst the improvement in the appearance of the work is minimal. With the exception of those works which are covered with a filthy but uncracked varnish, which in the ordinary run of things only happens in very small works, it is extremely rare that one can employ a universal cleaning fluid without diversification according to the various requirements that one has unearthed in different areas of any one painting. The principle which lies behind these variations is not dependent purely on the different techniques (*meccanismi*) employed by the artist in different areas of his work, nor on the variety of distinct effects that are caused by time (and the many different accidents which can have acted unequally in one and the same painting), but does depend strongly on the theoretical knowledge and the individual genius which have guided the thought and imagination of the artist himself in the unfolding of his work. There are few professors who possess all these sources of enlightenment to the required degree, but it is always preferable to opt for the more experienced than the most learned."

The cleaning methods to which Edwards then refers explicitly consist in applying a layer of egg-white onto a paint surface previously washed with water, and then to leave it for three or four days before proceeding to remove it with either warm water or milk, or with white wine where the egg-white might prove difficult to remove. One should only have recourse to the use of alcohol or soap "with great care". In the 1789 report on the canvases in the Sala del Maggior Consiglio, he observed that "because of the excessive blackness of some of the masses, and the dark tones of many of the others, one was not able to leave in all their beauty those several areas which were unaltered; thus, having cleaned such a huge painting with immense inexpressible difficulty, we had to leave several areas undercleaned, so as not to lose the most prized excellence (*pregio*) relating to the union of colours, that is their harmony. I do wish to speak of this at the end of the report, but as I have had to mention it at this juncture, I shall continue on the same subject: if the paintings of Francesco Bassano and those by Tintoretto could be seen in the disharmonious state in which they would find themselves if not cleaned in the fashion indicated above, they would excite the contempt (*dispetto*) of even the most mediocre connoisseur, even if during the cleaning, the original paint of the artist had rigorously been preserved with the greatest scruple."

Some of the observations on the risks of cleaning paintings have certainly not lost any of their relevance; cleaning is difficult "with regards to the overall harmony of the work, and the effects of foreground and background, the surface nature of the half-tints, the final glazes and localized strengthenings, especially in the heads of paintings of the Venetian or Lombard schools in the works of which the light, tiny touches are difficult to distinguish from external accretions. This is a crucial point as is the thinness of the paint, which in the practice of several artists only thinly covers the initial rough sketch (*abbozzo*)".

Moreover, "the masses of some of the strongest shadows as well as those of certain draperies which hardly contain any lead white in the paint mixture, in these old paintings will darken because of their nature, nor is there any hope of reviving them through cleaning, with the exception of some metal-based pigments which have corroded (*ossidato*) over the years. The liquids and the varnishes used in the restoration of these kinds of paintings, rather than reducing the darkness of those shadows, in fact increase their force. Therefore, if the practitioner begins and continues the operation cleaning the highlights and then the half-tints, cleaning them as one might say until they look freshly painted, the final result will be a severe loss of balance between the highlights which will appear exceedingly shrill and the deep shadows, without any intermediate gradation in tone. This can result in the necessity of weakening with so-called artificial *patinas* the most brilliant and conspicuous parts of the painting, and sweetening with opaque scumbles (*colori di corpo*) the harsh juncture between the shadows and the highlights, all of which are contrivances with unhappy results, to be used only when time has effectively corroded the surface of the painting in the lightest parts of the work".[28]

After retouching with varnish colours, the painting would be varnished in order to protect it, but also with a view to treating it with a material which, with its transparency and its yellowing with the passage of time, would accompany well the original characteristics of oil, but without the drawback of darkening.[29]

4. Considerations on the restoration of paintings

To the general report on the work carried out up to 1785 was attached a "Preliminary discussion for the conservation plan to be put in place for the possible preservation and the improved maintenance of public paintings" (*Dissertazione preliminare al piano di custodia da istituirsi per la possible preservazione e per il miglior mantenimento delle pubbliche pitture*). In this document, Edwards put forward his ideas on the behaviour of oil paintings and on the possibility of being able to slow down the deterioration process, and a dissertation to which it was to serve as an introduction: the "Practical plan for the general conservation of public paintings" (*Piano pratico per la general custodia delle pubbliche pitture*), in which he examined the necessary precautions to be taken for the good conservation of the paintings, for the elimination of infiltrations of humidity and water vapour and other incidents which might prove damaging, a complete and admirable programme for the maintenance of paintings and their environment.

From a position which considered time not as the cause of the ruin of paintings, but rather "a measure of the duration of the destructive action, no less than of that which preserves them", the *Dissertation* pondered the possible causes of the deterioration of paintings: in the case of Venice in particular, the climate full of "humid vapours" and "the wealth of salts in solution" which insinuated themselves into the porous fabric of the painting, corroding both the paint and the support.[30] The "seeds of decay" were hidden in the very "physical make-up" of the paintings executed in oil, the binding medium of which was responsible for the darkening of the colours and the loss of the mid-tones ("[neither of] which is found to be as fatal in any of the tempera binders[vi] nor in fresco") and to which can be imputed the "excessive desiccation, the loss of cohesion between the particles in the mixture, the rigidity of the painting, which almost acquires the characteristics of slate and can flake away in countless fractions; to the action of oil is also ascribed the coagulation (*rappigliamento*) of certain colours which then separate out into distinct globules, dark and very hard; a serious and insurmountable deterioration, known to artists by the term of "*sobbolimento*".[vii]

After the rapid evaporation of the oil, there only remained the "sediment which is incapable of subliming, which the chemists term *terra infiammabile* (inflammable earth)", and such are the alterations of the materials in the paint that chemical analysis finds elements present, such as sulphur, which were unquestionably absent when it was originally employed:

> "Amongst the intrinsic causes [of deterioration] which can be ascribed to errors on the part of the artist, some – if truth be told – can be radically removed by the means of ingenious discoveries; but this is only possible in a few cases, although they occur frequently and are very important, they only concern the support, the grounds and the original varnishes of the paintings, and involve the principal substance of the paint to a much lesser degree. How to increase the thickness of the paint layers in a painting? How can you extract from between the thinnest

---

[vi] *Tempera* in the general sense of the term means the binding medium, as in "tempered with". In this more restricted context, it refers to any of the media which uses water as their diluent, and are protein based: that is, egg-tempera, glue-size, casein. (See Glossary.)

[vii] There is no single term that corresponds to *sobbollimento*, which in Italian is highly descriptive, with evocations of bubbling paint; associated with tarry organic substances which dry with difficulty or not at all, resulting in the shrinkage of the paint, cracking, and a paint surface that is rough, bumpy and unpleasing to the eye.

layers that which keeps them apart and subdivided? How to reduce the unequal porosity of the mass to the uniform consistency of a body of paint fused together all at one time? How to change into something solid and resistant, the light and evanescent nature of the glazes? What means can be used to separate out from the mixture, specific unsuitable ingredients out of which it was composed? And with what secret solution will one disentangle the combination of materials which should have been used separately or in a different combination? Practically speaking, these are all complete impossibilities, however one might wish to boast to the contrary, abusing others' lack of skill or through the obstinacy of one's own ignorance. In almost the same way, one must reason in relation to the natural defects of the art. Oil painting remains painting in oil, before and after the poorly reasoned, puerile, and damaging operations put about by impostors: there is no power or skill which can ever extract from paint over two-hundred years old the solid and blackened part of the binder which has not been able to evaporate. The lead, copper and the mercury will continue to be subject to degradation however much the practitioners work on them: the alteration in these bodies which occurs frequently, especially in the case of lead, can take place repeatedly. Only with the greatest limitations should one think that some hues (and especially metallic greens which blacken through the excessive acid which combines to make a sulphurous compound with the oil), which at one time were brought back through the use of a suitable mixture of alkalis, are in any way improved durably in their condition. I am not asserting as an absolute that never, in no manner and to no degree can one ever decrease the strength of the inner agents; or to put it another way, that one can ever temper the bad characteristics of the paint. I know how far one can go with art, and I would willingly stop and discuss the distinctions put forward here in this brief report on the art of restoring: but there is too much left to say. I nevertheless maintain that you can never entirely alter the inherent defects of the mixture, and that the possible advantages one might draw from any such attempt are always limited in the extreme."

It is only through limiting the contact of the painting with air that one can hope to avoid these irreversible alterations, as one can easily verify in sections of paintings which have remained for long periods in close contact with their frames, where the colours have remained fresh and have not cracked. And it is in order to isolate paintings from the air that one has always resorted to the use of varnish, a method which can never give good results:

"Of the three kinds of varnish known today, spirit, oil-based (*crasse*) and mixed ones in which the drying oils are bound with volatile substances (*essenze*), there is not one which remains supple retaining a complete flexibility after it has dried: rather, the perfection of an optimal varnish requires it to harden and become as rigid as glass. One looks to this hardness as necessary requirement for its incorruptibility; if the most incorruptible varnish is also the hardest, it is this which makes the best varnishes completely unsuitable for our paintings on canvas, especially the very large ones. There is no way of controlling the movement in the canvas from the deformations, the contractions and expansions to which they are subject, the changes occurring in the stretchers and the supports, nor the necessity of their all too frequent removal, all of which can lead to the grinding down of this thin surface layer, which in breaking up brings away with it the paint, disfigures the work and causes the loss of the object one was defending …

The hardness produces a first reflection from the exterior surface, and its transparency allows the light to pass through and be refracted back; this means that the reflected and the refracted rays come back at different angles, which is at the root of the unwelcome confusion caused by the annoying resplendence (*tralucimento*) one finds in paintings, especially in those larger than so-called "cabinet pictures". If the varnish layer is very thin, then it does not fulfil its preserving function; if it is thick, then it embeds the painting as though in a crystal, and removes its natural grace and that bloom of beauty which enchants [the eye]. If it is a spirit varnish,[viii] it will crack more on a painting than when applied onto other bodies as experience shows, and is weak and insubstantial: if it is oil based,[ix] the painting will appear greasy and somehow muddied, the varnish always lacking a little in transparency, and it cannot be removed from the painting without removing the paint along with it; if it is of a mixed nature, it will remain soft or porous, and will also darken colours. All of them will also darken to some degree over a period of time, and for these reasons and many others, they were all excluded from use by good practitioners, and must remain so, as Watin notes in his book on varnishes. Occasionally, some particular disposition in a painting might make the use of either the second or the third type less improper, and there will no doubt be those who pretend to be in possession of secret ingredients that ensure against cracking or yellowing or something else besides. But there is no secret ingredient that can remove the consequences of rigidity, the darkening of colours, the forced and displeasing tone which varnish gives a painting nor the discomfort of its glare (*baglior della luce*).

It is out of place to put forward the practice of Flemish painters who varnished almost all of their little paintings. Those who speak of this do not realize that the *vernice commune* of these painters is only called varnish (*vernice*) because there is no technical term to describe this liquid by any specific name, just as one terms "varnish", that mixture used by our restorers which is similar to that employed by the Flemish painters, which is made up of oil of spike (*essenza di spico*) in which are dissolved some extremely soft resin gums, which are incapable of giving that solidity which is required in real varnishes; and when they give it increased tenacity by the addition of condensed oils, one is immediately aware of it through the darkening, or the yellow tint which the colours acquire,

---

[viii] A spirit varnish consists of a resin, traditionally mastic or dammar, although synthetic resin is also used nowadays, which is dissolved in a solvent (a "spirit"). Applied to a painting it will form a film through the evaporation of the solvent, and although it will change chemically over time (yellowing and becoming brittle or sometimes opaque to varying degrees according to its nature), its solubility will always be different from that of the underlying paint, with the proviso that no varnish was included in the paint by the artist, and therefore removable.

[ix] An oil varnish is made up of a "hard" resin such as one of the fossil resins (amber, copal) which will not dissolve in a spirit (solvent) but will dissolve in hot oil. They give a tough, highly coloured film which will darken greatly with time, and "dries" in the same way as the oil paint, by polymerization, requiring alkalis to break it down. In cleaning the danger is obvious: you are removing oil from oil, like cleaning a watercolour with water. Sometimes a proportion of oil was added to spirit varnishes to make them tougher.

quite apart from the great difficulty of removing it from the painting without causing damage …".

If restoration cannot give paintings the solidity and incorruptibility which they did not have even when they were created, nevertheless "it is not the ghostly creation of an over-heated imagination, but an incontrovertible fact known by all, that old paintings which have darkened to the extent that you can no longer recognize the subject matter, can be seen to be born afresh after they have been restored. And it is equally obvious and visible that colours which appear chilled (*assiderati*), broken up (*infranti*), having lost their binder (*slegati*) and flaking away, are brought back to a condition of stability and solidity through restoration. In these two operations which can in no way be contradicted by anyone who has eyes to see and hands to touch, is undoubtedly contained the essence of what one is trying to save in a painting: appearance and substance. And to these two principal objectives are also directed all the other processes in restoration which one might term accessory, the usefulness of which cannot be denied, and which have been demonstrated materially. Who cannot recognize that, by transferring the painting from a rotting canvas or from a worm-eaten panel full of salt deposits to a new suitably prepared support, one is insuring the painting from imminent destruction? Is there really the need for a long academic discussion in order to prove that a painting will increase in its longevity, and its condition will be improved, if one doubles up[x] the canvas on which it is painted? Or if one changes the old lining which is no longer keeping out the action of the salts which continuously attack it from the walls? Or if one straightens out the damaging creases in the surface of the painting? Or if one removes a varnish which has begun to yellow, to crack (*sobbollire*) and break up?"

That is, the "essence" of restoration is to "remedy the effects, not overcome the causes". Every now and then, it will again be necessary to restore the paintings when they have incurred damage, although the operations necessary will not be as long and (time-)consuming as those which were necessary in the first real restoration which was carried out on the public paintings.[31]

From these premises, one can understand the process by which Edwards would choose the paintings to be excluded from restoration. In the 1786 introduction to the general summary, he detailed the circumstances which determined whether or not restoration should be undertaken: "in the belief that the general restoration of public paintings was principally directed to the end of preserving these works inasmuch as they are to be considered as objects of intrinsic merit, and not because they are simply painted canvases …. I decided that restorations should be undertaken only on works that at least showed some degree of merit which could be considered of interest to public institutions. Convinced by this argument, I began to leave out in all the rooms seen until now, a great number of canvases not deserving, in my opinion, to be considered for restoration, and this was the rule I followed in making these exclusions. I felt that the public paintings could be separated into four categories. A few that have no real need of attention, and these – although few in number – are naturally excluded from the commission. Others, at the other extreme, have perished to such a degree that they are unrestorable; and the paintings belonging to this category, although not many, were also excluded because only with empty words could one promise their restoration. A third and more numerous order is that of the paintings which could be repaired, but which in the end are not worth the expense of the undertaking, considering their trivial merit; and these I excluded,

---

[x] Provides a lining.

considering them to be outside the objectives of the *Sovrana Risoluzione* (Royal Resolution). Finally, the fourth category of works, in which alongside the likelihood of a successful restoration, there was at least some value and merit in the paintings worthy of the attention of the public, and this was the only category from which I have so far chosen works."

At times the exclusions led to protests from the magistrates who would have liked to see the paintings in their offices put back into order, and at other times Edwards would relate the considerations which had led to works being restored although, in themselves, they would have been excluded; for instance, in order to avoid hanging them in a room alongside restored works, or, as was the case for a few paintings from the Magistrato al Sal taken down in 1780, because of the "desire to maintain without variation the same antique decoration". Certain paintings he was almost forced into take on: pressure from the magistrates of the Pro' fuori Zecca forced him into accepting two "*contorni*" (outlines) of a *Madonna* by Giovanni Bellini and a *Justice* attributed to one of the Vivarini, in addition to paintings by Bonifacio Veronese representing *Saint John the Evangelist* and *Saint Andrew and Saint Anthony Abbot* in which, although over half the picture surface was lost, he hoped to be able to recover what was left: "This, to tell the truth was what I had hoped before embarking on the cleaning of this work: but once I had brought it out of the deep blackness which covered it, I was better able to judge of its condition, and of the intrinsic merit of that which could be saved. As a result I ordered the suspension of the work, although a new lining had already been attached .... Nevertheless, I still thought that something needed to be done on the aforementioned *contorni* to make them fitting for their niches; in fact, for the painting by Vivarini, I saw to it that the assistants gave some added help to make the repositioning of these works back in their fixed places more decorous. I should however make clear that the little effort employed on these three paintings has not been included by me in any of the invoices, and therefore they should be considered as works which have been completely abandoned".[32]

Certain paintings by Bonifacio led to reflections of a more general nature on the subject of restoration:

"I would wish that those who are critical of the worth of our work, would deign to reflect that the judgement of the work should not be absolute, but relative. And if they no longer have a clear picture of the desolate state in which the work was handed to me and which was then made good (*risarcita*), they are, on the whole, not fit to pass judgement on the merit or demerit of our efforts ...

The most important operations which one needs to examine in the repair of the above mentioned paintings can be limited to the following: I) The solidity of the paint should be brought back to a stable consistency, and removed from the vulnerable state in which it was found ... II) The evenness of the surface, as well as the tension of the canvas, which in the present state is in places rigid and inflexible as though it were slate (*talco*). III) The complete accord (*unione*) in technique, colour and style between all the restored (*rifatte*) parts and the original. This holds good in the instance of the thousands of small losses which pepper the canvases, as well as for larger losses. IV) The general flavour of the work which must be removed not only from the crude appearance which is the result of the darkening of some of the colours, but which has also has been caused by past injudicious cleanings of the lighter areas, so that the painting now appears discordant and inharmonious. I should warn you though, that the large work by

Bonifacio representing the multiplication of the bread will never appear very harmonious; this is the result of the dispersal of small patches of highlight and minute areas of shadow, what professionals term a defect of distribution of masses in relation to the whole (*massa e partito*)".[33]

On 20 April 1781, taking charge of other paintings by Bonifacio and his school from the Governatori delle Entrate, Edwards pointed out that some of the errors in composition and perspective, as they were the author's own, could not be corrected. In *The Adoration of the Magi* by L'Aliense in the Sala del Consiglio dei Dieci, he noted: "Of the parts lost and replaced during restoration, that of the principal figure wearing yellow was treated with the utmost care; as this figure is one of the worst executed of the composition, during the restoration we were obliged to conserve traces which we would happily have erased, in order to improve the design somewhat as well as the fall of the drapery which are not at all consistent with the nude beneath. But the importance of not introducing this spirit of censure amongst the practition-ers, which could so easily degenerate into extremely dangerous licence, means that I often will respect mistakes in the original rather than correcting them with erudite falsifications, although, strictly speaking, I might presume that the artists themselves and the paintings would reap some advantage from allowing some corrections [to be made]".[34]

Elsewhere, the reports noted that the harmony of the work must be left as intended by the artist; a report of 1781, relating to various works by Bonifacio, observes: "Only remain a few words to say relating to the harmony of the aforementioned works after their restora-tion. This element cannot be as easily defined in words, as it can be felt in the flesh. Harmony in painting has not, as yet, been reduced to mathematical laws as has that of sounds; for almost all of men it is still a matter of feeling. Furthermore, as we are dealing with an old painting, we must not think to give back to the work a harmony of colour as this should be, intrinsically, but rather as it was practised by the author of the work, as it would have appeared according to his own judgement. Otherwise, we would be removing a characteristic differ-ence between the various styles of past masters".[35]

Respect for the author's intentions, and the desire to present the painting with the patina produced by time, whenever this is of benefit to the work, are the parameters within which good cleaning is carried out. The report on the work carried out in 1781 on the *Rape of Europa* by Veronese pointed out that: "The drapery has been cleaned in such a manner that, without touching the half-tints, care was taken to soften the impact of the strongest shad-ows, and the highlights were barely touched. The only area of flesh that we were able to clean completely was that of Europa's breast, a truly wonderful thing. We were able to treat this area of the flesh painting in this manner, unlike the rest, for two principal reasons: firstly, as this was the most important part of the main protagonist, the highlight could be stronger than in the rest of the work and secondly, because as the paint was much thicker, and applied in several thicknesses, it was resistant to the necessary operations".[36]

Edwards was emphatically against the application of artificial patinas; however, in order to harmonise his integrations he did have recourse to "simulations of discoloration" (*affumature*), as was the case for certain paintings by Bonifacio in the Decime del Clero: "We had the consolation of finding much of the original under the clumsily applied overpaint; and similarly, we had the satisfaction of bringing back to fitting beauty the darkened skies and all the green and blue drapery, without having to apply any new colour except in the lost or damaged areas, and this will be the third part of the work which I will describe. Of a hun-dred places in which it was essential for this work to be carried out, there are no more than two or three which might arouse the suspicion that they have undergone restoration, and this usually because of some particular circumstance which cannot always be avoided. The diligence with which the fillings perfectly matched the levels of the new with the old, as well as the matching of the style and the colours, and even the simulation of the discolorations, can leave no opening for criticism of the necessity of this work".[37]

5. Restorations after 1786

After the general report of 1786, it is more difficult to trace the reports on the restorations directed by Edwards, with the exception of the estimate for the paintings in the Church and the Sacristy of the Salute, and for two canvases by Bonifacio removed for further restoration in 1793 from the Magistrato al Sal, and the long reports on the canvases in the Sala del Maggior Consiglio.[38]

With the French occupation, the work was suddenly halted on 22 August 1797, when the inspector received the order to "immediately" clear out the refectory of the church of Santi Giovanni e Paolo which housed the restoration laboratory, as it was to be requisitioned as a military hospital for the occupying forces. This was not without damage to the large canvases which were being worked on [at the time], which Edwards managed to transfer into a room in Palazzo Grimani in the sestriere of San Luca. On 16 May 1798, after Venice was ceded to the Austrian Empire, Edwards compiled a list of these paintings, which also included the paintings which had been removed from offices or suppressed churches and deposited in his restoration studio. There were about fifty works, including a few removed from the Avogaria in 1783, of which Edwards had contested the need for restoration. It is in these circumstances that we find amongst their number various paintings from Madonna dell'Orto: the altarpiece attributed to Palma Vecchio, of which it is specified that the entire lower section had been repainted (*rifatta*) (including the strange parapet), five canvases depicting the *Virtues* by Tintoretto "painted with the utmost freedom (*trascuratezza*), and to be seen from a great distance" and, divided into three pieces, his vast compositions depicting *The Adoration of the Golden Calf* and *The Last Judgement*.[39]

Under Austrian rule, the restoration was completed of those works which could be replaced in their original positions; in 1803, twenty-eight paintings from the Ducal Palace which had suffered damage through the infiltration of rain were brought in for restoration. But restoration, as a sphere of activity, was not showing progress: Niccolò Baldassini had died in about 1786, and Bertani not long afterwards, "and inspector Edwards begged that after such a loss, no replacement should be made … as he found the choice of potential candidates too frightening …". Baldassini was replaced by his son Giuseppe, but the loss of these two practitioners meant that various works, such as the *Paradiso* by Tintoretto, were not restored although already under contract. Subsequent political events resulted in the breaking up of the laboratory; and the death of Giuseppe Diziani in 1803, in addition to the move to Rome of one of the other restorers (probably Giuseppe Candida), all contributed to the extinction of this tradition of restoration.[40]

Simultaneously, the public paintings were dispersed as a result of the new suppressions which occurred after Venice became part of the Kingdom of Italy (1805–1813). During this time, paintings were selected (largely by Edwards) from the old public palaces and the convents which had been suppressed, to be hung in the Royal houses in Venice and Strá,

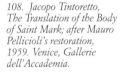

107. Jacopo Tintoretto,
The Translation of the
Body of Saint Mark; after the
adaptations of Giuseppe
Baldassini, 1816. Venice,
Gallerie dell'Accademia.

108. Jacopo Tintoretto,
The Translation of the Body
of Saint Mark; after Mauro
Pellicioli's restoration,
1959. Venice, Gallerie
dell'Accademia.

and the new Gallerie dell'Accademia. Apart from the works which passed into the collections of the picture galleries in Milan and Venice, or in the Royal palaces, a great number of the works from the institutions which were suppressed in these years ended up being stored, waiting to be sent to a church or to the Academy in Vienna, from whence many were returned after the 1919 Peace Treaty.[41]

107, 108   In the congestion of large canvases from the *scuole* and the altarpieces, the fate of Tintoretto's *Translation of the Body of Saint Mark*, cut down in 1816 in order to fit the architecture of the atrium of the Sansovino Library, is significant. The adaptation of paintings to different sizes, although rigorously excluded from the programme for the restoration of public works, must not have been unknown in the sphere of Edwards' activity: Lanzi, in a manuscript note in the library of the Uffizi, remarked that "the Venetians, even the modern ones, have an advantage over the other schools [of painting] in that they give unity to a work, imagining it as a whole with all its passages of light, so that the eye easily follows its lines and runs over the picture from top to bottom. Mister Pietro Edwards asserts that when having on occasion to cut down paintings because of the owners' will, it was as difficult to do on a work belonging to the Venetian school as it was easy to do it on works from other schools, where the composition is often piecemeal and not thought out in its integrity (*insieme*)".[42]

Moreover, the squaring up of certain arched canvases by Bonifacio, or some reductions in size such as that of the Tintoretto, allowed him to put these large works into safety, away from the disorder of the stores and away from the risk of being sent away to some far-flung destination. But the fate of the *Translation* can also be explained by the limited appreciation that Edwards had, alongside other Italian art critics such as Vasari, Lanzi and Longhi, of the worth of this sixteenth-century master. For example, in the instance of his paintings in the Sala del Collegio, he referred to "some crudeness in the tints, some little defects in the architecture and other little mistakes", as proof of the original condition in which they were returned, without any improvements added in restoration; elsewhere he noted the extravagance of the painting which made him unsure as to whether or not he should take into restoration the heavily damaged *Ascension* in the Church of the Redentore. With reference to a *Resurrection* by him which was included in a catalogue of the best paintings in the Ducal Palace in 1806, he observed: "A work full of enthusiasm. The overall effect is good: some of the attitudes and foreshortenings show not so much the masterly assurance but the negligence with which the master put his thoughts into practice. The whole of the painting is painted with boldness and good principles, but in the detail there are many shortcomings. One might say that as a stable rule, if you want works by Tintoretto, in each one you will have to live with some grave failing or a degree of boldness (*franchezza*) which at times borders on audacity".[43]

The last years of Edwards' guardianship of the Gallerie dell'Accademia saw him locked in battle with Leopoldo Cicognara over the restorations which, at the latter's request, had been hurriedly carried out in 1817 on such works as Titian's *Assumption*; the restorer was Antonio Florian, a practitioner active during the first decades of the nineteenth century, who had a completely different approach to that of the studio of Santi Giovanni e Paolo. He is remembered for having used rather less cautious methods of cleaning than those advocated by Edwards ["lye (*acqua di soda*)[xi] and walnut oil"] and was responsible for the enlargement of the panel attributed to Marco Basaiti, which replaced the altarpiece by Giovanni Bellini in San Zaccaria, after its requisition by the French.

One of the last manuscripts by Pietro Edwards which has come down to us, written after 1819, was the *Progetto per una scuola di restauro delle pitture* (Project for a school for the restoration of paintings), in which he advocated the necessity of training restorers in the style of the Old Masters, in the use of varnish colours and in the making of correct judgements during cleaning so as not to further unbalance paintings which have been already intrinsically altered by time. Amongst the characteristics of the styles of the Old Masters to which restorers must become accustomed, Edwards singled out feet and hands because, "even in chosen works of the Old Masters these parts retain much of the dry style which is typical of the second and third periods of art, and only rarely coincide with the ideal art of statues. Instead of which, they are rather modelled from nature with an accuracy which does not even omit the tiniest accidents of the skin. This, with only a few exceptions, can be considered the characteristic style of the time."

[xi] Lye, sodium hydroxide, is an alkaline reagent which will break down the oil medium of the paint layer, as well as any oil present in the varnish coating; because of this, oil would then be rubbed into the painting after cleaning to replace this, and give the painting a less parched appearance. This oil would itself darken and become insoluble with time; walnut or poppy oil at later dates would be chosen in preference to linseed oil for this rubbing in, because they yellow less.

He then advised that students should become accustomed to the physiognomies of the Old Masters, and should practise copying landscapes "with copious fronds", and the preparation of the typical primings (*fondi*) used by various masters, or the imitation of "hair-styles, wings, plumage or fronds" with the difficult medium of varnish colours. Moreover, he pointed out the various peculiarities in the draperies of the older masters which, even if highly finished (*elaborati*), did not vary much in their distinction between the individual qualities of different cloths; and the dry (*povere*) folds of the fourteenth-century masters which as time went on became richer, "carefully arranged without any attempt to hide the artifice, on puppets dressed with wet paper or with cloth soaked in clay dissolved in water …"; and finally the draperies of "the most accomplished century", which were copied from life with choices dictated by the natural inclination of the various masters.[44]

Little remained to be seen of the example set by Edwards in the work of nineteenth-century restorers in Venice: in 1849 Mary Merrifield would lament that a number of the restorers employed by the Venetian state were using linseed oil[xii] [to retouch], and in such circumstances it is not surprising that the Accademia di Venezia should have withheld consent for the publication of Edwards' writings which were, by implication, critical and which Giovanni Edwards had put together from his father's various manuscripts. One need only consider the rather sickly repaintings executed in the first half of the century on Giovanni Bellini's *Madonna* from the public offices of Monte Nuovissimo, or recall the paintings in the style of Placido Fabris to note to what extent, compared for instance to the reconstructions in the style of the original executed by Giuseppe Diziani on the work by Busati, the art of restoration in Venice had not really made any great progress.[45]

Pietro Edwards died on 17 March 1821.

Notes

1. Zanetti, 1733, p. 155; Edwards, 1778–1784, reports of 20 May 1780, 4 June 1784 and 25 February 1789 (Venetian calendar 1788); Moschini, 1815, I, p. 409; Edwards, in Olivato, 1974, p. 186.
2. Edwards, 1786; G. Edwards, in Merrifield, 1849, p. 867; Olivato, 1974, p. 21.
3. Zanetti, 1733, pp. 102, 131; Moschini, 1815, I, p. 414; Fulin, 1868, note 1, pp. 93–96; Olivato, 1974, pp. 19–29, 99–113; Merkel, 1981, p. 35; Nepi Scirè, 1984, pp. 22–28 (intervention on Veronese's *Last Supper* in the refectory of San Zanipolo in 1697; bibliography on Rossi as a painter). On Bambini, see also: Venice, Archivio di Stato, Compilazione Leggi, busta 303, cc. 791–793; Edwards, 1974, p. 160. A copy of Cecchi's inventory can be found in busta 'miscellanea' n. 49 of the Provveditori al Sal, Archivio di Stato di Venezia.
4. Fulin, 1868, pp. 94–96; Vianello, 1970–1971, pp. 136–138; Olivato, 1974, pp. 30–34, 113–119.
5. On Sebastiano Ricci, see: Edwards, 1778, II, p. 3; Moschini, 1815, I, p. 417 (restoration of the monochrome small figures painted on the ceiling of the Sala dell'Anticollegio); Olivato, 1974, pp. 36, 133; L. Olivato, *Sebastiano Ricci restauratore*, in "Atti del congresso internazionale su Sebastiano Ricci e il suo tempo" (Udine, 1975), Milan, s.d., pp. 20–28. On Pietro Cardinali, see: Edwards, 1786, p. 6; G. Edwards in Merrifield, 1849, p. 867; Marconi–Moschini, 1959, p. 69 and note 7; Olivato, 1974, pp. 36–38, 120–128, 187; Nepi Sciré, 1979, p. 86; Venice, Archivio di Stato, Compilazione Leggi, b. 303, c. 817.

[xii] Implicit in the use of varnish rather than oil-bound colours is a concern for both the ease of reversibility of the restoration and its longevity in terms of reduced alteration with time. The use of oil as a retouching medium shows a lack of concern or maybe a disregard for these issues, which are now central to restoration, as oil both darkens and becomes insoluble.

On Agostino Letterini: Moschini, 1815, III, p. 594; Edwards, 1778–1784, report of 15 November 1778 (amongst those who repainted the paintings by Veronese on the ceiling of the Sala del Consiglio dei Dieci); Moschini (1815, II, pp. 436, 594) also referred to the son of Agostino, Bartolomeo Letterini. See also Edwards, 1778, II; Edwards, 1785, D; Edwards, 1974, p. 160.

6. Moschini, 1815, I, p. 443; Olivato, 1974, pp. 38–39; Venice, Archivio di Stato, Magistrati al Sal, busta "miscellanea" 49: *Referte del Collegio dei Pittori*, 1728–1792; see p. 237 of the first edition of this volume for further information. Edwards, 1786, D.

7. Nicoletti, 1886, pp. 18–19, 19–21; Olivato, 1974, pp. 39–45. I refer you back to Olivato (notes on pp. 40–41) for information on the restorations executed by painters on this list. The paintings requiring restoration were as follows: Veronese's ceiling by Veronese in the Sala della Bussola which is now in the Louvre; two octagons by Francesco Bassano in the Sala del Maggior Consiglio; the *Raccolta della manna e delle coturnici* by Bonifacio Veronese and five other paintings in the Pro fuori di Zecca (Marconi–Moschini, 1962, nn. 81; 82, 94–96, 105, 106 as well as the *Nativity of the Virgin and the Saint Alvise* today in the Brera); also by Bonifacio, *Saint Mark between Justice and Peace* (Marconi–Moschini, 1962, n. 104). Edwards (1778–1784) refers to some of these paintings in the reports of 8 October 1778, 20 May 1780 and 12 June 1781.

8. On Domenico Maggiotto as a restorer, see Moschini, 1815, I, p. 83 (poor restoration on the *Baptism of Christ* by Cima da Conegliano in San Giovanni in Bragora); Olivato, 1974, note 89, p. 41. For Giuseppe Angeli: Moschini, 1815, II, p. 350.

9. Edwards, 1974, pp 157–160.

10. Moschini, 1815, I, pp. 133, 530; II, pp. 128, 610; P. Edwards, in V. Malamani, *Memorie del conte Leopoldo Cicognara*, Venice 1888, II, p. 370; V. Moschini, *Altri restauri alle Gallerie di Venezia*, in "Bollettino d'arte", 1960, pp. 362–363; *Arte a Venezia*, catalogue of the exhibition, Venice 1971, n. 27.

11. Moschini, 1815, II, p. 492; Marconi–Moschini, 1959; R. Palucchini–G. Perocco, *I teleri del Carpaccio in San Giorgio degli Schiavoni*, Milan, 1961, p. 93; Marconi–Moschini, 1962, note 275, pp. 166–167.

12. On collectionism in Venice at the end of the eighteenth century, after Haskell (1963), see: F. Haskell, *Some collectors of Venetian Art at the end of the Eighteenth Century,* in *Studies in Renaissance and Baroque Art*, London–New York, 1967, pp. 173–178; Olivato, 1974, pp. 49–50, 53–54. Also see Conti, 1973, p. 237, on the 1770 sale of Titian's altarpiece of San Niccolò dei Frari, which is today in the Pinacoteca Vaticana.

13. Zanetti, 1774–1778; Fulin, 1868, notes, pp. 97, 99–102; Vianello, 1970–1971, pp. 138–140; Olivato, 1974, pp. 53–66, 135–147; Olivato, 1975, op. cit., note 14 p. 28. In general, on the conservation undertaken by the Republic of Venice see also R. Palucchini, *Il problema della salvaguardia del patrimonio artistico veneziano,* in "Atti dell'Instituto Veneto di scienze, lettere ed arti", 1970–1971, pp. 158–160.

14. Mengardi, 1779–1795; Moschini, 1815, I, pp. 156, 560 (organ shutters by Sebastiano del Piombo in San Bartolomeo in Rialto); Moschini, 1817, p. 1 (adds the figure of an angel in Giandomenico Tiepolo's altarpiece in Sant'Agnese in Padua); Vianello, 1970–1971, p. 140; Olivato, 1974, pp. 85–89; his reports are to be found in the aforementioned b. 909 in the Inquisitori dello Stato. On Giovanni Maria Sasso as a restorer, see: Haskell, 1963, pp. 373–376; Moschini, 1806, III, p. 51; Cavalcaselle, 1871, I, note 1 p. 49 (he was responsible for the restoration of *The Death of the Virgin* by Bartolomeo Vivarini, now in the Metropolitan Museum, New York).

15. On the large canvases in the Scuola di San Giovanni Evangelista, there is also a record of a restoration by Matteo Zais, 1784 (Marconi–Moschini, 1955, p. 57); for the two altarpieces by Carpaccio and by the school of Bonifacio, see Marconi–Moschini, 1962, n. 114, pp. 68–69. On Bertani, see note 19 which follows.

16. Edwards, 1778–1792; Vianello, 1970–1971, pp. 140–141; Olivato, 1974, pp. 89–92, 200–208. The biographic note on Edwards in ms 787/4 in the Biblioteca del Seminario in Venice, mentions that he was consulted by the State Inquisitors in relation to the paintings in the churches, although they had Francesco Maggiotto as their inspector; see: Maggiotto, 1796–1797; Olivato, 1974, pp. 79–81, 178–183; for further details see Conti, 1973, p. 238.

17. On the restorations on the mainland, see: Brandolese, 1795, pp. 10, 21, 36, 64, 71, 76, 113, 114, 136, 168, 185, 231, 243; Moschini, 1817, pp. 1 (Mengardi, see A. Mariuz, *Giandomenico Tiepolo*, Venice 1971, p. 131), 20, 48, 62, 81, 83, 142, 155, 158, 164, 195, 217; Fulin, 1868, note 1, pp. 101–106; Cavalcaselle, 1871, II, note 1, p. 133; *Andrea Mantegna*, catalogue of the exhibition, Mantua, 1961, p. 113; L. Olivato, *Per una storia del restauro e della conservazione delle opera d'arte a Venezia nel '700,* in "Atti e memorie dell'Accademia Patavina di Scienze, Lettere ed Arti", LXXXII, 1969–1970, part III, pp. 53–62; Merkel, 1981.

18. G. B. Rossetti, *Descrizione delle pitture, sculture ed architetture di Padova*, Padua 1780, pp. 36, 41, 289; F. Beltrami, *Il forestiere instruito delle cose notabili della città di Ravenna*, Ravenna 1783, p. 126; Brandolese, 1795, pp. 7, 45, 158, 246, 307; Moschini, 1817, p. 105; Pietrucci, *Biografia degli artisti padovani,* Padua, 1858, p. 292;

Cavalcaselle–Crowe, 1864–1866, IV, note p. 149; Cavalcaselle–Crowe, 1877, I, note p. 138; A. Moschetti, *Gli antichi restauri e il ritrovamento degli affreschi originali della Sala della Ragione*, in "Bollettino del Museo Civico di Padova", 1910, pp. 35–52; S. Marconi–Moschini, in Thieme–Becker, 1947; A. Prosdocimi, *Restauro agli affreschi del Palazzo della Ragione*, in "Bollettino del Museo Civico di Padova", 1962, I, pp. 7–37; A. Prosdocimi, *La copia del monocromo giottesco con la "Stultitia" alla cappella degli Scrovegni*, ibid., 1964, I, pp. 91–96; A. Sartori, La cappella di San Giacomo al Santo, in "Il Santo", 1966, notes 2 and 3, pp. 298–299, 300–301 (Zannoni's observations on the harmony between architecture and fresco decorations in the fourteenth century), 351–353.

19. G. Edwards, in Merrifield, 1849, pp. 854–855; Edwards, 1974, p. 160; Olivato, 1974, pp. 42, 132–133; Venezia, Archivio di Stato, Senato Terra, register n. 380, 6 June 1771 and attachments to the relative file; idem. Compilazione Leggi, envelope 303.

On Bertani, see: Zanetti, 1774–1778, reports of 10 October 1774 and 5 April 1777; Edwards, 1778, II, cc. 3–4, 9; 1778, III, p. 4; Mengardi, 1779–1795, reports of 10 December 1783 and 1 June 1784; Moschini, 1815, I, p. 190; II, pp. 194, 564 (died in his eighties in 1797); G. Edwards, in Merrifield, 1849, pp. 854–855 and note 1 p. 856; Olivato, 1974, p. 42, note 88 pp. 40–41, p. 156; P. Edwards, ms 787/9 Seminario Venezia (Bertani died not long after Baldassini); P. Edwards, ms. Of the library of the Museo Correr P.D.G.C. 307, p. 13 (from it one can deduce that the *Pala Pesaro* had been restored in about 1750). See Conti, 1973, pp. 239–240 for the *Nota degli quadri da me sottoscritto Giuseppe Bertani restaurati …* from ms 787/7 of the Seminario di Venezia.

20. J. D. Fiorillo, *Geschichte der zeichnenden Künste … Göttingen*, 1798–1808, II, pp. 191–192; Millin, 1806, III, p. 435; Moschini, 1806, III, p. 54 (compare with Lanzi, 1809, p. 85), 126; Lanzi, 1809, III, pp. 291–292; Verri, 1814, p. 107; Moschini, 1815, I, p. 465, 511; II, pp. 11, 78; L. F., in "Il nuovo osservatore veneziano", 31 March 1821; Paillot de Montabert, 1829–1831, IX, pp. 693–694; E. A. Cicogna, *Delle inscrizioni veneziane raccolte ed illustrate*, IV, Venice, 1834, p. 227, note 340 pp. 385–391, p. 675; M. P. Merrifield and G. Edwards O'Kelly, in Merrifield, 1849, pp. 843–889; V. Malamani, *Un'amicizia di Antonio Canova, lettere di lui al conte Leopoldo Cicognara*, Città di Castello 1890, note 1 p. 85. C. A. Levi, *Le collezioni veneziane d'arte e di antichità dal secolo XIV ai nostri giorni*, Venice 1900, pp. XCVI–XCVIII; G. Lorenzetti, *Il 'Martirio di San Lorenzo' di Tiziano ed il soggiorno dei Conti del Nord a Venezia*, in "Fanfulla della Domenica", XXVII, 1915, nn. 10 and 11; Cagiano de Azavedo, 1950; N. Ivanoff, *I ritratti dell'Avogaria*, in "Arte veneta", 1954, pp. 272–283; Marconi–Moschini, 1955, pp. VIII–IX, XII; Muraro, 1962. Previtali, 1964, p. 242; Vianello, 1970–1971, pp. 141–142; Nepi Scirè, 1979, pp. 86–87 (see also the contributions of S. Sponza, P. L. Fantelli, A. Agati Ruggeri and A. Rizzi on the new restorations to the canvases in the Sala delle Quattro Porte in the same publication, n. 8 of the "Quaderni della Soprintendenza ai Beni Artistici e Storici di Venezia"). Particularly useful for a biography of Edwards are mss 787/4, 787/5 and 787/6, in the Biblioteca Seminario in Venice. In it various estimates on the occasion of the division of estates in mss 787 and 788.

21. Edwards, 1974; Edwards, 1778: *Ristaurazione delle pubbliche pitture assentita col decreto del Senato li 3 settembre 1778: Capitoli del progetto per il restauro dei quadri di pubblica ragione proposto dal professor Pietro Edwards, assentito dagli infrascritti professori e rassegnato, in relazione al decreto dell'Eccenllentissimo Senato 25 settembre 1777; Capitolare degl'offici ed incombence dell'ispettore al restauro dei pubblici quadri rassegnato da Pietro Edwards professor accademico collegiale*; 3 September 1778. The text for the decrees of the Senate on the organization of the restorations can be found in: Venice, Archivio di Stato, Senato Terra, 25 September 1777 and 3 September 1778.

On the restorers, with the exception of Bertani, see, for Giuseppe Diziani: A. P. Zugni Tauro, *Gaspare Diziani*, Venice, 1971, pp. 111–114; Edwards, 1778–1785, reports of 8 April 1783 and 10 June 1783; Venice, Archivio di Stato, Inquisitori di Stato, b. 909, "Miscellanea", 9 April 1774 and 2 January 1772/1773; G. Diziani, Alcuni quadri da me sottoscritto in diversi tempi accomodati …, in ms 787/8 in the Seminario di Venezia (in Conti, 1973, p. 240). For Niccolò Baldassini: ms Seminario 787/9–V (he died around 1786 and was replaced by his son Giuseppe, who restored Titian's *Saint John the Baptist*, in 1815; Moschini–Marconi, 1962, p. 259).

22. Edwards, 1778–1785, report of 8 October 1778, for the paintings from this ceiling, and for the continuation of the work, see 22 December 1778 and 7 June 1779.

23. The history of many of the paintings restored by Edwards, which are to be found in the Gallerie dell'Accademia, can be followed in Marconi–Moschini's catalogues (1955 and 1962), which also make reference to later restorations, and sometimes cite the eighteenth-century sources.

24. Edwards, 1778–1784, reports of 20 May 1780, 20 April 1781, 12 June 1781, 18 March and 2 October 1783; Moschini, 1815, II, p. 500; "Le arti", 1938–1939, newsletter pp. 39–40, 250; 1939–1940, pp. 253–255; *Mostra del Restauro*, Venice, 1949, p. 158; V. Moschini, *Nuovi aspetti di opera famose*, in "Bollettino d'Arte", 1949, pp. 167–168; Marconi–Moschini, 1955, nn. 66 and 67.

25. Edwards, 1778–1784, reports of 26 February and 10 June 1783 (Busati: Marconi–Moschini, 1955, n. 93); 14 July 1779 and 8 April 1783 (Metsys in the Ducal Palace, always cited as a Dürer); 18 April 1780 and 17 February 1780/1 (*Madonna dei tesorieri*: Marconi–Moschini, 1962, n. 402); 8 December 1778 and 23 March 1779 (Veronese on the north wall of the Sala del Collegio); 8 December 1778 and 7 June 1779 (large canvas depicting Doge Mocenigo, by Tintoretto); 18 March and 2 October 1783 (Bellini).

26. Merrifield, 1849, note 1 pp. 876–877; reports of 8 December 1778, 10 July 1781, 17 August 1787.

27. P. Edwards, *Progetto per una scuola di restauro delle pitture* (post-1819; Venice, Biblioteca del Seminario Patriarcale, ms 788/15), p. 10; Edwards, 1778–1784, reports of 14 July 1779 and 4 June 1784.

28. Olivato, 1974, pp. 84–85, 193; P. Edwards, ms 912/64 of the Biblioteca del Seminario Patriarcale di Venezia; Edwards, pp. 10–11 ms 788/15, op. cit. of the Seminario.

29. W. Goethe *Ältere Gemälde. Neuere Restaurationen in Venedig, betrachtet 1790, in Goethes Werke*, XXXI, Berlin–Leipzig s.d., pp. 51–58; P. Edwards, *Progetto per una scuola di restauro*, op. cit., pp. 9 (the necessity of training the students in the handling of varnish colours), 12 (lakes and other artificial colours which, exceptionally, must be bound in oil also for restoration).

30. The climate of Venice had already been described as damaging to paintings by Montesquieu in the journal of his visit to the city in 1728: "In Venice, the salty water (and the air which is impregnated with it) damages many things. It calcinates – so to speak – the walls; it ruins all the paintings. On the reverse of the paintings, one places a second 'wall', a tarred panel; nevertheless, the salty air passes through and ruins the paintings." (*Œuvres Complètes*, Paris, 1964, p. 224; see Lanzi, 1809, III, p. 173; Merrifield, 1849, p. 883).

31. Edwards, 1786, G.

32. For the criteria according to which restoration was to be excluded, see Edwards, 1778–1785, reports of 15 November 1778, 9 February 1778–1779, 18 April 1780, 20 May 1780, 20 April 1781, 12 June 1781, 10 July 1781, 30 November 1781, 21 December 1781, 3 October 1782, 18 March 1783, 15 December 1789; Edwards, 1786, introduction and points D and E, as well as the *Catalogo dei quadri ch'erano stati esclusi dall'ispettore Pietro Edwards a che gli fu appositamente commesso di prendere in consegna per la loro ristaurazione* (Catalogue of the pictures which had been excluded from restoration, and which he was specifically ordered to take in hand for restoration) (Conti, 1973, p. 242).

33. Edwards, 1778–1784, report of 20 April 1781.

34. Idem., 20 April 1781; 15 March 1782.

35. Idem., 10 April 1781.

36. Idem., 26 September 1781 (see Lanzi, 1809, III, p. 173); for the condition of the painting before the 1972 restoration, one should bear in mind that it had probably also undergone restoration in Paris, after the requisitioning of 1797.

37. Edwards, 1778–1784, report of 10 April 1781.

38. The reports that post-date the general report of 1786, which are to be found in ms 787/7 of the Seminario Patriarcale di Venezia, are: 26 August 1785; 17 August 1787; 25 February (Olivato, 1974, pp. 184–188), 15 December 1789 (Olivato, 1974, pp. 188–198); 1793, June; 8 June 1795; no dates on some [of the] works by Bonifacio.

39. Venice, Archivio di Stato, Direzione del Demanio, Economato, Edwards–Quadri, Corrispondenza 1797–1819, *Documenti comprovanti ricevimento e consegna degli oggetti, dal n. 1 al n. 40 inclusive, 1797; Ristauri, Ristretto delle pitture di pubblica ragione esistenti in mano dell'ispettore alle belle arti Pietro Edwards ora custodite nella sala superiore della casa Grimani a San Luca assegnata per un tal uso con intelligenza ed assenso del padrone e restaurata a pubbliche spese* (Documents proving the receipt and delivery of the objects, nn. 1–40 inclusive, 1797; restorations, summary of the public paintings held by the Inspector of Fine Arts Pietro Edwards, and which are now in the upper hall of the case Grimani in San Luca, which has been assigned to this use with the knowledge and consent of the owner, and has been restored with public funds). In the copy of this list presented to the Deputation of the Fine Arts 16 May 1798 (ibid.) is mentioned the altarpiece attributed to Palma Vecchio in the church of Madonna dell'Orto, specifically mentioning that the lower portion was modern.

40. G. Edwards, in Merrifield, 1849; Edwards, *Sommario di tutto l'occorso relativamente agli studi delle bell' arti del disegno nell'inter-regno democratico di Venezia l'anno 1797*, ms of the archive of the Accademia of Venice (cited in Marconi–Moschini, 1955, note 5, p. XXIX).

41. On the suppressions, and on Edwards' activity in these circumstances, see: C. Ricci, *La Pinacoteca di Brera*, Bergamo 1907, pp. 39–56; Marconi–Moschini, 1955, pp. VIII–IX, XIII, XV, note 9, p. XXX; A. Zorzi, *Venezia scomparsa*, Milan 1972, pp. 43–69, 106–120, 130–137. The *"buste"* Edwards of the Archivio di Stato di Venezia (Direzione Generale del Demanio, Economato, Edwards–Quadri), "Elenchi e inventari" (lists and inventories) and "Corrispondenza" (Correspondance) are an incomplete documentary source. On the objectives of the

activity of restoration, see ms 788/15 of the Seminario Patriarcale (*Progetto per una scuola di restauro delle pitture*, pp. 2–3).

42. Ms 36–37 of the library of the Uffizi, Florence (*Viaggio del 1793 per lo stato Veneto e Venezia istessa* … letter U, heading "veneti moderni"), a passage pointed out to me by Giovanni Previtali.

43. Marconi–Moschini, 1959; Edwards, 1778–1784, reports of 8 December 1778; 14 July 1779; 18 April 1780; 28 April 1780; 30 November 1781; 15 December 1789, pp. 5–6; Venice, Archivio di Stato, buste Edwards, op. cit. "Elenchi e inventari", *Catalogo estratto delle migliori pitture comprese nel catalogo generale dei quadri … con decreto del Magistrato Civile 10 Maggio 1806 consegnati all'ispettore delle belle arti Edwards* ….

44. Ms 788/15, op. cit. of the Seminario of Venice.

45. Moschini, 1815, I, p. 124; II, pp. 413–414 (Baldassini, who restored Bellini's *Mocenigo Altarpiece*); G. A. Moschini *Itinéraire de la ville de Venise*, Venice 1819, p. 19 (Floriani, who restored the Pala di San Zaccaria by Bellini, on its return from France); Merrifield, 1849, note 1 pp. 876–877; Venturi, 1882, p. 379 and note 5 (Baldassini restored the San Menna by Veronese, before its departure for Modena in 1811). On Floriani's methods, see Olivato, 1974, p. 84. Amongst the restorers working in Venice in the first half of the nineteenth century, a good level of practice was shown by Sebastiano Santi who, in 1827 and 1828, removed the sandarac varnish (which had been applied in Paris) from Veronese's *Feast in the House of Levi,* and enlarged Titian's *Presentation of the Virgin* (see Moschini–Marconi, 1962, p. 258; Nepi Scirè, 1984, p. 31).

7

From the eighteenth to the nineteenth century

1. The legacy of the eighteenth century

Those who regularly consult eighteenth-century texts or, referring to these sources turn to examine the works of these masters, will notice the particular concern shown towards the material aspects of the work and its technique, seen as elements which are intrinsic to the very nature of the painting; it is a serene vision of the relationship between materials and the image, which was unique and perhaps can never again be repeated. The nineteenth century did not lose this concern, but the Romantic cult of the will, combined with an idealistic vision of art as material expression of thought, meant that techniques were considered increasingly as an instrument; they would continue to be the subject of discussion, but the tone and contexts would be different.

This faith and confidence in technique can also be seen in the differing points of view which developed over the century with regard to the old theme of "Time the Painter". In step with a taste for paintings which were increasingly light in tone, no longer was it thought that the passage of time simply produced its own patina which added harmony and tone to paintings. Rather, Time put the capacities of the artist to the test, in his ability to choose materials which on ageing would not result in the tonal distortions that Hogarth lamented, but rather bring the painting to an optical and physical harmony which was better than that which the ground, the colours and the varnish possessed at the moment they were applied.

Amongst the evidence from this period collected by Otto Kurz, that of Joseph Vernet was probably the least ambiguous in showing us an artist who knew that he could programme the behaviour of the materials he used with this settling (*assestamento*) in mind. In 1781 the French Ambassador in Madrid wished to give as a gift to the Prince of the Asturias two works by Vernet; of the two which were proposed to him, he showed himself much pleased with one of the works, painted in 1769, but less so with the *pendant* which was of a more recent date, painted in 1777, which seemed to him rather monotonous. Nevertheless the paintings were acquired for the gift, but it was the artist himself who had to point out that his works had the merit (and he the satisfaction) of becoming more perfect with time. The time elapsing between 1769 and 1777 indicates it as a period of settling rather than deterioration of the materials, "which gives them increased vigour in colouring and greater harmony".[1] An effect, therefore, which is due to the settling of the oil medium, to patina and a slight yellowing of the varnish, in a measured equilibrium of transparency and saturation of tones.

Bearing in mind that this century opened with the unctuous paint of Crespi, and closed with the waxy spreads of so many of the Neo-classical masters, it is possible to frame in the right perspective three appraisals of the technique and the conservation of paintings by artists who were trained in this climate: David, Goya and Fuseli.

90   In 1794, during the controversies surrounding the management of museums, David denounced the restorers whose sacrilegious daubings on *The Holy Family of François I* had resulted in the loss of one of its most defining characteristics: the "sublime colouring" of Raphael.[2] This definition originated from a comparison with the precepts, sensitive to the tonality and the material qualities of a painting, which were common to all painters trained in the eighteenth century. The absence of a coloured ground, certain cold and at times dissonant tonalities which ensured the absence of any excessive seductiveness in the colouring of the painting, were all aspects which appeared to them outside the rules governing beauty and the allure of grace: their effect, if positive, could only be defined as sublime. To Raphael's rather wan light, well suited in its abstraction to the dampening of all chromaticism which might link the imitation of reality to an overwhelmingly optical perception, Longhi reserved the colloquial adjective *pisciosa*:[i] there is, indeed, a kind of opacity which stands in the way of the limpid results of the traditions of Piero della Francesca or Venetian painting, something rather fetid and polluted for those who cannot find within themselves an enthusiasm for the image as a sublime ideogram.

David also was an impassioned classicist, but through his technique and use of colour he was still linked to the traditions of a century in which painting qualified as such through its material aspects and its tonality: the dulled red and greyish browns he used neutralized more than one excess of green or blue (splendiferous ornamentation reserved to the *Sacre* or the *Oath of the Eagles*), but they never negated the very presence of colour, and were far removed from the sublime dissonances, the chromatic voids of Raphael, which an eighteenth-century eye could appreciate but not imitate.

In the letter of 1801 in which he refers to the restorations he had examined in the palace of Buen Ritiro, Goya confronted the problems relating to restoration and the materiality of painting even more directly. His observations take us back to a view of creativity in which the stroke (*gesto*) and the materials unequivocally characterize a painting: not even the authors, coming back to life, would be able perfectly to retouch their own colours which, through the effects of time, have taken on a yellowish tone; "it is not easy to retain the fleeting and momentary impulse of the imagination, and the harmony and concert which are found in the initial creation, and the change will be seen in the retouching".[ii] In the restoration were lost "the liveliness and vigour of the brushwork and the mastery of the delicate and learnèd touches of the original".[iii,3]

Leaving aside the problem of whether, and to what extent, such appraisals represented an opening towards a Romantic vision of artistic creativity, it is certain that they would not have been formulated in such terms without a deeply rooted habit of looking at paintings as material objects. The uniqueness of a painting is born of the momentary and unrepeatable

---

[i] That is, to put it crudely, piss like.
[ii] "*no es facile retenir el intento instantaneo y pasajero de la fantasia y el acorde y concierto que se propuso en la primera ejecucion, para que dejen resentirse los retoques de la variacion*".
[iii] "*el brio y la valentia de los pinceles y la maestria de delicados y sabios toques del original*".

intent of the artist no less than from the materials which he has used and time which has altered them, rendering them even more exceptional and impossible to reproduce.

Analogous considerations on the relationship between material and image and on the practice of artists who were well acquainted with the use of oilings, varnishes, bitumens, sullying and all the other improvised expedients used by artists to heighten or lower a tone, to bring forward or push back a mass, were at the root of Fuseli's criticism of the results of the restoration of Raphael's *Transfiguration* while the painting was in Paris. "These notes are based on the close examination of the painting in the laboratories of the 'Restauration' in 1802. The face of Christ not only did not appear as we all remembered it in San Pietro di Montorio, but appeared even inferior in quality to that in Dorigny's engraving: it had assumed a vulgar rather than dignified expression, lacking anything which might be called sublime, or austere or terrible. It is probable that these changes are due to the sacrilegious hands of the restorers who had already destroyed the best part of the Madonna di Foligno".[4]

One does wonder whether Fuseli could really have observed the large panel at such close quarters in San Pietro in Montorio, so as to draw of it an impression of the details that did not superimpose themselves on those of Dorigny's engraving, and if his disappointment was not rather born of the impossibility of recognizing in the original, the image which he had formed of it from this reproduction. However, what is certain and should make us take notice of his impressions is that the recent cleaning has revealed a painting from which the patina has been removed and that, as any enquiry into the practices of Napoleonic restorers will reveal, they were wont to clean thoroughly, trusting to glazing and artificial patinas to give back the original tonalities to the painting.

In their laboratories, the painting would emerge with an oily appearance (which would darken with time), and its surface – if it were not a painting which clearly relied on brushstroke for its effect – would be made as smooth as possible. One begins to notice that these interventions favoured (in the inevitable choices made in any restoration) the aspects which would prove the most useful to artists who, with their solid academic and classical roots, drew near in their desire of imitation of the great models: with eyes and hands trained in a manner similar to that required for the interpretation of a painting, with its light and shade, through Landon's line engravings which illustrated museum catalogues, they would be able to perceive the peculiarities in handling the small variations in colouring (*colorito*), that were hidden beneath the heavy glazings of the restoration. Secondary aspects these, when compared to the ideal composition, the outline (*contorno*) of a Raphael.

The results of a selection which followed such lines of thought could only perplex those artists who were more attentive to the specific technical aspects of painting, disposed to appreciate the accidental and non-repeatable creative aspects of the artist's touch and his materials: all those imponderables which made up the "best part" of the *Madonna di Foligno*. All Fuseli could see in the works of his contemporaries in England were the sullyings (*sporcature*), varnishes, bitumens, all those elements of finish which were so harmful to the good preservation of a painting, and of which the Redgrave brothers gave such a heartfelt and ardent account in *A Century of British Painters*. Reynolds himself would remind us of the importance of the accidental in certain material effects and, taking Rembrandt's handling of paint as his starting point (whether or not he had used a spatula to achieve these effects), observed: "Accident in the hands of an artist who knows how to take the advantage of his hints, will often produce bold and capricious beauties of handling and facility, such as would not have thought of, or ventured, with his pencil, under the regular restraint of his hand. However, this

109

109. Raphael, The Transfiguration,
detail; restored in Paris in 1802.
Rome, Pinacoteca Vaticana.

is fit only on occasions where no correctness of form is required, such as clouds, stumps of trees, rocks, or broken ground. Works produced in an accidental manner will have the same free unrestrained air as the works of nature, whose particular combinations seem to depend on accident".[5]

The "Nature" to which Reynolds referred here and elsewhere made one accept and value certain elements of chance which were outside the artist's programme, and to which "correctness of form" complied. It was something which gave spontaneity, a breath of fresh air, with effects which, because of that element of chance, could not be repeated. Choice, of a classical stamp, suggested to Napoleonic restorers which were the qualities that made the Raphael a masterpiece to be put forward as a model, and also offered consolation to Edwards for his replacement of elements lost in the Tintoretto in such a manner that "the author himself would have approved". Faith in spontaneity (*naturalezza*) (and how not to believe that all the Old Masters had indeed proceeded in the same way to give an air of spontaneity to their works?) led one to believe, instead, that it was this very "best part", that difficult balance between a figurative programme and the behaviour of the materials, that Fuseli no longer saw in the *Madonna di Foligno*.

This attitude of diffidence towards restoration, towards the confidence it showed in its knowledge of what to conserve in a work of art and how to do so, was also characteristic of Francesco Milizia who, in the entry for "retouching" (*ritoccare*) in the *Dizionario delle belle arti del disegno*, observed:

> "That the author retouch his freshly painted work, in order to correct it and adjust it, is a duty. But he must not retouch too much, if he does not wish the colouring to appear laboured. But to lay one's hands on another master's great work which has been altered by time is to deform it, which is worse than destroying it. If a painting which has lost its harmony and has been damaged by time is retouched with an expert hand, it will for a short time seem to have improved, but very quickly it will look worse than before, because the new colours alter and no longer match the original ones. And then one turns to another doctor, who promises miracles proportional to his ignorance: he applies new remedies, and soon the patient worsens. And here we come to the charlatan, who pitilessly scours (*scoria*), smears, rubs, grates (*raschia*), washes, smears again, varnishes, and goodbye painting. This fine art has made great progress as a result of the decadence of the fine arts".[6]

To the renovated, glossy picture was preferred the austerity of the Old Master; austerity which at times was achieved through halting the cleaning process at the right moment and, most importantly, avoiding the use of varnish, as we are reminded in the climate of Neo-classical Rome, by Ghelli's protestations against Hackert. Restoration always seemed to presuppose a trust in a series of precepts of good practice (*di buona scuola*) and in an academic tradition (with the characteristics of whatever school or style it had been formed in), which would enable it with absolute confidence both to define the rules with which to reconstruct the damaged or fragmentary image, and to give it a material apparel that would make it stand out more clearly and appear newer. At times it seemed that the restoration went beyond the effects which the materials and techniques of the time would have permitted (and, indeed, this can still be the case). I think it is from this perspective that one should understand why the Milanese Carlo Verri, who had visited Edwards' restoration laboratory in 1782, should refer to it as a place in which paintings were skinned despite the care and good precepts that Edwards followed in his practice, which nevertheless remained selective in relation to the imponderables of the creative act of painting. It was this confidence of the restorer which was to clash with Goya, Fuseli and David himself, and again Verri when he criticized the luxurious volume on the subject of Leonardo's *Last Supper* published in 1810 by Giuseppe Bossi.[7]

A great collector, knowledgeable connoisseur and central figure within the Lombard school of Neo-classical painting, Bossi had dedicated himself to a reconstruction of the terribly damaged masterpiece by Leonardo, and it is this copy which is thought to have served as model for the mosaic which is now in the Minoritenkirche in Vienna. His intention had been to make as accurate as possible a philological reconstruction, and with the volume of 1810, he provided the reader with the documentation on all the copies he had studied, discussing their reliability, and going back to Leonardo's own thoughts and drawings on the proportions and anatomy of the human body. Apart from the reproach of only having verified the original after having made the cartoon from the copies, Verri developed an entire critical debate on their reliability, with an enquiry worthy of a classical scholar reconstructing the origin and descent of an ancient text, even including a table with the distances between certain fixed points in the original and in the various copies, as proof of greater or lesser faithfulness to the original. But beyond all this philological effort, Verri's conclusion was that "Such research, and such studies will never be able to represent the manner of painting, and the technique of execution of the original; and it is this that we lament as lost, and which we would like to see imitated, remaining as there does, sufficient information in engravings and ancient copies so as to represent the composition of the work".[8]

Despite its inevitable selectivity, restoration had already by now focused on those ideas of respect for the work of art which required intervention, and which was also present in the activity of Edwards in Venice, and in the debate born in France on the restoration of the paintings in the Royal Collection. And then, if we begin to examine many of the criteria which are today fundamental to the concept of restoration, we will notice that these were already in place in the eighteenth century. Even in the case of reversibility, we need only consider Watin's observations on varnishes suitable for paintings, or the relationship between physical and chemical investigation and the conservation of paintings which was so very much present in Edwards' reports, as it was also, to varying degrees, in the French experiments in transferring paintings onto canvas.

We have already glimpsed a similar occurrence in the relationship between restoration and the sciences; in 1800, when it was decided to transfer *The Madonna di Foligno*, the work was planned with the assistance of the chemists Guyton and Berthollet. For the whole of the nineteenth century (one need only think as far as Secco-Suardo), scientific notions would be used to justify and characterize choices taken in restoration. Finally, if we consider the processes which would become characteristic of restoration, we find that they become so in the eighteenth century; from transfers, to the *strappo* of frescos and lining, to the misuse of varnish. If, in addition, we do not forget the concern for the material aspects of painting which characterized the entire century, we can only be encouraged to put our trust in their approach, bringing it up to date with our own requirements when need be, but without distancing ourselves from them.

It is obvious that the recognition of the principles which defined restoration did not mean that all paintings since that time have only undergone restorations which have been respectful of their status as true works of art. There were then, just as there are now, bad restorers, and we must also bear in mind those works which contemporary taste and critical judgement considered "production-line paintings" (*quadri di fabbrica*), as Forni would call them, or to use Horsin Déon's label, "*tableau à tournure*": minor works, which for commercial reasons were adapted to the style of a master or school in vogue at the time. Patel might be adapted à la Claude, or a sixteenth-century French painting altered in an attempt to glean an attribution to one of the more renowned Italian masters.[9]

If the French tradition of restoration seemed almost to want to guarantee an unlimited lifespan to the great masterpieces of art, from the *Grand Saint Michel* to the *Madonna di Foligno*, it was the very importance of these works and the impossibility of replacing this heritage which elsewhere had the effect of emphasizing the importance of maintenance, of conservation in the appropriate conditions, of the minor intervention which would avert the necessity of a restoration which could never be otherwise than selective. Although the routine of the Gallerie di Firenze seemed at times to be enclosed in its old habits rather than consciously maintaining the collection in order to prevent more serious restorations, Edwards would dedicate one of his most important texts, the *Piano pratico* of 1786, to the minor conservation practices and the controls necessary in order to prevent damage occurring to the pictures in the Ducal Palace, as well as subsequent and repeated interventions. Even within a more traditional context such as that of a family-owned picture gallery, we see how the *marchese* Giacomo Zambeccari, when drawing up deeds for the inheritance of the family gallery in Bologna in 1788, set down not only that the paintings could not be dispersed, and so on, but also that the heirs "must abstain from using as their living accommodation the aforementioned *appartamento nobile* and gallery rooms, so that in the winter months the paintings would not suffer the effects of smoke nor that of fireplaces"; and if then the public functions to which the apartment was dedicated occurred in the winter months, only certain fireplaces were to be lit and "that the brazier of the servants be placed only in the first hall before the great room".[10]

By now, the restorer was a figure already quite distinct from that of the artist, aiming at a different, but not lesser, professional prestige which was dealt with at length by Jean Michel Picault in 1793. Then, as now, there was no question that the figure of a great restorer would ever reach the stature of a great artist, but a great restorer could receive the recognition which would be considered preferable to that of a modest (even if not bad) artist. With Pietro Edwards, we saw how important the role played by an expert in restoration and conservation could be, when it came to decision making by the state on matters of conservation. With the onset of the French Revolution, the conservation of the Royal Collections (which were now national property) became a problem of cultural politics, to the extent of warranting an intervention within the political sphere by David himself in 1793. The restorer, as the demands made by Robert Picault revealed, could now hope for good professional remuneration and, in a context linked to the prestige of antiquity such as the restoration of antique statues in Rome, Bartolomeo Cavaceppi enjoyed a degree of comfort and a prestige which much exceeded that accorded to the majority of sculptors working in the papal capital at that time.

2. Antique statues and panel paintings by the Early Masters

At the end of the eighteenth century, the restoration of antique statues had taken on a different flavour to that which characterized seventeenth-century galleries. Obvious "pastiches" were avoided, as was the addition of new elements to antique groups (such as the putto added by Bernini to the *Ares Ludovisi*), although combinations of antique elements which did not belong together still continued. Of Bartolomeo Cavaceppi (1716–1799), Ennio Quirino Visconti said, "He introduced an improved manner to restorations, he adapted marbles which were completely disfigured by their condition, added the missing part without removing any of the original, introducing a new, more correct and truer method by which to return monuments to their antique splendour". Trusted by Winckelmann with the restoration of the Albani marbles, Cavaceppi was the most famous restorer of the century; his restorations were presented as though a broken statue had been put together again using the original pieces. Baroque in his own works, he based his integrations on models of Hadrian sculpture, the canon of beauty in Antiquity. This led to some perplexity in England when the state acquired the Elgin marbles (as Canova would call them), in that they were far removed from this canon of ideal beauty, which could be seen in collections of antique statues such as those at Holkham Hall and Petworth House, which were made up of pieces which Cavaceppi had re-elaborated.

110   Cavaceppi's restorations, such as the beautiful *Meleager* in Holkham Hall, were still strongly linked to a vision of the statue as part of a story in which it is a participant: busts in which the head turned towards a possible interlocutor, figures with an outstretched arm, a gesture or even the direction of a glance, all participated in an action, even if only potentially. Cavaceppi remained rooted to interpretations which sought to evoke mythological or historical figures: for Petworth House he restored a torso of a *Doriphoros* as *Dyonisus*, and for Bowood a *Discobolus* (sold by Gavin Hamilton in 1776) which he turned into a *Diomedes Fleeing with Pallas*.[11]

The surface of the marbles which he restored was often left rough (*scabra*), suggesting the authenticity of the original parts, which at times seem as though simply mounted onto the additions which support them. This approach was far removed from the vision of longed-for
111   perfection emanating from a statue such as the *Capitoline Antinous*, discovered in 1733,[12] the left leg of which was restored, and then the whole polished so that the marble almost seems to dematerialize, ready to seduce the spectator with an image of uncontaminated perfection and ambiguous beauty, such as only Antiquity could evoke. Cavaceppi, on the other hand, was able to win the good opinion of Winckelmann and then also of Ennio Quirino Visconti for the respect (albeit apparent) in which he held the original fragments which he completed, so that one forgave him more than one arbitrary judgement in the choice of attributes which he added in order to give a subject matter to his sculptures, which would then have to be presented as documents for the history of taste, and not only as examples of ideal beauty.

Not only did the completion of the statues discovered in the most recent excavations become ever more frequent, but so too did the replacement of old Baroque and sixteenth-century restorations with completions which, in their style and in the respect shown to their attributes, were more attuned to the antique. It was to the generation of restorers that followed Cavaceppi that we owe the rediscovery of some of the best known subjects of Greek sculpture: one of the first respectful restorations of the *Pothos* by Scopas was executed by Giovanni Pierantoni on a work in the Capitol, and the *Discobolus* discovered in Tivoli in 1792 (which is now in the British Museum) was, for the first time, integrated as such by Carlo Albacini.[13]

Cavaceppi's younger colleagues were now making reference to a more rigorous antiquarian tradition which guided them in the identification of subjects, but their interventions on the sculptures tended to be more imitative; this found favour amongst the public of cultured dilettanti, to the existence of which De Rossi could still testify in 1826, when he referred to this as the happiest epoch for the restoration of antique sculpture. In the Farnese statues which Albacini put in order before their departure for Naples, no restoration was visible which would allow one to detect the fractures and hence the evidence of Cavaceppi's handi-work. And how difficult it is to detect the extent of his interventions on a statue such as the *Venus Callipege*, or how coherent, figuratively speaking, is the *Satyr with the Child Bacchus*, restored by him in 1787, replacing the entire head and the hands of the satyr and all the upper portion of the child, resulting in one of the most pleasingly inventive restorations of the eighteenth century.[14]

However, the great novelty which we encounter in the field of restoration in these adventure-ridden years of the Napoleonic wars was the decision not to restore the Elgin marbles. During Elgin's visit to Rome in 1803, it was Canova himself who, having seen a number of casts and fragments of Phidias' sculptures, excluded the possibility of a restoration: under any circumstance, Flaxman added. He then estimated a cost of twenty-thousand pounds, but would later drop the offer. In the end, the committee dealing with the acquisition of the marbles in 1816 decided that no restoration was necessary, as there was no need to comply with the decorum required for sculptures in private homes: in a public institution such as the British Museum, they could contribute to the education of public taste and that of artists even in their fragmentary state.[15]

We seem to have run full course since the days in the sixteenth century, when the first sculptures in collections were completed in order to give them back that "grace" that Vasari observed to be the result of the restorations executed for cardinal Della Valle: in a public collection, Phidias' sculptures could retain their original, fragmentary state. There were precedents: partly by chance, and partly because of the suggestive power of its state, the *Psyche of Capua* remained mutilated after its breaks had been squared up ready for integrations to be attached. In 1787, Albacini left a torso in the "sublime" style unrestored (placing it within the same tradition as the *Torso Belvedere*) and, in theory at least, stated that attributes should not be added unless they were clearly identifiable and it was also clear that they would not lead to misunderstandings in the interpretation of the subject: "a sculpture exhibited to the public without the replacement of the attributes, allows the scholars to one day rediscover, as has so often happened in the past, the subject which is actually represented". The completion of sculptures was therefore abandoned in instances when one wished to display the beauty of the fragment (especially if of a sublime style), or through a sense of documentary rigour as when, in 1809, Edward Daniel Clarke would state that the *Ceres* in Cambridge would not be allowed to be disfigured by spurious additions. Publications which were explicit in their references to the extent of the restoration in antique gems and sculptures were already common at this time, ranging from those published by the Society of Dilettanti to the *Principi del disegno* of Volpato and Morghen.[16]

But the reasons for which Canova, or the committee deciding on the acquisition, turned away from a restoration of the marbles from the Parthenon was, I believe, the result also of a different vision of the unique status of these sculptures. The renowned Neo-classical sculptor was far from being a purist with regard to the completion of antique sculpture. For instance, although he was well aware of the original position of the arm of *Laocoon*, he did not consider altering the restorations of Montorsoli and Cornacchini; on the other hand, it was on the strength of his advice that the *Giustiniani Philosopher* changed aspect and became the *Euripides* of the Vatican Museums, whilst Antonio d'Este maintained that he was guided by him in the restoration of the arms and even the head of the *Lateran Antinous* discovered at Ostia. Finally, in the case of the sculptures from *Aegina*, Canova saw them more as a historical document than a perfect artistic exemplar and in Rome, under his very eyes

112

113

114

115

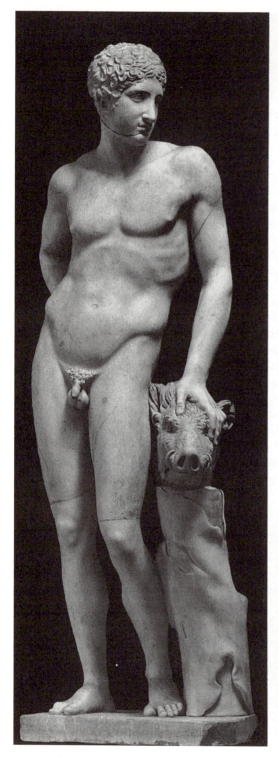 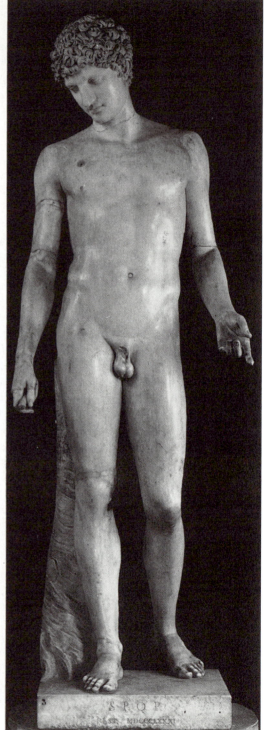

110. *Meleager; restored by*
Bartolomeo Cavaceppi. Holkham
Hall, Viscount Coke Collection.

111. *Capitoline Antinous;*
restored towards 1733.
Rome, Musei Capitolini.

112. *Satyr with the Child Bacchus;*
restored by Carlo Albacini
in 1787. Naples, Museo Nazionale
di Capodimonte.

*113. Three figures of goddesses from the
eastern pediment of the Parthenon
London, British Museum.*

and without giving rise to any controversy, Thorwaldsen would complete them, with an attitude towards the imperfections of the archaic style (showing considerable ability on his part
in their interpretation) which does not seem very far removed from the Peruginesque simulations towards which tended the empty romantic fancies of an Overbeck.[17]

Admiration for the Elgin marbles centred on their astonishing naturalism, a naturalism which was embodied in their anatomical perfection,[18] and in this sense beauty appeared
as never before, tied to the imitation of nature. Therefore, we are now leaving behind the
easily codifiable norms and precepts provided by a proportional model which the restorer
could emulate having first absorbed its principles. We are also outside the arbitrary free-
doms of the "sublime" style: Phidias' sculptures present us with an incomparable imitation
of the human body, of natural beauty, not of an abstract ideal. And, confronted with this
abstention from restoration, we must ask ourselves whether (in the wake of Winckelmann's
suggestions) these works do embody a relationship with nature similar to that of Shelley's
Greek urn, a nature which is different from that which we inhabit, and which therefore
dissuades us from empty attempts at imitation.

114. *Psyche of Naples (Capua);*
sculpture prepared for restor-
ation in the eighteenth century.
Naples, Museo Nazionale di
Capodimonte.

115. *Lateran Antinous;*
restored by Antonio d'Este
under the direction of Antonio
Canova. Rome, Musei Vaticani.

The clash between the idea of the reconstruction of a work according to a set of accepted rules, in the tradition of a Maratta who integrated Raphael's figures in the Loggia of the Farnesina, and the requirements of more receptive philology which paid greater attention to the inimitable aspects – whether the fruit of genius or of chance – of the original, by now dictated the judgements of those artists who were against restoration in general (or of a particular instance of it). Such were David, Goya and Fuseli. Canova himself, as a great artist confronting the problem of whether or not to intervene on great works of art, could only be of their number. However, the discussion on whether or not to restore and complete sculptures now became current, and would often refer to the relationship with the public, and to the didactic aspects (as we would say) of the presentation of works of art in museums.

Quatremère de Quincy favoured completions for their didactic aspect, and in his letters to Canova on the subject of the Elgin marbles, he enthused about the results obtained by Thorwaldsen on the statues from Aegina: in his view, he had succeeded in following the rigid and expressionless style, and in restoring the character of this school. "I am convinced – he declared – that the antique would never have produced such an effect on public taste in the last fifty years, had all the sculptures been left in their mutilated state", and that artists would have found it difficult to take pleasure in studying them in their fragmentary state. Quatremère showed himself to be diffident towards the idea that interpretation should be entrusted to the imagination: the public and even artists needed guidance from a good reconstruction; his solution for the Elgin marbles was to reintegrate them using casts, which would then be reassembled in the original disposition. It would be difficult, I think, not to see in these solutions a strongly Neo-classical prescriptive spirit, nor indeed not to read Wilhelm von Humboldt's protestations against the reconstructions in the Museum in Berlin in a Romantic key. Moreover, right from the early years of the century, had the latter not confessed to feeling a certain resentment against excavations, "a gain for erudition at the expense of fantasy?"[19]

In the field of painting, this newly developed philological attention led to a respect for the fragment, and to easily recognizable reintegrations of missing parts, but only in those restorations (usually frescos) overseen by artists, especially those from the Academies; within the sphere of collecting, on the other hand, we find a thick veil of secrecy shrouding the reconstructions, which collectors could not do without. In the eighteenth century, one was still able to discuss with a certain serenity the subject of reintegrations, and even the ability of the restorer who had executed them; think of the arm repainted in a Domenichino referred to by Giovanni Gherardo De Rossi in the debate surrounding varnishes in 1788. Now, however, non-authenticity would become an unforgivable sin to the extent of discrediting a painting, as Secco-Suardo would observe in the introduction to his manual.[20]

The increasingly frequent appearance of works by the Early Masters in galleries was a novelty which appeared at the end of the eighteenth century; there were precedents, of course, especially works presumed to be by Dürer and Mantegna, with real and apocryphal signatures, but it was around this time that was born the desire to have a historical series of Old Masters not only as a complement to the collections of the more important galleries, but also as autonomous collections. As far as the interpretation of this taste for the Primitives as a typically Romantic phenomenon, I think one should be aware, on the basis of Giovanni Previtali's research and the recent publication by Gombrich, that the very concept of primitive is linked to a long tradition already present in Latin writers; it refers not to a vision of art as intuition, but to a gradual conquest of a formal maturity which had not been available to earlier artists.[21]

Beyond the boundaries set by Classical precepts, the rediscovery of the Primitive would prove a useful counter-balance to the Baroque, introducing more austere principles on which to found a style which moved away from its licence. The link between Romanticism, nationalistic spirit and rediscovery in this key of the Gothic would lead in Germany and other European countries to concerns of varying nature; in Italy, however, the rediscovery of the paintings of the Early Masters was born of historical curiosity, and the anti-Baroque reaction of the eighteenth century.

Already in the middle years of the century, Hugford in Florence had succeeded in placing works by the Early Masters onto the English art market, and in the era of Pietro Leopoldo, one should remember how the librarian Bandini had brought together as a collection and adapted for the church of Sant'Ansano in Fiesole, a group of Primitive paintings, as well as the nucleus of the collection of Early Masters in the Uffizi, with works by Tuscan masters, and Memling and Dürer. In 1782, Lanzi described "the cabinet of ancient paintings" of the gallery in which, in the wake of Vasari, after a series of fourteenth-century Tuscan masters (including Giottino's *Deposition*), one passed to works by Fra Angelico, then Uccello's *Battle*, a predella by Neroccio ascribed to Andrea del Castagno, the series of *Virtues* by Pollaiuolo, and then a few works by Botticelli. We should not find it surprising that in Florence John Flaxman should have copied into his notebook a number of reliefs from the monument of the Torre in Santa Croce, and in Siena sketched the tomb of Cardinal Petroni by Tino di Camaiano: an eighteenth-century tradition of study had already opened the way to the Brancacci Chapel and the Camposanto in Pisa to all artists looking for representations of the sublime.[22]

The attention given to the Early Masters was also linked to a new attitude to colour. During the eighteenth century, we saw an acceptance of the inevitable yellowing of oil, but also the search for techniques which would ensure a greater stability both of the range of colours, and of chromatic variations themselves. There was a search for an encaustic medium which would not alter, and pastel and watercolour were used to achieve effects, the objective chromaticity of which would not be altered by the darkening associated with traditional techniques. It is difficult to pigeonhole this period of taste, which sits between Neo-classicism and the beginnings of Romanticism; it was a time of great upheaval that immediately involved oil painting itself, and which became a term of comparison for all nineteenth-century artists, but for which we have no stylistic label. To the darkened softness of oil painting which Vasari described with such enthusiasm as a characteristic of the third age of art, was often preferred the colouring of tempera and oil paintings which preceded the use of *sfumato*, and enveloping darkness. It is not by chance that the poor impression that made Carlo Verri so speedily pronounce a negative judgement on Edwards' restorations should be accompanied by a eulogy of the good state of preservation of lighter toned painting, to which fifteenth-century masters had entrusted their chromatic message.[23] The scholarly tradition of interest in the Early Masters was thus revived by an attentiveness to a completely different, new message, and one which was sought by many artists. And this new opening came about in the very decades in which the suppression of ecclesiastical bodies flooded the market with the paintings that had passed through the rather lax filtering of works selected for the public galleries.

The new fashion led to countless tamperings with paintings to remove or cover anything that might prevent an old painting from fitting into the furnishings of a private house, or within the programme of a picture gallery. Polyptychs and altarpieces were adapted in such a manner as to hide their liturgical function as large pieces of painted church furnishings, their partitions were often altered by the removal or the painting over of sections which were in poor condition or oddly shaped. The predellas were divided up into cabinet pictures. The new frames might be decorated *in stile*, but they avoided the placing of the predella, the subdivisions and the pilasters on different planes; for instance, the reclamation, without "pilasters" and with the predella pushed back, of Michele di Matteo's polyptych in the Accademia in Venice, carried out in 1829.

Similar adaptations had already begun with the suppressions in the eighteenth century, as could be seen from the Neo-classical frame on Agnolo Gaddi's *Tacoli Canacci Tryptych* in the Pinacoteca in Parma, which was, incredibly, removed; at a later date, and in the actual museum directed by Vivant de Denon, we could take as a typical example the *passe-partout* which was used to frame the disassembled fragments of one of the best pre-served paintings of the fifteenth century: the *Pala Barbadori* by Filippo Lippi. Atypical, in contrast, were the highly researched frames which Schinkel designed for the Altes Museum in Berlin, each individually adapted to the particular style of the painting, and with museo-graphically rigorous attention being paid to its presentation.[24]

3. Revolutionary vandalism

"Men make their own history, but not according to their own will, nor in circumstances that they have chosen for themselves, rather in the circumstances which confront them, deter-mined by events and tradition. The tradition of all the preceding generations weighs like an incubus on the minds of the living, and just when it seems that they are working towards a transformation of themselves and their circumstances, in order to create that which has never before existed, it is in these very times of revolutionary crisis that they evoke with anguish the spirits of the past to take them in their service; they borrow their names, pass-words to be used in battle, the customs so as to represent in this old and venerable disguise, and with these borrowed words, this new stage in history."[25]

A long literary tradition (reaching back as far as antiquity) and historical circumstances made Revolutionary France choose the disguise of the Republic and the Roman Empire. At the end of the eighteenth century, the Middle Ages did not as yet represent a world that could no longer be reproduced as was the case with Classical Antiquity; feudal institutions which had regulated this medieval world were being brought low only by the Revolution, and all that was linked to it was seen as an expression of barely conquered barbarism, still alive in other coun-tries and ready to irrupt into France itself to abolish the newly conquered freedom. Such a vision of the Middle Ages, as a past from which one had only recently freed oneself, would therefore often have the upper hand over the rules for the conservation of the objects considered to be of use to the sciences and the arts which the Constituent Assembly, the Legislative Assembly and even the Convention had programmed in view of the public use of the now nationalized heritage which had belonged to the Crown, to the ecclesiastical orders and to the *émigrés*.[26]

The legislation brought in for the conservation (*tutela*) of works of art which appeared during the Constituent Assembly often had the characteristics of a compromise, with the forces still favouring the king, bearing in mind the stature that was given to the paintings and sculp-tures of the Middle Ages and Renaissance as monuments to the French monarchy (consider, for instance, the work of Montfaucon published between 1729 and 1733: *Les Monuments de la Monarchie françoise*).[27] The transfer of some of the Royal tombs from the suppressed abbey of Royaumont at Saint Denis in August 1791 still bore the stamp of the old guardianship of ancient monuments linked either to the Monarchy or to the national past, as can be seen in the "*Instructions concernant les châsses, reliquaires et autres pièces d'orfèvrerie provenant du mobilier des maisons ecclésiastiques, et destinés à la fonte*" of March 1791 (the law of 23 October 1790 provided for their smelting), which planned for the safeguarding of all monuments pre-dating 1300, in which the excellence of the workmanship exceeded the value of the metal, and those which could be of interest because of their historical importance or for a history of customs.[28]

With the abolition of the monarchy, and with the antireligious campaigns which accompanied the various attempts to establish revolutionary cults, what we now consider works of art of the Middle Ages were only considered then as objects of curiosity, which could also be of historical interest, but had no role to play in the arts and were reminders of a past which, it was felt, must be erased. The 1794 reports drawn up by the abbot of the Constitution, Henry Grégoire, clearly defined which were the works of art which it was considered vandalism to destroy: just for Dijon (and without specifying the dates of the monuments), the reports lamented the damage to sculptures pre-dating the Renaissance; Grégoire deplored the mutilation or damage of the works of artists such as Germain Pilon, Jean-Baptiste Poultier and Edme Bouchardon. The conclusions as to why vandalism should be fought also throw considerable light on the considerations of the utility of the arts in the bourgeois revolution: although not always fervent patriots, scientists and artists would always bring benefits to their nation, and the commercial profit to England of Josiah Wedgwood's pottery was used as an example. Grégoire then went on to evoke the spirits of antiquity so dear to revolutionary rhetoric: the Romans who conquered Sparta took with them the painted walls which had adorned their council chamber; and, having mentioned the works of art that the republican armies had brought back from Belgium, with a patriotism which was by now imperialist in flavour, Grégoire went on to remind one that no conquest in Italy would ever be as beautiful as the *Apollo Belvedere* or the *Farnese Hercules*.[29]

Even taking into account the destruction carried out by the masses, one must admit that the losses to Medieval art which occurred between 1790 and 1794 were not disastrous to the degree represented in one of the most widespread clichés of the reactionary press. The most serious losses were those suffered by ecclesiastic goldsmitheries, and by the bronze artefacts that were requisitioned to be transformed into cannons, because of the war against Austria begun in March 1792. The material which did survive, whatever the gravity of the losses, allows one nevertheless to follow the developments in French art during the Romanesque and the Gothic periods, through to the Renaissance and the seventeenth century.

To use a summary example, one could observe that the Calvinist destruction in Holland, Switzerland and Germany, and even in England, left much larger and more serious lacunae in the knowledge of Medieval art than all the fury of the Revolution.

The law of 14 August 1792 programmed the destruction of all monuments of the feudal period, specifying that objects that were interesting to the arts and sciences should be respected, and an inventory presented to the legislative body; on 16 September it was specified that it was forbidden to destroy books and other objects useful to the arts and sciences even if these were adorned with crests. On 14 June, a two-year jail sentence was introduced for anyone damaging monuments of national importance: a situation which demonstrates the interest taken by the Convention for the safeguarding of that which, within the limits imposed by the taste of the time, was considered the artistic heritage, but also underlines how easy it was for vandalism to take place.

With the adoption of the new text on 25 November 1794, the reaction of the Thermidor clearly forbade grass-root initiatives for the destruction of monuments, as there were "persons to be recommended, because knowledgeable and public spirited", who were employed on the inventory and conservation of the monuments.[30] At this point in time, the destruction was no longer damage and mutilation caused during antifeudal turmoil, but the ordered and conscious work of private entrepreneurs who bought nationalized buildings that the state found difficult to use, in order to recover materials for use in construction work. Despois, in his book on the cultural politics of the Convention, published a table of the statistics relating to the demolition of ecclesiastical buildings which took place in Paris after 1790: none was registered in 1794, whilst the highest number was recorded in 1797, with eighteen demolitions. Demolitions taking place for private interest did not come to a stop either with the Empire, nor with the Restoration, and in 1833 Montalambert, as well as deploring the new "restoring" vandalism, also reviewed the whole of southern France, enumerating the numerous medieval monuments which had been destroyed over the past fifteen years.[31]

The official initiatives against feudal monuments were orderly affairs: the demolition of the kings on the façade of Nôtre Dame, voted by the Commune of Paris in October 1793, was carried out by a private entrepreneur between December of that year and September 1794.[32] The decree of the National Assembly of 14 August 1792 resulted in the removal of almost all the bronze monuments from Saint Denis: the only monuments surviving to this day are a few "gisants" and some inscribed slabs of the thirteenth, fourteenth and fifteenth centuries, the monument to Charles VIII by Guido Mazzoni and six figures from the tomb of Henry II by Germain Pilon. Before proceeding to the destruction of all the other monuments, on 1 May 1793, the municipality of Franciade (the new name adopted by the town) wrote to the National Convention to obtain an opinion from experts on the artistic value of these sculptures. The decree of 1 August following, ordered the destruction of all the Royal monuments in the anniversary year of the fall of the Monarchy (10 August), in the church of Saint Denis and over the whole of the national territory. Exhumations had already begun, and the first few days brought about the destruction of ten or so monuments. When, on 14 August, a small number of the members of the Commission for Monuments examined the remaining statues, only a few "gisants" of the fourteenth and fifteenth centuries (judged to be of interest for the realism of their lineaments and their costumes) were chosen for the depository of the Petits Augustins, and the stone sculptures of the previous century were abandoned to their fate, as it was decided that they did not offer anything of note "either for the arts or for history". More recent tombs were dismantled in October 1793. The architectural portions were not removed along with the statues, so that with the bases of the sepulchres of the first line kings, and with part of those of the second, the commune of Franciade erected a pyramid to Marat, and with other fragments erected a patriotic grotto dedicated to the spirits of Marat and Peltier.[33]

The figure who from 6 December 1790, flanked by the Commission for Monuments, was mainly responsible for the recovery of parts of these ensembles of sculptures and who continued in this task even after the selection by the Commission in 1794 and 1795, was Alexander Lenoir. To begin with, as the objects from the Royal residences became national property, those belonging to churches or *émigrés* were put up for sale, and it is thus that the furniture from Versailles found its way to England and St Petersburg, to be followed by paintings, usually by the hand of minor masters. Amongst all the vandalisms and disorders bringing grief to the artistic heritage, Grégoire would also condemn the sales which had taken place without adequate controls, often for prices much lower than the true worth of the works: as early as in year II, the *"Observations de quelques patriots sur la necessité de conserver les monuments de la littérature et des arts"* were already denouncing the damage these had produced.[34]

At first, from June 1791, Lenoir was the *"garde génerale"* for one of the various depositories for the sale of nationalized works, with its headquarters in the ex-convent of the

Petits-Augustins, where primarily paintings and sculptures from churches were assembled. Its promotion to the status of Museum occurred only on 29 Vendémiaire IV (21 October 1795), and not without protests from the Conservatoire du Musée Central des Arts which resided in the Louvre, which had until that time used the depository to fill in lacunae in its own collections (for instance, in August 1794, it had removed Michelangelo's two *Prigioni*).[35]

To a proposal for the transfer of the works collected in the Petits-Augustins to the Invalides, Bénézech (the Minister for the Interior) answered on 27 Germinal IV (8 April 1796) with the observation that this project of Lenoir's was at present impossible to put into practice, but that he did hope at some point in the future to gather together in the Louvre all the collections, in chronological order. In recognition of the zeal of Lenoir, he invited him to consult experts in antiquities and to hand over to the Musée Central and the Gallery of the Bibliothèque Nationale any objects which fell within their province.

Under the Restoration, the well-deserving Lenoir was often represented as the man responsible for saving the fragments of the glorious past of the Monarchy and its true national art from the fury of the populace, even at the risk of his own safety. The prefaces which he provided to the various editions of the catalogue of the museum demonstrate a facility in adapting himself to changing political climates, and therefore do not shed any light on his own cultural leanings. Nor is it easy to make out any specific scientific criteria beyond a vague chronological ordering of the museum, for which he used the restorations by the sculptor Beauvallet, and in which he combined in an arbitrary fashion many pieces from different monuments. It is not surprising that a connoisseur linked to the Musée Central such as Jean-Baptiste Lebrun should have severely criticized his catalogue when this was presented to the temporary commission for the arts in Thermidor of year II. The presence within the museum of an *Elysée*, a garden with funereal monuments surrounded by vegetation, allows one to perceive this collection as a place to be used for pre-Romantic meditations, quite different from the museum dedicated to the education of taste in young artists and the general public which was the aim of the museum to be opened in the Louvre. These were Viollet-le-Duc's comments:

> "It should be said that in this work it was the imagination rather than the knowledge or, critical spirit of the great curator that came into play. For instance, the Tomb of Abélard and Héloïse, which is now in the Eastern Cemetery, was made up with the arches and columns from the lateral naves of the Abbey church of Saint Denis, and bas-reliefs from the tombs of Philip and Louis (brother and son of Saint Louis), and masks from the Chapel to the Virgin Mary in Saint-Germain des Près, and finally two statues from the beginning of the fourteenth century. And it is in this manner that the statues of Charles V and Joan of Bourbon, originally from the tomb in Saint Denis, were placed above sixteenth-century wooden carvings taken from the Château de Gaillon, and then surmounted with a shrine dating from the end of the thirteenth century. In similar manner, the room dedicated to the fourteenth century was decorated with little arches removed from the rood-screen of the Sainte Chapelle, and with thirteenth-century statues backed onto columns also from the Sainte Chapelle: thus, in the absence of a Louis IX and a Marguerite of Provence, the statues of Charles V and Joan of Bourbon which had decorated the portal of the Célestins in Paris were rebaptized with the names of the saintly king and his consort."

116

On 21 February 1796, Lebrun intervened against this institution, with the proposal that the fine monuments dedicated to illustrious men should be removed from the shadows of the

116. *Alexandre Lenoir, tomb
of Abélard and Héloise;
reconstructed with Gothic fragments.
Paris, Cemetery of Père Lachaise.*

Petits-Augustins, and be brought together in the Pantheon a project which would be resurrected in 1806; as in 1811 that of returning the Royal tombs to Saint Denis, where the emperors of the new Napoleonic dynasty would also be buried. It was only with the Restoration that a project was resurrected which had been put into place by the sculptor Louis-Pierre Deseine as early as the year XI; not only were the royal tombs returned to Saint Denis but, closing the museum on 18 December 1816, the churches of Paris were authorized to take back the pieces which had been theirs, an operation which was carried out with a confusion that is readily confirmed by checking the original location of the sculptures and paintings.

The reassembly of the Royal tombs of Saint Denis was entrusted to the architect François Debret, who executed it according to the canons of the "restoring vandalism" lamented by Montalambert: the sixteenth-century monuments were reconstructed in the high church, the "gisants" piled up in the crypt, in the worst disorder, as in addition to the old monuments there now, those originally in other churches were also present. This situation, also grave because of the disastrous architectural restorations, was denounced by Montalambert to the Chambre des Pairs in 1847 with a speech which resulted in Eugène Viollet-le-Duc taking charge of the restorations in Saint Denis. It was only with him that under the Second Empire (between 1858 and 1867) the monuments of the basilica found an arrangement which was respectful to the sculptures: "This unfortunate church of Saint Denis was like a corpse on which the first artists on their way to becoming restorers, practised [their art]. For a period of thirty years, it suffered every conceivable mutilation, [so that in the end] its stability compromised, after the expenditure of huge sums, after the old order of architecture had been altered and all the fine monuments held within it disturbed, it became necessary to put a stop to this expensive experimentation in order to begin the programme established for the restorations by the Commission des Monuments Historiques".[36]

4. Restorations in the Musée Central des Arts

The Musée Central des Arts, that is the Louvre, created for the training of young artists and the education of public taste, was founded by the Republic, although attempts and suggestions for the exhibition of at least part of the Royal Collections pre-dated the Revolution: the Gallery which opened in the Luxembourg in 1750 closed to the public in 1779, when the palace became the residence of the Conte de Provence, and those projects (to which the *Encyclopédie* had already alluded) for a gallery in the Louvre remained exactly that: projects.

On 26 July 1791, the Constituent Assembly ordered that all artefacts deemed to be useful to the arts and sciences and belonging to the Crown should be gathered together in the Louvre and the Tuileries, a decision that was confirmed by the abolition of the monarchy in September 1792. On 8 November 1793, a museum was opened which left much to be desired as to its quality, so much so that on 28 Frimaire II (18 December 1793), David would demand the suspension of the governing committee, demonstrating with ease that it was formed neither of the best connoisseurs, nor indeed of people who were sufficiently guaranteed to run a revolutionary cultural programme. It was David himself who put forward the members of a new Conservatoire: for painting, the ageing Fragonard with the painters Bonvoisin, Le Sueur and Jean-Michel Picault, Robert Guillaume Dardel for sculpture, Delaunoy and Leroy for architecture, and Varon and Wicar (the painter known for his engravings in the Galleria di Firenze) for antiquities.[37]

David's criticism of the restorations was backed by Jean Michel Picault, and by the art-dealer and connoisseur Jean-Baptiste Lebrun. On the restorations, Picault's comments are of importance: in November 1792 he had succeeded in obtaining from the Museum the offer of the post of second restorer, after Hacquin and Martin de la Porte, with the obligation of putting back into order between forty and fifty paintings each month, a proposition he could only refuse. Jean-Baptiste Regnault, who as a member of the Commission was responsible for making him the offer, made it clear to him that the Minister wished to open the museum as quickly as possible, with all the paintings "restored", hence his opposition to the idea of a *concours* to decide who would be allowed to restore the public paintings, one of the points on which Picault was most insistent:

"I will do everything in my power to oppose the *concours*, because we are not looking for superior talents. Recognition of superiority of talent in one or more restorers would give them the right to some sort of supervisory role over less able [members of the profession]. The latter would find themselves criticized for the quality of their work, would be offended and would leave, and then we would have to entrust the restorations to anyone we could. This would be against the desires of the Minister who wishes to be able to enjoy the Museum this coming spring, which he would not be able to do if this came to pass".[38]

The idea of a *concours* (competition), whether for restoration in general or for one of its various specialities of lining, transfer, cleaning and pictorial restoration, was at the centre of the controversy between Picault and the Commission of the Museum until 7 February 1792 when, as well as trying to get the *concours* off the ground, Picault invited the Commission to examine his work in the Ponthièvre Gallery. Three members presented themselves (including Lenoir), "all undoubtedly very respectable, but without exception devoid of talent, and with no experience of painting, and without the slightest idea of the art of restoration". It was only because of David's encouragement that Picault persevered in his petitions to the Commission of the Museum and to the ministers, leading up to his intervention accompanied by an usher, amidst raised voices on both sides, at the Societé des Artistes on 23 February 1793, after which Picault (whose qualities as an artist were being contested) would be completely excluded from the Museum, until the time David included him in the new Conservatoire.[39]

Just as Pietro Edwards had done in Venice, but in a completely different climate and situation, during the course of this controversy Picault would insist on the necessity of distinguishing between the artist and the restorer. The usher who accompanied him to the Societé des Artistes in February 1793 read out the following observations: that "the art of painting and that of restoring, do not resemble each other in the least: that a painter who has the capacity of producing a masterpiece will destroy the masterpieces of another, wishing to restore them; that in a sick and damaged painting, the most renowned painter will substitute his style to that of Raphael, the Carracci or Titian; that his retouching will only result in the most monstrous assembly, the effect of which can only be to devalue the painting; that the painter has never occupied himself with this problem which requires long and careful studies, or else has only occupied himself with it in passing, and not thoroughly; that in order to restore successfully, specialized studies are necessary right from the very beginning, as is the knowledge of a series of operations which are both useful and indispensable, as well as consummate intimacy with the style and technique of the masters of every school to be able to recover them if they are lost, or conserve them if they are merely altered; in a word, one must be able to restore (*restituire*) even the most delicate nuances which are characteristic of a particular master or a particular school; and that the painter who is a stranger to this type of work and to its multiple aspects has seldom not adopted just one master or a single model that he has set himself to reach or surpass: this is a constant truth in the arts, which is confirmed by the experience of the painter who is in good faith, and by the admission of one of our most renowned artists; whilst the restorer who has studied all masters and all schools has not, and nor should he have, developed his own style. He has sacrificed his own ideas in order to bend to the ideas of others; he no longer has an existence of his own, he exists outside himself like one of these kings in a scene representing the rage of Achilles, or the pride of Agamemnon, he must be able to emulate the fierce and vigorous touch of Raphael, of Caravaggio, or the sweet and moving grace of Correggio, Titian, etc. .... And when there is nothing left of these masters, it is he and only he who can console you of their loss, bringing back to life the precious remains of their genius and talent, and even of their defects."

As an appendix to the account of his misadventures, Picault published the *Observations sur les inconvenients qui résultent des moyens que l'on employe pour les tableaux que l'on restaure journellement*, which had already been presented to the Royal administration in the spring of 1789. Alongside Edwards' reports, these are the most enlightened texts on what would be expected from a restorer at the end of the eighteenth century. Of lining he observed:

> "All paintings which are lined have lost their certificates of originality, the vigour of the handling of the masters, the freshness of touch and the very touches themselves ..., etc. Just look at the national pictures which hang in the Museum. Those who line paintings have no other means at their disposal but to iron their surface with hot irons. This operation which softens the paint flattens the touches of the masters, smooths paintings and in one fell swoop annihilates their beauty, their value, etc. Just look at the national pictures: amongst many, the portrait of the *Grand Master de Vignancourt*, painted by Michelangelo da Caravaggio, a painting irretrievably lost, along with many others, etc."

As a positive example he cites his own work on the paintings in the Galerie Penthièvre:

> "Most paintings which have been lined are just as covered with cracks now as they were before, but have in the meantime lost their freshness and the vitality of their touch. Look at the national paintings and the little Le Sueur from the Chartreuse, which is at present in the deposits of the Petits-Augustins, etc. .... All the paintings which are lined because of their cracks, do not lose them, and the cracks and delaminations (*sollevamenti*) do not augment and proliferate any less than before, depending on the nature of the ground and the movements which occur with the passage of time, etc. Look at the national paintings in the museum. The cracks in a painting which has been lined become hard without any possibility of change, without however being able to eradicate their traces as air has entered, and then the various varnishes, so that they all now have a blackish appearance which cannot be removed unless one were to melt the entire picture surface, which is not a possibility .... The paintings which have cracks, and these are wide ones, such as are found in the paintings of de la Hyre, de la Fosse, Parrocel, etc., have had them all filled and then retouched ...."

As far as transfers from panel and from copper are concerned (for transfers from canvas he prefers other methods of restoration), he noted that "all the paintings which have been transferred from panel onto canvas have lost the purity of their colours, their smoothness, the freshness of handling, their transparency …, etc. because the paint has taken on the imprint of the canvas weave for which it was not made. This canvas weave produces a multitude of deformations on the picture surface which enfeebles the handling and the touch of the master and destroys the painting's true worth. Look at the paintings transferred from panel onto canvas; look at the paintings from the Chartreuse and weep; examine the *Holy Family* by Raphael, and make an honest judgement. All the paintings which were painted on panel and that have deteriorated to the extent that one is forced to remove them from their original support should be transferred onto a similar support which has been appropriately prepared. Then they will not lose any of their surface finish. One must know this in order to believe it, and hence notice it: which is a fact of some importance. I can provide proof for all that I state."

Speaking of paintings on copper, he made the following observations: "pictures painted on copper in which only some parts are flaking and falling off, are restored in the most singular and truly incredible fashion. It is the custom, in these instances, to throw away all the parts that are about to be lost in the vulnerable areas (in that they can be detached without much effort). After which, all the parts that are missing the paint layer are filled and painted over, etc. Just look at all the paintings on copper which have been restored because they were in danger of losing paint, and judge for yourselves. One can reattach the parts which are threatening to come away and fall without transferring the painting from its support, unless complete and utter ruin is imminent: then one can transfer it from its copper support, then to reattach it".[40]

Hacquin published a brief response which was almost a personal attack on Picault, in which he attempted to turn attention away from some of the observations made by his competitor, remembering some of his less felicitous results, and pointing out that not all the linings of the paintings in the Museum were the work of Hacquin, and that in 1784 he had had to reline some paintings which had already been lined by Picault. Moreover, Robert Picault's transfers from panel had not been put back onto a similar support, but onto canvas. And finally, he reviewed some of the paintings in the Penthièvre Gallery, criticizing amongst others, Guido Reni's *Rape of Helen*: "The cracks are raised and open, the whole surface seems to have been punctured and torn away (*strappata*), the edges of the cracks are raised, the fills are lifting; all this you can check yourselves with both your eyes and hands".[41]

During the controversy, the administrators of the Museum reproached Picault with the poor outcome of the transfers carried out by his father (Hacquin reminded the reader of the "blackish and glutinous liquid" exuding from the cracks of Andrea del Sarto's *Charity*); the other polemicist who was attacking them, Jean-Baptiste Lebrun, lent himself to other criticisms for his activity as an art-dealer, probably not without foundation as, during the Revolution, he had been acting as an agent for the Empress Catherine II, and in 1792 was put on trial for being involved with the debts of an *émigré*.

Lebrun's principal argument against the administration of the Museum was that to hang the paintings and to oversee their restoration, connoisseurs were needed, not painters: it was not sufficient simply to hand over a painting to this or that liner, or to this or that painter, indifferently, in order to restore the image. Their work should always be supervised by a connoisseur: the artist "has never subjected himself to the often dry, almost repugnant, task of studying these paintings which are hidden beneath dust, disgusting varnishes, inept repaintings, until they have been freed of this ignominious and dreadful attire, allowing in the end a masterpiece or at least a good painting to be revealed".[42]

Recommended by David in November 1792 but to no avail, Picault stressed the necessity of the participation of connoisseurs in the organization of the Museum, publishing his *Réflexions sur le Muséum National*, in which he gave examples of painters who were poor connoisseurs, and protested against the methods used by Godefroid and Hoogstoel who were still working on the restoration of national paintings, as they had in the time of Pierre, the director of the national collections who favoured leaving paintings to die their natural death, as modern artists would be able to provide substitutes. During these clashes with the ministers and the administration of the Museum, Lebrun published his *Observations sur le Muséum National, par le citoyen Lebrun, peintre et marchand de tableaux*, in which he listed the bad restorations in the museum, insisting on the fact that painters had no knowledge of old techniques and, through boredom, would hand over restorations to their students to carry out, who then proceeded to ruin the paintings. Confirming this assertion, the administrative papers of the museum show Regnault the painter as a member of the directive committee, responsible in 1793 for the removal of the restorations from Rubens' *Village Fair* and the *Marie de'Medici* cycle, whilst his pupil Louis-Benjamin Devauges restored a *Marriage of the Virgin* by Philippe de Champaigne. Lebrun also demanded that there should be a *concours* in order to choose those allowed to restore paintings belonging to the nation.

Nor were the accusations against the museum restorers made by David in January 1794 (those mentioned above referring to Raphael's colouring) without foundation: of *La Sainte Famille de François I*, restored by Martin de la Porte, he said: "you will move your eyes away from this famous Raphael, which a heavy, barbaric hand has fearlessly profaned. Completely retouched, it has lost all that distinguished it not only amongst masters of that school, but within the œuvre of Raphael himself, that is his sublime use of colour." It is probable that David did not distinguish between irreparable damage and poor restoration: the restorer's report seems to suggest that the loss of Raphael's colour was mostly the result of overpaint, and to retouching along the cracks, as he noted: "Cleaned and integrated (*raccordato*) with the utmost care, the Virgin's head was particularly damaged by losses in the paint layer, splits and little holes which destroyed the harmony of this painting; it was retouched with lapis lazuli and with the utmost attention using a magnifier".[43]

Other observations made by David in his *Second report on the necessity of removing the commission of the museum*, dated 27 Nivôse II (16 January 1794), showed how the damages he lamented tallied with the condition of the paintings: in *Moses Trampling Pharaoh's Crown* by Poussin "you will not see anything more than a worn red and black canvas, destroyed by restoration". Although its condition may well have been caused by previous cleanings, the abraded state of Correggio's *Antiope* is still so evident as not to require further comment, and it is understandable that the great painter should be worried that already some works by Vernet were coming under the hands of restorers, being lined and covered with a thick varnish, "which removes from sight the excellence which lovers of his art are looking for".[44]

Finally, the Conservatoire, with the composition suggested by David, suspended all restorations from 26 Pluviôse II (14 February 1794), awaiting the *concours*. In June, by order of the Convention, the project of the decree drawn up by Gabriel Bouquier on behalf of the Committee of Public Instruction was published with an introduction discussing the necessity for Old Master paintings for the formation of taste of Republican artists, a taste which, if one were to visualize these programmes, makes one think more of Géricault than David, whose technique was still firmly attached to its eighteenth-century roots: "In order to paint the energy of a people who, breaking free of their chains, have chosen to dedicate themselves to the liberation of mankind, bold colours are required, a nervous style, a fear-less brush, a volcanic genius .... Let us dust down those superb paintings which, described as black pictures by our miniaturists, have been left to rot, forgotten, because of the iner-tia, the bad taste and the cowardice of courtiers responsible for the progress of the arts. Of these paintings which are rejected with such affectation by ignorance, it may well be that even if they cannot serve as a models through their subject matter, they can inspire young painters to use daring techniques, nervous draughtmanship, a virile handling, vigorous colouring, bold brushwork and a sure touch. And it is with this kind of painting, almost completely forgotten and neglected by the academic schools of painting which were ours, that we need to begin to revolutionize this fine art".[45]

The project for the *concours* extended beyond the thermidor revolt, when the Conservatoire of the Museum was purged of elements such as Wicar, and David himself was imprisoned. Criticizing the Conservatoire of 26 Pluviôse and David who had inspired it, the painter Guillaume Martin now became the spokesman for the project in *Un avis à la Nation sur la situation du Museum National*, and in November 1794 a definitive version was reached. The test restorations would be carried out on works chosen from the deposits, which were suitable for the various specializations (lining, transfer, etc.); for sculpture, it was envisaged that one could compete with both the execution of models of the parts to be integrated, and versions in marble. All the trial pieces would be tested for their reactions to variations in humidity and dryness; after six months, examining their condition after these tests, the jury would pronounce itself on the classification of the competitors.[46] However, the competition never took place. Picault remained in the Conservatoire until his substitution by a council of administration in Pluviôse of year V, when his duties were limited to restoration. In 1797, he was entrusted with another transfer of the *Grand Saint Michel*; the last report of his involve-ment with the museum is dated July 1803.

Lebrun was part of the Commission Temporaire des Arts (which replaced the Commission des Monuments) from August 1793; for it, he drew up various inventories of religious institutions and houses belonging to *émigrés*, whose collections were being requi-sitioned. In January, at the Société Républicaine des Arts, Le Sueur came under attack and found himself obliged to resign from the Commission. In April 1794, he was nevertheless chosen to be one of a number of judges charged with choosing and valuing the works which were becoming the property of the nation, and in November he once more became a mem-ber of the Commission Temporaire, as a deputy to the painting commission. At this time he published *Quelques idées sur les dispositions, l'arrangement et la décoration du Museum National*, where he put forward the best methods for illuminating the museum with sky-lights and the hanging of the paintings, and spoke of the dangers inherent in restoration, especially in cleaning, once again proposing a *concours* for the restoration of paintings belonging to the nation. When the administration of the museum was reformed in year V, Lebrun was nominated as expert member of the board, charged with valuing and classify-ing the works, and judging what the paintings required in the way of restoration. Finally, when Denon became director, he was replaced by Aubourg, becoming an honorary mem-ber, a sinecure which left him free to undertake commercial enterprises such as the journey of 1807 and 1808 though southern France, Spain and Italy, buying paintings and illustrat-ing them with a collection of engravings, an episode evoked by Roberto Longhi when he rediscovered a Pontormo which had been illustrated as an Andrea del Sarto. It was in this position that Lebrun received a pension from the museum until his final year, 1813.[47]

5. Napoleonic requisitioning

After the battle of Fleurus, on 8 Messidor of year II, the first of the works of art from an occupied territory, destined for the Central Museum in Paris, were requisitioned.

During Vendèmiaire of year III, Lebrun and Picault carried out the first interventions on the paintings by Rubens arriving from Belgium (the *Deposition*, the *Coup de lance*, *The Erection of the Cross*): a light cleaning and the reattachment of areas which were in danger of falling off. Over and above the intention of removing these paintings as useful contributions to the progress of the arts in France, what appears ever more clearly is the idea of these paintings, manuscripts and works of art as trophies, conquered not requisitioned. Already in the Fructidor of year II, Grégoire had been speaking of the glories of arms in Belgium, and looked forward to new arrivals from Italy; in year VI, Lebrun published a "critical examination" of the works brought from the peninsula, which began with a eulogy of the conquering heroes, and then referred to the deplorable condition of the paintings from Milan and Bologna. The new arrivals caused congestion both in the exhibition rooms and in the restoration laboratories, so much so that from 1801, many of the requisitioned works and others from the Royal Collection were sent to the new museums in the provinces, and in the new climate of Caesarist bonapartism, Napoleon's homes were decorated with public paintings and sculptures (mostly removed from the "museum of the French School" at Versailles). Amongst the works requisitioned from abroad, the *Battle of Issus* by Altdorfer was placed in the Emperor's bathroom at Saint Cloud.[48]

If we were to compare the capacities of the best restorers at the end of the eighteenth century as described by Picault in his *Observations* (capacities which were realized in much of the work carried out under the direction of Edwards in Venice, and expressly desired in the debates at the end of the century on the use of varnish) with those shown in the restorations in the Musée Central des Arts, their results were frequently rather modest (for instance, the transfer of Fra Bartolomeo's *The Redeemer Amongst the Evangelists*), and often had irreversible consequences, as was well demonstrated by the new restoration of Raphael's *Saint Cecilia*.

In May 1798, the objections levelled at his charges induced Hacquin to present two reports in which he described the methods he used to renew old linings, as well as to reline. He made a distinction between paintings which did not exceed five feet by four (one foot = 32.5 cm), for which he used stretchers and which would be the recipients of various facings and soakings (*imbibizioni*) of glues and varnishes; these he would then go over with irons and an especially constructed box-wood cylinder, always taking care to have made some marks to identify the position of the most prominent brush-strokes, so as not to flatten them. For big paintings, it was impossible to carry out such precise work: the painting was rolled onto a cylinder with a diameter of half a metre, and it was laid onto the new canvas (stretched on a stretcher) and ironed on, one foot at a time. But even with this method it was possible to avoid the defects of *en masse* linings which, with the glue applied over the entire surface of the canvas, in part dried too quickly or, when it was too thick, formed an intermediate layer between the old and the new canvas which cracked, transferring these cracks on to the picture surface; whilst if the glue was too dilute, it made the old canvas shrink, with the risk of the priming detaching. Moreover, with the old method, it was impossible to remove air bubbles, or to follow the heat of the iron with one hand left free whilst ironing with the other; and the stretcher bars and the seams in the canvas both left marks on the picture surface. Old linings of this type always required reworking.

In October 1799, the liner Foucque made the revelation that Hacquin had charged for the lining of Domenichino's *Madonna of the Rosary* and other paintings, as though lined with "*maroufle*" (at a cost of three francs fifty per square foot, according to the tariffs fixed by Lebrun), whilst in fact they had been lined using the old glue-lining system (one franc per square foot). Hacquin justified himself by saying that, not having been sufficiently remunerated, he could only carry out work in line with the payment received.

Hacquin's "*maroufle*" consisted of a mixture of gum elemi, mastic (tears of), oil of spike, white lead in pigment form and essence of turpentine. First, a glue paste lining was carried out in order to reduce the cracking and flatten the surface, then this first lining was removed, and a lining was carried out using the above mixture and a double canvas. This method was to be used on the more important paintings, with a view to its lasting a very long time. Extremely tough, this type of lining aimed to protect the painting from damage caused by humidity, but reversibility was very much a secondary consideration. Masterpieces of painting were therefore guaranteed a much longer life than that expected by their creators. However, should it become necessary to remove one of these linings, the process would endanger the paint layer itself, as it would be sensitive to the reagents which would have to be used to remove the "*maroufle*".[49]

Accidents occurring during the transport of the works also resulted in the restoration of many of the requisitioned works: the ship carrying *Saint Peter the Martyr* by Titian, with destination Marseilles, was struck by a storm, as a result of which the wooden packing crate as well as the panel became sodden, and the painting had to be transferred onto canvas, a task carried out by Hacquin. This became a test piece for the transfer of Raphael's panel requisitioned from Foligno, the famous operation which took place between May 1800 and December 1801, under the supervision of a commission nominated by the Institut National at the invitation of the Committee of the Museum (two chemists, Guyton and Berthollet, and two painters, Vincent and Taunay), and described in a report which was published several times from 1802 onwards.

A transfer was decided upon because of the severe flaking and the splitting of the panel. Hacquin flattened the panel with a series of incisions in the wood, not very dissimilar to those described by Secco-Suardo for the same end. But even after the panel had been flattened, and the split mended, the restorer carried on with its removal, cutting it into pieces by means of two saws working both perpendicularly to the painted surface and parallel to it. He then thinned it using planes, until the panel was the thickness of a leaf, and then removing what was left with moisture, "a small area at a time". At this point, Hacquin did not then confine himself simply to removing the old fills which had been introduced to consolidate the paint, but removed the entire original glue/gesso ground, in order "to make the paint rather more flexible as it had rather dried out with the passage of time, he wiped it with cotton-wool imbibed with oil, drying it with pieces of old muslin. Then white lead bound in oil was applied with a soft brush in place of the glue-based ground."

After leaving it for three months to dry out, he went on to glue a gauze and a canvas onto the new ground, then removed the "*cartonnage*"[iv] from the front, and ironed the whole

---

[iv] Facing. As the French term implies, paper, often in several layers, is attached to the front of the painting, to the paint surface. Especially when used for operations where the restorer is either working on the support (canvas, panel or wall) or in transfer operations, where the original support is being removed, it aims to provide a stronger support to the paint layer *from the front*, thus preventing, largely, its disintegration. The adhesive used to attach it must be soluble in a material which will not endanger the paint layer during removal of the facing, once the paint is attached to a new support.

of the painting to remove all traces of the "cupping" (*recoquillement*) of the craquelure which had formed on the panel. With the new lining on the reverse and a new lead white oil priming, the painting found itself "incorporated to a more lasting ground than its original [that is Hacquin's *maroufle*!] and so would be protected from the events that had caused it to deteriorate". The restoration of the image was carried out by Röser.

In the official publication, no mention was made of the objections put forward by Lebrun on the necessity of transferring panel paintings onto a new panel ("in order to preserve in panel paintings that smoothness that paintings on canvas lack"), an argument which was pushed aside by the consideration of the better reaction of canvases to changes in humidity. Not only was the work preserved, but technically improved: to the degree that in 1815 it would return to Rome rolled up. Maybe because it was considered such an obvious procedure, the report makes no mention of the cleaning which Hacquin carried out on all the paintings before applying the "facing", so that this would adhere better to the paint layer; in Floréal (may) of year VIII, amongst the operations to be carried out, he referred to

117. *Raphael, Madonna di Foligno; transferred by François-Toussaints Hacquin, 1800–1801. Rome, Pinacoteca Vaticana.*

118. *Raphael, Saint Cecilia; transferred by François-Toussaints Hacquin, 1803. Bologna, Pinacoteca Nazionale.*

119. *Raphael, Saint Cecilia,
detail. Bologna, Pinacoteca
Nazionale.*

120. Raphael, *Saint Cecilia,*
detail. Bologna, Pinacoteca
Nazionale.

"the procedure employed up to now to remove the varnish from paintings and especially those that are going to be transferred, so that the glue which is used can adhere better, and so that the humidity employed does not produce that blanching of the varnish which can be more difficult to remove than the varnish itself".[50]

117   In 1957–1958, the *Madonna di Foligno* underwent a clumsy and complete cleaning (*pulita a fondo*), and now has a sky which veers towards the turquoise, both of which are difficult to ascribe to Raphael. If it is permissible to compare works painted at different moments of his career, the *Pala Ansidei* in the National Gallery, London, seems to show what the intonation of the sky might be when cleaned of all varnish, but not denatured. In order to avoid such disharmonies, Napoleonic restorers used to patinate transferred paintings, as can be seen in the *Saint Cecilia* in Bologna, a painting which if completely cleaned might well reveal the livid tonalities of the *Madonna di Foligno*.

118   Rapahel's *Saint Cecilia* was transferred in 1803, in the climate of super-efficiency
119   which was created in the Museum under Vivant Denon, who was made director on 22
120   December 1802. After the Restoration, as soon as the painting was returned to Bologna, the altered oil retouchings which could be seen on the painting were removed, and the toned varnishes were reapplied, possibly many times, accentuating even more the oily appearance of the French restoration. But all of this also succeeded in preserving that polished appearance ("*poli*") of the surface, characteristic of paintings on panel, which could easily be disturbed by traces of the weave when transferred onto canvas. Peliccioli intervened on the painting without modifying its appearance, despite the widely held dissatisfaction with the leaden appearance of the sky. When Nonfarmale subsequently worked on it, he decided not to clean the painting to any greater degree; recognizing the technical excellence of the French transfer, he considered the alterations in the painting resulting from Hacquin's intervention as definitive and irreversible. The oil which had been applied to the reverse during the transfer had now permeated through the old cracks, and other oily deposits had gathered in the cracks formed in the new lead white priming. To remove them would have resulted in this network of cracks becoming more evident, with an overall effect probably not very different from that of the *Madonna di Foligno*.

The condition of the *Saint Cecilia* was described by Lebrun in the "critical examination" of the works of art brought from Italy in year VI: "This painting is extremely dirty, there are many areas of lifting paint on Saint Paul's green tunic, and on the neck, the chest and in the lower part of the saint's garment. Other areas of flaked or burnt paint have been poorly filled and repainted. And finally, the ground and the paint are strewn with wormholes, especially in the upper region. It has not incurred any damage during transport." Of the glazes, similar to those one can still see on the outer garment of the saint, Lebrun observed that "in all the areas in which Raphael has used glazes, these now have drying cracks (*sobbollito*), which can be ascribed to his use of some excessively fast drying material". Cavalcaselle would particularly refer to the loss of the glazes in the Gloria of angels in the top section, and others are noticeable too, in the shaded part of the faces of the two female saints, which appear flatter than in the lights, which may have proved more resistant because of the presence of lead white; and, as Picault had indeed regretted for transfers from wood to canvas, the paint has taken on the imprint of the canvas.

Passavant would recall that the retouchings executed in France were removed on the return of the *Saint Cecilia* to Bologna because, as was the case with all the Raphaels restored in Paris, they had darkened. The retouchings present at the time of writing have been executed with great ability: the candle burn described by Richardson can only be detected with difficulty in the shadows of the Magdalen's robe. And finally, we have the glossy, transparent patination which contributed to give the painting the appearance of a work with no thickness, as though it were a "mirror", as De Burtin would describe it when admiring the results of the French liners, and which was to be considered as amongst the achievements of a perfect restoration, giving back to the picture surface that *"poli"* of a painting on panel, which would have been too much altered by the weave of the canvas.[51]

Although it could be said that transfer was the preferred intervention amongst the restorers of the Museum, not all the paintings underwent this process automatically. On its arrival in Rome, Raphael's *Transfiguration* was only flaking in a few restricted areas: it was given a cradle with iron bars, which it still has, and it was cleaned and retouched by Röser, probably not without some additional glazing, those "light little tints" that Cavalcaselle noticed on it when bewailing its excessive cleaning. However, as we have seen, the cleaning had perplexed Henry Fuseli, and the raw (*spatinato*) state in which the panel presented itself after the 1976 cleaning would seem to show that his objections were not without foundation. David himself, according to a German traveller, deplored the fact that some restorers had repainted works by Domenichino, and that to remove the reddish tinge, they had rasped the surface of sculptures such as the *Apollo Belvedere*.[52]

We still do not know when exactly Hacquin's activity came to an end. When the Raphaels arrived from Madrid in 1810, the *Madonna of the Fish*, the *Visitation* and the *Spasimo di Sicilia* were all transferred by Féréol de Bonnemaison, who was also the Director of Restoration after the Restoration of the Monarchy; in fact, the latter painting was transferred in order to enable it to withstand the return journey to Madrid, which it finally made in 1822.[53]

Secco-Suardo would contrast the methods advocated by him for the transfer of panel paintings to those described and practised by the French, who were still considered to be the best in the middle of the century. Most of all, he criticized their overuse of oilings, which would lead to the darkening of the painting, and the employment of materials of disparate reactions to humidity for their "facings" and in their new supports. The description of the support onto which Paul Kievert had transferred the *Saint John the Baptist* and the *Saint Catherine* by Andrea Solario in the Poldi-Pezzoli collection, which was taken apart by Zanchi because it had not been successful, is one of the most important passages in his *Manuale*. In contrast, transfers such as the *Joan of Aragon* by Raphael and Giulio Romano (carried out at the time of Louis Philippe), after the recent cleaning, were seen to have been very well executed, without the painting losing the characteristics of a painting on panel.[54]

It was only in the second half of the nineteenth century that the fame of French (and Belgian) restorers for transferring paintings would be equalled by that of the Ssidorov in St Petersburg. Because of the climatic conditions within the Hermitage museum (the heating remained on for eight months of the year), they transferred all the new acquisitions onto canvas; amongst these were the *Madonna of the Book* by Raphael, and the *Madonna Litta* thought to be by Leonardo. The fame of the Ssidorov was such that, even in Belgium, it was they who were chosen for the transfer of the *Heads of Negroes* by Rubens from the Musées Royaux in Brussels.[55]

6. The world of the *"estrattisti"*

The technique of the *"strappo"*[v] of frescos, experimented with by Contri and carried out by Picault on the frescos by Primaticcio in the Chambre Saint-Louis in Fontainebeau, was developed in Italy in the eighteenth and nineteenth centuries. The most famous practitioners of this art were the Succi from Imola. In 1775 Giacomo, because of the reconstruction of the cathedral in his home town, detached a number of frescos by Bartolomeo Cesi, to which Lanzi referred; Secco-Suardo described some of the technical details of these transfers, and also that of a fresco by Andrea Camassei which was detached in Rome in 1792, all works that he was able to examine when they were in the hands of Michelangelo Gualandi in Bologna: "their surface is smooth, clean, without any signs of resin or any such material. They are lined onto a fine canvas, and are very flexible, which shows that the glue with which they were attached was very liquid, and could therefore be applied very thinly."

The fame of Succi's transfers was not confined, as was the case with Contri, to the limits of the Po valley. Cosimo Morelli, the architect for the new cathedral in Imola, in 1809 remembered that thirty years previously Giacomo Succi had offered his services in order to transfer the frescos by Cesi which would have been destroyed in the demolition of the old cathedral, and had referred to the success of the experimental tests carried out in Rome, despite the incredulity expressed by Mengs; [his renown was such] that a sinecure was created for Succi, the post of *"estrattista* of the paintings in the Sacro Palazzo Apostolico".

An inventory of the Accademia di Bologna drawn up between 1804 and 1808 related the failure of the *strappo* of two large-scale figures by Orazio Sammacchini, which had been detached from the church of Santa Maria degli Angeli; it is also likely that much was made of this failure, because of the antagonism towards the process of transfer of mural paintings which had become commonplace during the Napoleonic era, and because of the fear of the requisition of mural paintings which arose periodically, an attitude which was still very much present in the excellent article by Cicognara, published in 1825.

Two fragments from Cesi's frescos in Imola, depicting *Saint Anne* and a *Prophet*, which recently resurfaced in the municipal museum, are in too poor a state of conservation to be able to draw any conclusions as to the technical details of the transfer. More substantial evidence is provided by Guercino's frescos which were detached (so we are told by the engraver Francesco Rosaspina) in 1791, in Cento, and were at one time in the Aldovrandi collection in Bologna before moving to a private collection in Venice. The results of the transfer are different from those described by Secco-Suardo: the overmantel depicting *Venus* has a rigid support full of deformations, with the paint layer which is secure but lifting in large sections, whilst the surface has a grey finish broken up by countless little losses. The fine figure of a white mare in Casa Panini adheres in a more regular fashion to a support which is also more flexible, but shows the signs of an irregularly executed transfer as well as weave imprint. Therefore, both the fragments from Imola as well as the two Guercinos show results that seem to justify the diffidence

121

---

[v] There is no equivalent for either *"strappo"* or *"estrattisti"*, so when these terms occur, I shall leave them in the original Italian. "Strappo" (see diagram of the structure of a fresco, in the Glossary) refers to the detachment of the painted surface of the fresco, which remains attached to the paper or canvas which has been glued to it, and is "torn" (*strappato*) away in a similar way to that of a plaster from one's skin. *Estrattista* is the term applied to those who carry out transfers, particularly those of frescos, whether *strappo* (flexible, paint surface only) or *stacco* (rigid, with the plaster), or *a massello* (with part of the wall).

121. *Guercino, The White Mare; fresco transferred by Giacomo Succi, 1791. Cento, Pinacoteca Civica.*

122. *Prospero Fontana, fragment of a frieze; fresco transferred by Pellegrino Succi, around 1810. Bologna, Palazzina della Viola.*

felt towards these first *strappi*, and demonstrate that Giacomo Succi had not yet acquired that skill which his sons would later demonstrate on so many occasions.[56]

The fear of bad transfers which would result in the flaking of paint from the new support after a only a few years was not without foundation: Cicognara recalled (among others), a certain Madame Barret who, at the time of the Kingdom of Etruria, had carried out a poor transfer on a fifteenth-century *Madonna and Child* in Florence, and in Rome had been respon-sible for the loss of a fresco by Guido Reni in the Quirinale, when she transferred it onto a new support.[57] However, during the Napoleonic suppressions, the frescos which were brought together in the Brera Gallery in Milan, especially those from the Milanese convents which had been removed together with a portion of the wall (*a massello*), were only transferred onto can-vas after the unification of Italy, with at times excellent results, as for instance in the case of the *Madonna and Child* by Bramantino. In order to prevent the detachment of frescos for purely commercial ends, in 1818 the Reggenza Provvisoria del Governo Veneto issued a decree gov-erning the circumstances in which the transfer of mural paintings would be permitted: "It will not be possible to carry out these removals, unless it can be properly proven that the wall to which the painting is attached is in danger of falling, or else that it forms part of an edifice which is destined for demolition; or unless it can be proven that the painting will incur damage by remain-ing attached, and finally, unless there is some other grave motive necessitating its removal".[58]

Whilst the transfers executed by Giacomo Succi seemed fully to justify the diffidence shown in the first years of the nineteenth century towards the activity of the *estrattisti*, many of those carried out by his sons Pellegrino and Domenico seem, at times, to be preferable to those we sometimes see carried out in our times. The oldest is a portion of a fresco by

122   Prospero Fontana in the room with the *Stories of Constantine* in the Palazzina della Viola in Bologna, which was transferred by Pellegrino before 1812, peeling off (*strappando*) the pig-ment (*colore*) from the *intonaco* with a facing, as I was able to confirm in 1970 from a few fragments of paper remaining on the surface; the fresco was reattached in the Palazzina della Viola, but avoiding any intervention which might alter the character of such an impor-tant piece of evidence of the early days of the transfer of mural paintings.

123   The fresco depicting *Platina before Sixtus IV* from Forlì is the only one for which it is specifically mentioned that Domenico Succi alone was responsible for the transfer in 1826, when it formed part of a campaign of restoration of the public paintings in Rome, directed and overseen by Vincenzo Camuccini. Roberto Longhi was not wrong in citing this fresco as perhaps one of the best *strappi di colore* ever executed. Its present appearance is enhanced by the rigid support to which it has been attached in more recent times; the only shortcomings are some limited areas in which the canvas has imprinted its weave, maybe because these were painted in a glue medium. In the cutting down of the fresco for the transfer process, from which were excluded a large portion of the base and the frieze which would have completed it in the upper section, care was taken to preserve the entire thickness of the lateral pilasters, demon-strating an understanding of the importance of the perspective in the presentation of the scene.

It is, however, referring to this transfer that Horsin Déon lamented the loss of its per-fection in that the surface had been left rough, without giving it that *poli* so dear to French restorers (and this was still the case in the middle of the nineteenth century). The good result obtained by Domenico Succi was, on the other hand, confirmed, if indirectly, by William Dyce when he described the difference in the parts executed *a fresco* and *a secco* by Melozzo, without complaining of any alteration which impeded his appreciation of these peculiarities [in technique], even after the transfer. In Horsin Déon, we therefore find a survival of an operational model, based on the same lack of understanding of the nature of fresco as that demonstrated by Jean Michel Picault, when he observed that the process of transfer eliminated from the mural paintings the marks of the trowel from the plaster, and that, by taking on the imprint of the canvas, there was a hundred per cent improvement, the painting appearing "soft and smooth" ("*moelleux et suave*").[59]

123. *Melozzo da Forlì, Sixtus IV Nominates Platina as Prefect of the Biblioteca Vaticana, detail; fresco transferred by Domenico Succi, 1826. Rome, Pinacoteca Vaticana.*

Photographs taken before recent cleanings show some of the Succi's *strappi* masked by some material, possibly oil or wax, for instance the *Hercules* by Ludovico Carracci, transferred around 1839 and which is today in the Victoria & Albert Museum; or the cycle of frescos by Annibale and his collaborators, in the Herrera Chapel in San Giacomo degli Spagnoli, which was transferred between 1835 and 1842 and is today divided between the Prado and the museum in Barcelona. Such obfuscations are not, however, found on all transferred works, and must be due to the employment of materials which were only used in certain cases, or else have been applied subsequently. I believe the use of these materials, rather than a desire to adjust the painting to the model of other painting techniques, shows a desire to differentiate in the presentation of mural paintings which, successfully or otherwise, enhance the [original] characteristics of the final surface effects of frescos, which were known not to be the same in all instances. This is confirmed by the fact that in 1844 Pellegrino Succi used a mixture of walnut oil and spirits of turpentine (*acqua ragia*) on the frescos in the Basilica at Assisi to control the saltpetre, materials which he obviously felt were not incompatible with fresco technique.

There is no veil covering the *Platina* by Michelozzo, nor the two small Raphaelesque paintings depicting *Archers* and *The Wedding of Alexander and Roxane* which came into the Borghese Gallery in 1836, where they were framed and put under glass as though easel paintings; nor is there any of this cloudiness of surface in Domenichino's frescos which are now in the National Gallery in London and were removed from the Villa Belvedere in Frascati, nor, in the same gallery, the frescos by Pinturicchio and Signorelli which were originally in the Palzzo del Magnifico in Siena, from whence they were removed for a French collector between 1842 and 1844.[60]

To the exceptionally good results achieved by the Succi in the transfer of mural paintings, corresponds the extraordinary capacity for both observation and understanding of mural painting that is demonstrated by Leopoldo Cicognara in the article published in 1825 in "Antologia".

For example, on the difference in the *intonaci* used: "in Tuscany one sees old paintings, and especially those by Andrea del Sarto, executed with unparalleled preciosity, but because of their enamel-like surface without facility of touch. Why this should be the case was made clear from the results of the analysis undertaken by the diligent signor Fabbrini, a painter, which showed that the *intonaco* in the cloister of the Nunziata was composed only of lime and powdered marble, without sand, and therefore he obtained from the mason's trowel a much smoother finish than the plaster used in Rome which was made with volcanic lime (*calce puzzolana*). In Bologna and Rome, more singularly, a coarser sand was preferred which was thought to provide more tooth, so to speak, thus retaining the pigment and receiving on the very surface a verve of finishing touches and rapid glazings, produced more by the vivacity of creative energy rather than the industriousness of diligent practice."

Against the practice of the transfer of frescos, in addition to the arguments relating to the impoverishment of the artistic heritage, Cicognara also put forward observations of a technical order: on the lime which makes a sort of veil, a layer of natural patination, on the surface of the fresco and which the *strappo* shatters, thus losing the fresco's transparency; on the needlessness of detaching too thin a layer, and against the use of sulphuric acid to facilitate the detachment of the paint layer, all observations which have lost none of their pertinence today:

> "I should like to now also reveal one of the pernicious discoveries with which some
> thought to prevent in some degree the above drawbacks: in order to avoid the frac-
> ture of the crystallized surface, and to procure a good adhesion of this surface to

the first canvas used to detach it from the wall, they have thought it advantageous to wet it with milk mixed with concentrated sulphuric acid. But they did not realize that the action of the concentrated sulphuric acid on the calcareous plaster was to convert the calcium carbonate into the sulphate, thus decomposing the surface of the painting; and there are other effects, all very grave. First of all, the mixing of the colours at the slightest motion or rubbing on the part of the practitioner, or even by the inevitable effervescence; secondly, the loss of all transparency which brings an immediate visible opacity; thirdly, the conversion into sulphate of only the top layer of pigment, so that it can occur that only this layer will detach, adhering quickly to the glue applied to it, leaving behind part of the paint attached to the plaster, as one has often seen in places where this method has been used for the transfers."

As these pages show, the examination of wall paintings was accompanied by chemical investigations which led to the identification of pigments or of the components of the *intonaco*. Giuseppe Branchi, professor of chemistry at Pisa, analysed a few fragments taken from the frescos of Niccolò di Tommaso and Antonio di Vita in the chapel of San Jacopo in the Duomo of Pistoia; Giuseppe Zeni stated explicitly that the *intonaco* in Mantegna's frescos in the Eremitani was composed of four parts plaster and one part sand, and gave various analyses of the behaviour of the pigments on the *intonaco*, and of the new supports onto which he transferred them.[61]

Other practitioners of transfers (*estrattisti*) active in this period tended to be amateurs, and never achieved the renown of the Succi. The Paduan pharmacist Giuseppe Zeni transferred a number of frescos from the Carraresi tombs in Sant'Agostino del Guariento, a fresco by Parentino from the cloister of Santa Giustina (1820), and the fragments of the school of Mantegna from the Oratory of San Sebastiano which now can be seen in the Museo Civico in Padua; one of his texts, in which he refers to his subject matter as (very scientifically) "calcareous hydropaintings" (*idropinti calcarei*), was only published in 1840.[62]

Of greater renown was Count Filippo Balbi who, between 1817 and 1818, transferred more than a hundred frescos by Veronese from the Soranza, near Castelfranco Veneto, one of the many villas which, during the period of crisis which was the Republic of Venice, found themselves without owners able to maintain them, and were sold for building materials. Many of these fragments of frescos can no longer be traced, others are known to be in museums and private collections, and others again were given as a gift by Balbi himself to the Duomo of Castelfranco; from their appearance, having been put back in order for the Veronese exhibition of 1939 (Cicognara was critical of their alteration due to the presence of some "liniment"), they can be considered as some of the best of nineteenth-century transfers. A celebratory pamphlet published in 1819 described the method used by Balbi, only veiling in secrecy the actual components of the materials used by him: "... he first covers the fresco with finest soft cambric which he has prepared with a particular mixture which attaches it strongly [to the fresco]. It dries slowly, little by little, depending on the temperature of the air, until – having become completely dry, it detaches itself of its own accord removing with it the coloured surface, of which only the barest trace remains on the untouched *intonaco* on the wall. In that moment one can see and admire what Paolo himself neither saw, nor could ever have believed would be seen, that is the reverse of his paintings. In order to straighten it once more, he covers the reverse of the painting with another piece of muslin, soaked in a preparation which you can well imagine is different from the first, and places the whole under even weights, leaving it until it has thoroughly dried out. Then one can see the painting flattened

124

124. Paolo Veronese,
Temperance; fresco transferred
by Filippo Balbi, 1817–1818.
Castelfranco Veneto, Duomo.

125. *Bernardino Luini, Putto;*
fresco transferred by Stefano
Barezzi, 1822. Milan,
Pinacoteca di Brera.

126. *Bernardino Luini,*
The Crossing of the Red Sea;
fresco transferred by Stefano
Barezzi, 1822. Milan,
Pinacoteca di Brera.

out and strongly secured to the second cambric, the first one having once again become white. With a new adhesive he then adheres the overflexible cambric to a stronger canvas, thus ensuring a work which will last through time".[63]

In Milan, we find Stefano Barezzi working as an *estrattista*, who was remembered by Secco-Suardo as a bad practitioner. He probably compensated for his lack of practical skill with an ability for self-advertisement, as Paillot de Montalbert would speak of him as the inventor of the technique of *strappo*. His most important undertaking was the transfer of the frescos by Bernardino Luini in the Villa Pelucca in Monza, which were transferred onto panel in 1822, and are today mostly housed in the Brera Museum in Milan. Not only were they cut into pieces of no more than half a square metre in order to carry out the transfer (compare this to the transfer of the Camassei by Giacomo Succi in 1792, which was 1.25 metres high and 5.60 metres long), but they were also cut down in a completely arbitrary fashion, leaving out the marginal sections, so that the individual stories now lack their original proportions and perspective.[64]

125,
126

Amongst the practitioners who were thought to have contributed to the progress of the art of transfer of frescos, Secco-Suardo also referred to Antonio Boccolari from Modena; Giordani specified that his method (which was a *strappo* technique) was different from that practised by either Contri or Succi. Notwithstanding the positive judgement of Secco-Suardo, who particularly mentioned the octagonal ceiling from Scordiano, recent restorations resulted in some reservations as to the effects and the technique of his transfers. In the *strappo* of the frescos by Garofalo in the Corte Ospitale di Rubiera, he even limited the transfer to the sole head of the figure of Moses, and half the figure of the horseman plus the head of the princess in *Saint George and the Dragon*.[65]

In 1842, when the Parliamentary Commission was investigating which technique (oil or fresco) was best suited for the decoration of the Houses of Parliament in London, taking into consideration the aspects of durability and conservation of mural paintings, it illustrated a method of *strappo* similar to that practised by Balbi, which had been put into practice in 1829 in Brescia by Ludwig Gruner on the frescos by Lattanzio Gambara in the convent of Saint Eufemia; and the information on which techniques could be used for the transfer of mural paintings in the Select Committee's Report always refers to Italian practitioners. The methods which developed, and consisted rather in the demolition of the supporting wall than in the detachment of the layer of painted plaster, must have originated from different sources than the expedient of the *strappo* of the sole paint layer. Horsin Dèon described one which, with the help of large panels of wood which were anchored to the painting as a support, still appeared in his manual of 1855, whilst the vitality which the transfers *a massello* still enjoyed in the nineteenth century was well attested by the space which Forni devoted to this practice, in 1866.[66]

Notes

1. X. de Salas, *Miscellanea goyesca*, in "Archivo Español de Arte", 1950, p. 338; Kurz, 1962, p. 59; Mahon, 1962, pp. 467–468; Kurz, 1963, p. 95. The text quoted by Salas observes that the painting of 1777 "was painted eight years after its pendant, a drawback which time will put right, as my paintings have the advantage, and I the satisfaction, of seeing that my works improve with time, which gives them vigour in colouring and greater harmony" (*a ... huit ans de moins que son pendant, défaut que le temps corrige, car mes tableaux ont l'avantage, et j'ai la satisfaction de voir que mes ouvrages gagnent par le temps que leur donne de la vigueur de couleur, de l'harmonie*).

2. David, 1794, ed. 1909, p. 269.

3. F. Zapater y Gomez *Colleccion de ... cuadros ... de Goya precedidos de un epistolario*, Madrid, 1924, p. 63; Kurz, 1962, p. 59. Here is the text of Goya's letter:

"No puedo ponderar a V. E. la disonancia que me causò el cotejo de las partes retocadas con las que no le esteban, puen en aquéllas se habla desaparecido y destruido enteramente el brio y valentia de los pinceles y la maestria de delicados y sabios toques del original que se conservaban en éstos; con mi franqueza natural, animata dal sentimiento, no le oculté lo mal que me parecia ... porque además de ser constante que cuanto más se toquen las pinturas con pretexto de su conservación mas se destruyen, y que los mismos autores, reviviendo ahora, no podrían retocarlas perfectamente a causa del tono rancio de colores que les da el tiempo, que es también quien pinta, segun máxima y obsevación de los sabios, no es fácil retener el intento instantáneo y pasajero de la fantasía y el acorde y concierto que se propuso en la primera ejecución, para que dejen de resentirse los retoques de la variancíon. Y si esto se cree indispensable en su artista consumado, ¿qué ha de suceder cuando le emprende elque carece de sólidos principios? Por lo tocante a la naturaleza de los ingredientes con que se da el lustre a las pinturas, aunque pregunté de cuáles se valia, sólo me anunció que era clara de huevo, sin otra explicacíon; de suerte que conocí desde luego se formaba misterio y había interés en ocultar la verdad; pero intiendo no merece el asunto ningún examen, y que, como todo lo que huele a secretos, es poco digno de aprecio."

"I cannot begin to tell Your Excellency of the unease which I felt comparing the areas which had been retouched with those which were not, because in the former the vigour and liveliness of the brushwork has been destroyed and have completely disappeared, as well as the delicacy and well-judged touches which are still present in the untouched areas. With the frankness which is in my nature and moved by my feelings, I cannot hide from you the awfulness of what I beheld. ... besides, whenever one touches a painting under the pretext of its conservation, one always destroys it; and even the authors themselves, coming back to life, would not be able to retouch them perfectly because of the yellowish tone which they acquire with Time, who, as the sages have observed, is also a painter, because it is not easy to retain the fleeting and momentary impulse of the imagination, and the harmony and concert which are found in the initial creation, so that the retouching does not stand out. If this cannot be otherwise for the consummate artist himself, how can somebody lacking the basic principles succeed? As far as the nature of the materials used to give a shine to paintings, when I asked him what he used, he said only white of egg, without any further explanation, so I understood of course that he was creating a bit of a mystery, and was intent on concealing the truth, but I do not think it is worthwhile pursuing the examination, as with everything which is shrouded in mystery, it is not worthy of consideration."

4. J. Knowles, *The Life and Writings of Henry Fuseli*, London, 1831, III, p. 268, nota.
5. J. Reynolds, *Discourses on Art*, ed. New Haven–London, 1975, p. 223 (Discourse XII, read on 10 December 1784)
6. F. Milizia, *Dizionario delle belle arti del disegno*, Bologna, 1802, II, p. 200; see also: II, pp. 4–5.
7. C. Verri, *Saggio elementare sul disegno*, Milan, 1814, p. 107; G. Bossi, *Del Cenacolo di Leonardo da Vinci*, Milan, 1810, p. 199; C. Verri, *Osservazioni sul volume intitolato del Cenacolo di Leonardo da Vinci*, Milan, 1812; G. Bossi, *Postille alle osservazioni sul volume intitolato del cenacolo di Leonardo da Vinci*, Milan, 1812. Ugo Foscolo's lively observations on Bossi's "restoration" have something of a criticism of taste, see *Ipercalisse*, Zurich, 1815, XII, 22–24, in G. Rocchi, *Camillo Boito*, in "Restauro", n. 15, 1974, p. 9.
8. *Osservazioni*, pp. 73–74.
9. Dèon, 1851, pp. 123–124, 125–126, note 1 p. 162; Forni, 1866, pp. 160–163.
10. Edwards, 1786, H; Incerpi, 1979 and 1982.
11. Cavaceppi, 1768; 1769; 1772; E. Q. Visconti, *Opere*, Milan, 1818, III, p. 400; De Rossi, 1826, p. 32; S. Howard, *Bartolomeo Cavaceppi Eighteenth Century Restorer* (thesis, Chicago 1958); S. Howard, *Boy on a Dolphin: Nollekens and Cavaceppi*, in "The Art Bulletin", 1964, pp. 177–189; S. Howard, *Bartolomeo Cavaceppi and the origins of Neo-classic sculpture*, in "The Art Quarterly", 1970, pp. 120–133; S. Howard, *ad vocem*, in *Dizionario biografico degli italiani*, XXII, 1959; Ferretti, 1981, pp. 161–162; Rossi Pinelli, 1981, pp. 41–48; Picon, 1983; Rossi Pinelli, 1986, pp. 232–239.
12. Haskell–Penny, 1981, n. 6
13. Cagiano de Azavedo, 1948, p. 64 (restoration of the *Pothos* by Giovanni Pierantoni); Howard, 1962.
14. On Albacini see: De Rossi, 1826, pp. 34–35; F. de Navenne, *Rome, le Palais Farnese et les Farnese*, Paris s.d., p. 463; *Museo Nazionale di Napoli – Guida. Parte prima. Antichità*, Naples, 1911, pp. 71, 78–79, 90, 105, 169, 181, 188; A. De Franciscis, *Restauri di Carlo Albacini*, in "Samnium", 1946; Howard, 1962, note 30 pp. 333–334; Pepe, 1960. Richly illustrated documentation allows one to follow the Farnese sculptures before

and after restoration by Albacini in *Le Palais Farnese*, Rome, 1980–1981, illustrations, 1980 (see R. Vincent, *Les antiques*, pp. 331–351, on the history of the collection). For other restorers active in Rome at the end of the eighteenth century, see in "Memorie enciclopedie romane", III, 1806, pp. 84–93 (Vincenzo Pacetti); De Rossi, 1826, pp. 33–36 (reintegration of the *Nile* by Gaspare Sibilla; drapery by Giovanni Pierantoni on the Braschi *Antinous*; restorations of sculptures of animals by Francesco Franzoni; Cagiano, 1948, pp. 57 (Piranesi), 63; Howard, 1962; D. Irwin, *Gavin Hamilton: Archeologist, Painter and Dealer*, in "The Art Bulletin", 1962, pp. 90–92.

15. A. Michaelis, *Ancient Marbles in Great Britain*, Cambridge, 1882, p. 68; De Rossi, 1826, pp. 25–26, 37, in particular; M. Pavan, *Antonio Canova e la discussione sugli "Elgin Marbles"* in "Rivista dell'Istituto di Archeologia e Storia dell'arte", 1976; pp. 219–244; Conti, 1981, pp. 69–70; Rossi Pinelli, 1986, pp. 239–244.

16. Rossi Pinelli, 1981, Fig. 3; Haskell–Penny, 1981, p. 124.

17. L. O. Larsson, *Thorvaldsens Restaurierung der Aegina-Skulpturen*, in "Konsthistorisk Tidskrift", 1969, pp. 23–46; Oechslin, 1974, quoted in Pavan, 1976, p. 242; L. Beschi, editor D. Ohly, *Die Aegineten*, I, Munich, 1976, in "Prospettiva", n. 11, 1977, pp. 62–66; Rossi Pinelli, 1986, pp. 242–246.

18. Such was Robert Haydon's opinion in particular (Pavan, 1976, p. 229). On Canova and anatomical knowledge, see M. Ferretti, *Il notomista e il canonico*, in *I materiali dell'Istituto della Scienza*, catalogue of the exhibition, Bologna, 1979, pp. 110–112.

19. A. C. Quatremère de Quincy, *Lettres écrites de Londres à Rome et addressées a Mr Canova sur les Marbres d'Elgin à Athènes*, Paris, 1818, pp. 20, 81, 82, 87; W. von Humboldt, *Briefe 1802–1805*, Munich, 1952, pp. 241, 262, 270; Rossi Pinelli, 1981, pp. 50–51; E. and J. Garms, *Mito e realtà di Roma nella cultura europea*, in "Storia d'Italia – Annali 5", Turin, 1982, p. 646; Rossi Pinelli, 1986, pp. 241–245.

20. *Lettera di G.G.D.R.*, 1788, pp. 247–248.

21. Previtali, 1964; E. H. Gombrich, *Il gusto dei primitivi. Le radici della ribellione*, Naples, 1985.

22. On Ignazio Hugford, also as a restorer, see: A. Comolli, *Vita … di Raffaello*, Rome, 1790, note 62, pp. 50–51 (restoration of the Rinuccini copy of the *Holy Family of Canigiani*, see: Cavalcaselle, 1882–1885, I, note 3, p. 307; von Sonnenberg, 1983, p. 16); M. Marangoni, *La pittura fiorentina del Settecento*, in "Rivista d'Arte", 1912, p. 100; J. Fleming, *The Hugfords of Florence*, in "The Connoisseur", 1955, II, pp. 106–110; Previtali, 1964, pp. 222–223. Lanzi, in a letter added by Ticozzi to Bottari (1754–1773, ed. 1825, VIII, pp. 7–8), referred to the fact that Hugford had been the consultant of Richa for "pictorial judgements" expressed in his work on the churches in Florence. For other episodes linked to the fortunes of Primitive paintings in Tuscany, see: L. Lanzi, *La real galleria di Firenze*, Florence, 1782 (from volume XLVII of the "Giornale de'letterati"; facsimile copy, Florence, 1982), pp. 67–72; A. Lumachi, *Memorie istoriche dell'antichissima basilica di San Giovanni Battista di Firenze*, Florence, 1782, pp. 136–144 (restoration of the mosaics in 1781–1782); Cicognara, 1825, p. 9; Forni, 1866, p. 22; Milanesi, I, 1878, note p. 645; *Pacini, Sante*, entry for, in Thieme–Becker, 1932; U. Procacci, *L'incendio della chiesa del Carmine del 1771*, in "Rivista d'Arte", 1932, pp. 218–223; R. Longhi, *Il più bel frammento degli affreschi del Carmine di Spinello Aretino*, in "Paragone", n. 131, 1960, pp. 33–35; in *Opere complete*, VII, Florence, 1974, pp. 101–103; Previtali, 1964, pp. 86–92, 175–184, 221–226.

23. C. Verri, 1814, pp. 107–108.

24. A. O. Quintavalle, *La. R. Galleria di Parma*, Rome, 1939, p. 5; F. Zeri *Diari di lavoro*, Bergamo, 1971, pp. 13–14 and note 6, pp. 14–15; on the Tacoli Canacci collection I have taken account of the verifications carried out by Alessandria Talignani (*La collezione Tacoli Canacci*, thesis, sup. M. Ferretti, 1984–1985), while for the frames on paintings by the Early Masters, in eighteenth- and nineteenth-century collections, I should like to mention the verifications carried out by Caterina Pieri in her thesis, of which I was the supervisor in 1987.

25. K. Marx, *Il 18 brumaio di Luigi Bonaparte*, trad., Rome, 1964, pp. 44–45; the text was quoted in relation to the nineteenth-century "revivals" by Enrico Castelnuovo (*Arte e rivoluzione industriale*, in "Paragone", n. 237, 1969, p. 22; reprinted in "Arte, industria, rivoluzioni", Turin, 1985, pp. 93–94).

26. E. Despois, 1868 (on Eugene Despois, 1818–1876, anti-Bonapartist under the Second Empire, see *Dictionnaire de biographie française*, XI, 1967, pp. 6–7); L. Courajod, 1878–1879; S. J. Idzerda, *Iconoclasm During the French Revolution*, in "The American Historical Review", October 1954; L. Reau, 1959; E. Castelnuovo, *Arte e Rivoluzione. Ideologie e politiche artistiche nella Francia rivoluzionaria*, in "Ricerche di storia dell'arte", n. 13–14, 1981, pp. 5–20; in *Arte, industria, rivoluzioni*, pp. 125–158. See Conti, 1973, p. 345, for further information on these texts.

27. B. de Montfaucon, *Les monuments de la monarchie françoise*, Paris, 1729–1733 (one should remember its singular importance for the fortunes of Medieval art, also for examples of graphic interpretation such as its reproduction of the Bayeux tapestry).

28. On the fusion of Medieval goldsmitheries, see: L. Courajod, 1878–1879, pp. 174–175, 179–181, 182–183.

29. H. B. Grégoire, *Rapport sur les destructions opérées par le vandalisme et sur les moyens de le réprimer*, Paris, 1794; on the origin of the term "vandalisme", see Réau, 1959, I, p. 13.

30. Despois, 1868, pp. 203, 222; Courajod, 1878–1879, note 1 p. 489, p. 522; *Procés verbaux de la Commission des Monuments*, in "Nouvelles Archives de l'Art Français", III, XVII, 1901, pp. 16–19; Réau, 1959, I, pp. 362, 380–382.

31. Victor Hugo, *Guerre aux Démolisseurs*, in "Revue des deux mondes", V, 1832, I, pp. 607–622 (I ed. 1825); C. de Montalembert, 1833, and *De l'attitude du Vandalisme en 1838*, in *Du Vandalisme et du Catholicisme dans l'Art (fragments)*, Paris, 1839, pp. 1–69, 205–243; Despois, 1868, p. 221; Réau, 1958, I, pp. 267–268, 382, II, pp. 14–43.

32. Courajod, 1878–1879, pp. 172–173; Cabanes–Nass, *La névrose révolutionnaire*, Paris, 1924, note 1, p. 4; Réau, 1959, I, p. 230–231. On the recently recovered fragments used as material for foundations, see: A. Erlande Brandenbourg–M. Fleuty–F. Giscard d'Estaing, *Les rois retrouvés*, Paris, 1978. On David's project to build, with these and other fragments of overturned feudality, a colossus dedicated to the *French People as Hercules*, see; L. Courajod, *La statue de Louis XV execute par J. B. Lemoine*, in "Gazette des Beaux-Arts", 1875, II, note 3 pp. 52–53.

33. Despois, 1868, pp. 198, 203–214; Courajod, 1878–1879, pp. 490, 543–547; P. Vitry–G. Brière, *L'Eglise Abbatiale de Saint-Denis et ses Tombeaux*, Paris, 1906, pp. 90–95; Cabanes–Nass, 1924, cit. II, pp. 7–11, 59–60; Réau, 1959, I, pp. 226–227.

34. Courajod, 1878–1879, p. 520; Réau, 1959, I, p. 217; on the instance of the sale of works of art requisitioned from the Florence Gallery, see: P. Rosenberg, in *Pittura francese nelle collezioni pubbliche fiorentine*, catalogue of the exhibition, Florence, 1977, pp. 95–98.

35. E. Viollet-le-Duc, 1866, p. 22; Courajod, 1878–1879, pp. 186, 201–204, 205–206, 210–211, 524–525, 547, 553; F. Benoit, *L'Art sous la Révolution et l'Empire*, Paris, 1897, pp. 119–120; Vitry–Brière, 1906, op. cit., pp. 95–98; M. Beaulieu–M. Aubert, *Musée National du Louvre – Description raisonné des sculptures …*, I, *Moyen Age*, Paris, 1950, pp. 197–198; Emile-Mâle, 1956, pp. 388–389; Réau, 1959, II, pp. 226–227.

36. Viollet-le-Duc, 1866, pp. 22–23; Vitry–Brière, 1906, op. cit., pp. 94–104; Beaulieu–Aubert, 1950, op. cit., pp. 11–12; Réau, op. cit. II, pp. 48–50, 65–72, 107–109; *Eugène Viollet-le-Duc*, catalogue of the exhibition, Paris, 1965, pp. 78–81; Castelnuovo, 1981, op. cit., ed. 1985, pp. 147–148.

37. F. Villot, *Notice des tableaux exposés dans les galéries du Musée Imperial du Louvre*, I, ed. 1861, pp. XXXI–XLII; E. Despois, 1868, pp. 169–176; L. Courajod, 1878–1879, p. 494–500; F. Benoit, *L'art sous la Révolution et l'Empire*, Paris, 1897, pp. 110–113; *La Commission*, 1909; David, 1793.

38. Picault, 1793, ed. 1859, IX, pp. 515–516.

39. As above, p. 508 in particular.

40. Picault, 1793. In 1853 (*Report*, 1853, p. 91), the art dealer John Nieuwenhuys, referring to Claude's *Embarcation of the Queen of Sheba*, remarked that the linings executed in France at the end of the eighteenth century would often come away from the original canvas, because of the poor adhesion of the glue or the paste that was used in the process.

41. F. T. Hacquin, *Un mot au citoyen Picault sur son mémoire relatif à la restauration des tableaux du Muséum*, Paris, l'an II. On the paintings of the Ponthièvre Gallery, see W. Vitzthum, *La Galerie de la Vrillière*, in "L'œil", December 1966, pp. 23–31.

42. On J.-P. Lebrun, see *La Commission du Muséum*, 1909, pp. 97, 102–104; Emile-Mâle, 1956. Of his writings dealing with the activities of the Museum, refer to: *Réflexions sur le Muséum National par le citoyen Lebrun*, Paris, 1792; *Quelques idées sur la disposition, l'arrangement et la décoration du Muséum National …*, Paris, l'an III (on pp. 20–21, his ideas on cleaning which are similar to those put forward by Edwards, as well as the details of the actual methods employed and their possible dangers, on p. 19).

43. On David, and the intervention with which he puts an end to the Commission of the Museum, see: David, 1793 and 1794; D. L. Dowd, *Jacques Louis David, Artist Member of the Committee of General Security*, in "The American Historical Review", 1951–1952, pp. 871–892; D. L. Dowd, in *Studies in Modern European History in Honor of Franklin Charles Palm*, New York, 1956, pp. 105–128.

44. David, 1794. For the restoration work carried out at the time of the Commission of the Museum (for some references see Conti, 1973, p. 246), see: Engerand, 1900, p. 532; *La Commission*, 1909. Martin (1794) accused David of inaccuracy over his denunciation of the lining of the paintings by Vernet, attributing the cracking (*sbollature*) to the poor priming containing too much litharge. However, the index of the "Archives de l'Art Français" of 1909 listed several payments made for interventions on Vernet's paintings.

45. G. Bouquier, *Rapport et projet de decret relatifs à la restauration des tableaux et autres monuments des arts, formant la collection du Muséum National*, Paris, l'an II (1794), pp. 2–4.

46. In addition to the writings of Picault and Lebrun, on the projects for the *concours*, also see: Bouquier, op. cit.; Martin, 1794; L. Tuety, *Procès verbaux de la Commission Temporaire des arts*, Paris, 1912–1917, pp. 667–673.

47. *La Commission du Muséum*, 1909, pp. 97, 102–104; Emile-Mâle, 1956; R. Longhi, *Pontormo: un ritratto giovanile*, in "Paragone", n. 217, 1968, pp. 58–60; in *Opere Complete*, VII, Florence, 1976, pp. 93–94.

48. On the requisitioning of works for the Musée Central des Arts, see: M. L. Blumer, *Catalogue des peintures transportées de l'Italie en France de 1796 à 1814*, in "Bulletin de la Société de l'Art Français", 1936, II, pp. 244–348; C. Gould, *Trophy of Conquest. The Musée Napoléon and the creation of the Louvre*, London, 1965; Haskell–Penny, 1981, pp. 132–143 (the problem is well set out by the authors, in their discussion on antique statues). On methods of restoration, and in particular on transfers: Millin, 1806, III, pp. 435–438; J. D. Fiorillo, *Geschichte der zeichnenden Künste*, Göttingen 1798–1808, III, pp. 403–412; Steinmann, 1917; Incerpi, 1979; Emile-Mâle, 1983; Nonfarmale, 1983. On the restoration of these first paintings coming out of Belgium, and the resulting congestion in the laboratories: Emile-Mâle 1956, p. 409; Emile-Mâle, 1964, pp. 156, 165–166; C. Gould 1965, op. cit., pp. 74–75.

49. Hacquin's "mémoires" on lining methods are referred to by Gilberte Emile-Mâle (1956, note 1, p. 409) and can be found in the archives of the Administration du Musée central des Beaux-Arts (pp. 16, 14 and 27 May 1798); the method is described, again, by Gilberte Emile-Mâle, 1983, p. 228. See Icerpi, 1979, p. 223, for the different adhesive used in the transfer from canvas to canvas, in *Cardinal Bentivoglio* by Van Dyck.

50. G. Mengozzi, *Lettera intorno alle pitture di Raffaello esistenti in Foligno*, in *Antologia romana*, III, 1776–1777, pp. 321–325; *Notice de plusieurs précieux tableaux recueillis à Venise, Florence, Turin, et Foligno*, Paris l'an X (1802), pp. 43–52 (report on the transfer, translation in M. Prunetti, *Saggio Pittorico*, Rome, 1818, pp. 139–145), 63; Forni, 1866, p. 107; Cavalcaselle, 1882–1885, II, note 2 p. 189; D. Redig de Campos, *La "Madonna di Foligno", di Raffaello. Nota sulla storia e i suoi restauri*, in "Miscellanes Bibliothecae Hertzianae", Munich, 1961, pp. 184–197. The *Rapport à l'Institut National sur la Vierge de Foligno par les Citoyens Guyton, Vincent, Taunay et Berthollet*, in a more amplified form than in the 1802 report, has been published by P. Lacroix, *Restauration des tableaux de Raphael*, in "Revue universelle des arts", IX, 1859, pp. 220–228; in J. D. Passavant, *Raphael*, II, Paris, 1860, pp. 622–629; passages and extracts can also be found in: Paillot de Montabert, 1829–1830, IX, pp. 704–707; Horsin Déon, 1851, pp. 6–11.

51. Richardson, 1728, III, p. 144; J. B. P. Lebrun, *Examen historique et critique des tableaux exposés provisoirement venant des premier et second envois de Milan, Crémone, Parme, Plaisance, Modène, Cento et Bologne…*, Paris, l'an VI, pp. 18–21; Passavant, 1839, II, p. 172; Cavalcaselle, 1882–1885, III, note 1 p. 79; G. Emile-Mâle, 1983; A. Mazza, in *L'Estasi di Santa Cecilia di Raffaello da Urbino nella Pinacoteca Nazionale di Bologna*, Bologna, 1983, pp. 94–98; Nonfarmale, 1983.

52. U. Hegner, *Auch ich war in Paris*, in *Gesammelte Schriften*, Berlin, 1824, p. 308 (David's reservations about museum restorations); J. Knowles, *The Life and Writings of Henry Fuseli*, London, 1831, III, p. 268; A. D'Este, *Memorie di Antonio Canova …*, Florence, 1864, p. 243; Passavant, 1839, trans. 1882–1891 II, p. 334; Cavalcaselle, 1882–1885, III, note 1 p. 262 and pp. 247–248; G. Emile-Mâle, *La Transfiguration de Raphael, quelques documents sur son séjour à Paris (1798–1815)*, in *Rendiconti della Pontificia Accademia Romana*, 1960–1961, pp. 225–236.

On Mathias Bartolomeus Röser, see: *La Commission*, 1909, pp. 166–171; Passavant is critical of the almost without exception, unsuccessful retouchings in the Napoleonic museum, see 1839, cited translation, II, pp. 16, 172, 311.

53. Passavant, 1839, II, pp. 145, 281–282, 284, 288; Geffroy, in Thieme–Becker 1907; Steinmann, 1917 p. 14. On the important transfer executed by Hacquin on Raphael's *Coronation of the Virgin* (and this was confirmed by Gilberte Emile-Mâle on 27 January 1971), we have no information on the technical details of the process; see D. Redig de Campos, *L'Incoronazione della Madonna di Raffaello ed il suo restauro*, in "Fede ed arte", 1958, pp. 343–348. Amongst the other paintings transferred after their removal to Paris, one could mention the Giovanni Bellini from San Zaccaria, the altarpiece by Garofalo from the Este Gallery, and the *Immaculate Conception* by Gerolamo Mazzola Bedoli in the Pinacoteca Nazionale in Parma, which has recently been retransferred by Silvia Baroni and Camillo Tarozzi.

In the context of the activity of the museum, there was a probable restoration by Lebrun, of Raphael's *Madonna dell'Impannata* (Steinmann, 1917, p. 23), which had already been restored by Vittorio Sampieri in 1796 (*Raffaello a Firenze*, catalogue of the exhibition, Florence, 1984, p. 168). For the restoration of the paintings coming from Florence, see Forni, 1866, p. 107; F. Beaucamp, *Le peintre Lillois Jean-Baptiste Wicar*, Lille, 1939, notes on pp. 316–318; Emile-Mâle, 1979; Incerpi, 1979.

54. De Burtin, 1808, I, pp. 422–423, 438, Secco-Suardo, 1866, Ch. II; M. Hours, *Radiographies des tableaux de Léonard de Vinci*, in "Revue des arts", 1952, p. 234.

55. B. Marconi, *The Transfer of Panel Paintings on Linen by Ssidorov*, in *Application of Science in Examination of Works of Art*, Boston 1965, pp. 246–254; Marijnissen, 1967, I, pp. 46–49, II, notes 150–183 (with information and bibliography referring to nineteenth-century transfers in Belgium).

56. On Giacomo Succi (who died in Rome in 1809) see: *Maniera di trasportare in tela le pitture a fresco*, in "Antologia romana", III, 1776–1777, pp. 361–362; Lanzi, 1809, V, p. 278; G. Alberghetti, *Compendio della storia di Imola*, Imola 1810, II, p. 128; *Due lettere critiche sull'opuscolo Descrizione del giardino della Viola della città di Bologna*, Imola, 1816, pp. 15–19; Cicognara, 1825, pp. 10–11; Giordani, 1840, pp. 11–18 and notes 15 and 20; G. Gioradani in Baruffaldi, *Vite de' pittori e scultori ferraresi*, Ferrara, 1844, II, note 1 pp. 40–41; M. Gualandi, *Tre giorni a Bologna*, Bologna, 1850, p. 20; Secco-Suardo, 1866, ed. cit., pp. 219, 229, 245–246 and note; A. Presenzini, *Vita ed opera del pittore Andrea Camassei*, Assisi, 1880, pp. 94–97, 247, 248; G. Villa, *Guida pittorica d'Imola dell'Abate Giovanni Villa con note aggiunte di Guido Gambetti*(1794), Bologna 1925, pp. 26 (ceilings painted by Giacomo Succi in Palazzo Sassatelli), 29–30; *Omaggio al Guercino*, catalogue of the exhibition, Cento, 1967, p. XXVII; A. Emiliani *La Pinacoteca Nazionale di Bologna*, Bologna, 1967, p. 58, n. 209; Conti, 1973, pp. 248–249; O. Baracchi Giovannardi, *Il modenese Antonio Boccolari e l'arte di "strappare" gli affreschi dal muro*, in "Atti e memorie", department for native history of the ancient provinces of Modena (*dep di storia patria per le antiche provincie modenesi*), 1984, p. 333; A. Mazza, in *Il museo come programma*, catalogue of the exhibition, Imola, 1985, pp. 66–67.

57. Cignora, 1825, pp. 9–10; Giordani, 1840, pp. 10–11; Ufficio Regionali, 1906, note 1 p. 26; E. Castelnuovo, *Un pittore italiano alla corte di Avignone*, Turin, 1962, p. 160 (in 1819 he offers his services to undertake transfers in Avignon); Incerpi, 1979, p. 220 and note 17 p. 226; Conti, 1981, p. 71. The experiment carried out by Signora Barrett, can be identified as a Madonna which is in the deposits of the Gallerie di Firenze, attributed to Sebastiano Mainardi, n. 6106 in the inventory of 1890.

58. Cicognara, 1825; Malaguzzi Valeri, 1908, pp. 10–14, 21, 23, 26; F. Mariotti, *Legislazione delle belle arti*, Sezione Provincie Venete e Lombarde, n. 2490–240, quoted in Muraro, 1960, p. 32.

59. *Descrizione delle pitture del Giardino della Viola nella città di Bologna*, Venice, 1812, p. 23; *Due lettere critiche sull'opuscolo descrizione del giardino della Viola nella città di Bologna*, Imola, 1816, pp. 13, 14, 16; G. Melchiorri, in "L'ape italiana", Rome, 1835, plates XVI and XXXI; M. Gualandi, in "Il solerte foglio settimanale", 1839, n. 47, p. 128, note 6; Giordani, 1840, pp. 17, 18, 21–22; Zeni, 1840, note 2 p. 9; C. d'Arco, *Istoria della vita e delle opere di Giulio Pippi romano*, Manua 1842, appendices, pp. L–LII; Dyce, 18147, note p. 17; Forni, 1866, p. 22; Secco-Suardo, 1866, ed. cit., p. 229; Milanesi, 1878–1885, III, p. 229; Milanesi, 1878–1885, III, 1878, p. 702; VI, 1881, note 3 p. 466; Cagiano de Azavedo, 1948, pp. 72–73; A. Prandi–T. Steinby, *Villa Lante al Gianicolo*, Rome, 1954, pp. 13–15; Della Pergola, *Galleria Borghese. I dipinti*, II, Rome, 1959, pp. 128, 227; D. Posner, *Annibale Carracci and his School. The Paintings of the Herrera Chapel*, in "Arte antica e moderna", 1960, p. 397; Hueck, 1980, p. 6 and note 25 p. 10; Hueck 1981, pp. 144–147, 149–152. The activity of Pellegrino Succi seems to have been continued, tiredly, within the context of the politics of conservation of the Pontifical State, see F. Buranelli in *La tomba François di Vulci*, catalogue of the exhibition, Città del Vaticano, 1987, pp. 183–184 (in 1863, transfer of the frescos of the François Tomb).

60. *Segreto chimico per trasportare le pitture dal muro sulla tela*, in "Memorie enciclopediche romane sulle belle arti, antichità ecc", II, 1806, pp. 37–41 (on the transfers carried out by the doctor Nicola Martelli, with an attitude very similar to that later shown by Horsin Déon in respect to the material qualities of frescos: "the roughness, the dullness, and the *secco*, all effects integral to the nature of plaster, are the original sin of fresco painting. Now he, with his remedy, has given it unaccustomed qualities, making it appear colourful, soft and mellow, emulating the nature of oil painting"); *National Gallery Acquisitions 1953–1962*, London, 1963, note 1 p. 27; Hueck, 1981, pp. 145, 149.

61. G. Branchi, *Lettera del Prof. Branchi al Sig. Sebastiano Ciampi sopra gl'ingredienti di vari musaici e di varie antiche pitture*, in S. Ciampi, *Notizie inedite della segrestia de' belli arredi*, Florence, 1810, appendix, pp. 3–25; Cicognara, 1825, pp. 3–4; G. Branchi, *Sopra alcuni colori che nei secoli XIV e XV furono adoperati per le pitture dell'insigne Camposanto di Pisa, e sulla composizione dell'intonaco che fu fatto per le pitture medesime*, in "Nuovo giornale de'letterati", Pisa, 1836, pp. 95–116; reprinted in "Bollettino dell'Istituto centrale di restauro", n. 7–8, 1951, pp. 85–98; Zeni, 1840; Botti, 1864, pp. 30–39.

62. Zeni, 1840; G. Fiocco, *Un affresco di Bernardo Parenzano*, in "Bollettino d'arte", 1931–1932, pp. 433–439; there is a considerable amount of information on Zeni in the Ms P. D. 307 XVII of the library of the Museo Correr in Venice, see Conti, 1973, p. 250.

63. *Omaggio di riconoscenza al nobile signore Filippo Balbi …*, Venice, 1819, p. 8. On him, and on the frescos in the Villa Soranza, see: Cicognara, 1825, pp. 11–12; L. Cicognara, *Lettere inedite … ad Antonio Canova*, Padua,

1839, p. 31; R. Palucchini, *Mostra di Paolo Veronese*, Venice, 1939, pp. 37–43; R. Palucchini, *Restauri verone-siani*, in "Le ari", 1939–1940, pp. 29–30; G. Bordignon Favero, *La villa Soranza di Michele Sanmicheli a Castelfranco Veneto*, Treviso, 1958; L. Crosato, *Di un putto della Soranza*, in "Arte Veneta", 1959–1960, p. 202; G. Bordignon Favero, *Le opera d'arte e il tesoro del duomo ...*, Castelfranco, 1965, pp. 41–43; B. Rupprecht, *Sanmichelis Villa Soranza*, in "Festschrift Ulrich Middeldorf", Berlin, 1968, pp. 324–332; G. Schweikhart, *Paolo Veronese in der Villa Soranza*, in "Mitteilungen des Kunsthistorischen Institutes in Florenz", 1971, pp. 187–205.

64. S. Stratico, ms It. IV, 334 of the Biblioteca Marciana in Venice (1820), cc. 524–525; Paillot de Montabert, 1829–1830, IX, pp. 707–708; Curti, 1864, p. 359; Secco-Suardo, 1866, ed. cit., p. 220; Ufficio Regionale, 1906, pp. 22–36, 40–54; L. Beltrami, *Il Cenacolo di Leonardo ...*, Milan, 1908, pp. 35–37; Malaguzzi Valeri, 1908, p. 33; L. Beltrami, *I dipinti di Bernardino Luini alla villa Rabia detta "la Pelucca"*, Milan, 1911, pp. 55–58, 61; Cavenaghi, 1912, p. 495; A. Ottino della Chiesa, *Bernardino Luini*, Novara, 1956, pp. 99–100; Conti, 1973, p. 250.

65. "Gazzetta di Bologna" n. 85, 24 October 1806; Cicognara, 1825, p. 10; Giordani, 1840, pp. 18–19; Secco-Suardo, ed. cit., 1866, p. 220; Venturi, 1882, pp. 377–378, 424, 430; R. Palucchini, *I dipinti della Galleria Estense di Modena*, Rome, 1945, pp. 48–49; C. Caccia Scarafoni, *Un affresco ritrovato del Garofalo*, in "Bollettino dell'arte", 1958, pp. 88–92; A. C. Quintavalle, in *Arte in Emilia 1960–1961*, catalogue of the exhibition, Parma 1961, pp. 62–64; S. Béguin, in *Mostra di Niccolò dell'Abate*, catalogue of the exhibition, Modena, 1970, pp. 16–27, 32–49; Conti, 1973, p. 251; O. Baracchi Giovannardi, op. cit., 1984, pp. 319–410.

66. *Report from the Select Committee on Fine Arts*, London, 1842, p. 31 (see also the mention of a method in which absorbent paper was put into direct contact with the painting to be transferred); Déon 1851, pp. 14–15; Secco-Suardo, ed. cit., 1866, pp. 222–228.

8

Restoration: from the Academies to Romanticism

1. Restoration and the Papacy

The sad climate which reigned over Rome, no longer the European capital of Neo-classicism as it had been under Pius VI and despoiled of its masterpieces which had been ceded to France with the treaty of Tolentino, can be perceived through the fate of Daniele da Volterra's *Deposition*. It was the restorer himself, Pietro Palmaroli, who evoked the circumstances which led to the decision to carry out the transfer of this painting, only second in esteem to Raphael's *Transfiguration* (which nobody could envisage ever returning from Paris). After a disastrous attempt to remove it along with part of the wall (*a massello*) in 1798 (this had been carried out "without knowledge or understanding of the art"), which had resulted in the caving in of the vault, the work had then been left to the mercy of the weather, the rain and the rubbish which the soldiers billeted in the ex-convent threw into the ruins.

127

What took place between this first attempt and the time when Palmaroli worked on the painting (1809–1810) is not clear. What is clear, however, is that the painting remained exposed to all weathers for a period of eleven years, and that the Roman restorer transferred it onto canvas using a technique which preserved some of the underlying plaster. Unable to use either oil or mastic varnish for the restoration (as both would have been absorbed by the wall, leaving the paint layer as powder), he resorted to using an "encaustic medium"; it was this, the "liniments of grease and oil (*untume*)", which Cigognara deplored. This treatment remained on the painting until, according to Zeni, Camuccini had it cleaned off, thus returning it to its original state "of faded (*sparuta*) but not counterfeit existence".[1] We will understand Palmaroli's technique better once the observations which enabled the recent intervention by Jéraldine Albers on the lunette with the *Marriage of the Virgin* have been published[i]; this fresco was transferred by Palmaroli from the della Rovere chapel in Trinità dei Monti, as a trial run for the more difficult transfer of the Daniele da Volterra.[2]

128

The earliest measures for conservation taken by the Church in the wake of the treaty of Tolentino (with the handwritten Chiaromonti document of 1802) sought to limit the impoverishment of the artistic heritage, which had occurred as a result of the French requisitions. The events surrounding the *Deposition* serve as a reminder of the less than happy state of affairs in which this heritage found itself, when Rome became the "second city of

---

[i] Now published.

127. *Daniele da Volterra, Deposition; fresco transferred by Pietro Palmaroli, 1809–1810. Rome, Trinità dei Monti.*

*128. Pellegrino Tebaldi and Marco
Pino, Marriage of the Virgin; fresco
transferred by Pietro Palmaroli,
1809. Rome, Académie de France.*

the Empire". The Restoration, with the unhoped-for return of the works of art, seemed to also restore to Rome its old role of capital of the arts of Neo-classical Europe, and with this was born a veritable programme of reappraisal and re-evaluation within the administration of the artistic heritage. The paintings which were returned on the request of the allies now formed the new Pinacoteca Vaticana, an institution which would therefore facilitate the study of these works by artists. A proper restoration programme was also put into place to put lie to the statements so often made by French publicists, which had presented the requisitions as a rescue operation of masterpieces from the neglect of the Papal Curia.

In his capacity of Inspector of Public Paintings, a position he held from 1814, and fulfilled in much in the same way as Pietro Edwards had in Venice supervising and controlling not only the work but also the categories of expenditure, Vincenzo Camuccini had the "ill-advised daubings" removed from Daniele da Volterra's *Deposition*. The interventions on the paintings were carried out in conjunction with the architectural restoration of the buildings, as well as the new decorations, which would become characteristic of so many Roman churches; the scope of these can be gauged immediately, by comparing the works which are found in them now with those cited in Titi's eighteenth-century guide. The interventions fitted within a real programme of reappraisal and modernization of buildings used for worship, evidently discharged selectively, but never forgetting Rome's prestigious position as the artistic capital of Europe.

It may be because of this that only the best masterpieces from each style were chosen for restoration. Between 1814 and 1823, simply to list them, we find Reni and Domenichino, the *Sybils* by Raphael and Sebastiano del Piombo, Caravaggio's paintings in Santa Maria del Popolo and the Van Baburen in San Pietro in Montorio, or the frescos by Mattia Preti in Sant'Andrea della Valle. Nor were examples of fifteenth-century mural painting overlooked, such as the Filippino Lippi in the Minerva, or the works by Pinturicchio in the Aracoeli and Santa Maria del Popolo. In the Cappella Brada di Castiglione in San Clemente, Pietro Palmaroli restored the frescos by Masolino, with the vast integrations and areas of repainting which characterized them until the more recent interventions, and which still remain in the damaged sections of the *Crucifixion*.[3]

In addition to Camuccini himself, and his brother Pietro, the restoration work was carried out by either Palmaroli or Giuseppe Candida, a restorer and *estrattista* who we know was trained in Venice; paintings such as the Van Baburen in San Pietro in Montorio, and the restoration of the works by Caravaggio in Santa Maria del Popolo, bear testimony to the seriousness with which the work was executed, as is the good result obtained with the transfer of Melozzo da Forlì's fresco of *Platina*. Linked, as they were, to programmes of reappraisal of the environment and the furnishings of the churches of Rome, the restorations of cycles of frescos or mosaics all shared a strong element of reconstruction. The uncommon skill shown by the interventions directed by Camuccini in integrating the restorations with the

129, 130 original mosaics can be seen clearly in the ring vault of Santa Costanza (1834–1840), an integration exceptional both in the sheer scope of the reconstruction of the missing areas and in its understanding of the art of mosaic of Late Antiquity.[4]

In other cases, such as the Terze Loggie restored by Filippo Agricola between 1838 and 1842, the location of the reconstructions can only be determined from the descriptive documentation, and only for the areas reconstructed *ex novo*, not in the case of those insidious retouchings with which the damaged paintings were refreshed.[5] This type of restoration seems to be a re-elaboration of Maratta's precepts, by which – with an attitude which is academic rather than Neo-classical – the restorer felt entitled to interpret what was missing or what required "refreshment", according to recognized precepts. It should not be forgotten that these works were seen from the perspective of their function as decoration, and as didactic objects for artists, and therefore had to comply with specifications which made them suitable to these ends. Moreover, by means of these rules and precepts, it was always going to be possible to find a solution which would restore the formal and decorative whole, and which would fulfil the same function as the missing original, although not corresponding to it in every detail.

The climate in which these restorations took place is well exemplified by Agricola's observations on the finishing touches executed *a secco*[ii] in the Stanze di Raffaello (which he had restored in 1839), in opposition to those who maintained that the paintings were executed entirely *a fresco* (befitting a Romantic model of impulsive creativity). He replied that

---

[ii] *A secco*, in contrast to *a fresco*. "Secco" literally means dry; these were the finishing touches which were executed on top of the dry plaster, which had been painted first when wet (*a fresco*). Because applied on top of dry plaster with a binding medium such as glue, casein or egg-tempera, these finishing touches were often lost, as they would flake off.

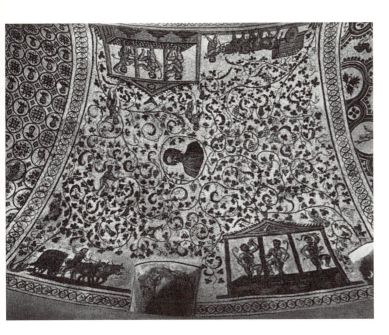

129. *Detail of the Early Christian mosaics; restored under the direction of Pietro Camuccini, 1834–1840. Rome, Mausoleo di Santa Costanza.*

130. *Diagram showing the original portions of the mosaic integrated during the restoration directed by Pietro Camuccini (from G. Matthiae, Rome, 1967). Rome, Mausoleo di Santa Costanza.*

Raphael did not follow his "first immediate idea", but "whilst working, used to improve on it at times". The Stanze were "indeed painted in fresco technique, but retouched with mixtures of which we have lost all knowledge, and in many places even with hatched coloured strokes, and by the artists themselves, with the intent of bringing harmony to such large works, which they could not create all in one go, as is maintained by certain modern artists".[iii],[6]

The restoration of paintings which had attained recognition as works of art could only take place with the consent of the inspector, that is, Camuccini. Agricola himself found himself in an ambiguous position within the direction of the work in the Stanze; when we follow the activity of the best-known restorer working in Rome after the Restoration, that is, Pietro Palmaroli, it is always the figure of Camuccini which we encounter directing the work. Palmaroli's activity was supported by publications propounding his fame as a highly skilled restorer, such as the *Saggio analitico chimico sui colori* by Lorenzo Marcucci, which owed to him the information on the techniques of the Old Masters, or the *Saggio Pittorico* by Michelangelo Prunetti, in which the generalized eulogy was accompanied by reservations with regard to the results of the restoration of the famed fresco in Trinità dei Monti.

Palmaroli was most famed for his interventions on the paintings of the Dresden Gallery, carried out between 1826 and 1827, becoming not only renowned throughout Europe, but also a favourite target in controversies, for the new generation of connoisseurs. Eastlake had seen him work in Rome, and knew his German restorations, and quite explicitly affirmed that he restored badly. In 1853, Cavalcaselle reproached him for the plasterings on Raphael's *Madonna di San Sisto*, and did not attempt to hide his doubts concerning the restorations, especially in his monographs on Raphael and Titian. In the *Sibyls* of Santa Maria della Pace, he recognized what was left of Palmaroli's restoration of 1816 from the pointillist retouching and integration, a technique analogous to that used by miniaturists, which he used to integrate the chromatic values, thus avoiding the application of layers of new paint: this was his habitual working method, also noticeable on the *Meeting of Jacob and Rachel* by Palma Vecchio in Dresden, the same method that Simon Horsin-Déon mentioned as being characteristic of Italian restorers, to the degree of giving a family air to the paintings on which it was used in a gallery.[7]

Artists, on the other hand, even as a body such as the Accademia di San Luca, tended to request simple conservation or non-intervention, which by now was the current stance amongst artists elsewhere as well. On 23 November 1825, the academicians declared themselves opposed to the cleaning of Michelangelo's *Last Judgement*, which was nevertheless entrusted to Pietro Camuccini:

"The undersigned professors of the Accademia di San Luca, having examined closely not only the group and the other sections of the *Last Judgement* cleaned by Signor Camuccini, and by him indicated in his last report, but also the whole of the painting of the Judgement, have come to the conclusion that this painting has not only been repeatedly cleaned before but also restored, because of which this great work has suffered much damage. Now, being cleaned again, it is inevitable that these old areas of damage will be revealed which at present are hidden by the soot. Once this old damage is revealed, it will become necessary

---

[iii] "*sono bensì dipinte a fresco, ma ritocche assolutamente con mestiche che più non conosciamo, ed in moltissimi luoghi anche a tratti colorati, dagli autori medesimi che così intendevano armonizzare siffatte opere di tanta grandezza, non potendole condurre di un getto, come da qualche moderno artefice si pretende*".

to retouch and restore the painting, which is what we do not want. And nor is there any guarantee that a new cleaning would not engender new damage".[iv] They concluded, therefore, that the fresco "is not to be touched in any way, nor at any time", and doubted that a cleaning would bring the advantages expected by Cavalier Camuccini. After a thorough attempt to convince, Giambattista Wicar remained nevertheless convinced of the contrary, and he wrote thus to the President of the Accademia on 27 November 1825:

> "Mr President – in fulfilment of the decision taken at the general assembly of the twentieth of this month, I took myself to the Sistine Chapel, where I examined more closely and with the most careful attention the portion of the Judgement recently cleaned by Mr Pietro Camuccini. It was with pleasure that I observed that not only had it not suffered, but that it had rather gained; moreover, I remarked that the modern cleaning had revealed certain damage, not caused by the much-praised Mr Camuccini, but by those who had attempted to clean this immortal painting previously and with less caution, which will not be so clearly visible at a greater distance and without scaffolding. This incident, and the well-founded fear of revealing during the cleaning other major areas of damage (again the result of old restorations), make me wish that not only this painting, but all frescos would be properly respected and never touched."

On the other hand, Frederick Overbeck, in 1836, revealed his preoccupations at the possibility of an intervention on the frescos of the Basilica at Assisi, turning to the President of the Accademia di San Luca in order to prevent the "danger that they may perish under barbarous hands", and hoping that the Accademia itself would take the cue from this occasion in order to "publish the correct principles of this very important subject, that is that restoration, especially when dealing with paintings executed in fresco or tempera technique, should absolutely refrain from anything which is not merely the conservation of the state in which the works to be restored find themselves at that moment in time, ensuring to this end that they do not suffer any further deterioration or damage of any kind, without the presumption of wishing, in whatever way, to replace that which no longer exists, nor of reviving colours which have faded with time".[v,8]

The restoration campaign directed by Camuccini was the most systematically organized of the first half of the nineteenth century, and should be seen against the background of the legislation of which the Pacca Edict of 1819 was the most important and well-known manifestation. Flying the flag for conservation and against the free commerce of works of art, for the entire second half of the nineteenth century, until the Italian State passed (and this only in 1902) a new law for the conservation of artistic heritage, the authoritarian and

---

[iv] *"Avendo ben esaminato li sottoscritti professori dell'Accademia di San Luca non solo il gruppo e le altri parti ripulite dal Sig. Camuccini, e da esso indicate nell'ultimo suo foglio, ma tutta insieme la dipintura del Giudizio, hanno rilevato che questo dipinto è stato non solo ripulito ma restaurato altre volte, per cui la grande opera sofferse molti danni. Ora, ripulendosi di nuovo, si va incontro inevitabilmente a scoprire questi danni antichi, i quali al presente restano ottenebrati dal fumo, ed una volta che questi danni antichi fossero scoperti, si saria alla necessità di ritoccare e restaurare il dipinto, ciocchè non si vuole. E niuno poi potrebbe garantire che con un nuovo ripulimento non uscissero altri danni."*

[v] *"pubblicare i giusti principi in questa si importante materia, cioè che il restauro, specialmente trattenendosi di pitture a fresco e a tempera, dovrebbe assolutamente contenersi nei limiti d'una mera conservazione nello stato in cui le pitture da restaurarsi attualmente si trovano, assicurandole a questo fine da ogni ulteriore deterioramento e offesa qualunque, senza pretender di voler in verun modo o rifare quello che non esiste più, oppure di ravvivare i colori svaniti dal tempo".*

antiliberal (certainly not "democratic") spirit of these politics can be inferred from Paolo Marconi's recent observations regarding Carlo Fea, the civil servant who drew up the edict, and his position on the rebuilding of the Basilica of San Paolo fuori le Mura.

On this occasion he vindicated the directing role of the archaeologist against the author of a booklet inspired by Valadier, and signed by a self-styled stone-cutter. The "calloused" hands of craftsmen and architects should not attempt to write about the rules of art. The only person who had this knowledge, relative to antiquity and through Winckelmann's *History*, was the archaeologist: a figure qualified with a term which links him to the antiquarianism of the eighteenth century. Here, we are confronted with the complete reversal of the spirit of the *encyclopédistes*; Fea even succeeded in completely ignoring the value of the old rhetorical fiction of attributing to a simple character, in this case the stone-cutter, observations which the author would be at pains to indicate had their origins in plain common sense. The reference to Winckelmann, in 1826, clearly underlined the antiquated reference to guiding principles, which were aiming to set dogmatic rules which would prevent all innovation.[9]

The actual effectiveness of the edict was to be very limited. With hindsight, it becomes obvious that it did not succeed in halting the dispersion and the expatriation of the great collections put together in Rome in the nineteenth century: the Fesch collection, that belonging to Luciano Bonaparte, the Campana Collection. Its usefulness was perhaps that of limiting exports at a public level and for the private gain of civil servants, with one of those laws that the precepts of enlightenment absolutism advised not to promulgate, because of the damage suffered by the dignity of the State when laws were infringed too frequently.

The spirit of these politics of conservation, the nostalgia for a time in which Rome had been the capital of European Neo-classicism, the search for a set of rules which could be codified once and for all, seems also to be behind the regression towards a desired regularity of approach which can be seen in the two differing solutions which were adopted for the restoration of the Colosseum. In 1807, Raffaello Stern worked on the side of the Colosseum facing the Lateran, indulging in a taste for ruins that seemed to block the monument in the very instant of its collapse; he did not touch the original materials, the fragments remained in the position they had settled in, with Stern limiting himself to consolidating the structure, and then blocking them in place with the new walling. In 1826, the now aged Valadier built on the brick buttress towards the Forum, with a rigidity and an adherence to the rules, which not even the accidental nature of the ruins could check. Here, nothing of the ruins was preserved: the well-conserved portions were kept, but the ruins replaced with the new brick structure which was destined to be distressed to look like travertine stone.

Even the famous restoration of the Arch of Titus, which was begun by Stern and completed by Valadier between 1819 and 1821, responded well to this prescriptive spirit. His solution, which left the integrations visible, was long admired as the first example of the scientific restoration of a building; this desire for regularity, the rules which inevitably guided the reconstruction were not accepted by one onlooker, perhaps rather distracted but nevertheless discerning, that is Stendhal, who, in his *Promenades dans Rome*, defined the spirit of this restoration when he wrote that Valadier, protected by the conservative party, had dared to "cut some travertine blocks in the shape of the old stones, and then substitute them for the originals, which now cannot be found", taking a position for which he would be reproached for being overly Romantic.[10]

131. *Colosseum, with the restoration*
by Raffaello Stern, 1807.

132. *Rome, Arch of Titus; restored*
by Giuseppe Valadier, 1819–1821.

2. Romantic restoration

By this time, the position of the restorer had become clear-cut, as had also the risks attached to his activity. In 1803, Julius Caesar Ibbetson had described an imaginary cleaner, Colliveau, at work on a Dutch painting from which he was removing a wall bringing to light ... a sleeping beauty, and then finally an inscription which admonished him for the irreparable damage he has caused. Eastlake, during the 1853 inquiry on the administration of the National Gallery, recalled an incident of a picture cleaner who was wont to point out details which appeared clearer after his intervention, but on one of Eastlake's paintings had in fact brought to light details that he himself had not intended should be seen.[11]

A lively panorama of the practitioners of the Restoration and their methods emerges from the manual written by Giovanni Bedetti, published in Paris in 1837. Of Piedmontese origin, he had particularly worked in Vercelli, on the *Madonna della Grazia* by Bernardino Lanino in San Paolo, on the frescos (retouching in casein) as well as the *Madonna degli Aranci* by Gaudenzio Ferrari in San Cristoforo. It is likely that his restorations formed part of the same campaign for the recovery of municipal monuments during which Carlo Emanuele Arborio Mella restored (1823–1830) the abbey of Sant'Andrea, with an end result which made of it one of the most significant examples (and not only within the confines of Italy) of the dawning consciousness of the values of medieval architecture.[12]

133

133. *Bernardino Lanino,*
Madonna della Grazia, detail;
restored by Giovanni Bedotti,
1820. Vercelli, San Paolo.

As a restoration manual quite distinct from the more general treatises on painting, Bedotti's book is only pre-dated by that of Köster, which appeared in 1827. For the first time, the Piedmontese restorer formulated some of those interpretative artistic rules for cleaning which were already beginning to emerge in Edwards' reports: possible disharmonies were to be compensated by leaving some of the original discoloured varnish or dirt already present on the painting; thanks to the patina, a painting could become even more harmonious than when it had first been painted. With complete openness towards the requirements of the commercial market, Bedotti also observed that often, a touch or two of the brush was sufficient for a painting to find a buyer; he therefore advised that errors should be corrected, care being taken, however, to conserve those errors which were typical of the style of the master and of his epoch. Repainting became a necessity in such cases as the darkening of the sky because of a poor preparatory layer, which could then be covered over with paint soluble in spirits of turpentine,[vi] and then patinated with a mixture of soot and ash.[13]

According to Giovanni Bedotti, the best restorer in Italy was Giuseppe Guizzardi from Bologna; his skill was such that he could repaint heads by Guido Reni, Domenichino and Albani, deceiving even the most expert eye. In a letter to the Count Teodoro Lechi, his brother Pietro described the extraordinary manipulations of which he was capable:

"If you should then wish to be broadly instructed in this art, you should come to Bologna and frequent his studio as do so many foreigners, and particularly the English, both dealers and art-lovers, who pass many hours there. You would then see things which you have never seen before, for example a painting with a sacred subject becoming profane, and vice versa. Paintings cut into pieces so as to place the figures differently, and thus alter the composition completely. Removing figures from one painting to put them in another in order to improve the composition and make it more interesting. When the need arises, prostrate figures made upright. Transferring canvas paintings onto panels, and panel paintings onto canvas. Making three or four paintings out of one large one, adding figures, landscapes, etc., according to the subject one wishes to represent: in other words, many such operations which are so well executed, that no eye nor lens can reveal them."

Over and above this letter, which deliberately emphasized extreme cases in which Guizzardi could show his prowess, his professionalism can be better evaluated in a brief exchange of letters with Secco-Suardo, between 1852 and 1854, in which he discussed at some length the preparation of the oil suitable for retouching, or else when he pointed out that the retouching on a painting belonging to the Count, which the latter had not liked, could be removed with "a few drops of spirits of turpentine": "Therefore, you will have lost nothing, and only it is I who will be left with the displeasure of your anxiety, and, for having shown too much devotion to the painting, the regret of so many analyses, observations and reproaches, which in your generosity you saw fit to dress with unnecessary and unmerited praise, for which you will have to forgive me for not thanking you".[14]

It is from one of these letters, dated 8 January 1854, that one learns that the town of Forlì had entrusted him with the restoration of a panel by Cotignola, the *Immaculate*

[vi] That is, colours bound with varnish, which can therefore be easily removed. The principle of reversibility seems here to compensating for that of covering original paint.

Conception in the municipal gallery. Newly restored in 1975, all that can be seen now of the nineteenth-century restoration is the sheer extent of Guizzardi's reintegrations which corresponded to the losses that are now so clearly visible, revealing a taste which is closer to that of a dental technician than to that of a restorer.

The new meaning of the term "patina" is the strongest indication of the direction taken by restoration in the first half of the nineteenth century. No longer did it refer to the darkening of oil, the effects of "Time the Painter", but rather to the golden brown tonalities given to paintings by the varnish altered by time, as well as the various mixtures which could be used to imitate it on the retouchings, and in areas which had been overcleaned.[15] A desire for a contact with the past is clear in this taste for patinas, no longer seen simply as the effect of time, but rather guaranteeing a "beauty" belonging to antiquity which had to appear as such, and which, through its power of suggestion, was preferable to the freshness of a work, especially as the works of early fifteenth-century artists and other Early Masters, with their piercing colours (to which collectors had not as yet become accustomed), were now beginning to appear in galleries.

Eastlake, in his *Materials for a History of Oil Painting*, had concluded that the varnishes used by the Early Masters would have had to have been dark in colour, and that artists would not have considered their painting finished without this kind of overall glazing, which they had borne in mind when applying their colours. He reached this conclusion through examining source material and through experimental data, similar to those which in our times have convinced restorers with quite different tastes to his of the necessity of total cleaning in the "cleaning controversy".[vii]

For patination, Secco-Suardo principally advocated amber varnishes, or the extract of the skins of fresh walnuts or the bark of the black alder, all substances which give a golden tone to the painting, with effects which would not have differed greatly from those found on the *Madonna and Child* in the Poldi-Pezzoli Museum in Milan, restored by Giuseppe Molteni in about 1860.[16]

The National Gallery restorations which came under review by the 1853 Select Committee inquiry represent the best known example of the controversies which were also bound up with the taste for what was the newly defined patina. Considering the taste for the early works of the Pre-Raphaelites, it is not surprising to find Eastlake (despite the timidity of his own works) favouring total varnish removal. From his answers during the inquiry, and certain private letters, one can only deduce that he favoured the removal of yellowed varnish; different conclusions were, however, reached, on the conservation of some of these paintings after their cleaning, a subject which drew Cavalcaselle in a letter

---

[vii] "Total cleaning", as the term suggests, refers to the complete removal of all the discoloured varnish layers on a painting, and usually implies the removal of any discoloured earlier restorations as well, revealing the painting in its present physical condition, and has an aura – misplaced – of "objectivity". As an approach to cleaning, it is associated largely with Anglo-Saxon countries. The other options are what Gerry Hedley, in *On Humanism, Aesthetics and the Cleaning of Paintings* (Measured Opinions, UKIC, 1993), termed "selective cleaning" and "partial cleaning": the former implies a choice – usually aesthetic – made by the restorer as to the levels of varnish removed in different areas of the painting, while the latter implies an overall thinning of the varnish layers present, and thus a less subjective practice. Both these approaches are associated with continental practice. It should be borne in mind that the application of any solvent, irrespective of what varnish layers are removed, and to what degree, will always affect the physical structure of the underlying paint layers.

appended to the acts of the Commission. In *Hagar in the Desert* by Claude Lorrain, for example, he observed the loss of the glazes which would have allowed the blue of Hagar's drapery to reflect, in the figure of the angel, its complementary – orange. It is easy to take this as excessive fastidiousness on the part of Cavalcaselle, but it is in other works by Claude, such as the *Apollo and Mercury* in the Galleria Doria Pamphili, that we see the effects which the nineteenth-century historian lamented as lost in the English painting: that of an atmosphere represented not in its limpidity but through a kind of chromatic satura- tion, of enchanting mistiness.[17]

In the sphere of this sensibility to paintings toned and patinated by time, artistic cleaning would go as far as was necessary to achieve the particular effect sought by the restorer, with a subjective interpretation linked to purely figurative considerations and to the desire to allow future darkening or yellowing to "improve" the intrinsic appearance of the painting. The risk of this approach is obvious: that of becoming a restoration aiming to please the art-collector (*restauro amatoriale*), which tries to make indifferent paintings more attractive, with all the implications that this holds for a professionalism which easily veered away from being that of the restorer, towards brokerage and the commercial aspect of paintings.[18]

3. Restorations in Tuscany: from academy to purism

In Florence, after the arrival of Vittorio Sampieri from Rome in 1796, gallery restoration found a good practitioner in Francesco Assai, a figure who has emerged only gradually from documentary research, and whose good interventions and reconstructions we can perceive in such works as the *Storie della Beata Umiltà* by Pietro Lorenzetti, or the *Coronation of the Virgin* by Botticelli, on which he worked in 1830 and on which he reconstructed the hand of Sant'Eligio, demonstrating an unusual sensibility to Quattrocento painting.[19]

In the domain of fresco restoration, the figure dominating the Florentine scene was that of Antonio Marini; his biographer Cesare Guasti would present his purism enrobed in an aura of Neo-Guelphism, and he was remembered with sympathy even by Niccolò Tommaseo. In 1853, the future bishop Ferdinando Baldanzi would present Filippo Lippi's frescos in the Duomo of Prato which Cesare Guasti had just restored, with a series of observations on the "essential similarities" of the *arti del disegno* of a particular epoch. These observations were not novel, but nor were they without merit in the years which saw the destruction of the remains of Giotto's frescos which had reappeared from under the plaster in the Giugni and Tosinghi chapels in Santa Croce, to be replaced with modern decorations.

In Antonio Marini's restorations, there was a clear intention of making the early work harmonize with the Gothic architecture, but the painting was still considered in isolation rather than as part of the polychromy of the whole. This approach is clearly evident when (with the lucky discovery of the giottesque *Portrait of Dante* in the Bargello Chapel in 1840), he recov- ered the wall-paintings in the Peruzzi Chapel in Santa Croce as individual scenes: in 1841 he brought to light *Herod's Banquet*, and then in 1848 *The Ascension of Saint John the Evangelist*, leaving the other frescos to be brought back to light in 1862 by his pupil Pietro Pezzati, well after Gaetano Bianchi had recovered the frescos of the Bardi Chapel. It is difficult not to link a taste such as that shown by Marini in these reconstructions with that found in these verses

134

*134. Giotto, The Announcement to
Zacharias, restored by Pietro Pezzati,
around 1862. Florence, Santa Croce,
Peruzzi Chapel.*

from *La scritta* pointed out to me by Roberto Longhi, in which Giusti described a fourteenth-century forebear, merchant and money-lender, appearing in a dream to a ruined noble:

"His appearance was such that an artist

could not find a model at the time of masks,

if he needed to repaint a fourteenth-century man.

Smooth-shaven, short hair and his head covered with a hood …".[viii]

The recuperation of Ghirlandaio's angels in the apse of the Duomo in Pisa was described in a letter to "Antologia" at the end of August 1828, as carried out by Marini with great philological modesty in the reconstruction of their original appearance. The entirely purist characteristics of their present appearance makes us understand that this was simply a case of the recovery (*ripristino*) of the image, over and above the conservation of the materials of which the image was made up.[20]

[viii] My translation is particularly free: "*Era l'aspetto suo quale un artista/non trova al tempo degli Stenterelli/se gli tocca a rifare un trecentista /Rasa la barba avea, mozzi i capelli,/e del cappuccio la testa guernita …*". "Stenterello", was one of the "masks" (*maschere*) of the Commedia dell'Arte.

Alongside Marini, working on the transfer of frescos, was Giovanni Rizzoli da Pieve di Cento, collaborator if not pupil, of the Boccolari of Modena. During the restoration by Gaetano Baccani, when Marini handled almost all of the paintings in the Duomo in Florence, he was responsible for the transfer of the equestrian portraits in fresco by Paolo Uccello and Andrea del Castagno, whilst his disastrous intervention on Domenico Veneziano's tabernacle in the canto dei Carnesecchi (now in the National Gallery in London) was completed by Marini's pictorial restoration. The transfers of the Andrea del Castagno and the Paolo Uccello were notable by their sheer size, but the paint layer in both is now full of pit-holes (*sgranature*). In Ferrara, the unsuccessful transfer of Garofalo's *Last Supper* in the convent of Santo Spirito in 1874 would continue to cause problems right up to the end of the century, when Filippo Fiscali would attempt to deal with them. 135–137 139

Secco-Suardo related a completely different method which was used in the transfer of Andrea del Castagno's *Illustrious Men* series (detached by Rizzoli in 1850) and a *Crucifixion* by Palmezzano in the museum of Forlì. The transferred frescos in Florence "are completely different in their nature from those executed by Succi, in that they are not thin, flexible and light but rather heavy, thick, extremely hard and dry to the point that they warp, even distorting the stretchers on which they are mounted which themselves are extremely strong, and in some cases even splitting them. From an examination of the surface, which on the whole presents itself as smoother and shinier than is customary with frescos, it seemed to me that certain colours had been completely lost, without being able to understand either how or when; and I had the very strong impression that the practitioner had detached the painting from the wall using resins to attach the canvas facing, as in some areas I found what I took to be traces of turpentine resin (*trementina*). A doubt which was reinforced by the presence of the aforementioned gloss, which is perhaps the result of the use of spirits of turpentine (*acqua ragia*) to wash it, and the considerable thickness of the plaster which is pre-sent on the reverse. What I observed in Forlì, on the other hand, although of much larger dimensions (5.10 metres in height and 3 metres in width), was much thinner, nor did it have the same thickness of plaster on the reverse as in the examples above. Which is why, although one cannot say that these frescos have the flexibility and the thinness which it is possible to achieve, and are still hard and rigid in a way that does not allow them to be rolled, I must confess that they are nevertheless greatly superior to those I examined in Florence".[21] 138

Michele Ridolfi, a purist like Marini and one of the principal protagonists in the restorations carried out in Lucca every year from 1824 onwards, nevertheless directed and executed these restorations with a quite different philological respect. Having laid aside the tiresome and binding programmes of making inventories of the works of art, these interventions began with the restoration of the works by Fra Bartolomeo in San Romano by the hand of the Florentine Luigi Nardi. These interventions stand out by the care taken to restore altarpieces which had been enlarged, back to their original dimensions, or else to leave figures which had been cut down exactly as they were, without completing them, such as in the *Marriage of the Virgin* by Agostino Marti in San Michele, a decision taken at what is still the astonishingly early date of 1832. 140

Within the context of monuments, in 1834 the whitewash which hid the stonework in Santa Maria Forisportam was removed and, in 1841, the same occurred with the walls of San Giovanni: these are the earliest examples in Europe of bareness in the presentation of medieval buildings. Taking into consideration the fact that in monuments "one can be sure that any additions made will always be damaging", in 1838 the Commission had the

135. *Andrea del Castagno, Monument to
Niccolò da Tolentino, detail; fresco trans-
ferred by Giovanni Rizzoli and restored by
Antonio Marini, around 1842. Florence,
Cathedral.*

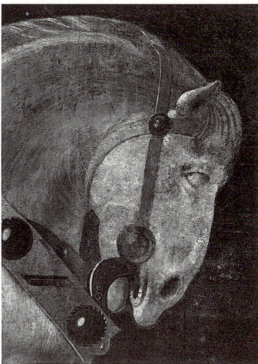

136. Paolo Uccello, Monument to Sir John Hawkwood (Giovanni Acuto); during the removal of the adhesives and the retouching of the Rizzoli-Marini restoration of around 1842. Florence, Cathedral.

137. Paolo Uccello, Monument to Sir John Hawkwood (Giovanni Acuto), detail; after the removal of the adhesives and the retouchings of the Rizzoli-Marini restoration. Florence, Cathedral.

seventeenth-century figures removed from the Tempietto del Volto Santo in Duomo, but then opted to have it regilded, by analogy, from documents which referred to other instances. What emerges from Ridolfi's periodic reports is a gradual museification of the churches themselves: the removal of Baroque altarpieces, paintings moved so that they could be seen in better light, the repositioning of Jacopo della Quercia's *Ilaria del Carretto*, or else the putting behind glass of Ghirlandaio's predella in the new marble frame in the sacristy in the Cathedral.

This remarkable philological attention to the retrieval (*ripristino*), and especially to the conservation of fine art monuments, went as far as to leave completely visible the losses in the frescos by Amico Aspertini da Frediano in the vault of the chapel, in the 1831 restoration carried out by Ridolfi. The rigorously purist intervention which forbade any interpretative restoration was born of the dicta of the Commission for the Fine Arts (*Commissione delle Belle Arti*) of the small Duchy; following a practice which had been in place since the first half of the nineteenth century, the restoration of works of art in the public domain was placed under the control of artists, unlike works which belonged to private collections or which were part of the commercial market.[22]

DOMINVS PHLIPPVS HISPANVS DESCOLARIS RELATOR VICTORIE THEVCRO3

*138. Andrea del Castagno, Pippo Spano,
raking light photograph; fresco transferred
by Giovanni Rizzoli, 1850. Florence,
Galleria degli Uffizi.*

139. *Domenico Veneziano,*
Head of a Saint; fragment
restored by Antonio Marini.
London, National Gallery.

140. *Agostino Marti, The Marriage of the Virgin; restored in 1832. Lucca, San Michele.*

For the consolidation and the conservation of the frescos by Amico Aspertini, Ridolfi had applied wax (*encausticazione*). The practice of waxing the surface of frescos is a very ancient one, possibly handed down in traditional practice from antiquity, and still used today in marbling. In the same way that applications of glue, oil or lime water were originally used for the finishing of mural paintings, waxing was used on frescoed surfaces which had evidence suggesting that they had originally been treated in this way. But the use of wax also followed in the wake of eighteenth-century studies on the painting of Antiquity, making it the preferred treatment for the protection and finishing of fresco surfaces and, as Daniele da Volterra's *Deposition* showed, on mural paintings which had been transferred.

In 1836, the practitioner working on the Duomo of Pisa came into conflict with the curator of the Camposanto, Carlo Lasinio, because, in line with the advice received by Professor Branchi, he had been using skimmed milk (that is, casein) to consolidate the frescos, rather than the wax used on the wall paintings from Pompeii.[23] However, in 1857, a return to the use of wax was sanctioned by Guglielmo Botti for the restoration of the frescos by Benozzo Gozzoli; the Commission of the Accademia di Pisa, which was overseeing the work on the paintings in the Camposanto, discussed the operation with a very real sense of the material qualities of the paint, and an awareness of the inevitably selective aspects of restoration, which it would be good to think was still part of the present heritage of those in charge of the present-day direction of the restoration of frescos:

141

> "It is true that the fresco painting will thus be changed in its appearance. This is because that varnished appearance which is given it by the wax makes it resemble oil painting and, according to the different nature and density of the colours, will alter the value of certain tones to the detriment of the harmony of the whole; but it is also true that, although wax alters true fresco, it does not alter either the design, or the composition. Now, who is not aware that the principal excellence of paintings of this century lies more in the purity of line and the truth of expression, than in the mastery of chiaro-scuro or the artifices of colour?"[ix]

The use of wax was considered inevitable in order to consolidate Benozzo Gozzoli's painting, which was extensively finished *a secco*; on the other hand, for the transfer of the figure of a woman by Ghirlandaio, which is now in the museum at Pisa, Botti avoided the alterations caused by the use of this fixative, because the figure was completely executed in fresco technique, and therefore he was able to detach it without needing to fix a tempera layer. His restorations in the Camposanto in Pisa, which are perhaps better known through the booklet which he wrote on the subject rather than any direct examination of the paintings themselves, would become some of the most esteemed of the nineteenth century. With its origins in the academies of the mid-nineteenth century, the restoration which consolidated but no longer resorted to the use of the brush, which left losses visible and renounced the deceit of restorations directed to the art-lover (*restauro amatoriale*), had all the elements which were destined to become the heritage of a new vision of the work of art as a document, a vision which would characterize the approach to conservation of a Cavalcaselle.[24]

142

[ix] "*È vero che la pittura a fresco viene così a cangiar fisionomia; perchè quella specie di vernice che le dà la cera, la rende somigliante alla pittura a olio e secondo la diversa natura o densità dei colori, altera il valore di alcuni toni a carico dell'armonia generale; ma è altresì vero che se l'encausto altera il buon fresco, non altera però il disegno o la composizione. Ora chi non sa che il pregio principale della pittura di quel secolo consiste più nella purezza del disegno, nella verità dell'espressione che nel magistero del chiaroscuro o nell'artificio del colorito?*"

141. *Benozzo Gozzoli, Il ratto*
di Dina, detail; restored by
Guglielmo Botti, 1856.
Formerly Pisa, Camposanto.

142. *Domenico Ghirlandaio, Figure of a Woman; fresco transferred by Guglielmo Botti, around 1856. Pisa, Museo di San Matteo.*

Another technique which would become characteristic of conservation–restoration (*restauro di conservazione*)[x] would be experimented in Pisa on a vast scale: that is, the partial detachment of the vulnerable portions of the fresco which were coming away from the wall (the "*spanci*"), the renewal of the arriccio[xi] and then the reattachment of the fresco in its original position. Such techniques were already known: Pellegrino Succi in 1844 had detached and then replaced the head of Christ the Redeemer in the *Coronation of the Virgin* by "Stefano" – Puccio Capanna in the Lower Basilica in Assisi. One of the many examples which followed was the detachment and reattachment by Giovanni Spoldi, in 1895, of the head of Giorgione's *Nude* in the Fondaco dei Tedeschi in Venice.[25]

4. Aesthetic restoration:[xii] Molteni and Secco-Suardo

When we admire the extraordinary clarity which characterizes Secco-Suardo's manual, and makes it even now relevant to those involved in whatever capacity in restoration, one must not forget that unlike the authors of other nineteenth-century treatises, the Count was not bound by work deadlines and had the time to put into order, compare, verify and select all that he himself had experienced and amassed in the studios of restorers or through the observation of their work. His field of enquiry was northern Italy, and his challenge was directed at the methods used in Paris which had been eulogized by de Burtin and Horsin-Déon in the 1851 manual. His letters reveal the names of some of the restorers with whom he corresponded: Giuseppe Guizzardi, Giuseppe Fumagalli and Michele Ridolfi (and this at a formal meeting, which stands alone in the manual).[26] The restorers who do not appear, however, were those to whom he was closest, and with whom he must have had continuous personal contact: that is, the *estrattista* from Brescia Bernardo Galizzioli, Alessandro Brison, Antonio Zanchi and Giuseppe Molteni.

The personality of Molteni, pupil of Guizzardi, esteemed and fashionable portrait-painter, "matador" of all the exhibitions in the Brera (he was thus remembered by Rovani), is well known. Exceptionally, for the middle of the nineteenth century, in him we find the two professions: confirmed artist and restorer, side by side. The world in which he worked was that of the great connoisseurs Eastlake, Mündler and Morelli, who still saw in Lombard painting of the Renaissance an important source of supply for the great foreign museums and,

---

[x]I have opted for the rather clumsy expression of conservation–restoration as there is no direct equivalent in English for *restauro di conservazione*. This is because, historically, there has been no philosophical and theoretical structure to the various approaches to restoration, and no real definitions of the terms used.
"Conservation–restoration" implies that the work of art is simply "conserved" in its present state, ensuring its best preservation for posterity, with no attempt to "restore" its original or intended appearance; that is, no interpretative intervention on its "aesthetic" entity. It is what Conti refers to as a purist approach, treating the work of art as a historical document, the authenticity of which must not be impaired by any intrusion from our times.
[xi]The first, coarser, more granular layer of plaster which is applied to the wall, and which will be covered by the layer of finer plaster, the *intonaco* which will be painted on while still wet: this is what is known as *buon fresco* technique.
[xii]I have used the term "aesthetic restoration" for the Italian "*restauro amatoriale*" to define an approach which is diametrically opposed to that of conservation–restoration ("*restauro di conservazione*"). Directed to the "art-lover", it gives precedence to the aesthetic qualities and legibility of a painting, at the expense of its historical and authorial authenticity. There are degrees in its practice, now as in the past, so that what is carried out by a restorer for the "commercial" market is not equivalent (in intent as well as materials) to what is carried out within a museum or gallery, although both may be aiming to "please" the art-lover.

in a manner which leaves one somewhat perplexed, he combined the office of controller of the export of works of art from Lombardy, not only the profession of restorer, but also with that of dealer in Old Master paintings.[27]

Highly esteemed by Eastlake, Molteni was entrusted with the restoration of many of the pictures acquired in Italy for the National Gallery; and it is only relatively recently that some of the restorations (*rifacimenti*) have been removed; these showed that he conformed to the principle of correcting defects which were not characteristic of the style of a painting, a flaw linked to his academic education, wanting to correct the *"naives incorrections des anciens maîtres"*, as Giovanni Morelli would observe. In *Christ on the Road to Emmaus* by Altobello Melone, he had modified the general tonality to make it more even, and corrected some of the details which were furthest removed from accepted precepts; in Romanino's *Nativity*, he hid the rather bothersome and irreverent ox in the foreground. In Lotto's double-portrait in the Louvre, rather than recovering or replacing the original head, his solution for the head of the young della Torre was to replace earlier reconstructions with a typically six-teenth-century model. In 1865, he restored for Austen Layard a portrait from the Casa Lupi del Morone, adding a thin band of background to the top (necessary in order to provide the correct scale), but also altered the costume, which seemed to him to overwhelm the figure. The restoration (which was also carried out for Layard) of Andrea Busati's *Deposition* clearly showed the solutions which he was able to propose to his clients, and which they were more than happy to accept; he "improved" the panel with small corrections, and removed the two sorrowing little angels seated in the foreground on the balustrade, which he maintained were restorations. At least he did not destroy them, and simply painted them over, overpaint which was removed during the 1980 restoration of the painting.

143, 144

In a letter to Morelli dated 1865, he revealed his exquisitely refined taste for Lombard painting, requesting the renowned connoisseur to allow him to restore Moretto's *Christ Blessing Saint John the Baptist* (now in the National Gallery, London) as a reward for having had to restore a "weak Botticelli" belonging to him, the grotesque face of which he had found repugnant, "for which I have to ask your forgiveness as I have allowed myself, without your express permission and order, to lay my hands, or rather my brush, upon it …".[28] The very same tradition of Lombard connoisseurship would later distance itself from the practices of this great mid-nineteenth-century restorer. Referring to the small panel by Pisanello (at that time known as a Vittorio Pisano) depicting *The Virgin Appearing to Saints Anthony and George*, also in the National Gallery, Gustavo Frizzoni remarked that: "It is a shame that this work, the only panel in existence of this renowned master, should have undergone after its acquisition in Ferrara, a restoration which corresponds rather to a complete reworking of the painting; a repainting which however accurately executed, is not for us as welcome as the original would have been. To the extent that the restorer, who was Professor Molteni, a character as facetious as he was knowledgeable and refined in his tastes, believed that he had so immersed himself in the spirit of the artist that having accomplished his work, he was wont to say amongst friends, that he no longer called himself Giuseppe Molteni, but Vittorio Molteni."

His retouching of the Pisanello had probably been a question of spotting in and bring-ing together the worn areas in the sky and the armour of the saintly knight, at one time splendidly detailed but which had become, according to Eastlake in 1858, almost invisible.[29] Above all, Molteni restored Renaissance paintings and, on the whole, did not seem to embark on restorations weightier than those to be found on the Pisanello. Alongside this little panel, in 1860 Eastlake had also acquired the other work by Pisano with the signature of Bono da

143. *Lorenzo Lotto, Della
Torre portrait; restored by
Giuseppe Molteni.
London, National Gallery.*

144. *Lorenzo Lotto, Della Torre portrait; after the removal of Giuseppe Molteni's restoration. London, National Gallery.*

Ferrara, as well as the *Saint Jerome* by Cosmè Tura and an altarpiece by Garofalo, which are all now part of the National Gallery. These paintings were immediately sent to Molteni, who would leave the eighteenth-century enlargement on the sixteenth-century painting, and give the two works depicting Saint Jerome a golden transparent tonality which they still have.[xiii] In the painting sporting the apocryphal signature of Bono, or rather the "autumnal melancholy of the young Bellini", the echo of which was identified in 1958 by one of the greatest connoisseurs of Italian painting, how much of this was Pisanello's intent rather than the expression of Giuseppe Molteni's exquisite taste? Remaining in the field of Ferrarese painting, it is difficult not to admire his solution in the varnishing of Cosmè Tura's *Venus*, which passed from the Layard collection to that of the National Gallery.[xiv, 30]

Many of Molteni's restorations were of paintings in the Poldi-Pezzoli collection in Milan; we know of his restoration of Mantegna's *Madonna* and of the *Rest on the Flight into Egypt* by Andrea Solario, which both still appear in the splendidly patinated robes in which he clothed them. Of two other small panels by Andrea Solario, depicting *Saint John* and *Saint Catherine*, Secco-Suardo himself described the inspection undertaken by Molteni and Antonio Zanchi on the transfer carried out on these paintings by Paul Kiewert in Paris, despite which paint was still lifting away (*sobollarsi*). A new direction can be seen here in the presentation of paintings belonging to collections, in that these were both transferred onto wooden supports, in order to preserve the characteristic external appearance of works painted on panel.[31]

In the Brera, Molteni restored both Mantegna's *Dead Christ* and Raphael's *Marriage of the Virgin*. His 1858 report on the restoration of this panel is one of the finest documents on nineteenth-century approaches to restoration, and is a good introduction to the idea of patina as a deposit left by Time as well as an alteration in the original materials, and on cleaning carried out with the aim of an aesthetic recovery. Having described the work carried out on the wooden support, Molteni observed that "it was even more important to proceed first and foremost and with the utmost care with the cleaning of the patina produced by Time which had left large patches in various areas, cleaning with restraint and to different levels according to the need and always trying to leave as much as was possible, not reducing it unseemingly, according to the rules of 'good restoration'", continuing:

> "On all the flesh and the light parts I did not touch the patina, but began by cleaning the great paved area (of pale red and white marble slabs) which lay before the temple. At this point it is worth noting that in this paved area, it is the white parts which prevail, and that it is against these that all the figures are set; it is also worth noting that the patina on this paved area, if compared to that on the heads, could be quantified as ten to one; so that by not touching the flesh painting whilst cleaning the pavement, this became so light that the original effect of the painting (which had been inverted as I mentioned before by the imbalance in the patina) once more became apparent, and – in my opinion – wonderfully so. In fact, before [the cleaning] most of the figures would stand out lighter relative to the general tonality of the background, or in other parts shared the same tonality. Once the paved area had been cleaned (on which

145, 148

146, 147

149

[xiii] No longer; they have both been restored since the time of writing.
[xiv] This work has also now been restored, so Molteni's varnishing is no longer visible. The subject matter of the painting has been changed from *Venus* to *Allegorical Figure*.

145. *Andrea Mantegna, Madonna and
Child; restored by Giuseppe Molteni,
around 1860. Milan, Museo Poldi Pezzoli.*

146. *Andrea Solario, Saint*
John the Baptist; transferred by
Antonio Zanchi. Milan, Museo
Poldi Pezzoli.

147. *Andrea Solario, Saint*
Catherine; transferred by
Antonio Zanchi. Milan, Museo
Poldi Pezzoli.

148. *Andrea Solario, Rest on the*
Flight into Egypt; restored by
Giuseppe Molteni, around 1860.
Milan, Museo Poldi Pezzoli.

remains however at least the same of amount of patina as is present on the flesh), the figures detached themselves by their tonality, and appeared more highly coloured and saturated. The change was such that now from the point of view of colour, one would be fully justified in comparing the *Marriage* by Raphael to the paintings of the greatest colourists and masters of the Venetian school".[xv]

Having recovered the temple and freed the sky from excesses of both patina and overpainting ("it appeared cloudless and beautiful and *sfumato*, the glowing azure bringing a resplendent warmth to the rest of the painting"), he proceeded to the cleaning of the draperies, which gave him the opportunity of lingering on the "luscious emerald green of sixteenth-century painters, that is, the colour which consists of an opaque straw coloured underlayer, then glazed with a copper green, and finally with asphaltum.[xvi] Will someone explain to me why this glorious piece of drapery in which I found no evidence of damage, was painted over? This is why. Every restorer is aware that these sixteenth-century greens are overwhelmingly difficult and desperately hard to clean, because they either lose their asphaltum glaze and then clash, or else they remain black because of the accumulation of asphaltum. And this is why even the most expert restorer, when cleaning this colour, will have a patchy result."

And, finally, Molteni left the panel unvarnished, "because the painting after the cleaning has a beautiful and modest sheen, the fruit of the good varnish which Raphael must have originally applied warm, as was the custom in those times".[xvii]

149   Admired by Passavant, the restoration of the *Marriage of the Virgin* was criticized by Cavalcaselle, who did not find the relationship between the figures and the now lighter background to be correct.[32] His dissent should be seen against the backdrop of his rivalry with Morelli and the circle to which Molteni himself belonged. However, the level of

---

[xv] *"fosse ancora più importante di procedure per la prima cosa e colla massima attenzione alla pulitura della patina prodotta dal tempo che formava grandi macchie in vari punti, praticandola parcamente ed in grado diverso secondo che ne ravvivasse il bisogno e lasciandone però sempre quanto era possibile, non stando nelle regole delb buon restauro di menomarla sconvenevolmente".*

"Su tutte lecarni e sulle vesti chiare non toccai la patina, e mi diedi a pulire delicatamente il grande lastrico (raffigurante marmo bianco e rosso pallido) posto davanti al tempio. Qui giova osservare che in detto lastrico predominano le parti bianche e che su di esse campeggiano tutte le figure; è pure a notarsi che la patina di detto lastrico a confronto di quella delle teste poteva considerarsi come dieci ad uno quindi non toccando le carni ed invece ripulendo la patina del lastrico questo a confronto andò facendosi chiaro in tal grado che l'originale effetto del quadro (invertito, come io accenava, dallo squilibrio della patina) ricomparve in modo, a mio giudizio, meraviglioso. Infatti dapprima per rispetto al tono del fondo il maggior numero delle figure vedevasi generalmente staccare alquanto in chiaro ed in qualche parte di esse erano col fondo a pari d tono. Invece dopo pulito il lastrico (sul quale pure rimane ancora almeno tanto patina quanto ve ne è sulle carni) le figure al confronto staccarono per tono, e si fecero più colorite e più succose. Il cambiamento fu tale che ora dal lato del colore ben a ragione si può paragonare lo Sposalizio del Sanzio ai dipinti dei più grandi coloristi e sovrani maestri veneziani."

[xvi] Which corresponds exactly to contemporary documentary evidence provided in G. B. Armenini's *De Veri Precetti della Pittura*, 1586 (Einaudi, 1988).

[xvii] *"verde smeraldo e succoso dei cinquecentisti, quello cioè fatto prima di color paglierino a corpo, poscia velato di verde di rame e per ultimo di asfalto. Non trovando nessun guasto in questo grandioso panneggiamento mi si dirà perchè venisse ridipinto? Eccone la spiegazione. Ogni restauratore sa che questi verdi del Cinquecento sono di una durezza e di una difficoltà disperante per chi deve pulirli perchè o perdono la velatura dell'asfalto e allora stonano, ovvero rimangono ancora neri per l'accrescimento dell' asfalto stesso. Questo è il motivo per cui anche ai più esperti restauratori la pulitura di quell colore riesce quasi sempre macchiata".*

"attesoché il dipinto dopo la pulitura, presenta un lucido bello e modesto, frutto della buona vernice originale che Raffaello avrà dato probabilmente a caldo come si costumava in quei tempi".

149. *Raphael, Marriage of the
Virgin, detail; restored by
Giuseppe Molteni, 1858.
Milan, Pinacoteca di Brera.*

professionalism of the great Milanese restorer should not let us forget that the pleasurable enjoyment to which he predisposed paintings through his restorations did not coincide with the vision of works of art as historical documents held by that great historian of Italian art, Cavalcaselle: his distrust was not, therefore, the result only of party politics, but also of a fundamentally different vision of the function of the work of art.

Of a quite different order to the restorations carried out by Molteni were the repaintings, the completions and even the signatures added according to the attributions given by the collector, linked to the nineteenth-century tradition of aesthetic restoration, the *restauro amatoriale*. In a letter of 1855 to Secco-Suardo, Giuseppe Fumagalli would ask what date he was to add to a *Sacra Conversazione* by Andrea Previtali, which he had restored with huge areas of retouching and to which he had already added a *cartouche* with the signature, which in fact would prove not to be to the satisfaction of the "restorer Count". This is an important document as it serves to explain certain strange signatures, which are typical of paintings which passed through the art market and collectors' hands in northern Italy towards the middle of the nineteenth century: the astonishing Giovanni da Udine dated 1517 in the Accademia Carrara in Bergamo, the famous signature of Bono da Ferrara on the *Saint Jerome* by Pisanello, and that of Giovanni Oriolo on the *Portrait of Lionello d'Este* (so close to Jacopo Bellini) in the National Gallery in London.[33]

The picture-gallery painting (*quadro da galleria*) restored according to Secco-Suardo's directions would be retouched accurately with restorations (*risarcimenti*) which must on no account be recognizable as such, executed using either oil or varnish as the medium, depending on the requirements of the technique; the surface of the painting would be absolutely flat thanks to various operations using the introduction of inserts, or the securing of panels to stretchers, and that *parquetage*[xviii] which, already in use in the eighteenth century, would almost label the panel painting as coming from a collection.[34] The kind of restoration discussed in the manual, was one which, with the exclusion of the compromises found in the restoration of production-line paintings ("*quadri di fabbrica*"), dealt exclusively with works of a certain value, which justified the long and often expensive procedures which were necessary for a "correct" intervention (*a regola d'arte*). A restoration, moreover, as suggested by the invitation to secrecy with which the manual begins ("a painting is like a single woman, whose honour can be sullied with a single word"), that is linked to a rather hedonistic enjoyment, and to the exploitation, which was also financial, of works of art in the collectors' market.

When faced with the conservation of original materials so far degraded that they disturbed this enjoyment, Secco-Suardo would move with complete confidence in his own ability to make the correct choice, deriving from the correct precepts[xix] (and these were not necessarily academic rules in a traditional sense) which every painter must possess. Respect for the figurative elements of a painting were beyond discussion, but excessive deterioration should be corrected, in the same way as any defect in technique which prevented the solidity and legibility which – according to those very rules – were desirable. A borderline case would be that of the "overabundant oil" ("*olio esuberante*"), used by the painter which formed a crust on the surface: the employment of "*l'acquetta Lechi*" would enable one to "give back to

---

[xviii] Cradling; that is, securing a wooden armature of vertical and horizontal members to the reverse of the panel, which was often thinned before the operation, in order to keep the panel flat.
[xix] "*norme di buona scuola*"

the colours their natural vivacity", that is, the characteristic hue of an optimum ratio of oil to pigment. In whatever painting, the darkening of greens would be removed using alkaline substances, unlike Molteni's solution for the Raphael in the Brera in Milan. A brush, "well and prudently employed", would then remedy "the loss of some of the hues and the alteration of others, always so long as it is not the case of the whole painting, but only of specific areas." Secco-Suardo's typically nineteenth-century gratification with the amber tones of old paintings, and his advice on artificial patinas with which to imitate this age, were therefore due to a criterion of taste which found more enjoyment in darkened paintings. In this search for an aura of antiquity, "patina" had definitely lost its meaning as an exudation of the oil medium, or alteration of the original materials, to take on the vaguely emotional overtones romantic in the negative sense so dear to Roberto Longhi.[35]

Cleaning would be resorted to, in order to compensate for "the natural and induced sullying which a painting suffers, which results in the loss of its liveliness, and which at times so deadens the painting that one can no longer comprehend its subject matter. The alteration of the varnishes applied to it in the past, some of which have yellowed to an exceptional degree, others darkened, and yet others which have become whitish and completely opaque. The poor retouchings and restorations applied to improve and restore the painting, which now disfigure it; sometimes, because executed by an inexperienced hand, and on other occasions because they have altered to such a degree because they were executed with inappropriate techniques."

Secco-Suardo's knowledge of chemistry was very carefully and clearly directed to the understanding of the behaviour of the original materials. He referred to the resinification of oils in order to clarify the behaviour of certain reagents, and underlined the risk of their saponification by the use of certain alkaline reagents which would destroy "the gloss and transparency" characteristic of oils. His observations are therefore still pertinent: one would have to be particularly obtuse not to deduce that the alkaline reagents so much in use today could have a similar effect, without actually destroying the paint layer. Varnish was by this time a means of maintenance and restoration so widespread that Forni would record how even the *tempere grasse*[xx] of the Early Masters were originally varnished, with substances which would allow them from afar to take on the tonalities of a picture painted in oil: "either to fix the colours solidly and prevent their contact with the air which makes them fade, or to obtain a certain brilliance and fire (*fiammeggiante*) in the colours which would be impossible to obtain without its use."

Faced with this rather simplistic statement, Secco-Suardo launched into a detailed series of objections, with the polemical tones which he always used when confronted with the Tuscan restorer. He noted, for example, with reference to Mantegna, that there were many old tempera paintings (on canvas as well as panel), that were not varnished, or else only varnished after a lapse of time which was proven by the dirt layer present under the varnish, and insisted that the technique of tempera painting was different to that employed in miniatures: "all paintings which have as their medium animal or vegetable glue, and specially containing the milk of the fig-tree, are well suited to having a varnish, especially if it is an oily varnish, and they acquire through it an extraordinary brilliance in their colours. Whilst those

---

[xx] A term which refers to a technique which was half-way between egg-tempera and oil painting, although it is not clear even now whether oil would be added to the egg-yolk medium, or whether top layers would be painted in oil over initial layers in egg.

150. Floriano Ferramola,
fragment of a fresco from
Casa Bergondio della Torre;
transferred by Bernardo
Gallizioli, around 1845.
Brescia, Pinacoteca Tosio
Martinengo.

151. *Moretto da Brescia, Prophet; fresco
transferred by Bernardo Gallizioli, around
1861. Brescia, private collection.*

bound with a gum, alter, lose their harmony and become distorted in the most horrible manner; the colours which have little body, such as lakes and the *stil de grain*[xxi] become excessively transparent, whilst others such as all the mineral pigments and those which have great covering power, leap out excessively. And this is why *miniatures on parchment are never varnished, and never could be varnished*,[xxii] as Forni asserts without putting forward any substantiation."

Secco-Suardo was still tied to the taste and the restoration practices of the first half of the nineteenth century, when a finish which made the Early Masters resemble oil paintings more closely was certainly favoured, because it facilitated their insertion within private and public collections, which could only gradually come to accept characteristics which were so far-removed from those of the customary gallery picture. The distinction between *tempere grasse* and gums is, however, correct. And on the same panel one might find pigments tempered with egg, glue or fig milk (*lattifico*) and others with "gums" which easily altered when, as would often happen, they were then varnished.[36] Frescos were required to retain their opacity but, relinquishing the wall, they had to adapt to the flexible structure of canvas. The transfers which Secco-Suardo always had before him were those carried out by Bernardo Galizzioli in Brescia: no resin residues were present on the surface, they were "thin, light and flexible" and on the reverse "an ashy coloured layer" hid the method used to attach the *strappo* to the new canvas.

Gallizzioli was undoubtedly very proficient at detaching frescos, even though his *strappi*, rather more than those by Succi, show the imprint of the weave, as for instance in the *Madonna degli Angeli* by Bergognone in the Brera, Milan, which was transferred in 1847 from Santa Maria dei Servi in Milan. It was also Galizzioli who, sometime before 1845, transferred the works by Ferramola in Casa Bergondio della Torre in Brescia: the fragments in the Tosio Martinengo Gallery in Brescia, and the large fresco in the Victoria and Albert Museum, London, depicting the scene of a tournament in the square in Brescia. Technically, a perfectly executed *strappo* of a mural painting is that of Moretto's *Prophets*, detached from the Palazzo Martinengo Cesaresco, which received a prize at the Italian Exhibition of 1861.[37] In Secco-Suardo, the split between *intonaco* (the conservation of the plaster layer was of no interest) and the painting was total, even when the paintings were to be reattached to a wall, as was the case with those by Giovan Battista Castello, which were removed from Gorlago by Antonio Zanchi, and then used in the decoration of the hall of the new *prefettura* in Bergamo in 1866.[38]

150

151

152

5. Ulisse Forni, Gaetano Bianchi and restoration in Florence

When, in 1864, Secco-Suardo was invited (at the suggestion of Giovanni Morelli) to run a course in Florence on the techniques used to transfer paintings, this initiative was taken entirely over the head of the gallery restorer, the capable Ulisse Forni who had just presented his publisher Le Monnier with the manuscript of *Il Manuale del pittore restauratore*, which was destined to see the light of day at the same time as the first part of Secco-Suardo's manual. It is hard to establish all the details (with all the adaptations, retouchings,

---

[xxi] An organic yellow.
[xxii] In italics in the original.

*152. Giovan Battista Castello,
Stories of Ulysses; fresco trans-
ferred by Antonio Zanchi, 1866.
Bergamo, Prefettura.*

etc.), but not to imagine what form this race for priority between the two restorers took, in
a climate which led to paradoxes such as that of Pietro Pezzati affirming (wrongly), that he
was the only one in Florence capable of carrying out a *strappo* on a fresco, and therefore
demanding compensation for the loss of income which would result from Secco-Suardo's
public communication of the method.[39]

Of the tests carried out during the course, so far we know of the transfer from panel
onto canvas of the *Madonna with Child and the Young Saint John* by Michele di Ridolfo del
Ghirlandaio, of a Peruginesque tondo and also a sixteenth-century Florentine portrait, in addition to the three *strappi* of frescos from the Chiostro degli Aranci in the Badia Fiorentina:
two sections of the decoration of the base from the workshop of Giovanni di Consalvo, and
the lunette by Bronzino depicting the *Penitence of Saint Benedict*. The partial failure of the
latter transfer, as Secco-Suardo was himself to point out in his manual, was the result of the
canvases used for the removal from the wall not having been wetted prior to the operation.

153, 154

153. *Agnolo Bronzino, The Penitence of Saint Benedict; fresco transferred by Giovanni Secco-Suardo, 1866. Florence, Chiesa di Badia, chiostro degli Aranci.*

154. *Agnolo Bronzino, The Penitence of Saint Benedict; imprint remaining on the wall after the "strappo" by Giovanni Secco-Suardo. Originally from Florence, Chiesa della Badia, Chiostro degli Aranci.*

However, it is not at Secco-Suardo's feet that we should lay the present poor state of conservation of the paint layer, which in recent times has fallen victim to some new restorer's ill-placed trust in the painting's execution entirely in *buon fresco*.[40]

The context of the paintings dealt with in Forni's text was quite different from that of other treatises on restoration available until then. Frescos and their transfer were dealt with at length, seemingly following the advice of Guglielmo Botti or Gaetano Bianchi, rather than from personal experience. In the wake of the practices in vogue at the beginning of the century, he also gave ample space to the transfer of frescos *a massello*, of which he had seen some noteworthy examples in Siena, carried out between 1841 (Sodoma's *Christ at the Column*) and 1854 (the frescos by Pietro and Ambrogio Lorenzetti in San Francesco).   156
Considerable time was also spent discussing the *tempera grassa* used by the Early Masters, and there was no shortage of advice on treatments for gilded backgrounds. Before discussing the subject of cradling, Forni discussed "how to repair large panels in which the planks have come apart and are warped, as well as small warped panels". The manual reveals a sound knowledge of both Italian and French treatises, takes its bearings from chemistry, but mostly follows a practical slant, without inhibitions and without imposing on itself any questions of professional ethics when expounding, for instance, on the methods useful in quickly putting back into order the lower commercial rungs of painting, much as Horsin-Déon had also done. The experience of the poor results achieved with the wax used by Ignazio Zotti on the *Cenacolo di Foligno* by Perugino disenchanted him completely with the use of encaustic, and he made use of the poor results of the restorations executed in this medium by Michele Ridolfi on the work by Aspertini in San Frediano in Lucca. If, from a technical point of view, there is a myth in the book, it is that of the egg-tempera medium used by the Early Masters.[41]

For patination, Ulisse Forni's choice of ingredients was of a much more domestic nature than the amber varnish recommended by Secco-Suardo: liquorice, soot, tobacco water, coffee and diluted asphaltum, all materials which could at times lead to that opacity of effect sometimes found on the paintings which he restored, such as *The Adoration of the Magi* by Cosimo Rosselli in the galleries in Florence, which was restored, spotted and repainted to such a degree that it is easy to understand why he should have wanted to restore some "antiquity" to it. This is what Cosimo Conti had to say about Forni:

"He lacked none of the practical qualities necessary to be a good restorer, but alas, he was also possessed by that disastrous propensity which, in order to hide a restoration carried out in one area, retouches and spots in a whole figure. Completely invisible! … and of course it could not be seen, because the whole thing appeared restored. On the other hand, with Forni the art of restoration had made some progress; the repair of panels in his time improved, cleaning sometimes, but most of all he is to be praised because with his methods, one can remove his restoration with the greatest ease without damaging the original".[42]

Secco-Suardo, on the other hand, pointed out with contempt the succession of recipes which were in essence identical, not checked, copied from other manuals, and the many contradictions found in the Tuscan restorer's book. One should also not forget that Forni, because his principles were always in direct relation to the need to find work, which is the lot of being a craftsman, always relied on the skill and the experience of the restorer reading his manual; it is according to these same principles that he also counselled the use of cleaning methods

*155. Marco d'Oggiono, Madonna with
Saints; transferred by Alessandro Brison
and Giovanni Secco-Suardo. Milan,
Sant'Eufemia.*

156. *Sodoma, Christ at the
Column; transferred "a mas-
sello" in 1841. Siena,
Pinacoteca Nazionale.*

which were undoubtedly dangerous or poorly tested, because he knew that he was address-
ing expert craftsmen who were able to evaluate and master the risks involved.

The incompatible character of these two restorers is well highlighted by their respective accounts of the discovery of the Pettenkofer method which, between 1865 and 1866,
was a novelty officially promoted by Charles Vogdt, an agent from Geneva representing its
inventor. Secco-Suardo contacted him through Eastlake himself, in whose gallery the
method of regenerating old varnishes had been tried out on Titian's *Bacchus and Ariadne*.
In the 1866 edition, Secco-Suardo did not reveal any of the details of the procedure which
were kept secret by its inventor. Forni, on the other hand, was part of the commission which
met in 1865 with Vogdt in order to assess the discovery on behalf of the Ministry. After a
private meeting, and without any mention of this appearing in the official report, he proved
his perspicacity by presenting two trials identical to those presented officially by Vogdt. He
concluded by emphasizing the limitations of the Pettenkofer system, and also suggested its
use in softening varnishes which then would become soluble in simple spirits of turpentine
(*acqua ragia*).[43]

Without the pressures of having to reply with facts to the Florentine course run by Secco-
Suardo, and then the haste to get the manuscript published, Forni would probably have elaborated his manual with more thought. His campaign against the "restorer Count" (as Valentino
Bernardi called him) is manifest in the preface to the 1866 volume, which appeared dated
1863, and in the opening page addressed a warning to the reader[xxiii] in which he stated specifically that he, "Forni, was present at the classes given in Florence by the aforementioned
Count, not as a pupil, but charged with the task of observing the procedures and methods used
by him to transfer paintings, and then to write a report, which he did, for the commission which
was elected to this end."

Ulisse Forni was to die in 1867; the recriminations indulged in by Secco-Suardo
throughout the second part of the manual (published in 1894 but written before 1873, the
year in which Secco-Suardo died) were reproaches addressed to one who no longer had the
possibility of responding. Moreover, as can be seen in Guizzardi's letters, it was frequently
the case that the activities of Secco-Suardo (as both collector and restorer) lent themselves
to misunderstandings such as those leading to the mutual estrangement in Milan between
himself and a respected restorer such as Alessandro Brison, with whom he had tried out
methods of transfer which differed from those practised by the French, on a panel attributed to Palma Vecchio, and on the altarpiece by Marco d'Oggiono in Sant' Eufemia.[44] We
find confirmation of the practical usefulness of Forni's advice on the various methods
which can be used to transfer frescos, when Girolamo Botter and Antonio Carlini have suddenly to become experts in the technique in order to rescue from demolition what
remained of the mural paintings by Tommaso Modena (*The Stories of Saint Ursula*) in
Treviso; dissatisfied with the *strappo* advised by Secco-Suardo, they decide to follow Forni's
precepts. One of the most justified objections which can be levelled at the manual of the
"Count-restorer" is that *strappo* was the only method he advised for the transfer of frescos;
it was a choice linked to the practices of the first half of the century, and which already
appeared out of date at the time of publication, when the recovery of monuments as a
whole, or the imitation of what one presumed to be the original appearance, was no longer

155

<hr>

[xxiii] "*per norma di lettore giova avvertire*".

a novelty. In a space which retained the style of the original, a *distacco*,[xxv] which preserved all the irregularities of the plaster surface, was preferable to a mural painting with a perfectly smooth and regular surface, such as that acquired after it has been transferred onto canvas. It is noteworthy that as late as 1898, a booklet appeared dealing with this problem, in which the habitual restorer and director of the Accademia Carrara in Bergamo, Valentino Bernardi, propounded his criticisms of the "Count-restorer", and in particular of his advice to paint the reverse of the fresco paint layer (detached with the *strappo* technique) with pigments bound in casein.[45]

The point of reference put forward by Bernardi was that of the work of the "king of restorers", the Florentine Gaetano Bianchi. Having abandoned the heroic *trasporti a massello* of the forties described by Forni, one of his favoured methods was to detach all the *intonaco* and transfer it onto a stretcher previously prepared with lathes. This preserved not only the imprints from the cartoon, as in the best examples of *strappo*, but also all the irregularities of the *intonaco* and the junction marks from the various *giornate*.[xxvi] The frescos were therefore particularly well adapted to be reinstalled within a building, whether within the same monument or in new complexes, such as was the case with the restorations from the Bargello (where his reconstructions "in the style of" deceived the Turinese Massimo D'Azeglio) or the Castello di Vincigliata, for which Bianchi adapted certain mediocre frescos from the end of the fourteenth century which he had detached from a convent in via Scala in Florence.[46]

Bianchi's renown is most strongly linked to Giotto's frescos in the Bardi Chapel in Santa Croce, which had been recovered from beneath the whitewash in 1852, and the recriminations aimed at his reconstructions, which were obviously not of the standard of the originals. The *Saint Louis the King* which Ruskin admired so much as a masterpiece 157, 158 of Early Christian art, and which Van Marle would still describe as an example of the school of Giotto, was in fact entirely by the hand of Bianchi. He had patinated these pictures, lowering them in tone, which helped the integrations to merge with the original, as all will remember who saw the paintings before Leonetto Tintori's restoration.[47]

If we were to take as indications of the procedures employed by Bianchi what Forni advised for the restoration of mural paintings, we would find ourselves confronted with an extremely rich and well-calibrated array of the finishing techniques and treatments for mural paintings; of their possible *a secco* finishes, varnishings which they may have suffered and which may mean that no intervention is possible, advice as to the techniques to be used for the retouching and toning in of areas which are reconstructed *ex novo*, all of which constitute a useful guide for the recognition of the various ancient techniques of mural painting.

Between 1858 and 1861, Gaetano Bianchi restored Piero della Francesca's frescos with 159–161 different techniques from those used on Giotto's paintings in Santa Croce. Cavalcaselle commented that "the work was conducted by Bianchi with much care and devotion: a new *intonaco* was made for the missing parts, giving it a colour which would not offend the eye

---

[xxv] Literally, detachment; the painting is detached along with the plaster. Also known as *stacco*.
[xxvi] *Giornata* refers to the work of a single day. Only enough wet plaster (the *intonaco*) would be applied onto the underlying *arriccio*, which could be painted in a single day. The evolution of the execution of a fresco can be followed through the overlapping areas of the *giornate*. The area painted in a single day would obviously vary in size depending on the detail and difficulty of the composition – a single head might be a *giornata*, as indeed may be a large section of landscape or background.

*157. Gaetano Bianchi,
San Luigi; 1852.
Florence, Santa Croce,
Bardi Chapel.*

158. Giotto, *The Funeral of Saint Francis; restored by Gaetano Bianchi, 1852. Florence, Santa Croce, Bardi Chapel.*

159. *Piero della Francesca, Battle of Constantine; with the integrations by Gaetano Bianchi, 1858–1861. Arezzo, San Francesco.*

160. *Piero della Francesca,*
Prophet; with the restorations by
Gaetano Bianchi.

161. *Piero della Francesca,
Prophet; after the removal of
the restorations by Gaetano
Bianchi. Arezzo, San Francesco.*

of the beholder." It is likely that Cavalcaselle himself was not entirely absent from the final choices made in the treatment, especially those pertaining to the integration of the losses. If in some areas, for instance in the young prophet positioned at a height to the right of the window, Bianchi has dealt in a rather summary fashion with the blue area which had lost the shadows of its modelling, when he integrated *The Battle of Constantine*, he executed those easily recognizable but toned reconstructions which were so helpful in the legibility of Piero della Francesca's masterpiece. But, without finding out about the date of these integrations, and hence their historical importance, these were destroyed during the unsuccessful restoration of around 1960. What the frescos in Arezzo have recently undergone, and not only with reference to the integration of the losses, can only make one appreciate all the more the skill of Gaetano Bianchi, when compared to the presumptuousness of his twentieth-century successors.[48]

Moreover, if we look at Bianchi's interventions as examples of a restoration (*ripristino*) of the whole space in its original polychromy, we realize that we are in fact dealing with an exceptionally interesting figure linked to a vision of restoration which presupposed a knowledge of Viollet-le-Duc. The aim was to recapture a general polychromy made up of coats of arms, imitation marble, decorations and figures; to reconstruct the decoration in false marble of San Miniato al Monte (1859–1861) according to the original "cartoon", or else to restore to the transept of Santa Croce the appearance it had in the fourteenth century. With the aid of the remains of the original (which were only preserved if in good condition, otherwise they were traced and made *ex novo*), in 1870 the Florentine restorer was so successful in the external decoration of the chapels that even recently this had to be tested in order to establish the date of the frescos, forgetting to verify the amplitude and nature of his intervention.[49]

Notes

1. P. Palmaroli, letter of 10 September 1810, in "Memorie enciclopediche romane", V, 1810, pp. 127–128. Some of the events relating to the transfer of the *Deposition* are not entirely clear, even when comparing the sources, see: Cicognara, 1825, p. 11; [T. Wright], *Advice to Proprietors, on the Care of Valuable Pictures Painted in Oil with Instructions for Preserving, Cleaning and Restoring them by an Artist*, London, 1835, pp. 25–26; Zeni, 1840, note 8 p. 12 ("The calcareous water-paintings are only attacked by acids, in contact with which they actually decompose completely. But with alkalis, one is able to clean them when they have been covered by oleo-resinous substances such as smoke, for instance. It was this method which was used in Rome to clean the famous fresco by Daniele di Volterra, which had been sawn from the wall by order of General Miollis in the early years of the [nineteenth] century, and then covered with wax, varnishes, etc. But this method cannot be employed for frescos which have been transferred using such substances."); F. Bonnard, *Histoire du Couvent Royal de la Trinité du Mont Pincio à Rome*, Paris, 1933, pp. 222, 253–254; Scicolone, 1981–1982.
2. The restoration, which has respected in a truly admirable fashion the evidence of Palmaroli's intervention, is illustrated by Philippe Morel in an article in the "Bollettino d'Arte" (*Pellegrino Tibaldi e Marco Pino alla Trinità dei Monti, un affresco ritrovato, Pietro Palmaroli e le origini dello stacco*).
3. On Pietro, and on Vincenzo Camuccini and the interventions they directed, see: Cicognara, 1825, pp. 18–19; C. Falconieri, *Vita di Vincenzo Cumaccini*, Rome, 1875, p. 123; F. Noack, in Thieme–Becker, 1911; Biagetti–de Campos, 1944, pp. 187–191; G. Bandinelli, *Critici romani del primo Ottocento intorno a un quadro celebre. La Danae della Galleria Borghese*, in "L'Urbe", 1952, V, pp. 3–10; P. della Pergola, *Galleria Borghese. I dipinti*, II, Rome, 1959, pp. 116, 226; Corbo, 1969; A. Bovero, *Camuccini Pietro*, in *Dizionario biografico degli italiani*, XVII, 1974. Of the restorers who were working under the direction of Pietro Camuccini, Giuseppe Candida is cited by Bedotti (1837, p. 13) because he carried out his retouching using varnish as the medium,

according to the Venetian tradition; in 1839, he was granted the licence to transfer paintings (as an *estrattista*). (*La tomba Franîois di Vulci*, catalogue of the exhibition, Città del Vaticano, 1987, p. 183).

4. For the restoration of the mosaics, see Matthiae, 1967, pp. 399–423; for different interpretations of the restored sections, see: J. Wilpert, *Die römischen Mosaiken und Malereien der Kirchlichen Bauten von IV bis XIII Jahrhundert*, Freiburg im Brisgau, 1917.

5. F. Agricola, *Relazione dei restauri nelle terze logge del Pontificio Palazzo Vaticano*, Rome, 1842.

6. Agricola, 1839, pp. 5, 17.

7. On Palmaroli, apart from the intervention on the Daniele da Volterra, see: Marcucci, 1816; Guattani, in "Memorie enciclopediche sulle antichità e le belle arti di Roma per il" MDCCCCXVI, Rome, 1817, pp. 61–62; C. L. Eastlake, in *Report*, 1853, pp. 278, 285; J. Hübner, *Catalogue de la Galerie Royale de Dresde*, Dresden, 1863, pp. 62–63; Cavalcaselle–Crowe, 1877, I, p. 121; Milanesi, VII, 1881, note 2 p. 571; Cavalcaselle–Crowe, 1882–1885, II, note 2 p. 71 and note 1, pp. 254–257; Stübel, 1926, p. 129; Scicolone, 1981–1982. For comparison with the methods employed by Palmaroli, one can use the somewhat negative judgements passed on the restorations in the private galleries in Rome, as found in William Coningham's statement in the first National Gallery inquiry (*Report from the Select Committee on the National Gallery ...*, London, 1850, p. 51).

8. De Campos–Biagetti, 1944, pp. 189 (letter of 23 November 1825 signed by: Girolamo Scaccia, Tommaso Minardi, Andrea Pozzi, Filippo Agricola, Agostino Tofanelli, Luigi Durantini, Giovanni Silvagni, Carlo Viganoni, Alberto Thorvaldsen, Antonio d'Este, Antonio Solà, Giuseppe Camporese, Gaspare Salvi, Pietro Bracci, Missirini, chief secretary), 189–190 (letter from Wicar); Hueck; 1981, p. 149.

9. Marconi, 1979; O. Rossi Pinelli, *Carlo Fea e il chirografo del 1802: cronaca giudiziaria e non, delle prime battaglie per la tutela delle "belle arti"*, in "Ricerche di storia dell'arte", n. 8, 1979, pp. 27–41. On the reconstruction of San Paolo fuori le Mura, see M. F. Fischer, *Classicism and Historicism in 19th Century Roman Architecture*, in *Actes du XXIIme Congrès international d'histoire de l'art* (1969), Budapest, 1972, pp. 603–608.

10. G. Valadier, *Narrazione artistica dell'operato finora nel restauro dell'Arco di Tito in Roma*, Rome, 1822; Stendhal, *Promenades dans Rome*, Paris, 1829, 30 June 1828; G. Giovannoni, *Questioni d'architettura*, Rome, 1929, II, pp. 161–162; Marconi, 1979, pp. 63–64.

11. J. C. Ibbetson, *An Accidence or Gamut of Painting in Oil and Watercolours*, London, 1803, ed. 1828; note pp. 3–4; cited by Gombrich, 1962, p. 53; C. L. Eastlake, statement in *Report*, 1853, p. 276 (more generally, refer to this source for a wealth of information on methods of cleaning employed by English restorers in the mid-nineteenth century).

12. Bedotti, 1837, pp. 14–21; on these restorations see: *Cultura figurative negli stati del re di Sardegna (1773–1861)*, catalogue of the exhibition, Turin, 1980, n. 324, pp. 348–349 and 1387–1388; P. Astrua, in *Bernardino Lanino*, catalogue of the exhibition, Vercelli, 1985, p. 123; A. Quazza, in *Bernardino Lanino e il Cinquecento a Vercelli*, a cura di G. Romano, Turin, 1986, p. 274.

13. Bedotti, 1837, pp. 32–34, 44–46. Again in 1862, the director of the Uffizi Paolo Feroni would state that "the restorer must confine himself to lightly cleaning the painting and scrupulously restoring also the missing parts but leaving those defects which are part of the original" (letter of 21 November in A.C.S., I vers., b. 246, f. 114, discovered by my student Dora Gabito).

14. Bedotti, 1837, pp. 8–9, 11–12; Secco-Suardo, 1894, ed. cit., pp. 369–370, 499; Lechi, 1968, pp. 107–109; Ferretti, 1981, p. 163; letters from 3 July 1852 to 12 June 1854, in the archives of the Secco-Suardo family. Modern documents of the family "Conte Girolamo"; letters, recollections.

15. Bianchi, 1984, pp. 108–113.

16. Eastlake, 1847, pp. 255–256, 271–272; Secco-Suardo, 1894, pp. 539–540.

17. *Report*, 1853; G. B. Cavalcaselle, letter of 9 June 1853, pp. 784–787 of the same publication; Marijnissen, 1967, II, note 306, pp. 364–366 (letter from Eastlake of 1847 on the cleaning of some of the paintings by Rubens in the National Gallery).

18. Bedotti, 1837, pp. 26–28.

19. Forni, 1866, p. 2; *Notiziario*, in "Bollettino d'Arte", 1907, n. 8, p. 31; Marcucci, 1965, p. 153; Conti, 1981, p. 82; Incerpi, 1982, pp. 333–334 and notes 45–47, pp. 343–344.

20. *Pittura a buon fresco*, in "l'Antologia", 1828, November–December, pp. 90–95, facsimile edition, III, Florence, 1975; F. Baldanzi, *Delle pitture che adornano la Cappella del Sacro Cingolo di Maria Vergine nella Cattedrale di Prato*, Prato, 1831; F. Baldanzi, *Delle pitture di Fra Filippo Lippi nel coro della Cattedrale di Prato...*, Prato, 1835; N. Tommaseo, *Della bellezza educatrice, pensieri*, Venice, 1838, p. 147; F. Fantozzi, 1842, p. 773; Wilson, 1843, note 29; C. Pucci, *All'anonimo articolista difensore di un recente vandalismo commesso nel convento di*

Santa Croce, in "La rivista di Firenze", 21 August 1847; Botti, 1864, p. 34; A. F. Rio, *De l'Art Chrétien*, Paris, 1861, I, pp. 232–233; C. Guasti, *Antonio Marini, pittore*, Florence, 1862 (reprinted, editors M. Bellandi e C. Paoletti, *L'opera di Antonio Marini pittore 1788–1861*, Florence, 1961); Cavalcaselle–Crowe, 1864–1866, V, note p. 131; VI, note p. 68; VIII, note, pp. 29–30; C. Guasti, *Belle arti …*, Florence, 1874, pp. 5–6; A. Bellini Pietri, *Guida di Pisa*, Pisa, 1913, p. 140; Longhi, 1960–1961, p. 15; Conti, 1973, pp. 252–253.

21. Giordani, 1840, pp. 27–29; notes in Malvasia, 1678, ed. 1841, II, pp. 65, 278; G. Atti, *Sunto storico della città di Cento*, Cento, 1853, p. 69; Forni, 1866, p. 23; Secco-Suardo, 1866, ed. cit., pp. 220, 230–231; Milanesi, 1873–1885, II, 1878, note 1 p. 675; R. Palucchini, *I dipinti della Galleria Estense di Modena*, Rome, 1945, pp. 49, 109; C. Grigioni, *Marco Palmezzano*, Faenza, 1956, p. 384; L. Tintori, *Methods used in Italy for Detaching Murals*, in *Recent Advances in Conservation*, London, 1963, caption on p. 120; R. Roli, *I fregi centesi del Guercino*, Bologna, 1968, p. 59; Ferrara, Archivio della Pinacoteca Nazionale, Belle Arti XIX century, cartella 3 (traced in the thesis of Paola Mingozzi, *Restauri a Ferrara: 1861–1915*, University of Bologna, supervisor A. Conti, academic year 1984–85).

22. M. Ridolfi, *Scritti vari riguardanti le belle arti del dipintore M.R.*, Lucca, 1844, (pp. 29–33, 214–218 on Aspertini); M. Ridolfi, *Scritti d'arte e d'antichità*, Florence, 1879; Ferretti, 1979.

23. Various details on the waxing of frescos emerged from the controversy over who had made the discovery, Andrea Celestino or Giovanni Fabbroni; Guglielmo Botti referred to them when detailing the advice given by Fabbroni to Luigi Ademollo in 1794 for the frescos of Giovanni di San Giovanni in the villa Pozzino at Castello (1864, pp. 9–10).

24. *Il Camposanto e l'Accademia di belle arti di Pisa dal 1806 al 1838 nelle memorie e nelle carte di Carlo Lasinio*, Pisa, 1923, pp. 30–33; Cavalcaselle, 1863, pp. 35–36; Botti, 1864; Forni, 1866, pp. 23–24, 37–38.

25. G. Nepi Sciré, in *Giorgione a Venezia*, catalogo della mostra, Venice, 1978, note 50 pp. 128–129; Hueck, 1981, pp. 144–145, 149.

26. Thanks to the courtesy of the much missed Count Suardino Secco-Suardo, in 1976 I was able to examine the letters of Giovanni Secco-Suardo in the family archives; ample, although not exhaustive, references are made to them by Cristina Giannini (*Giovanni Secco-Suardo restauratore e teorico …*, in "Paragone", n. 437, 1986, pp. 68–75). The letters to Guizzardi are dated 20 May 1852 to 12 June 1854, those to Giuseppe Fumagalli from November 1847 to 4 September 1859; two letters from Michele Ridolfi (23 October 1853 and 9 May 1854) are requests for information on the restoration of Leonardo's *Last Supper*, which had been entrusted to Barezzi (on this, see Ufficio regionale, 1906, pp. 40–54).

27. On Giuseppe Molteni, see: G. Rovani, *Le tre arti considerate in alcuni illustri italiani contemporanei*, Milan, 1854, pp. 163–164; Secco-Suardo, 1866, ed. 1927, pp. 190–193; A. Caimi, *Commemorazione del Cav. Giuseppe Molteni*, in "Atti dell'Accademia di Belle Arti di Brera in Milano", 1867; Malaguzzi Valeri, 1908; Venturi, 1912, pp. 448–452; *The National Gallery, January 1965–December 1966*, London, 1967, pp. 68–69; J. Fleming, *Art Dealing and the Risorgimento*, I, in "The Burlington Magazine", 1973, pp. 5–6, note 47, p. 8; *I maestri di Brera*, catalogue of the exhibition, Milan, 1975, pp. 244–246; D. Robertson, *Sir Charles Eastlake and the Victorian Art World*, Princeton, 1978, pp. 153–154, 175, 176, 306, 322; *Cultura figurativa negli stati del re di Sardegna (1773–1861)*, catalogue of the exhibition, Turin, 1980, pp. 419, 707, 1466; A. Zanni, *Note su alcuni restauratori a Milano: Cavenaghi e Molteni*, in *Zenale e Leonardo*, catalogue of the exhibition, Milan, 1982, pp. 250–253; Anderson, 1987.

28. Venturi, 1912, p. 450; C. Gould, *Eastlake and Molteni: The Ethics of Restoration*, in "The Burlington Magazine", 1974, pp. 530–534; Anderson, 1987, pp. 111, 115–116, 123–124 and note 43 p. 130.

29. G. Frizzoni, *Arte italiana del Rinascimento*, Milan, 1891, p. 303; M. Davies, *National Gallery Catalogues. The Earlier Italian Schools*, London, 1961, pp. 439–440.

30. Anderson, 1987, p. 114; C. Volpe, review to the exhibition *Da Altichiero a Pisanello*, in "Arte antica e moderna", 1958, p. 413.

31. A. Mottola Molfino–M. Natale, in *Museo Poldi Pezzoli. Dipinti*, Milan, 1982, p. 17 and index.

32. The complete text of the 1857 report is published in C. Bertelli–P. L. De Vecchi, *Lo Sposalizio della Vergine di Raffaello*, Treviglio, 1983, pp. 76–80; on this restoration, see also: Passavant, 1839, cited translation, II, 1889, p. 23; Cavalcaselle–Crowe, 1882–1885, Italian translation, p. 170 note 1; M. Olivari, in *Raffaello e Brera*, catalogue of the exhibition, Milan, 1984, pp. 32–34.

33. On the letters in the Secco-Suardo Archive dated 28 March 1855 and 22 March 1856, see my observations in *Una miniatura e altre considerazioni sul Pisanello*, in "Itinerari", I, 1979, p. 74.

34. Marijnissen, 1967, pp. 35, 190–191.

35. Longhi, 1940, p. 121, ed. 1985, p. 2.

36. Forni, 1866, p. 72; Secco-Suardo, 1894, ed. cit., pp. 455–456.

37. F. Odorici, *Guida di Brescia*, Brescia, 1853, pp. 188–189; Curti, 1864, pp. 359–360; Forni, 1866, note 3 p. 23; Secco-Suardo, 1866, ed. cit., pp. 220, 231–232; Bernardi, 1898, p. 98; Maleguzzi Valeri, 1908, pp. 6–7, 36; Longhi, 1957, p. 4; Paolucci, 1986, p. 12.

38. Antonio Zanchi was the restorer who carried out the new transfer of the small panels by Solario Poldi Pezzoli, and also removed the *beverone* from the *Madonna with Child and Saint Anne* by Girolamo dei Libri, which was bought by the National Gallery in 1864; see Secco-Suardo, 1866, ed. cit, pp. 191–195; 1894, ed. cit., note pp. 390–391, pp. 554–555; Malaguzzi Valeri, 1908, pp. 17, 176. Some of the transfers carried out under the direction of Secco-Suardo can be traced to the Accademia Carrara in Bergamo (see Giannini, 1986, cit., p. 71).

39. Secco-Suardo, 1866, introduction to the original edition; G. Secco-Suardo, *Della pittura ad encausto, ad olio e a tempera*, in "L'arte in Italia", 1871, pp. 83–84; Secco-Suardo, 1894, ed. 1927, pp. 362–363, 369, 393–394; Conti, 1981, p. 81; Incerpi, 1982, p. 337; draft of a letter of presentation from Giovanni Morelli in the Biblioteca Comunale in Bergamo (ms 5/281); request for compensation from Pietro Pezzati dated 1 July 1864, in the Secco-Suardo family archive. Pezzati, a pupil of Marini, and a good painter in the purist tradition (see Thieme–Becker, 1932), was nevertheless an interesting figure as a restorer; see: C. Guasti, *Antonio Marini pittore*, Florence, 1862, pp. 19, 38, 42, 43; C. Guasti, *Belle arti. Opuscoli descrittivi e bibliografici*, Florence, 1874, pp. 53–68; V. Lusini, *Storia della Basilica di San Francesco a Siena*, Siena, 1894, note 1, p. 217; G. Marchini, in *Due secoli di pittura murale*, catalogo della mostra, Prato, 1969, p. 132; Hueck, 1980, p. 4; Paolucci, 1986, p. 14.

40. Secco-Suardo, 1866, ed. cit., p. 239; Conti, 1981, pp. 81–82; C. Giannini, *Note sul restauro italiano del secondo Ottocento …*, in "Paragone", n. 391, 1982, pp. 44–45; Paolucci, 1986, note 19 p. 18. On the course of 1864, see A.C.S., vers. I, b. 385, fasc. 22. In addition to the Florentine transfers, we know of the one from canvas, carried out in Bergamo in 1864 on a *Madonna and Child* by Antonio Maria da Carpi (F. Rossi, *Accademia Carrara di Bergamo. Catalogo dei dipinti*, Bergamo, 1979, p. 73).

41. Forni, 1866, pp. 2, 29–33, 59–62 in particular; Incerpi, 1982, note 59 p. 346. The sequence of frescos which were transferred *a massello* in Siena, and to which Forni refers, include: the *Christ at the Column* by Sodoma (1841, architect Lorenzo Doveri; see Wilson, 1843 p. 31 on the technique of this fresco); *Crocifissione e Resurrezione* di Girolamo di Benvenuto al Monistero (1841, mason Lorenzo Lotti); frescos by Genga and Signorelli for the Palace of Lorenzo il Magnifico which are today in the picture gallery; the *Resurrection* by Sodoma in the Palazzo Pubblico (1842, engineer Maurizio Zanetti); frescos by Pietro and Ambrogio Lorenzetti in San Francesco (mason Giovanni Vestri, 1854).

42. Cavalcaselle–Crowe, 1864–1866, ed. cit., VI, note pp. 11–12; Conti, 1879–1882, sezione III, cc. 3–4; Gaetano Milanesi (1878–1885, VI, p. 292 and note 3 p. 294) refers to the restoration of the *Venus* by Pontormo from a cartoon by Michelangelo, in the Florentine Galleries.

43. Forni, 1866, pp. 429–434; Secco-Suardo, 1866, ed. 1927, note 1 p. 265; 1894, ed. cit., pp. 408–420.

44. We have information on the following transfers executed by Brison: the transfer of a Longhi in the Lochis Collection in Bergamo (canvas to canvas); in 1857 on a Cima da Conegliano in the Brera (which had already been transferred previously); in 1862 on a *Noli me tangere* attributed to Palma il Vecchio (through Secco-Suardo, they both received a silver medal), and finally on the altarpiece by Marco d'Oggiono in Sant'Eufemia in Milan (together with Secco-Suardo). The debate with the Count is revealed in the article by Curti (note 1 pp. 364–364) and is confirmed in A.C.S., vers. I, b. 385, fasc. 22; also, the fact that Brison should only feature in 1856 as the restorer for the *Three Saints* by Montagna suggests a gradual deterioration in the relationship with the group headed by Morelli and Secco-Suardo. On him, see Curti, 1864; Secco-Suardo, 1866, pp. 7, 8, 10–11 of the first edition; Venturi, 1912, pp. 449–450.

45. L. Bailo, *Degli affreschi salvati nella demolita Chiesa di S. Margherita in Treviso*, Treviso 1883; Bernardi, 1898; M. Botter, in M. Muraro, *Tomaso da Modena. Le storie di Sant'Orsola*, Villorba, 1987, pp. 27–37.

46. G. B. Uccelli, *Il Palazzo del Podestà*, Florence, 1865, p. 198 (see G. Previtali, *Giotto e la sua bottega*, Milan, 1967, p. 341, for the *Madonna* transferred on this occasion); Forni, 1866, pp. 23–24, 27–29; M. D'Azeglio, *Intorno al restauro del Palazzo del Podestà a … Firenze 1870;* A. Gotti, *Le gallerie di Firenze*, Rome, 1872, pp. 235–239, 266; Milanesi, I, 1878, note on p. 679; Conti, 1879–1882, c. 50; A. Alfani–P. Ferrigni, *Gaetano Bianchi pittore a buon fresco commemorato nella Società Colombaria*, Florence, 1892; Secco-Suardo, 1894, pp. 486–487; Bernardi, 1898, pp. 14–16; G. Tutino, in Thieme–Becker, 1909; S. Meloni Trkulia, in *Dizionario Biografico degli Italiani*, XI, 1968, pp. 95–96; Conti, 1981, pp. 86–87; R. Signorini, *Opus hoc tenue*, Mantua, 1985, p. 262.

47. G. Morelli, *Lettera al signor professore a Roma riguardante le pitture di Giotto nella Cappella di San Francesco*, Florence, 1851; Cavalcaselle–Crowe, 1864–1866, I, pp. 522–528; J. Ruskin, *Mornings in Florence*, 1875–1877, I, 8–9; R. Van Marle, *The Development of the Italian Schools of Painting*, III, The Hague, 1924, pp. 136–138; Conti, 1973, p. 254.

48. Cavalcaselle–Crowe, 1864–1866, VIII, n., p. 214.

49. C. J. Cavallucci, *Dei restauri operati nella chiesa di Santa Croce*, in "L'Arte in Italia", 1871, pp. 54–56; J. Gardner, *The Early Decoration of Santa Croce in Florence*, in "The Burlington Magazine", 1971, pp. 391–392. A letter of 14 October 1869 from the mayor of Florence to the Prefettura of Verona on the recovery of whitewashed frescos tells us that the removal of the whitewash was carried out by two ex-monks on behalf of Bianchi (Verona, Archivio di Stato, Fondo della Prefettura, Commissione consultativa conservatrice delle belle arti e antichità, b. 2, cited in the thesis of Giuliana Sona, *Per una storia della tutela a Verona …*, University of Bologna, academic year 1986/87, sup. M. Ferretti).

9

Restoration in Italy after the Unification

1. Frescos and polychromy

The campaigns of restoration which took place in the churches in Rome in parallel with the restoration of paintings under the direction of Camuccini did not make any attempt to recover the original decoration or polychromy. Single works of art would be restored, but the interiors were decorated with Baroque splendour, and in a style which remained consistently Neo-classical. As late as 1847, the new decoration of Santa Maria sopra Minerva was adapted to the Gothic nave and vault, but with its gold and bright colours, it was a perfect illustration of the exhibitionism that Ruskin reproached in the decoration of Papist churches.[1]

A more rigorously Neo-classical interpretation of the Gothic monument can, on the other hand, lead to an effect of bareness, to the stone mouldings standing proud of the walls, to whitewashed vaults, which is what Gaetano Baccani proposed with his restoration of the Duomo in Florence between 1841 and 1842. One perceives a desire to give the monument an arrangement in which the stylistic elements are in tune with the original – Gothic – construction, and not one of recovering an interior of the Middle Ages.[2] During this restoration, the sixteenth-century altar by Bandinelli was partially destroyed, the large sixteenth-century canvases which are referred to in old guides were dispersed, and the monuments in fresco were detached and then put back in an orderly fashion; the frescos of *Sir John Hawkwood* and *Niccolò da Tolentino* were transferred by Rizzoli so that they might be placed symmetrically, as decorations of the interior façade of the Duomo.

The undoubted quality of Baccani's planning has always made his intervention on the Duomo acceptable; quite other are the results of the restoration of Santa Maria Novella carried out by Enrico Romoli in the years straddling the Unification, in no way attuned to the expectations held of the manner in which one should, or must, intervene on a medieval building: the old pavement was replaced with a new one made up of small grey and white bricks; the windows along the nave were moved and altered with respect to the original design; the polychromy of the mouldings was hidden beneath brown plastering; Vasari's altars were destroyed, and the altarpieces presented within vaguely Gothic niches, which "not only are out of tune – as Cosimo Conti was to remark – but say nothing, and rather than referring to altars they resemble mirror frames".[3]

The purist response to these restorations, which did not renovate the Gothic architecture but limited themselves to reinterpreting it according to a decorative system of a Gothic rather than Classical order, can be found at their highest level in the restorations executed in Lucca under the direction of Ridolfi beginning in the 1830s. Instead of white-washing or adding decorations which did not respect the character of the original architecture, it was decided to lay bare the original masonry, in a search for a bareness which perhaps never existed, but somehow seemed in keeping with the medieval monument, coherent with a taste also shown by Eugène Delacroix when he protested against the Nazarene spirit of the new polycromies in Cologne Cathedral:

> "The more I witness the efforts which are made to restore Gothic churches, and particularly to paint them, the more I persist in my taste for finding them all the more beautiful the less they are painted. And it is useless telling me or proving to me that indeed they were so originally (of which I am convinced, as traces still exist of this painting), I still feel that they should be left as time has made them; this nudity adorns them sufficiently; the architecture has its full effect, whilst all our efforts, we men belonging to another time, wanting to deco-rate these beautiful monuments, instead cover them in nonsense, make them a travesty, and render the whole false and hateful. The windows which the King of Bavaria has donated to the Cathedral at Cologne are another unhappy exam-ple of our modern schools. All this resounds with the talents of the Ingres and Flandrin of this world. The more one wishes to resemble the Gothic, the more one veers towards the religious knick-knack, the small-scale neo-Christian painting, and its modern practitioners. What folly, and what misfortune that this fury, which could harmlessly be expended and then seen in our exhibitions, should be turned to ruin such glorious works as these churches!"[i,4]

When Delacroix launched this protest in 1850, the taste for integrating restorations (*restauri di completamento*) and the renovation (*rifacimenti*) of more or less documented polychromies was in full swing (the restoration of Saint-Germain-des-Prés, for instance, enriched with the compositions of Hippolyte Flandrin, dates from 1845), running parallel to a vision of restoration which Viollet-le-Duc was developing. The latter made reference to Ludovic Vitet's report in which he requested, as early as 1831, the restoration of the monuments in northern France, reinvoking the taste for polychromy which the restoration would recover:

> "It came to pass that at the end of the sixteenth century, in part due to Protestantism, to Classicism, and for a variety of other reasons, as our imagina-tion became increasingly dulled, and less natural, more deadened one might say, so it became the custom to whitewash these beautiful painted churches; a taste developed for walls and wooden panelling left bare, and if the interior were decorated at all, this would only be on a small scale. As things have remained thus for the last two- to three-hundred years, one has become accustomed to thinking that they have always been so, and that these poor monuments have

---

[i] *"Plus j'assiste aux efforts qu'on fait pour restorer les églises gothiques, et surtout pour les peindre, plus je persévère dans mon goût de les trouver autant plus belles qu'elles sont moins peintes. On a beau me dire et me prouver qu'elles l'étaient, chose dont je suis convaincu, puisque les traces existent encore, je persiste à trouver qu'il faut encore les laisser comme le temps les a faites; cette nudité les pare suffisamment; l'architecture a tout son effet, tandis que nos efforts, à nous autres hommes d'un autre temps, pour illuminer ces beaux monuments, les couvrent de contresens, font tout grimacer, rendent tout faux et audieux. Les vitraux que le roi de Bavière a donnés à Cologne sont encore un échantillon malheureux de nos écoles mod-ernes; tout cela est plein du talent des Ingres et des Flandrin. Plus cela veut ressembler au gothique, plus cela tourne au col-ifichet, à la petite peinture néo-chrétienne des adeptes modernes. Quelle folie et quel malheur, quand cette fureur, qui pourrait s'exercer sans nuire dans nos petites expositions, est appliquée à dégrader de beaux ouvrages comme ces églises!"*

always been seen so pale and bare as they are today. But if you look carefully, you will quickly discover some remnant of their former clothing: wherever the whitewash is peeling, you will find the original polychromy [beneath] ...."[5]

Gaetano Bianchi's restorations are linked to this new position, that is, distancing itself from the purist taste for bareness as well as from romantic attitudes which were ready to accept overt signs of the consuming nature of time. The preference was now for a monument which was restored in its entirety, which encouraged almost a flight from contemporary society, a journey into the past suggested by a decoration which faithfully reconstructed the "original" aspect, recovering the decorations which had been whitewashed, reconstructing fragmented polychromies or, simply, proposing new ones reconstructed from ancient models. The restorer became an artist who not only knew how to document himself in order to reconstruct and renew (*ripristinare*), but also was able to invest himself with the spirit of the Gothic architect every time he had to intervene on a functional level, where it was necessary to invent *ex novo* and find old forms to fit new functions.

The furniture also would have to be coherent with the unity of the new space, whether newly built or rebuilt in the "style of"; after the period of the suppressions, and the collectionism which ensued from it which saw panels or fragments from polyptychs adapted and turned into gallery pictures, one began now to consider the small collectors' painting as a small altarpiece, an object with its own *boiserie*, as can be seen in the most discerning collectors such as Poldi Pezzoli or the Carrand. One also began deliberately to reconstruct ensembles "in the style", for instance the *Demidoff Polyptych* by Carlo Crivelli, assembled with individual panels from two separate altarpieces which he had painted for San Domenico in Ascoli Piceno. In Santa Croce, to accompany Gaetano Bianchi's restoration of the polychromy, Vasari's baldachin was removed, a high altar "in the style" was constructed, and a search began for a polyptych of the right dimensions for the Franciscan Basilica. Once the polyptych by Pietro Nelli and Pietro Mazza dell'Impruneta was no longer a possibility, the problem was resolved by the assembly of a polyptych using panels from a variety of different sources, ranging from some early fourteenth-century saints by the "Master of the Cappella Medici" to the principal figures by Giovanni del Biondo and Niccolò di Pietro Gerini, and the small *Triumph of Death* by Lorenzo Monaco, which was inserted into the middle of the predella.[6]

162

The restoration "*à la* Viollet-le-Duc", with which Bianchi would insert imitation Gothic polychromies, would be strongly contested, leading to a revision of its margins of interpretation in the wake of the events surrounding the restoration of the south front of the Basilica of Saint Mark's in Venice. The observations on the damage suffered by the ancient marbles in an intervention which was carried out in a spirit of excessive zeal, and which appeared in the *Osservazioni intorno ai restauri interni ed esterni di San Marco* by Alvise Pietro Zorzi in 1877 (the introduction written by Ruskin), the appeal to the Italian Government by the Society for the Protection of Ancient Buildings under the impetus of William Morris, all clashed with the old spirit of intuition which felt authorized to carry out functional adaptations, and to use new materials and new techniques once the spirit of the original creator had been fully absorbed.

In 1872, Viollet-le-Duc himself commented favourably on the management of the worksite of Saint Mark, but dwelling on an analysis of the technique of the marble facing of the ancient Romanesque brickwork, with the aim of setting it as an example to modern architects; in truth, he did not discuss the essential problem at the heart of the controversy, that is, the character and nature of the substitutions which were being made on the site. Whilst if we

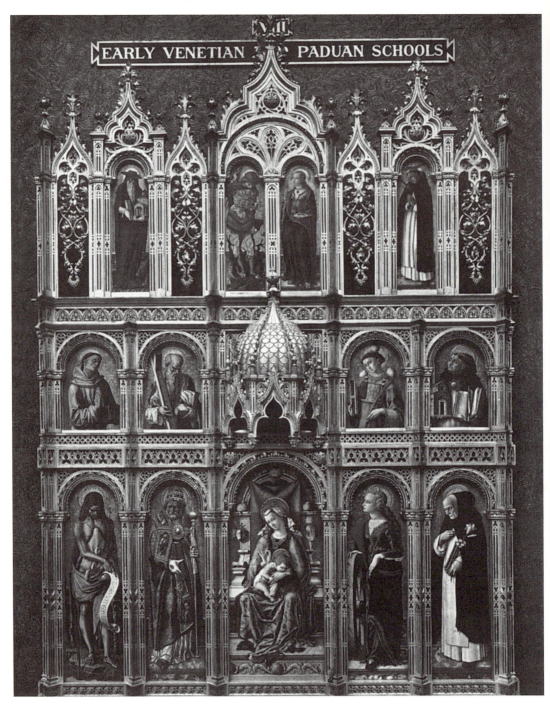

162. *Carlo Crivelli, The
Demidoff Polyptych; mid-
nineteenth-century framing.
London, National Gallery.*

consider the nature of the restoration carried out, and bearing in mind how a monument reflects a particular set of human conditions which can never be repeated, tied to religious and moral values higher than our own as Ruskin had been at such pains to point out, the sub-stitutions, the reconstructions (*rifacimenti*), the new regularity imposed on the structures which had degraded and subsided over time could not appear other than arbitrary: an inter-vention on which none of "the seven lamps of architecture" had shed the smallest ray of light. The work being carried out on Saint Mark's seemed to want to illustrate what Ruskin had stig-matized as early as 1849, when observing what the term *restoration* implied:

> "[Neither by the public, nor by those who have the care of public monuments, is the true meaning of the word *restoration* understood.] It means the most total destruction which a building can suffer: a destruction out of which no remnants can be gathered: a destruction accompanied with a false description of the thing destroyed. Do not let us deceive ourselves in this important matter: it is *impossible*, as impossible as to raise the dead, to restore anything that has ever been great or beautiful in architecture. That which I have above insisted upon as the life of the whole, that spirit which is given only by the hand and eye of the workman, can never be recalled. Another spirit may be given by another time, and it is then a new building; but the spirit of the dead workman cannot be summoned up, and com-manded to direct other hands, and other thoughts. And as for direct and simple copying, it is palpably impossible; what copying can there be of surfaces that have been worn half an inch down? The whole finish of the work was in the half-inch that is gone; if you attempt to restore that finish you do it conjecturally: if you copy what is left, granting fidelity to be possible (and what care, or watchfulness, or cost can secure it?), how is the new work better than the old? There was yet in the old *some* life, some mysterious suggestion of what it had been, and of what it had lost; some sweetness in the gentle lines which rain and sun had wrought. There can be none in the brute hardness of the new carving."

Ruskin's vision of the monument required that it should be accepted with the alterations produced upon it by time; an incipient aestheticism was already leading towards an appre-ciation of ancient marbles in their current state, streaked and time-darkened, recognizing an inseparable bond between form and materials. It is within the sphere of these controver-sies, that Giacomo Boni was formed:[7] a player in the field of restoration as conservation and of stratigraphic investigation.

The doubts associated with Romantic intuitionism would become more and more evi-dent as restoration turned to Romanesque and Byzantine buildings, for which the collections of models which had suggested so many solutions for Gothic architecture were useless. This was also true for more recent monuments, towards which one turned with a new spirit which accepted the fragmentary nature of their decoration and their [inherent] stratification.

2. Giovanni Battista Cavalcaselle and restoration as conservation

When we look at the well-known publication by Giovanni Battista Cavalcaselle of 1863, dedicated to the conservation of monuments and art objects, we notice that his enquiry focused not on the restoration of buildings as a whole, but rather on the pictorial monu-ments on which he had concentrated as a historian, monuments belonging for the most part to the Middle Ages and the fifteenth century. In this publication, conservation problems are, significantly, discussed alongside reforms of the academic system, museum organization, the creation of schools of restoration and, because of the necessity for documentary verification which in those years led to the great archival explorations of Campori or Milanesi, the search for new documentary material which would illuminate the history of art.

After a succession of temporary posts and the position, most certainly inadequate, as inspector at the Museo Nazionale di Firenze, in 1875 Cavalcaselle became Inspector General for painting and sculpture, a position which he would hold until 1893, and which would frequently find him, because of his choice of restorations deliberately and solely limited to conservation, at the centre of controversies involving the practitioners of restoration in the private field (*restauro amatoriale*), a type of restoration which, despite its limitations and its deceits, was frequently of a higher professional standard than that of the restorers who were entrusted with work from "the Ministry".[8]

Giovanni Morelli made no attempt to hide his opinion when confronted with this position or with Cavalcaselle, who was its champion, when he observed that Filippino Lippi's frescos in the Minerva "in our times, were restored under the eyes of the Ministero di Pubblica Istruzione, that is, they were disfigured in the most pitiless manner, as indeed was the case later with Raphael's frescos in Perugia, those by Titian in the Scuola del Santo in Padua, and especially those by Mantegna in the Ducal Palace in Mantua, under the auspices of the Inspector General G. B. Cavalcaselle".[9]

The didactic function of works of art was no longer linked, obviously, to its liturgical function, as it had been for the Pontifical curators who until this time had been responsible for the most organic programme of conservation of the artistic heritage; all the more since now Cavalcaselle had identified another public alongside the student from the Academy: the historian, for whom works of art were first and foremost documents. In preference, they should be housed in a great museum, school by school: the Florentine school in the Tuscan capital, the Umbrian school in Perugia, and that of the Marche in Urbino. The work of art inserted within the cultural programme of the lay state was presented for study, often detaching it from the stratifications of its original context, which was almost invariably a church, for historical verification.

The most ancient works were no longer described as "primitive", despite their defects, but as instances within a dialectic, testimonies of a period which was the most fruitful and lively in Italian art, which had an intrinsic value, and were not only important in the context of future developments. In the slim publication on conservation, there was a fleeting mention of the decadence of the figurative arts in Italy after Michelangelo, organically linked to an interest strongly focused on the Middle Ages and the Renaissance, and on the problem of considering as true works of art (and not simply as polychrome decoration of a monument) the cycles of frescos and mosaics, and this at the time when the firm of Salviati were working at San Marco, and Felice Kibel was rampant in Ravenna.

Fixing with metal staples, filling losses, and the whole or partial transfer of mosaics were operations which were already technically feasible, but which would only become the norm at the end of the century, putting in place the restoration of the mosaic complexes according to the principle of the conservation of the individual tesserae and their inclination (but still without giving any importance to the nature or the even at times the colour of enamel), a principle which is still characteristic of the restoration of mosaics today. In 1863, it was still necessary to make the point that such restorations should not consist in the reproduction of the cartoon (actual or presumed) from which the mosaic had been executed, but rather in the conservation of the materials, the tesserae of which it was made. In a situation which still bore the imprint of the tradition of the Vatican school of mosaics, which specialized in the reproduction of altar-pieces using tesserae of vitreous paste, the only solution was to tackle the training of future restorers on new bases, and to propose the creation of new specialized schools.[10]

When dealing with cycles of frescos, artists were required who were capable of understanding whether a mural painting "should be left as it is, rather than lose its harmony either completely or in part". Cavalcaselle certainly understood better than many who supervise today's restorations, that "not all wall-paintings are frescos, as one is wont to say. There are paintings executed on walls with glue, other paintings which are partly in fresco and partly in tempera, or fresco retouched or finished *a secco*, finally *buon fresco*, and even paintings in oil. *Buon fresco* is the most resistant of all, but the mixed fresco and tempera technique commonly used by painters in the fourteenth and fifteenth centuries, who would use tempera for the accessories, the draperies, the background and even sometimes to retouch the flesh, is not so resistant. The parts in tempera easily come away from the plaster on the wall, and fall, as can be seen in almost all paintings from that time, which cannot be cleaned without removing some of the original paint in the process."

As an example of method, Cavalcaselle cited the work of Guglielmo Botti, which was overseen by the commission of Pisa, and which included Professor Savi and the architect Bellini: Italy should be grateful to them for the new pilot method demonstrated in the conservation of the mural paintings. Respect for the original painting also dictated that when integrating the losses, the retouching should not overlap so as to better harmonize the new parts with the original; for worn parts which still had the original *intonaco*, he suggested leaving visible the incisions from the cartoon used as guides during the composition, rather than intervening in any manner with the application of colour: respect for the authenticity of the authentic part "should be inculcated in the public who usually prefer a completely repainted fresco to one which is missing some parts".[11]

In his research as a historian, Cavalcaselle was in the constant position of having to verify the limits of authenticity in the works that he examined; his notes on the state of conservation of these works are often the most intelligent accounts of them to have been made. A work of art which is first and foremost seen as an historical document must be preserved in this condition of authenticity, and the limits [of this authenticity] must be drawn with absolute clarity, to ensure that its limitations as a document source are known. Such a position must inevitably lead to different choices from those suggested by the needs of the enjoyment of the image by the art-lover and the collector of the Molteni–Secco-Suardo–Morelli tradition. Better to have a darkened than a damaged painting, a loss that is recognizable as such rather than the invisibility achieved through repainting. It is because of this that it was important to educate public taste to follow the original even through its damage, without deception.

Works of art were also irreplaceable in the training of restorers. Their training should include the making of copies, some of which could also be used alongside a damaged work in order to facilitate its reading, for example the cartoon which was traced in 1871 from Fra Bartolomeo's *Last Judgement*, which was transferred by Guglielmo Botti, and the missing parts 163, 164 completed on the tracing only, leaving them as they were on the fresco, in accordance with the principles formulated in 1863: "For ancient works of art one should observe the same practice as in public libraries, where a visitor is presented with an ancient parchment, partly worn away and worm-eaten under glass, and at the same time with a copy in which the missing parts have

163. *Fra Bartolomeo, The Last*
Judgement; fresco transferred
by Guglielmo Botti, 1872.
Florence, Museo di San Marco.

164. *Telemaco Buonaiuti, recon-*
struction of The Last Judgement
by Fra Bartolomeo, 1872.
Originally in Florence, Museo di
San Marco.

been filled with legible characters. One should take copies of frescos and complete the missing parts; in this way, the ancient original would be saved for the scholar, and the copy would satisfy the curiosity of the visitor, and would help to make the original intelligible for him."[12]

As far as cleaning was concerned, Cavalcaselle was prepared to accept a loss in legibility in a fresco as long as authenticity was respected; with paintings he was able to accept them being somewhat dirty rather than damaged through cleaning, his stance lacking, however, the rich and well-analysed survey which aesthetic restoration (*restauro amatoriale*) demonstrated in the text of Secco-Suardo, for instance. For him patina just seemed to be an irritating alteration, rather than an element which further harmonized the painting:

"In general, before starting on the restoration of a painting, it was common practice to remove together with the varnishes the patina given by time; but it is not always possible to execute this operation without damaging the painting, as together with the patina one often also removes the finishing touches and those thin, transparent glazes which are not always well fused with the body of the paint, but rather with the varnish that the artist applied to his painting.

"Sometimes, the paintings were deliberately toned with a coloured varnish, and it was necessary to be very experienced in order to take decisions about the cleaning, so that the process should not lay bare the body colour only to then proceed to tone it with new varnishes; those who admire the results of paintings which appear as though they have only just left the artist's studio do not realize that they are discrediting the very thing they want to exalt, in that the ancient painting is wholly adulterated or hidden by the new paint with which it is covered".[13]

The risks of a rather ingenuous and over-rigorous philological bent which wants to leave losses actively visible according to criteria which we still meet today, and the objections of an aesthetic

taste which wants to exploit a more hedonistic enjoyment of the work of art, are clearly formulated in the controversy surrounding a restoration carried out by Guglielmo Botti: the
transfer of a panel by the workshop of Ghirlandaio from Vallombrosa, carried out in Florence   165
in 1871. The President of the Accademia delle Arti del Disegno, Niccolò Antinori, protested
strongly against this restoration and, following directly in the traces of Secco-Suardo, he
remembered the lectures on transfer given in Florence in 1864, and those executed to such
a degree of perfection in Paris by Kiewert, and suggested Zanchi as a person suitable for the
execution of such operations. Botti, on the other hand, was obviously thinking of the defects
of the transfers carried out in the Napoleonic era and, confusing these with the methods
referred to by Secco-Suardo, noted:

> "The method of transfer – *distacco* – carried out by me is not known to these
> practitioners, because it is new and different from the methods practised until
> now, which on the whole have the defect of then being altered in tone, and of los-
> ing their original character; Ghirlandaio's painting on the other hand still has, and
> always will have, the original tonalities, transparency and freshness of colouring.
> This is a result of the system used by me for the transfer because I have preserved
> the entirety of the original ground, which I then secured together with the paint
> layers, onto the canvas. The strength of the glue and the thickness of the ground
> have resulted in those almost invisible cracks which, as I have already said, do not
> produce nor will they produce any alterations, as everything is very strongly
> bonded to the canvas, and will remain thus for centuries".[14]

This episode is a good illustration of the methods of the restorers chosen by Cavalcaselle: the
choice of minor alteration (the new cracks) in order to guarantee the painting planned and
secure longevity, and over a considerable period; preservation of the original ground despite
the irregularity thus produced on the picture surface and, as we can easily judge, integration
with a neutral tone of all areas, including those which could have easily been reconstructed
using other works from the Ghirlandaio workshop. It is a restoration which looks to conserve
and recover the document without any formal allurements, and almost takes pleasure in the
display of its losses, to the point of falling into a rigidity of presentation which does not facilitate the legibility of the work, and which, in certain situations of managerial disorder, can lead
to an oversimplified choice being made between that which is preserved and that which the
restoration feels authorized to sacrifice, in order to ensure a longer and more secure life for the
work of art.

For the great historian of Italian painting, the possibility of an intervention on the
Basilica in Assisi had particular significance (also in relation to the old Pontifical administration). In 1863, he had noted that several of the figures had been re-outlined in pencil (in
particular in the Chapel of San Martino painted by Simone Martini) by those who, with the
permission of Rome, had sought to make copies; during some festivities, he had also been
present when fragments of the painted plaster had come away after the explosion of fireworks ("one must therefore order that the fireworks should not be let off from the tower,
and I would propose that – to remove all danger – they should be let off in the square, further down near the arcade").

In 1871, he approached the restoration of the Basilica with principles aimed at retriev-
ing the paintings of the famous Franciscan church, and the aim of increasing their intrinsic
worth rather than restoring them as part of the decoration and polychromy of the architecture.
In order to recover the thirteenth-century transept in its correct architectural proportions and
in the most correct relationship to the paintings, he ordered the removal of the choir stalls

*165. Workshop of Domenico Ghirlandaio,
Madonna and Child with Saints; transferred
and restored by Guglielmo Botti, 1871.
Florence, gallery, deposits.*

made in 1501 by Domenico del Sanseverino: "because of their dark colour, they are detrimental to the optical effect and the eurythmics of the church, because they diminish the space, and because when you see them on entering the church, they appear as a dark band separating the base of the building from the rest. And this drawback increases the damage, in that it draws away from the effect of the artifice employed by the artist who (in addition to the good and overall proportions of the building) was able to add from the entrance door, those particular excellent modifications in proportions by means of which the spectator, on entering the church, embraces – so to speak – the entire building, receiving a pleasurable impression".[15]

The removal of the stalls gave rise to heated debate, fuelled by what seemed as an intrusion of the State within a religious building, which considered the Basilica as a simple monument in all its interventions, but also because of the new taste for furnished architectural [spaces], by now very far removed from the purist matrix which is easily discernible in Cavalcaselle's programme.[16] When putting in place the restorations at Assisi, he had in mind interventions similar to those executed by Botti in the much praised restorations in the Camposanto in Pisa: vulnerable areas secured with copper staples and injections with cement, partial transfer and re-adhesion onto a new support of the larger vulnerable areas, and the most absolute respect of the original parts, however deteriorated these might appear, demanding that integration be rigorously confined to simple monochrome fills of a "neutral" tint.

Between 1872 and 1874, Botti worked on the first two bays of the Basilica Superiore, all those of the upper part by the young Giotto and certain followers of Cimabue, including

166. Giotto, *The Deceit of Jacob, after Guglielmo Botti's restoration, 1872. Assisi, Basilica Superiore di San Francesco.*

the Volta dei Dottori; he probably also worked on the *Stories of Saint Francis*, although the notes in the archive only show him to have worked on the *Madonna* on the inside of the façade, the *Sermon to the Birds*, the *Death of the Cavaliere di Celano*, and the first frescos on the right as one enters the church. In the lower Basilica, he worked on the cells of the vault of the chapel of the Magdalen with the figures of the Redeemer and the Saint, and on the fresco with her *Communion and Ecstasy*, from which he extracted the copal varnish with which it had been treated. He also restored the fresco by Cimabue, and the Franciscan figures by Lorenzetti below. On 14 February 1874, the architect Alfonso Brizi, who was in charge of the restoration of the building, wrote to Cavalcaselle to tell him that when the seventeenth-century altar which backed onto Pietro Lorenzetti's *Crucifixion* was moved, "sixteen heads came to light, and a magnificent Saint Francis in the lower section of the [fresco of the] Virgin". Botti secured the fresco, and then carried out the monochrome reintegration of the losses caused by the attachment of the altar to the wall.

The interventions in the Upper Basilica would undergo a radical revision under the direction of Giuseppe Sacconi, who had the 1501 choir put back into the transept, stopped the work on the frescos, and imposed new rules which allowed misinterpretation of the original restoration programme as set out by Cavalcaselle. Sacconi underlined various negative aspects of the work which had already, unfortunately, been carried out by Luigi Muzio, and which were far removed from the original criteria: as was the norm for restorers working until the beginning of the twentieth century (and as can be seen in old photographs of the *Stories of Isaac*), the decorative parts were painted anew, *ex novo*, or overpainted; the repainting (*rifacimento*) of these decorative bands made the poor condition of the frescos all the more evident, and it now became necessary to remove all this overpaint, taking care not to go over the edges, and not cause drip marks over the paintings.

It also remained to find a different solution to the problem of neutral integration [of losses]; these were Sacconi's observations on one of the losses in Giotto's fresco depicting *Saint Claire Embracing the Bier of Saint Francis*: "This instance is a clear example of how false is the criterion that a neutral tint, used over the whole picture, can be a reasoned choice; in many areas, it will appear dark against light, and vice versa, or else of a contrasting colour in comparison with paint surrounding it, and will be more disturbing to the eye than simple a loss of paint from the *intonaco*".[17]

The integration of losses was consistently at the centre of the controversies surrounding restorations directed by Cavalcaselle; the ministerial circular dictated by him on 30 January 1877 on the restoration of paintings confirmed that: "Where the paint is missing, lay a colour or several colours which are similar to the originals in the painting, keeping them always lower in tone to the brightness of the local hues and so as not to disturb the eye of the onlooker. Where the priming is also missing, fill those losses with a new priming layer, and then pass over it with a tint as I have described above. It is of no consequence that the restoration is visible, indeed it should be visible; the important point is, that one should respect the original in the painting. The lie, to put it nicely, should be removed from its midst. And with this, the scholar will be able, in a restored painting, to distinguish that which is original from that which is new, and extract useful precepts".[ii,18]

[ii] *"Dove mancassero i colori, stendere una tinta o tinte che si avvicinino ai colori originali della pittura, tenendole sempre qualche poco al disotto della vivacità delle tinte locali e tanto quanto non offenda l'occhio del riguardante. Ove mancasse anco l'imprimatura, riempire quei vuoti con una nuova e poi passarvi sopra una tinta nel modo sovraccennato. Poco rileva*

Such rigorous guidelines would continually be eluded; the drawbacks so clearly underlined by Sacconi for the frescos in Assisi, the stance linked to the methods used by the great restorers from Lombardy which transpires through the criticisms directed at Botti's restoration of the panel by the school of Ghirlandaio, all these things resulted from the demands of the professional prestige of restorers who also worked in the private sector. On 3 March 1879, Cosimo Conti wrote to the director of the Academy of Fine Arts of Florence refusing, on the grounds of his professional pride and in "the interests of art itself", to restore the famous cassone with the *Nozze Adimari*, and the *Deposition of Santa Maria della Croce al Tempio* by Fra Angelico along the guidelines set out by the Ministry which imposed a visible restoration of the losses:

"… you, Dear Director, will no doubt remember how astonished I was to hear of these conditions, because it seemed to me that when a commission of the most distinguished artists proposed me as suitable in order conscientiously to execute such restorations, and that I in my report promised to only touch with the brush those areas which were lost, *without invading to the slightest degree* what is original, one should have shown faith in my promise. Instead, by imposing on me that I should only carry out the conservation repairs (*reparazioni*), apart from removing *any artistic quality* from the work entrusted to me, it would place me in an impossible position as an artist for the reasons which I permit myself to enumerate to you.

As far as the restoration of the front of the cassone depicting the Marriage of Boccaccio Adimari which you wish me only to secure and fill, then placing a local colour in the missing portions, which are only very simple folds in the drapery, I will say that any able craftsman or even a *wood-worker* under the eye of a painter would be able to do this. But when it is a question of painting by Beato Angelico, which has been restored on other occasions, the case is quite different and demonstrates the impossibility of following the guidelines set out by the Ministry. Because in that painting there are not only several areas of paint lifting and coming away from the panel, but also blots which disfigure it, it is certain (or at least very probable) that in the operations required to make it secure and remove the blots, some of the earlier restorations will also come away, and the painting will show the losses which it had had previously. In this case, I would be obliged to fill these with a *local tint* leaving Fra Angelico's painting *apparently* in worse condition than that in which it was consigned me. My conscience would be at peace, but there would be no-one to defend me from the attacks of the malicious who would say that these losses, which now are not visible, were caused by me. How can I remove these restorations, when I am not permitted to execute the very simple ones on the front of the cassone? …". [iii,19]

---

che apparisca il restauro, anzi dovrebbe apparire; ma quello che conta è che si rispetti l'originale della pittura. La bugia, detta ancora con bel garbo, dovrebbe essere tolta di mezzo. E con ciò lo studioso potrà distinguere in un dipinto restaurato in questa guisa quel che è originale da quello che è nuovo, a cavarne utili ammaestramenti".

[iii] *"… Ella, Signor Direttore, rammenterà come io mi meravigliassi nel sentire quelle condizioni, poichè sembravami che quando una commissione di artisti distintissimi proponeva me come adatto aad eseguire coscienzosamente tali restauri, e che io nella mia relazione prometteva di limitarmi a porre il pennello solamente sulle parti mancanti, senza invadere menomamente ciò che è di originale, si dovesse aver fede nella mia promessa. Ma coll'impormi invece di eseguire semplicemente le*

167. *Giotto, Saint Claire Embraces the*
Bier of Saint Francis, after the revision
of the losses carried out in the early
twentieth century. Assisi, Basilica
Superiore di San Francesco.

168. *Giotto, The Mission to Gabriel,*
detail; with the partial transfers by
Guglielmo Botti, 1868–1871. Padua,
Scrovegni Chapel.

169. *Giotto, the Annunciate Virgin;*
photograph by Naya, as part of the
documentation prior to restoration,
1868.Padua, Scrovegni Chapel.

3. Guglielmo Botti and Cavalcaselle's restorers

Guglielmo Botti was one of the restorers whose practical skills and critical orientation were best suited to the requirements of Cavalcaselle. Originally a painter of stained-glass windows, his first interventions took place in Pisa where, in 1856, he had been entrusted with an experimental intervention on the *Ratto di Dina* by Benozzo Gozzoli in the Camposanto: fixing (*fissaggio*)[iv] with "punic wax", removal of the vulnerable areas of the *intonaco*, replacement (*rifacimento*) of the *arriccio* and reattachment to the wall. In the purist climate of a restoration directed by a painting academy in the mid-nineteenth century, not even the cuts made to allow the partial transfer of the bulges (*spanci*) were hidden by any retouching, and it was mentioned as a particular merit of the restoration that it was executed without the use of the paintbrush.[20]

Between 1868 and 1871, Botti was commissioned by the municipality of Padua to intervene on the Scrovegni Chapel and in 1873, under the direction of Cavalcaselle, he began the restoration of the Upper Basilica in Assisi. The famous paintings by Giotto in Padua were found to be executed in fresco technique, with the exception of the ultramarine which he fixed using a glue solution (*colletta*) made according to Cennino Cennini's recipe. The first partial transfers of the vulnerable areas of the *Last Judgement* received the commendation of Selvatico himself. One is still struck by the way in which the supervising commission and Botti programmed and carried out the work. The frescos were photographed before the restoration by Naya in Venice; the losses were left visible, but they were filled with a brownish coloured plaster which made them less prominent; in the *Annunciation* around the triumphal arch, the blue background was retouched [to unify it] (*ripreso*), as were also some of the architectural elements.

The restoration was interrupted by the most wretched incident: Botti, instead of using copper nails to secure the detached frescos to the wall (and as indeed he was using at the time on the fresco by Altichiero in the Oratorio di San Giorgio), had used iron ones, thus exposing the frescos to the danger of rust and its expansions. He was therefore sacked, and replaced by the Paduan Antonio Bertolli at the beginning of 1872. The restoration of Giotto's frescos continued according to the same principles, to the extent that one almost has the impression that the restoration no longer reflected the character of the practitioner (a skilled technician, not an artist of the type of Gaetano Bianchi), so much as that of the commission directing the work.[21]

168

169

---

pure reparazioni. Oltre a togliere ogni qualità artistica *al lavoro che mi si affida, mi si porrebbe in una situazione impossibile come artista per le ragioni che mi permetto di enumerarle. Quanto al restauro del davanti del cassone esprimente le Nozze di Boccaccio Adimari che io dovrei solamente assicurare e stuccare ponendo una tinta locale nelle parti mancanti, le quali non sono altro che pieghe di vestimenti molto semplici, dirò allora che qualunque capace* conrattelatore *ed anche un* legnajuolo *sotto la sorveglianza di un pittore può eseguirlo. Ma quando si tratta di un dipinto dell'Angelico, il quale è stato altre volte restaurato, il caso è ben diverso e dimostra l'impossibilità di attenersi a quanto il Ministero prescrive. Poichè riscontrandosi in quel dipinto oltre numerosi sollevamenti e distacchi dalla tavola, anche delle macchie che lo deturpano, è certo, o almeno probabilissimo, che nella operazione da farsi per assicurarlo e smacchiarlo, vengano via in parte i precedenti restauri ed il dipinto si mostri colle mancanze che precedentemente a quelli esistevano. In tal caso io sarei obbligato a riempire con una* tinta locale *queste lacune lasciando la tavola dell'Angelico apparentemente* in peggior condizione di quando mi venne consegnata. La mia coscienza sarebbe tranquilla, ma nessuno potrebbe difendermi dagli attacchi dei malevoli che attribuirebbero* a me *quelle* mancanze *che ora non appariscono. Posso io rimuovere questi restauri quando non mi si permette di eseguire quelli semplicissimi del davanti di cassa?...."*

[iv] The most commonly used term today would be "consolidation", although technically there is a difference in that fixing of detached plaster is adhesion (with an adhesive) of a layer which has detached, while "consolidation" deals with the cohesion of a layer, that is, replacing whatever substance held together the particles, for instance if the layer is crumbling away. Wax would in fact perform both of these functions.

The methods used by Bertolli were similar to Botti's, even though he seemed to insist rather mechanically on the partial transfers which are then put back together on the original wall or on wooden or metal stretchers with lathes made of copper, with a gesso ground of which no contemporary restorer could approve. In 1888, he executed the transfer – in pieces, with the joins left deliberately visible – of the fresco depicting the *Assunta* by Mantegna in the Ovetari chapel, but in 1886 he had confined himself to cutting Mantegna's *Martirio di San Cristoforo* into only four sections, and in 1892 the frescos of the Scrovegni Chapel depicting *Jesus Amongst the Doctors* and *The Road to Calvary* were detached in a single piece.[22]

170

Despite having been sacked by the municipality of Padua, in 1873 Botti became Inspector of the Gallerie dell'Accademia in Venice, a city in which he had already restored Veronese's frescos in San Sebastiano. Contrary to the methods then in use in the city on the *laguna*, which were often a degenerate form of those practised by a Floriani or a Fabris during the Restoration years, he appears as a figure completely turned towards conservation. An intervention such as the one he carried out in 1871 in Florence on the panel of the School of Ghirlandaio might leave one somewhat perplexed when compared with the best examples of aesthetic restoration (*restauro amatoriale*) in the Lombard tradition, but not when compared with the interventions of a Tagliapietra, the restorer whose name is sadly linked with the poor conservation of the *Pietà Donà dalle Rose* or the *Madonna degli alberetti* by Giovanni Bellini.[23]

The way in which Botti confronted conservation can be followed from the description made by him in 1879 of the work carried out on the altarpiece of Santa Cristina al Tiverone by Lorenzo Lotto: "Because this panel (or rather, two panels, as the semicircular upper portion is separate from the principal panel) was extraordinarily worm-eaten, I have had a skilled carpenter plane away almost half of the thickness of these panels in order to destroy the majority of the infested wood. As well as this calamity there was also another problem, not inconsiderable, in that some of the panels making up the altarpiece have warped badly, so that they must be straightened out in accordance with the precepts guiding this sort of work; having strengthened these panels with good bars made out of larch, these are now held in place by over three-hundred walnut clamps fixed within the body of the original panel with strong glue and screws; thus the many bars attached in this manner serve a double function – they both keep the panel flat and allow it to move as it wishes thus avoiding splits …. In order to preserve this monument of painting, it was also necessary to destroy all the living woodworm remaining in the body of the panel, and this I achieved by making the reverse of the panel, after the chiselling down, absorb a large quantity of almost boiling mineral spirits (*petrolio*), which most satisfactorily penetrated the thickness of the panel to kill all those insects once and for all. After this, I once again make the panel absorb [a mixture] of boiled linseed oil, minium and wax, then immediately setting the bars into place as explained above; and only then could the work be suspended, to be taken up again in the good season, and thus I secured the conservation of this monument."

The attention given to the conservation of the panel also involved the environment in which it was to be displayed, which had to be improved: "it is necessary to remove all the plaster from the wall of the tribune of Santa Cristina, both internally and externally; on the exterior, on the right, the wall itself is also worn away. It is necessary to replaster with good mortars (*cementi*), and then polish it like imitation marble. Before replacing the painting, it is necessary to reinforce the back of the old altar, so that it is able to take the increased weight of the panel. It is also necessary to place between the wall and the painting, a wooden panel which is bigger than the painting, well varnished, in order to keep humidity away".[24]

*170. Giotto, The Road to Calvary, detail;
photograph prior to Antonio Bertolli's transfer
of 1892. Padua, Scrovegni Chapel.*

*171. Andrea del Castagno, Crucifixion
with Saints; fresco transferred by
Alessandro Mazzanti and Filippo Fiscali,
around 1876. Florence, Cenacolo di
Sant'Apollonia.*

Lotto's altarpiece then remained in its seventeenth-century frame, despite the problems which the cradling must have presented; I think that this, rather than being the result of a question of taste or a respect for historical documentation, was dictated by a deliberate lack of interest in presentation, which is unlikely to have been missing in the sphere of aesthetic restoration. The network of scrupulous observance and connivance which one catches sight of in 1883 behind the suspension of Antonio Zambler's restoration of Lorenzo Lotto's *Elemosina di Sant'Antonino* in San Zanipolo helps us to understand why in Venice, the good precepts of Botti and Cavalcaselle often resulted in poor restorations, to such a degree as to make Adolfo Venturi and Giulio Cantalamessa transfer Botti to the Egyptian Museum in Turin, with the idea that he would cause less harm to the country's artistic heritage amongst "the basalts and the sycamore cases".[25]

The durability of many of Botti's restorations helps us to understand the trust in which he was held by Cavalcaselle; nevertheless, even in the interventions in the Camposanto in Pisa, one can see parts of the fresco which after transfer have been incorrectly repositioned, differing levels with the surrounding fresco, irregularities and defects in the execution. It would be true, at least in part, that the renown of this restoration as exemplar of a new philosophy of conservation was born more of a reading of the publication which accompanied it than from a close inspection of the restored works themselves.[26] If one were to make a direct comparison with the work of the great figures of the Lombard school of aesthetic restoration (Giuseppe Bertini and, now that Giuseppe Molteni was dead, Luigi Cavenaghi), it was easy to see in the work of Botti a "state restoration", which (as collectors, amateurs and art-dealers love to say) was simply bad.

In 1882, it was Bertini himself whilst on a tour of inspection in Venice who wrote to the Ministry that he thought that Tintoretto's *Crucifixion* in the Accademia was best left unrestored as it only seemed to be afflicted with "parched varnish" ("*arsure di vernice*"), and that natural degradation was in any case preferable to "that caused artificially by an unskilled restorer". On this occasion Botti, with the repainting of the sky in the *Martirio di Sant'Orsola* by Carpaccio, found himself associated in Bertini's negative opinion with a representative of the traditional craft, Paolo Fabris, who had just completed his second intervention on Titian's *Pala Pesaro*.[27]

The Botti episode brings to light another problem which would very much come to the fore with interventions for the conservation[v] of the artistic heritage, that is, to find "repairers" willing to move periodically (and continuously). It would be interesting to discover more about the activity of Luigi Missaghi, who in 1881 worked on various cycles of frescos of which we can still admire the perfect condition, such as those by Melozzo da Forlì in Loreto and, probably, the *Madonna del Belvedere* by Ottaviano Nelli in Gubbio, whilst in 1882 he transferred and repositioned a number of the *Storie della Vergine* by Andrea Delitio in the Duomo at Atri.[28]

Filippo Fiscali had a very widespread activity, especially in Emilia-Romagna and in the smaller centres of central Italy; in Florence in 1879 he transferred the *Cristo Deposto* by Andrea del Sarto, along with its supporting plaster, onto metal netting. In 1887 he carried out the same operation on the *Pestapepe* attributed to Melozzo da Forlì. Many cycles of frescos owe to him their late nineteenth-century apparel, from those by Salimbeni in the Oratorio di San Giovanni in Urbino (1881) to the chapel by Mantegna in Mantua, and the Brancacci Chapel, which he cleaned in 1904. Between 1889 and 1891, he restored the cycles by Benozzo Gozzoli and the fresco by Perugino in San Francesco in Montefalco and in Ferrara, he worked on the *Last Supper* by Garofalo (which had been poorly transferred by Rizzoli). A multifaceted restorer, he transferred Pietro Lorenzetti's *Pala del Carmine* in the Pinacoteca in Siena, and lined the *Pala dei Mercanti* by Francesco del Cossa in Bologna, where he was also to be found working on the tempera paintings by Costa in San Giacomo Maggiore and on the *Pala Bevilacqua* in San Petronio. He restored the panel by Perugino in Fano, in Urbino "the small panel by Piero della Francesca", that is, the *Flagellation* which he recorded as having restored in 1881.

To the trust shown towards Fiscali by Cavalcaselle, we find a diametrically opposed position held by Adolfo Venturi; in 1896, he blocked the restoration of the Garofalo in Ferrara, thus initiating a series of events which would have legal consequences. The following year he would point out that Fiscali's requests for work to the Ministry could not be complied with since work was not given to restorers who were better qualified than he, such

171

---

[v] "*restauro di tutela*": restoration as an intervention on the work of art to ensure its conservation, but with no aesthetic intervention on the image. (See Glossary.)

172. *Benozzo Gozzoli, Il miracolo del Cavaliere di Celano; restored by Filippo Fiscali, 1889–1891. Montefalco, San Francesco.*

as Orfeo Orfei or Sidonio Centenari. In 1898 he stressed the poor quality of the marbling carried out by Fiscali in the chapel decorated by Mantegna, as well as that of the fills with which he had hidden the graffiti. A host of (negative) criticisms is also found in 1907, when Fiscali complained about the decision made to exclude him from the work on the frescos by Ghirlandaio in Santa Maria Novella, which were entrusted solely to his son Domenico. Again, Adolfo Venturi brought to the fore the work on the Mantegna chapel, the Garofalo in Ferrara and the poor lining of the *Pala dei Mercanti* by Cossa, while Ugo Ojetti made even greater protestations on the grounds of the restoration on the painting by Benozzo Gozzoli in Montefalco, where Fiscali was supposed to have renewed all the halos and painted in black the　172 window openings. The poor reputation and bad image which Fiscali seemed able to construct around his capacities as a restorer were confirmed in 1911 by Venturi's description of him in his *Memorie autobiografiche*: the allusions to the work in which he had been found wanting identify him as the restorer who had started his career as a simple varnisher of carriages, and who neglected his work on Mantegna in the chapel in order to make tomato preserves.

However, the material condition of the frescos by Benozzo Gozzoli in Montefalco, even after all these years, is excellent: the black tints, although arbitrary, are not out of keeping with the ensemble of the polychromy; the halos have been given a dark tonality [in their losses], in order to be in keeping with the effect of the deteriorated metallic leaf, whilst visible integrations using a neutral tone are some of the happiest solutions left to us of Cavalcaselle's philosophy of restoration, who indeed had been very appreciative of the "degree of care and diligence" taken by Filippo Fiscali in this restoration. In a letter to Bruno Toscano, Roberto Longhi himself was to cite Fiscali's work in the Umbrian citadel as exemplary. It is important, therefore, that further research be carried out on him, so as to have a better picture of differing visions of the restoration held by Cavalcaselle and Venturi.[29]

4. Science and restoration: experiments with the Pettenkofer method

One of the aspects which made a controversial figure such as Botti appear acceptable and professionally serious up to the point of enjoying the trust of Cavalcaselle was undoubtedly his interest in the Pettenkofer method. The non-intervention dictated by a purist respect towards the work of art now turned towards a positivist faith in science, and the method perfected by the German professor seemed to offer one of the most desirable instruments [to this end].[30] The treatment had already been very well described, in its chemical and physical characteristics, by Secco-Suardo: "Professor Pettenkofer, with the help of the specialist in optics Steinheil, observed that varnishes applied to oil paintings bloomed and became opaque, because of the formation of a myriad of tiny fissures visible only under the microscope, and caused by the continuous alternation of humidity and dryness in the atmosphere. These begin to appear on the surface of the varnish, and then multiply to infinity, always deeper into the varnish layer until they reach the paint layer, penetrating to the extent of reaching either the panel or the canvas, so long as the ground is an oil-based ground. Through these microfissures, air penetrates, and the resulting flakes reflect the light and hence the colours in a manner different from the norm, in a similar way as happens to oil which, when beaten, loses all its transparency. This is the cause of the blanching of varnishes, that fogging that merges everything together, which is so often seen on paintings. Alcohol vapours have a great effect both on resins and fatty materials, and therefore on oils: and when a painting which has deteriorated in this manner is exposed to their action, the solvents penetrating into those microfissures replace the air, and softening the interfaces of the flakes which air kept apart, these come back together and fuse, once more forming a single body, as they did originally. As a result of this, light once more behaving with the varnish and the colours in a similar way to how it behaved before the alteration, the colours are now reflected as they had been before, and the false effect produced by the altered method of reflection caused by the fissures, disappears."

It was a method which opened the way to the possibility of intervention without chemical alterations and avoided the subjectivity and the risks involved in manual intervention. Indeed, the regeneration of the varnish with alcohol became an excellent instrument of verification – scientifically objective – of the actual state of conservation of the painting. Secco-Suardo recorded an experiment that he had carried out on a small painting by Giulio Romano representing the *Feast of the Gods* in his possession: "the effect of making the retouchings appear is so constant and so effective, that Sir Charles Eastlake writing to us, is of the opinion that the Pettenkofer method is very useful in order to verify whether or not a painting has been restored, adding that a wise restorer should never begin to clean a painting without having first used the method on the painting, to avoid the danger of wasting time in matching false or altered hues".[31]

Secco-Suardo died in 1873, and therefore could only refer to the early experiments with the method, before the limited duration of the treatment had been observed, and before the potential for damage to the glazes and even to the body of the painting, if this had been executed with varnish, had been recognized. The fact that: "if the painting is left exposed to the alcohol vapours too long, the varnish contracts into blobs (*peduncoli*) which will remain for ever", or the fact that the copaiba balsam tended to become blue and matt; Cavalcaselle himself knew that the method had limitations and drawbacks.[32]

These defects were already well known in 1874 when Count Giusumberto Valentinis (landscape painter from the Friuli region, pupil of Carlo Markò in Florence, and friend and correspondent of Cavalcaselle, but above all impassioned defender of the method and translator of the literature published by Max Pettenkofer on the method of varnish regeneration with alcohol) proposed to run a course to bring practitioners up to date, at the Ministero di Pubblica Istruzione.[33] The Pettenkofer method, over and above the simple process of regeneration described by Secco-Suardo, had in the interim developed into an entire system of restoration with scientifically tested materials, but limited in its scope, as is inevitable in any choice in restoration. The old system of "feeding" paintings with oils and varnishes had been taken up once more but using copaiba balsam, which seemed to prevent the whitening of the picture surface, and to homogenize and increase the durability of the effects of the regeneration. The balsam would take on such a characteristic role that in 1876 the commissioners, following Valentinis' demonstrations in Venice, seemed to recognize in this the element characterizing the process, rather than the application of alcohol vapours. In fact, they observed that:

> "The alcohol vapours help the balsam to penetrate through the fissures on the surface, and reach the molecules of colour, adhering them to one another and to the ground, and bring back the brightness they had before losing their cohesion ….
> It is, however, necessary that Regeneration be the first process to which ancient paintings should be subjected, in whatever condition they are …. Copaiba balsam is then applied to the surface of a painting, or from the reverse if on canvas; this is a material which binds once more together the molecules of colour which have lost cohesion, attaches them to the ground and which conserves its great elasticity with time. After this initial operation, should the canvas be torn, carry out a lining, and whether on panel or canvas, fill the damage and then proceed to the restoration."

In order to free paintings from oil-based varnishes and put them into a state in which they could be exposed to alcohol regeneration, Pettenkofer himself proposed, in 1887, the use of a soap composed of copaiba balsam and ammonia which, although properly dosed and its preparation verified chemically, was nevertheless a soap; Valentinis would prefer a mixture of the same balsam but with alcohol. And it is to this method that he refers, which is a partial re-elaboration of old methods of m tures and soaps, availing themselves of the presence of copaiba balsam.[34]

The authority of the great hygienist to whom was owed the discovery of the method nevertheless meant that there was a certain difficulty in officially voicing reservations which any good restorer could easily have formulated. Almost all the testimonials and reports accompanying the minutes of the work of the Venetian commission were ten years old, from Liebig's declarations to the report of the Commissione di Sorveglianza (23 February 1865), which had admired the result of the regeneration of the blue attacked by ultramarine sickness in Mabuse's *Danae*. Only the declarations of the Director of the Munich Gallery, Ignaz Frey, and the retractions of Friedrich Pecht, who had initially been against the Pettenkofer process, were more recent. The most up-to-date information which the ministry had sought in Munich on the eve of the course was of a different tenor: Geppi, the envoy or attaché from the Embassy, wrote as follows on 3 April 1874:

> "Professor Pettenkofer enjoys a very high reputation in the scientific world, in particular for his work on chemistry applied to hygiene, and now, in his capacity as court pharmacist, he is also held in high esteem in those circles, so that it was not an easy task to obtain, through official routes, an exact judgement on his discovery for the restoration of paintings. I therefore decided to consult the judgement of a foreign artist who kindly, in the paper I have the honour of including here, gave me his opinion, supporting it with details which – in my opinion – give weight to his opinion. The aforementioned artist, having offered to substantiate his observations with practical demonstrations, offered to be my guide in the Royal Gallery, and there pointed out to me some paintings restored according to the system under discussion. Even to the inexperienced eye, which in these matters I freely confess mine is, it was quite obvious that not only in many instances the Pettenkofer method proved inadequate, but that it was actually harmful to the paintings, creating bluish patches, removing from the painting its brightest tints, and leaving the outlines blurred …."

The foreign artist, that is not a Bavarian, made his notes anonymously on an crested sheet of paper, with the emblem representing the painters' tools surmounted by the crest of a Marquis. The note is written in a rather generic French, but records unequivocally that the exposure of a painting to alcohol vapour will dissolve the varnishes used in the painting itself, transforming them into a soft and amorphous mass. As it is not possible to know in advance whether or not a painter has used varnishes in his paint, one must proceed with tests which in themselves are also dangerous, especially for Dutch masters who have a predeliction for varnish colours.

Valentinis himself was aware of the risk: and it is for this reason that he had perfected the method using cases which, unlike those described by Secco-Suardo, kept the painting horizontal and placed the flannel soaked with the alcohol on the lid. Had the painting been held "on its side", then the glazes applied with varnish "would have suffered and moved"; but as the painting was horizontal he was not worried, as the latter would have readhered to the painting of their own accord.[35]

The Venetian course of 1876 concluded with the recognition of the advantages of a process which was already known, and the use of which was limited. Count Valentinis, however, saw the scientific character of the new method as something to place in opposition to the casualness and haphazard nature of the materials used, with little verification, in traditional restoration; in his activity of diffusion, he seemed to see in the Pettenkofer method an instance of the fight of the progress of science against ignorance, and put himself forward once again to demonstrate the utility of the system.

In Florence in 1891, he obtained good results with the method on the *Venere di Urbino* in an intervention overseen by him and carried out by Alessandro Mazzanti; he then received a new ministerial commission to hold another course in Venice, in which to communicate his system to the restorers there. It was not that in the Florentine galleries the method was a novelty: the fact that one had recourse to Valentinis for the restoration of such a famous painting, speaks rather of a formal recognition towards him, or towards the Ministry which was putting him forward. Regeneration with alcohol was at this time a current option, and already in 1887 Cosimo Conti's estimates would propose this treatment for paintings as varied as ones belonging to the French school, to Barocci, and to Van Dyck and other Dutch and Flemish masters. *The Martyrdom of Saint Catherine* by Francesco Bassano, the treatment of which by the Pettenkofer method was proposed in 1888, clearly showed that it had been treated because of the opaque striations of the copaiba balsam which had altered with time, which were visible until they were removed in the recent restoration.[36]

The course held in Venice would have a very different outcome. After initial serious misunderstandings with the local restorers Giovanni Spoldi and Giovanni Zennaro on paintings of the Sala dello Scrutinio (Vicentino, Aliense, Pietro Bellotti, Camillo Ballini), the course would take place at the end of the year with the restorers Sidonio Centenari, Vinceslao Bigoni and Secondo Grandi also gaining admission. Botti would take part as a member of the commission overseeing the project. Spoldi and Zennaro tried out the regeneration with alcohol on some large canvases of the Ducal Palace, such as *Battle of Lepanto* by Andrea Vicentino, or the *Battle of Zara* by Tintoretto in the Sala dello Scrutinio; but the results of the restoration immediately inflamed a series of controversies, which had not occurred with the treatment of a much more demanding painting such as Titian's *Venere di Urbino* in Florence.

It is obvious that the vast canvases in the Ducal Palace, which were not well preserved, as was the case with the painting from the Uffizi, and had undergone previous restorations, were not ideal candidates for an overall treatment of regeneration, especially if they had been retouched with varnish colours. But at the heart of the scandal which erupted at the close of Valentinis' second Venetian course lay the repainting with which he had covered a presumed pentiment[vi] in the canvas representing *La giustizia che scopre la verità* by Filippo Zaniberti of the Quarantina Civil Nova. Faced with such an episode (although it is not difficult to imagine the level of consideration in which seventeenth-century Venetian painters were held in 1892), all declarations of a scientific approach floundered miserably; the local press, which from the very first meetings had been critical of Valentinis, now found echoes in the pen of such prestigious characters as Angelo Conti. The latter wrote an open letter to the minister, Pasquale Villari, noting the irreversibility of the alteration of the oil colours used, and being highly critical of the result of the restoration. On the agenda of the Chamber of Deputies of 23 February 1893, appeared the following question from Pompeo Molmenti to the minister: "Whether having taken action so that the masterpieces of Italian art did not leave the country, he would now safeguard the rights of the great Masters of the past, from the pernicious activity of restorers".

[vi] Pentiment; *pentimento* in Italian comes from the word *pentire*, to repent, that is, to change one's mind. It is used to describe what are now visible alterations in a composition, by the artist's hand, which lie beneath the final paint layer. On completion of the painting, these would have been invisible. As oil becomes more transparent with time, these *pentiments* become visible and can be disturbing. To cover one is nevertheless to cover original paint, by the hand of the artist himself, although not part of the final composition.

The official defence of the restorations carried out during the ministry (but how could one now put one's trust in one who had carried out the repainting on the Zaniberti?) also required a verification which the minister, Paquale Villari, addressed to the chemist Stanislao Cannizzaro, whom he provided with the appropriate documentation, including the translation of a letter from the new director of restoration in Munich, the famous Aloïs Hauser, who ably summarized what had already come to pass by the end of the century as a result of using regeneration with alcohol:

> "We no longer use the Pettenkofer method except extremely rarely, and only when the varnish of the painting has completely disappeared, or become dull (*fosca*). Experience has shown that the regeneration is not long lasting and that, depending on the nature of the varnishes of the individual paintings, after a few months the paintings are as they were before; more robust varnishes might last a year or two. My predecessors, having noted that the Pettenkofer method was not long lasting, covered the regenerated paintings several times over with copaiba balsam, but with no greater success. The balsam gives the paintings a glassy appearance, and makes them flake and more fragile, as well as accumulating resinous material on their surface."

This was the only variant which a typically nineteenth-century faith in science had put forward in addition to the materials and methods found in the eighteenth century, when restoration as such was born; the more this faith turned to the Pettenkofer method as to a panacea, seeing in it the point of departure of a new system, the more its limits had become apparent, reaching the point where now there is an almost excessive diffidence with regard to regeneration with alcohol.

For Angelo Conti, "this word *regeneration* is, in the present instance, synonymous with destruction. A German chemist, Pettenkofer, furnished the destroyers with the arms, and these are the corroding sublimate and copaiba balsam. And this is how one wrecks Italian paintings: one first repeatedly washes the painting with a soap containing the sublimate, and then – in order to halt the corrosion, one has recourse to the balsam. With every wash, a more intensely coloured liquid leaves the painting, which contains – as one might expect – the colour from the glazing, and traces of the uncovered body paint. In such a manner, after two or three washes, one destroys what might be considered the final wishes of the artist, his final brush-strokes, maybe the supreme effort to which was tied the mystery and magic of the work of art. With this done, one then arrests the action of the corrosive sublimate with the copaiba balsam. With the copaiba, polished and fragile as a crystal. Now, as must be evident, this also damages the work of the artist to no small degree – first with the yellowing, and then with its brilliance".

The doubts shown by Angelo Conti, or by Giacomo Boni for whom the Pettenkofer method changed the paintings into "resplendent mummies", were shared by the author of a letter written on behalf of the minister Villari to Stanislao Cannizzaro, asking with reference to "the embalming of paintings" (that is, the "nourishing" with copaiba balsam), "if and in what instances the painting should be allowed to lose the appearance of what it is, in order to take on the appearance of a work of art obtained by the use of completely other methods and materials, and if, just as one would not introduce changes in the building materials used for a monument, which were not considered to be contemporary, should not the embalming of paintings, if indeed one can rely on it, be considered an extreme remedy?"[37]

The episode of the Venetian course, alongside the failures of Botti or the revision of the restorations at Assisi, takes its place amongst the episodes marking the end of the structure and position which Cavalcaselle had tried to give to restoration as conservation (*restauro di conservazione*). Realistically, faced with the modesty of the salaries and career prospects of restorers within the State system, this position had come up against the impossibility of creating a series of operators of the same rich and articulated professionalism as that found amongst the professionals operating in the private sector, whether in the much lauded restoring tradition found amongst Lombard collectors or within the collecting, commerce and falsification of the Early Masters which had its small capital in Florence. The new generation of State civil servants (and Adolfo Venturi amongst their number) turned indeed to this circle of restorers in order to find operators able to carry out philologically accurate and respectful interventions, which were technically beyond criticism, as was required for a work of art belonging to the State.

5. Mosaics and polychromy in monuments of the Middle Ages

Giacomo Boni, with his extraordinary capacity to distinguish and appraise the different materials employed in a building or a work of art, in his stratigraphic analysis of any excavation report, embodied a symbiosis between aestheticism and positivism which made of him one of the most significant figures in the decades spanning the turn of the twentieth century. For many, his personality is still one awaiting discovery; the generation of swift excavators of the 1930s would not have been able to recognize themselves in his methodical stratigraphic analyses, whilst later, his sympathies for Fascism and his theories of racial pollution as a cause for the fall of the Roman Empire were not beneficial to his popularity. The idealism characteristic of much of Italian culture in the first half of the twentieth century and the vision of archaeology as the history of the art of antiquity, were therefore cultural directions which fitted ideological prejudices. The search for scientific positivism, which in him was linked to a root of Ruskinian origin, led him to enquire into evolutionary aspects of the perception of colour. This then led him onto areas which were more specifically anthropological during the excavations which he undertook in the valley of the Forum and on the Palatine, resulting in the famous discoveries of the origins of Rome. In the restoration of monuments, this climate induced him to give preference to the testimonies of races and civilizations which were far removed from the compass of interests of the vision of history inherited from De Sanctis which we find in Cavalcaselle: buildings, mosaics, the tessellated pavements of Late Antiquity – Byzantine, barbarian – would focus an interest which was already used to the irregularities of the Romanesque, and which would then direct its interests towards the art of the Late Middle Ages.

The restoration of mosaics finally moved away from a vision of mosaics as more durable and precious versions of painting, a vision which even Cavalcaselle had not succeeded in leaving behind. Indeed, it is some observations made by Boni which are a good indication of the moment in which a respect for the original comes into being, recognized in all its material aspects. The occasion is his article published in 1894 on the mosaics of the unredeemed [basilica of] Parenzo, which the Austrian government was having restored by the same Pietro Bornia, who in 1886 had made anew (rather than transferring) the mosaic 173 of the demolished apse in San Giovanni in Laterano:

"Even if when reforming (*rimaneggiando*) a mosaic, it were to retain its original
form, it will always lose something when it does not keep its original structure or

173. *Detail of the Byzantine mosaics;*
restored by Pietro Bornia, around
1894. Parenzo, Basilica Eufrasiana.

this has been tampered with, which will make us suspicious even of what remains of the original work. Authenticity, and it is worth repeating this once again, is not the main quality of monuments, but it is a necessary condition if they are to have any quality or excellence at all. And what possible authenticity could the mosaics of the Triumphal Arch of Parenzo possibly have, when the figures were made flat, transferring them onto canvas, when the tesserae were replaced closer together, or other coloured enamels were introduced where the Byzantine artist had left a gap at the join (*commettitura*)! When the sixth-century gold background, made up of tiny tesserae inserted at an angle, was destroyed in order to be replaced with a gold background manufactured with modern methods, unsympathetic and monotonous in its effect! Or when the hunt began for the gold tesserae in the apse mosaics, in order to remove with a scalpel those which one presumed had lost their gold leaf or else the covering glass, taking no account of the fact that in certain of the gold backgrounds of antiquity, we find

mixed in [with the gold ones] coloured tesserae and even ones inserted head
down, that is with the gilded surface embedded into the mortar!"[38]
It was in these years that the mosaics in Saint Mark's began to be restored by Saccardo
according to criteria which preserved the original tesserae, whilst Edoardo Marchionni put
the finishing touches to the techniques with which the Opificio delle Pietre Dure would
intervene on the mosaics of the cupola of the Baptistry between 1898 and 1906. In this   174, 175
instance, the mosaics were transferred, in pieces, using facings which preserved the position
and the original angles of the tesserae, with similar cuts to those used by Botti and Bertolli
in the transfer of frescos. However, during the execution of this work, the *sinopie* were
destroyed, and the original plaster was replaced with a different mixture (one part lime to
one part of sand, mixed with two of slow-setting cement) which was applied to the walls having introduced nails and a copper netting in order to ensure that there would be no losses
from the plaster. However, the luminosity of mosaic within the space suggests that a mimetic
solution was found when integrating the losses, in contrast to the solution used for frescos
at this time. The old repairs painted onto the plaster were replaced with mosaic and, in the
three lost sections with the stories of Cain and of Noah, the cartoon for the new stories was
entrusted to Arturo Vigilardi, in consultation with Pietro Toesca on matters iconographic.[39]

The mosaics in Ravenna also finally received a duly respectful restoration, at the hands
of Alessandro Azzaroni and Giuseppe Zampiga. In their campaign of restoration, the losses
were accurately reintegrated with retouching on plaster in imitation of mosaic; the restoration
was directed by Corrado Ricci from Ravenna, who was the first Soprintendente ai Monumenti
(1898–1906) of the city. During this campaign, there was a strong bias in the classification of
the monuments in Ravenna, towards those belonging to Late Antiquity. The most recent
events in the history [of the monuments] almost become a parenthesis, and in 1910 there came
the famous project which proposed the destruction of the eighteenth-century frescos in order
to return the cupola of San Vitale to its original bareness: with this in mind, Ricci made an
appeal which would be signed by all the most famous intellectuals of the day, from Berenson
to Croce and D'Annunzio. However, once testing had revealed the poor reversibility of the
whitewash which the restorer Venceslao Bigoni was going to use in order to cover the frescos
of Giacomo Guarana and Serafino Barozzi, it was decided to leave the frescos as they were,
confining the work to the installation of opaque glass in the upper register of the windows of
the Basilica, which would make their presence less evident within the Byzantine architecture.[40]

At the end of the nineteenth century, the debate surrounding the restoration of monuments was very rich, and the themes which Alois Riegl expounded in his *Denkmalkultus*
also give a good idea of the state of the debate on the conservation of monuments which
had been reached in Italy at this time. A moderate "historical standpoint" (*istanza storica*),
to use a particularly felicitous expression of Cesare Brandi's, was already part of the current
terminology in use for ideas on restoration, in which one could find observations on the
importance of context. For instance, Giacomo Boni's observations that the "rapid and
superficial comparisons which museums allow are not sufficient to compensate for the loss
of the relative values of the objects, removed from their place of origin, and dispersed."

In 1892, Luca Beltrami gave some thought to the damage caused by the destruction
of the original context: "The vast and intelligent comprehension of art has become so fragmentary, so broken up into small pieces and so atrophied in its few manifestations, that it
has lost its essential quality, its perfume one might almost say, that is that indefinable and
continuous vibration which knows how to capture in each aesthetic form, the individual atom

174. *From a model by Cimabue,*
L'imposizione del nome di Battista,
detail; photograph documenting
the transfer directed by Edoardo
Marchionni, 1898–1906. Florence,
Baptistry.

175. *From a model by Cimabue, Saint*
John Retires to the Desert, detail; photo-
graph documenting the transfer directed
by Edoardo Marchionni, 1898–1906.
Florence, Baptistry.

176. *Giovanni Battista Giovenale, project for the restoration of the polychromy of Santa Maria in Cosmedin, 1893.*

177. *Rome, interior of Santa Maria in Cosmedin; before the restoration by Giovanni Battista Giovenale.*

178. *Rome, interior of Santa Maria in Cosmedin; after the restoration by Giovanni Battista Giovenale, 1894.*

of a complex and strong organism. It has become transformed, rather, into conventional admiration, disciplined by guides and art tracts, excited not so much by a sincere emotion of the soul, but more by the curiousness of a formal element, the strangeness of a composition, or the material impact of a mass. The secondary monuments, which in our everyday lives suddenly appear and from time to time lift our minds out of their daily preoccupations, are becoming ever scarcer, and can no longer prepare us and educate us for the gradual comprehension of the major forms of art; and these, in the continuous dissolution of the environment from which they were created, remain lost in the turbulent atmosphere of modern civilization, and no longer address the soul with their powerful language, because we increasingly feel the presence of something which inexorably separates us from them. Thus, we are daily brought closer to that time when each artistic manifestation will have become the mute page of a catalogue, which will indicate the value of each work, and will thus gauge our degree of admiration".[41]

179. *Rome, interior of Santa Sabina; before the restoration by Antonio Muñoz.*

180. *Rome, interior of Santa Sabina; after the restoration by Antonio Muñoz, 1919 and 1936.*

An enquiry into the ideas which guided the restoration of monuments at the turn of the twentieth century would bring to light a highly articulate panorama, containing elements which we would find surprising, after decades of an idealistic position in restoration, which had proposed both "historical" and aesthetic elements placing them in a falsely dialectic position. The comparison between the restoration of two Roman basilicas should serve, I think, to give an understanding of the criteria which were guiding restoration (*restauro di ripristino*) in the first half of the twentieth century.

176–178   Between 1894 and 1899, Giovanni Battista Giovenale brought the interior of Santa Maria in Cosmedin back to its medieval appearance. Its restoration is remembered rather for the destruction of the fine eighteenth-century façade by Giuseppe Sardi, for which Giovenale was responsible following a sense of the organic wholeness of the building in the wake of Viollet-le-Duc, than for the good result obtained in the restoration of the interior. The polychromy which had originally been part of the project was abandoned after the first unsuccessful attempts, and the stories containing figures were not reconstructed; rather, bays which would contain stories are suggested, and the walls toned down to be in keeping with the few remains of medieval painting: the result is one of a cautious renovation, demonstrating a great understanding in its choice of materials.

179, 180   The other Roman basilica to use as a reference is Santa Sabina, which was restored by Antonio Muñoz between 1919 and 1936, pushing the renovation to the extent of rebuilding, *ex novo*, a false ceiling. The marbles used to line the apse, similar to those cited in the documentary sources, the insertion of a multiple series of windows in the walls, make of it the luminous Early Christian basilica with which we are familiar from textbooks, in which spaces and materials have all been reconstructed by analogy or from suggestions from the sources, rather than through completion from existing fragments or recovery of original portions. If we look at the interventions of Muñoz and Giovenale in perspective, it is not difficult to recognize in the restoration of Santa Sabina the burgeoning of a spirit of discrimination in which Viollet-le-Duc is read in what is already an idealistic key, giving preference to the retrieval of an idea of the original (not by chance Early Christian), and to a luminosity of materials which not even the similarity with the results of Poletti's restoration in San Paolo fuori le Mura could lead one to suspect. It is a new kind of discrimination in which the life of the building through time is completely secondary to the importance and the value of that which one wishes to recapture in terms of the poetic and historical "message" of the original, in a way that would have been completely inconceivable at the end of the nineteenth century.[42]

6. The years of Adolfo Venturi and Luigi Cantalamessa

The most important inheritance that Cavalcaselle left to his successor Adolfo Venturi in many of his directorial roles (in that he was charged with the cataloguing of the national heritage of works of art) was a series of restorers willing to move periodically as well as continuously. As was eloquently demonstrated by the continuous invectives directed towards Filippo Fiscali, Adolfo Venturi was not overimpressed by Cavalcaselle's most trusted restorers and, even in 1911, he would distance himself from him, as well as from Gaetano Bianchi, and in particular Botti: "When one thinks that one entrusts masterpieces to the hands of such people, one is appalled: Botti, for example, would use iron staples rather than the copper ones paid for by the State, in order to prevent the *intonaco* from falling away in Giotto's frescos in the Arena chapel in Padua. One day I saw him restore with oil colours a tempera painting by Bartolomeo Vivarini; on another occasion, stain, rubbing with oil the very centre of the great frieze by Tiepolo which is in the Venetian Gallery. Terrified by that Attila, I firmly told the chief of the personnel in that museum that that overesteemed restorer, who was also inspector of the Royal Galleries, should be sent to the Egyptian Museum in Turin".[43]

The panel by Bartolomeo Vivarini retouched in oil paint, the varnishing of which resulted in the transfer of the old restorer, was the *Sant'Agostino* in San Zanipolo, which we now see in the apparel given it by Mauro Pelliccioli's restoration: without saturations which disturb, it is however covered with a varnish, as is almost always the case with the paintings of the Early Masters in the early years of the twentieth century. A circumstance which helps us to understand how restoration was at that time still far removed from the criteria leading to a recovery of the original whatever the cost, to which we are tied to this day, lies in the fact that the discussion at the time never touched on the question of the recovery of the original gold background of the *Sant'Agostino*. The green repainting of the background still remained, as well as the additions. Moreover, one of the reasons for undertaking the restoration had in fact been the necessity of securing the side additions which were coming away from the central panel.[44]

With Cantalamessa, who replaced Botti in the direction of the Venetian galleries, a good management of the restorations is established, which used the services of Giovanni Spoldi, Giovanni Zennaro, and then Luigi Betto, whilst to begin with restorers from other cities, such as Centenari, were also present. Despite the fact that Spoldi and Zennaro signed themselves "painter restorers", the term used when referring to them, and to an activity far removed from the criteria of aesthetic restoration and guided by civil servants, was that of "repairers". This definition well suited the spirit with which one intervened on these paintings at this moment in time, which is, possibly, the best that restoration in Italy had seen.[45]

The restoration logbooks which now accompanied each intervention were models of their kind and should be borne in mind, as indeed should their clarity. In 1895, Sidonio Centenari returned Titian's *Presentation of the Virgin* to its original format, removing the 181, 182 inserts over the old openings for the doors, as well as an addition which ran the length of the upper part of the painting. With a mixture of spirits of turpentine and alcohol, he removed a "an aged and rank glaze" (*velatura irrancidita*) which had darkened "the limpidity of a cloud" (lamented since the end of the eighteenth century by Zanetti), and the one which lowered the tone of the white dress of the woman in the centre of the painting. Cantalamessa had in fact already abandoned the nineteenth-century taste for artificial patinas; referring to the fragment of the *Consecration of Saint Nicholas* by Veronese, he observed that "a fanatical loathing of the luminous and fresh tonalities in this case was the inspiration, as in so many other cases, to cover the surface of the painting with a crass varnish mixed with I do not know what yellow foul matter, and to lower the light tones of the wandering clouds".

The *San Giobbe Altarpiece* by Giovanni Bellini, *The Incredulity of Saint Thomas* by Cima da Conegliano, had severe problems caused by woodworm. Adolfo Venturi's observations on Botti make one realize that in the filling of the tiny holes, and their subsequent retouching, lay one of the most vexing aspects of his restorations. The problem was now confronted not only through seeking the advice of Centenari (mixture of spirits of turpentine, camphor, siccative aloe and santonin;[vii] the holes would then be blocked with a filling material bound with

---

[vii] *"acqua ragia, camphor, aloe siccativo and santonina"*.

181. Titian, Presentation of the Virgin;
after the restoration by Sebastiano Santi,
1828. Venice, Gallerie dell'Accademia.

182. Titian, Presentation of the Virgin;
after the restoration by Sidonio Centenari,
1895. Venice, Gallerie dell'Accademia.

fish-glue), but also the Ministry and its consultant, Professor Filippo Trois, who had indicated a solution of an arsenical acid which one feared might damage the priming layer.

The problems of Giovanni Bellini's altarpiece were very well expressed. For example: volatile cedar oil would be a solution for the woodworm which would not damage the paint layer, but it was no longer efficacious after seven years, with obvious drawbacks "for a painting of this size". Extracts from the restoration logbook give a very clear picture of the difference in position between Centenari, confronting the restoration of the large panel with the co-operation of Mariano Fortuny for the art-historical aspects, and Botti, who was working on the restoration of the Lotto in Santa Cristina al Tiverone. In order to straighten the warped planks of wood, he made use of a method similar to that advised by Secco Suardo, and then: "for several days he directed the work of the carpenter who was charged with making a rational framework on the reverse of the panel. This additional support, considering the vast surface area to protect, was a demanding piece of work, made up of transverse members and wedges secured with 848 brass screws, so assembled as to allow the natural movement of the panels of which the painting is made up." On the surface of the painting, the intervention seemed to be fairly limited: small retouchings with colours bound in honey, local regeneration of degenerated varnish with "the evaporation system", and presentation of the surface "with a light coating of mastic".[46]

Once the most heated moments of the criticisms against Botti had passed, Cantalamessa chose to protect with varnish two panels not very far removed in either style or technique, from the work of Vivarini, the two pairs of saints by Carlo Crivelli, from the Duomo of Camerino. The report on the work executed in 1895 by Giovanni Spoldi made no mention of varnishes, and this only a year after the events surrounding Botti: it did, however, mention in passing a "light rubbing with essence of turpentine, with an eighth of mastic varnish".

Giovanni Spoldi is the easiest figure from this context to reconstruct. As well as the Crivellis and other paintings in the Galleria dell'Accademia, we know of his restorations in the Palazzo Ducale between 1886 and 1891: the *Ecce Homo* by Quentin Metsys, Titian's *Faith*, Giovanni Bellini's *Deposition*, Tiepolo's *Neptune Paying Homage to Venice*, the Veronese in the ceiling of the Sala del Maggior Consiglio and *The Battle of Lepanto* by Andrea Vicentino on its return from the course organized by Valentinis. In 1900, Spoldi worked on some paintings from the Pinacoteca di Ferrara, documenting his work, as was his wont, with a detailed logbook. In Ferrara, he worked on paintings which were still well preserved, such as the *Massacre of the Innocents* by Garofalo, or the *Angelo Custode* by Carlo Bonone, as well as difficult cases such as the reintegration of the losses in Ortolano's *Deposition*, which has recently received the attentions of Mirella Simonetti. The impression one receives, of great professionalism and great attention to detail, can also be felt in his exhortations to prudence when faced with a proposal to transfer Titian's *Deposition*, a painting which, he says, was "painted at different times and on three or four different types of canvas, which probably would all have received different priming layers".[47]

Cantalamessa's final years were embittered by the failure in 1902 of the cleaning of Giovanni Bellini's *Madonna degli Alberetti*. It is difficult to judge to what degree the painting had been damaged, previously, by Tagliapietra, but it is Cantalamessa's name which is usually associated with this restoration, rather than to everything he had done to ensure the best level of practice (which was clearly of a standard to be in competition with that of private restorers such as Cavenaghi), notwithstanding the difficulties in the administration of the restoration of public works.[48]

Sidonio Centenari, the painter Orfeo Orfei and Venceslao Bigoni, all of whom appear during these years, were restorers who slotted into State commissions with restorations guided by the conservation principles characteristic of Cavalcaselle, but were able to present the works in a less unforgiving manner than Botti. In a very fine report on the paintings of the Pinacoteca di Ferrara, dating from 1896, Bigoni listed all the defects of the routine restorations typical of the second half of the nineteenth century which, thanks to the work of the above restorers, were now being left behind.

"Take cleaning for instance, often it was taken too far, methodically trying (because this is the case in each and every one of the paintings which were

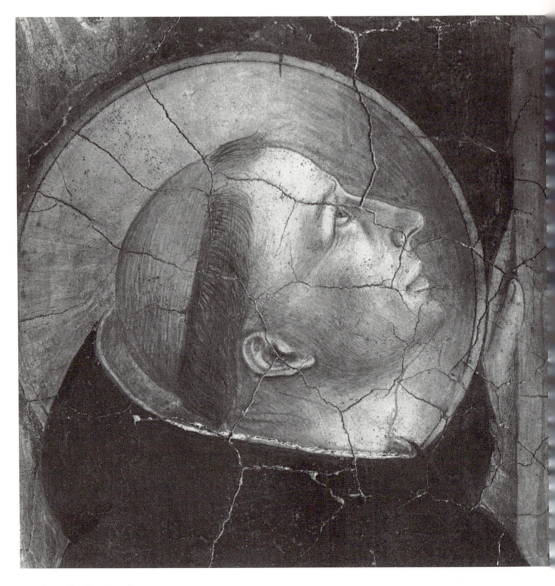

183. *Beato Angelico, Crucifixion,*
detail; fresco transferred for Stefano
Bardini, around 1879. Paris,
Musée du Louvre.

184. *Sandro Botticelli, fresco from Villa*
Lemmi, detail; transferred for Stefano
Bardini, around 1882. Paris, Musée du
Louvre.

185. *Simone Martini, Saint Catherine; before restoration, carried out for Stefano Bardini. Ottawa, National Gallery of Canada.*

186. *Simone Martini, Saint Catherine; after the restoration carried out for Stefano Bardini. Ottawa, National Gallery of Canada.*

treated) to thoroughly clean the light parts to make them whiter (*biaccose*), thus removing any final glazes applied by the artist, as well the patina given by time. As far as the varnish is concerned, this was applied thickly and not always very well, because in many instances under the varnish we can see some sort of deposit – now greyish, now yellowish – a clear sign that it was either applied over deteriorated varnish, already present over the painting, or that – once the painting had been cleaned – the deteriorated varnish decomposed by the agents used in the cleaning was not completely removed".[49]

In the field of fresco restoration, whilst Fiscali's activity and that of other practitioners of the old school continued, we meet Valentino Bernardi, the future director of the Accademia Carrara, to whom we owe some delightful tracts on restoration and on the transfer of mural paintings and, again in Bergamo, the Steffanoni family. Their activity extended widely, reaching as far as Catalonia, where, for American clients, they transferred certain Romanesque frescos, which in fact would be prevented from leaving the country, and can now be found in the Museum of Romanesque Art in Barcelona.[50]

Very good results were also achieved in the transfer of mural paintings in the private antiquarian sector (*restauro antiquariale*); Cosimo Conti described the technique used by Stefano Bardini in the transfer of Beato Angelico's *Crucifixion*, which he then sold to the Louvre. It was removed from the convent of San Domenico by demolishing the wall on which it was painted from behind, in order not to alter the appearance of the paint with glues, and then transferred onto metal netting. Among the transfers executed for Bardini, who probably used the services of Cosimo Conti, with whom he seems to have collaborated in various ways, there were also the paintings by Botticelli from Villa Lemmi now in the Louvre, and it is with techniques very similar to theirs that Domenico Ghirlandaio's *San Cristoforo* was admirably transferred (in the Metropolitan Museum of Art, New York, as early as 1880).[51]

With such a famous antique-dealer as Bardini, one finds oneself in an environment open to the practices of commercial restoration and of falsification. One cannot help but be astonished when confronted with the photograph of Simone Martini's *Saint Catherine* in Ottawa, Canada taking into consideration the scale of the reintegrated losses, compared with its appearance before it was sold to the Prince of Liechtenstein. Demonstrating such skill, with a full understanding of the technique of Trecento painting, reconstructing the pouncing, imitating the drapery painted with transparent glazes on gold of the saint's mantle, a true masterpiece which must make us reflect on the skill of these restorers linked to the commerce of art, working at the very limits of falsification. The fake that Bardini executed, or commissioned, of Simone dei Crocefissi's *Madonna dell'orecchio* employs all the necessary devices in its use of an old panel, and of a frame in perfect keeping with a fourteenth-century Bolognese painting, which blur the limits between excessive restoration and falsification, even if they do not justify the awkward official defence of the panel as a work of the fourteenth century.[52]

The logic behind these operations, already implicit in the Lombard tradition of aesthetic restoration, was that the art-lover desired a work which, for his pleasure and as a question of prestige, answered to certain requirements of quality and style. The work of art as a historical document remained either completely outside his considerations or only marginal, should a date or a document provide some detail of additional interest. If the imitation was a complete success, so that it was accepted as an original by Bode, Horne or Berenson, without damaging their good name, it then answered all the criteria required of an original: and there seemed no reason why a collector should be wary of it, nor why an art-dealer should

183

184

185, 186

not put it on the market for the same price as an original. In fact, falsifiers, art-dealers and the connoisseurs who had to unmask them, engaged in a kind of friendly competition: it was understood that if for some element of weakness the painter "in-the-style-of", or the restorer who had gone too far in his "adaptation" or in the aesthetic recovery of a work, revealed his limitations either in the quality or in the recent date of execution of the painting, then the connoisseurs would be compelled to recognize him [as its author].[53]

7. Luigi Cavenaghi

The years in which Adolfo Venturi was at the Ministry, were a period characterized by the good administration of the artistic heritage; when the director of the Uffizi, Enrico Ridolfi, was looking for new and skilled restorers, he was confronted with failure both with Elia Volpi and Luigi Grassi. These restorers (who would soon become art-dealers of some standing) were unwilling to give up the revenues of private work for the modest salaries of a State income. Elia Volpi had worked for Bardini for a long time, and Bode himself could guarantee the quality of his work; in 1894 he restored the canvas painting by the workshop of Botticelli which had just been recovered from Castello del Trebbio, but he almost immediately stopped frequenting the laboratory in the Gallery. Luigi Grassi worked on more demanding problems: in 1895 he consolidated the paint on Titian's *Venere con l' amorino*, thus avoiding the transfer advised by Cavenaghi; in 1897, he worked on Perugino's *Deposition* in the Pitti Palace, and lined Rubens' large *Battle* as well as Sustermans' *Oath to Ferdinand II*. However, after that, his involvement with the Galleries seems to have been limited to the acquisition of paintings.[54]

In these years in which the State attempted, with limited means and difficulty, and it must be said not always successfully, to guarantee the presence of able restorers, Luigi Cavenaghi remained the practitioner of greatest renown. From the confines of aesthetic restoration, he turned to an increasingly diverse relationship with the Ministry, to the point that he was asked to curate the new hanging of the Brera under the direction of Corrado Ricci, and to be part of the *Consiglio superiore* of antiquities and works of art.[55]

A pupil of Molteni, at his death Cavenaghi began to work alongside Giuseppe Bertini, but always autonomously, so that Secco-Suardo already remembered the cleaning and removal of an oily and hard crust of varnish and dirt which covered a Madonna in the style of Botticelli, which was bought in 1868 by the National Gallery in London. Gradually, he emerged as the successor to Giuseppe Molteni, inheriting from him clients such as Layard, thus continuing the prestigious tradition of Milanese restoration.[56] Cavenaghi was part of the circle linked to Morelli, and it is through the latter and Marco Minghetti that in 1874 he was entrusted with the restoration of the frescos in the Oratorio di Santa Cecilia in Bologna. It was also through Morelli that he was chosen for the restoration of Mantegna's Camera degli Sposi. As a result of a series of misunderstandings resulting in the removal of the Senator from the direction of restorations, the commission remained his even under the direction of Cavalcaselle, and in 1876 he removed the repainting carried out by Martino Knoller from most of the frescos on the shortest of the walls in the Sala. The reintegration of the two heads of *canettieri* to the left of the door are his work.[57]

Cavenaghi, who was himself a painter of frescos, was nevertheless mostly a restorer of panel and canvas paintings. Initially, the major impediment to his employment by the State was that he insisted on working in his own studio in Milan. The transfer of Titian's

187. *Workshop of Botticelli,*
Madonna and Child with Saints;
restored by Luigi Grassi, 1894.
Florence, Galleria dell'Accademia.

Martyrdom of Saint Lawrence in Venice (which was carried out between 1878 and 1880) was entrusted to Botti because of the impossibility of agreeing to Cavenaghi's request to carry out the work in Milan; but it was to Milan that the Madonna by Jacopo Bellini was sent, on which he worked in 1895, by which time his renown was beyond discussion. The work of art was now considered beyond the problems that its conservation might present in its normal environment, and transfer onto canvas became a preventive measure. In 1912, Cavenaghi himself would observe that paintings on panel were much more prone to damage and deterioration than those on canvas:

"However, this truth is now so widely held, especially abroad, where not only the climate but also the prices are less moderate, that in the past few years I have

188. *Giovanni Bellini, Madonna di*
Alzano Maggiore; restored by Luigi
Cavenaghi, around 1884. Bergamo,
Accademia Carrara.

189. Giovanni Bellini, detail of the Madonna di Alzano Maggiore; restoration by Luigi Cavenaghi, around 1884. Bergamo, Accademia Carrara.

noted that the majority of paintings on panel sold by the great art-dealers in Paris and London, on leaving for America, are transferred onto canvas, the buyers for reasons of safety, renouncing the visible appearance of age which the panel gives the painting. Panels are prone to flaking of the paint, to splitting, warping and a host of other afflictions …".[58]

*190. Giovanni Bellini,
Madonna and Child with
Donor, detail. London,
Harewood Collection.*

The question of Cavenaghi's links with the repaintings characteristic of the aesthetic restorations of the first half of the twentieth century is presented in a slightly enigmatic manner by the *Madonna di Alzano Maggiore* by Giovanni Bellini, which he restored around 1880. It is difficult to establish whether all that one sees now is the result of Cavenaghi's restoration or of an earlier one. Morelli, who owned the panel, used to affirm that he did not know of another painting by Giovanni Bellini in a better state of conservation, but the cleaning test

188–190

carried out not so long ago showed that the painting was to a great extent masked by restorations. The appearance of the Virgin is too thoughtful for the hand of Giovanni Bellini, and there are incongruities: for instance, in the landscape to the left, the even application of paint (*campitura*) (perhaps a base of copper green and lead white or lead tin yellow?) which does not vary in tone between the earth, the fields, the mirror-like water beneath the walls of the city, something one never sees in a background by Giovanni Bellini. And the collaborator to whom (quite rightly) has been ascribed the landscape to the right: when was he painting? All these questions will find an answer the moment when, rather than hagiographic reports on the state of conservation of the panel which are worthy of an American foundation, a decision is made to publish the appropriate scientific documentation of X-radiographs and other analyses. It is likely that Cavenaghi will emerge as a restorer who conserved a pre-existing equilibrium, and put into relief the resplendent material qualities of the painting, rather than as the author of reconstructions.[59]

In fact, he is the first restorer to break with the tradition which always preserved the whole painting in the state in which it had been entrusted to the restorer, whose job it was to integrate but not remove. The events surrounding Bartolomeo Vivarini's *Saint Augustine* remind us of the fact that even Botti (and this was already in 1893) did not deviate from this rule, which had received the approval of Secco-Suardo, when he remarked that "the less one torments a painting, the less risk one runs of damaging it", and he would then advise on methods to be used in reintegrating and toning in old restorations. In 1885, Cavenaghi brought to light the original paint in Mantegna's *Madonna coi cherubini*, whose clothing had probably been altered in the early sixteenth century, in order to give the Virgin a more nun-like mantle, in consideration of the destination of the painting: the nuns of Santa Maria Maggiore in Venice. Another famous retrieval was the one which gave back the Dionysiac appearance to Giovanni Bellini's *Portrait of a Humanist* in the Castello Sforzesco, Milan, and in 1911, Cavenaghi would recover the original apparel of Raphael's *Portrait of a Man* in the Galleria Borghese, Rome.[60]

Beyond the tradition of aesthetic restoration, in Cavenaghi one detects the emergence of the necessity of recovering the original, which brings him closer to the appreciation of the work of art as a document, suggesting different solutions for restorations depending on whether the works belonged to private individuals or were in the public domain. The vast reconstruction through analogy which he carried out around 1910 on Carlo Crivelli's *Pietà*, which is now in the Fogg Art Museum in Boston, is usually discussed in texts relating to fakes rather than in relation to restoration practices, and this is a section of his activity which has as yet received no attention. The choices he made were quite different when he was putting back together Antonello da Messina's *Polittico di San Gregorio*, which was caught up in the earthquake in Messina, or when he avoided the reconstruction of areas which would be too hypothetical in Antonello's *Annunciation* in Syracuse, where he nevertheless reconstructed all that was necessary in order to reinsert the figures in perspective within the space, as Antonello had intended.[61]

Our vision of the Renaissance has been largely built on the appearance of works restored by him. Even outside Lombardy and the Veneto, around which his activities were centred, one need only think of Florentine panels such as Filippo Lippi's *Hertz Annunciation*, Pesellino's *Storie di Griselda*, Botticelli's *The Last Communion of Saint Jerome*, the *Madonna dell'Eucarestia* or the *Storie di Virginia*, the *Profilo Poldi Pezzoli* which was reattributed to Pollaiuolo thanks to his suggestions, Piero di Cosimo's *Magdalen* or the *Tondo Visconti Venosta* by Fra Bartolomeo.

If his fame was confirmed, almost, by the fact of his being trusted with the restoration of Giorgione's *Tempest* or the *Portrait of a Young Man* in Berlin (the latter we now see after a subsequent restoration by Ruhemann), and Titian's *Schiavona*, the new directions of taste which was increasingly directed towards fifteenth-century painting made Cavenaghi the choice for works by Giovanni Bellini, from the *Frizzoni Madonna* and the *Madonna Greca* of the Brera to the *Santa Giustina* by Bagatti Valsecchi, in the very years when Berenson first proposed, and then revised, an attribution to Alvise Vivarini. In the *Saint Francis* in the Frick collection, New York, he accurately preserved the varnish glazes on the green drapery, although these had darkened and spread over the surrounding paint; if the painting had not undergone subsequent treatments, it would have been interesting to see what solution the great restorer would have found, so that the blue with which the rocks were painted did not appear as such, but rather as a shadow, cold in tonality, enshrouding the cave with the saint, with an effect which we now only see in the layered rocks in the upper part on the right, and in the more shaded part, between the posts which are supporting the vine.

Berenson would remember Cavenaghi as the most cultivated and skilful restorer that he had ever met, and entrusted him with paintings from his own collection; when in 1900 the civil servants from the Ministry, having been alerted by Adolfo Venturi to the fate of Domenico Veneziano's *Madonna* after the Panciatichi sale, asked for news of it from Berenson, he assured Ridolfi, the director of the Uffizi, that "the painting was one which he had desired for many years, and that now that it was his he could not part with it, and hoped to enjoy it for many years to come". In the meantime, it was being restored in Milan by Cavenaghi.[62]

In the domain of mural paintings, having found the impression of the figure of *Santa Caterina portata in cielo dagli angeli* by Luini, which had been badly transferred by Barezzi from the Villa Pelucca in Monza, he reintegrated it, recovering the decorative effect of the whole; at times, however, rather than intervening directly, he supervised the work of other restorers who executed the transfer or carried out other operations, for instance the Annoni who, in 1901, transferred Bramante's *Uomini illustri* to the Brera, from casa Panigarola. As was inevitable in his position as "prince" of Lombard restorers, it was to him that in 1908 was entrusted the umpteenth restoration of Leonardo's *Last Supper*; in this instance, the results were not to be as good as usual, and they would require the further intervention by Oreste Silvestri in 1924.[63] The recent intervention which removed his 1912 restorations from the fragment of the *Pala di San Nicola da Tolentino* by Raphael in the Pinacoteca Tosio Martinengo in Brescia, helps us to understand the way in which Cavenaghi presented the 191, 192 paintings he restored. He had removed the dark repainting from the background, which covered all those details that revealed the fragmentary nature of the figure. In the resulting figure, the verdigris of the wing which we see on the right (unlike the other one) was skinned in appearance, and moreover, if the cleaning has progressed further, the preparatory drawing for the hair of the angel would have come to light on the forehead: an effect which Cavenaghi certainly, unlike the previous restorers, would have felt unable to accept. He had therefore chosen to attenuate, by means of appropriately toned varnishes, all the irregularities (such as the overbright pink of the cheeks, the hardness of the foreshortening in the eyes) which occur in this painting, as they do in the fragment in the Louvre; even the skinned verdigris became acceptable without the use of pigmented glazings. The image, once all hardness of technique or poor conservation was toned down, fitted perfectly within the development of the young Raphael, maybe with some generalization, but completely in keeping with his early masterpieces.[64]

191. Raphael, fragment of the Pala di San Nicola da Tolentino; after the restoration by Luigi Cavenaghi, 1912. Brescia, Pinacoteca Tosio Martinengo.

192. Raphael, fragment of the Pala di San Nicola da Tolentino; present state. Brescia, Pinacoteca Tosio Martinengo.

The presence of Cavenaghi (who was already part of the *Consiglio superiore delle antichità delle belle arti*), in the commission brought together in 1910 to give its opinion on some of the paintings cleaned in the Florentine galleries by Otto Vermehren, was therefore to be expected. The varnishes had been removed, presenting the paintings without any artificially applied patinas, leaving them in strong contrast to the taste for a golden tonality typical of nineteenth-century collectors. A group of local artists had been greatly offended by the new appearance of the paintings, giving birth to a controversy which put under discussion the administration of the galleries by the Ministry's inspectors, which was not to be without wider political repercussions.

Cavenaghi found himself part of the commission alongside Ludovico Pogliaghi, with whom he drew up a joint report, and Giulio Aristide Sartorio, who was not disposed to take a conciliatory position in relation to the results of the new restorations. The terms of the debate can be clearly perceived from what Cavenaghi observed with reference to the *Portrait of Pietro Secco-Suardo* by Giovan Battista Moroni:

"The portrait of Secco-Suardo painted by G. B. Moroni shows a dissonance of tonalities which is really offensive to an eye which has been educated to the enjoyment of Old Master paintings. And this sensation is accentuated by its present position in the Gallery, surrounded as it is by works which have a golden or low tonality. There is an obvious lack of balance (*squilibrio*) between the light tones of the flesh and the landscape background, the black of the gentleman's garment and the grey tints of the background. Nevertheless, to the careful

193. Alessio Baldovinetti,
Adoring Saints, detail; documentation photograph taken
during Otto Vermehren's
restoration, around 1910.
Florence, Sant'Ambrogio.

observer, with the exception of some superficial damage to the paint, there appears to be no loss in the original paint. The modelling and highlights of the black garment are still present although, as often happens in paintings which are centuries old, these are partly absorbed by the general tint of the drapery or, to use the jargon, they have receded (*sono rientrate*), an effect which is all the more disturbing because of the cleaned tonality of the surrounding background. It was not the glazes which were removed in this painting, nor any other original physical material, so it is not really correct to say that the painting has been ruined. Rather, one should lament, and this is also valid (although to a lesser degree), for the other paintings with which we are dealing, that the restorer – either through an excess of scruple or because deficient in sensitivity for art – but in any case failing in his duty, was not able to restore to the painting, after cleaning, the balance of its overall harmony. In Old Masters, it is only very exceptionally that the tonalities retain their original relationship and, whilst the tints containing lead white alter only slightly, the more intense hues darken and therefore it is inevitable that their original harmony is altered. Mr Otto Vermehren himself asserts in his report that the paintings restored by him, after the cleaning, filling and retouching of the colours, were varnished with mastic varnish tinted with yellow lake to a greater or lesser degree according to the tonality of the painting. Now, there is nobody who would think that an overall varnish would compensate for the imbalance produced by the unequal alteration of the hues over the years, and which the cleaning of the varnishes does not always remove to the same degree; whilst this operation, the most delicate and difficult of the art of restoration, must be wisely and with exquisite sense of artistry be limited to lowering the over-bright tones to [re-establish] their natural harmony with those which are fatally altered."

Cavenaghi's evaluation was then confirmed with an examination of the paintings themselves. Sartorio, on the other hand, began his report with observations on the Van Eycks' invention of painting with soft resin varnish (*la vernice emolliente*) and the inevitable use of this medium in good painting. His diffidence was such that even in the case of the repainting removed from Titian's so-called *Portrait of Vincenzo Mosti*, he asked himself whether it was justifiable to alter the appearance by which the painting had been known for the past two-hundred years. The "airiness" which he lamented as having been lost in the Moroni is not the limpidity of the somewhat cold tonalities, but rather that effect of saturation which Cavalcaselle mourned the loss of in Claude Lorrain's *Hagar*; when missing, it could be obtained by fogging (*inebbiamento*) of the darkened varnishes, which therefore constituted an artificial patina replacing the one originally present. Some of Vermehren's paintings, in the Galleria d'Arte Moderna in Florence, executed in the style of Fuerbach, have precisely this brownish tonality which Sartorio finds absent, and shows us that with these cleanings he had attempted, with objectivity, to bring to light the taste of the masters he was restoring.[65]

Over and above the importance which the episode had as a verification of methods of restoration, the small-scale enquiry on the Florentine paintings had the specific aim on the part of Corrado Ricci (the Director General of Antiquities and the Fine Arts) of creating a precedent, in order to establish who would be responsible for taking decisions in the field of restoration. This episode would create a precedent for future decision making; this he had attempted also in 1910, without success, for the problem of the integrations in Botticelli's *Coronation of the Virgin*.[66]

However, now it became a case of protecting the civil servants in the Administration of the Department of Antiquities and the Fine Arts from the external interference of artists, whether or not gathered under the banner of an academic commission who, throughout the nineteenth century, had participated in the direction of restorations. The system of having one artist as a consultant for every restoration, which Cantalamessa had set up so successfully in Venice, was certainly put into question by the unfounded character of some of the objections of the Florentine artists, and by the modest stature of many of them. The decision, which will become the norm and the validity of which is still unquestioned, is that the restorer must be "followed" (or "directed" as some prefer to emphasize) by the art historian civil servants of the Soprintendenze. The episode of the Florence cleanings shows us, very clearly, the origins of the present system of administration of restorations by the administrating conservation bodies, and not only in Italy. It is a tradition to which it is easy, but in many cases gratuitous, to attribute an idealistic core, and the principal characteristic of which is to have excluded the presence of artists from the process of decision making in restoration.

Corrado Ricci, who was at the helm of this inquiry, did not have a cultural background with specific idealistic connotations; in fact, it is rather difficult to work out precisely what exactly were his cultural leanings, as he moved between different areas in art, history, music and theatre. Trained as a lawyer, with his somewhat eclectic and almost accidental culture, he had overtaken Adolfo Venturi to become (1906–1919) Director General, organizing the new structure of the Soprintendenze, concentrating the decision-making powers in the hands of State employees and leaving behind the old nineteenth-century provincial commissions.[67]

Wishing to carry on with the history of restoration in the twentieth century, one would continue to meet great restorers, such as Mauro Pelliccioli, who wanted to interpret the figurative values of a painting and show them to their best advantage with the correct material apparel. However, one would gradually find oneself confronted with examples of astonishing deafness to these aspects of painting: one need only mention how varnish is considered as a protective layer, without asking oneself any questions as to the degrees of saturation it causes in different colours; or else the definition of "consolidation", and its subsequent preventive use in a treatment of frescos which is highly selective, such as with barium hydroxide. Attention to the painting technique and to the material qualities of the image often becomes a laborious personal adventure requiring research back to the sources or to the evidence provided by the materials themselves, leaping over statements made by restorers and sometimes in direct opposition to important governing bodies. It is essential, therefore, that we return to the sources, to the eighteenth-century discussions on varnish, to the nineteenth-century debates on the transfer of frescos, to Cavenaghi's reflections on the cleanings of 1909. Along the road which is lit for us by these sources, we may, perhaps, be able to begin the time-consuming recovery of all those parameters of perception of the material aspect of images, which are indispensable if restoration is to preserve a good, working functionality, and become an instance of the conservation of the original materials, rather than simply an updating to new visual demands.

Notes

1. *The Seven Lamps of Architecture*, I, VIII.
2. See Fantozzi, 1842, pp. 775–777.
3. Cosimo Conti, 1879–1882, c. 45 of the first section.

4. *Journal de Eugène Delacroix*, Paris, 1996, p. 257 (6 August 1850); the purist restorations on the monuments of Lucca met with the approval of Carlo Cattaneo; see Levi, 1988, note 46, p. 356.

5. E. Viollet-le-Duc, 1866, pp. 17–20; see also note 1, pp. 28–29. One should also see this attitude of intentional retrieval in the light of the state of complete abandon and dilapidation in which many of the medieval monuments found themselves after the Revolution; see Montalambert, 1833, ed. cit., p. 6.

6. C. J. Cavallucci, *Dei restauri operati nella chiesa di Santa Croce*, in "L'arte in Italia", III, 1971, pp. 54–56; R. Offner, *A Corpus of Florentine Paintings*, sect. III, vol. II/I, New York, 1930, p. 78; F. Zeri, *Cinque schede per Carlo Crivelli*, in "Arte antica e moderna", 1961, pp. 162–163.

7. J. Ruskin, *The Seven Lamps of Architecture*, VI, XVIII; E. Viollet-le-Duc, *De la restauration des anciens edifices en Italie*, in "Encyclopédie d'Architecture", 1872, pp. 15–16, 57–59; in Zorzi, 1877, pp. 161–167 (see *Le voyage d'Italie d'Eugène Viollet-le-Duc 1836–1837*, catalogue of the exhibition, Paris–Florence, 1980, pp. 223–224; translation in Dalla Costa cit., 1983, pp. 109–114); Zorzi, 1877; C. Boito, *I restauri di San Marco*, in "Nuova antologia", 15 December 1879, pp. 701–721; in *Architettura del Medioevo in Italia*, Milan, 1880, pp. 299–381; C. Yriarte, *Les restaurations de Saint Marc de Venise*, in "Revue des deux mondes", XXXVIII, 1880, pp. 827–856; Conti, 1892, pp. 8–9; E. Tea, *Il carteggio Boni-Caroë sui monumenti veneziani: 1881–1889*, in "Archivi", 1959, pp. 234–254; C. Robotti, *Le idee di Ruskin e i restauri della Basilica di San Marco*, in "Bollettino d'Arte", 1976, pp. 115–121; S. Boscarino, *Il primo intervento della S.P.A.B. all'estero*, in "Psicon", January–March 1977, pp. 110–118; J. Clegg, *Ruskin and Venice*, London, 1981; M. Dalla Costa, *La Basilica di San Marco e I restauri dell'Ottocento*, Venice, 1983.

8. The frequently apologetic character of much of the literature dedicated to him does not help when one is trying to focus on the culture of Cavalcaselle; to begin with it is spoiled by the somewhat nationalistic character of the comparison with his colleague Crowe, and then by the taste for restoration as conservation which renounced all attempts to integrate losses, etc., and which saw in Cavalcaselle a precursor to its approach; see, rather: D. Levi, *L'officina di Crowe e Cavalcaselle*, in "Prospettiva", n. 26, 1981, pp. 74–87; D. Levi, *Cavalcaselle e Crowe: analisi di una collaborazione*, in "Annali della Scuola N. le Sup. Di Pisa" (classe di lettere), 1982, pp. 1131–1171 (note 9 is specifically dedicated to Crowe's poor following in Italy and Germany); D. Levi, *Sui manoscritti friulani di Cavalcaselle: una storia illustrata*, ibid., 1983, pp. 239–307. On Cavalcaselle, and also to access the vast existing bibliography, see: *G. B. Cavalcaselle, Disegni da antichi maestri*, catalogue of the exhibition (Venice–Verona, 1973), edited by L. Moretti; for the themes I have been treating, I have leant heavily on the excellent thesis which I have discussed with Patrizia Poletti (1982–1983). I should also like to mention the newly published work by Donata Levi (1988), which I was not able to refer to adequately when drawing up these notes.

9. G. Morelli, *Della pittura italiana* (1890), Milan, 1897, p. 76. I have not been able to trace any restorations carried out on the frescos by Filippo Lippi in this period. The restorations on the Camera degli Sposi are documented in 1876–1877 (A.C.S., vers. I, b. 476; very informative is the illustrated article on the events in "La Gazzetta di Mantova" of 2 March 1877); Morelli's dissent had its origins in the bad effects of the oil and wax mixture which Antonio Bertolli had used in order to consolidate the detached sections then re-adhere them to the vault, effects which would be remedied by Gaetano Bianchi's intervention (see "La Gazzetta d'Italia", 17 September 1877). The interventions on the frescos in the Scuola del Santo were also by the hand of Bertolli (1877 and 1879; see the same versamento, b. 499).

10. Cavalcaselle, 1863, ed. 1875, pp. 31–34. On the restoration of the mosaics of San Marco and Torcello, see: P. Saccardo, *Saggio di uno studio storico-artistico sopra i mosaici della chiesa di S. Marco in Venezia ...*, Venice, 1864; Zorzi, 1877, pp. 54–55, 121–160; P. Saccardo, *Mosaici e loro iscrizioni*, in *La Basilica di San Marco a Venezia*, Venice, 1988, III, pp. 329–333; P. Saccardo, *La basilica di San Marco e il suo pavimento e i restauri dell'ultimo ventennio*, Venice, 1901; I Andrescu, *Torcello I, II*, in "Dumbarton Oak Papers", 1972, pp. 182–223; I. Andrescu, *Torcello*, III, ibid., 1976, pp. 247–341; O. Demus, *The Mosaics of San Marco in Venice*, Chicago–London, 1984, I, pp. 14–17; amongst the documents traced in the thesis by Francesca Luzi (discussed with me) (*Mosaici e rivestimenti marmorei nei restauri ottocenteschi di S. Marco* (academic year 1983/84), see: A.C.S., vers. I, b. 608, 609 and 612. On the restorations in Ravenna, see Gerola, 1917, pp. 142–181; Ricci, 1930–1937. In the problematics of the restoration of mosaics before the end of the nineteenth century, the best standard was that shown by Gaetano Riolo in 1870.

11. Cavalcaselle, 1863, ed. 1875, pp. 34–37. Very appropriately, Cavalcaselle insisted on the necessity of good maintenance (*manutenzione*) of the buildings which housed the frescos, as later in the circular of the Ministero della Pubblica Istruzione, 9 January 1879; *Norme per lavori di restauro dei dipinti a fresco* (published in L. Magagnato, *G. B. Cavalcaselle a Verona*, Verona, 1973, pp. 37–38; minutes in A.C.S., vers. I, b. 385, fasc. 22–9).

12. Cavalcaselle, 1863, ed. cit., pp. 36–37. On the *Last Judgement* by Fra Bartolomeo, which has lately undergone an intervention which has removed it from the support given it by Botti, see C. J. Cavallucci, *Distacco dell'affresco*

rappresentante il Giudizio Universale ..., in "L'arte in Italia", 1872, pp. 11–12; letter from G. Botti of 20 August 1870: A.C.S., vers. I, b. 450.

13. Cavalcaselle, 1863, ed. cit., pp. 38–39.

14. Conti, 1982, pp. 132–133; Levi, 1988, pp. 329–330; see A.C.S., vers. I, b. 450, fasc. 268.

15. Cavalcaselle, 1863, ed. cit., p. 30; letter of 7 December 1872, in "L'arte in Italia", 1872, pp. 166–167. Of the restorations which were carried out during the pontifical period, one notes the reconstruction (*rifacimento*) "*in stile*" of some of the Cimabuesque figures in the decoration in the transept, dating from before the drawings from it by Anton Ramboux (*c.* 1835–1836); see Hueck, 1980, p. 2; the interventions of Pellegrino Succi of 1844 (head of the Redeemer in the *Coronation* by Puccio Capanna, and on one of the *Angels* by Cimabue in the transept: Hueck, 1981, pp. 144–145, 149) and those of 1847–48 and 1851 (Chapel of San Martino, *Stories of Saint Francis* by Giotto, single figures in the Cappella della Maddalena and *Saints* by Simone Martini in the right transept: here, pp. 146–147, 150–152). On the important restoration of the stained-glass windows by Giovanni Bertini (1839–1844), see Hueck, 1979.

16. *Restauri* (reprint of the letter from Cesare Cantù of 5 December, and Cavalcaselle's reply of 7 December 1872), in "L'arte in Italia", 1872, pp. 166–167; G. Biscarra, *Restauri dell'antica basilica di San Francesco in Assisi*, here, pp. 38–40; G. Rossi-Scotti, *Sull'avvenuta rimozione del coro di Maestro Domenico da Sanseverino*, Perugia, 1873; G. Rossi-Scotti, *Ancora due parole sul rimosso coro di S. Francesco in Assisi*, Perugia, 1874; G. Rossi-Scotti, *Dibattito del giornalismo italiano intorno alla rimozione del coro di Maestro Domenico da Sanseverino ...*, Perugia, 1874; G. B. Cavalcaselle, letter of 15 December 1892, p. 445; Hueck, 1981, pp. 147–148; Levi, 1988, pp. 335–340.

17. G. Sacconi, *Relazione dell'ufficio regionale per la conservazione dei monumenti delle Marche e dell'Umbria*, Perugia, 1903, p. 72 (see pp. 57–82, 70–72 on the basilica and its frescos). Sacconi himself seemed to show a rather ambivalent approach with regard to original materials, proposing to remove the lead white retouchings which had blackened, knowing that these were by the hand of the authors of the frescos, in the hope of finding the white underlayer. Numerous documents relating to this restoration can be found transcribed in the theses of Paola Irene Canu and Patrizia Poletti (1982–1983), see: A.C.S., vers. I, b. 526, (restoration of the stained-glass windows), 527, 528; letters from the architect Alfonso Brizi, from 29 April 1872 to 16 August 1878, in the Cavalcaselle correspondence.

18. *Riparazione ai dipinti*, circular from the Ministry of Public Instruction, 30 January 1877 (minutes in A.C.S., b. 385, fasc. 22–3); in 1863, Cavalcaselle went no further than insisting that the integration of losses should not "spill over" onto the original paint surface, without, however, suggesting any norms that should be followed in their execution. A slightly less rigorous attitude in the painting in of losses was discerned by Marina Cesani (1986–1987) in the restorations of Domenico Fiscali in San Giminiano, which were supervised by Cavalcaselle.

19. A.C.S., vers. I, b. 197, fasc. 44–9; in this, see Conti's estimate of 10 April 1878, and the reply of 21 March, in which Cavalcaselle proposes Filippo Fiscali for the Adimari Cassone.

20. On Botti, in addition to the information and comments relating to the restoration of the Camposanto in Pisa, see: L. Rotelli, *Delle invetriate dipinte da Guglielmo Botti*, Pisa, 1868 (extract from the "Rivista Universale"); Breda, *Sul nuovo sistema del Cav. Guglielmo Botti, pittore, per distaccare gli affreschi dalle pareti*, in "La Gazzetta di Mantova", 8 July 1870; G. Botti, *Sulla riparazione del Cenacolo di Leonardo da Vinci*, Assisi, 1874; A. Rondani, *Sul distacco e trasporto di un affresco di A. Allegri da Correggio in Parma*, Venice, 1876; F. della Rovere, *Un dipinto a tempera di Bartolomeo Vivarini ...*, in "Gazzetta di Venezia", 4 May 1877; M. Sernagiotto, *Il Cavaliere Guglielmo Botti di Pisa, professore di pittura*, Treviso, 1879; G. Botti, *Cose locali: lo stato della nostra Pinacoteca*, in "La Gazzetta ferrarese", 6, 7, 8, 9 and 10 June 1891; A. De Gubernatis–U. Martini, *Dizionario degli artisti italiani viventi*, Florence, 1892, pp. 70–72; Secco-Suardo, 1894, p. 548; Ufficio regionale, 1906, pp. 53–58; A. Venturi, 1911, pp. 133–134; E. Bassi, entry for *Botti, Guglielmo* in *Dizionario biografico degli italiani*, XIII, 1971; Conti, 1981, pp. 89–90; G. Curto, in *Alfredo d'Andrade*, 1981, pp. 284–293; Moro, 1981–1982; Conti, 1982, pp. 131–136; for the transcription of documents and bibliographical checks, I availed myself of the thesis of Paola Irene Canu (*Guglielmo Botti: un restauratore dell'800*, Pisa, faculty of letters, academic year 1980/81, supervisor D. Devoti).

21. P. E. Selvatico, *Sulle reparazioni dei celebri affreschi di Giotto detti dell'Arena in Padova*, Pisa, 1870; E. Prosdocimi, *Il Comune di Padova e la Cappella degli Scrovegni nell'Ottocento*, special edition of the "Bollettino del Museo Civico di Padova", XLIX, 1960. In here (pp. 77–79), a report by Cavalcaselle on the conservation of the frescos in 1857, which took as its model Förster's intervention in 1837 on the Oratorio di San Giorgio (see Förster, 1846).

22. On Bertolli see: A. Moschetti, *Per l'integrità della Cappella Ovetari e di un affresco di Andrea Mantegna*, in "Bollettino del Museo Civico di Padova", 1930, pp. 1–33; A. Moschetti, *L'ultima parola intorno all'integrità della Cappella Ovetari ...*, ibid., 1931, pp. 153–163; *Pitture murali*, 1960, p. 46; Prosdocimi, 1960, op. cit.; A. Sartori,

La Cappella di San Giacomo al Santo, in "Il Santo", 1966, n. 2–3, pp. 302, 356; Conti, 1981, p. 91; letters from 1882 to 1885 in Cavalcaselle's correspondence. In A.C.S., vers. II, p. 1, b. 322, fasc. 5821/6 contains a report by him, dated 1891, on the conservation of Titian's *Saint Christopher* in the Ducal Palace in Venice, which one can compare with the different methods of intervention proposed by Botti and Giovanni Spoldi.

23. On the restoration of Veronese's frescos, see A.C.S., vers. I, b. 616 (where you also find the documentation on Botti's restoration of Pordenone's frescos in the cloister of Santo Stefano, carried out between 1875 and 1877). On Tagliapietra, see Marconi–Moschini, 1956, pp. 71, 75; for the ill fame of Venetian restorers, see the letter from Saverio Cavallari to Austen Layard, which is quoted in Venturi, 1912, p. 449.

24. Conti, 1982, p. 134 (A.C.S., vers. I, b. 600); on the various stages of the conservation of the panel, see A. M. Spiazzi, in *Lorenzo Lotto a Treviso*, catalogue of the exhibition, Treviso, 1980, pp. 113–117.

25. As can easily be seen by the unfortunate outcome of the mosaics of Saint Mark in the nineteenth century, Venice was the only city in which the management of the restorations under the direction of the local academy regularly led to poor results. We have information on Zambler's restorations as early as 1843; Camillo Boito alludes to this restoration when referring to the abrasions suffered by an altarpiece by Lorenzo Lotto (*I restauratori*, Florence, 1884, p. 25); see Conti, 1982, p. 135.

26. P. d'Achiardi, *I restauri agli affreschi di Benozzo Gozzoli nel Camposanto di Pisa*, in "L'Arte", 1903, p. 121; Conti, 1982, p. 135.

27. F. Valcanover, *La Pala Pesaro*, in "Quaderni nella Soprintendenza ai Beni Artistici e Storici di Venezia", n. 8, 1979, pp. 63–64 (also on the earlier restoration carried out by Fabris in 1842); Conti, 1982, pp. 135–136 (see A.C.S., vers. I., b. 355).

28. See Cavalcaselle's correspondence for his letter of 2 October 1881, and those from Gabriello Cherubini da Atri of 26 August 1882 (transferred and then reattached, the *Nativity of the Virgin*, and the *Cacciata di Gioacchino dal Tempio*, the *Presentation at the Temple*) and 30 November 1882. In 1879, Missaghi is the restorer of the Galleria Capitolina in Rome (A.C.S., vers. I, b. 434, fasc. 120, memorandum of 20 April).

29. The information I have gathered on Filippo Fiscali is somewhat fragmentary, see: Cavalcaselle–Crowe, 1864–1866 (but the ed. cit.), VIII, p. 15; A. Santarelli, *Un affresco di Melozzo da Forlì*, in "Arte e storia", 1887, p. 5; Papini, 1909, pp. 454–455; Venturi, 1911, pp. 137–139; Longhi, 1957, p. 6, ed. 1985, p. 56; L. Moro, in *Il Museo Civico di Ferrara. Donazioni e restauri*, catalogue of the exhibition, Ferrara, 1985, pp. 267–269; A.C.S., vers. I, b. 197, fasc. 44/7; b. 434, fasc. 120 (interventions in Bologna, 1878–1879, in the Cappella Bentivoglio in San Giacomo Maggiore, and on many works in the picture gallery); deposit II, p. 2, b. 214; Ferrara, Arch. Storico Com., sec. XIX, p. 1, cartella 2 (segnalata da L. Moro, 1981–1982); letters from 1881–1889 in the correspondence of Cavalcaselle.

His son, Domenico Fiscali, as well as directing the cleaning of the Ghirlandaio in Santa Maria Novella which began, after a whole year of discussion, in 1907, then carried out a *strappo* on the *Last Judgement* and the *Sacrifice of Noah* in the Chiostro Verde of Santa Maria Novella. Also his work, and executed between 1915 and 1916, was the restoration of the Piero della Francesca's frescos in Arezzo, with the partial transfer of various sections in which the wall had to be consolidated, for instance the group on the right in *The Death of Adam*. He also had the chains, which in the earliest photographs cut across some of the stories, moved in relation to the framing. At Monterchi, in 1910 he transferred the *Madonna del parto*, and in Sansepolcro he restored the *Resurrection*, which is still in good condition: see *Cronaca*, in "Bollettino d'Arte", 1917, pp. 11–13; L. T.-E. B., *Il restauro degli affreschi di Piero della Francesca*, in "Il Vasari", XXII, 1963, n. 4, p. XI; A.C.S., vers. III p. 2, b. 248; vers. IV, div. I, 1908–1924, b. 95, 820, 441. On his activities in San Gimignano (from 1886), see now Cesani, 1986–1987; correspondence relating to his intervention at Monterchi is also to be found in Anna Maria Quartili (1986–1987).

30. On Botti's experiments, see Levi, 1988, pp. 346–347; A.C.S., vers. I, b. 355, fasc. 246; b. 385, fasc. 22/5.

31. Secco-Suardo, 1894, ed. cit., pp. 410, 412–413.

32. Cavalcaselle, minute of 5 February 1879 in A.C.S., vers. I, b. 197; the opinion of Ludwig Passiny is related in Pasquale Villari's letter to the chemist Cannizzaro, dated 9 March 1892 in A.C.S., vers. II, p. 1, b. 322, fasc. 5521/5; here is also quoted one of Eastlake's old opinions: "To give a single recipe for the conservation of paintings would be like giving one recipe for the painting of them. The methods to be employed must necessarily vary from case to case, and according to the condition of the painting. The Pettenkofer method was experimented with here from 1865, but it is a dangerous expedient, and under the Directorship of Sir Frederic Burton, it was not deemed safe to adopt it. We now do not restore paintings but only carefully conserve them, only doing what is necessary to keep them in good order. At times they are put under glass to protect them from the influence of London air."

33. Biographical details on Count Giuseppe Umberto Valentinis (1819–1901) can be found in G. Marchetti, *Il Friuli: uomini e tempi*, II, Pordenone, 1979, and the collaboration with Cavalcaselle in the frequent references which appear in *La pittura friulana del Rinascimento*, Venice, 1974, and in the letters overflowing with information of the Cavalcaselle correspondence (1877), which are known to me through Patrizia Poletti's thesis (now see Levi, 1988, pp. 344–347). For the tracing of documents and for their transcription, I have used Raffaella Bruschetta's thesis, which I supervised (*La rigenerazione dei dipinti: Max von Pettenkofer in Italia*, Univ. di Bologna, academic year 1983/84).

34. Valentinis, 1891; report of 12 May 1876, and report of 10 May 1876 (attachment *i*) in A.C.S., vers. I, b. 385, fasc. 22/5.

35. Valentinis report of 9 April 1876 and attachments, in A.C.S., vers. I, b. 385, fasc. 22/5 cit.

36. G. Marcotti, *La Venere rigenerata*, in "L'illustrazione italiana", 8 November 1891 (journalistic in character); A.C.S., vers. II, p. 1, b. 77, fasc. 1373/1; estimate for regeneration interventions by Cosimo Conti, and various documents illustrating the activities of Alessandro Mazzanti in A.C.S., deposit I, envelope 197. Of Mazzanti, born 1824 and died 1893, we know that apart from working for the Galleria degli Uffizi, he was the trusted restorer of the Archispedale of Santa Maria Nuova, where he transferred (together with Filippo Fiscali) Andrea del Castagno's lunette of the *Crucifixion* (moved to the Cenacolo of Sant'Apollonia; see, A.C.S., vers. I, b. 434, fasc. 120, letter from Antonio Ciseri of 18 July 1876); we also have information on an intervention of his on the *Ritratto Martinengo* attributed to Moroni, which is now in the North Carolina Museum of Art, Raleigh, USA, on which he tested the authenticity of the signature, see J. Fleming, *Art dealing in the Risorgimento*, III, in "The Burlington Magazine", 1979, p. 577 and note.

37. Conti, 1892, pp. 10–11; Tea, 1932, I, p. 395; quotations from the letter written on behalf of Villari, dated 9 March 1892 (and further clarifications in the minute of 19 March) in A.C.S., vers. II, p. 1, b. 322, fasc. 5521/5, in which can be found all the documentation relating to the Venetian Course of 1891–1892; Ferrara, Archivio Storico Comunale, XIX century, p. 1, cartella 4, fasc. 7 (letter from G. Botti dated 22 September 1891). On the final verdict on the Pettenkofer method, see Venturi, 1911, p. 137; Marijnissen, 1967, pp. 60–61, 76–78.

38. Boni, 1894, p. 361; Tea, 1932, I, pp. 131–132. On Giacomo Boni see: Venturi, 1911, p. 107; Beltrami, 1926; L. Beltrami, *Il sacrario di Vesta*, in "Il Marzocco", 7, 14 and 21 April 1929; Tea, 1932; P. Romanelli, in *Dizionario biografico degli italiani*, XII, 1970 (with preceding bibliography); A. Carandini, *Archeoogia e cultura materiale*, Bari, 1979, pp. 47–48, 300–304; D. Manacorda, *Cento anni di ricerche archeologiche italiane …*, in "Quaderni di storia", n. 16, 1982, pp. 86–92; Conti, 1983, pp. 32–36. Amongst the works of Boni which deal more directly with the problems relating to conservation and restoration, see: *Scavi nel Foro Romano: Aedes Vestae*, in "La Nuova Antologia", 1 August 1900, pp. 426–444; *La torre di S. Marco*, in *Atti del Congresso internazionale di scienze storiche*, V, Rome, 1904, pp. 585–610; *Esplorazione del Forum Ulpium*, in "Notizie degli Scavi", 1907, pp. 361–427; *Colonna Traiana*, in "Nuova Antologia", 1 January 1912, pp. 49–64; *Il "metodo" nelle esplorazioni archeologiche*, in "Bollettino d'Arte", 1913, pp. 43–67.

39. Ponticelli, 1950–1951, II, pp. 52–53; A. Pampaloni Martelli, *Edoardo Marchionni. La trasformazione dell'Opificio delle Pietre Dure in laboratorio di restauro*, in *Scritti … Procacci*, 1977, pp. 630–676. The restoration methods are described by Marchionni in an unsigned manuscript with a preface dated 4 August 1921, *Norme per il restauro dei mosaici*, which is to be found in the Opificio.

40. Gerola, 1917, pp. 182–194; Ricci, 1930–1937; Bencivenni–Mazzei, 1982.

41. Boni, in Tea, 1932, I, p. 56; L. Beltrami, *La conservazione dei monumenti in Italia nell'ultimo ventennio*, in "Nuova Antologia", April 1892, pp. 447–449.

42. G. B. Giovenale, *La basilica di Santa Maria in Cosmedin*, Rome, 1927; R. Longhi, *La toilette de Sabina e altre cose*, in "Tempo", 8 July 1919; in *Opere Complete*, I, Florence, 1961, pp. 437–440; A. Muñoz, *Il restauro di Santa Sabina*, Rome, 1938.

43. Venturi, 1911, pp. 133–34. The Tiepolo alluded to by Venturi is the *Bronze Serpent*, restored in 1893.

44. Conti, 1982, pp. 137–138; A.C.S., vers. II, p. 2, b. 628.

45. In order to understand the certain degree of disorder which reigned in the Academy under Guglielmo Botti, de Valentinis' suggestions in the 1892 pamphlet are useful. For the new administration under Luigi Cantalamessa, see: A.C.S., vers. II, p. 1, b. 563; here, busta 346, in particular the report dated 18 May 1895.

46. On Titian's *Presentation at the Temple*, see: A. M. Zanetti, *Della pittura veneziana*, Venice, 1771, pp. 113–114; G. Cantalamessa, *R. R. Gallerie di Venezia*, in *Le Gallerie Nazionali italiane*, 1896, pp. 40–41; Moschini–Marconi, 1962, p. 258; G. Nepi Scirè, 1983; A.C.S. vers. II, series I, b. 346 (in this is also to be found the daily logbook of work on the *Pala di San Giobbe*). On Veronese's *Consacration of Saint Nicholas* which was restored by Zennaro, see Conti, 1982, p. 140; A.C.S., vers. II, p. 2, b. 207.

47. On the restoration of the paintings by Crivelli, see A.C.S., vers. II, p. 1, b. 343, request for the balance for the work carried out on the Crivelli, dated 21 January 1896. On Spoldi, see A. Droghetti, in "La Gazzetta Ferrarese", 27 September and 11 October 1901; Conti, 1982, pp. 138–140 and note 4, pp. 131–132; L. Moro, in *Il Museo CIvico di Ferrara. Donazioni e restauri*, catalogue of the exhibition, Ferrara, 1985, pp. 269–270. On the restorations in the Ducal Palace, see A.C.S., vers. II, series 1, b. 322; for restorations at the Accademia between 1895 and 1898: vers. II, series 1, b. 343 and 346; vers. III, p. 2, b. 209; see also, here, b. 216. On the condition of the works by Ortolano and Bonone da Ferrara, at the time of Mirella Simonetti's restoration, see M. Sarti, in *Un palazzo, un museo*, edited by J. Bentini, Bologna, 1981, pp. 114, 125–126.

48. C. Ricci, *La Madonna degli alberetti*, in "Rassegna d'arte", 1902, pp. 125–126; Venturi, 1911, pp. 134–135; G. Fogolari, *I restauri del Giambellino delle Gallerie dell'Accademia di Venezia*, in "Le arti", 1939–1940, pp. 251–255; Conti, 1982, pp. 140–141; A.C.S., vers. III, p. 2, b. 207.

49. Ferrara, Archivio Storico Comunale, XIX century, p. 1, cartella 2 (report by V. Bigoni, 15 October 1896; noted by L. Moro, 1981–1982) and see Venturi, 1911, p. 46 on the poor restorations of the gallery owner Droghetti. On these restorers, see: E. A. Marescotti, *Cronaca*, in "Rassegna d'Arte", May 1903; E. Camesasca in L. Coletti–E. Camesasca, *La Camera degli Sposi del Mantegna a Mantova*, Milan, 1959, p. 67 (the intervention of Bigoni and Centenari in 1893–94); C. Mossetti, in *Alfredo D'Andrade*, 1981, p. 342; Quartili, 1986–1987; A.C.S., vers. III, p. 2, b. 216 and 219 (Bigoni and Orfei active in Piedmont between 1901–1903); A.C.S., vers. III, p. 2, b. 205: Orfei's restorations in Turin; recollections of the restoration can be found in envelope 226 of the same holding.

50. Bernardi, 1898; V. Bernardi, *La chiesetta di San Bernardino da Siena in Comune di Lallio …*, Begamo, 1900. Valentino Bernardi's letters in the Ricci correspondence, dated from 1904 to 1911. On the Steffanoni see: C. Ricci, *La Pinacoteca di Brera*, Bergamo, 1907, pp. 188–189 (transfers of the figures of female saints by Bergognone in San Satiro); Malaguzzi Valeri, 1908, p. 17; *Catalèg del Museu d'art de Catalunya*, Barcelona, 1936, p. 11; V. Viale, *I dipinti*, Vercelli (Civico Museo F. Borgogna) 1968, pp. 19, 46, 48, 54, 57, 60; C. Mossetti, in *Alfredo d'Andrade*, 1981, pp. 342, 346–348; A. Quazza, in *Bernardino Lanino e il Cinquecento a Vercelli*, Turin, 1986, pp. 270, 272, 276, 279; A.C.S., vers. III, p. 2, busta 173 (Giuseppe Stefanoni's transfers of the *Storie delle Sante Liberata e Faustina*, and other frescos in Como, 1897–1899).

51. C. Bon, entry for *Conti, Cosimo*, in *Dizionario biografico degli italiani, XXVIII*, 1983; *Omaggio a Donatello*, catalogue of the exhibition, Florence, 1986, pp. 115, 433 (removal of the whitewash from the Cavalcanti *Annunciation* by Donatello in 1886, and from the terracotta acquired by the National Museum in 1893); Conti, 1879–82, c. 26 terza num., for Conti the *strappo* technique is acceptable only for works of a purely documentary interest.

52. Ferretti, 1981, p. 178; F. Scalia–C. De Benedictis, *Il Museo Bardini a Firenze*, Milan, 1984, pp. 52–62, illustration on p. 109, n. 3, pp. 227–229.

53. See Ferretti (1981, pp. 164–166) on the dialectics of falsification; pp. 170, 187–189 on Ioni; pp. 168–169 on Cavenaghi. The figure of Ioni, in comparison to the usual figures of copyist and imitator of Sienese panels which are easily identifiable as such, becomes more interesting thanks to the recent documents which have emerged permitting Colin Simpson (*Artful Partners*, New York 1986) to recognize in Ioni the restorer who in 1899 intervened on the Gardner *Annunciation* (pp. 88–89) by Piermatteo d'Amelia, who turned a Baldovinetti into a Pier Francesco Fiorentino which then passed to the National Gallery in Washington (p. 184), and who owned and probably restored the two fragments of Fra Angelico's *Annunciation* (p. 194) in the Ford Collection in Detroit. Riccardo Nobili (*The Gentle Art of Faking*; London, 1922) gives a rich panorama in which one still sees the constants pertaining to the nineteenth century, but which already reflects the situation at the beginning of the twentieth century.

54. A.C.S., vers. II, p. I, b. 77, fasc. 1373/1 (Luigi Grassi's intervention on Titian's *Venus* in 1895); vers. III, p. 2, b. 249 (Ridolfi's letter of 17 October 1897 on Grassi, and the work he was carrying out); in 1906, he would buy the two shutters by Merlozzo da Forlì in the Uffizi (idem., b. 181).

55. On Luigi Cavenaghi (selecting from among the many bibliographic entries that Alain Tarica has been kind enough to indicate to me during his impassioned research on the figure of Cavenaghi as restorer and falsifier), see: A. de Gubernatis, *Dizionario degli artisti italiani viventi*, Florence, 1889, p. 113; E. Verga–U. Nebbia–E. Marzorati, *Milano*, Milan, 1906, pp. 63–69; Malaguzzi Valeri, 1908, pp. 94, 111, 166, 193; L. Callari, in Thieme–Becker, VI, 1912; Venturi, 1912, p. 457; G. Cagnola, *Luigi Cavenaghi*, in "Rassegna d'Arte", 1918, pp. 67–68; G. Frizzoni, *Luigi Cavenaghi*, in "Il Marzocco", 21 April 1918; E. Modigliani, obituary in *Cronaca delle belle arti*, supplement to the "Bollettino d'Arte", 1918, pp. 37–39; G. Frizzoni, *Luigi Cavenaghi e i maestri antichi*, in "La Nuova Antologia", 1 January 1919, pp. 94–103; C. Ricci, entry for *Cavenaghi, Luigi*, in *Enciclopedia*

italiana, IX, 1931; A. Lancellotti, *Centenari*, in "La Nuova Antologia", December 1945, pp. 424–425; B. Berenson, *Estetica, etica e storia delle arti della rappresentazione visiva*, Florence, 1948, pp. 424–425; G. Rosso del Brenno, entry for *Cavenaghi, Luigi* in *Dizionario biografico degli italiani*, XXIII, Rome, 1979; Conti, 1981, pp. 95–97; Ferretti, 1981, p. 168; Anderson, 1987, pp. 118, 125. Many of Cavenaghi's restorations, which fortunately are still in existence, are referred to by Malaguzzi Valeri, 1908, and in A. Mottola Molfino–M. Natale, *Museo Poldi-Pezzoli. Dipinti*, Milan, 1982.

From among Cavenaghi's publications, see: *I dipinti di Boscoreale e la loro tecnica*, in "Rassegna d'Arte", 1901, pp. 5–7; *Antichi affreschi nel Duomo di Atri*, in Bollettino d'Arte", 1907, n. 3, pp. 14–18; *Le malattie delle pitture e la loro cura*, in "la Lettura", 1908, pp. 903–912; *Relazione sul consolidamento eseguito al dipinto nel MCVIII*, in L. Beltrami, *Vicende del Cenacolo vinciano*, Milan, 1908, pp. 321–323; in "Raccolta vinciana", 1908–1909, pp. 95–103); Cavenaghi, 1912.

56. The Madonna in the National Gallery can be identified as n. 782; see Secco-Suardo, 1894, ed. cit., p. 460. The restorations for Layard go back to 1880–1881, and they involved the Jacometto Veneziano, and two other paintings which had already received the attentions of Pinti: Bartolomeo Montagna's *Three Saints* and the *Adoration of the Magi* attributed to Gentile Bellini; see G. Frizzoni, 1919 op. cit., p. 96; A.C.S., div. I, 1916–1919, b. 475.

57. G. Frizzoni, *Gli affreschi di S. Cecilia in Bologna*, in "Il Buonarroti", July 1876, p. 125; A.C.S., deposit I, b. 476, see note 9, p. 355; in March 1877, Cavenaghi had moved on from the Camera degli Sposi to work on other restorations, and Knoller's retouchings remained on the *Incontro col cardinale*. See Cavenaghi, 1912, p. 497, for his opposition to Bertolli's wholesale (*a campitura*) retouchings.

58. Cavenaghi, 1912, p. 490; Marconi–Moschini, 1955, p. 25; Conti, 1982, p. 136 and note 17; for the documentation, see A.C.S., vers. I, b. 355 (fasc. 246/I) and 605; vers. II, p. I, b. 346.

59. G. Frizzoni, *La Galleria Morelli in Bergamo*, Bergamo, 1892, p. 33; F. Zeri–F. Rossi, *La raccolta Morelli nell'Accademia Carrara*, Bergamo, 1986, p. 128.

60. Secco-Suardo, 1894, ed. cit., pp. 403–404; Cavenaghi, 1912, p. 497; E. Modigliani, *Il ritratto del Perugino della Galleria Borghese*, in "L' Arte", 1912, p. 70.

61. On Crivelli's *Deposition* see: H. Tietze, *Genuine and False*, New York, 1948, pp. 62–63; Ferretti, 1981, pp. 168–169; the two panels were restored once more at the Istituto Centrale di Restauro, and exhibited in 1942; see C. Brandi, in *Mostra dei dipinti di Antonello da Messina*, Rome, 1942; on their vicissitudes, see *Antonello da Messina*, catalogue of the exhibition, Messina, 1981–82, pp. 146, 150.

62. H. P. Horne, *Alessandro Filipepi Commonly Called Sandro Botticelli*, London, 1908; G. Frizzoni, 1919, op. cit.; R. Longhi, *Il carteggio Morelli-Richter*, in "Paragone", n. 137, 1961, p. 54; in *Opere complete*, XIII, Florence, 1985, p. 220; C. Simpson, *Artful Partners*, New York, 1986, p. 86; A.C.S., vers. III, p. 2, b. 246.

63. L. Cavenaghi, *Relazione*, cit., 1908; Cavenaghi, 1912, p. 495; G. Frizzoni, 1919 cit., p. 99; *Mostra di Bernardino Luini*, catalogue, Como, 1953, p. 40; S. Matalon–P. Brambilla Barcillon, in *Donato Bramante, gli uomini d'arme*, "Quaderni di Brera", n. 3, Florence, 1977, p. 20.

64. *Raffaello a Brescia. Echi e presenze*, catalogue of the exhibition, Brescia, 1986, pp. 15–31; for the history of the fragments of the Pala di San Nicola da Tolentino, see S. Béguin, in *Raphael*, 1983, pp. 69–75.

65. *Per alcuni restauri di quadri della Galleria degli Uffizi*, in "Bollettino d'Arte", 1910, pp. 69–77. The events with all the repercussions in the press and the highly interesting figure of Otto Vermehren, father of Augustus, the restorer who was to play such an important role *vis à vis* the works in the Florentine gallery, have recently been pieced together by Caterina Caneva (*I "lavati" degli Uffizi*, in "Antichità viva", 1986, n. 1, pp. 34–40). On Vermehren see also A.C.S., vers. I, p. 1, b. 77, fasc. 1373/1–2 (1894; a request for work, in which he declared himself a pupil of Aloïs Hauser "the foremost restorer in Germany"), vers. III, p. 2, b. 181 (cleaning of Lorenzo Costa's *Saint Sebastian* after its acquisition by the Uffizi in 1905); div. I, 1908–1912, b. 41 (he restored Dosso Dossi's *Nymph and Satyr* in the Pitti, in 1908). One of his letters dated 9 October 1911 in the Ricci correspondence in the Classense Library in Ravenna refers to his restoration of Baldovinetti's panel which had just been rediscovered by Horne in S. Ambrogio, and speaks of his difficulties in adapting to both the remuneration and the delays in payment when working for the State.

66. *Cronaca delle belle arti*, in "Bollettino d'Arte", 1907, n. 8, p. 31; Paolucci, 1966, p. 15; A.C.S.; div. I, 1908–1912, b. 42.

67. The figure of Ricci is sometimes evoked with nostalgia, especially by civil servants in the *soprintendenza* who admired his indisputable qualities as an organizer; his many reports are focused on admirably in *In memoria di Corrado Ricci*, Rome, 1935 (one should also, however, see the most conspicuous lacunae in a negative light); for a profile of the figure from the point of view of one sympathizing with Adolfo Venturi, and with the teachers who were his pupils, see Conti, 1983, pp. 22–27.

Final essay: "A serene vision of the relationship between material and image"

Massimo Ferretti

> *"I confess that I love the conservation of buildings,*
> *and especially of the most ancient,*
> *which must be the best possible evidence*
> *of the strength of which human nature is capable,*
> *which in itself is so fragile and so transient, in this world."*
>
> Pietro Giordani

In 1973, when this book was published for the first time, its author was only twenty-two. When it was enlarged, trimmed here and there, made both more compact and more fluent, he was forty-two years old. This biographical material is evidence of the astonishing precocity and the no less precocious didactic maturity of Alessandro Conti (Florence 1946–Siena 1994); I use the word didactic because, in its definitive version, to those who witnessed it, this book is indissolubly linked to the great work carried out with his students at the University of Bologna.

It was Longhi who was at the root of it all. "This book was the wish of Roberto Longhi; he set out its broad editorial outlines, and followed it with great attention to detail and youthful enthusiasm over a period of some years before his death": the opening phrase of the anonymous editorial introduction of 1973. The author echoed this in the acknowledgements at the end of the book: "Roberto Longhi ... thought of entrusting me with a work on the history of restoration, with the specific intent of accompanying it with a text written by himself as an introduction". The promise was kept. Antonio Boschetto (Longhi's trusted editorial collaborator, and probably the author of that note, as well as guide for the young author) took charge of publishing the notes taken during and after the 1956 Paris conference on *Problems of interpretation and problems of conservation* (*Problemi di lettura e problemi di conservazione*).[1] Longhi's teaching showed itself in its most direct form, "spoken", with that typical discursive rhythm which regulated the pace of the succeeding slides. And it is one of Longhi's examples, that of the *Kress Madonna* by Bartolomeo Vivarini, gradually freed from all its repainting which had completely altered the style of its appearance, which would provide the cover of the book. The true identity of its author, despite the indication "essay by Roberto Longhi" (referring precisely to that unpublished lecture, although lacking any form of introduction), was clear. A double signature? And, perhaps, one of them apocryphal? Rather, Longhi's name makes one think of the signature of the Master on a painting executed in the workshop, under his strict supervision.

It is clear that the 1973 frontispiece reflected a preoccupation which occupied more and more of Longhi's attention with the passing years. Already as a young man, using a title which seems to be the title of a painting somewhere between the Metaphysical painters and the twentieth century, *La toilette di Sabina*, he had shown himself to be against the principle of removal of layers of historical importance, against the "obsessions of restoration".[2] A more purposeful attention to these questions and their history began with the Second World War, and would recur in the years that followed. The war was not only a chronological reference, it was the wound that, for Longhi as it was for other art historians, conditioned the very terms of what they understood by restoration and preventive conservation.

Antonio Bertolucci provides good evidence of these concerns. In 1963, Longhi's ex-pupil attempted an interview with the master. He quickly realized how difficult it would be to keep the interview running along the pre-arranged lines. With one exception: "where it is always possible to keep hold of Longhi, is on the subject of the conservation of our cultural heritage". (Unfortunately, the particular occasion was the restoration of the cupola of San Giovanni in Parma, which Longhi approved of; as he had also made himself the champion of the *strappo* of frescos, a practice which today survives mostly as a pretext for expenditure.[3]) Bertolucci therefore noted: "How loquacious Longhi becomes if he has to speak of *intonaco*, bricks, infiltration of water, etc. The frail physical nature of those sublimely spiritual objects which are works of art, their transience, profoundly moves him, and then, in order to ward off that dreadful thing which might be their end, he further sharpens his intellect on matters pertaining to carpentry and masonry, or the micro-chemistry of pigments and varnishes".[4]

It is true that the first idea for this book, however incomplete, does indeed go back to Longhi, writing in 1940: "Unfortunately, the history of restoration is one of few benefits and huge injuries; and, if one were to place statistically the causes of the loss of works of art on a scale over time, after the wear of centuries with all their cataclysms, wars and then iconoclasm, restoration would come a close fourth. That modern criticism of art has resulted in the progress of the techniques of restoration is certain; in fact, if one were to compare that statistic with past epochs, one could set against it a very fine book which would re-evoke the successes obtained in the last century, and the works which have solemnly been brought back from history and taste".[5]

And again, many years later, in the editorial of "Paragone" which took its cue from the Florentine exhibition of detached frescos, transforming itself into that historiographic trail of those responsible for the detachment of frescos (the *estrattisti*) which would become fundamental for Conti, Robert Longhi made the following observation: "we are talking of a history which is already long, and which it would be profitable to run through and look into in more detail [...]. I think it would make a very fine book (let us hope that some young person may do it)".[6]

Several years went by before Longhi found the young man to whom he could entrust such a book. It was not one of his university students who took it on (in 1970, having reached the appropriate age, Longhi had retired from university teaching). Alessandro Conti became one of his students in Via Fortini, the house in which his books and pictures can still be found. As far as I can work out, he was introduced by Giovanni Previtali, who Longhi had met at the University of Florence. Previtali, a communist, was a natural focal point for a student such as Conti, who was socially anomalous (during this period it was still young ladies from good families who would qualify with a degree in the history of art), but their closeness was consolidated by their shared passions in the figurative arts. It is true that Conti would be one of the few art historians of his generation with the capacity to move across the centuries, from miniatures to gardens, from goldsmithery to sculpture, from the social themes of art (the image of the artist) to those of collectionism; but still, the miniatures and painting of the thirteenth and fourteenth centuries would always hold a privileged place.

In this also, we can see a Longhian inheritance, and the mark of a generation. To the generation of students growing up in the 1950s and 1960s, during the time he was drawing close once again to his first teacher, Toesca, Longhi had repeatedly stated that the fourteenth century, and its paintings, was "perhaps the greatest century for our art".[7] On this subject, Conti was reflecting something which was even more specifically associated with Previtali. It had been Previtali in his *Fortuna dei primitivi*, travelling back to the earliest period of Italian art, in a lay and rational spirit, who had reawakened interest in this period. While still a student, Conti had collaborated in the preparation of Previtali's monograph on *Giotto e la sua bottega*, and maybe this was his first "workshop" as an art historian. In Previtali's *Giotto*, there was not the slightest whiff of spiritualism. Giotto had indeed been a "Guelf", as shown by the social and economic history [of the times], and Giotto had been part of this economic and social dimension. However, in order to see this, it had been necessary to look with "lay" eyes, or rather, through the eyes of historical materialism; although it should immediately be said that there was no doctrinarian element in this repositioning of Giotto within the organization of his productive output: the figurative evidence from his paintings always took precedence. It has been necessary to refer to the idea of the painting of the "Early Masters" within which Conti came to maturity so quickly because, even in the more stagnant moments in Tuscan thirteenth-century art, the expressiveness of those paintings always relied on the use of good materials, on the utmost craftsmanship, on all those aspects (frames, supports, etc.) which would become the object of later removals, and not simply in a Freudian sense. So, his special attention for that moment in the history of art was at one with his systematic curiosity as to the choices made in the use and handling of materials, the transformations undergone [by the work of art] and the history of conservation.

Behind all this, there was of course the Longhi we find in *Qualità e industria in Taddeo Gaddi* (Quality and industry in Taddeo Gaddi) or *Una cornice per Bonifacio Bembo* (A frame for Bonifacio Bembo); but for Conti, history of art had come long before Longhi, so that he made absolutely no effort to write as Longhi did. His deskmate at the Liceo remembers Conti's "almost furious and devouring dedication to art and the history of art, which were so typical of his character, and which made him even in those early days, because of the vast scope of his knowledge, a master able to enchant and transmit to others his passion for the object of his passion".[8]

And one should also bear in mind what we read on page 313 of this volume, with reference to the Bardi Chapel in Santa Croce: "[Bianchi] had patinated these pictures, lowering them in tone which helped the integrations merge with the original, as all will remember who saw the paintings before Leonetto Tintori's restoration". He could not have been more than eleven, in order to have this memory. He did not brag, and those who felt they had an equally precocious interest in the figurative arts, knowing him at the age of twenty and beginning to accompany him round churches and museums, would be surprised by the way his attention would always, and instantly, be drawn to the material signs of conservation.

With the exception (as always) of an adolescent facility in drawing, which (as is almost always the case) would not be cultivated, I believe that at the root of such a precocious passion was the discovery of the city, his own city. He never did anything to lead one to think this, and although he was often ironic, if not completely intolerant, with regard to "Florentinity", Conti was passionately tied to Florence. In any case, that history of art should begin to speak to him through the shapes and forms of the city he lived in, in the museums in which he was at home every Sunday (when entry was free), had all the more immediacy, or popularity in the real sense of the word. And if one should happen to speak of this in the past tense, it is because with the passing of one or two generations, the culture industry has succeeded in interposing its own less spontaneous filters, with its exhibitions and other ritualistic obligations, so that at times one almost has the impression of having lived through an anthropological mutation.

Later, Conti would take part in art-historical research "in the field", the aspect of recent historiography of art which was the most originally Italian. He carried out a series of research projects in the zone of Figline Valdarno, and co-ordinated and partly wrote a guide to the *Dintorni di Firenze* (The surroundings of Florence), a guide which was almost the exact opposite of those compilations prepared in a library.[9] Of course, on such occasions his links with older friends, masters from more recent generations (Castelnuovo, Romano, Toscano, as well as Bellosi), become more evident. But his way of questioning objects remained that of his early years: the sense of the link between objects and place, or the relationship between centre and periphery, between Florence and Figline, between Florence and Rignano, spoke as powerfully in the archival papers as in the objects dispersed in the churches in the countryside. It was not by chance that the humble labour of a guidebook (which in reality is the great eighteenth-century precedent for art-historical knowledge) was not that of the city expropriated by the tourist industry, but of places which he had got to know in his boyhood wanderings on a bicycle, as a boy, interested more in the history of art than in the bicycle (an object of devotion in the family, just as in popular tradition throughout Tuscany). I have always felt that it was his uncle Leo who had directed his enthusiasm for the history of art towards useful reading: Leonardo Mattioli, the graphic designer to whom we owe some of the finest bookcovers to come out of Florence, in the last period in which Florence was a great publishing centre.[10]

The 1966 flood, a ruinous moment also for Florentine publishers, confronted the twenty-year-old Conti with the physical reality of works of art, bringing him into contact with restorers and laboratories. In the memory of Paola Barocchi, Conti has remained "the young art historian" prepared to raise the alarm with regard to the fate of Cimabue's *Crucifix*.[11] It is this which gave birth to his first important publication: the identification of the paintings which were flood damaged in 1333 and 1557. At twenty-two he made his debut in "Paragone", in answer to a solicitation by Longhi in an earlier edition of the publication dedicated to the flood and the policies of conservation. And thus was born the book which would see the light five years later, the book which Longhi had imagined so many years before.

In the meantime, as a result of the rather stormy period within the Institute of History of Art of the University of Florence, Previtali had finished up by teaching in Messina and Conti went to take his degree in Bologna under Francesco Arcangeli, who had only recently entered the arena of university teaching. He went there on the advice of Longhi, who had gone as far as to warn him about those who he called *"polpetta"* (another example of supreme lexical mimetism). The alternative, had he remained in Florence, would have been to take his degree with Emanuele Casamassima: that is, to write a thesis on the history of the miniature (the 1981 book on *La Miniatura bolognese. Scuole e botteghe, 1270–1340* had deep roots). The Bolognese thesis was concerned with the very theme of the research which many years previously Longhi had wished for. Its subject was *Gli estrat-tisti. Precisazioni e problemi sull'origine del trasporto dei dipinti murali.*[i] Although Arcangeli probably did not have simply to submit to the choice of his Florentine undergraduate (to a fellow student he had assigned a thesis on the "*stacco a massello*" of the frescos which were subsequently moved to the Certosa di Bologna), the thesis was explicitly understood to be directed towards this book, which had already been commissioned. Having received his degree, already bearing the physiognomy of a researcher, Conti might have seemed to have been less influenced by Arcangeli than the rest of us. But I think that the teaching of that unforgettable man, used to looking at paintings in artists' studios, over time came to have an influence on the student interested in restoration; especially in the last years, when Conti turned to look more closely at the material nature, the technical choices made by contemporary painters, and, when speaking of varnishes, writing: "contemporary painting teaches you to appreciate the relationship between colour, gloss and surface, which a varnish is not always able to preserve".

Even in the two years following his degree, when he won the postgraduate award to the Scuola Normale di Pisa where he had the guidance of Paola Barocchi, the labour of this book coincided with a "scholastic" itinerary. In fact, that became another decisive factor in the maturing of this history of restoration, tied of course to the material evidence which had survived (whatever its form) but also to the ancient literature on art. In the interweaving of written information and material evidence, the history of restoration became a decisive articulation of the idea of a history of art criticism, expressing itself outside the limitations of theoretical pigeonholes, which Longhi had set in his *Proposte* in 1950.

Should this book then be entirely inscribed under the great name of Longhi? First of all, it would be quite easy to show that Conti never subscribed, either in this book or in any other, to Longhi's recommendations for a systematic campaign to detach frescos from their original supports (that obsession with preserving the most important works in a kind of Noah's ark, which was so strong in the generation which had witnessed the destruction of the Second World War). Rather, if it were possible to distinguish the different stages of Longhi's intellectual interests in the succession of different generations of students, then Conti, in this first book, could be seen to reflect suggestions of his *maggior maestro*,[ii] but through his own energy. Longhi, as we have already said, in that student arriving to him out of season, found himself guiding an intellect which was already very much alive; and an intellect which looked to be explicitly anti-idealistic, adhering to the physical presence of works of art. It seems natural that he should have found greater encouragement in the empiricism of one (Longhi) who had written: "the original of a figurative text is always a single example: an 'object' which has its own material, corporeal existence, and – because of this – is victim to all the vicissitudes of time",[12] rather than in the greater theoretical approach to the problems of restoration, with its distinctions between "extrachronological moment of the *time* that is enclosed in the rhythmic consonance" (true history of art), and the "the history of *chronological time*, which gathers the finished and immutable work of art into its flow" (a history of taste, with the relative "the fortunes and misfortunes, over the centuries,

---

[i]The *estrattisti.* Clarifications and problems on the origins of the transfer of mural paintings.
[ii]An allusion which all Italian readers would understand: Virgil was Dante's "*maggior maestro*" (literally greater master), who was his guide through the circles of hell, in the *Inferno.*

of Giotto or Raphael").[13] History of art and history of taste seemed in fact to depend on the same evidence, in which they were made one.

I am thinking of the proofs of the first edition of *Storia del restauro* (the author was doing his military service, so I was lending a hand). There were sections which had been cut at the last minute, because the text exceeded the word limit. Even though texts and facts which had been gathered with great effort were abbreviated, the book was not changed radically, and in fact was reprinted in that same format. But it was only the suggestion of a new edition, in 1988, which allowed a reconsideration of its structure.

In the interim, Conti had already been teaching *"Storia e tecnica del restauro"* (History and practice of restoration) for some years at the University of Bologna (DAMS course[iii]). He had landed the post not yet thirty, and at thirty-five was awarded a full professorship, remaining for a considerable length of time the youngest within the disciplines related to art or history. The environment was still lively: it suited him. Or rather, he felt at home with some of his colleagues and with the more motivated of his students, especially the under-graduates. In order to prepare the new edition of *The History of Restoration* he asked for a year off, but the work had been prepared over a period of fifteen years, teaching and super-vising theses. When the book appeared, Conti had just moved to the Università Statale di Milano, where he taught "History of Modern Art". The subsequent move to the University of Siena and to the teaching of "History of Art Criticism" was mostly linked to the illness which little by little brought his life to an end at the age of forty-six, without having suc-ceeded in stopping him from working: which he did, right to the end.

Longhi's essay was no longer present in the second edition: by then both the author and the book were standing on their own two feet. The only mention of the previous work was on the reverse of the dustjacket. In general, in similar situations, the author advises that the previous edition (tied to a particular moment in time, etc.) really needed to be rewrit-ten, but that one was only able to make some slight alterations, adding a "hand" or two of bibliographic varnish. Because, as is well known, after publication a book belongs not only to the author, but also to the readers. Alessandro Conti was sufficiently narcissistic to exclude any suggestion that "that book" was not, first of all "his" book, and also to put it in perspective, at a certain distance. He used it as a first draft on which he carried on work-ing. Therefore, it was never a book completely different from the first one, but nor was it the same, notwithstanding the similarity in the titles and the different sections, often left unchanged. It was a polished, more accomplished book, and not only because of the two final chapters which he added, bringing the chronological arc nearer to our time: a consid-erable addition, almost a third of the whole. The change also affected the form, and by that I do not just mean the writing, but also the organization, the interlinking of the argument. This argument now had the benefit of the wide-ranging didactic approval received by the first edition, which the author now returned to with a myriad of small cuts, adjustments, moves and final touches. He mostly concentrated on the introductions and on the articu-lating joins, seeking additional synthesis and greater efficacy of argument. He translated and often lightened the flow of the quotations, respecting, however, the integrity of those which bore an overwhelming weight of evidence (such as Maratta and Edwards). He did much the same in the restoration reports, with that reciprocal cross-checking between documentary

---

[iii] Discipline dell'Arte, della Musica, dello Spettacolo.

sources and the physical object which remained the fundamental basis of his methodology. Naturally, several things were brought up to date, and new restorations and archival discoveries were also put to good use, but always along the streamlines which make of this book a historiographic construction, and not a *pot-pourri* on the subject.[14] There were frequent references to what had emerged from the Bolognese theses. The bibliography was better articulated, without the commentary which in some instances had accompanied the entries in the first edition. End notes were inserted, in the place of the rather consistent bibliographic elucidations, which had been inserted to provide further elements of information. The notes also included references to the first edition, and this remains an important source for certain aspects of research.

What becomes more explicit in the new shape taken by the book is the importance of eighteenth-century materialism as the turning point [in the history of the subject]. It would be well to mark page 221, which was added both to recapitulate and to introduce the two new final chapters: "Those who regularly consult eighteenth-century texts or, referring to these sources turn to examine the works of these masters, will notice the particular concern shown towards the material aspects of the work and its technique, seen as elements which are intrinsic to the very nature of the painting; it is a serene vision of the relationship between materials and the image, which was unique and perhaps can never again be repeated. The nineteenth century did not lose this concern, but the Romantic cult of the will combined with an idealistic vision of art as material expression of thought, meant that techniques were considered increasingly as instruments [to an end] ...."

It was already the case with the first edition that an extract from the programmatic preface to the *Encyclopédie* corresponded to a fundamental passage in the book; but that same passage now had a counterweight in the considerations on Carlo Fea, who had drafted the Pacca edict which, because of a certain seasonal optimism, was running the risk of being considered the work of a Jacobin. However, the dialectic tension was treated lightly, and not allowed to obscure the structure of the information given: in other words, there was no ideological distortion.

On one occasion, I happened to remind Conti of a passage in which Pietro Giordani speaks, using expressions reminiscent of Leopardi, of conservation and restoration as of a link binding men and generations [through time] against the destructive force of Nature.[15]

I had read the passage in the Giordani anthology of the "Carducciana", reprinted with an introduction by Sebastiano Timpanaro, in which it was noted, however, that the old anthologist had devoted too many pages to the subject of art. But how could one ask of him an understanding of Neo-classical taste, if such prejudices were also prevalent amongst art-historians? Alessandro immediately established that I should be thinking of an essay on materialism and antimaterialism, or something similar, in the history of restoration. I do not know why he did not say that he should be writing such an essay, but I can imagine the reason. What interested him most, rather than the ideological aspects of the question, was the direct recognition of that "serene relationship between material and image" which had affirmed itself in the eighteenth century, on the works of art themselves. Confronted with the inextricable entanglement which the objects of art history form with their physical entity in posterity, Brandi's articulation between "*istanza storica*" (historical standpoint) and "*istanza estetica*" (aesthetic standpoint) is undoubtedly an elegant conceptualization of the problem, but it becomes dangerous in the hands of people who lean too heavily on binary shortcuts [to problems].[16] Conti preferred to insist on the fact that each process through which the work of art succeeds in surviving its various original functions implies a process of selection, the making of an aesthetic choice.

Between the two editions, Conti had continued to involve himself with techniques, materials, conservation and cleanings, and he continued afterwards as well. Unless I have miscalculated, a good third of his publications (which are numerous!) are devoted to restoration or similar subjects.[17] It is not simply a question of numbers. Indeed, it would be senseless to keep apart this third of his output because the particular field of study which was defining itself (largely thanks to this book) as the history of restoration was not seen by him as something distinct to be cut out of a larger field of research: for him, it was a more direct way of being an art-historian. In order to gather the facts for such a history, one would need to make use of not only the figurative elements, but also the historical evidence, with its particular vocabulary.

In the years between the first and second editions what had also grown, and to an astonishing degree, was the symbolic investment in restorations, so that any opinion expressed on a particular cleaning in no time at all found itself moving on to much larger fields of battle. There is more than a trace of these differences of opinion in this book. Sometimes, they seem to be the result of a reconsideration of what had been written several years before: the *Madonna di Foligno* "cleaned thoroughly" (*pulita a fondo*) in the first edition, in the second edition becomes "*sgarbatamente pulita*", that is, gracelessly cleaned. But even in the harshness of certain judgements, each case is always considered separately: if the work on the restoration of Raphael's *Saint Cecilia* is considered with attention (*considerato con attenzione*), of another restoration carried out in the same laboratory, he laments in no uncertain terms the "losses" presented with the taste of an "odontological technician rather than a restorer". When it was necessary to disagree, Conti never drew back, and always dissented without any tactical calculation. He would never have done so temperamentally, and would have found it inconceivable that anyone should do so for questions of such importance. It was his principal opponent in the Sistine Chapel controversy, who in the same breath as labelling him as an "individual against cleaning on principle" (which was not true), would add "because he has seen many bad ones, as indeed there are [many]", ending up by naming other examples of destructive cleanings, with great intellectual honesty.[18]

In this aspect also, Conti felt himself to be on the side of Longhi. Longhi who, pressing for a great exhibition of the restorations carried out in the second quarter of the twentieth century (an occasion for inspection, not a parade!), would not allow that "some dirty laundry [...] could have been washed at home"; of Longhi who, with unusual nineteenth-century emphasis, had written: "with holy violence hold back the arm of the restorer".[19] Or who, at the end of the 1956 Paris conference, had confessed: "... restorers! I honour and admire them, but I have no intention of aiding their progress". Longhi's expressions reflect the idea of the restorer as subaltern to the art historian which, at least in the illusions of the latter, was current when the Istituto Centrale di Restauro was founded. This was not a tenable position, without sounding outmoded, in the years that Conti was growing up; he did not, however, think that such a relationship should simply be turned over. What was at stake was not simply the idea of belonging to one "job" rather than another. The demands of both approaches to the work of art had to combine together; not that this was always easy (one could almost say as a rule of thumb: if there was complete harmony, one needed to ask if one approach has not squashed the other). Perhaps, the dedication of the new edition to the memory of a restorer, Memo Galli, one of the friends he listened to most (disagreeing on one or two occasions), was not simply a personal gesture.

It may seem strange to some (let us hope not) that it should be an art historian who always worked within a university who is discussing restoration: but one who would find every possible occasion to go and lecture in churches and museums. The anomaly, if it really is such, would be even more glaring if we think of the book symmetrical to this one, and not only because it is the last, posthumous one, just as this is the first: *Il manuale di restauro* (Manual for restoration).[20] In the *Manuale*, one is not confined to the operational field as the title might suggest, but the attempt is made to link together different fields, different areas of reading, responsibilities right up to the political level, and analyses of a more broadly cultural nature. It is a book against the risks of specialization, against the arrogance of narrow sections of experience (I was thinking of this when I said earlier that Arcangeli's teaching emerged in Conti with time). It is certainly not a book against restoration, but against the pretensions of self-sufficiency of those who are under the illusion of being scientifically exonerated from being part of the broad visual culture in which we are all immersed: to an experience made up of images rather than of matter, of images devoid of a physical body, as though they were a transparent and coloured screen. With regard to Longhi's reproach to restorers, that they "followed a predetermined taste which could not be other than modern taste", the problem has now worsened, not so much in terms of size, but in its very nature. Cruel fate has at least spared Alessandro Conti from hearing the solemn proclamation in the faculty of a new institution, that in "conservation, science has now replaced history" (the same faculty in which, apparently, subjects for research theses have had titles such as "Methods and materials used in the cleaning of museum environments"). The separation between science and history would immediately have labelled it as anti-Enlightenment, as well as far removed from the very essence of conservation. The critical responsibility of those who wish to remove themselves from the dominant spirit of simplification becomes even more difficult, and exact, detailed and correctly structured documentation all the more necessary. And it was he who would censure any personal input to the extent of not even attaching to the new edition of *Storia del restauro* any mention of the updating undertaken; he who would certainly not have welcomed the reminiscences which appear in these pages ended his book with this invitation to a critical understanding, this almost autobiographical confession: "the attention to the technique of paintings and the material qualities of the image often becomes a personal adventure [...] it is essential therefore that we go back to the sources".

Notes

1. The lecture, which was not included in the second edition of the book, will appear in Volume XV of *Opere Complete di Roberto Longhi*, which will contain his unpublished and posthumous material.
2. *La toilette di Sabina, e altre cose* (1919), now in *Scritti giovanili, 1912–1922* ("Opere complete", I), Florence, Sansoni, 1961, pp. 437–440, takes its title from the archaeological conservation of the Roman basilica of Santa Sabina.
3. Later, Conti would forcefully attack (and with some justification) the last of the interventions on the Correggio carried out in Parma by the same restorer: *Diario Correggesco*, in "Ricerche di Storia dell'arte", 13–14, 1981, pp. 105–110. Today the inclination to detach frescos has on the whole come to an end, in fact one detects diametrically opposed risks, over-corrective in their tendency (L. Bellosi, *Come un prato fiorito. Studi sull'arte tardogotica*, Milan, Jaca Books, 2000, p. 11). Bellosi's considerations, dictated by good sense, will not, however,

serve as justification for those who only a few years back had a cycle of frescos detached and transferred in order for them to be sent on exhibition, nor for those who consented to the rolling up of important frescos in restoration studios, where they remained for years, until such time as finance was found for them to be remounted. In this way, the transfer of frescos became a kind of interest-bearing security, suitably index-linked.

4. A. Bertolucci, *Non intervista a Roberto Longhi*, in *Aritmie*, Milan, Garzanti, 1991, p. 165, now in *Opere*, edited by P. Lagazzi and G. Palli Baroni, Milan, Mondadori, 1997, p. 1141 (one should remember that Bertolucci dedicated to Longhi the poem *Gli imbianchini sono artisti*, in which he speaks of manual pleasures and of the quality of everyday things).

5. *Restauri* (1940), now in *Critica d'arte e buongoverno, 1938–1969* ("Opere complete", XIII), Florence, Sansoni, 1985, p. 121.

6. *Per una mostra storica degli "estrattisti" (1957)*, now in *Critica d'arte* …, op. cit., p. 53.

7. This affirmation occurs several times, but I am quoting from *Letteratura artistica e letteratura nazionale* (1952), now in *Critica d'arte* …, op. cit, p. 195. On at least one occasion, Alessandro Conti himself reiterated the same thing, *Il "Maestro di Figline": 1980–1985*, in C. Caneva, editor, *Capolavori a Figline. Cinque anni di restauri*, Florence, Opus Libri, 1986, p. 61, now in *Scritti figlinesi*, edited by A. Natali and P. Pirillo, Florence, Opus Libri, 2001, p. 53 ("maybe the greatest century in Italian painting").

8. V. Valoriani, *Presentazione* ad A. Conti, *Scritti figlinesi* …, op. cit., p. V (in the introduction by Antonio Natali, one can read a friendly and impassioned – but not blind – intellectual evaluation of Alessandro Conti).

9. *I dintorni di Firenze. Arte, storia, paesaggio*, edited by A. Conti, with the collaboration of F. Petrucci, P. Pirillo and G. Ragionieri, notes on the environment by G. Campioni and G. Ferraresi, Florence, La Casa Usher, 1983.

10. There has been a recent exhibition dedicated to his work in Florence and Siena, with a catalogue edited by L. Fontanelli and G. Mattioli, *Leonardo Mattioli. Illustrazione e visual design nella communicazione di cultura*, Florence, Centro Di, 2001.

11. P. Barocchi, *Ricordo di Alessandro Conti*, in "Prospettiva", 73–74, 1994, p. 189.

12. R. Longhi, *Restauri* (1940), op. cit., p. 25.

13. C. Brandi, *Theory of Restoration*, Nardini Editore/Istituto Centrale del Restauro, 2005, p. 62.

14. It is mostly for this reason, with the agreement of the editor, that it was not felt necessary to add any additional up-to-date bibliographic details to this reprinting.

15. P. Giordani *Scritti*, edited by G. Chiarini [1890], new presentation by S. Timpanaro, Florence, Sansoni, 1961, pp. 82–83 (for the judgement on Neo-classical taste, "inevitably old-fashioned", p. XX). The essay reappears, reworked and bearing the title *Giordani, Carducci e Chiarini*, in S. Timpanaro, *Classicismo e illuminismo nell'Ottocento italiano*, Pisa, Nistri–Lischi, 1965, pp. 119–132.

16. A more explicit contradiction of Brandi's two standpoints which he saw in opposition to one another in restoration work was formulated by Conti in the slim volume with the title *Restauro*, Milan, Jaka Books, 1992, p. 14 (a "false dialectic" in that "the historical aspects, and the aesthetic ones, and indeed their distinction, belong to the culture of the individual carrying out the restoration").

17. The list of publications can be found in F. Caglioti, M. Fileti Mazza, U. Parrini, editors, *Ad Alessandro Conti (1946–1994)*, Pisa, Scuola Normale Superiore, pp. XI–XXVI.

18. B. Zanardi, *Conservazione, restauro e tutela. 24 dialoghi*, Milan, Skira, 1999, p. 320 (interview with Gianluigi Colalucci on *Restauro e restauratori*).

19. R. Longhi, *Restauri* (1940), op. cit., pp. 5, 121.

20. *Manuale di restauro*, Turin, Einaudi, 1996 (and 2001). Conti finished writing the book a few days before his death. He had been commissioned and then warmly pressed to write it, by Paolo Fossati, a friend from the Bologna days, also prematurely deceased.

Bibliography

M. Vitruvius Pollio, *De architectura libri decem.*

C. Plinius Secundus, *Naturalis historia.*

1500–1700

M. Michiel, *Notizie di opere di disegno pubblicate e illustrate da D. Jacopo Morelli (c. 1521–1543)*, op. cit., ed. G. Frizzoni, Bologna, 1884.

G. Vasari, *Le vite de' più eccellenti architetti, pittori et scultori italiani*, Florence, 1550.

L. Dolce, *Dialogo della pittura intitolato l'Aretino*, 1557, op. cit., ed. P. Barocchi, 1960, pp. 143–206.

G. Vasari, *Le vite de' più eccellenti pittori, scultori et architettori*, Florence, 1568.

R. Borghini, *Il Riposo*, Florence, 1584.

Carel van Mander, *Der Schilderboek*, Alkmaar, 1604, op. cit. in *Le livre des peintres* (trans. H. Hymans), Paris, 1884.

G. Celio, *Memorie fatte dal sig. Gaspare Celio delli nomi degli artefici delle pitture che sono in alcune chiese, facciate e palazzi di Roma*, Naples, 1638.

G. Baglione, *Le vite de' pittori, scultori et architetti. Dal pontificato di Gregorio XIII del 1572 infino a' tempi di papa Urbano VIII nel 1642*, Rome, 1642.

C. Ridolfi, *Le maraviglie dell'arte*, Venice, 1648.

M. Boschini, *Carta del navegar pitoresco*, Venice, 1660.

G. P. Bellori, *Vite de' pittori, scultori et architetti moderni*, Rome, 1672, op. cit., ed. E. Borea, Turin, 1976.

G. B. Passeri, *Il libro delle vite de' pittori, scultori et architetti*, Rome, 1673.

G. P. Bellori, *Vite inedite* (1672–1696), op. cit., ed. Turin, 1976.

C. C. Malvasia, *Felsina pittrice*, Bologna, 1678, op. cit., ed. Bologna, 1841.

F. Baldinucci, *Notizie de' professori del disegno da Cimabue in qua* (1681–1728), op. cit., ed. Florence, 1845–1847.

C. C. Malvasia, *Le pitture di Bologna*, Bologna, 1686.

C. Celano, *Notitie dell'antico, del bello e del curioso della città di Napoli*, Naples, 1692.

G. P. Bellori, *Descrizione delle immagini dipinte da Raffaelle d'Urbino nelle Camere del Palazzo Apostolico Vaticano*, Rome, 1695.

1720

F. Bonanni, *Trattato sopra la vernice detta comunemente cinese*, Rome.

1728

J. Richardson, *Description de divers fameaux tableaux, dessins, statues, bas-reliefs etc. qui se trouvent en Italie*, in *Traité de la peinture et de la sculpture*, III, Amsterdam.

1730

G. Bottari, introduction and notes to R. Borghini, *Il Riposo*, ed. Florence.

L. Pascoli, *Vite de' pittori, scultori ed architetti moderni*, Rome, 1730–1736.

1733

A. M. Zanetti, *Descrizione di tutte le pubbliche pitture della città di Venezia*, Venice.

1742

B. De Dominici, *Vite de' pittori, scultori e architetti napoletani*, Naples, 1742–1743.

1743

Castelli e ponti di maestro Niccola Zabaglia, Rome.

1753

J. Gautier d'Agoty, *Observations sur la peinture et sur les tableaux anciens et modernes*, Paris.

1754

G. Bottari, *Dialoghi sopra le tre arti del disegno*, Lucca.

L. Crespi, Lettere a Francesco Algarotti (1756), in G. Bottari, *Raccolta di lettere sulla pittura, scultura ed architettura*, Rome, 1754–1773, ed. S. Ticozzi, Milan, 1822–1825, III, pp. 387–417, 419–443.

1758

C. N. Cochin, *Voyage d'Italie*, Paris.

1759

G. Bottari, notes in Vasari, *Le Vite…*, Rome, 1759–1760.

1763

F. Titi, *Descrizione delle pitture, sculture e architetture esposte al pubblico in Roma*, Rome; eds B. Contardi and S. Romano, Florence, 1987.

1768

B. Cavaceppi, *Raccolta d'antiche statue, busti, bassirilievi ed altre sculture restaurate*, Rome.

G. Piacenza, notes to F. Baldinucci, *Notizie…*, Turin, 1768–1820.

1769

B. Cavaceppi, *Raccolta d'antiche statue, teste cognite ed altre sculture antiche*, Rome.

J.-J. de la Lande, *Voyage d'un françois en Italie fait dans les années 1765 et 1766*, Venise, op. cit., ed. Yverdun, 1786–1788.

J. Reynolds, *Discourses on Art*, 1769–1790, op. cit., ed. New Haven–London, 1975.

1772

B. Cavaceppi, *Raccolta d'antiche statue, busti, teste cognite ed altre sculture*, Rome.

1773

Watin, *L'art du peintre, doreur, vernisseur*, 2nd ed., Paris.

1774

A. M. Zanetti (the younger), *Riferte dell'Ispettore Zanetti*, Venice, Archivio di Stato, Inquisitori di Stato, busta 909 (Quadri–Ispezione, inserto miscellanea), 1774–1778.

1775

A. Pasta, *Dell'amoroso e diligente governo dei quadri*, in *Le pitture di Bergamo*, Bergamo; reprinted by R. Longhi, in "Paragone", n. 179, 1964, pp. 48–52.

1778

P. Edwards, Relazioni e minute del 1778, Venice, Biblioteca del Seminario Patriarcale, Ms 787, inserto 7.

P. Edwards, *Riferte ai Provveditori al Sal*, 8 ottobre 1778–7 giugno 1784; Venice, Biblioteca del Seminario Patriarcale, Ms 787, inserto 7.

P. Edwards, *Riferte dell'Ispettore Pietro Edwards*, Venice, Archivio di Stato, Inquisitori di Stato, busta 909 (Quadri–Ispezione, inserto miscellanea), 1778–1792.

1779

G. B. Mengardi, *Riferte dell'Ispettore Mengardi*, Venice, Archivio di Stato, Inquisitori di Stato, busta 909 (Quadri–Ispezione, inserto miscellanea), 1779–1795.

1781

F. Algarotti, *Opere*, Cremona.

1783

A. R. Mengs. *Opere*, ed. Bassano.

J. J. Winckelmann, *Storia delle arti del disegno presso gli antichi*, ed. C. Fea, Rome.

1786

P. Edwards, Relazione presentata ai Provveditori al Sal il 6 aprile 1786, Venice, Biblioteca del Seminario Patriarcale, Ms 787, inserto 7. Include: A-B, catalogo delle opere restaurate dal 1778 al 1785 e dei loro autori; C, sommario delle fedi di collaudo; D, elenco delle opere "rinunciate"; E, elenco delle opere che si potranno escludere dal lavoro di restauro; F, elenco delle opere da restaurare; G, *Dissertazione preliminare al piano di custodia da istituirsi per la possibile preservazione e per il miglior mantenimento delle pubbliche pitture*; H, *Piano pratico per la generale custodia delle pubbliche pitture rassegnato agli Eccellentissimi Signori Provveditori al Sal ed Eccellentissimo Savio Cassier del Collegio in ordine alle commissioni dell'Eccellentissimo Senato 3 marzo 1785*.

1788

[R. Ghelli], *Risposta alla lettera del Sig. Filippo Hackert*, in "Giornale delle belle arti", pp. 266–274, 287–291.

Ph. Hackert, *Lettera a Sua Ecc. il Sig. Cavaliere Hamilton […], sull'uso della vernice nelle pitture*, Naples; reprinted in "Giornale delle belle arti", Rome, pp. 255–261, 263–265; reprinted with preface by R. Ansidei, Perugia; German edition, *Ueber den Gebrauch des Firnis in der Malerei*, Dresden, 1800.

Lettera di G.G.D.R. al Ch. Sig. Filippo Hackert celebre pittore, sul restauro dei quadri e sopra l'uso della vernice su di essi, in "Memorie per le belle arti", pp. 247–248.

1793

L. David, *Rapport sur la suppression de la Commission du Muséum par le citoyen David*, Paris year II [8 dicembre], reprinted in *La Commission*, 1909, pp. 353–361.

J.M. Picault, *Observations sur les inconvenients qui résultent des moyens que l'on employe pour les tableaux que l'on restaure journellement*, in *Observations de Picault […] sur les tableaux de la Republique*, Paris year II; reprinted in "Revue universelle des arts", 1859, IX, pp. 504–524; X pp. 38–47; in "Archives de l'art français", n.s., 1901, pp. 288–297.

1794

L. David, *Second rapport sur la nécessité de la suppression de la Commission du Muséum … par David …*, Paris year II [16 gennaio], reprinted in *La Commission*, 1909, pp. 365–374.

G. Martin, *Avis à la Nation sur la situation du Museum National*, Paris.

1795

P. Brandolese, *Pitture, sculture e architetture di Padova nuovamente descritte*, Padova.

1796

F. Maggiotto, *Riferte dell'Ispettore Maggiotto*, Venice, Archivio di Stato, Inquisitori di Stato, busta 909 (Quadri–Ispezione, inserto miscellanea), 1796–1797.

1803

J. C. Ibbetson, *An Accidence or Gamut of Painting in Oil and Watercolours*, London.

P. F. Tingry, *Traité théorique et pratique sur l'art de faire et d'appliquer les vernis*, Genève.

1806

A. L. Millin, *Dictionnaire des Beaux-Arts*, Paris.

G. Moschini, *Della letteratura veneziana del secolo XVIII*, Venice.

1808

F.-X. de Burtin, *Traité théorique et pratique des connoissances qui sont nécessaires à tout amateur de tableaux*, Paris.

1809

L. Lanzi, *Storia pittorica dell'Italia dal risorgimento delle belle arti fin presso la fine del XVII secolo*, Bassano, 1809, op. cit., ed. M. Capucci, Florence, 1968.

1814

C. Verri, *Saggio elementare sul disegno etc. con alcune avvertenze sull'uso dei colori ad olio*, Milan.

1815

G. Moschini, *Guida per la città di Venezia all'amico delle belle arti*, Venice.

1816

L. Marcucci, *Saggio analitico – chimico sopra i colori minerali*, Rome.

1817

G. Moschini, *Guida per la città di Padova*, Padova.

1818
M. Prunetti, *Saggio pittorico*, Rome.
1826
G. G. De Rossi, *Lettera sopra il restauro di un antica statua di Antinoo e sopra il restauro degli antichi marmi nei tre secoli precedenti il nostro*, in "Nuovo giornale de' letterati", XIII, Pisa, pp. 23–38.
1827
C. Köster, *Über Restaurierung alter Ölgemälde*, Heidelberg.
1829
J. N. Paillot de Montabert, *Traité complet de la peinture*, Paris.
1837
J. Bedotti, *De la restauration des tableaux*, Paris.
1839
F. Agricola, *Alcune osservazioni artistiche fatte dal cavaliere Filippo Agricola […] in occasione di aver tolto l'ingombro della polvere che offuscava i famosi dipinti di Raffaello nelle Camere Vaticane*, Rome.
C. Cattaneo, *Del restauro dei monumenti e della loro conservazione*, in "Il Politecnico", n. 1, pp. 58–66; in *Scritti sulla Lombardia*, Milan, 1971, II, pp. 685–696.
C. de Montalambert, *Du Vandalisme en France, lettre à M. Victor Hugo* (1833), in *Du Vandalisme et du Catholicisme dans l'Art*, Paris, pp. 1–69.
J. D. Passavant, *Raffael* … (1839), op. cit., trans., *Raffaello d'Urbino e il padre suo Giovanni Santi*, Florence, 1882–1891.
1840
G. Giordani, *Cenni sopra diverse pitture staccate dal muro e trasportate su tela*, Bologna.
G. Zeni, *Sul distacco delle pitture a fresco. Lettera di Giuseppe Zeni ad un amico*, Padova, 1840.
1842
F. Fantozzi, *Nuova guida ovvero descrizione storico-critica della città e contorni di Firenze*, Florence.
1843
C. H. Wilson, *Mr. Wilson's Report*, in *Second Report of the Commission on the Fine Arts*, London, pp. 16–40.

1846
W. Dyce, *Observations on Fresco Painting*, in *Sixth Report of the Commission on the Fine Arts*, London, pp. 11–19.
C. L. Eastlake, *Styles and Methods of Painting Suited to the Decoration of Public Buildings*, in *Fifth Report of the Commission on the Fine Arts*, London, pp. 11–25.
E. Förster, *I dipinti nella Cappella di San Giorgio in Padova*, trans. Padova.
M. P. Merrifield, *The Art of Fresco Painting as Practised by the Old Italian and Spanish Masters*, London.
1847
C. L. Eastlake, *Materials for a History of Oil Painting*, London, 1847–1869; facsimile reprint with the title *Methods and Materials of the Great Schools and Masters*, New York, 1960.
1853
S. Horsin-Déon, *De la conservation et restauration des tableaux*, Paris, 1851. *Report from the Select Committee on the National Gallery […], Ordered to be Printed by the House of Commons*, London.
1863
G. B. Cavalcaselle, *Sulla conservazione dei monumenti e degli oggetti d'arte e sulla riforma dell'insegnamento accademico*, in "Rivista dei Comuni italiani"; cit. ed. Rome, 1875.
1864
G. Botti, *Della conservazione delle pitture del Camposanto di Pisa*, Pisa (1st ed. 1857).
P. A. Curti, *Del trasporto dei dipinti antichi e del nuovo metodo di eseguirlo usato dal pittore Alessandro Brison*, in "Il Politecnico", XXI, Milan, pp. 353–369.
G. B. Cavalcaselle–J. A. Crowe, *A New History of Painting in Italy from the Second to the Sixteenth Century*, London, 1864–1866.
1866
U. Forni, *Manuale del pittore restauratore*, Florence.
G. Secco-Suardo, *Manuale ragionato per la parte meccanica dell'arte*

del ristauratore dei dipinti, Milan, op. cit. from *Il restauratore dei dipinti*, ed. Milan, 1927.
E. Viollet-le-Duc, ad vocem *Restauration*, in *Dictionnaire raisonné de l'Architecture Française du XI au XVI siècle*, VIII, Paris, pp. 14–34.
1868
E. Despois, *Vandalisme révolutionnaire. Fondations littéraires, scientifiques et artistiques de la Convention*, Paris.
R. Fulin, *Studi nell'archivio degli Inquisitori di Stato*, Venice.
1869
L. Courajod, *L'Administration des Beaux-Arts au milieu du XVIIIme siècle. La Restauration des tableaux du Roi*, in "Gazette des Beaux-Arts", II, pp. 372–376.
1870
G. Riolo, *Notizia dei restauri delle pitture a mosaico della R. Cappella Palatina in Palermo*, Palermo.
1873
G. U. Valentinis, *La rigenerazione dei dipinti per Pettenkofer*, Udine.
1874
G. U. Valentinis, *Il restauro e la rigenerazione dei dipinti a olio di Massimiliano de Pettenkofer*, Udine.
1876
B. Orsini, *Risposta ad una lettera sull'uso della vernice …*, in "Giornale di erudizione artistica", pp. 248–256; *Si dà conto del ristauro della tavola di Pietro Perugino a chi desidera conservare le altre*, ibid., pp. 300–303.
1877
G. B. Cavalcaselle–J. A. Crowe, *Titian: His Life and Times*, London.
1878
L. Courajod, *La révolution et les musées nationaux*, in "Revue des Questions historiques", XXIII, pp. 488–554; XXIV, 1879, pp. 154–216.
G. Milanesi, notes and commentary to G. Vasari, *Le Vite …*, Florence, 1878–1885.
1879
C. Conti, *Del restauro in generale e dei restauratori*, ms. 280 della Biblioteca degli Uffizi a Florence, datable to 1879–1882 (cfr. Conti, 1973, p. 258).

J. J. Guiffrey, *Restauration des tableaux de Raphael représentant saint Michel et saint Jean par Picault*, in "Nouvelles Archives de l'Art Français", pp. 407–417.

1882
A. Venturi, *La R. Galleria Estense in Modena*, Modena.
G. B. Cavalcaselle–J. A. Crowe, *Raphael: His Life and Works*, London.

1884
C. Boito, *I restauratori*, Florence.

1885
M. Ruggiero, *Storia degli scavi di Ercolano*, Naples.

1886
G. Nicoletti, *Documenti tolti dal Magistrato del sale relativi a restauri di quadri dei palazzi Ducale e di Rialto*, Venice.

1891
G. U. Valentinis, *La riparazione dei dipinti secondo il metodo Pettenkofer*, Udine.

1892
L. Beltrami, *La conservazione dei monumenti nell'ultimo ventennio*, in "La Nuova Antologia", April, pp. 447–470.
A. Conti, *Per l'arte italiana. Lettera a Pasquale Villari*, in "Il Fanfulla della domenica", XIV, n. 8, and as an extract, Rome.
G. U. Valentinis, *Il governo razionale delle pinacoteche desunto dalle teorie e pratiche di Massimiliano dottor Pettenkofer*, Udine.

1894
G. Secco-Suardo, *Il restauratore dei dipinti*, Milan, cit. ed. Milan, 1927; facsimile reprint, Milan, 1979.

1898
V. Bernardi, *Rimozione, consolidamento, ristauro dei dipinti a fresco*, Bergamo (for the exhibition "Esposizione di arte sacra").

1899
F. Engerand, *Inventaire des tableaux du Roi [...] redigé en 1709 et 1710 par Nicolas Bailly*, Paris.

1900
F. Engerand, *Inventaire des tableaux commandés et achetés par la direction des bâtiments du Roi (1709–1792)*, Paris.

1901
T. Turquet de Mayerne, *Pictoria, sculptoria et quae subalternarium artium* (ms dated 1620), in E. Berger, *Quellen für Maltechnik*, IV, München, pp. 100–363.
E. Steinmann, *Die Sixtinische Kapelle*, München, 1901–1905.

1903
A. Riegl, *Der moderne Denkmalkultus, sein Wesen und seine Entstehung*, Wien–Leipzig.

1906
Ufficio Regionale per la conservazione dei Monumenti della Lombardia, *Le vicende del Cenacolo di Leonardo da Vinci nel secolo XIX*, Milan.

1908
F. Malaguzzi Valeri, *Catalogo della R. Pinacoteca di Brera*, Milan.

1909
La Commission du Museum et la création du Musée du Louvre, ed. A. Tuetey and J. Guiffrey, in "Archives de l'Art Français", n.s. C. Lupi, *I restauri delle pitture del Camposanto urbano di Pisa*, in "Rivista d'Arte", pp. 54–59.
R. Papini, *Il deperimento delle pitture murali nel Campo Santo di Pisa*, in "Bollettino d'Arte", pp. 441–457.

1911
A. Venturi, *Memorie autobiografiche*, Milan.

1912
L. Cavenaghi, *Il restauro e la conservazione dei dipinti*, in "Bollettino d'Arte", pp. 488–500.
A. Venturi, *La formazione della Galleria Layard a Venezia*, in "L'Arte", pp. 449–462.

1917
G. Gerola, *La tecnica dei restauri ai mosaici di Ravenna*, in "Atti e memorie della R. Deputazione di Storia Patria per le Romagne", series IV, II, pp. 101–194.
E. Steinmann, *Raffael im Musée Napoléon*, in "Monatshefte für Kunstwissenschaft", X, pp. 8–25.

1926
L. Beltrami, *Giacomo Boni*, Milan.

M. Stübel, *Gemälderestaurierung im XVIII Jahrhundert*, in "Der Cicerone", XVIII, pp. 122–135.

1930
C. Ricci, *Tavole storiche dei mosaici di Ravenna*, Rome, 1930–1937.

1932
E. Tea, *Giacomo Boni nella vita del suo tempo*, Milan.

1937
A. Fogolari, *Lettere pittoriche del Gran principe Ferdinando di Toscana a Niccolò Cassana*, in "Rivista del R. Istituto di archeologia e storia dell'arte", VI, pp. 145–186.

1938
K. Clark, *The Aesthetics of Restoration*, in "Proceedings of the Royal Institution", XXX, pp. 382–397.
R. W. Kennedy, *Alesso Baldovinetti*, New Haven.

1940
R. Longhi, *Restauri*, in "La critica d'arte", pp. 121–128; in *Opere complete*, XIII, Florence, 1985, pp. 119–127.

1944
D. Redig de Campos–B. Biagetti, *Il Giudizio Universale di Michelangelo*, Rome.

1948
M. Cagiano de Azevedo, *Il gusto nel restauro delle opere d'arte antiche*, Rome.
R. Longhi, *"Buongoverno": una situazione grave*, in "Proporzioni", pp. 185–188; in *Opere complete*, XIII, Florence, 1985, pp. 1–5.

1950
P. Cellini, *Una Madonna molto antica*, in "Proporzioni", pp. 1–6.
P. Marot, *Recherches sur les origines de la transposition de la peinture en France*, in "Annales de l'Est", n. 4, pp. 241–283.
L. Ponticelli, *I restauri ai mosaici del Battistero di Firenze*, in "Commentari", pp. 121–129, 187–189, 247–250; 1951, pp. 51–55.

1952
M. Cagiano de Azevedo, *Conservazione e restauro presso i greci e i romani*, in "Bollettino dell'Istituto

Centrale di Restauro", IX–X, pp. 53–60.

1953

U. Procacci, *Distacco di due tempere duecentesche sovrapposte*, in "Bollettino d'Arte", pp. 31–33.

1955

C. Brandi, *Chiarimenti sul Buon governo di Ambrogio Lorenzetti*, in "Bollettino dell'Istituto Centrale di Restauro", n. 21–22, pp. 3–10 ed. in "Bollettino d'Arte", pp. 119–123.

S. Marconi Moschini, *Gallerie dell'Accademia di Venezia. Opere d'arte dei secoli XIV e XV*, Rome.

1956

Y. Bruand, *La restauration des Sculptures du Cardinal Ludovisi*, in "Mélanges de l'Ecole Française de Rome", LXVIII, pp. 397–418.

G. Emile-Mâle, *Jean-Baptiste Pierre Lebrun (1748–1813). Son rôle dans l'histoire de la restauration des tableaux du Louvre*, in "Mémoires de Paris et lle-de-France", VIII, pp. 371–417.

G. Mancini, *Considerazioni sulla pittura (1614–1621)*, ed. A. Marucchi–L. Salerno, Rome.

U. Procacci, *Il Vasari e la conservazione degli affreschi della Cappella Brancacci al Carmine e della Trinità in Santa Maria Novella*, in *Scritti in onore di Lionello Venturi*, Rome, I, pp. 211–222.

1957

R. Longhi, *Per una mostra storica degli estrattisti*, in "Paragone", n. 91, pp. 3–8; in *Opere complete*, XIII, Florence, 1985, pp. 53–58.

1959

S. Marconi–Moschini, *Revisione di due Tintoretto*, in "Bollettino d'Arte", pp. 69–81.

L Réau, *Histoire du vandalisme – Les monuments détruits de l'art français*, Paris.

1960

P. Barocchi (edited by), *Trattati d'arte del Cinquecento fra manierismo e controriforma*, Bari, 1960–1962.

M. Pepe, ad vocem *Albacini, Carlo*, in *Dizionario biografico degli italiani*, I, Rome.

Pitture murali nel Veneto, catalogue of the exhibition, Venice.

R. Longhi, *Problemi di lettura e problemi di conservazione*, course lectures, Università di Firenze, academic year 1960/61.

1962

E. H. Gombrich, *Dark Varnishes: Variations on a Theme from Pliny*, in "The Burlington Magazine", pp. 51–55.

S. Howard, *Some Eighteenth-Century Restorations of Myron's "Discobolos"*, in "Journal of the Courtauld and Warburg Institutes", pp. 330–334.

O. Kurz, *Varnishes, Tinted Varnishes and Patina*, in "The Burlington Magazine", pp. 56–59.

D. Mahon, *Miscellanea for the Cleaning Controversy*, in "The Burlington Magazine", pp. 460–470.

S. Marconi Moschini, *Gallerie dell'Accademia di Venezia. Opere d'arte del secolo XVI*, Rome.

M. Muraro, *Notes on Traditional Methods of Cleaning Pictures in Venice and Florence*, in "The Burlington Magazine", pp. 475–477.

J. Plesters, *Dark Varnishes. Some Further Comments*, in "The Burlington Magazine", pp. 452–460.

S. Rees Jones, *Science and the Art of Picture Cleaning*, in "The Burlington Magazine", pp. 60–62.

1963

C. Brandi, *Teoria del restauro*, Rome; Turin, 1977.

F. Haskell, *Patrons and Painters*, London.

R. Longhi, *Piero della Francesca*, op. cit. Florence.

1964

G. Emile-Mâle, *Le séjour à Paris de 1794 à 1815 de célèbres tableaux de Rubens. Quelques documents inédits*, in "Bulletin de l'Institut Royal du Patrimonie Artistique", VII, Brussels, pp. 153–171.

J. Guillerme, *L'atelier du temps*, Paris.

G. Previtali, *La fortuna dei primitivi dal Vasari ai neoclassici*, Turin.

1965

F. Abbate, *Idee cinquecentesche e seicentesche sul restauro; Molano,*

Marino, Celio, Baldinucci, in "Paragone", n. 181, pp. 35–51.

M. Cagiano de Azevedo, ad vocem *Restauro in Enciclopedia dell'Arte Antica*, VI, Rome, pp. 655–657.

L. Marcucci, *Gallerie Nazionali di Firenze. I dipinti toscani del secolo XIV*, Rome.

1967

R. H. Marijnissen, *Degradation, conservation et restauration de l'oeuvre d'art*, Brussels.

G. Matthiae, *Mosaici medievali delle chiese di Roma*, Rome.

1968

A. Conti, *Quadri alluvionati*, in "Paragone", n. 223, pp. 3–22, n. 225, pp. 3–27.

S. Howard, *Pulling Herakles' Leg*, in *Festschrift Ulrich Middeldorf*, Berlin, pp. 402–407.

F. Lechi (edited by), *I quadri delle collezioni Lechi di Brescia*, Florence.

1969

A. M. Corbo, *Il restauro delle pitture a Roma dal 1814 al 1823*, in "Commentari", pp. 237–243.

A. Esch, *Spolien. Zur Wiederverwendung antiker Baustücke im mittelalterlichen Italien*, in "Archiv für Kulturgeschichte", LI, pp. 1–64.

1970

M. Vianello, *Documenti per la storia della tutela a Venezia nel '700*, in "Atti dell'Istituto Veneto di scienze, lettere ed arti", 1970–1971, pp. 135–142.

1973

A. Conti, *Storia del restauro e della conservazione delle opere d'arte*, Milan.

A. Emiliani, *La Collezione Zambeccari nella Pinacoteca Nazionale di Bologna*, Bologna.

1974

[P. Edwards], *Privata informazione preliminare al progetto del ristauro generale di tutte le pitture di pubblica ragione. Commesso agli Eminentissimi Signori Riformatori dello Studio di Padova con decreto dell'Eccellentissimo Senato 6 giugno 1771 [1777]*, in Olivato, pp. 157–165.

W. Oechslin, *Il Laocoonte. O del restauro delle statue antiche*, in "Paragone", n. 287, pp. 3–29.

L. Olivato, *Provvedimenti della Repubblica Veneta per la salvaguardia del patrimonio pittorico nei secoli XVII e XVIII* (Istituto Veneto di scienze, lettere ed arti, Memorie, XXXVII, I), Venice.

J. Paul, *Antikenergänzung und Ent-Restaurierung*, in "Kunstchronik", n. 4, pp. 85–112.

1975

G. Emile-Mâle–D. Pignerol, *Etude historique des vernis à tableaux d'après les texts français de 1620 à 1803*, Comitè pour la conservation de l'ICOM, Venice.

1976

H. Jedrzejewska, *Ethics in Conservation*, Stockholm.

Neri di Bicci, *Le ricordanze*, ed. B. Santi, Pisa.

S. Tschudy-Madsen, *Restoration and Antirestoration*, Oslo–Bergen.

1977

M. M. Gauthier, *Antichi ripristini e restauri moderni su smalti e oreficerie medievali*, in *Il restauro delle opere d'arte*, acts of the conference (Pistoia, 1968), Pistoia, pp. 251–261.

P. and L. Mora–P. Philippot, *La conservation des peintures murales*, Bologna.

Scritti di storia dell'arte in onore di Ugo Procacci, Milan.

1978

O. Boselli, *Osservazioni della scoltura antica*, edited by Ph. Dent Weil, Florence; extract on restoration, in "Studies in Conservation", 1967, pp. 81–101.

A. De Nicolò Salmazo, *Richieste e segnalazioni di restauri delle "pubbliche pitture" di Padova nelle relazioni degli ispettori della Repubblica Veneta*, in "Arte veneta", pp. 448–452.

P. Marconi, *Roma 1806–1829: un momento critico per la formazione della metodologia del restauro architettonico*, in "Ricerche di storia dell'arte", n. 8, 1978–1979, pp. 63–72.

1979

S. Baroni–M. Sarti–M. Simonetti–C. Tarozzi–L. Vanghi, *Considerazioni sulle tecniche della pittura*, Parma.

A. Conti, *L'evoluzione dell'artista*, in *Storia dell'arte italiana*, II, Turin, pp. 117–264.

G. Emile-Mâle, *Le sejour à Paris entre 1799 et 1815 de quelques tableaux du Palais Pitti*, in *Florence et la France ...*, acts of the conference, Florence, pp. 237–249.

M. Ferretti, *Politica di tutela e idee sul restauro nel Ducato di Lucca*, in "Ricerche di storia dell'arte", n. 8, pp. 73–98.

G. Incerpi, *I restauri sui quadri fiorentini portati a Parigi*, in *Florence et la France ...*, acts of the conference, Florence, pp. 215–227.

S. Howard, ad vocem *Cavaceppi, Bartolomeo*, in *Dizionario biografico degli italiani*, XXII, Rome.

I. Hueck, *Le vetrate di Assisi nelle copie del Ramboux e notizie sul restauro di Giovanni Bertini*, in "Bollettino d'arte", pp. 75–90.

P. Marconi, *Roma 1806–1829: un momento critico per la formazione della metodologia del restauro architettonico*, in "Ricerche di storia dell'arte", n. 8, pp. 63–72.

S. Nepi Scirè, *La "Fede" di Tiziano*, in "Quaderni della Soprintendenza ai Beni Artistici e Storici di Venezia", n. 8, pp. 85–88.

1980

M. L. Barreno Sevillano, *La restauración de pinturas de las collecciones reales durante el siglo XVIII*, in "Archivo Español de Arte", pp. 467–490.

Il Cardinal Alessandro Albani e la sua villa. Documenti (Quaderni sul neoclassico, n. 5), Rome.

I. Hueck, *Le copie di Johann Anton Ramboux da alcuni affreschi in Toscana ed in Umbria*, in "Prospettiva", n. 23, pp. 2–10.

Palazzo Vecchio: committenza e collezionismo medicei, catalogue of the exhibition, Florence.

Standing Commission on Museums and Galleries, *Conservation*, Report by a Working Party, London. *Viollet-le-Duc*, catalogue of the exhibition, Parigi.

1981

Alfredo d'Andrade tutela e restauro, catalogue of the exhibition, Turin.

E. Castelnuovo, *Arti e rivoluzione. Ideologie e politiche artistiche nella Francia rivoluzionaria*, in "Ricerche di storia dell'arte", n. 13–14, pp. 5–20; in *Arte, industria, rivoluzioni*, Turin, 1985, pp. 125–158.

A. Conti, *Vicende e cultura del restauro*, in *Storia dell'arte italiana*, X, Turin, pp. 39–112.

M. Ferretti, *Falsi e tradizione artistica*, in *Storia dell'arte italiana*, X, Turin, pp. 115–195.

F. Haskell–N. Penny, *Taste and the Antique. The Lure of Classical Sculpture 1500–1900*, New Haven–London.

I. Hueck, *La Basilica francescana di Assisi nell'Ottocento: alcuni documenti su restauri progettati ed interventi eseguiti*, in "Bollettino d'arte", pp. 143–152.

E. Merkel, *I due primi restauri della pala Costanzo di Giorgione*, in *Giorgione e la cultura veneta tra '400 e '500* (acts of the conference, Rome, 1978), Rome, pp. 35–40.

Il monumento e il suo doppio – Firenze, catalogue of the exhibition, ed. M. Dezzi Bardeschi, Florence.

O. Rossi Pinelli, *Artisti, falsari o filologhi?*, in "Ricerche di storia dell'arte", n. 13–14, pp. 41–56.

L. Moro, *Pinacoteca di Ferrara. Testimonianze e documenti sui restauri 1891–1933*, unpublished final year dissertation, Università di Bologna, sup. A. Conti, academic year 1981/82.

G. Scicolone, *Pietro Palmaroli, restauratore a Roma negli anni della Restaurazione*, unpublished final year dissertation, Università di Bologna; sup. A. Conti, academic year 1981/82.

1982

A. Angelini, *I restauri di Pietro di Francesco agli affreschi di Ambrogio Lorenzetti nella Sala della Pace*, in "Prospettiva", n. 31, pp. 78–82.

M. Bencivenni–O. Mazzei, *La cultura del "restauro": alla ricerca della "Felix Ravenna"*, in *Ravenna, la*

Biblioteca Classense, I, Bologna, pp. 203–309.

A. Conti, *Fra conservazione e restauro amatoriale, in La grande vetrata di San Giovanni e Paolo*, catalogue of the exhibition, Venice, pp. 131–143.

A. Conti, *La patina della pittura …*, in "Ricerche di storia dell'arte", n. 16, pp. 23–35.

G. Emile-Mâle, *La première transposition au Louvre en 1750: La Charité d'Andrea del Sarto*, in "Revue du Louvre et des Musées de France", n. 3, pp. 223–231.

G. Incerpi, *Conservazione e restauro dei quadri degli Uffizi nel periodo lorenese, in Gli Uffizi: quattro secoli di una galleria; Fonti e documenti*, Florence, pp. 315–357.

Patrizia Poletti, *Giovanni Battista Cavalcaselle: carteggi con i restauratori*, unpublished final year dissertation, Università di Bologna, sup. A. Conti, academic year 1982/83.

1983

A. Conti, *Storia di una distruzione*, in L. Barroero–A. Conti–A.M. Racheli–M. Serio, *Via dei Fori Imperiali*, Venice, pp. 3–60.

M. Cordaro, *Il problema dei rifacimenti e delle aggiunte nei restauri*, in "Arte medievale", pp. 263–276.

G. Emile-Mâle, *Le transport, le séjour et la restauration à Paris de la Sainte Cécile de Raphael 1796–1815, in Indagini per un dipinto. La Santa Cecilia di Raffaello*, Bologna, pp. 217–235.

G. Nepi Scirè, *Il restauro della "Presentazione di Maria al Tempio" di Tiziano*, in *Studi veneziani*, suppl. n. 5 to "Bollettino d'arte", pp. 151–164.

O. Nonfarmale, *Il restauro della Santa Cecilia di Raffaello*, in

Indagini per un dipinto. La Santa Cecilia di Raffaello, Bologna, pp. 239–249.

C. A. Picon, *Bartolomeo Cavaceppi*, catalogue of the exhibition, London. *La pittura nel XIV e XV secolo, il contributo dell'analisi tecnica alla storia dell'arte*, acts of the conference C.i.h.a. 1979, Bologna.

Raphael dans les collections françaises, catalogue of the exhibition, Paris.

H. von Sonnenburg, *Raphael in der Alten Pinakothek*, München.

1984

M. Bianchi, *"Patina": appunti per una definizione*, in "Itinerari", III, pp. 105–115.

M. Greenhalg, *"Ipsa ruina docet": l'uso dell'antico nel Medioevo*, in *Memoria dell'antico nell'arte italiana*, I, Turin, pp. 115–167.

G. Nepi Scirè, *Il "Convito in casa di Levi": di Paolo Veronese, vicende e restauri*, in "Quaderni della Sopr. ai Beni Artistici e Storici di Venezia", n. 11, pp. 13–53.

G. Romano, *La ricerca scientifica per la storia del restauro*, in *Chimica e restauro*, Venice, pp. 27–31.

1985

M. Collareta, *Michelangelo e le statue antiche: un probabile intervento di restauro*, in "Prospettiva", n. 43, pp. 51–55.

1986

A. Conti, *Michelangelo e la pittura a fresco. Tecnica e conservazione della Volta Sistina*, Florence.

A. Paolucci, *Il laboratorio del restauro a Firenze*, Turin.

O. Rossi Pinelli, *Chirurgia della memoria: scultura antica e restauri storici*, in *Memoria dell'antico nell'arte italiana*, III, Turin, pp. 183–250.

S. Settis, *Continuità, distanza, conoscenza. Tre usi dell'antico*, in *Memoria dell'antico nell'arte italiana*, III, Turin, pp. 375–486.

G. Torraca, *Momenti nella storia della conservazione del marmo*, in "OPD. Restauro" (Restauro del marmo. Opere e problemi), pp. 32–45.

1987

M. Cesani, *Restauro e tutela a San Gimignano, 1875–1915*, final year dissertation, Università di Bologna, sup. A. Conti, academic year 1986/87.

A. M. Quartili, *Lettere di restauratori nel carteggio di Corrado Ricci*, final year dissertation, Università di Bologna, sup. A. Conti, academic year 1986/87.

J. Anderson, *Layard and Morelli*, in *Austen Henry Layard tra l'Oriente e Venezia* (acts of the symposium), Rome, pp. 109–137.

1988

Sul restauro, edited by A. Conti, Turin.

D. Levi, *Cavalcaselle, il pioniere della conservazione dell'arte italiana*, Turin.

Thieme–Becker, *Allgemeines Lexikon der bildenden Künstler von der Antike bis zur Gegenwart*, edited by Thieme and Becker, Leipzig, 1907–1950.

Abbreviations used when citing archival sources:

Seminario: Venice, Biblioteca del Seminario Patriarcale.

A.C.S.: Rome, Archivio centrale dello Stato, Ministero della Pubblica Istruzione, Direzione generale Antichità e Belle Arti.

Carteggio Cavalcaselle: carteggio di Giambattista Cavalcaselle, Venice, Biblioteca Marciana, Ms It. 2035 (=12276).

Index of Names

Index of place names and works

Glossary of technical terms

1. Terminology used to describe the materials and techniques of paintings

Wall paintings (frescos)

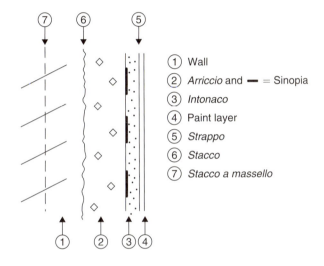

Fig i Schematic diagram showing the structure of a fresco indicating the level at which the various techniques of transfer occur.

(Adapted from *The Conservation of Wall Paintings*, Mora, Mora and Philippot)

Arriccio
The first coat of rough-cast plaster or rendering applied directly to the wall to create a uniform surface onto which to apply the subsequent finer layer of plaster, the *intonaco*. It usually consists of one part lime plaster to three parts coarse sand.

Intonaco
The surface layer of lime plaster, usually containing more finely ground sand to give a smoother finish (but not always). For a fresco, enough would be applied to remain wet for the duration of the day's painting.

Fresco
As the etymology of the word indicates (*fresco* means fresh, therefore still wet), when pigments simply mixed with water are painted onto freshly applied plaster (the *intonaco*), the

421

technique is called *fresco* or *buon fresco*. The calcium hydroxide (CaOH) in the wet plaster is drawn to the surface by the evaporation of the water, enveloping the pigments on its way out. This then carbonizes in contact with the carbon dioxide (CO_2) in the air, eventually forming a pigmented crust of calcium carbonate ($CaCO_3$) on the surface which slows down the reaction in the body of the layer. There is therefore a discrete paint layer, which is what is removed with the "*strappo*" technique.

Secco

A secco, in contrast to *a fresco*. "*Secco*" literally means dry; some wall paintings were executed entirely in this technique, or else these are the finishing touches which were executed on top of the dry plaster, which had been painted first when wet (*a fresco*).

Some artists would use both techniques in their paintings. Pigments which could not be used within the plaster because of their chemical nature (lapis lazuli, for instance) would be applied *a secco*, once it had dried. Because these layers were applied on top of dry plaster with a binding medium, such as glue, casein or egg-tempera, they were particularly vulnerable, and would flake if moisture seeped through the wall, for instance. The different chemical and physical natures of *secco* and *fresco* techniques also require special care during conservation treatments.

Sinopia

A full-scale preparatory drawing, usually executed on the *arriccio*. *Sinopia* refers to the red ochre which is usually used for the drawing, although it can also be in yellow ochre or black.

Giornata

The term refers to the work of a single day (*giorno*). Only wet plaster (the *intonaco*) that could be painted in a single day would be applied onto the underlying *arriccio*. The evolution of the execution of a fresco can be followed through the overlapping areas of the *giornate*. The area painted in a single day would vary in size depending on the detail and difficulty of the composition: a single head might be a *giornata*, as indeed might a large section of landscape or background.

Easel paintings
Support

All paintings are painted on a support which is, traditionally, either rigid (stone, brick, metal, wood) or flexible (woven fabric, usually canvas). The physical nature of the support cannot but influence the appearance of the painting: its surface, the way the paint handles and is applied, but also in the way the materials settle or deteriorate with time.

Size

Water-based glue, traditionally made from parchment clippings and more recently from rabbit skin (rabbit-skin glue). Up to the nineteenth century, it was applied warm, in liquid form, to make the support, whether wood or canvas, less absorbent; when canvases began to be prepared commercially, especially at the end of the nineteenth century, this layer would be applied cold, as a jelly, on top of the canvas (see Fig. ii). This led to serious conservation problems for works painted on these canvases in later years, as the jelly (not having impregnated the canvas) would swell, and the paint and ground would come away from the canvas.

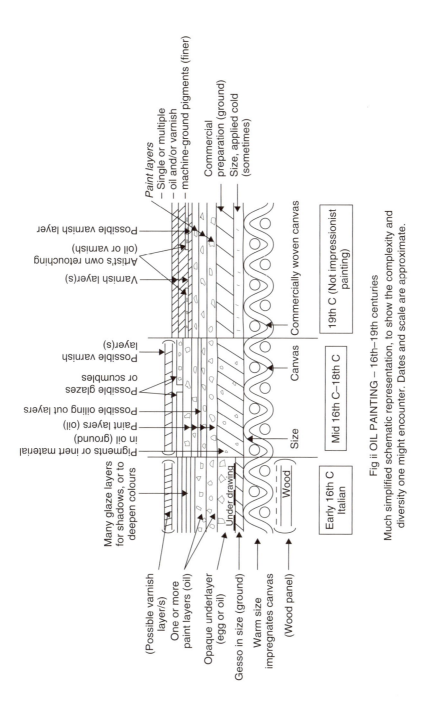

Paint layers
– Single or multiple
– oil and/or varnish
– machine-ground pigments (finer)

Commercial preparation (ground)
Size, applied cold (sometimes)

Possible varnish layer

Artist's own retouching (oil or varnish)

Varnish layer(s)

Commercially woven canvas

19th C (Not impressionist painting)

Possible varnish layer(s)

Possible glazes or scumbles

Possible oiling out layers

Paint layers (oil)

Pigments or inert material in oil (ground)

Canvas

Size

Mid 16th C–18th C

Many glaze layers for shadows, or to deepen colours

(Possible varnish layer/s)

One or more paint layers (oil)

Opaque underlayer (egg or oil)

Gesso in size (ground)

Warm size impregnates canvas

(Wood panel)

Under drawing

Wood

Early 16th C Italian

Fig ii OIL PAINTING – 16th–19th centuries

Much simplified schematic representation, to show the complexity and diversity one might encounter. Dates and scale are approximate.

Ground

Whatever its nature, the support will require preparation to provide a suitable surface for the paint. This priming layer is usually referred to as the ground layer in paintings which have wood, metal or canvas as their support. It can differ in its components, absorbency, texture, colour and hence visual role within the painting. Its physical nature and aesthetic effect will affect the ultimate durability of the painting, as well as influencing all aspects of subsequent conservation and restoration interventions.

Early Italian panels were prepared by applying several layers of gesso (see Fig. iii), increasingly fine, which were smoothed down to give a white, reflectant, polished ivory-like surface on which to paint. Up to the last quarter of the sixteenth century, this gesso layer would also incorporate a layer of canvas. Later Italian panel paintings do not have this layer, and it is also absent from panel paintings in northern Europe which were prepared with a similarly smooth white layer but made up of chalk (calcium carbonate rather than the sulphate) and size.

During the sixteenth century, paintings on canvas would also be prepared with a thin layer of this ground. Because the gesso is bound together with a water-soluble binder (size), paintings with this kind of preparation were particularly vulnerable to humidity, and therefore posed, and pose, particular conservation problems. As a result, as early as the sixteenth century, grounds prepared with earth pigments bound in oil began to be applied to canvases as a preparatory layer, and this continued throughout the seventeenth century. These grounds are responsible for the dark appearance which at times appears to engulf paintings from this period, and led to problems both structurally and visually in their conservation and restoration. Some artists would apply an additional lighter layer to counteract this.

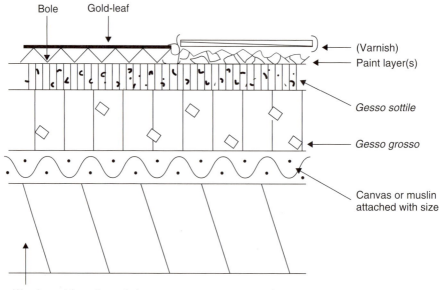

Fig iii Simplified section through an Early Italian panel painting.

By the eighteenth century, the perception of these problems led artists to prepare their canvases with lighter oil-based grounds: pink and grey. Although artists were able to buy ready prepared canvases as early as the seventeenth century (many additional conservation problems were caused by the painter not being able to control the nature and quality of the materials used), the nineteenth century saw further problems for the restorer caused by the widespread use of commercially prepared canvases.

Paint

With the exception of *fresco* technique, all paint consists of powdered coloured material (pigment) and a more or less fluid material (medium) which binds all the particles together, and which after application will "dry" to form a film. When one speaks of the technique of a painting, what is usually referred to is the nature of the binding medium of the paint, and the support onto which the paint has been applied: oil on canvas, tempera on panel, etc.

In order to apply the paint, the pigment/medium mixture would be made less intractable and easier to apply by adding a suitable diluent, which would then evaporate completely (this is not true, however, of all diluents). The handling properties of the paint would influence the way in which it was applied, especially in earlier times, before paint began to be manufactured commercially and to be available in tubes (the 1840s) with largely uniform consistencies.

Pigments

Pigments are the coloured particles which are then mixed with a medium (binder) and applied as paint with the help of diluent if necessary. Pigments have a variety of different sources (mineral, vegetable, synthetic) and all have different chemical make-ups which dictate not only their hue, but also how they behave when mixed with a particular medium, and how they will age on exposure to light and air. Some are inert and others reactive; some are gritty and others have almost invisible particles. They all deteriorate in different ways and at different rates, if at all.

Every pigment has a defined refractive index, which gives an indication of its inherent transparency or opacity, although one pigment can be transparent in one medium and opaque in another (because of the difference between their relative refractive indices).

Some pigments will react chemically and deteriorate if certain materials are used in the cleaning of the painting.

Medium or binder
Size

Traditionally, size is a glue made from animal skin or bones and water (parchment size, rabbit-skin glue, etc.). It was also used as a binding medium on canvas, giving a very matt, non-saturated appearance. It is vulnerable both in the qualities of its appearance (its mattness and unsaturated colour are both liable to be lost through lining and varnishing), and in its materials (vulnerability of the glue-bound paint to moisture).

Tempera

Traditionally, the word "tempera" is associated with the medium of egg-tempera, although in the context of paintings "tempered" literally means "bound with". More generally, it has been used to describe any of the old techniques which used water as their diluent and were protein based: for instance, casein (from milk) or size (from the skin and bones of animals).

Pigments tempered with any of these protein-based binding media were used for painting *a secco*, on walls, and size was used to paint on canvas from a very early date.

Casein

A binding medium used from very early times, made from the "skim" on milk and lime. It produces a very opaque, very hard and insoluble and, in itself, potentially durable paint film.

Egg

Egg-yolk is perhaps the most durable paint medium, both because it alters least in colour with time and because it produces a very tough paint film. It is an emulsion of oil droplets in water (like milk), so by adding water it becomes more liquid, and by adding oil thicker, more like mayonnaise. It was the medium used by the Early Italian Masters to bind their pigment particles. The characteristic hatched appearance of the paint is due to the fact that the water used by the artist to make the egg-yolk and pigment mixture more fluid is immediately drawn into the absorbent gesso ground, so that the brush effectively becomes a pencil and the paint is hatched in, as the paint is so quick to dry that the artist cannot "blend", but can only hatch.

Oil

Not all oils can be used as a medium for painting. The oil has to be an unsaturated "drying oil", that is, one which will form a film by polymerizing through the action of light and oxygen. "Drying" is not really the correct term for what happens to oil; once the diluent, turpentine or white spirit evaporates, the oil film continues to alter chemically, becoming stiffer and more rigid. The process of polymerization takes some time to complete, and the oil paint film will remain flexible for some time owing to the presence of small sections of saturated oils within the structure of the polymerized oil film. These small flexible components are at risk during cleaning. The slow drying of oil allows the artist to blend colours, but also means that enough time must be allowed between applications of paint to ensure that the underlying layer is properly "dry".

On ageing the oil darkens, and becomes more brittle, more transparent and insoluble in all but the most active solvents. Linseed oil dries the most quickly of the drying oils commonly used in painting, and also yellows the most. Artists would use walnut or poppy oil in preference for whites and blues (cool colours most altered visually by the yellowing).

Each pigment requires a different proportion of oil to bind it (one of the skills which, until the seventeenth century, artists would learn in their seven-year apprenticeships in the studio), and every pigment/oil mixture would have its own characteristic texture due to the different chemical and physical natures of pigments.

Wax

Natural beeswax is used as a medium in encaustic painting, as a consolidant and an adhesive in the conservation of easel paintings, and as a finish after restoration of frescos and some paintings. It gives a sheen rather than a gloss, but will nevertheless saturate and alter the tonality of poorly bound surfaces such as frescos.

Diluent

A liquid used to make paint more fluid. Its nature depends on the chemical nature of the binding medium. Water is the diluent for size and egg, for example, and spirits of turpentine and now white spirit are used to thin oil paint. The diluent usually evaporates completely, although turpentine, and the earliest diluents such as oil of spike, left residues in the paint.

Varnishes

Varnishes have throughout time fulfilled a dual function, both as a protective layer and as a substance which would saturate the underlying paint. They have not always been applied over the entire painting.

A "spirit varnish" consists of a resin, traditionally mastic or dammar (although synthetic resins are also used nowadays) which is dissolved in a solvent (a "spirit"). Applied to a painting it will form a film through the evaporation of the solvent, and although it will change chemically over time (yellowing and becoming brittle or sometimes opaque to varying degrees according to its nature), its solubility will always be different to that of the underlying paint, and therefore removable, with the proviso that no varnish was included in the paint by the artist.

An oil varnish is made up of a "hard" resin such as one of the fossil resins (amber, copal) which will not dissolve in a spirit (solvent) but will dissolve in hot oil. It gives a tough, highly coloured film which will darken greatly with time; this film will "dry" in the same way as the oil paint, by polymerization, requiring an alkali reagent to break it down. In cleaning the danger is obvious: you are removing oil from oil, like cleaning a watercolour with water. These varnishes can in no way be considered reversible. Sometimes a proportion of oil was added to spirit varnishes to make them tougher, so that they would offer better protection to the painting: these would have the same problems of darkening and reversibility as oil varnishes, but to a lesser degree.

Varnishes can be, and are, also used as a painting medium.

Perception and optical effects
Refractive index

All materials to be found in the paint layer have a refractive index (RI). This is a measure of how much a beam of light is deflected when travelling through a material, in relation to such a beam travelling through a vacuum. What one sees is dictated not only by the RI of any individual material, but also by the relationship between the RI of that material and the RI of the material which surrounds it. Therefore, what one sees is as much due to the relationship between two materials as to the individual nature of either. The RI of a material can also change over time: for instance, that of oil appears to increase, bringing it nearer to that of some pigments, which means that oil paint appears more transparent on ageing.

Opacity

Opacity is a measure of the extent to which a material will cover and obscure an underlying layer. A pigment can be opaque in itself (have a high RI, that is deflecting the light falling onto it) or because the difference between its RI and that of the medium in which it has been applied is so great as to render it opaque. Therefore, some pigments (chalk, for instance) can be opaque in one medium (glue) and transparent in another (oil), a property which artists have exploited throughout time.

Varnishes can become opaque when they break up with age, white light being diffracted off the irregular surface of the fragmented varnish (the same effect obtained by breaking and grinding down a glass bottle: transparent when whole, and white when ground down) (see Fig. iv).

Transparency

Transparency is a measure of how much a material will allow light to travel through it. This can be because the RI of a pigment is itself low (a lake pigment, for instance), or because the difference between the RI of the pigment and the medium is slight.

Pentiment

Pentimento in Italian comes from the word *pentire*, to repent, that is, to change one's mind. It is used to describe alterations in a composition, by the artist's hand, which lie beneath the final paint layer. On completion of the painting, these would have been invisible, but as oil appears more transparent with time, these *pentiments* have become visible and can be distracting.

Colour (see also Introductory essay)

Without light, there would be no colour. The colour of the pigment will depend on what portion of the visible spectrum is absorbed and what is reflected. The colour we see is the portion of the spectrum which is reflected. Colours can be classed as warm (red end of the spectrum) and cool (violet/blue end).

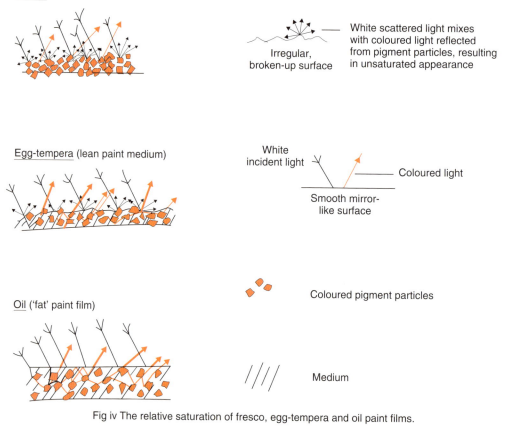

Fresco

Irregular, broken-up surface

White scattered light mixes with coloured light reflected from pigment particles, resulting in unsaturated appearance

Egg-tempera (lean paint medium)

White incident light

Coloured light

Smooth mirror-like surface

Oil ('fat' paint film)

Coloured pigment particles

Medium

Fig iv The relative saturation of fresco, egg-tempera and oil paint films.

An exceptionally complex phenomenon, colour can be considered both as a material (in that pigments are in themselves coloured) and as perception. Perceived colour depends not only on the nature of the pigment and medium, the colour of the underlayers and the surface texture of the paint (see Fig. iv), but also on the context in which it is seen: the colours we see will appear different according to the lighting and to the colours which surround them, for instance.

The degree of saturation of a colour will also be influenced by the light in which it is seen, but depends largely on the surface texture of the paint. The mirror-like surface provided by a varnish will saturate a pigment, making it darker and richer in colour, by eliminating the surface scattering of white light. Irregular surfaces, such as pastel or fresco will appear more matt and scatter white light; this mixes with the light-reflecting colour from the pigment particles, so the painted surface has a paler appearance. Painters throughout the ages have manipulated these aspects of colour and saturation and differences in mattness and gloss. Conservation and restoration treatments need to consider these perceptual elements as well as the material aspects.

A colour can be achieved either by physically mixing the pigments (subtractive colour mixing) or by the reflected coloured light from the pigments mixing optically in the eye of the observer (additive colour mixing) (glazing, scumbling, hatching, etc.).

Scumble and glaze

Eastlake[i] defines these, respectively, as "dynamic coolness and warmth", in that they are produced by the effects of seeing one layer through another, rather than by a physical mixture.

A scumble is produced by passing a light, semi-transparent or semi-opaque tone over a darker one; this will always result in coolness of effect, which "has much more power of freshness than a solid cool tint". First fully described and used in painting by Leonardo, it is now known as Rayleigh scattering, and is the optical effect which makes the sky (and veins) appear blue. This is also known as "turbid medium effect".

A glaze can be termed a layer which is more or less transparent, but which is darker than the layer on which it has been applied, and therefore appears warm; and "there is more real warmth in a glazed colour than what professes to be its equivalent in an atomic mixture".[ii] The pigments in a glaze are usually of a transparent and often organic nature, and bound in oil or varnish, or both.

These are the "finishing touches" which are particularly vulnerable during cleaning, because of their thinness, of their application, their medium, or because they are applied over a varnish layer which is in itself vulnerable to cleaning agents.

2. Deterioration, conservation and restoration terminology

Deterioration and ageing

Patina

Perceived but not generally measurable. Its definition changes according to culture and perception, and can accordingly have positive or negative connotations. Common to all

---

[i] Sir John Lock Eastlake.
[ii] As above.

definitions is the fact that it is not something associated with a freshly executed work, and its perception denotes either the passage or the presence of "Time" on the painting, or indeed a sculpture.

Blooming

Not completely understood as a phenomenon, this is the cloudiness, opalescence and at times completely opaque appearance of a varnish. It is thought that humidity plays a role in its appearance. Natural resin varnishes are prone to blooming, mastic in particular. In the past a little drying oil would be added to the mastic varnish to prevent blooming. When blooming occurs in the varnish layer only, it will disappear with cleaning. It can also occur in the paint layer, when the oil medium has been broken down by the use of a strong reagent.

Yellowing and/or darkening

This occurs in both varnish and paint layers as they age and oxidize. Because this happens in the varnish layer, the original colour harmonies as well as the actual composition can become obscured or illegible. Because the yellowed surface layer affects colours differently although it is even itself, colour relationships indicating depth and volume can become completely distorted. For instance, the misty blues of distant landscapes are "warmed up" by the yellow/brown varnish, taking on the tone of the warm hues used to indicate midground and foreground. All drying oils used in painting also yellow and darken with age; linseed oil more than either walnut or poppy.

Cracking

This occurs in both varnish and paint layers as they age. The cracking of the varnish is induced by light, which makes it more brittle (varnish protected by the frame rebate has neither yellowed nor cracked to the same degree). It will also crack on a bigger scale from movement of the paint following movement of the support and ground.

Cracking in the paint can be the result of poor technique on the part of the artist (sometimes referred to as drying cracks) when either incorrect proportions of pigment and medium have been mixed, or paint has been applied on top of underlayers which were insufficiently dry and are still shrinking. This same kind of cracking can occur if paint has been applied thickly, and dries first on the surface.

Paint and ground will both crack as they become more brittle with age, and the pattern of the craquelure will reflect the nature of the support: wood, canvas or wall. The transfer of paintings onto different supports has in certain cases led to distortions of visual effects, surface image and physical make-up being at odds with one another.

Flaking

In time, continued movement of the support in reaction to changes in humidity can lead to the detachment of the cracked ground and paint layers. The detachment will occur at the weakest point of the structure. The use of organic materials in linings (organic material swells in high humidity) exacerbates the problem. Canvas, although organic, because it is a woven material will become taut or even shrink in high humidity (washed T-shirt effect).

Flaking, or delamination between layers, can also occur when the material make-up of the layers is incompatible (oil over wax, for instance).

3. Structural conservation: wall[iii] and easel paintings

Transfer (see Fig. i)
Detaching a painting from its support, and reattaching it onto another support. At times, when paintings were detached from a wall, they might be replaced in the same position, once the stability and conservation of the original wall or plaster had been attended to. Wall paintings were transferred using one of three techniques: *strappo*, *stacco* and *a massello*.

Paintings on panel could be either transferred onto canvas or onto another panel (in modern times, not made of wood). Paintings on canvas would be transferred onto a new canvas. In both cases the paint layers (the image) could be transferred either along with the ground layer, or without. Transfers are rarely carried out today, and only if no other option is viable to preserve the painting for posterity.

Strappo
The surface paint layer of the fresco is peeled off the plaster (*intonaco*).

Stacco
The frescoed surface is detached along with the *intonaco*.

A massello
The fresco is detached with the plaster layers and also part of the supporting wall.

Cradling
Cradles are a wooden armature which used to be attached to the reverse of a panel (often thinned right down) which had warped, in order to keep it flat. Although the vertical members which were glued on along the grain were fixed, the transverse members were theoretically mobile, allowing the wooden panel its natural movement in response to changes in humidity. Unfortunately, the wooden transverse members were also prone to these movements and would therefore lock, causing the original panel to split. Today, this practice has largely fallen into disuse, and cradles are being removed by restorers.

Lining
The attachment of a painting on canvas onto a new canvas with some form of adhesive. At times this was carried out to provide additional support to a weak, damaged or deteriorated original canvas; the heat, moisture and pressure used in the traditional lining process could also be used to reduce prominent cracking, or to reattach paint which was flaking. Other adhesives (wax, for instance) would be introduced to replace the medium which was no longer binding together the pigment particles – the action of the adhesive would be more exactly described as cohesive (that is, binding together). The term relining implies the removal of a previous lining and adhesive, before attaching a new one. In the early days of the practice, it was sometimes carried out locally, as patches. This practice has largely fallen into disuse, as the imprint of the patch would appear after a time, on the front of the painting.

Facing
A protective layer, canvas or paper, which is attached to the paint surface. An adhesive is used which forms a very strong bond, stronger than that of the paint layers to the support,

---

[iii] I am deeply indebted to the volume devoted to the *Conservation of Wall Paintings* (Mora, Mora and Philippot).

to enable the latter to be detached from it without causing, or at least minimizing, damage. A facing is also sometimes used during lining. The adhesive used to attach it must be soluble in a material which will not endanger the paint layer during removal of the facing, once the paint is attached to a new support.

Adhesives and consolidants

The most commonly used term today would be "consolidation", although technically there is a difference in that fixing of a layer which has detached (detached plaster, for instance, or blistering paint) is adhesion (with an adhesive). "Consolidation" deals with the cohesion of a layer, that is, replacing whatever substance held together the particles (the medium or binder), for instance if the layer is crumbling away.

Cleaning

Removal (to varying degrees) of surface layers which are not considered to be original to the work, and which visually distort or obfuscate the painting. These can be grime and soot, varnishes, paint, oils and other substances applied during previous restorations.

There is, and always has been, dissent as to the nature of that which is removed, and the degree to which this should take place (if at all): at what point do "history" and "time" become an integral part of the original object, whether materially or in its perception? Caution is dictated by the fact that what is removed cannot be put back.

Traditionally, reagents, solvents and other materials carried in solution or dispersion in water would be used for the removal, although this can also be carried out mechanically.

"Total cleaning", as the term suggests, refers to the complete removal of all the discoloured non-original layers on a painting, and usually implies the removal of any discoloured earlier restorations as well, revealing the painting in its present physical condition, and has an aura (misplaced) of "objectivity". As an approach to cleaning, it is associated largely with Anglo-Saxon countries. Gerry Hedley, in *On Humanism, Aesthetics and the Cleaning of Paintings* (Measured Opinions, UKIC, 1993), rationalized the other approaches, giving them the terms "selective cleaning" and "partial cleaning".[iv] The former implies a choice made by the restorer as to the levels of varnish removed in different areas of the painting, whilst the latter involves an overall thinning of the varnish layers present, implying a less subjective practice. Both these approaches are associated with continental practice. It should be borne in mind that the application of any solvent, or reagent, irrespective of what varnish layers are removed, and to what degree, will always affect the physical structure of the underlying paint layers.

Paint surfaces which were not originally varnished are problematic in that whatever the material one is trying to remove can have penetrated or at least interacted with the original paint.

Solvents

Organic solvents, which have a chemical structure similar to that of the varnishes they are used to remove, are probably the most used substances for the removal of discoloured varnishes. "Spirit of wine" is likely to have been the earliest form used (an alcohol). The strength of the solvent is not an absolute, but relative to the chemical structure of the substance removed, and sometimes adding a "weaker solvent" to dilute or slow down the action of the main solvent, can

---

[iv] He is referring in particular to easel paintings and therefore to the cleaning of varnishes, but the principles are the same for wall paintings.

in fact make it "stronger" in that it has a greater effect on the underlying paint film. The solvent will affect the underlying paint, extracting the soluble elements and making the paint film increasingly brittle, whether the varnish is completely or only partially removed. That means that every time a painting is cleaned the paint film becomes more fragile.

Reagents

Reagents are alkali substances in solution (such as lye or ammonia) which will remove oily substances and varnishes, whether these are present in the paint medium or in surface varnishes. They have to be used with great skill and caution. When used to clean paintings in the past, oil would then be rubbed into the surface of the painting after cleaning in order to replace lost medium, and give the painting a less parched appearance. This oil would itself darken and become insoluble with time, causing problems for subsequent restorers. Walnut or poppy oil would at later dates be chosen in preference to linseed oil for this rubbing in, because they darken less with time.

Mechanical removal

At times it is safer for the original paint to remove old restorations and tough varnishes mechanically, with a scalpel and the aid of a stereomicroscope, rather than by using a solvent or a reagent.

Friction

At other times the discoloured surface varnish is so brittle that it can be removed by gentle friction with the fingers. Early examples of cleaning involve friction as well as a substance which would either dissolve or break down the varnish layers. These substances would be used with rags or sponges, and therefore the peaks of the cracked paint were liable to abrasion. Nowadays solvents are applied with cotton swabs on sticks which are rolled over the surface, minimizing abrasion.

Retouching
Filling

Losses in the ground and paint layer are filled by the restorer in order to provide a continuous surface with the paint film. The surface texture of the paint film is imitated in the fill if the restorer is aiming to make his or her intervention invisible to the observer, as difference in texture between original paint and the restoration leaps to the eye even more than a colour incorrectly matched.

Fills are made up of an inert filler material mixed with a medium; for instance, chalk mixed with gelatine or with an acrylic resin. In the past, oil was added to fills to make them more plastic and less absorbent, and often overlapped the surrounding paint. These have darkened with time and have proved very difficult to remove.

The restorer usually applies a layer of isolating varnish over the painting, either before or after it is filled, to saturate the picture surface after cleaning and so that the restoration is physically distinct from the original painting, and to facilitate matching of the colours, as these alter in appearance when varnished (see Fig. iv).

Retouching materials
Retouching medium

Reversibility of the paint medium of the restoration is a prerequisite in our times, as is minimal alteration, so that the restoration does not have to be carried out again (in theory) as a result of the aged retouchings standing out as blemishes on the painting (as happens when retouchings are carried out in oil).

Future restorers should be able to remove present restorations without damaging the original paint. As Conti has shown, the concept of reversibility is not new: Maratta in the seventeenth century used pastel to this end, and Edwards in the eighteenth insisted that the restorers under him should use easily soluble varnish colours in their work. As always in restoration, there have been cycles; oil paint has been much used as a retouching medium, and there are still instances of its use. It is not reversible. It quickly darkens, becoming tough and insoluble, leaving future restorers the problem of removing oil paint from oil paint.

Retouching pigments
Restorers are often asked whether they use the same pigments as the artist whose painting they are restoring. The answer is on the whole negative: they *imitate* the effect of those pigments, and usually their deterioration as well, but with pigments which are known not to deteriorate, so that, again theoretically, they will not alter with time.

Reversibility is a requirement of all restoration materials; that is, one should be able to remove all paint applied by the restorer with solvents which are "weak" in relation to the painting, and will not damage the original. A further (theoretical) requirement is that no original paint should be covered.

In-painting
As opposed to retouching by the restorer which covers original paint. The requirement of all museum-standard interventions is that neither the fill nor the paint applied by the restorer should cover "the pure brushwork" of the artist. The practice of glazing worn areas of paint is a compromise.

Glazing
Not to be confused with the insertion of a piece of glass within a frame. Literally, this means the application of a transparent layer. In the context of restoration this refers to the practice of applying localized areas of pigmented varnish over original paint where this has been abraded or is damaged without actual loss of a discrete area of paint, so that it does not stand out from the rest of the painting.

Toning
Again, the application of a pigmented and therefore coloured varnish, but implied is a more wholesale application, and also a desire to tone down the freshly cleaned appearance. In the nineteenth century it would have been a layer containing maybe liquorice and soot to impart an Old Master "glow".

Restoration
Aesthetic restoration (*restauro amatoriale*)
I have used the term "aesthetic restoration" for the Italian *"restauro amatoriale"* to define an approach which is diametrically opposed to that of archaeological restoration, *"restauro di conservazione"*. Directed to the "art-lover", it gives precedence to the aesthetic qualities and legibility of a painting, at the expense of its historical and authorial authenticity. There are degrees in its practice, now as in the past, so that what is carried out by a restorer for the "commercial" market is not equivalent (in intent or materials) to what is carried out within a museum or gallery, although both may be aiming to "please" the art-lover by reconstructing missing areas and removing signs of age deterioration. This restoration aims to be invisible, and

to restore an original appearance which is now lost. Reconstruction of missing areas is interpretative, and controversial on many counts.

Visible or harmonizing restoration (*restauro d'accompagnamento*)

Literally, "which accompanies", that is, a restoration which is in harmony with the original, but is making no attempt to be mistaken with it. It is not invisible, and makes no attempt to be so. The technique of *tratteggio* (reconstructing missing areas with hatched strokes which are clearly visible from close to, but do not disturb from the appropriate viewing distance) is a rationalized attempt at such an intervention. Based on the principles of Gestalt psychology, it looks to put losses into the background, so that the painting can be appreciated aesthetically despite its damage, without compromising its historical authenticity.

Archaeological restoration (*restauro di conservazione – di tutela*)

I have opted for this rather interpretative expression for the practice of restoration as conservation, as there is no direct equivalent in English for *restauro di conservazione*. This is because, historically, there has been no philosophical and theoretical structure to the various approaches to restoration, and no real definitions of the terms used to provide direct counterparts to the Italian terminology.

"Conservation–restoration" implies that the work of art is simply "conserved" in its present state, ensuring its best preservation for posterity, with no attempt to "restore" it to anything approaching its original or intended appearance; that is, there is no interpretative intervention on its "aesthetic" entity. It is what Conti refers to as a purist approach, treating the work of art simply as a "historical" document, the authenticity of which must not be impaired by any intrusion from outside. The losses are left as they are, or else filled with a toned fill, or retouched with a "neutral" colour which usually corresponds to the colour of either the ground or the support. These interrupt the picture surface, putting the painting into the "background" and the damage into the "foreground".

Neutral retouchings

There is no such thing as a neutral colour and tone. A colour can only be "neutral" in relation to the colours in its immediate vicinity. It is relative, not absolute. It has often been associated with mixtures of colours which have no particular hue but verge on the grey/beige: the implication is always that such a tone, a "neutral" tone, will not stand out but merge in, so that the losses are less disturbing to the onlooker.

Varnishing

Varnishing is now an integral part of restoration. It is applied both as a measure of conservation, to protect the picture surface, and as a final saturating layer. The painting is varnished after cleaning (not always) and receives a final varnish, one or more coats, which can be either brushed or sprayed. The principle of reversibility requires that the varnish remain easily soluble in a "weak" solvent, that is, a solvent which will minimize the effects of its removal on the physical make-up of the painting.

The natural resin dammar is still often used for its aesthetic qualities, although it yellows with time. Synthetic varnishes are also used, which alter less. Evenness of finish is sought by the restorer, and this as well as the desired degree of glossiness can be controlled either in the brushing or by applying it as a spray. There are occasions when the restored painting has not received this final varnish, either because of technique or because of the known intent of the artist to leave his work unvarnished.

Photographic credits

Jörg P. Anders, Berlin; Bayerische Staatsgemäldesammlungen, Alte Pinakothek, Munich; Osvaldo Böhm, Venice; Photographie Bulloz, Paris; British Museum, London; Chomon-Perino, Turin; Erzbischöfliches Diözesan-Museum, Cologne; Electa, Milan; Fogg Art Museum, Cambridge (Mass.); Fotofast, Bologna; Fototeca Alessandro Conti; Gabinetto Fotografico Nazionale, Rome; Gabinetto Fotografico, Soprintendenza alle Gallerie di Firenze; Giraudon, Paris; Foto Grassi, Siena; Antonio Guerra, Bologna; National Gallery, London; Musées Nationaux, Paris; Musées Royaux, Brussels; National Gallery of Ireland, Dublin; Musei Capitolini, Rome; Narodni Galerie, Prague; Photo Service Gruppo Editoriale Fabbri, Milan; Pinacoteca Vaticana, Vatican City; Fotostudio Rapuzzi; Scala, Florence; Soprintendenza ai Beni Artistici e Storici, Parma; Soprintendenza Archeologica di Roma; Soprintendenza alle Antichità della Campania, Naples; Staatliche Museen Preussischer Kulturbesitz, Berlin-Dahlem; Università di Pisa.

With thanks to the author and the museums who kindly allowed their photographs to be used.